ANTOINE PREDOCK

65 YEARS OF ARCHITECTURE

First published in the United States of America in 2024 by
RIZZOLI INTERNATIONAL PUBLICATIONS, INC.
300 Park Avenue South, New York, NY 10010
www.rizzoliusa.com

Photography credits appear on page 688.

Publisher: Charles Miers
Editor: Douglas Curran
Production Manager: Colin Hough Trapp
Managing Editor: Lynn Scrabis
Design Manager: Olivia Russin
Proofreader: Sarah Stump

Edited and designed by Group C Inc. New Haven, CT (BC, TK, LT)

Cover: Canadian Museum for Human Rights, Winnipeg, Manitoba. Photograph by Alex Fradkin.

Printed in Hong Kong
2024 2025 2026 2027 2028 / 10 9 8 7 6 5 4 3 2 1

ISBN-13: 978-0-8478-9951-7
Library of Congress Control Number: 2023940893

Visit us online:
Facebook.com/RizzoliNewYork
Twitter: @Rizzoli_Books
Instagram.com/RizzoliBooks
Pinterest.com/RizzoliBooks
Youtube.com/user/RizzoliNY
Issuu.com/Rizzoli

ANTOINE PREDOCK
65 YEARS OF ARCHITECTURE

New York · Paris · London · Milan

ARTIS

The Ride

The beginning is an opening, an unexpected recognition that has worked its way through layers of habit—habits of thinking, habits of behavior and cultural expectation. That point of light is the beginning. And the most difficult thing for many is to recognize it and jump on it, take a ride on it. Subsequent development sometimes leads to the elaboration of a narrative, but half the time I simply make something I like. The narrative doesn't rule. I don't test every move against it. If it is there, it is open-ended, it is malleable, like the clay of the models that I make. I can change it or scrap it or reverse it. At the end you wonder what it was that started it all—what was the beginning, the so-called inspiration. It just seems to show up, as in Garcia Lorca's notion of "duende."

Development, exploration, is a voracious notion. It is being a cosmic omnivore. It is a kind of benign pathology. With every project, there is an attempt to digest and consume—to find, but not entirely burn up, the right kind of fuel. On the ride there have to be quiet points of reference, pauses that allow the opportunity to appreciate, to understand—like eddies that reside in the flow of the deeper channel, each possessing a different manifestation as a river moves through space and time. To move from one eddy to another, you have to reenter the main current.

The explorations come back to a consistent impulse of mine—to encounter the subject deeply, empathetically; to get out of my head and back to some original impulse, some original power that touches different chords rather than work that is more cerebral. The intellectual component, the rational component, is there in my work and in my life, but it is tempered and balanced by this impulse to go deeper each time.

These explorations result in the discovery, the unearthing, of geomorphic and cultural deformations or indicators that act independently or intersect and animate one another. So many of the buildings are examples, of really looking at the underlying strata and the history of the larger geographic and cultural environment, over not just centuries but millennia: upheavals in the land, the changing course of water, paths that people have traveled—both physical and spiritual. These all become primary indicators for architecture.

With each project, with each process, this underlying impulse to explore humanity at-large and the specificity of site is neither program-driven nor budget-driven. It is about creating a different conceptual foundation each time out, a foundation that grows out of an understanding of the importance of all the elements. There are impulses that resurface in different ways in different projects, but it is not a matter of applying those to different programs. It is more a matter that the underlying discoveries lead toward certain gestures in the work that are fundamental to how people move through and around not only buildings, but different cultures in the world.

These are timeless impulses that get beyond the meaning "contextualism" has come to have—a word I rarely use because it has been trivialized by nostalgic readings. It has to do with a larger arena, a deeper arena. You have to spin around 360 degrees and imagine what has evolved and will evolve on the site, figure out what the platform is that is now available to ground a building on. That, for me, is context.

The Pantheon was a pagan temple, then it became a church; that's a rather traumatic shifting of gears. The ethos of the space changes—you can call that program—but in changing, the essential power of the space remains unaffected. In this way, buildings can exist out of time. If the south transept in my Saint John the Divine proposal became a market or a bazaar, it would be a wonderful one, a kind of twenty-first-century mall. Its cosmological rootedness would remain intact because the sacred numbers that ground the scheme converge on numbers that come from the Fibonacci series, revealing the overlaps and congruencies between the sacred, the scientific, and the organic, a kind of DNA that engenders a timeless quality. The time travel that buildings can engage in, paralleling or independent of programs, is fundamental to me.

Architecture is a performance. It is a cat with nine lives, and those lives start with some nebulous urge. It may stop there, it may develop into the beginnings of a project, or it may develop into a completed project. Even if it is not built, it has a life. We do our best to play out the lives that are latent, awaiting construction, and let that become subject, rather than only the realized building becoming the subject. Then, the next idea you build. It has a life, and you talk about it afterward, you give a lecture, you write a book—those are lives, they are all part of the performance. The reality, though, is the building riding out the ages.

Each of the nine lives is significant. My lectures about architecture are performances. They aren't about my buildings. Buildings are about themselves. So, in a way, this book is a vast disclaimer. When you go to the Louvre, why is there a tour group in a frenzy around the *Mona Lisa*, listening to the guide talk about it, figuring out the right angle for their videos or photographs so they won't see their reflection in the protective Lexan? What is it that Leonardo instilled in the *Mona Lisa*? It has nothing to do with what the guide says, or what the photographs look like later. It is its intangible quality that has created the frenzy. Because we have seen its likeness so often, it's hard to really see it, even when we are standing there in front of it.

When I'm at the Louvre, I beeline to the *Mona Lisa*; rather than look at it, I watch the behaviors associated with it. And of course, the *Mona Lisa* is moving me, mystically and unconsciously, as I watch the performance. This aspect of performance has much to do with architecture. The cat's nine lives that accrue around the process of making and experiencing a particular architecture are fundamental to it. But where is its deepest reality?

If we think about the performance aspect of architecture, we think of it not only as an actor but as a stage. That is something that I am aware of and act on: the building is not simply an artifact; it is a stage. In many of my buildings people physically engage them as a "ride," but there isn't a single way of moving through, there isn't a single way of encountering. It is the process of encounter that creates the building for each person. There is a physical stage and a conceptual stage—the latter made of vapor, not hard architecture.

A building has as many lives as encounters: not only is a new building created as each person comes to it; each time one comes to it one creates yet another building. During a single trip a person may create more than one building. It's like walking through the wall at the Dance Facility and being open to possibility, to the potential of choreography. Of the nine lives, for me, that is the crucial life: the life of encounter with the constructed thing.

Choreography most often suggests the ordering of the body in space and the recording of it—a repeatable formal exercise. In that sense it is a dangerous word, a loaded word. But choreography can also be thought of, in a John Cage sense, as the recognition of a behavior in the world and seeing that behavior differently, of creating a datum or frame to understand the behavior, not out of habit but in the present moment. Architecture can be that datum or frame. It can have that kind of choreographic impulse.

This indeterminacy is more interesting to me than any kind of locked-in choreography. Even though there is an indeterminate aspect to any work of art that is repeatedly interpreted, at a deeper level, indeterminacy can be a strategy rather than a response. In architecture, one can organize processional routes internally and externally, and imagine the body occupying those spaces, in somewhat expected ways, but it never turns out that way. An open-ended narrative falls into step with the open-ended choreographic intention. In my work, possibilities are provided for people to take advantage of in different ways. Encounters with buildings invite the discovery of a personal procession, the creation of a personal pattern of experience.

Indeterminacy is one end, the ongoing end, but it's not a matter simply of creating or accommodating patterns that are open-ended. Recognizing patterns is critical to my process—understanding that individual patterns of encounter are often continuations of patterns that preexist. My response to these patterns results in a matrix of intersections and trajectories, a loosely organized three-dimensional spatial matrix that isn't prescriptive—you don't have to follow it; you can short circuit it. The matrix isn't prescriptive because it isn't just physical. It is a conceptual field that includes a physical component.

I like to think of my buildings as pinball machines, advancing the participant unexpectedly from one possibility to the next, in the context of a program that has been dealt with pragmatically, but not perfunctorily. It is never "here's the front door, here's the back door, here's the most efficient route in between." My work isn't about that. It is about the possibilities of personal journeys—the trajectories that you don't take, inner journeys. If the building is successful there is an intuitive connection to the possible. It is living, open-ended choreography in an open-ended narrative.

So, a "narrative" is not a recitation; it is an invitation to participate—a story-telling that involves the listener in the creation of the story. Architects can invent any story, there is no one out there to say the story is right or wrong. Still, architects have to satisfy the program, the practical aspects—the building has to work. But there is the timeless responsibility that transcends program because programs change—they are ephemeral.

Architects are double agents in an ongoing balancing act, balancing inner and outer worlds. Much of the discussions that surround the making of a building are about ephemera. To ignore the ephemera is an abnegation of responsibility. But to ignore the inner world, to brush over content, and give ephemera priority leaves the essential power of architecture unexplored.

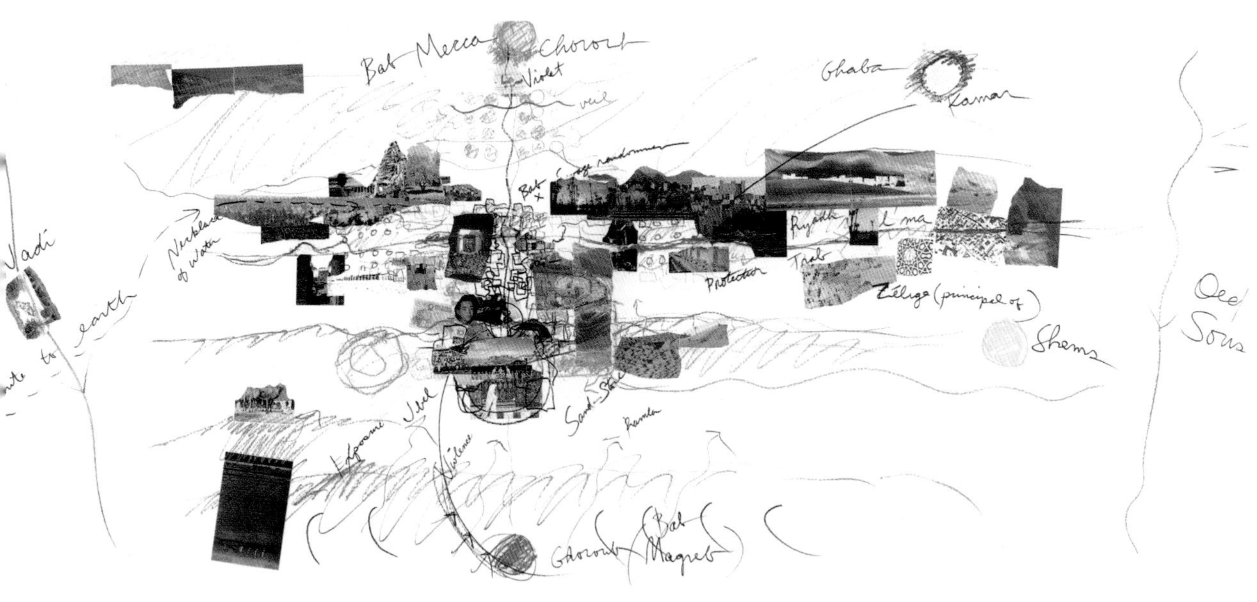

arley-davidson
brembo

Inner Life

In the late 1950s, as an engineering student at the University of New Mexico, I was playing out my studies, successfully, albeit aimlessly—the only exciting part was summer jobs in the aircraft industry and becoming enamored of its technology and the exotica of jet aircraft materials. Then, by chance, or I should say, by destiny, I landed in an engineering drawing course taught by a young architect. Meeting him turned out to be a pivotal point in my life. Without any architectural proselytizing, he ignited some latent flame within me. He projected an enthusiasm that showed me that it was possible for work to be life, not merely a job. I switched to architecture, understanding through him that I had a previously unimagined mission. That encounter was with Don Schlegel. It reinforced my reliance on, and trust in, an inner truth—to be always true to an inner life. This has made all the difference in understanding the necessity even to walk away from uninspiring projects and to always choose the option of adventure. Architecture is a ride—an intellectual and physical ride—with the adrenalin of a roller coaster and the thrill of a motorcycle on the open road.

Twenty years into my practice, the Rome Prize allowed me to study as a Fellow at the American Academy, extracted from my everyday life and immersed in a new (old) world, amid the strata, where the man-made dissolves through time into a geological blur, where natural landscapes have had order imposed upon them that is subtle and extraordinary, and an ancient presence is always haunting.

The deepest, most lasting thing I brought away was a vision of a kind of time travel. In Rome I found myself exposed, physically and conceptually, to the process of excavation. Ushered into the basement of an apartment building, I discovered the subterranean water of the Tiber flowing over gigantic stones with Latin inscriptions on them. It was the great Sundial Field of Augustus of which the gnomon, the sundial pointer, was an Egyptian obelisk, now in the Piazza Montecitorio. Shuffling through the accretions, I experienced the collapse of time and timelessness so vividly—like a sci-fi movie.

This Roman blurring of geology, landscape, and building has had a profound effect on my approach to architecture and has propelled me to seek the spirit of those layers, to delve into and explore the accreted deep time of every site—even where not so obviously present as in Rome. This curiosity and desire to be immersed in the essence of site continues to be at the heart of my process.

With a primitive video camera, I made a piece on Rome—nonstop, Andy Warhol/Blair Witchesque footage. Anywhere I'd go, I'd take my camera, pastels, and brush pen. I had a mixed-media, complete immersion experience. With daily practice drawing, I learned to trust in the innocence of an encounter and the translation of that encounter into an innocent mark. Capturing essences of this surreal landscape through pastel on paper and through time slices on video, I was able to grasp, within two dimensions, the truth of four dimensions.

Long before the Rome experience, evolving as an architect in New Mexico, I saw highway roadcuts, real and imagined, that diagrammed deep geologic time, capped with the thin layer of human occupation—the magical traces in the American Southwest of the Anasazi, the Mimbres people, the later Tewa, Keres, and Navajo Nations. Living in the West has shown me that we don't have to learn just from Europe. Working in New Mexico, creating a built architecture, you have no choice but to deal with wind direction, the movement of the sun, and the iconic landscape. Working in the Southwest has engendered the self-mandated ethos of environmental responsiveness well before the terms green architecture and sustainability had been coined. The Southwest offers so many examples—like Acoma, as a radical diagram of sustainability on an acropolis, or Pueblo Bonito in Chaco Canyon, a sophisticated twelfth-century urban diagram of living, sustenance, and worship. Learning from these, I haven't come away with stylistic trappings, only fundamental power.

These cumulative experiences have led me to look for deeper continuities when working elsewhere—like the Kolomoki Mound in southwest Georgia, in relation to the Flint RiverQuarium; travels to the ancient Turfan oasis on the far reaches of the Silk Road in Central Asia, in relation to the National Palace Museum in Taiwan; the American industrial landscape in the tough port vernacular of Tacoma, in relation to the Tacoma Art Museum; and the sociopolitical consensus building of First Nations chiefs at the forks in Winnipeg and how their symbolic stones, used in nonviolent dispute resolution, could help inform the design of the Canadian Museum for Human Rights. The power of these geologic and cultural strata collapses in time toward topicality, viscerally connecting to people and the landscapes they inhabit.

My work has always been about creating landscapes—physical and psychological—that invite myriad modes of inhabitation. I like to think of my buildings as processional events, choreographic events; they are an accumulation of perceptual and experiential vantage points. My work is inspired by an immersion—by necessity passionate, intense, and experiential. It is about the importance of private and shared journeys, and about creating glimpses of the present and into hidden aspects of the past, connecting the timeless to time beyond. It is about the vastness of landscape, whether natural or urban, about an acknowledgment of the physicality of the world, and the body and self—concurrent in a moment and in space. It is about an optimistic

predicting of the future. It is not just an architecture about building or sculpture; it is a practice informed by a belief in spirit manifest in the built environment.

Emerging from saturation in place, my team (a band of kindred-spirit charrette animals) and I are equipped with instinctive responses to human and natural forces. Serving both client and the gods of architecture, we have, in affirming place, defined a portable regionalism that we take with us as process anywhere we work.

Deeper connections to site and their manifestation in the making of architecture depend on and derive from a client's program. But we know that the function of buildings changes through the ages. This ephemeral aspect of program has to do with political overlays, cultural norms, and evolutionary changes. Tremendous reversals of function are a part of the possibility. Because of this, any piece of architecture must have a life of its own, independent of program, yet fully expressive of it. When a building becomes only program-driven and is merely a functional diagram without the admixture of spirit, it becomes a body without a soul.

In my work, paralleling the translation of the client's program requirements, is the inhabitation of site and the development of a preliminary understanding of what the building may be. It is a kind of DNA encoding that begins with cryptic, anticipatory drawings and continues with the assembly of annotated collages in which the poetic,

physical, and cultural issues of site are diagrammed. It is a process through which the essence of place is derived. This kind of mixed-media saturation is something I have always done. The collages are essential to exploring a project with my team and

having them live it with me. They constitute a critical starting point in the collective process. This leads to what I consider my most significant medium: the clay model. Compared to sketches, the models are very real; they *are* the building. The gestural imperative of making a clay model is like drawing, is as fluid as a drawing. This hands-on process, in amazing and unexpected ways, flows into the realm of digital collage. It's so important to me that the tactile physical process is not overwhelmed by the digital—they seamlessly become one, the nineteenth century merges with the twenty-first.

Receiving the iconic American Institute of Architects Gold Medal, the aura of which carries the aspirations, achievements, and spirit of those previously recognized, was such a phenomenal, momentous, and humbling event. That recognition speaks to me as a validation of my life in architecture; as an acknowledgment that has nothing, in a sense, to do with specific work.

Coinciding with the Gold Medal was the next realm of exploration—Asia, and the establishment of my Taipei studio. The cultural time, geological time and non-linear, episodic space of China is similar to Rome's in its depth of history—from the Shang bronze masterpieces, to the Terracotta Warriors in Xian of the Qin Dynasty, to the Northern Song Dynasty hand scrolls. The commission for the National Palace Museum in Chiayi was a milepost, an Asian geographic dislocation. I embarked on a reapplication of the immersive process to a new body of experience charged with potential.

In my travels—above the ground, on the ground, and underwater—I see endless site-specific richness to interpret, differentiate, and celebrate. Like my scuba diving, this adventure into Asia is a new kind of plunge. Continuing to live and work in New Mexico, 65 years after my architectural epiphany, my world has expanded, but we continue the dance of Architecture between the topical and the timeless.

THE WORLD
POLITICAL
ARCTIC OCEAN
PACIFIC OCEAN
NORTH ATLANTIC OCEAN
SOUTH ATLANTIC OCEAN
RUSSIA
U.S.A.
CANADA
GREENLAND (KALAALLIT NUNAAT)
ICELAND
IRELAND
PORTUGAL
MOROCCO
MAURITANIA
CAPE VERDE
SENEGAL
SIERRA LEONE
LIBERIA
MEXICO
CUBA
THE BAHAMAS
HAITI
DOMINICAN REPUBLIC
JAMAICA
HONDURAS
GUATEMALA
EL SALVADOR
NICARAGUA
COSTA RICA
PANAMA
VENEZUELA
COLOMBIA
ECUADOR
PERU
BRAZIL
BOLIVIA
PARAGUAY
URUGUAY
ARGENTINA
CHILE
KIRIBATI
SAMOA
TONGA
FIJI
COOK ISLANDS
FRENCH POLYNESIA
PITCAIRN ISLANDS
NEW ZEALAND
BERING SEA
GULF OF ALASKA
HUDSON BAY
BAFFIN BAY
LABRADOR SEA
GULF OF MEXICO
CARIBBEAN SEA
SARGASSO SEA
WEDDELL SEA
Maps International
Cartographic excellence from Lovell Johns
VAN DER GRINTEN PROJECTION

RUSSIA
SIBERIA
KAZAKHSTAN
MONGOLIA
GOBI DESERT
CHINA
XIZANG ZIZHIQU (TIBET)
INDIA
PAKISTAN
AFGHANISTAN
IRAN
IRAQ
SAUDI ARABIA
YEMEN
OMAN
TURKEY
GEORGIA
UZBEKISTAN
TURKMENISTAN
KYRGYZSTAN
TAJIKISTAN
EGYPT
LIBYA
TUNISIA
SUDAN
SOUTH SUDAN
CHAD
NIGER
NIGERIA
CAMEROON
CENTRAL AFRICAN REPUBLIC
DEMOCRATIC REPUBLIC OF THE CONGO
CONGO
GABON
ETHIOPIA
SOMALIA
KENYA
UGANDA
TANZANIA
ANGOLA
ZAMBIA
MALAWI
MOZAMBIQUE
ZIMBABWE
BOTSWANA
NAMIBIA
SOUTH AFRICA
LESOTHO
SWAZILAND
MADAGASCAR
COMOROS
SEYCHELLES
MAURITIUS
NORWAY
SWEDEN
FINLAND
DENMARK
POLAND
BELARUS
UKRAINE
ROMANIA
HUNGARY
CZECHIA
BULGARIA
ALBANIA
CYPRUS
SYRIA
LEBANON
ISRAEL
JAPAN
NORTH KOREA
SOUTH KOREA
MYANMAR (BURMA)
THAILAND
LAOS
VIETNAM
CAMBODIA
MALAYSIA
SINGAPORE
INDONESIA
PHILIPPINES
SRI LANKA
MALDIVES
BANGLADESH
NEPAL
AUSTRALIA
NEW ZEALAND
PAPUA NEW GUINEA
SOLOMON ISLANDS
VANUATU
NEW CALEDONIA
FEDERATED STATES OF MICRONESIA
MARSHALL ISLANDS
NORTHERN MARIANA ISLANDS
PALAU
NAURU
KIRIBATI
EAST TIMOR
U.S.A.
ALASKA
BROOKS RANGE
ALASKA RANGE
PACIFIC OCEAN
INDIAN OCEAN
ARCTIC OCEAN
BARENTS SEA
KARA SEA
LAPTEV SEA
EAST SIBERIAN SEA
CHUKCHI SEA
BERING SEA
SEA OF OKHOTSK
SEA OF JAPAN (EAST SEA)
EAST CHINA SEA
SOUTH CHINA SEA
PHILIPPINE SEA
ARABIAN SEA
BAY OF BENGAL
ANDAMAN SEA
CORAL SEA
ARAFURA SEA
TIMOR SEA
TASMAN SEA
BLACK SEA
CASPIAN SEA
MEDITERRANEAN SEA
RED SEA
MICRONESIA
MELANESIA
BRITISH INDIAN OCEAN TERRITORY
FRENCH SOUTHERN AND ANTARCTIC LANDS
GREAT SANDY DESERT
GIBSON DESERT
GREAT VICTORIA DESERT
Great Australian Bight
Taymyr Peninsula
Kamchatka Peninsula
Novaya Zemlya
Franz Josef Land
Svalbard
Severnaya Zemlya
Novosibirskiye Ostrova (New Siberian Islands)
Aleutian Islands
Stanovoy Range
Chersky Range
Verkhoyansk Range
Koryak Range
Yablonovyy Range
Chukot Range
ANTARCTICA
Enderby Land
Queen Maud Land
MOSCOW
BEIJING
TOKYO
Shanghai
DELHI
Mumbai
Karachi
Kolkata
DHAKA
BANGKOK
MANILA
JAKARTA
KUALA LUMPUR
SINGAPORE
Ho Chi Minh
HANOI
CAIRO
KHARTOUM
RIYADH
TEHRAN
BAGHDAD
KABUL
TASHKENT
ANKARA
DAMASCUS
BEIRUT
ADDIS ABABA
NAIROBI
MOGADISHU
KAMPALA
KINSHASA
LUANDA
HARARE
MAPUTO
CAPE TOWN
Port Elizabeth
Chennai
Bengaluru
Colombo
Harbin
Tianjin
Chongqing
Hong Kong
Shenzhen
Perth
Adelaide
Newcastle
Brisbane
Tasmania
North Island
South Island

ANTOINE PREDOCK
65 YEARS OF ARCHITECTURE

BEGINNINGS

BORN IN THE OZARKS
MOTHER, FATHER, SISTER SALLY

Poetic Mom Ruth.
Pragmatic Dad Tony.

A kid during WWII. A baseball fanatic, with Stan Musial of the St. Louis Cardinals as my hero. Learning to cuss, and drag racing my hot rod Plymouth in high school. My life on two wheels begins. Couldn't wait to graduate and escape Missouri.

BRILLIANT SISTER SALLY—SARAH PREDOCK BURKE-LUPINSKI PROFESSOR EMERITA OF MODERN LANGUAGES AND LITERATURES AT TRINITY UNIVERITY IN SAN ANTONIO, TEXAS, GRADUATED MAGNA CUM LAUDE FROM THE UNIVERSITY OF TEXAS AT AUSTIN IN 1962 WITH A BACHELOR'S DEGREE IN RUSSIAN AND ENGLISH. IN 1966, DR. BURKE-LUPINSKI RECEIVED A WOODROW WILSON DISSERTATION FELLOWSHIP, AND THAT SAME YEAR SHE EARNED HER PH.D. IN RUSSIAN LITERATURE AND LINGUISTICS FROM THE UNIVERSITY OF TEXAS.

AFTER SHORT STINTS AT OTHER UNIVERSITIES, DR. BURKE-LUPINSKI JOINED THE DEPARTMENT OF MODERN LANGUAGES AT TRINITY UNIVERSITY IN 1973, WHERE SHE TAUGHT RUSSIAN LANGUAGE, LITERATURE, ART, AND CULTURE. SHE WAS ESPECIALLY INTERESTED IN LITERATURE AND ART OF THE SILVER AGE OF RUSSIAN CULTURE FROM THE LATE 19TH CENTURY TO THE 1930S AND SERVED FOR MANY YEARS AS A CO-DIRECTOR OF THE INSTITUTE OF MODERN RUSSIAN CULTURE AT TRINITY UNIVERSITY.

Highway 66 in 1946

MY HOMETOWN—LEBANON, MO

HOUSE WHERE I GREW UP IN FERGUSON, MO

TWA FLIGHTS TO ARIZONA TO SPEND SUMMERS WITH AUNT ADALINE AND UNCLE ELLIOT

ENGINEERING FALSE START

UNIVERSITY OF NEW MEXICO 1954 MECHANICAL ENGINEERING
ALBUQUERQUE, NEW MEXICO

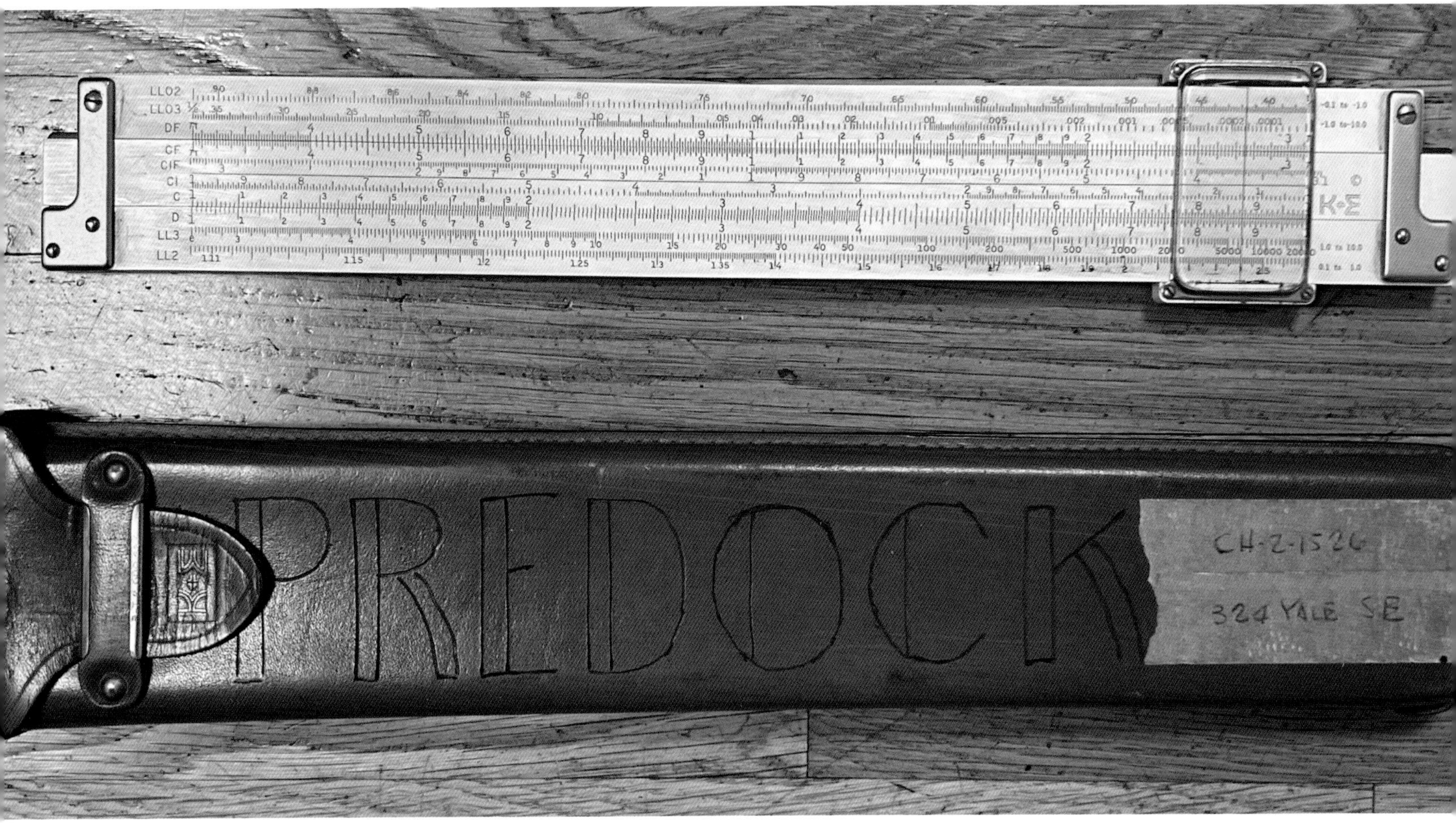

With Highway 66 and desert summers in my blood, I drove my 1940s Plymouth to Albuquerque and the University of New Mexico to begin Engineering studies mandated by my father. I learned enough engineering that my dad got me a summer job at McDonnell Aircraft, doing weight and balance calculations for jet fighters—precursors of the iconic F-4. That was far more rewarding than any engineering courses—the howl of jet engines, the smell of jet fuel, the technological exotica of the materials, afterburners blasting at takeoff were all adrenaline for a kid who had worked on the other side of Lambert Field during high school, gassing and maintaining private aircraft, and learning to fly with free lessons from an alcoholic flight instructor in a Piper J-3 Cub. Meanwhile, at the University, I moved through all the engineering courses—integral and differential calculus, physics, chemistry—quite successfully, but uninspired.

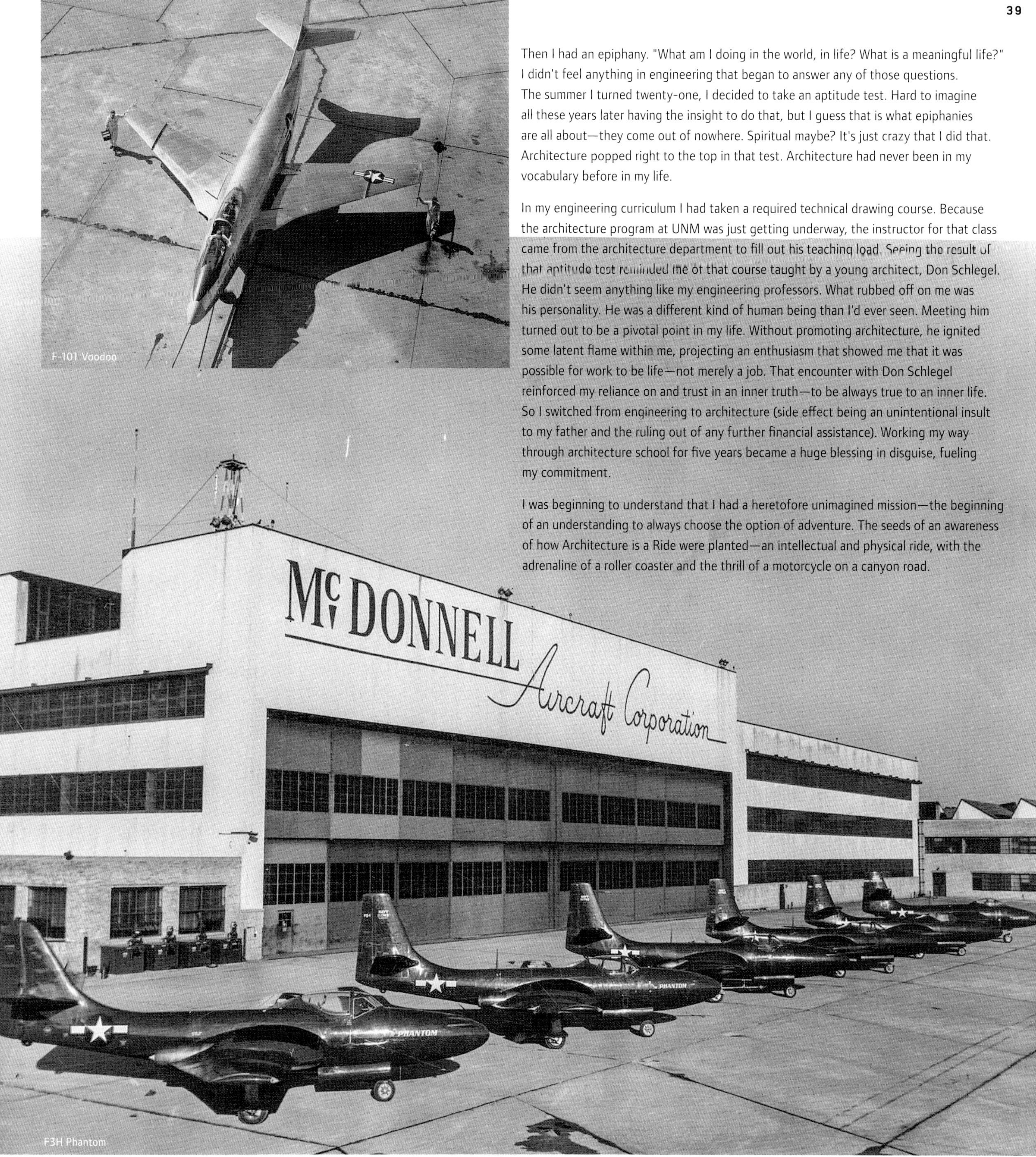

F-101 Voodoo

F3H Phantom

Then I had an epiphany. "What am I doing in the world, in life? What is a meaningful life?" I didn't feel anything in engineering that began to answer any of those questions. The summer I turned twenty-one, I decided to take an aptitude test. Hard to imagine all these years later having the insight to do that, but I guess that is what epiphanies are all about—they come out of nowhere. Spiritual maybe? It's just crazy that I did that. Architecture popped right to the top in that test. Architecture had never been in my vocabulary before in my life.

In my engineering curriculum I had taken a required technical drawing course. Because the architecture program at UNM was just getting underway, the instructor for that class came from the architecture department to fill out his teaching load. Seeing the result of that aptitude test reminded me of that course taught by a young architect, Don Schlegel. He didn't seem anything like my engineering professors. What rubbed off on me was his personality. He was a different kind of human being than I'd ever seen. Meeting him turned out to be a pivotal point in my life. Without promoting architecture, he ignited some latent flame within me, projecting an enthusiasm that showed me that it was possible for work to be life—not merely a job. That encounter with Don Schlegel reinforced my reliance on and trust in an inner truth—to be always true to an inner life. So I switched from engineering to architecture (side effect being an unintentional insult to my father and the ruling out of any further financial assistance). Working my way through architecture school for five years became a huge blessing in disguise, fueling my commitment.

I was beginning to understand that I had a heretofore unimagined mission—the beginning of an understanding to always choose the option of adventure. The seeds of an awareness of how Architecture is a Ride were planted—an intellectual and physical ride, with the adrenaline of a roller coaster and the thrill of a motorcycle on a canyon road.

LIFE BEGINS IN ARCHITECTURE AND ART

UNIVERSITY OF NEW MEXICO 1957
ALBUQUERQUE, NEW MEXICO

I found home, finally, at the age of 21.

I knew nothing about architecture—zero. I thought "Architect, oh like a doctor or a lawyer, there's some prestige in that. That sounds pretty good." What turned up second to architecture as a career, was being a teacher, in the aptitude test. Those two things kind of stopped me in my tracks and I immediately enrolled in architecture at the University of New Mexico. I was 21 and had enough hours already to probably have some kind of BA in something. I landed in my first architectural design class back at UNM, taught by Don Schlegel of all people! It felt so comfortable connecting with him again—so natural, everything about it. It was nothing like engineering. It was deeply fulfilling, I wouldn't have been able to articulate it at that time, but looking back it was transformational.

DON SCHLEGEL WHEN FRANK LLOYD WRIGHT VISITED UNM IN THE '50s... I MET WRIGHT AT TALIESIN WEST SHORTLY BEFORE HIS DEATH—HE WAS GRACIOUS AND WELCOMING, AND I STUMBLED FOR WORDS.

PROJECTS AT UNM WHILE WORKING MY FULL-TIME EMPLOYMENT SCHEDULE AROUND MY COURSES.

The University of New Mexico, at the time I was there, had a very strong art department. Because I came from engineering, I had completed all of my technical courses—far beyond those normally required in the architectural curriculum. So I had an open slate for electives. I took electives in literature, poetry in particular, music appreciation and, above all, art classes one after the other—painting, sculpture, drawing, watercolor—with real masters that maybe weren't on the map yet but would be. One of my painting teachers was Elaine de Kooning, Willem de Kooning's wife—a strong painter making her way under his shadow. Abstract expressionism, action painting, was in the air. I also had Bay Area devotees of Clifford Still, like Walt Kuhlman, as instructors. Richard Diebenkorn had just completed his master's degree at UNM, and his paintings were in the halls; the sensuality and physicality of oil painting was so powerful for me. We even had field trips to the richly colored clay strata of La Bajada to collect material to use as pigment for making our own paint (which ended up on big canvases, like the one shown above).

I was in the midst of intertwining love affairs with art and architecture and at one point I really felt I could go either way with my life. They were both shockingly wonderful for a kid from the Ozarks, and created an unimagined new world for me. I went through the UNM architectural design courses like they were second nature, but painting was a seductive path also. In my fourth year of design studios I received a scholarship from the AIA. Don Schlegel had been my mentor all along. Just before my fifth year he took me aside and said, "We can't teach you any more here. You need to leave." He aimed me toward Penn, Harvard, Columbia, and the University of North Carolina, which was a hot spot at that time. I got accepted to all of them.

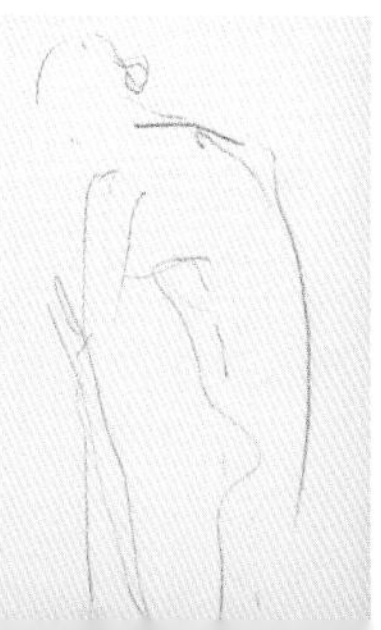

COLUMBIA UNIVERSITY SCHOOL OF ARCHITECTURE AND NEW YORK CITY

COLUMBIA UNIVERSITY 1961/63

I was at a Robert Frost–like fork in the road.
I could have chosen artist or architect.
(But true architects are artists.)

My painting life continued, but only around the edges—and I studied sculpture at Columbia with Peter Agostini.

Columbia was my choice. I had never been east of the Mississippi and I landed in a dream world of urban excitement and art. Architecture at Columbia was a graduate program. Everybody in my class had an undergraduate degree, but I was accepted without one—I was in graduate school without being a graduate, I think that shocked my classmates. During all my time at UNM, four solid years I was there, I worked 40-hour weeks because my father no longer supported my education. At first, I gassed airplanes, and then I got a job with an architect. I was gifted the opportunity to work with a master draftsman to learn drafting, as we called it then. I learned to be a hardcore doer. Not just a thinker. I was so honored to be working with John Hawkins. It was mind-blowing that I was doing complete buildings when I was a junior in architecture. Warehouse buildings, and office buildings, doing working drawings for them. Not flunky stuff, but serious stuff, enabled by my engineering skills. Because this firm didn't think much about the art of architecture, I worked on projects that were kind of modern—with some conscience about them, but nothing deep. My drawing/ technical abilities, learned while studying and working in Albuquerque, invaluably set the stage for me at Columbia. Those Ivy Leaguers didn't scare me at all.

I learned to be a hardcore doer.
Not just a thinker/talker.

MY CLASSMATE STEVE AND PROFESSIONAL PRACTICE CRITIC THOMAS CREIGHTON. DISCOVERING D'ARCY THOMPSON...

Riverside Church

116 and Broadway

I aced Columbia in every way, and loved it. I really had to be on my toes intellectually and critically compared to UNM, and I had fantastic instruction—James Marston Fitch, the Wrightian Harwell Hamilton Harris, Frank Schlesinger, and the landscape architect Arthur E. Bye. Minoring in landscape architecture, I received the William Alciphron Boring Medal for landscape architecture. Then on graduation, a handful of us became William Kinne Fellows—we were given stipends to do personal projects anywhere we wanted. Of course, we all flocked to Europe. I got my degree, a Bachelor of Architecture, because I didn't have the underlying degree. The other guys got Master's.

Living in New York City I was exposed to the avant-garde, as was my girlfriend Jennifer Masley. Her grounding was in ballet—the Metropolitan Opera ballet master, Antony Tudor, pulled her out of Julliard to join the Met Ballet Company. But she was also into literature and poetry. That's how we met, in a poetry class at UNM. Her strong connection to New York was one of the reasons why I chose Columbia. She had a small apartment with another dancer from the Met and a Julliard cello student, who later became the famed Martha Gerschefski, along. That was quite a mix of exchanges, with those artists from other fields. All of this was overlaid on the city, a giant performance art event unto itself.

AND AVERY HALL FOR MY CLASSES AND THE LEGENDARY AVERY ARCHITECTURE LIBRARY

MY NEW YORK PAINTING STUDIO

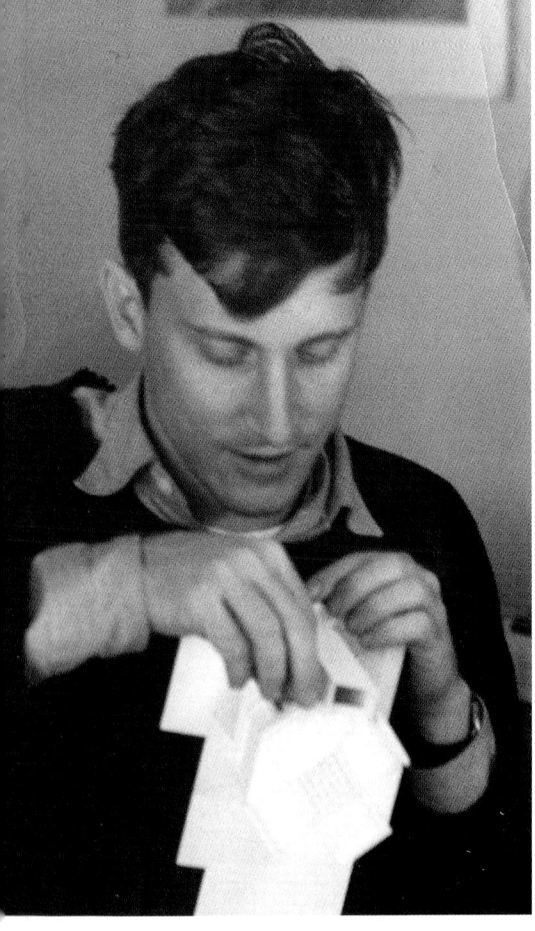

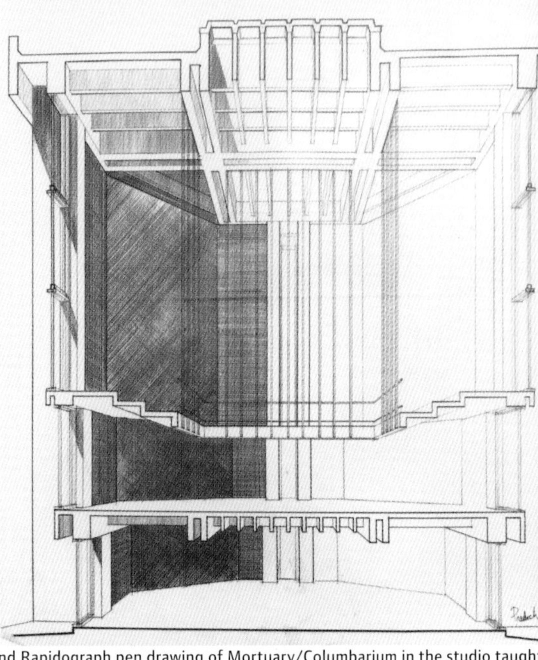

Judson Church addition model and sketches in Frank Schlesinger's studio—and Rapidograph pen drawing of Mortuary/Columbarium in the studio taught

While at Columbia I kept working—my scholarship money wasn't enough. I got a job with I.M. Pei in his model shop and worked on some high profile projects—the Everson Museum, Tel Aviv Urban Design Project, and Mile High Center, Denver. The model shop, supervised by Paul Crocker, was very high tech for the time—with German goldsmiths (literally) working with materials and techniques I had never experienced. From my UNM studies I knew that model building was everything in architecture, which my experience with Pei emphatically confirmed.

THE '60s IN NEW YORK SKETCHING ALL AROUND THE CITY—THE VIEW OF THE BATTERY FROM THE STATEN ISLAND FERRY, THE GEORGE WASHINGTON BRIDGE FROM RIVERSIDE PARK, THE VERRAZANO-NARROWS BRIDGE UNDER CONSTRUCTION...

critic Harwell Hamilton Harris—inspired by Evelyn Waugh's *The Loved One*.

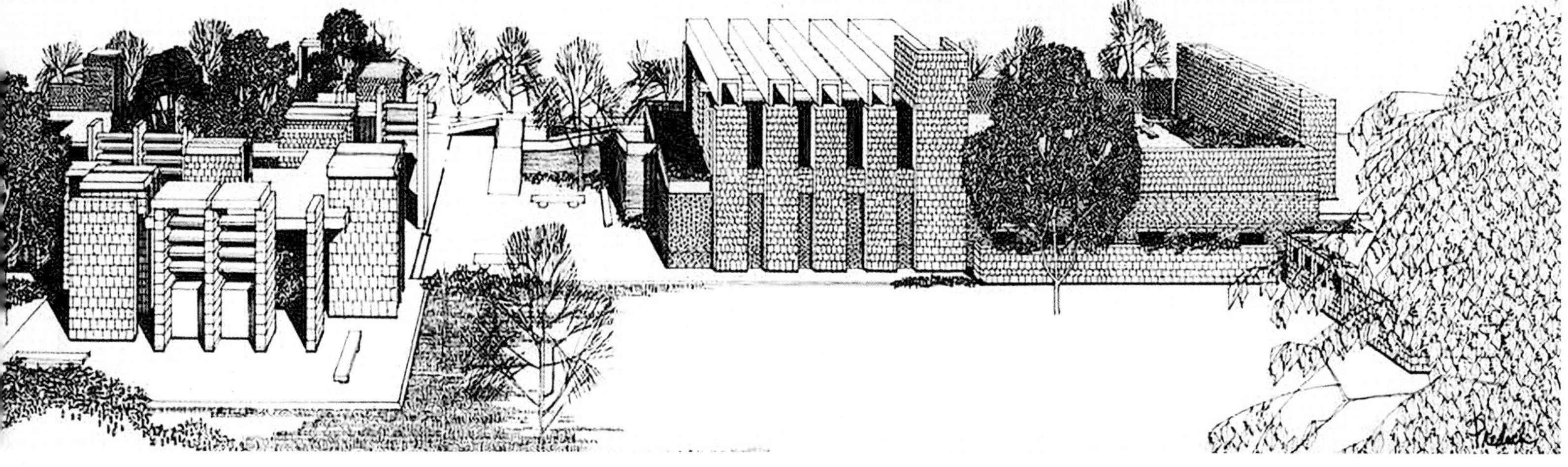

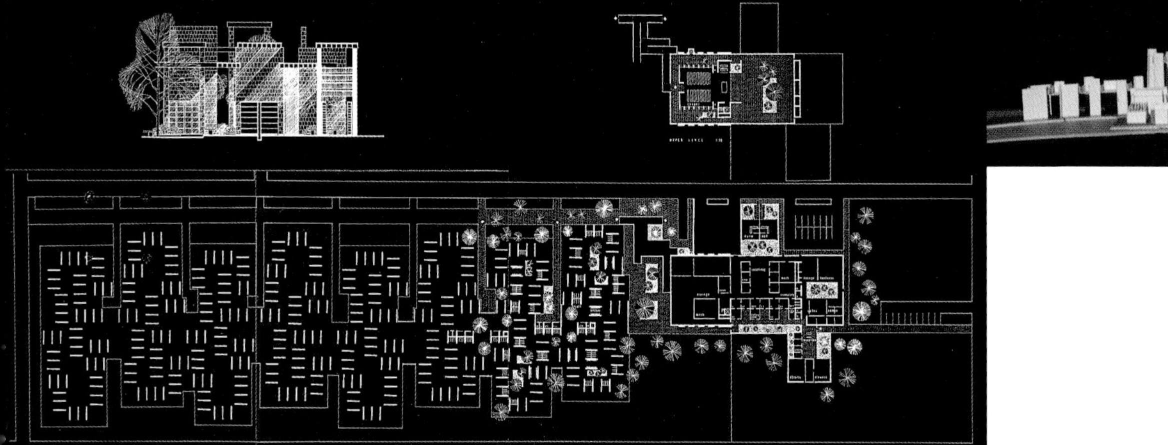

THE WORLD OF THEATER AND DANCE OPENED TO ME—SAMUEL BECKETT, BERTOLT BRECHT, THE METROPOLITAN OPERA BALLET COMPANY MASTER ANTONY TUDOR, MERCE CUNNINGHAM, RUDOLF NUREYEV, THE LIVING THEATER OF BECK AND MALINA... SEEING THE YOUNG ACTOR JAMES EARL JONES ON STAGE... HEARING "A HARD RAIN'S A-GONNA FALL" DRIFTING OUT OF THE RADIO, BOB DYLAN JOINED MY PANTHEON OF HEROES, FOLLOWED THROUGH THE YEARS BY ANNA HALPRIN, FEDERICO GARCIA LORCA, FRANCESCO BORROMINI, ISABEL ALLENDE, JORGE LUIS BORGES AND, OF COURSE, FRANK LLOYD WRIGHT.

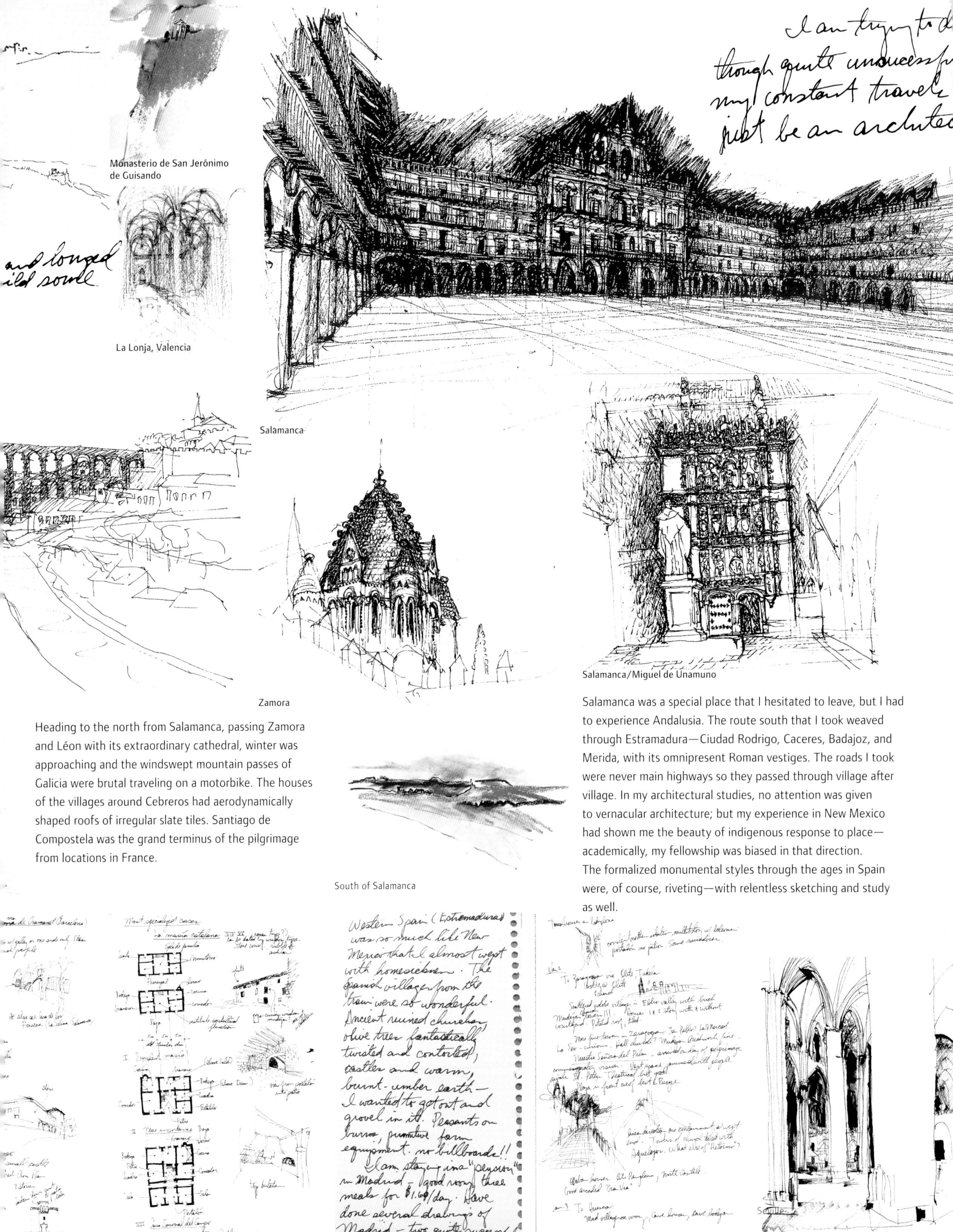

Monasterio de San Jerônimo de Guisando

La Lonja, Valencia

Salamanca

Zamora

Salamanca/Miguel de Unamuno

South of Salamanca

Seville

Heading to the north from Salamanca, passing Zamora and Léon with its extraordinary cathedral, winter was approaching and the windswept mountain passes of Galicia were brutal traveling on a motorbike. The houses of the villages around Cebreros had aerodynamically shaped roofs of irregular slate tiles. Santiago de Compostela was the grand terminus of the pilgrimage from locations in France.

Salamanca was a special place that I hesitated to leave, but I had to experience Andalusia. The route south that I took weaved through Estramadura—Ciudad Rodrigo, Caceres, Badajoz, and Merida, with its omnipresent Roman vestiges. The roads I took were never main highways so they passed through village after village. In my architectural studies, no attention was given to vernacular architecture; but my experience in New Mexico had shown me the beauty of indigenous response to place—academically, my fellowship was biased in that direction. The formalized monumental styles through the ages in Spain were, of course, riveting—with relentless sketching and study as well.

La Granja

Toledo

Trujillo

Segovia

With months ahead of me on Fellowship, my first base was Madrid, with time spent at architecture libraries, the Prado, and endless city explorations. Side trips from Madrid to Toledo and Segovia, passing Ávila on my way to Salamanca, where I settled in for a couple of months. Salamanca had the dramatic Plaza Mayor, along with a beautifully preserved Roman Bridge and the haunting Romanesque Catedral Vieja. Not far from the Portuguese border, it provided access to Extremadura and the city of Trujillo. This was the time of Franco, and my local student roommates at the boarding house where I stayed cautioned me about how I spoke in public, because the Guardia Civil was omnipresent. Another aspect of Franco's iron hand was that the country was frozen economically—there was little modern construction, so I experienced the purity of untouched villages and landscapes.

Plaza Mayor, Madrid

Ayuntamiento

Segovia

Guadarrama Mountains

El Prado, Madrid

Segovia

Sidewalk café sketches

Segovia

Aragon

Atlantic crossing on the Danish freighter *Agnette Torm*

WILLIAM KINNE FELLOWSHIP— COLUMBIA UNIVERSITY SCHOOL OF ARCHITECTURE

EUROPE 1962/63

Immediately after graduating from Columbia with my Kinne Fellowship, I booked passage on a freighter from Brooklyn to Lisbon. With my Fellowship stipend I could have flown to Europe, but there was something about experiencing the drama of the slow motion freighter passage where the sheer distance of intercontinental travel was hard to ignore. The ship was the *Agnette Torm* under Danish registry. On the 4th of July, 1962, we sailed from the Brooklyn docks, paralleling the Long Island coast with endless fireworks displays. The open Atlantic had so many different aspects—the variations of the surface, ranging from a quiet lake to a raging torrent, an occasional bird in flight in the middle of the ocean...

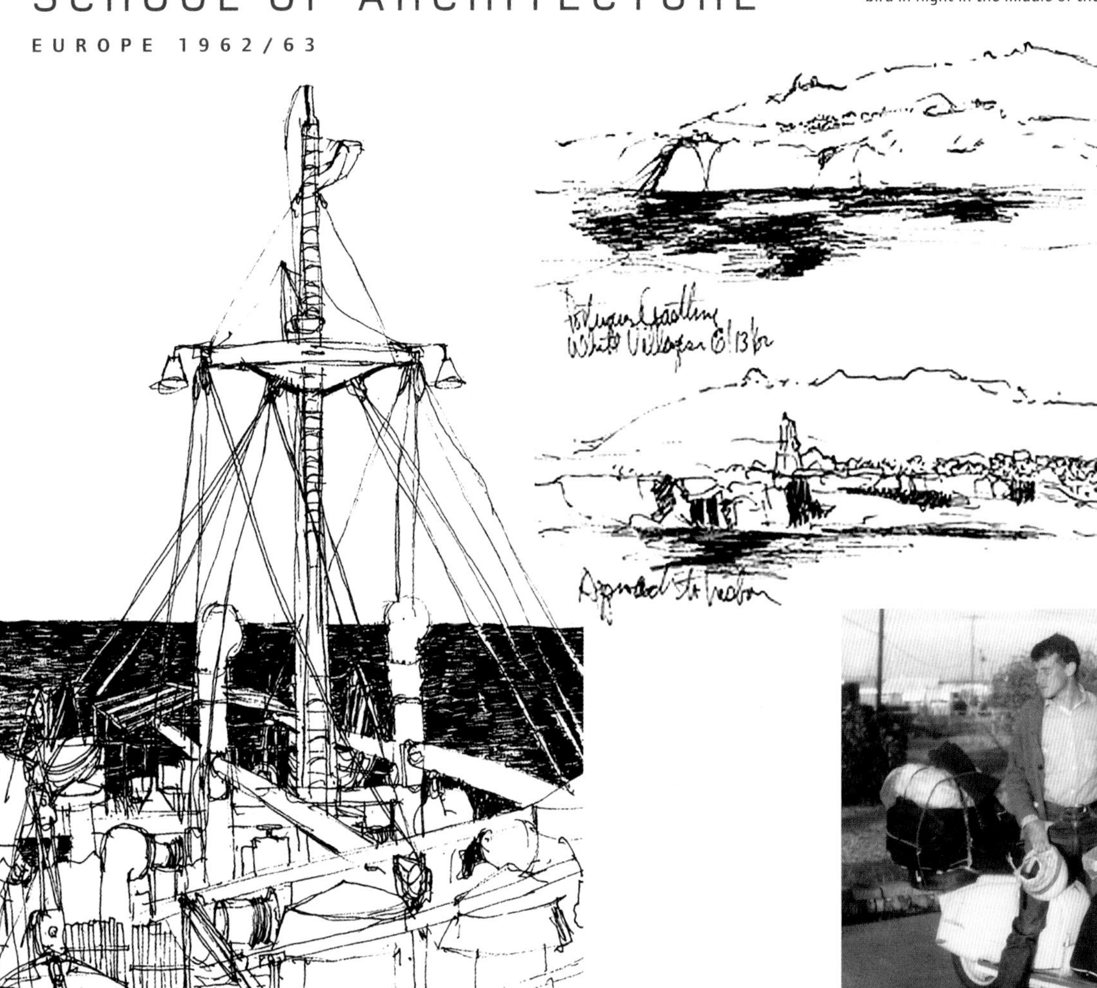

Arriving in Lisbon, with its wonderful urban elevator, then quickly across Spain by train to the Lambretta factory in Genoa.

The powerful harbor of Genoa with the legendary lighthouse and, most importantly for me, the Lambretta factory—picked up my TV-175 motorbike and headed across the Alps to Paris.

The Atlantic crossing was magnificent. The vast loneliness of the ocean is rivaled only by certain remote areas of New Mexico. I sunbathed every day and sketched the ship. Saw sharks, porpoises, giant turtles. The sea has an infinite number of moods. The Danish food was excellent - smorgasbord and Danish beer every day. I could roam around the ship at my pleasure. The first sight of Europe

were the mountains of Portugal. They were very hazy for a long time then I could make out white villages ranging up and down the mountainsides. I could see the ruins of a Moorish castle atop one of the peaks. ↓

The approach into the Lisbon harbor was fantastic. The ship entered the mouth of the Rio Tejo from the

HENRY MILLER WASN'T FAMOUS FOR BEING A MEDITERRANEAN TRAVEL WRITER, BUT MAYBE HE SHOULD HAVE BEEN.

THE COLOSSUS OF MAROUSSI

HENRY MILLER

"Paris is a divine section of eternity."
E. E. Cummings

Notre-Dame

Paris

Chartres

"That city, placed at the junction of two seas and two continents, seemed like a diamond set between two sapphires and two emeralds, to form the most precious stone in a ring of universal empires."
Osman's Dream of Constantinople, 1280

Iconic stops along the way to Paris from Genoa, culminating with the "Mothership"—Chartres Cathedral. Chartres communicated an ineffable deep-time Druid kind of presence beyond its mere liturgical/Christian purpose. I involuntarily fell to my knees and tears came to my eyes.

Notre-Dame, another "Mothership," and the panorama of the architecture of Paris—on to Istanbul, crossing the Alps again to Brindisi, the realm of the venerable Trulli architecture. Took the transport ship with my Lambretta to Piraeus, Port of Athens—passing Delphi, Olympia through the Corinth Canal; then Athens, Thessaloniki and Kavala, arriving in Istanbul.

From Istanbul to Naples on a cargo ferry and after on the Lambretta—Spain via Rome, Florence and the Rivieria with a pause at Sete, then straight to Madrid and the panorama of Spain.

Istanbul

Delphi

Rome Zoo

Rome from St. Peter's Dome

Corinth

Trulli

Acropolis, Athens

Acropolis, Athens

I left Córdoba via Málaga for Granada—and the Alhambra.

"...the Alhambra is a composite of sequential spatial perfection with layers of detail, formidably executed by Moorish master artisans. The Alhambra doesn't have an obvious "front door"…. Rather, there is an immediate sense of the prioritization of non-hierarchically linked spatial sequences with the linkages-cum-chambers—for me, as charged as the "star" spaces they serve. These shadowy transitions to open courts never suggest an overly determined intention about entry, rather a quietly morphing condition in total contrast to the Platonic sequencing of the renaissance palace of Carlos V, which is intrusively embedded in one flank of the Alhambra."

Antoine Predock, *Architects on Architects*, 2002

Alhambra

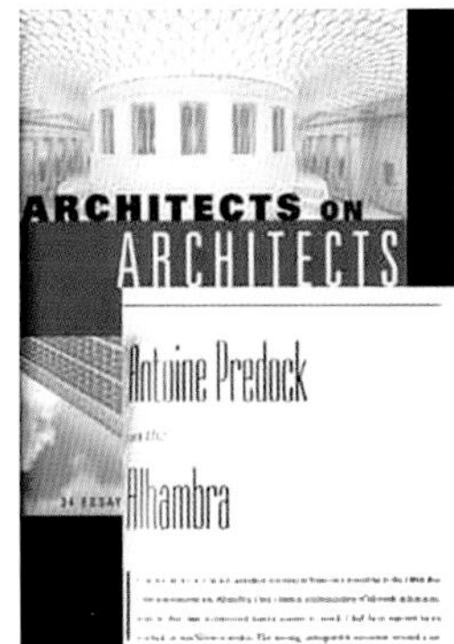

Kind of speechless after visiting that masterpiece, then north to Baeza/Úbeda and then up the coast at Alicante, Benidorm Valencia, Cuenca, then Zaragosa, arriving in Barcelona in Spring of 1963—next, back to the New World.

Barcelona

I had seen hints of Moorish architecture prior to arriving in Seville, but the "fusion" of the ex-minaret La Giralda becoming the bell tower of the Cathedral was a mixed message. From Seville to Córdoba—García Lorca's poetry became even more alive to me—"Sevilla para herir, Córdoba para morir…" The Great Mosque in Córdoba dramatized the concept of Zélige, intense repetition of abstract surface patterning (like Talavera tiles), into three-dimensional space in the forest of compartmentalizing arches.

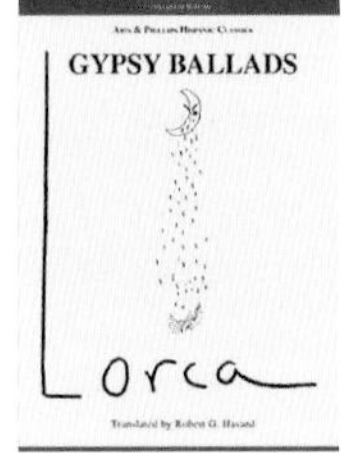

Aragon

Barcelona

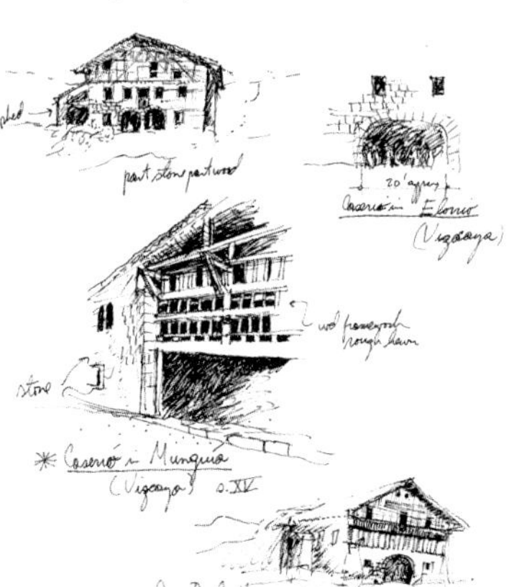

Estremadura

Santiago de Compostela

Santiago de Compostela

Léon

Córdoba

Rio Ebro

El Pardo

Castilla la Vieja

Málaga

Satrustegui

Boarded the cargo/passenger freighter *Satrustegui* in Barcelona to cross the Atlantic—with stops in Tenerife, Canary Islands, La Guaira the Port of Caracas Venezuela, Curacao, Santo Domingo—landing in Veracruz, Mexico, then Orizaba Puebla, Cholula, Oaxca and Mexico City. The Lambretta was scuffed up at that point, but none the less alive and well, taking me north to the border crossing at Reynosa/McAllen. My sister Sally was a graduate student at University of Texas, Austin—and I rested at her apartment. Then from Austin to Albuquerque to get my bearings and make relationships between Spain and this colony of New Mexico after those glorious months in Spain—spending the summer of '63 living in an adobe apartment on the edge of Spanish "Old Town" with its church and plaza.

Santo Domingo

Santuario de Chimayo

MEXICO/NEW MEXICO

1963

Oaxaca, Mitla a Mixteca Site

Monte Albán, Zapotec Site

Teotihuacan

Quarai

Oil Still Life

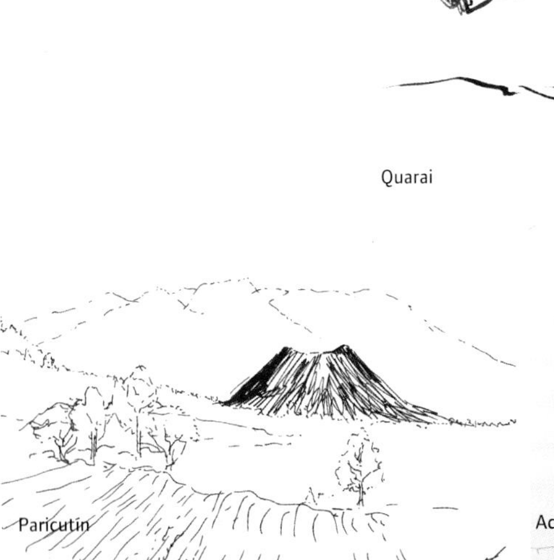
Paricutin

Acoma

Hopi First Mesa

Second Mesa

Chetro Ketl, Chaco Canyon

Las Trampas

Pueblo Bonito, Chaco Canyon

My painter life was rekindled that summer, but I knew by then that I was an architect, so painting stayed around the edges from then on. During that summer of 1963 I resolved to pursue graduate studies and was accepted at Harvard. The Lambretta was still running, so I left Albuquerque for Cambridge. There were no interstate highways then, so I was on Highway 66, then other combinations of routes until I reached the Pennsylvania Turnpike. At the toll booth I was informed that scooters weren't allowed on the Turnpike. I pointed out the top speed on the speedometer (which was in kilometers which the guy obviously didn't notice) and he let me on, continuing to Cambridge, Massachusetts.

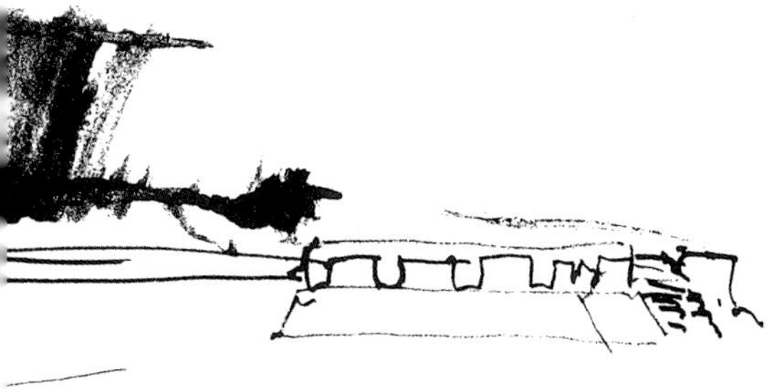

Rio Grande Valley

Shiprock on Highway 666

Pueblo Bonito, Chaco Canyon

Antoine Predock '63
Chaco Canyon

THE WONDERFUL DINÉ NATION

BACK FROM THE EURO ODYSSEY TO A SMALL APARTMENT IN OLD TOWN ALBUQUERQUE WITH FRANCISCO AS NEIGHBOR. PETE, MY LANDLORD, RODE HORSES AND AFTER GETTING TO KNOW EACH OTHER THAT SUMMER, GIFTED ME A HORSE NAMED STREAK. I KEPT STREAK IN AN IMPROVISED CORRAL AND TOOK DAILY RIDES ALONG THE ACEQUIAS. THE I-40 HADN'T BEEN CONSTRUCTED YET SO I COULD FREELY RIDE NORTH ALL THE WAY TO CORRALES. I GOT AWAY WITH THAT FOR A COUPLE OF MONTHS UNTIL THE CITY FINALLY CAUGHT ON THAT I WAS ILLEGALLY KEEPING A HORSE IN THE CITY WHEN THEY SPOTTED THE MANURE PILE... SO I HAD TO RESORT BACK TO THE LAMBRETTA.

HARVARD GRADUATE SCHOOL OF DESIGN (DROP OUT) CAMBRIDGE, MASSACHUSETTS

1963

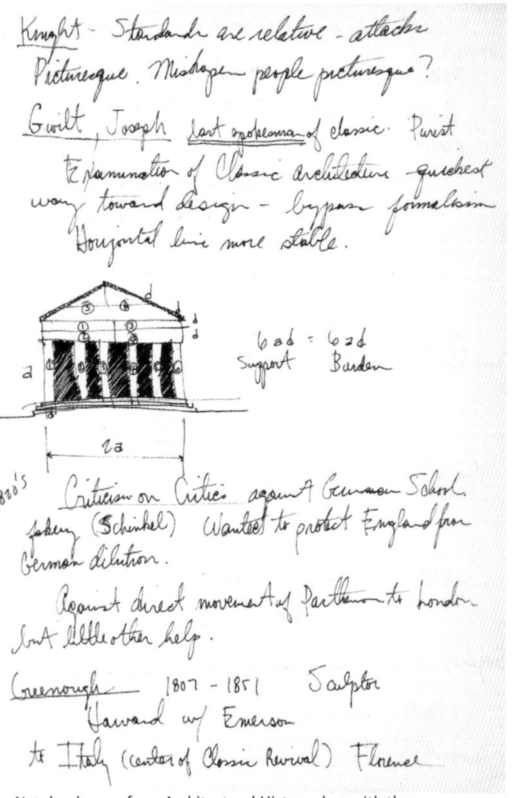
Knight - Standards are relative - attacks
Picturesque. Misshapen people picturesque?
Gwilt, Joseph last spokesman of classic. Purist
Examination of Classic architecture quickest
way toward design - bypass formalism
Horizontal line more stable.

6ad = 6ad
Support Burden
a
2a

1820's Criticism on Critics against German School
[illegible] (Schinkel) Wanted to protect England from
German dilution.
Against direct movement of Parthenon to London
but little other help.
Greenough 1807 - 1851 Sculptor
Harvard w/ Emerson
to Italy (center of Classic Revival) Florence

Notebook page from Architectural History class with the legendary historian Edouard Seckler

Memorial to Miguel de Unamuno, Salamanca, Spain—clay model from studio with Josep Lluís Sert

Charles River

Henry Hobson Richardson

I arrived in Cambridge and stayed in a rooming house, beginning my studio and class work at the Graduate School of Design. The studio that I took, taught by Josep Lluís Sert, was uninspiring, but my housemates—a nurse, a secretary working in Boston, and a mixed bag of students in various areas of study—made up for it. This included a student studying psychedelics with Timothy Leary and Richard Alpert who were teaching a graduate program there. I became intrigued with their accounts, which included readings from the Tibetan *Book of the Dead*, that they were using as a kind of guide book to their drug trips. Drugs had never interested me because I was taking a very strong one already—Architecture. During my studies earlier at UNM a classmate and I were discussing the expanded state of consciousness described in Huxley's *Doors of Perception*. So in Cambridge, studying at Harvard, that interest in an expanded state of consciousness was rekindled. I dropped out, quit my part-time job with Benjamin Thompson of The Architects Collaborative, bought a BMW motorcycle, and headed to San Francisco, thinking that Esalen in Big Sur would be a controlled approach to trying LSD—something I had so far stayed completely clear of. The Lambretta, worn out, was left in the backyard of the rooming house.

That was November of 1963. Taking the southern route back to Albuquerque on the way to San Francisco, I encountered lots of anti-Kennedy and Jesus bumper stickers and billboards. On November 22, I pulled into a Dallas gas station moments after Kennedy had been shot. In disbelief, I kept riding on to Albuquerque where I traded in my "gutless wonder" BMW R-26 for a high-performance BMW R-69S/2—my current 70-year history of riding and traveling on two wheels had a big upgrade moment in 1963.

MIT viewed from across the Charles River

BMW R-26

SAN FRANCISCO

1964/65

At Golden Gate Bridge with David Cantrell

The search for something beyond what I was getting in engineering—which I found in architecture—didn't stop me from looking under rocks for inner meaning. I pulled into San Francisco on my BMW completely disoriented in that new world. A guy standing on the street corner was obviously scoping out my bike, so I stopped to ask him if he knew a cheap part of town to stay. After discussing the bike, he pointed in the direction of the edge of the Filmore area. That turned out to be an auspicious meeting with David Cantrell. At that time the architecture program at Berkeley was a hotbed and there was a lot of architectural talent around San Francisco. I got a job as a principal designer working on BART for Gerry McCue, who later went on to be Dean of the GSD at Harvard. One day, David Cantrell mysteriously showed up with some blueprints on his delivery motorcycle. Then, later, there he was again, photographing my motorcycle, which he recognized, parked in front of San Francisco City Hall as Jennifer and I walked down the steps having just gotten married. David and I had a "There's something going on here" moment. We were both wondering if we were stalking each other. That made us want to get to know each other a bit more.

My Esalen/LSD quest had never left my mind. I still hadn't touched drugs, but as it turned out, without any proselytizing, David introduced me to a spiritual practice, something far more powerful—that jump-started my life in a new way. I had no religion in my life then; and now, decades later, I still don't—but I am deeply religious.

In 1964 all I needed was architecture... and the new life that was opened for me in San Francisco.

BMW R-69S/2

Big Sur

BMW

Fort Ross, Russian church

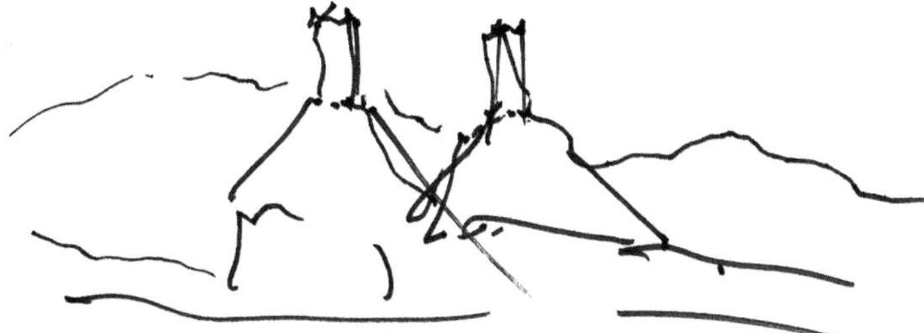

Sonoma hops-drying sheds

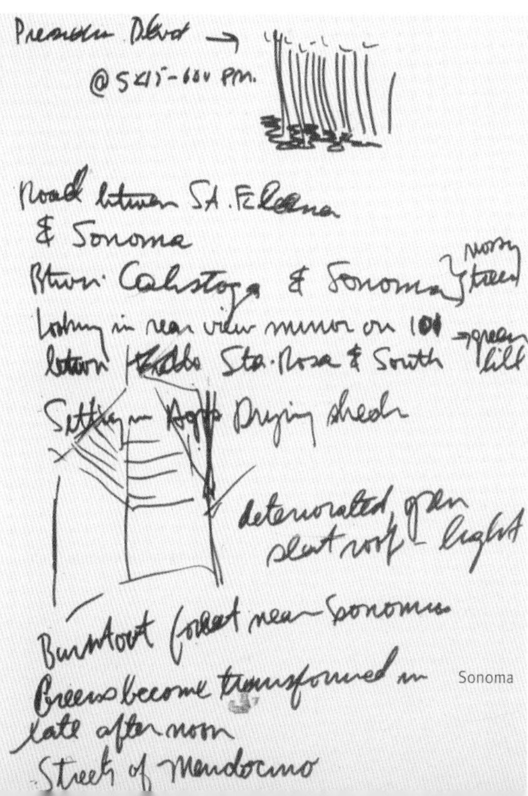

Sonoma

SAN FRANCISCO

GERALD McCUE AND ASSOCIATES
OAKLAND, CA 1964/65

My principal role was designer on the Oakland 12th and 19th Street stations and entry plazas. Toward the end of my tenure, I designed an ancillary structure, a Portal, at the point where the ground-level tracks between Berkeley and Oakland went underground—a concrete structure that guided and buffered rarification waves that are driven into a tunnel ahead of a speeding train. The geometry of the tapering walls and soffits facilitate the aerodynamic transition.

The urban archaeological excavation for the stations seemed Egyptian in scale and scope—keeping the buried utilities operating, dealing with hydrologic lateral forces, avoiding flanking building foundations, etc.

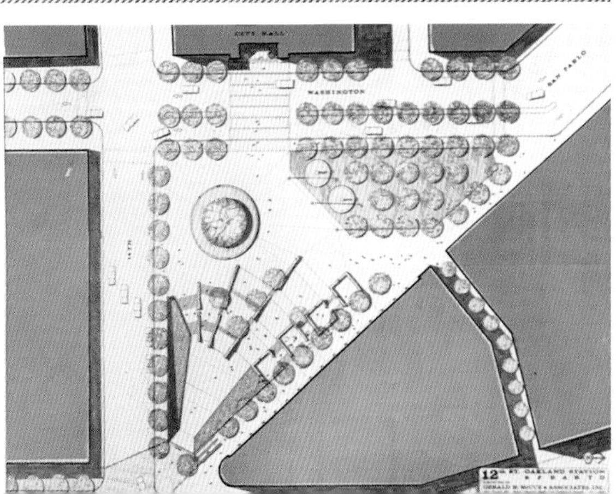

THIS VERSION OF THE MAIN BART ENTRY PLAZA NEVER GOT BUILT. IT WAS FIBONACCI SERIES BASED, LOW WALL BENCHES FLUNG OUT TO DEFINE STAIRWAYS AND RAMPS, EACH WITH A DIFFERENT ELEVATIONAL RELATIONSHIP, FUNNELING INTO THE STATION ENTRY.

STATION-LEVEL ARRIVAL ZONE

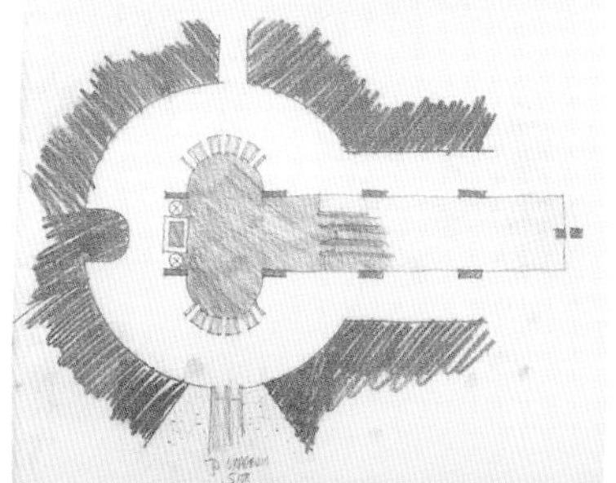

I sensed a career black hole opening up called B-A-R-T; and said to myself, "That's not for me; doing this forever, no way." I hit the road, and put that all behind me.

Lykes Lines freighter

Shoreline of France on arrival

BACK TO EUROPE

1965

Leaving San Francisco on the big BMW R69S/2 was a great relief. I made a stop in Albuquerque where Jennifer was still in graduate school, then continued to New Orleans to depart on a Lykes Lines freighter to Le Havre, France. Jennifer would fly over when the semester was done.

From La Havre I traveled through France to Munich and the BMW factory to take care of a persistent problem on the bike. My mentor Don Schlegel and his family were spending the summer in Tutzing on the Starnberger See and I explored Bavaria with Don. I then crossed the Alps into northern Italy with the intention of riding in North Africa while waiting for Jennifer to arrive. But the heat drove me back north ending up in London meeting her plane at Gatwick. Built my first project in Europe, a garden shed for a couple who hosted our stay in Lowestoft, Suffolk. Roland Starr loved to ride on the back of my bike and we collected driftwood scraps that I used to construct the shed. Jennifer and I toured northern Europe, finally departing Rotterdam to cross the Atlantic on the Belgian freighter *Stad Ghent*. It was a titanium ore hauler traveling back and forth to Canada—the empty ship was like a bobber in the giant winter waves of the north Atlantic.

ROLAND AND ALLISON STARR PEERING OUT OF THE SHED—IT WAS PRETTY COOL ACTUALLY. I WAS VERY PROUD OF IT SINCE IT WAS MY FIRST PIECE OF "ARCHITECTURE" IN EUROPE—THE FIRST "BUILDING" I EVER BUILT WITH MY OWN HANDS.

The Varieties of Religious Experience

WILLIAM JAMES

The famous classic on the psychology of religion

With a Foreword by JACQUES BARZUN

ROLAND WAS A PHILOSOPHER, A GURU OF SORTS, AND HE CREATED A KIND OF SPIRITUAL BIBLIOGRAPHY FOR ME. ONE OF THE BOOKS WAS WILLIAM JAMES' *THE VARIETIES OF RELIGIOUS EXPERIENCE*. IT WAS A VERY ENLIGHTENING SUMMER, BUT IT WAS ALSO HARD BECAUSE HE HAD A CAPTIVE AUDIENCE AND HE WORKED MY ASS OFF AROUND THE PROPERTY.

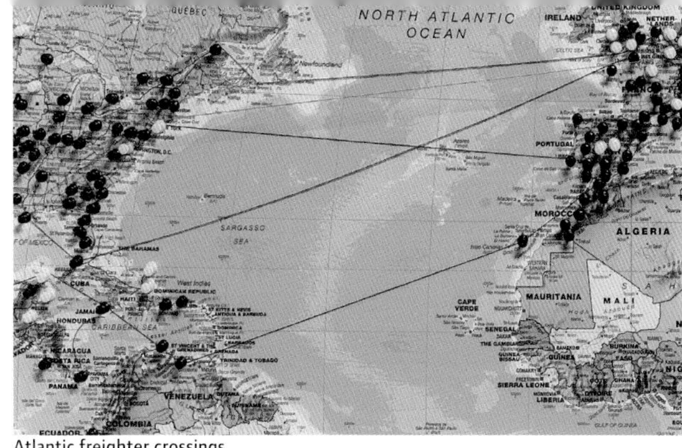

Atlantic freighter crossings

1965 was the last of my trans-Atlantic freighter crossings, shown here in the northern-most route via the St. Lawrence Seaway to Sorel, port of Montreal—juxtaposed to the lines of previous voyages. The thin yellow line comes later and honorifically represents Paris to New York flights on the Concorde in the '80s/'90s.

Reims Cathedral

Passing Quebec on the St. Lawrence Seaway

Holland

Captain of the *Stad Ghent* in port

Trafalgar Square, London

Sulfur mountains in the Port of Rotterdam

Stad Ghent and the huge north Atlantic waves

Casey and Blair Darnell Ranch—our cottage

BACK TO NEW MEXICO

1965

Casey and Blair Darnell Ranch

To save money, we lived for free in a bunkhouse/cottage at the Casey and Blair Darnell horse ranch in Alameda in exchange for our labor, while I worked with Tim Vreeland who was Chair of Architecture at UNM. So at 5:30 a.m. we were up feeding and watering horses and shoveling manure—then on to work—with Jennifer transitioning her career as a Julliard-trained soloist with the Metropolitan Opera Ballet when we were in New York, into modern dance and teaching ballet classes for income.

Lots of joy living on the ranch—from shoveling manure to surplus aircraft landing drag parachutes suspended in the Cottonwood trees

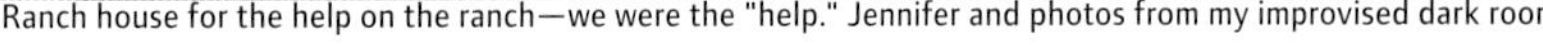

Ranch house for the help on the ranch—we were the "help." Jennifer and photos from my improvised dark room.

"Ribbon Wrapped Trees"

JENNIFER'S DISCOVERY OF THE SAN FRANCISCO DANCERS WORKSHOP LED BY ANNA HALPRIN CHANGED HER LIFE IN DANCE IN MANY WAYS—THE INTENSE DISCIPLINE OF A LIFE OF BALLET TRAINING MERGED WITH NOTIONS OF INDETERMINACY AND CHANCE OPERATIONS IN TERMS OF CHOREOGRAPHIC CONSTRUCTS. EVENTS SUCH AS "RIBBON WRAPPED TREES" COMBINED CONTACT IMPROVISATION AMONG THE DANCERS WITH URBAN INTERVENTION.

MOVEMENT RITUAL BY ANNA HALPRIN

ANNA HALPRIN INVESTIGATED CHANCE OPERATIONS IN COLLABORATION WITH JOHN CAGE AND OTHER ARTISTS—RECOGNIZING THAT A HUMAN BEING, AS A "TUNING FORK" EXPERIENCING EVERYDAY SOUNDS, COULD BE AN END IN ITSELF. ANNA ALSO EXTRAPOLATED "EVERYDAY" NON-FORMALIZED MOVEMENT INTO DANCE AND PERFORMANCE STRATEGIES.

THE ICONIC ANNA HALPRIN PASSED AWAY IN 2021 AT THE AGE OF 100.

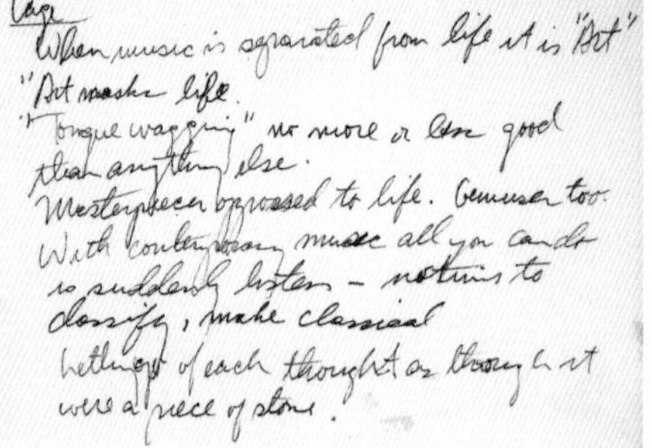

Cage
When music is separated from life it is "Art"
"Art masks life.
"Tongue wagging" no more or less good
than anything else.
Masterpieces opposed to life. Geniuses too.
With contemporary music all you can do
is suddenly listen – nothing to
classify, make classical
Letting go of each thought as though it
were a piece of stone.

Workshop—architecture and dance students exploring membrane spatial phenomena

Jennifer performing in "Greening"

Workshop—Vicki exploring tensile response

JENNIFER AND I CO-DIRECTED A DANCE COMPANY—"HERE AND NOW DANCE THEATER"—WITH MY RESPONSIBILITY BEING SCENIC DESIGN, LIGHTING AND "OVER HER SHOULDER" COLLABORATION ON SOME OF THE CHOREOGRAPHIC STRATEGIES. WE CO-TAUGHT A WORKSHOP FOR ARCHITECTURE AND DANCE STUDENTS THAT EXPLORED THE DIFFERING SPATIAL AWARENESS THAT ARCHITECTS AND DANCERS CARRY WITH THEM, IN ADDITION TO COLLABORATIVE ARCHITECTURAL CONSTRUCTS. THIS WORKSHOP LEAD TO A PERFORMANCE AT THE UNIVERSITY.

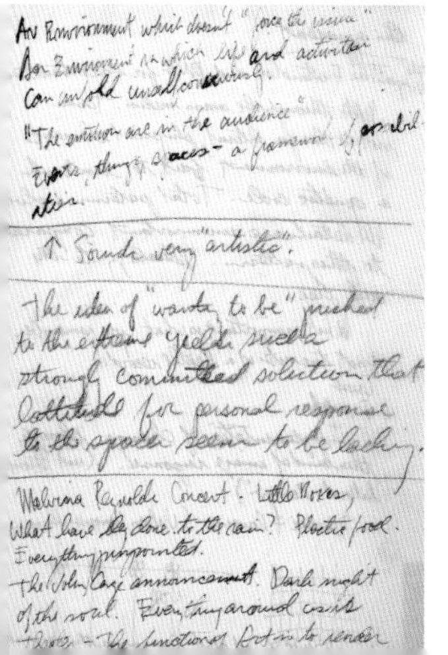

Workshop—collective spatial awareness manipulations

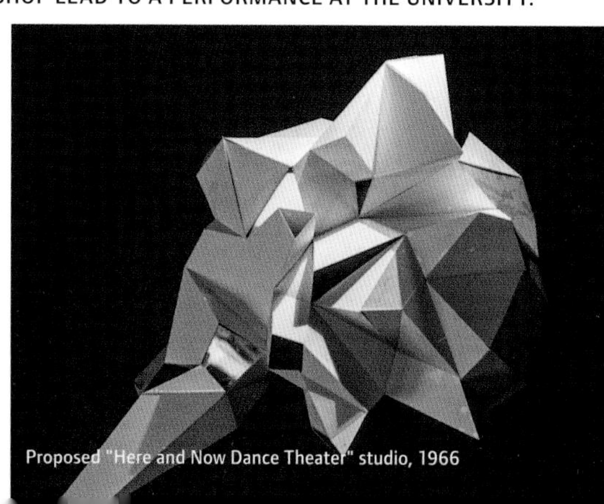
Proposed "Here and Now Dance Theater" studio, 1966

BACK TO WORK

PROJECT DESIGNER/ASSOCIATE WITH GEORGE WRIGHT ARCHITECT 1965

From my job with Tim Vreeland, I moved on to a "real job" with George Wright, as lead designer on projects ranging from the Albuquerque Zoo to various schools in Albuquerque and elsewhere—culminating in what at that time was, for me, the project of a lifetime—the University of New Mexico Law School.

Beginning work on the Law School, I wanted to understand the culture of the study of Law—so I audited law classes at UNM, observing that apart from the formal pedagogy, the classes spilled out into the corridors of the existing building with intense debate continuing among the students. I imagined classrooms embracing a wide-open circulation central forum, instead of compartmentalized corridors, the symbolic center of the space—the Moot Courtroom surrounded by a beehive of spill-out activity. The Moot Courtroom positioning gave the students a centralized reminder of real-life cases, but the lifeblood of the Law School was most certainly the law library, with the geometry of the building anchoring it to a panoramic view of the Sandia Mountains from an open reading area. We constructed a huge model and had endless back-and-forth critiques with Professor Fred Hart and the faculty along with student input.

THE ALBUQUERQUE ZOO ENTRY PAVILION LEAD TO OTHER ZOO PROJECTS LIKE THE PRIMATE HOUSE, WHICH WAS CONCRETE, AKIN TO THE BART PORTAL STRUCTURE.

ALBUQUERQUE ZOO
ENTRY PAVILION, PRIMATE HOUSE
ALBUQUERQUE, NM 1966

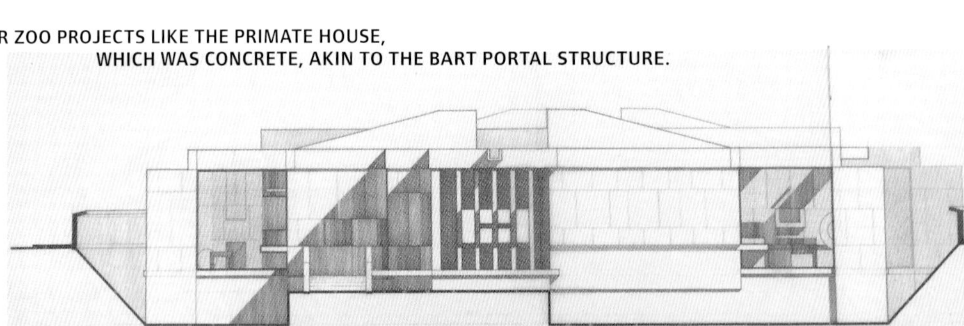

With renewed confidence in the George Wright firm, and poised to become a partner, I was ready to move forward full blast on other projects. Then, akin to meeting David on the street corner in San Francisco, Didier Raven comes along. I had gotten to know Didier casually as a fellow New Wave Cinema fan at the UNM film series, understanding that he was painting at the time. Out of nowhere, he made a proposal to me to become the architect of a New Community project that he and his financial partner, Ray Graham, were embarking upon. Neither of them seemed like "developers" and what they proposed, at first glance, was absolutely "pie in the sky." But after my switch from being secure in engineering to architecture, I knew that life could be an ongoing adventure so I said "I'm in," and left the safety of guaranteed major-project partnership to work on some houses.

DESIGNING THE SANTA ROSA HIGH SCHOOL WAS A HIGH POINT BUT ENDED UP BEING A BAD EXPERIENCE—WRIGHT ALLOWED CHANGES THAT COMPROMISED THE PROJECT, SO I BEGAN TO QUESTION MY COMMITMENT TO HIS FIRM. THE WEST SIDE ELEMENTARY SCHOOL IN LAS VEGAS, NEW MEXICO, CAME THROUGH CONSTRUCTION FAIRLY UNSCATHED GIVING ME HOPE.

SANTA ROSA HIGH SCHOOL
SANTA ROSA, CA 1965

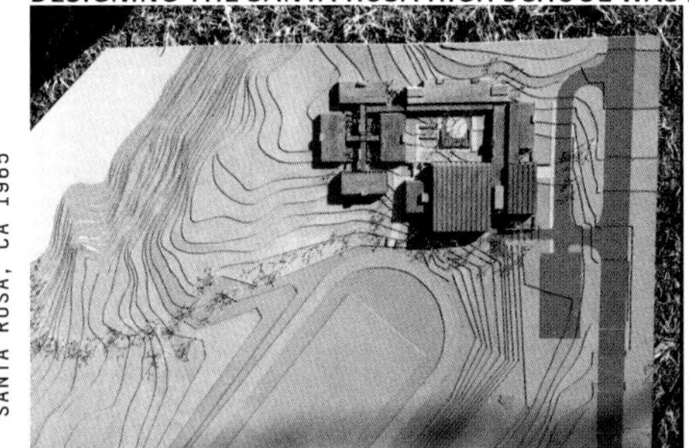

WEST LAS VEGAS ELEMENTARY
LAS VEGAS, NM 1966

I NEEDED A TALENTED UNM STUDENT TO HELP ME WITH MODEL CONSTRUCTION ON THIS PROJECT AND LUCKILY FOUND GEOFF BEEBE. GEOFF WENT WITH ME WHEN I LEFT GEORGE WRIGHT, WORKING DECADES WITH ME BEGINNING WITH LA LUZ AND ON TO OUR INTERNATIONAL PROJECTS. HE DEVELOPED CONSUMMATE DESIGN DETAIL SKILLS ALONG WITH HIS X-RAY EYE ON CONSTRUCTION SITE OBSERVATION, MENTORING MY YOUNG TEAM.

ANTOINE PREDOCK ARCHITECT

1967

LA LUZ COMMUNITY

ALBUQUERQUE, NEW MEXICO 1967/74

JUST LICENSED, LA LUZ UNEXPECTEDLY FALLS INTO MY LAP

Architect
registered in
New Mexico

Pursuant to an Act by the Legislature of the State of New Mexico approved March 18, 1931, entitled "An Act to Provide for the Registration of Architects and Regulate the Practice of Architecture in the State of New Mexico", the New Mexico State Board of Examiners for Architects, after due examination, hereby grants a certificate to

Antoine S Predock

to practice Architecture in the State of New Mexico in accordance with the provisions of said Act. Issued and attested to by the New Mexico State Board of Examiners for Architects this 27th day of January, 1967

CHAIRMAN

Certificate Number 401

SECRETARY

Many become one—100 connected townhomes form a surrogate escarpment. Blank walls to the west, the project turns its back to the invasive, low summer sun and dust storm winds—blasting open to views to the east across the Rio Grande valley to the Sandia Mountains.

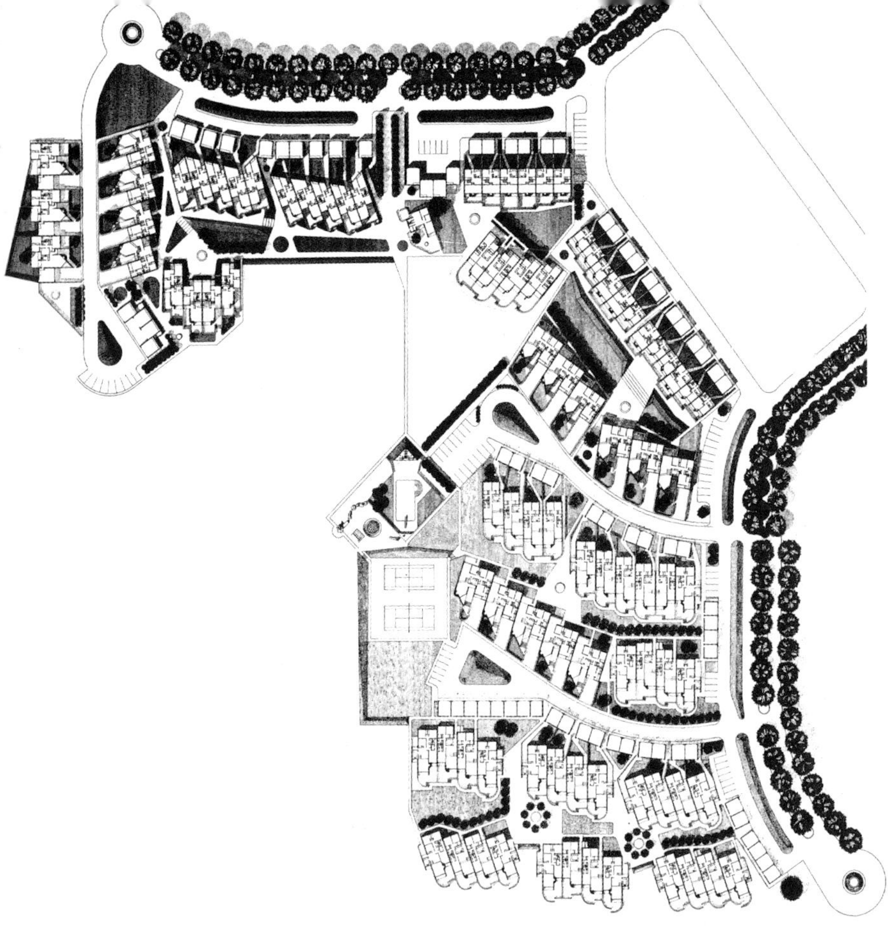

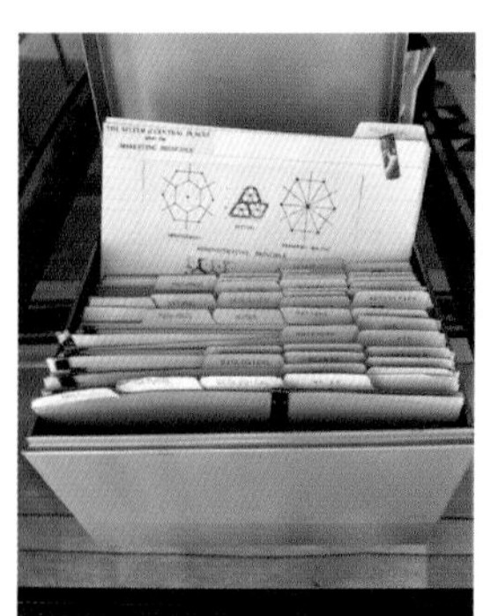

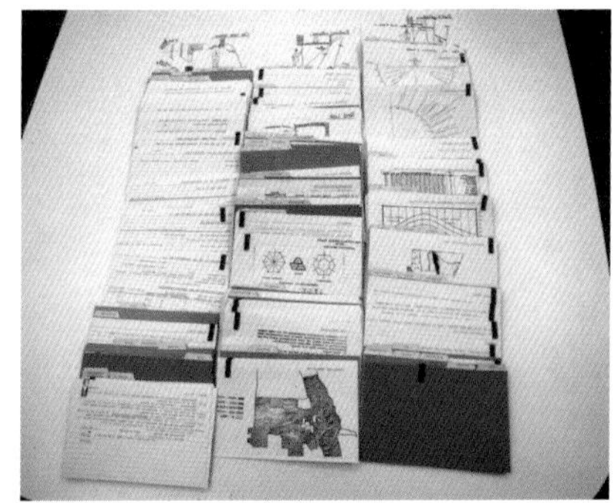

"When he began the project with a box of index cards, he collected relevant climatic, topographic, and geological data. Before the practice got its name, Predock had anticipated what Kenneth Frampton later called 'critical regionalism'—an architecture whose close attention to 'topography, context, climate, light, and tectonic form' could reintegrate the binary terms of nature and culture by once again grounding buildings in a coherent sense of place."

Christopher Mead, *Roadcut*, 2012

OUR MASTER PLAN FOR THE 500-ACRE SITE WAS PREDOMINANTLY FOR HOUSING BUT INCLUDED NEIGHBORHOOD COMMERCIAL ZONES AND AN ELEMENTARY SCHOOL. THE CENTRAL AREA WOULD RETAIN 55 ACRES OF NATURAL OPEN SPACE.

Z, I JUST USED
THE CLIMATE

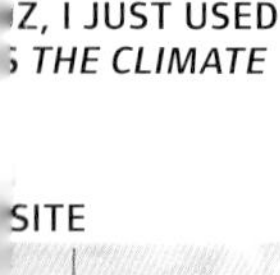

SITE

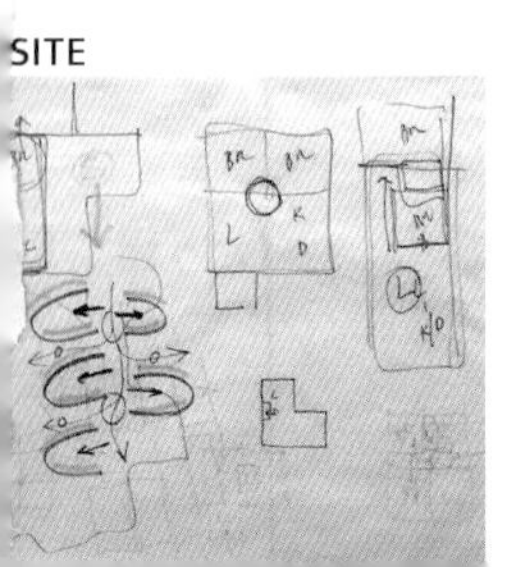

The first step for Didier, Ray, and me, was to find the perfect site for the project. We looked up and down the Middle Rio Grande Valley and landed on a site west of the river—within the Albuquerque city limits, yet completely undeveloped. The 500-acre parcel was owned by a wizened old cowboy, Joel Taylor, who had been running cattle on the property for years. Everything was wonderful about the site, especially the full frontal view of the Sandia Mountains across the Rio Grande.

On the mile-high altiplano of central New Mexico, on this semi-arid mesa above the west bank of the Rio Grande Bosque, we envisioned a close-knit community of townhouses and supporting structures, an intimate private realm that would conserve major areas of open space.

The concept of a community within which the townhouses are sited involved a basic attitude toward the land—that an urban environment and open natural areas can and should coexist, especially in New Mexico; that existing natural patterns should be recognized and reinforced. These factors demanded a concentration of development on the high ground of the site, completely avoiding the flood plain below. These massed townhouses recognize particular landscape and view nuances and climatic forces, generating a man-made "escarpment-like" landscape event.

Building forms and materials provide protection from wildly varying seasonal and diurnal climate shifts. Glass areas are deeply recessed beneath concrete facias. The massive adobe walls serve as heat reservoirs and form acoustical barriers. Some adobe walls are stuccoed white to bounce light into a patio or room. High adobe walls protect outdoor yard areas from wind and provide privacy between units. All exterior walls are earth-colored, stuccoed adobe with sand-blasted concrete lintels spanning openings. Horizontal roof framing is wood joist. Living area ceilings are gapped white fir planks. The floor is earth-colored brick.

These earth-bound houses face either private cul-de-sac streets or pedestrian courts. Glass walls aim east at mountain and city views. The west walls of the townhouses are predominantly solid to reduce the impact of the afternoon sun and the spring dust storms. The patios provide shelter from winter winds, yet act as receptors for trapping solar radiation. Following the existing topography, the units step down the hillside, each with views over the next.

THERE WERE NO SUSTAINABILITY BUZZWORDS AT THE TIME—I DIDN'T KNOW WHAT TO CALL LA L PHRASES LIKE ECOLOGICAL PLANNING/SITE SPECIFICITY/CLIMATIC RESPONSE. RUDOLPH GEIGER *NEAR THE GROUND* AND IAN McHARG'S WRITINGS WERE IMPORTANT RESOURCES.

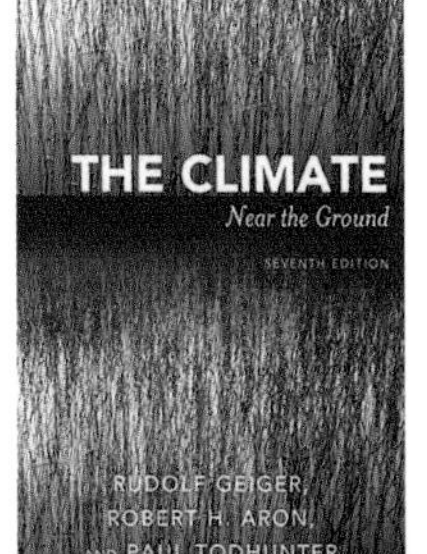

A NUMBER OF PLAN RELATIONSHIPS WERE DEVELOPED RESPONDING TC SLOPE CONDITIONS AND WE LANDED ON SIX DIFFERENT "MODELS."

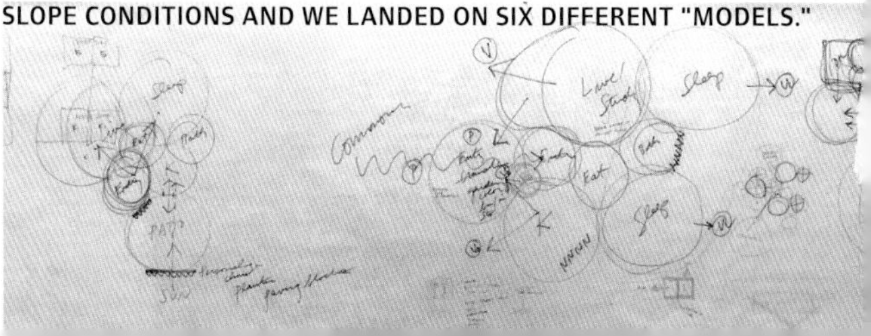

"The essence of Predock's architecture can be simply stated: He has found original ways to connect dramatic, abstract forms with both the natural and cultural conditions of a particular place. Predock's best buildings tell stories in memorable forms and spaces, and this makes him different from most other modern architects."

Benjamin Forgey, "In the High Desert, An Oasis of Design," *The Washington Post*, September 30, 2001

COMPACT CLUSTERING OF THE TOWNHOUSES WAS STUDIED WITH CLAY ON THE TOPOGRAPHIC BASE, THEN LARGER-SCALE INDIVIDUAL MODELS WERE CONSTRUCTED LEADING TO THE CONSTRUCTION DRAWINGS.

OUR ON-SITE "ADOBE FACTORY" UNDER THE GUIDANCE OF ERNIE SANCHEZ—ADOBE BRICKS RIGHT OUT OF THE EARTH OF THE PROJECT SITE AND STRAIGHT INTO THE TOWNHOUSE WALLS.

Didier Raven standing in his living room

Interior of art historian Peter Walsh's townhouse

"CRIB CUBED," WHICH I DESIGNED AND BUILT FOR MY TWO SONS HADRIAN AND JASON, EVOLVED FROM "FLAT ON THE BACK" MANIPULABLES SUSPENDED FROM A PLASTIC TRAY WITH AN ACTIVE FISHBOWL AND BRIGHT OBJECTS. THE LARGER GRAPHIC IMAGES ON THE REMOVABLE ACRYLIC SIDE PANELS REINFORCED MY SONS' EARLY EYE ACCOMMODATION PHASE AND WERE REPLACED ON ONE SIDE WITH WOODEN DOWELS AS THEY BEGAN TO PULL THEMSELVES UP. THE CRIB WAS THE BEGINNING OF A SERIES OF SINGULAR DESIGN OBJECTS LIKE THE PANTHEON WATCH, BASEBALL CAPS, ETC.—AND THIS INCENSE BURNER, AN ABSTRACTION OF VOLCANO, LAKE, ISLAND, AND TREES...

CONTINUING THE "DESIGN OBJECT" FLOW—FOR THE FACETED PIECE, AND SHAPED THE

Hadrian

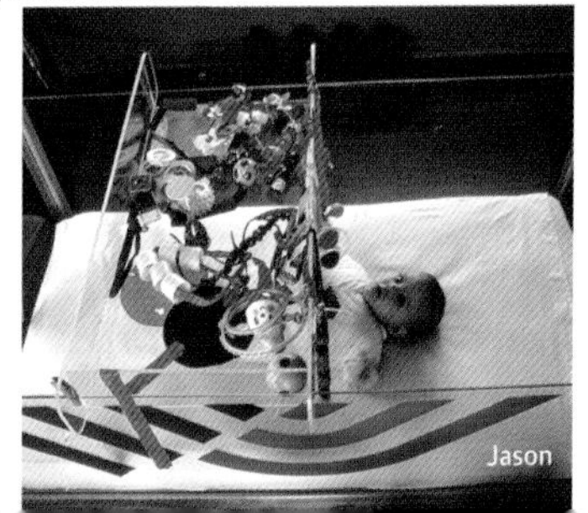
Jason

Planning for the 100 townhouse units separated cars from pedestrians while enclosing intimate courtyards. Intertwining passageways between units followed the topography down the slope. The cross section through the units allowed for unobstructed views toward the river and the mountains over successive townhouse arrays.

Everything was done incrementally, never knowing when or if the next phase was going to happen.

It was so adventurous of Didier and Ray to do this project—it was in the middle of nowhere. Realtor: "What? You going to do a project on the west side of town, no way that'll happen."

Well, there's a whole second city out there now surrounding the project.

ASSISTED BY THE LA LUZ CONTRACTOR TEAM, I CONSTRUCTED THE ARMATURE FOR THE COMMUNITY PLAY STRUCTURES, WE USED EXPANDED POLYSTYRENE PANELS EARTH FOR THE CLIMBABLE SECTIONS. THEN WE SPRAYED GUNNITE CONCRETE OVER THE FORMS.

"La Luz is not only a demonstration in creative conservation, architecture, and planning. It is, also, a show of courage. Most suburban development around Albuquerque is plain awful—imitative of the worst that has despoiled Southern California."

Peter Blake, *Architectural Forum*, July/August 1969

ON THE EASTERN EDGE OF THE 55 ACRE RIPARIAN PRESERVED OPEN SPACE, A GROUNDWATER WETLAND MARSH WITH BEAVER DAMS.

DIDIER, JACK AND DONNA RUST, AND NEIL KAMINSKY CELEBRATING FOURTH OF JULY AT LA LUZ

Not sure how word about the project got out, but Peter Blake the editor of *Architectural Forum* magazine in New York came to check it out, published it, and suddenly there was global awareness of it—book/exhibition at Centre Pompidou, Paris—*Des Architectures de Terre*, and many other publications.

SUSTAINABILITY MAKES *GOOD MORNING AMERICA*

OUR FIRST STUDIO AT 1313 12TH STREET, WHICH LED TO THE DISCOVERY OF THE 300 12TH STREET PROPERTY IN 1970.

"La Luz asserted not just modern but avant-garde principles of open space and community planning, and of the response of building to climate and site, wind direction, heating and cooling systems, views, composition of public and private realms."

Edna Heatherington, "The Mystique of La Luz," *Pueblo Style and Regional Architecture: The Mystique of New Mexico*, 1998

THE LA LUZ RECREATION CENTER WAS ENTERED PAST THE EARTH-SHELTERED SUPPORT BUILDING—A SLOPING "NON-FAÇADE" GUIDING PREVAILING WINDS UP AND OVER THE POOL.

PREDOCK COMPOUND

ALBUQUERQUE, NEW MEXICO 1970

The work on La Luz was done in Didier's kid's playroom in Corrales to begin with, then we rented an office at 1313 12th Street, where we worked through the late '60s. Because I drove back and forth on 12th Street to get to Central Ave/ Highway 66, I routinely passed by the corner of 12th and Marquette where a "For Sale" sign had popped up. It was a disheveled complex of three buildings: a house, a contractor's office, and a two story storage building on the alley at the rear of the property. The price was $25,000. Our family was living month-to-month on my earnings from La Luz, but after a discussion with one of the financial advisors to La Luz I figured out a way to buy it on a real estate contract since I couldn't get a mortgage—I had no collateral. That became the Predock Compound—with living quarters for the family and the alley building adaptable to become a dance studio for Jennifer. The corner building which stretched from 12th Street to the alley was perfect for the design studio. The property had commercial zoning, which allowed for walls around the perimeter—so it became an enclosed realm of interconnecting courtyards linking the three buildings. On through the years two other houses along 12th Street were purchased and tied into the courtyard network. The studio space was a relatively easy, quick fix-up. The night after refinishing the floor we all went to a Janis Joplin concert at the Civic Auditorium in nearby downtown Albuquerque. We carried the crazy energy of Janis Joplin sliding all over the stage back to our new floor, sliding all over it like she did while playing her music.

The compound, with both parents' workplaces merging with our home, was an exhilarating and challenging hotbed of activity, our two sons growing up in a mix of artistic energy—a commingling of architects and dancers, with, at times, 24/7 charrettes; dance celebrities like Tim Wengerd of the Martha Graham Dance Company; local students; and friends. No surprise that our son Hadrian became an architect, and that Jason works in film and photography. Embedded in our move was the realization that "living over the shop" had the added advantage of zero commuting and minimal need for a car—with the implicit, associated energy conservation.

The house prior to renovation

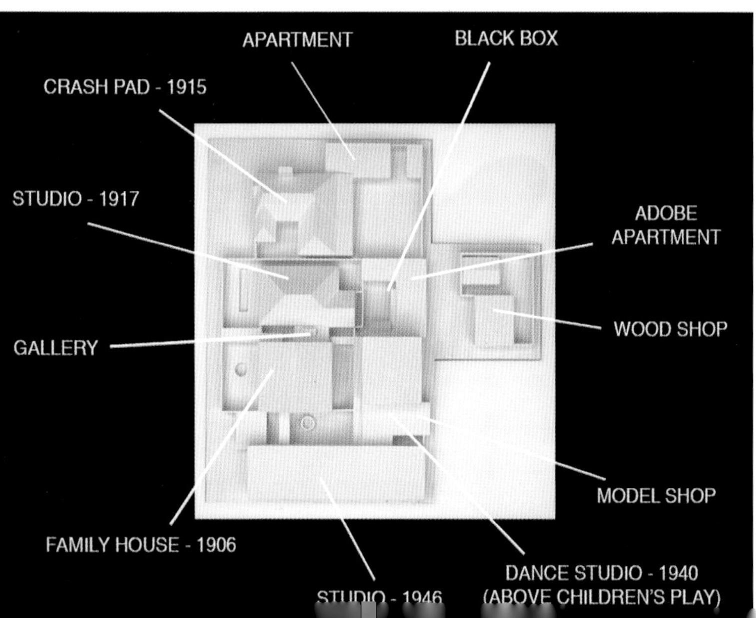

INHABITING THE ATTIC OF THE ORIGINAL HOUSE

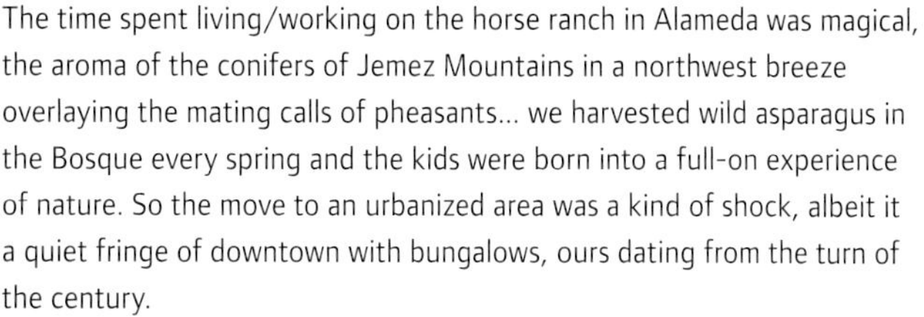

The time spent living/working on the horse ranch in Alameda was magical, the aroma of the conifers of Jemez Mountains in a northwest breeze overlaying the mating calls of pheasants... we harvested wild asparagus in the Bosque every spring and the kids were born into a full-on experience of nature. So the move to an urbanized area was a kind of shock, albeit it a quiet fringe of downtown with bungalows, ours dating from the turn of the century.

Rear garden access to Blue (Play) Room, past the Kinetic Tree House that I built for Hadrian and Jason.

MARTHA GRAHAM DANCE COMPANY SOLOIST TIM WENGERD IN OUR DANCE STUDIO

FIRST NATIONAL BANK—SANDIA PLAZA

ALBUQUERQUE, NEW MEXICO 1970/72

ALONG WITH SANDIA PLAZA, THERE WERE FOUR OTHER BRANCHES OF FIRST NATIONAL BANK: WEST CENTRAL, EUBANK AND TWO MODULAR MOBILE BRANCHES.

ADDITIONAL BANK BRANCHES
ALBUQUERQUE, NM 1968

I was approached by the CEO of First National Bank to design several branch banks scattered around the city. The flagship of those was Sandia Plaza. I didn't want customers to just drive up, park, and walk in the front door—as is the case in most precedents. So a low wall wraps a courtyard with a central fountain—a psychological deceleration from the traffic. Entering the banking hall, all-pervasive panoramic views back to the Sandia Mountains for bank workers and customers lock the project into the site.

The massive concrete structure communicated permanence and security, but with refined wood detailing for furniture and fixtures. We found a perfect Italian tile that mirrored the sandy earth color of the New Mexico terrain and covered the entire plaza and interior floor plane. The truncated rotated pyramidal form of the building had the same earth-color tile roof.

THE SIX-FOOT-SQUARE MODEL WAS LARGE ENOUGH TO LOOK AT STRUCTURAL SYSTEMS AND INTERIOR DETAILS—THE BANKING HALL WITH OFFICER WORK STATIONS, SYMBOLIC MASSIVE CONCRETE VAULT, AND A MULTI-USE MEETING ROOM THAT SPILLED OUT INTO THE COURTYARD.

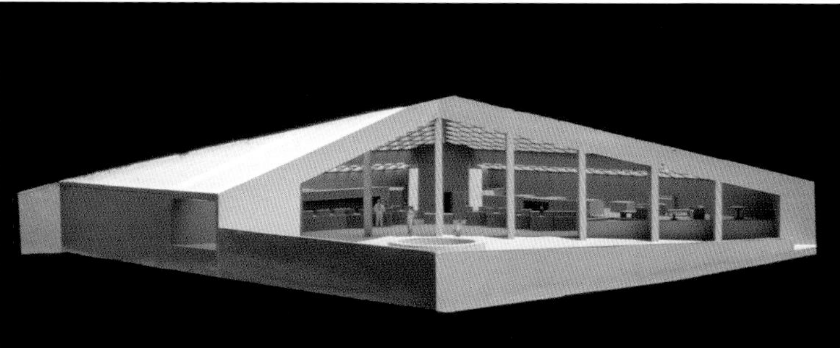

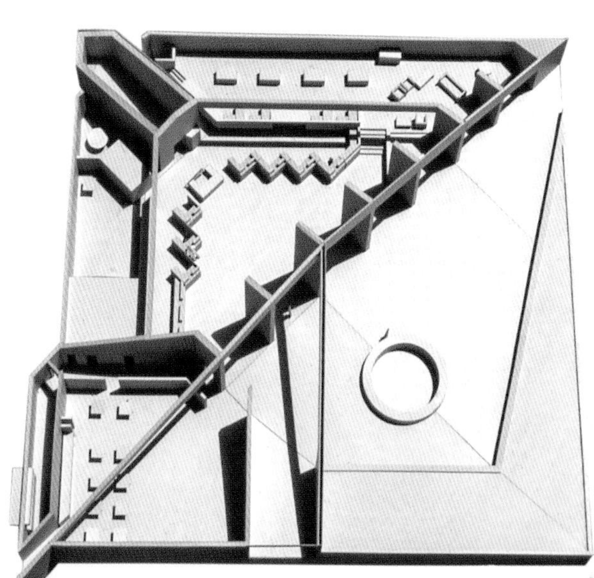

Hand-painted Modena tile—1971

This was the first emergence of commercial scale work for me after La Luz. Sandia Plaza was a breakout project, even though I had designed far larger projects, such as the University of New Mexico Law School, when I was an associate with George Wright.

I thought the indoor/outdoor application of the sand-colored Italian tile was so strong I decided to let it become the finished roof as well, so the whole structure appeared to be a concrete-and-tile monolith. This project was published and it seems that Italy noticed, subsequently inviting me to Modena, center of the Italian tile industry. A five-star itinerary with stops at various tile factories, at one of which they gave me the opportunity to design a ceramic tile unit, so they made a prototype tile and I drew a sketch of Parma directly on the tile before firing. We did a special tour of the Ferrari factory in Modena and I was first introduced to the magic of balsamic vinegar and Parmigiano Reggiano. (Riding Ducatis came a bit later.)

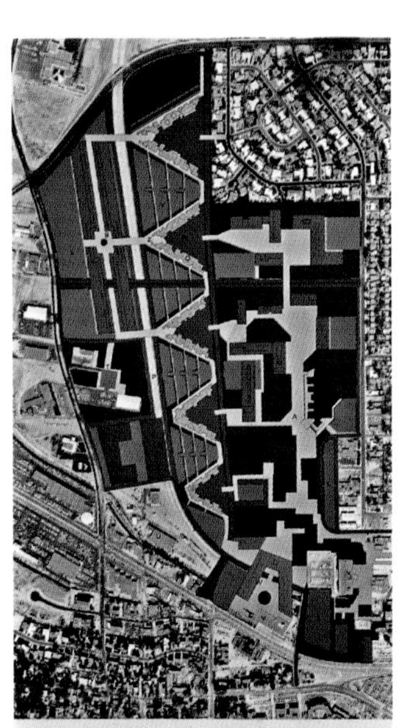

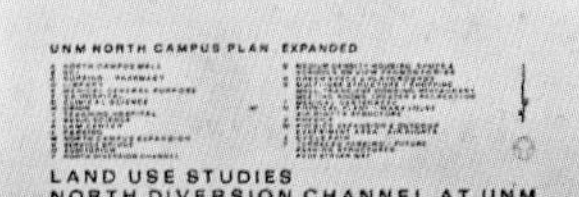

UNIVERSITY OF NEW MEXICO
NORTH CAMPUS PLAN/
STUDENT HOUSING
ALBUQUERQUE, NM 1974

LAS BARRANCAS WAS TO BE A MIXED-USE NEW COMMUNITY—POSITIONING OF THE HOUSING UNITS WOULD FOLLOW THE TOPOGRAPHY, LIKE LA LUZ.

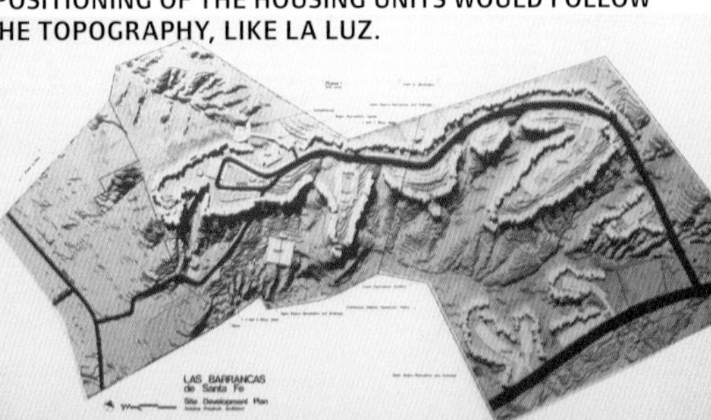

LAS BARRANCAS OF SANTA FE
NOT BUILT 1971

"In this growing suburban section of the city, the bank wanted its customers to feel they weren't just going into a check-cashing mill, but that they were going into a special environment where they could discuss and work out their financial problems. In addition, the building was to be an oasis in the strip environment."

Progressive Architecture, 1974

THE CLAY MODEL SHOWS A PERIMETER RIDGELINE ENCLOSING A SOFTBALL FIELD THEN MEANDERING TO DEFINE BASKETBALL COURTS, PLAYGROUND, AND INTIMATE PICNIC AND GATHERING AREAS. IT WAS A CITY PARK DEVELOPED WITH SIGNIFICANT COMMUNITY INPUT. ACTIVIST EMMA CHAVIRA CONVINCED EVERYONE TO NAME IT TIGUEX PARK, HONORING THE INDIGENOUS TRIBES.

IN 1972 I BEGAN TEACHING A DESIGN STUDIO AT THE UNM SCHOOL OF ARCHITECTURE. I WAS INSPIRED TO DO IT AND IT CONNECTED WITH THE RESULT OF THE APTITUDE TEST I TOOK WHEN I LEFT ENGINEERING—ARCHITECT/TEACHER. IT SEEMED LIKE A FIT AND I LOVED BONDING WITH THE STUDENTS, SHOWN HERE CONSTRUCTING A PROTEST PIECE CALLING ATTENTION TO NIXON'S CAMBODIA BOMBINGS. MILITARY SURPLUS FORMED THE MATERIAL PALETTE. BUT AS TIME WENT ON IT WAS DIFFICULT TO RECONCILE TEACHING WITH A FULL BLAST ARCHITECTURAL PRACTICE, SO I DID NOT RENEW MY CONTRACT. (I WAS REMEMBERING FRANK LLOYD WRIGHT'S ONE LINER—"THOSE WHO CAN, DO. THOSE WHO CAN'T, TEACH.") TEACHING CERTAINLY DIDN'T STOP OVER THE YEARS, BUT WOULD BE SHORTER GIGS—ACADEMIC CHAIRS, WORKSHOPS, AND U.S. AND INTERNATIONAL LECTURES: HARVARD, CLEMSON, UCLA, SCI-ARC, COLUMBIA, CAPRI ITALY, CORNELL, TECHNICAL UNIVERSITY TOKYO, STANFORD, YALE, RISD; CENTRE GEORGES POMPIDOU, PARIS; THE GRAHAM FOUNDATION, CHICAGO; BUENOS AIRES; THE MALAYSIAN INSTITUTE OF ARCHITECTS, KUALA LUMPUR; GUANGZHOU, CHINA; DOHA, QATAR...

KAMINSKY HOUSE

LATER PREDOCK HOUSE

ALBUQUERQUE, NEW MEXICO 1971/73

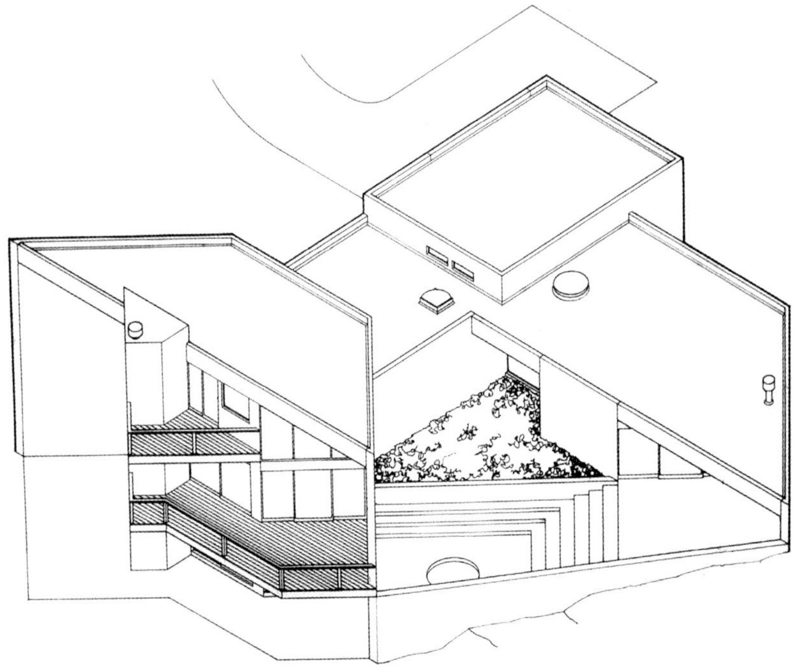

A landmark project because it came right after La Luz. This was my first single-family house. In the mid '90s I purchased it from my original client, renowned endocrinologist Neil Kaminsky, and have been living in it ever since. Then, decades later came Kaminsky II.

Motorcycles in living room came 2 decades later.

The stepped section of the house follows the existing slope, yielding a one-story façade on the west while three levels command panoramic views to the east. The house has essentially blank south and west walls to reduce solar impact on the interior while also buffering spring dust storms from that direction. The splayed walls channel sweeping views and divert prevailing winds out and around the east terrace and deck areas.

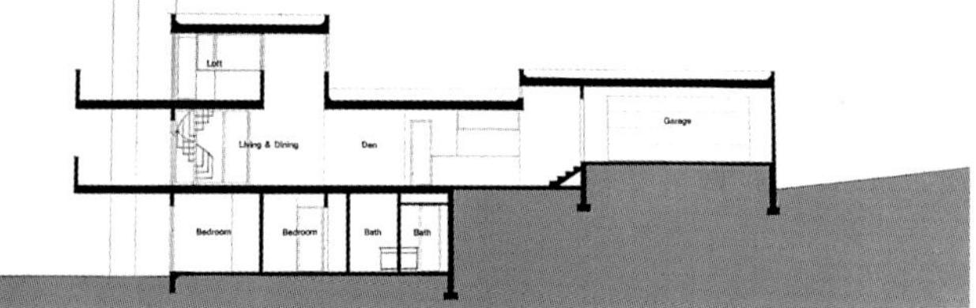

INDIVIDUAL HOUSE COMMISSIONS FOLLOWED FROM LA LUZ—SUTIN HOUSE AND RUST HOUSE.

THEN CITADEL—MORE URBANIZED MULTI-FAMILY HOUSING THAT WAS SHOWN ON THE COVER OF *PROGRESSIVE ARCHITECTURE*—FACILITATING AN ENCOUNTER THAT PROVED TO BE THE BEGINNING OF A DECADES-LONG FRIENDSHIP WITH CRITIC/WRITER/EDITOR DAVID MORTON.

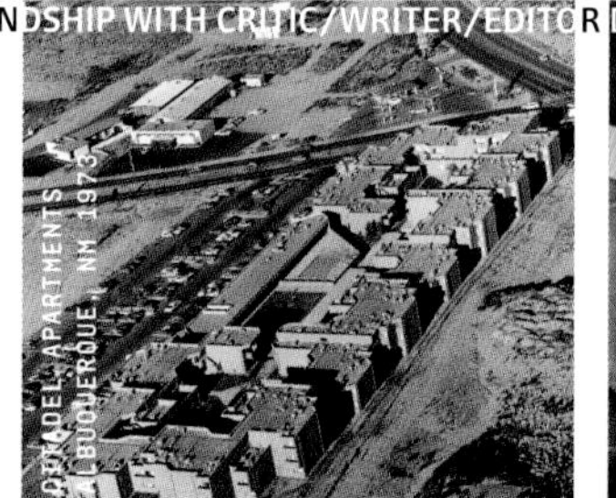

WE TOOK OUR FIRST VACATION IN 1973 TO MOROCCO—MY FIRST TRANS-ATLANTIC FLIGHT. PREVIOUS CROSSINGS HAD ALWAYS BEEN BY FREIGHTER... FEZ, MARRAKESH, RAMMED-EARTH CONSTRUCTION AND A FABULOUS OASIS VERGING ON THE SAHARA AT ZAGORA.

A SITE-PLANNING STUDY FOR THE COCHITI PUEBLO LANDS AS PART OF A DESIGN TEAM THAT INCLUDED FRANK GEHRY WHO DESIGNED THE COMMUNITY CENTER WHILE I DID MASTER PLANNING AND THE BUILDOUT OF A FEW TOWNHOUSES.

COCHITI MESA TOWNHOUSE
COCHITI, NM 1973

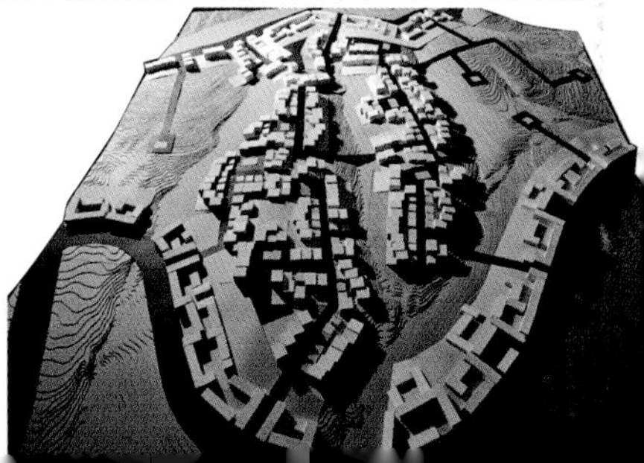

The haunting power of the Sandia Mountains with ever-changing light on this giant 10,000 foot altitude projection screen... overpowering the Northeast Heights "developerville."

MORE INTERNATIONAL TRAVEL IN LATE 1973 WITH MY FRIEND MUNEO (SIMON) MATSUSHIMA TO JAPAN: EXPLORING TOKYO, SKETCHING THE WILDNESS OF KABUKI THEATER AND THE AUSTERITY OF NOH PLAYS, THE SOBRIETY OF TAKAYAMA WITH ITS IMMACULATE TIMBER DETAILING AND BEAUTIFUL OPEN STORMWATER CHANNELS. CAPPING THE TRIP IN ISE AND KYOTO WITH THE SILENCE OF SAIHO-JI AND THE QUIET POWER OF RYOAN-JI.

A VERY EARLY EXAMPLE OF ACTIVE SOLAR HEATING.

PECOS NATIONAL MONUMENT VISITOR'S CENTER & MASTER PLAN 1973

DESIGNED AT THE SAME TIME, WITH STEPPING CLERESTORIES FOR NORTH LIGHT TO THE STUDIOS AND BRIDGES LINKING TO THE EXISTING FINE ARTS CENTER.

UNIVERSITY OF NEW MEXICO
ART BUILDING
ALBUQUERQUE, NM 1974/76

BOULDER HOUSE

ALBUQUERQUE, NEW MEXICO 1975/76

A SUCCESSION OF PROJECTS FLOWED THROUGH THE 1970s...

UNIVERSITY OF NEW MEXICO
STUDENT HOUSING
ALBUQUERQUE, NM 1974

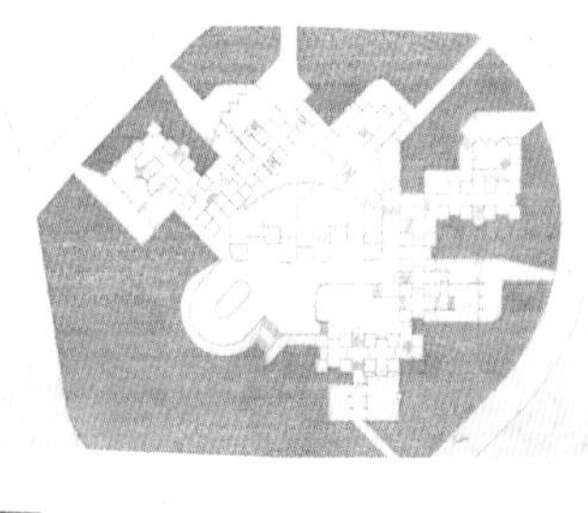

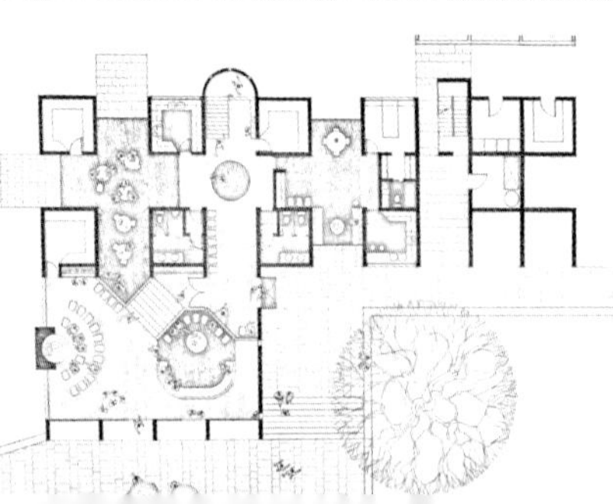

"In its massing, the house responds to the traditional architectural forms of the region, and the admittedly difficult geometry of arc segments and triangles is sufficiently resolved to create highly interesting spaces and forms that fit this high desert site."

Architectural Record, Mid-May 1977

DIDIER RAVEN, FROM LA LUZ, COMMISSIONED THIS MAJOR HIGHWAY 66/RAILROAD CROSSROADS MIXED-USE DEVELOPMENT.

GRAND CENTER
ALBUQUERQUE, NM 1975

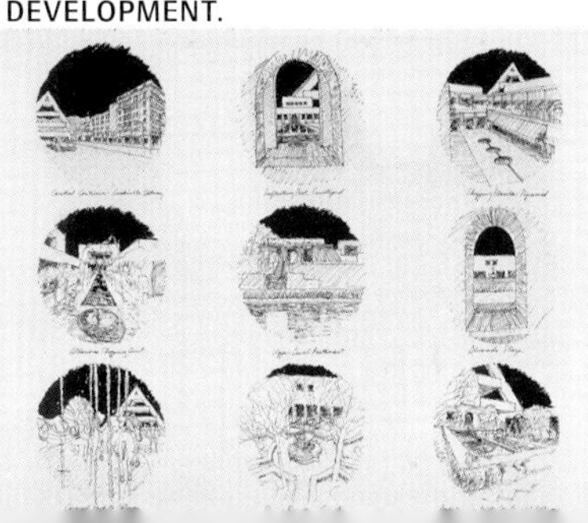

Boulder House locks in to the Precambrian granite talus that was shed off the west face of the Sandia Mountains. Active and passive energy strategies shape its form—the steep collector slope to the south and the radial floor-to-ceiling apertures to the northwest calibrate protection from the very low summer sun angles, while focusing particularized views across the Rio Grande Valley.

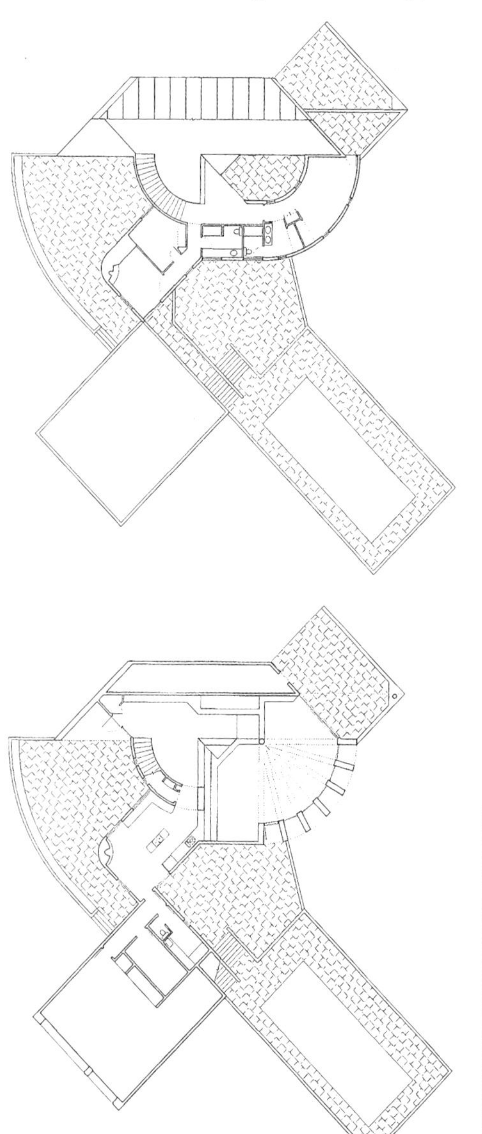

TWO STUDENT UNION PROJECTS, ONE AT UNM CAMPUS IN ALBUQUERQUE THE OTHER AT NEW MEXICO TECH IN SOCORRO—AND A MASTER PLAN FOR NMT.

UNM STUDENT UNION BUILDING
RENOVATION AND ADDITION
ALBUQUERQUE, NM 1977

NEW MEXICO TECH STUDENT
UNION & MASTER PLAN,
NEW MEXICO INSTITUTE OF
MINING AND TECHNOLOGY
SOCORRO, NM 1975

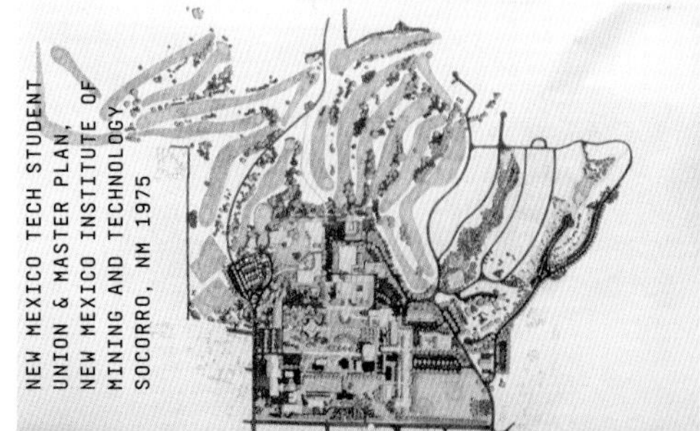

TOM, LARRY, STAN, GLADE AND PATRICK LINED UP IN THE STUDIO.

FOR THE CORP OF ENGINEERS, A RECREATIONAL MASTER PLAN FOR ABIQUIU LAKE, NOT FAR FROM GEORGIA O'KEEFFE'S LEGENDARY HOUSE/STUDIO

ABIQUIU LAKE RECREATIONAL
MASTER PLAN
ABIQUIU, NM 1976

"The Rio Grande Nature Center is a building about movement, movement across the landscape and into the water, movement that enhances the educational function of the center. It is sited in a wetlands preserve in Albuquerque, a place where water management has been practiced for over a hundred years. Albuquerque architect Antoine Predock, FAIA, says that his building celebrates the site's history while providing a connection between the visitor and the water."

Michael J. Crosbie, "Nature Center Stands in the Water Like a Sculpted Dam," *Architecture*, Dec. 1984

MAKING ARCHITECTURE IN A COMMITTED, UNCOMPROMISING WAY IS AN ENDURANCE CONTEST. CHALLENGING PHYSICAL ACTIVITY PREPARES ONE FOR THE NEVER-ENDING ARCHITORTURE THAT ACCOMPANIES MANY PROJECTS, STARTS IN ARCHITECTURE SCHOOL... WITH THE ALL-NIGHTER CHARRETTES (WHAT BUILDING ON CAMPUS DO YOU NOTICE THE LIGHTS ON ALL NIGHT? THE BUSINESS SCHOOL?—NO. THE LAW SCHOOL?—NO.)

Fiesta Bowl Marathon
803
adidas

10 L.A.'s LARGEST RUN
1876

The Rio Grande Nature Center and Preserve is a symbol of a profoundly important but rapidly diminishing New Mexico ecosystem. The open fields are vestiges of a beautiful pastoral setting that once stretched the length of the city. The natural wetlands still harbor a diverse set of environments that sharply contrast with those of the upland semi-arid mesas. Acquisition of the site by the State of New Mexico offered a unique opportunity to maintain the important connections between the city and the river, its symbiotic agricultural development and a prime wildfowl preserve located on the Rio Grande Flyway.

In response to these resources and intents, we developed the master plan. Environmental, legal, historical, and recreational concerns were incorporated into the planning, phasing, and design criteria established for the various components of the site. In recent history, the river had been difficult to access and the Bosque del Rio Grande had become a trash-filled "backyard/UNM party central." So the first step was a massive cleanup of the Bosque area with city and state personnel joining neighborhood forces. We wanted to keep the agricultural life of the land working for the farmers that had been leasing the fields alive and well. We devised a legal framework so they would continue as partners, benefiting from the yield with the requirement to plant a percentage of forage for the big birds—the sandhill cranes and the Canadian snow geese. The historic wetland area of the site was reaffirmed with the construction of a major pond.

We then designed an interpretive exhibition building for the 170-acre site that was completed in 1982. The Nature Center acts as an unobtrusive "blind," affording visitors discrete panoramic views of the wildfowl areas. Viewed on the approach path: earthen berms, bunker-like concrete structure, and a human-scale entry—a sliced 8-foot-diameter, corrugated drainage culvert forms and frames the tunnel entry into the Center, adding an element of "river-edge vernacular."

"The building itself becomes a medium both to introduce natural relationships to visitors and to introduce visitors to the site. Its presence as part of the initial development of the preserve was also to caution the dirt-bikers and chainsaw-firewood collectors who had progressively ravaged the woodlands. Its imagery was, in this respect, somewhat deliberately chosen; its bunkerlike appearance shows that the naturalists mean business."

Peter C. Papademetriou, "Blind Trust"
Progressive Architecture, March 1984

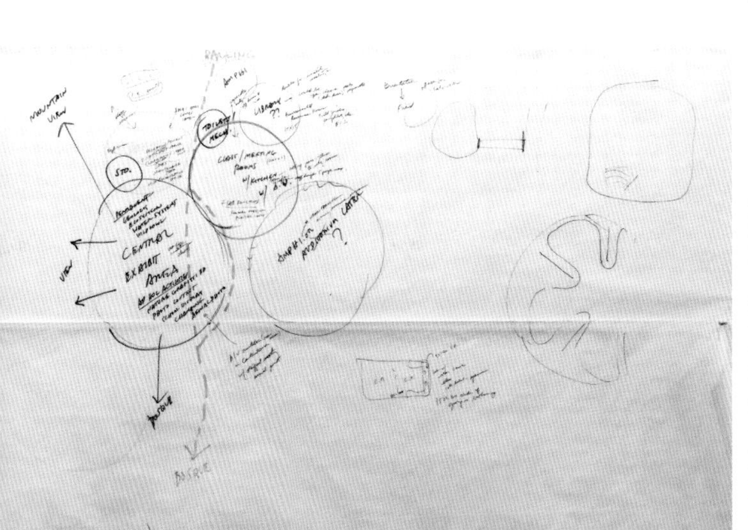

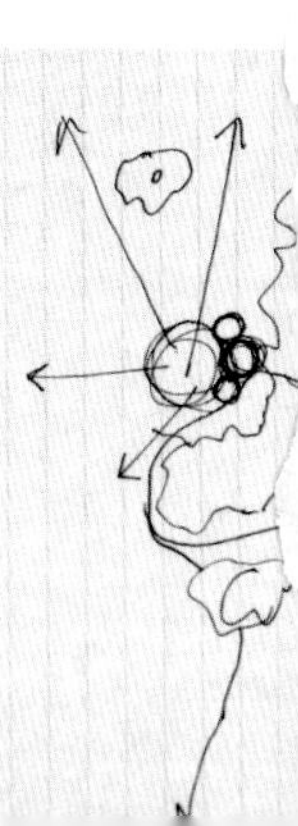

RIO GRANDE NATURE CENTER MASTER PLAN AND VISITOR CENTER

ALBUQUERQUE, NEW MEXICO 1978/82

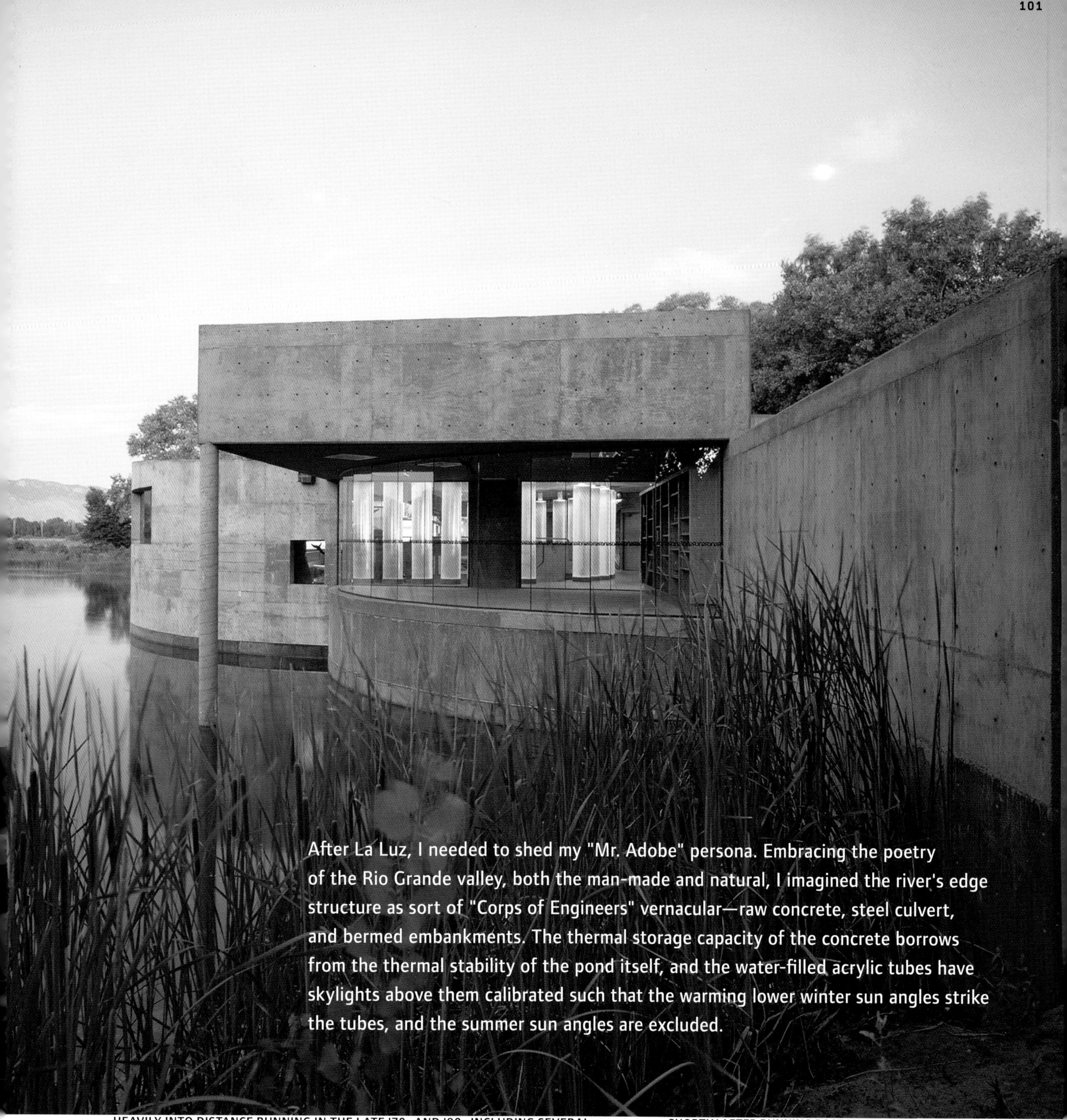

After La Luz, I needed to shed my "Mr. Adobe" persona. Embracing the poetry of the Rio Grande valley, both the man-made and natural, I imagined the river's edge structure as sort of "Corps of Engineers" vernacular—raw concrete, steel culvert, and bermed embankments. The thermal storage capacity of the concrete borrows from the thermal stability of the pond itself, and the water-filled acrylic tubes have skylights above them calibrated such that the warming lower winter sun angles strike the tubes, and the summer sun angles are excluded.

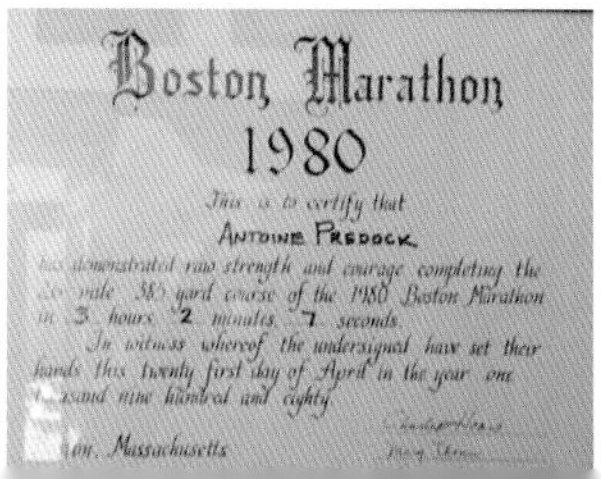

HEAVILY INTO DISTANCE RUNNING IN THE LATE '70s AND '80s INCLUDING SEVERAL MARATHONS, WITH BOSTON AS THE CROWN JEWEL—THE CROWDED START IN HOPKINTON, PASSING WELLSLEY COLLEGE WHERE WE WERE CHEERED ON AND SPRAYED WITH WATER, THEN AT AROUND 20 MILES, HEARTBREAK HILL—EXACTLY WHAT THE RUNNER DOESN'T NEED AT THAT MILEAGE. FINISHING IN 3 HOURS AT THE PRUDENTIAL, COOLING OFF AND RECOVERING IN THE PARKING STRUCTURE BENEATH.

1980 BOSTON MARATHON

V 61

TIGER SHOES

Boston Marathon

1980

This is to certify that

Antoine Predock

has demonstrated raw strength and courage completing the 26 mile 385 yard course of the 1980 Boston Marathon in 3 hours 2 minutes 7 seconds.

In witness whereof the undersigned have set their hands this twenty first day of April in the year one thousand nine hundred and eighty.

...ton, Massachusetts

SHORTLY AFTER RUNNING BOSTON, WHILE I WAS DOING INTERVAL TRAINING WITH ELLEN HART, AN OLYMPIC TEAM CANDIDATE, I TORE MY HAMSTRING ELIMINATING MY RUNNING THE NEW YORK CITY MARATHON AND LAUNCHING ME INTO A BICYCLE TRAINING LIFE WHICH IS STILL ALIVE AND WELL.

FIRST MAJOR PUBLIC COMMISSION—SOLAR HEATED, INTERNAL COURTYARDS, VIEW CORRIDORS DOWN THE OLD TOWN PLAZA ACCESS LANES.

ALBUQUERQUE MUSEUM
ALBUQUERQUE, NM 197[illegible]–79

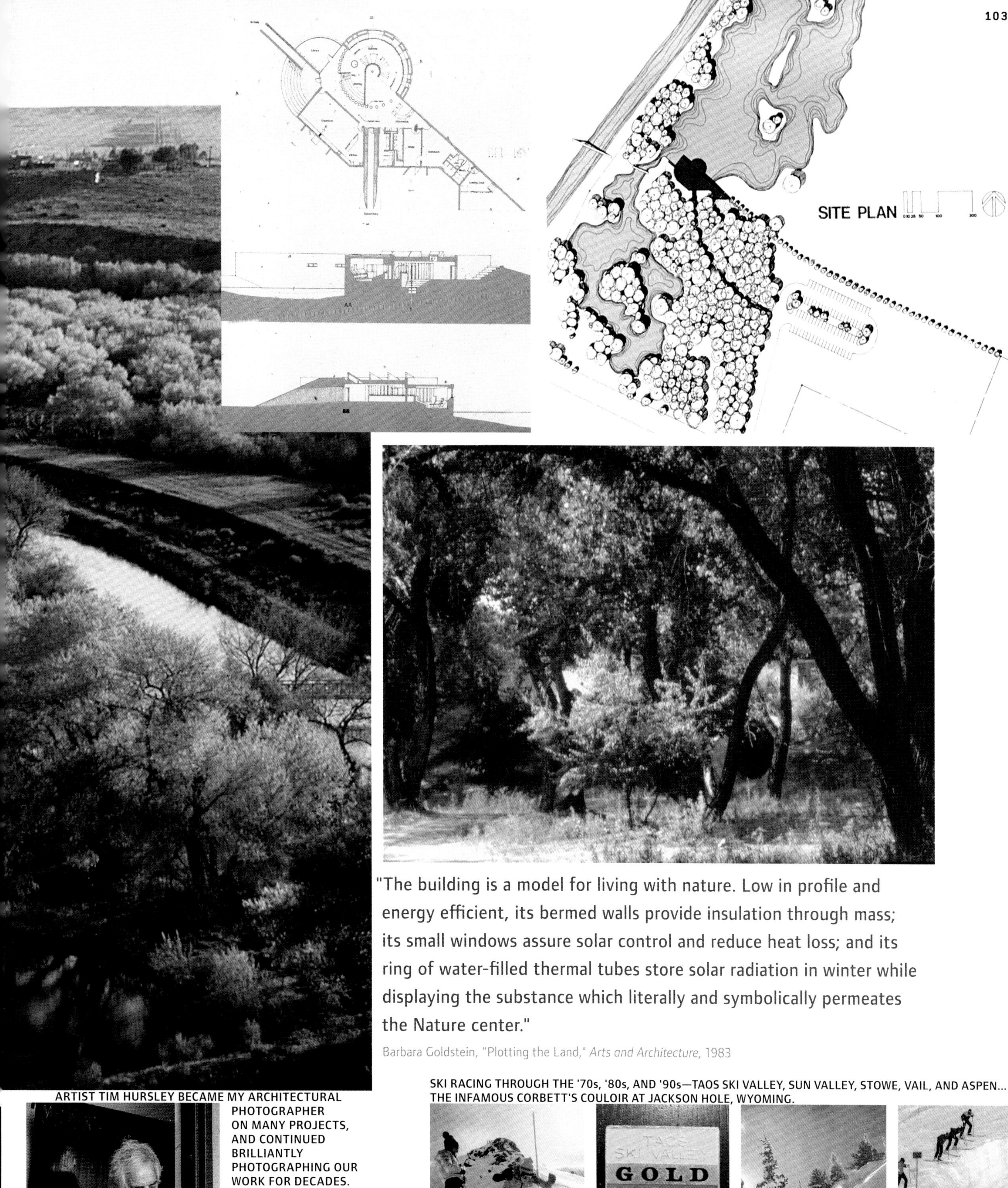

"The building is a model for living with nature. Low in profile and energy efficient, its bermed walls provide insulation through mass; its small windows assure solar control and reduce heat loss; and its ring of water-filled thermal tubes store solar radiation in winter while displaying the substance which literally and symbolically permeates the Nature center."

Barbara Goldstein, "Plotting the Land," *Arts and Architecture*, 1983

ARTIST TIM HURSLEY BECAME MY ARCHITECTURAL PHOTOGRAPHER ON MANY PROJECTS, AND CONTINUED BRILLIANTLY PHOTOGRAPHING OUR WORK FOR DECADES.

SKI RACING THROUGH THE '70s, '80s, AND '90s—TAOS SKI VALLEY, SUN VALLEY, STOWE, VAIL, AND ASPEN... THE INFAMOUS CORBETT'S COULOIR AT JACKSON HOLE, WYOMING.

A psychological deceleration—coming down the approach road from Rio Grande Boulevard, parking in the cottonwoods, walking a curvilinear path through the Bosque—then unexpectedly greeted by a drainage culvert entry.

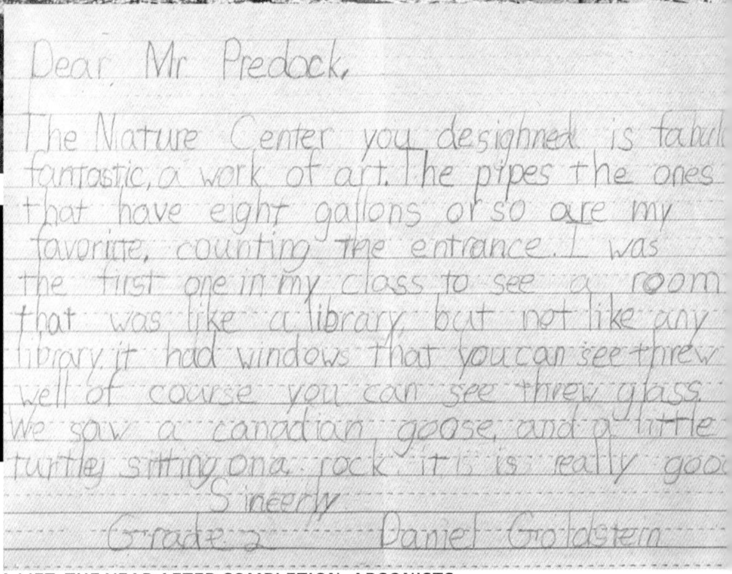

Dear Mr Predock,

The Nature Center you desighned is fabul fantastic, a work of art. The pipes the ones that have eight gallons or so are my favorite, counting the entrance. I was the first one in my class to see a room that was like a library but not like any library it had windows that you can see threw well of course you can see threw glass. We saw a canadian goose and a little turtley sitting on a rock. it is really goo

Sincerly

Grade 2 Daniel Goldstein

DESIGNED THE SCHWENDI ON-SLOPE LODGE AT TAOS SKI VALLEY AT THE BOTTOM OF THE KACHINA LIFT. THE YEAR AFTER COMPLETION, ARSONISTS SET IT ON FIRE AT 3 A.M. THE HEAT-SOFTENED, METAL ROOF DRAPED OVER THE CONCRETE BLADE.

SCHWENDI RESTAURANT & LODGE
TAOS SKI VALLEY
TAOS, NM 1978/80

Passing through the entry culvert, visitors become aware of a significant feature of the building: vertical, 8-foot-high, water-filled solar receptor tubes encircle a sunken, ramped exhibit and viewing area. Light striking from skylights shimmers through these tubes to create an underwater effect. The ramp descends physically and symbolically, aiming "view rays" toward the vast forage areas, the marshlands and a reverse-periscope underwater image of the pond. At each stage along the ramp, interpretive displays augment the views; the exhibits complement the trails that lace the refuge per our master plan.

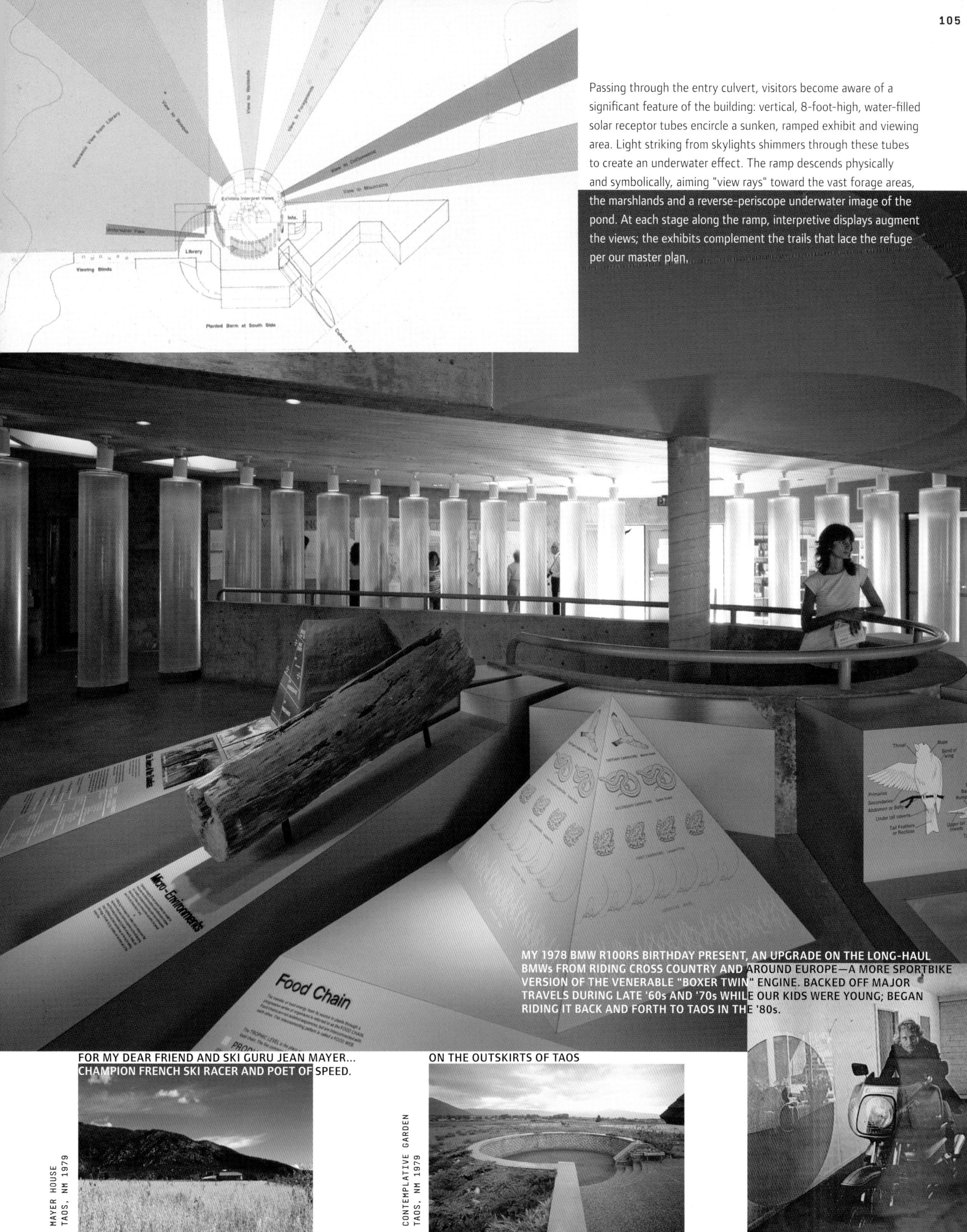

MY 1978 BMW R100RS BIRTHDAY PRESENT, AN UPGRADE ON THE LONG-HAUL BMWs FROM RIDING CROSS COUNTRY AND AROUND EUROPE—A MORE SPORTBIKE VERSION OF THE VENERABLE "BOXER TWIN" ENGINE. BACKED OFF MAJOR TRAVELS DURING LATE '60s AND '70s WHILE OUR KIDS WERE YOUNG; BEGAN RIDING IT BACK AND FORTH TO TAOS IN THE '80s.

FOR MY DEAR FRIEND AND SKI GURU JEAN MAYER... CHAMPION FRENCH SKI RACER AND POET OF SPEED.

MAYER HOUSE
TAOS, NM 1979

ON THE OUTSKIRTS OF TAOS

CONTEMPLATIVE GARDEN
TAOS, NM 1979

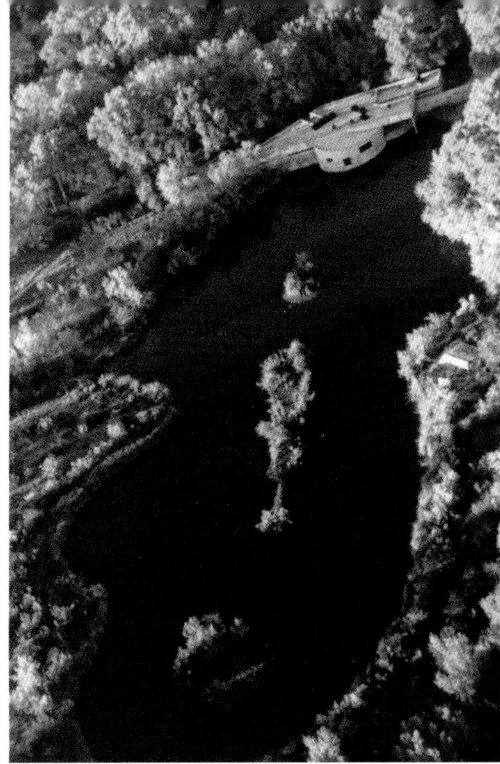

"The building's hard-edged geometry and industrial materials ... expose the inherent tension—and collaboration—between technology and nature that comes with preserving a wildlife sanctuary in the middle of a city."

Christopher Mead, *Roadcut*, 2012

MULTI-TOWNHOUSE PROJECT, FOLLOWED LA LUZ ON THE HIGH SAGE BRUSH PLAIN BELOW VALLECITO PEAK. TOWNHOUSE GROUPINGS AIMED AT MOUNTAIN VIEWS BUFFER PREVAILING WINDS WHILE DEFINING TENNIS COURT PLACITAS.

TENNIS RANCH OF TAOS
TAOS, NM 1980

"The natural wetlands ecosystem harbor an incredibly diverse set of processes that contrast dramatically with the upland semi-arid mesas. Predock's Rio Grande Nature Center and Preserve, with its 170-acre site on the Rio Grande Flyway for migratory wildfowl, stands as a symbol of the importance these wetland areas have in Albuquerque's past, present, and future developments."

Kevin J. Lorenz, "Passive Solar in the Land of Adobe," *Texas Architect*, March/April, 1983

I EXCHANGED A PORTION OF MY FEE FOR OWNERSHIP OF ONE OF THE UNITS. MY CLIENT INSISTED ON PUTTING TRADITIONAL WOOD PANEL ENTRY DOORS ON THE UNITS. I LOST THAT BATTLE, BUT ON MY UNIT I USED A FLUSH MODERN DOOR I PAINTED PURPLE, WHICH WASN'T APPRECIATED.

PREDOCK CONDOMINIUMS

PREVIOUSLY ST. BERNARD CONDOMINIUMS

TAOS, NEW MEXICO 1979/1982

At Taos Ski Valley, following The Tennis Ranch of Taos, as I settled in as a regular during ski season, I developed a lifelong friendship with Jean Mayer—designing a house for his family. Jean owned a beautiful undeveloped site there that clients of mine purchased to construct the St. Bernard Condominiums. Jean held a minority ownership and linked management of the condos to his famed St. Bernard Hotel. Decades later the condominium owners association decided to rename the project after me.

MY SON JASON TOOK THIS SHOT OF ME SKIING THE CONDO ROOF IN 1984.

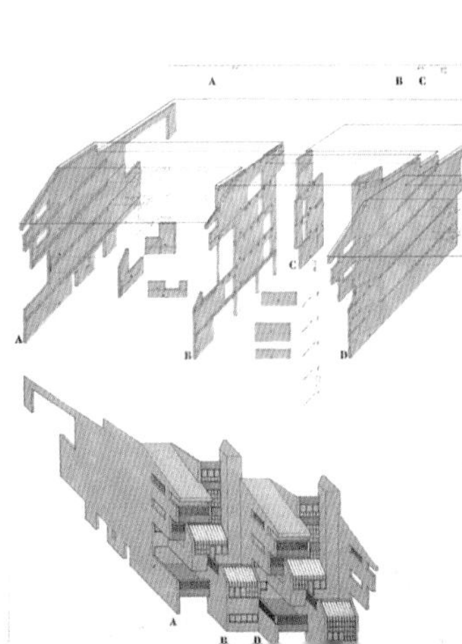

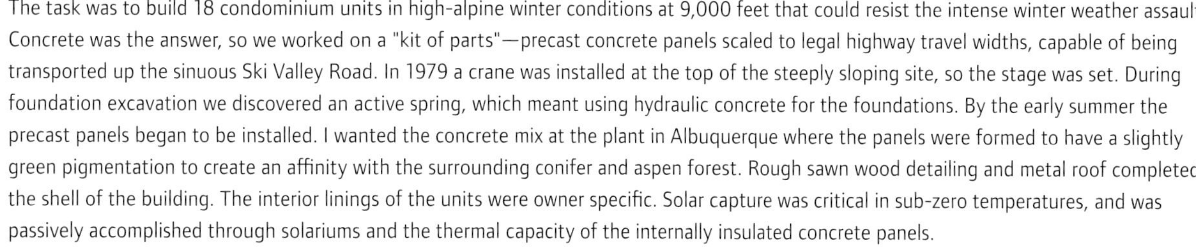

The task was to build 18 condominium units in high-alpine winter conditions at 9,000 feet that could resist the intense winter weather assault. Concrete was the answer, so we worked on a "kit of parts"—precast concrete panels scaled to legal highway travel widths, capable of being transported up the sinuous Ski Valley Road. In 1979 a crane was installed at the top of the steeply sloping site, so the stage was set. During foundation excavation we discovered an active spring, which meant using hydraulic concrete for the foundations. By the early summer the precast panels began to be installed. I wanted the concrete mix at the plant in Albuquerque where the panels were formed to have a slightly green pigmentation to create an affinity with the surrounding conifer and aspen forest. Rough sawn wood detailing and metal roof completed the shell of the building. The interior linings of the units were owner specific. Solar capture was critical in sub-zero temperatures, and was passively accomplished through solariums and the thermal capacity of the internally insulated concrete panels.

HADRIAN, SARAH, STEVE, AND NEPHEW ANDREW AT THE STUDIO IN THE '80s

UNITED BLOOD SERVICES

ALBUQUERQUE, NEW MEXICO 1980/82

GROUP OF BICYCLE RACERS I RODE WITH—CALLED TEAM FARMACIA DEL MUNDO. HOUSE/CLINIC FOR THE TEAM DOCTOR—NEVER BUILT.

CLINICO EQUIPO
ALBUQUERQUE, NM 1980

TRAVELS TO PARIS AT THE TIME—NOTRE-DAME AND PARIS PANORAMA—NOTRE-DAME,

Jerry Bednorz wearing a blood red tie, director of United Blood Services, drove up to my Studio in a bright red car.

I said "The building should be red, reflecting its purpose." He replied "Go for it!"

LA SAINTE CHAPELLE, PANTHÉON AND SAINT EUSTACHE.

AN EARLY SANTA FE SOLAR HOUSE—PASSIVE SOLAR HEAT EXCHANGE AUGMENTED THE MECHANICAL SYSTEMS.

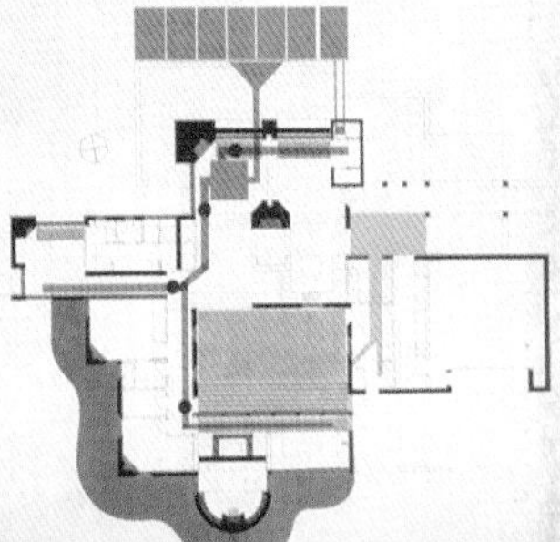

LA LUZ IN CENTRE POMPIDOU EXHIBIT OCTOBER 31, 1981

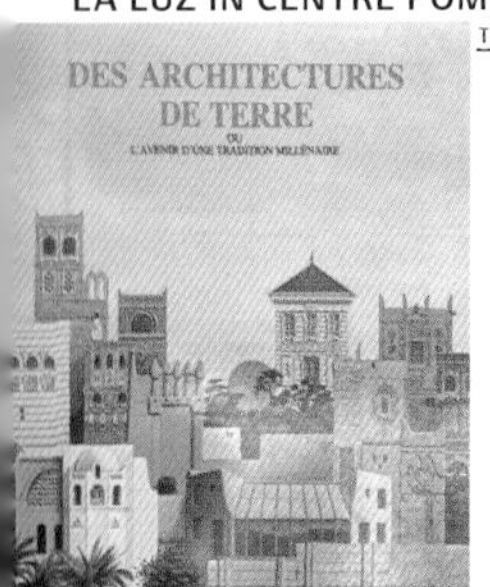

Trois séminaires sur l'architecture en terre

. L'actualité et l'avenir des architectures de terre (adobe) (adobe) aux Etats-Unis

samedi 31 octobre 1981 ; de 14h30 à 18h30
Centre Pompidou - Petite salle
Entrée libre dans la mesure des places disponibles

- Antoine Predock, architecte à Albuquerque (New-Mexico), auteur du quartier urbain de "La Luz" édifié en adobe en 1975.

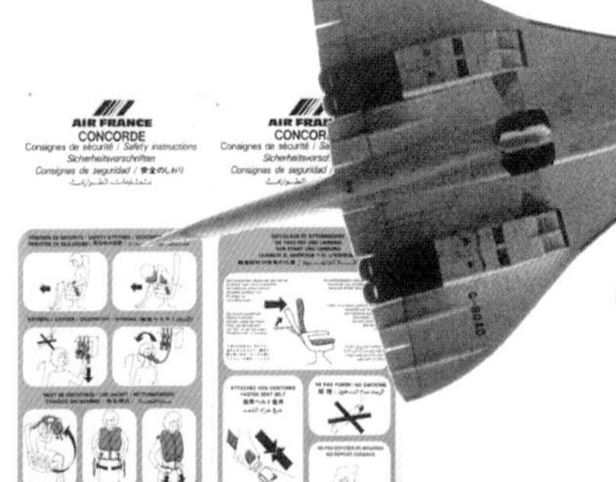

MY FIRST TRIP TO EUROPE BY FREIGHTER IN THE '60s,

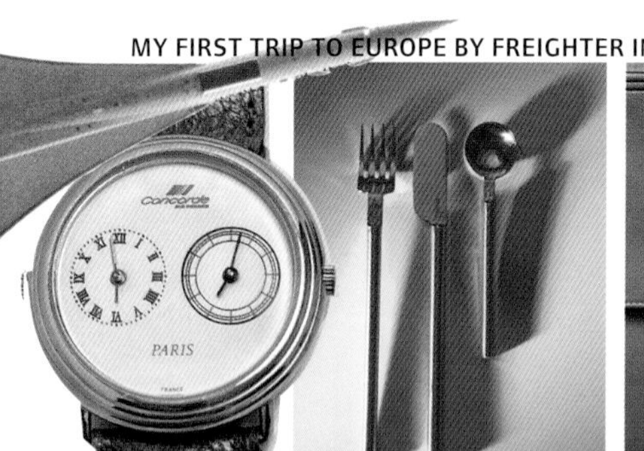

One day Mayor Kinney called and asked,
"Is that red just the color of the primer."
I said "Nope Harry, what you see is what you get."

TOOK 10 DAYS. IN THE '80s—3.5 HOURS AT MACH 2 ON THE CONCORDE. AT 65,000 FEET ALTITUDE, THE CURVATURE OF THE EARTH WAS VISIBLE. SEVERAL FLIGHTS THROUGH THE '80s AND '90s, CHRISTOPHER WALKEN WAS A FELLOW PASSENGER, AND ON ANOTHER FLIGHT RUDOLF NUREYEV AUTOGRAPHED MY LEFT ARM... AND I GOT A FREE WATCH...

CHINON, FRANCE LOIRE VALLEY, 1982

ABU SIMBEL AND KARNAK, 1982

Post-Nuclear Vision

DESERT HIGHLANDS

PHOENIX, AZ 1983

The linking of attached housing units defines outdoor placitas and entraps natural features. These outdoor areas inform the housing precinct with rituals of the desert—campfires, sunset and night sky viewing.

"... it's a project in which the process of arriving at its forms is almost as important as the forms themselves. Given its location, the aridity of the place, and the fact that these are in the desert ... it achieves a remarkable sense of place and of privacy."

James Stewart Polshek, *Progressive Architecture*, January 1984

VENICE BEACH WITH HADRIAN AND JASON, EARLY '80s

A significant part of the house is set partially underground—providing thermal stability while capturing eye-level views of the desert landscape. The higher vantage points, like the sunset tower, have views across the valley to the night lights of Phoenix, the sunset in the west, and the mountains in the east.

"Like the bones of the landscape, the building must stand forth in its own structural right—but not too much. Thus the architect balances on a knife-edge between building too forcefully (against his surroundings) and building too self-effacingly (so that his work disappears into the surroundings). The house built on the out-skirts of Phoenix, Arizona, for Gene and Donna Fuller by Antoine Predock not only treads that knife-edge, it transforms the balancing act into a deliberate, graceful dance."

GA House, December 1986

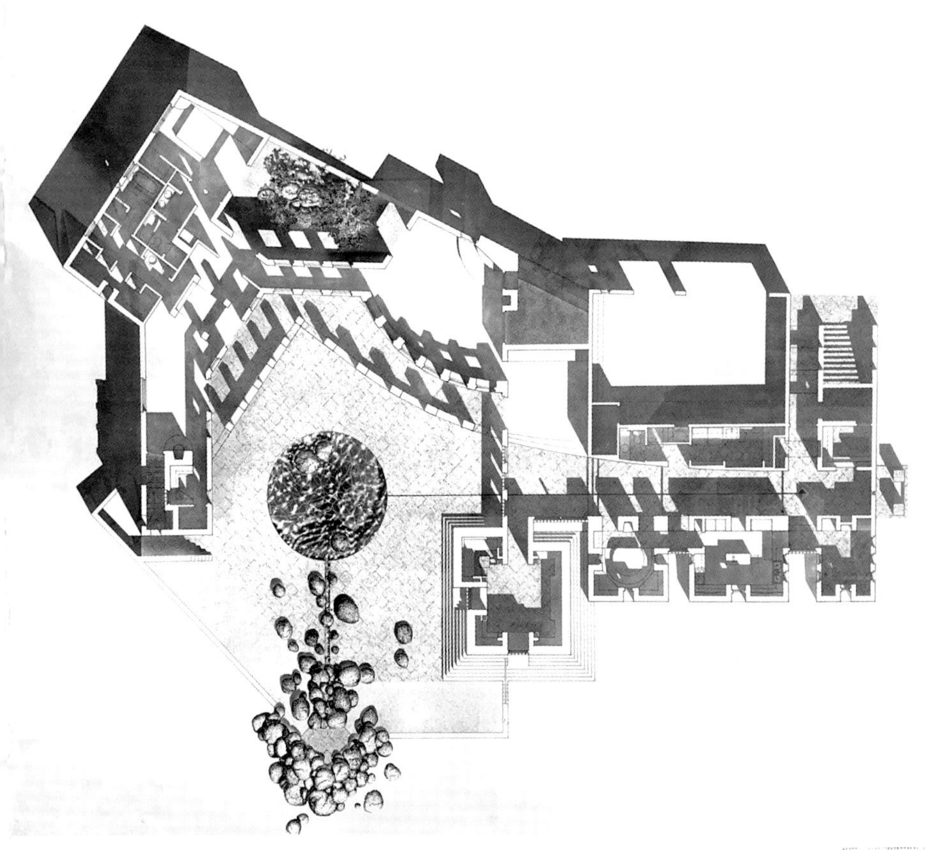

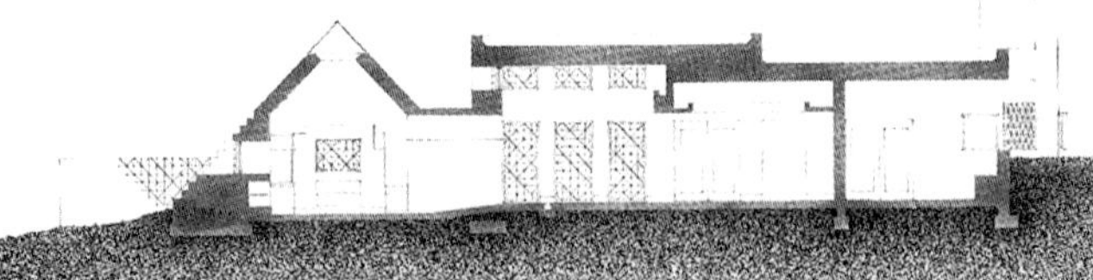

This High Sonoran desert site is enclosed by peaks and eroded granite ridges. Below this encircling rim, sparse vegetation, at once hardy and fragile, surrounds the house and speaks of the adaptations necessary for life beneath an unremitting sun.

In this desert environment, architecture, landscape, and human procession join in a synchronous dance. The low, weighty perimeter of the house connects in its massiveness and its color to the powerful geologic context. Contrasting brittle steel shade structures create shadow patterns that recall the tracery cast on the site by the lacy branches of the Ocotillo and Palo Verde. The house is axially positioned in relation to the east-west travel of the sun. Daily living patterns shift from morning to evening. A sunrise viewing pavilion is situated above the breakfast room; an interior "canyon," a gallery with centered, sequential water system, leads past kitchen and dining fragments as the "mountain," the pyramidal study, introduces the "valley," the central courtyard; across the "valley" a trellised, sunset tower completes the track of the sun. Inside the house, water issues from a black granite block and runs through a channel parallel to the east-west axis. The water's path culminates in a quiet pool in the courtyard.

The gentle standoff between built form and desert environment is expressed as a poetic tension. The line of demarcation between the house and the terrain becomes ambiguous. At certain places the desert enters—boulders tumble into the courtyard. Refuge in this arid precinct has been created by the presence of water, shade, and enclosure. Looking out from this sequestered desert retreat, the majestic landscape and the vast sky become theater.

FULLER HOUSE

SCOTTSDALE, ARIZONA 1984/87

"Predock is ... creating a remarkable body of work—tough and sensual, fabulously imagined, altogether persuasive."

Kurt Andersen, "Design: An Architect for the New Age," *Time Magazine*, April 11, 1988

"Not since Frank Lloyd Wright first ventured into Scottsdale in 1932 ... has ANY architect evoked with comparable intensity the myth of America's aboriginal past and of the desert in which it is inscribed."

Kenneth Frampton, *American Masterworks*, 1995

"Yet for all the house's risky paradox—B-movie imagery conceived with restraint and accomplished with first-rate production values—it succeeds breathtakingly."

Kurt Andersen, "Design: An Architect for the New Age," *Time Magazine*, April 11, 1988

In the Southwest, I always think of the fundamental connection between earth and sky, through the mute blank adobe walls that you find here. This has influenced me enormously. There is such a completeness in adobe architecture; the wall acts as a bridge between earth and sky. It is of the earth, an extension of the earth aspiring toward the sky; and any sort of decorative addition, a cornice or a stringcourse, would feel secondary and half-hearted compared to the power of the wall itself.

Sometimes a building's connection to place starts with a silhouette. When we come to the West for the first time and try to get our bearings, there is a daunting confrontation of the limitless landscape, a limitless sky, distant mountain ranges iconically marking the land. I understand the tendency toward monumentality, ersatz monumentality, when confronted by the onslaught of this infinite space. How does one go up against a mountain range? One option is to make something comfortable like a classical pediment, the impulse that had traditionally been followed in false-front western towns. Another option, one that I have chosen, is to make buildings that suggest an analogous landscape.

THE PROJECT STRADDLES A CULTURAL FAULT LINE BETWEEN THE TERRAIN OF THE LOWRIDERS AND THE FAIRWAYS OF THE ALBUQUERQUE COUNTRY CLUB GOLFERS. IMPLICIT IN THIS

BEACH APARTMENTS
ALBUQUERQUE, NM 1983/86

JUXTAPOSITION IS THE LOCATION OF THE COMPLEX ON HIGHWAY 66—A 3D BLANKET-LIKE EVOCATION OF THE IMAGERY OF THE POIGNANTLY SURVIVING MOTELS (TOURIST COURTS), CAFÉS, AND FILLING STATIONS—REMNANTS OF A PASSAGE IN AMERICAN LIFE.

"Predock's central axis is a water channel that leads from east to west, tracking the path of the sun. As Predock describes it, this channel of water 'is a stream, discharging into a valley, then into a lake, with the mountain as witness.' He creates his own 'mountain as witness' in the pyramid, echoing the shape of the peaks around the house, anchoring the house in the realm of the mountain.... And Predock's court, with its pool and boulders, can be associated with Japanese gardens, each device extending the architecture into a 'universal frame.' ... Predock somehow manages to combine gravitas with a light touch that stems from a celebration of the joy of life itself."

Geoffery Baker, *Antoine Predock*, 1997

HONORING THE MAJESTY AND HISTORY OF THE RIO GRANDE VALLEY

ROBINSON-BURNEY HOUSE
ALBUQUERQUE, NM 1983/85

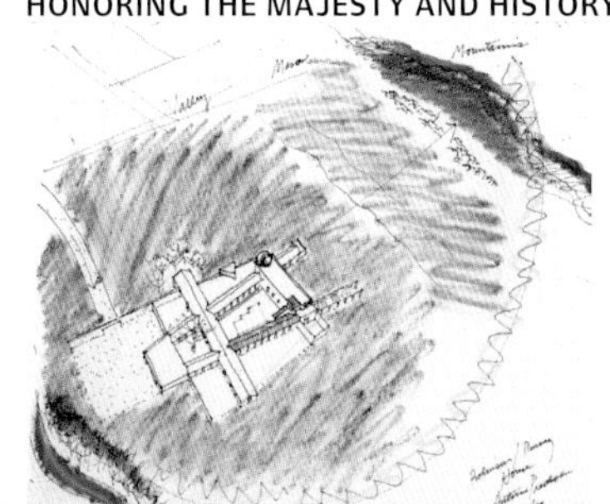

"The most dramatic and most symbolic aspect of the house is the central pyramid.... At once all-seeing eye and pyramidon, the top of this pyramid forms the pyramidal skylight to the study beneath. According to Egyptian legend, this is the point at which the Phoenix alights at dawn at the beginning of each day. Irrespective of such associations, this aperture clearly functions as an inverted sundial, since the sunlight that enters the study also effectively registers the time of day until it drops so low as to disappear from view."

Kenneth Frampton, *American Masterworks,* 1995

SOUTHWEST D.C. SECTOR PLAN "GATEWAY TO THE REST OF AMERICA"

SMITHSONIAN URBAN DESIGN CHARRETTE, WASHINGTON, D.C. 1984

UT AUSTIN SCHOOL OF ARCHITECTURE—STUDIO DESIGN

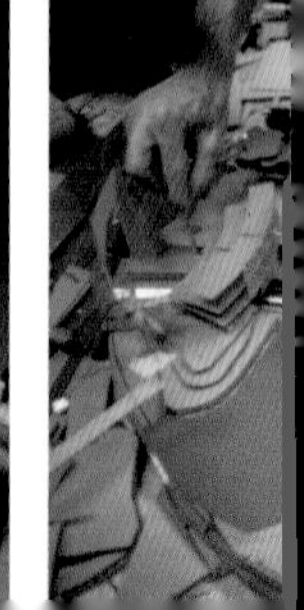

The house is axially positioned in relation to the east-west travel of the sun. Daily living patterns shift from morning to evening.

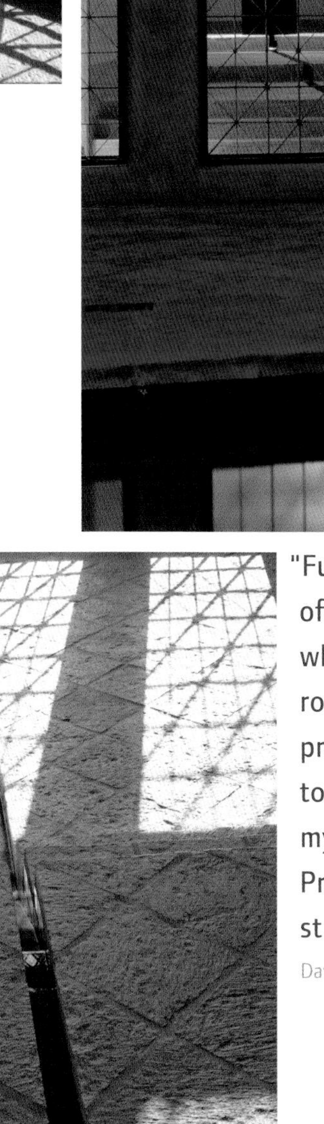

"Fuller House ... marked the emergence of a bolder, more diagrammatic idiom in which the conventional procession from room to room was transformed into a procession from season to season, earth to sky, and matter to spirit. ... It is more mystical and more overtly theatrical than Predock's previous houses, and it set the stage for later projects."

David Dillon, "Border Crossings," *Architecture*, August 1991

CHARRETTE WITH SUPERSTUDENTS LIZ AND HYPATIA

TRIP TO TALIESIN WEST WITH KEVIN KELLOG AND PERRY BECKER, WHILE A VISITING PROFESSOR AT ASU.

SKI MOUNTAINEERING ABOVE TAOS SKI VALLEY IN THE '80s.

"Architecture as a defense system against a hostile environment is appropriate in the Sonoran desert. The potential claiming of architecture by the landscape sets into motion a dance between building and site. The gentle standoff between the two is expressed in the project as a poetic tension. Project edges are somewhat ambiguous—at times allowing the desert to enter, other times setting a tight line of defense. Refuge is created by the presence of water, shade, and enclosure. Looking out from this sequestered desert retreat, the vast landscape scale can be better comprehended."

GA Houses Special, Masterpieces 1971-2000, 2000

PANTHEON CAP, PANTHEON BEANIE MODELED BY JEAN NOUVEL, THEN A PLATE, THEN A WATCH...

Twenty years into my practice, the Rome Prize allowed me to study as a Fellow at the American Academy, my everyday life on pause, immersed in a new (old) world, amid the strata, where the man-made dissolves through time into a geological blur, where natural landscapes have had order imposed upon them that is subtle and extraordinary, all haunted by an ancient presence.

The deepest, most lasting thing I brought away was a vision of a kind of time travel. In Rome I found myself exposed, physically and conceptually, to the process of excavation. Ushered into the basement of an apartment building, I experienced the groundwater of the Tiber flowing over gigantic stones with Latin inscriptions on them. It was the great Sundial Field of Augustus, of which the gnomon, the sundial pointer, was an Egyptian obelisk, now in the Piazza Montecitorio. I experienced these accretions throughout the city vividly, over and over again, the collapse of time into timelessness—like a sci-fi movie.

This Roman blurring of geology, landscape, and building has had a profound effect on my approach to architecture and has propelled me to seek the spirit of those layers, to delve into and even further explore the accreted deep time of every site, every Roadcut—even where not so obviously present. This curiosity and desire to be immersed in the essence of site/Roadcut continues to be at the heart of my process.

With a primitive video camera, I made a piece on Rome—nonstop, Andy Warhol/Blair Witchesque footage. Anywhere I'd go, I'd take my camera, pastels, and brush pen. I had a mixed-media, complete immersion experience. And with this opportunity to sketch on a daily basis, I learned to trust in the innocence of encounter and the translation of that encounter into an innocent mark. Capturing essences of this surreal urban landscape through pastel on paper, through time-slices on video, I was able to document, within two dimensions, the truth of four dimensions.

THE VIEW FROM MY TOP FLOOR STUDIO AT THE AMERICAN ACADEMY IN ROME

ROME PRIZE

ROME, ITALY 1985

OMNIBVS·AD·QVOS·HAE·LITTERAE·PERVENERINT
NOTVM·SIT·NOS·PRAEPOSITVM·ET·CVRATORES
ACADEMIAE·AMERICANAE·ROMAE·SITAE

ANTOINE PREDOCK

QVI·ROMAE·IN·ACADEMIA·NOSTRA

ARTES ELEGANTIORES

COLVERIT·OMNIBVS·MVNERIBVS·OFFICIISQVE
ACADEMICIS·RITE·CONFECTIS·SOCIVM
ACADEMIAE·ROMAE·SITAE·COOPTAVISSE·EVMQVE
AD·OMNIA·IVRA·PRIVILEGIA·INSIGNIA·AD
HVNC·HONOREM·PERTINENTIA·ADMISISSE

NOVI EBORACI AD MDCCCCLXXXV

ACADEMIAE DIRECTOR

CVRATORVM PRAEPOSITVS

ACADEMIAE PRAESES

Announcement for the centennial celebration of the American Academy in Rome used my Pantheon sketch from 1985.

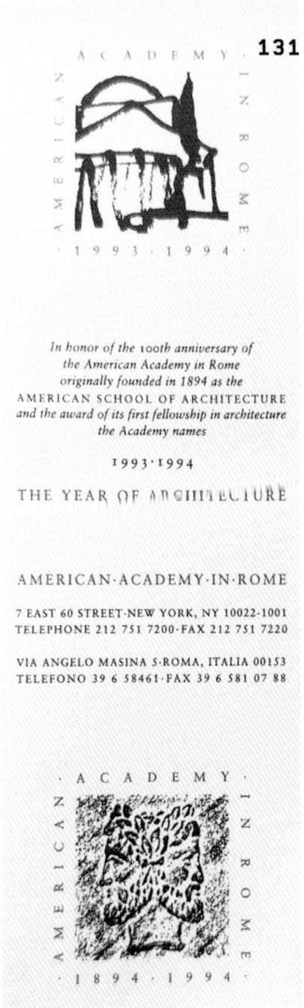

· 1 9 9 3 · 1 9 9 4 ·

In honor of the 100th anniversary of the American Academy in Rome originally founded in 1894 as the AMERICAN SCHOOL OF ARCHITECTURE *and the award of its first fellowship in architecture the Academy names*

1993·1994

THE YEAR OF ARCHITECTURE

AMERICAN·ACADEMY·IN·ROME

7 EAST 60 STREET·NEW YORK, NY 10022-1001
TELEPHONE 212 751 7200·FAX 212 751 7220

VIA ANGELO MASINA 5·ROMA, ITALIA 00153
TELEFONO 39 6 58461·FAX 39 6 581 07 88

· ACADEMY · IN ROME · AMERICAN ·
· 1 8 9 4 · 1 9 9 4 ·

The enigmatic Pantheon is of such a different order than "architecture"— it exerts transformational power on the viewer that is undeniable. One can talk about the highly advanced engineering strategies used by the Romans but it blasts beyond all of that into a cosmic blur.

On one trip to Rome I returned to the "Mothership" as always— it was a rainy day and standing directly under the open-to-the-sky oculus was a Japanese couple, umbrella unfurled. "It's raining in the Pantheon."

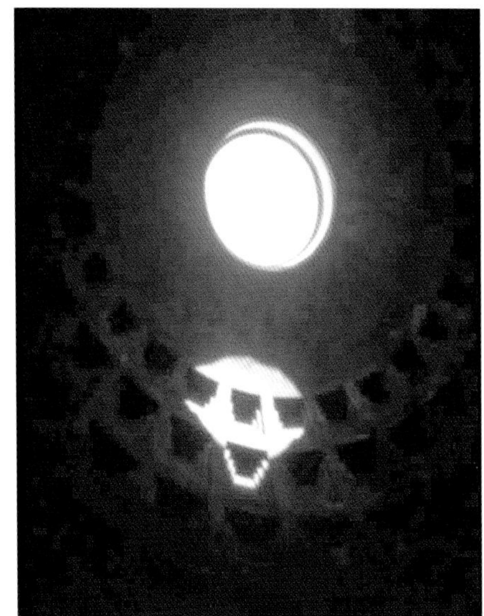

WHILE IN ROME, BACK IN NEW MEXICO PROJECTS PROGRESSED, WORKING ON THEM REMOTELY.
I RAN UP THE HILLSIDE SITE OF THE HOUSE, SPINNING AROUND TOWARD THE DISTANT VIEWS—I RECORDED IT IN A DIAGRAM THAT BECAME THE FRAGMENTED HOUSE.

TREASTER-GREY HOUSE
TESUQUE, NM 1984/86

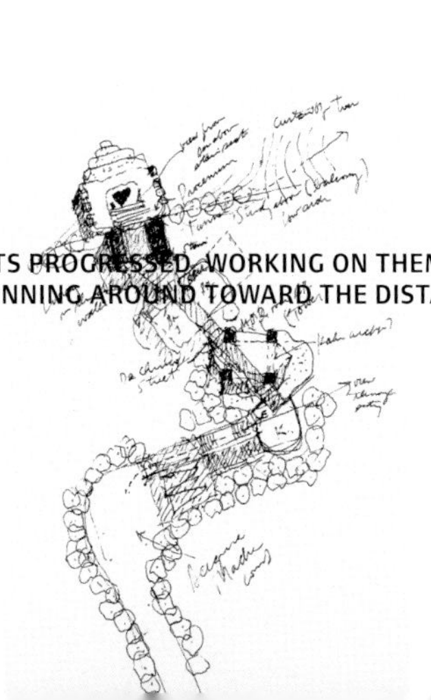

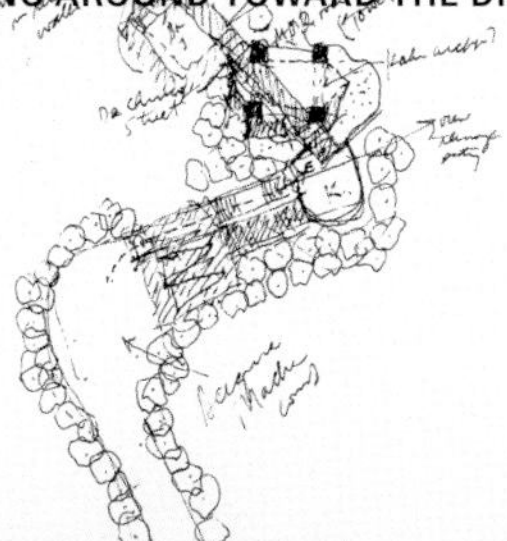

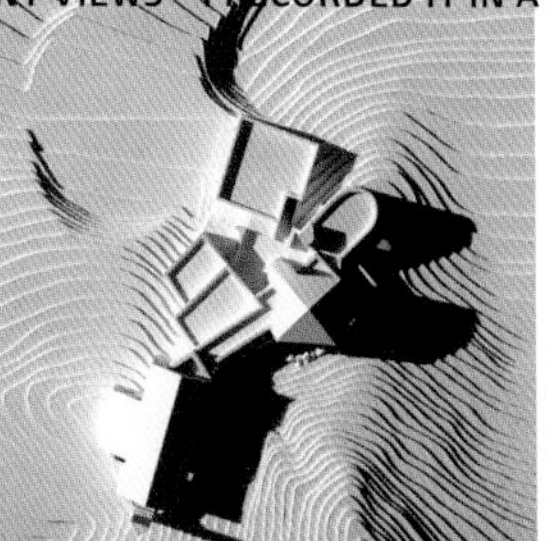

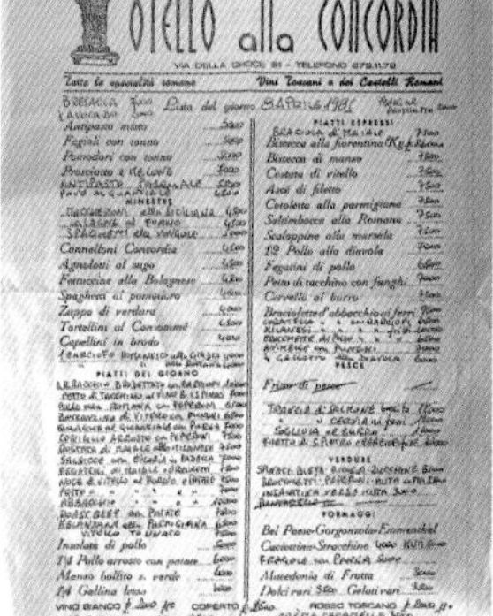

TRATTORIA

OTELLO alla CONCORDIA

VIA DELLA CROCE 81 - TELEFONO 679.11.78

Tutte le specialità romane — Vini Toscani e dei Castelli Romani

Lista del giorno

Antipasto misto
Fagioli con tonno
Pomodori con tonno
Prosciutto e
MINESTRE
Cannelloni Concordia
Agnolotti al sugo
Fettuccine alla Bolognese
Spaghetti al pomodoro
Zuppa di verdura
Tortellini al Consommé
Capellini in brodo
PIATTI DEL GIORNO
Insalata di pollo
1/4 Pollo arrosto con patate
Manzo bollito s. verde
1/4 Gallina lessa
VINO BIANCO — COPERTO — ROSSO TOSCANO

PIATTI ESPRESSI
Bistecca alla fiorentina
Bistecca di manzo
Costata di vitello
Asso di filetto
Cotoletta alla parmigiana
Saltimbocca alla Romana
Scaloppine alla marsala
1/2 Pollo alla diavola
Fegatini di pollo
Petto di tacchino con funghi
Cervello al burro
Braciolette d'abbacchio ai ferri
PESCE
Frittura di pesce
VERDURE
FORMAGGI
Bel Paese-Gorgonzola-Emmenthal
Caciottina-Stracchino
Macedonia di Frutta
Dolci vari — Gelati vari

MENU FROM MY FAVORITE TRATTORIA

Porta Maggiore becomes a bauble on the necklace-like Aurelian wall, predating Marcus Aurelius with its brutal Claudian masonry. And then juxtaposed to it, cheek by jowl, was the Baker's Tomb—very ancient and beautiful with the appearance of a kind of Italian rationalist abstraction of circular baker's ovens. When you view the Porta Maggiore, the Baker's Tomb is adjunct to it, side-stepping the Aurelian wall, which absorbs and incorporates existing monuments like the pyramid of Caio Cestio and the Amphitheatrum Castrense, etc. along its wandering trajectory.

Rome goes every which way—not only in what is in front of you, but to the sky in the case of the sundial of Augustus, and deep into the earth as in the subterranean Mithraic chambers.

HOUSE FOR PAUL LAZARUS POISED ON THE EDGE OF A RIDGE ABOVE TESUQUE, NEW MEXICO. A LINEAR PROCESSION LINKS CORRAL/GARAGE TRELLIS PASSAGEWAY THROUGH

LAZARUS HOUSE
TESUQUE, NM 1984/86

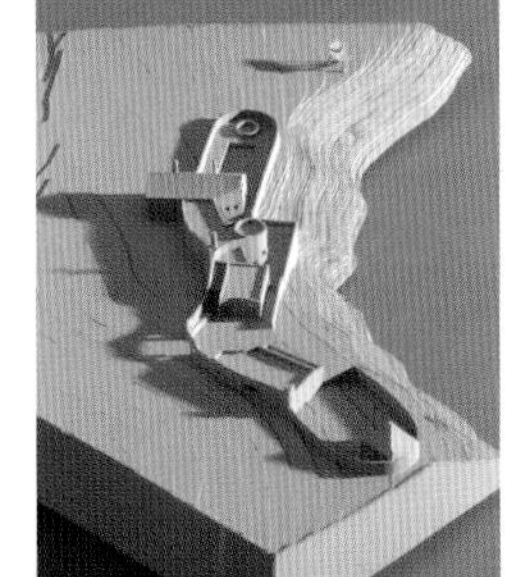

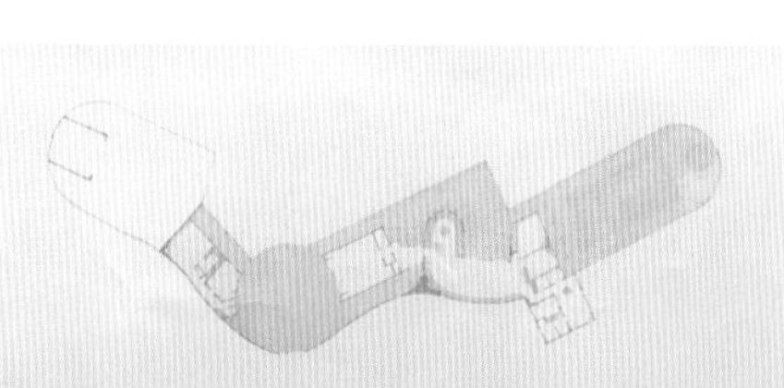

Imagine coming down the Palatine Hill—from Renaissance to the time of Christ, it "is a pile of emperors"—imperial residue, imperial accretion. Weaving our way down through time, each emperor erasing whoever preceded him—emperor after emperor erasing, and at the bottom is a delicate entablature, a beautifully crafted marble mantlepiece for the evil Nero.

LIVING/SLEEPING SPACES TO THE POOL AT THE END OF THE NECKLACE.

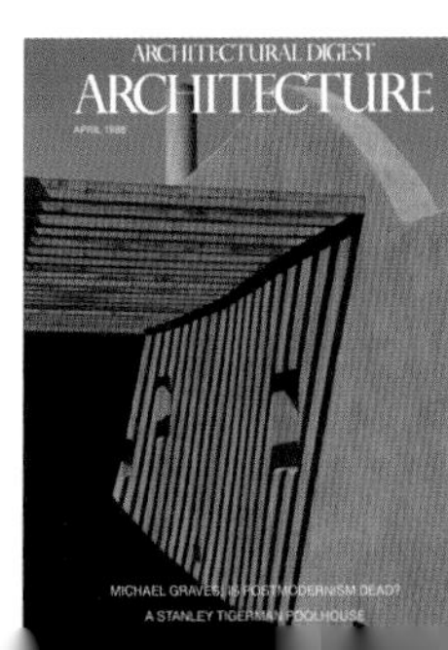

Bramante's
"Little Caged Beast"

Borromini, Bramante... and Turandot and
Aida, with elephants, in the Baths of Caracalla

Across a web of converging roads and a trolley track that accidentally formed a plaza, there is a strange little shack containing a stairway. With an Academy "permesso," we were able to access a subterranean Mithraic Basilica—in the deep strata of Rome, pagan temples, later co-opted as Christian chapels. The Latin cross plan of churches comes from the pagan Basilica plan.

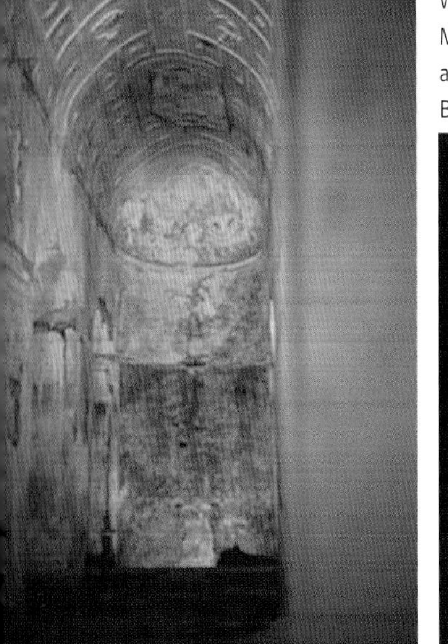

BORROMINI BLASTING OUT OF ST. IVO

Trips out of Rome—Villa Lante, Assisi, Orvieto

NEW MEXICO HEART CLINIC
ALBUQUERQUE, NM 1984/86

WHILE I WAS IN ROME, THE HEART BUILDING

Spanish Steps—Times Square of Rome

FOR BARRY RAMO'S CARDIOLOGIST GROUP PROGRESSED—A VILLAGE OF OFFICES AND EXAM ROOMS EMBRACED BY A MASSIVE MASONRY WALL ALONG THE I-25.

Florence had me with the raw power of the Cimabue Crucifix at Santa Croce—not for Christian reasons.

India ink and saliva wash Duomo

"Ducati City"

TROY HOUSE COMPLETES THE "X" OF VALLECITO MOUNTAIN AND TAOS MOUNTAIN IN ROBERT RECK'S BEAUTIFUL SHOT.

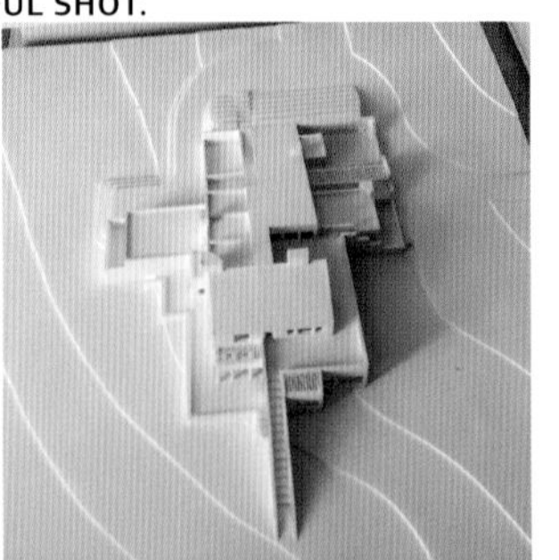

TROY HOUSE
TAOS, NM 1985/91

Taormina and spooky Etna

Roman architecture is so full of surprises—like the Grotto of Tiberius where the dialectic play of man-ordered water and the surf of the Mediterranean is made so explicit—water to water, imperial intention creating an aperture to the realm of the sea.

San Leo, where the imprisoned scoundrel/fornicator Cagliostro spent his days with a cross atop the village church the only view from his cell.

Umbria

The surrealism of Italy—Fellini-like juxtapositions, like the ski area on Mt. Etna, cables and lift towers memorialized in the lava.

VESUVIUS FROM HERCULANEUM—THE OTHER SIDE OF POMPEII

Venice—on a vaporetto around the island, not going anywhere in particular, I noticed an inconspicuous passage through a big wall labeled "Ospedale." Hopping off the vaporetto, I passed through a weathered stucco wall into a garden occupied by patients of the hospital—a wonderful place of echoes and hollow sounds, evoking a peaceful vibe of compassion and warmth. Molto Italiano.

Fontana Acqua Paola—marble facing cannibalized from Trajan's Market.

Vatican City—how kind and minimal and austere Jesus was—in appearance and message—contrasted with Popes and all of their treasures and private villas. I tried wrapping my mind around it. In the Belvedere Garden of the Vatican Palace, the famous Apollo sculpture under a fine mesh overhead, protecting it from all the birds that come from around the world to crap on the Apollo Belvedere...

Casina Pio—Pope Pio IV's crash pad in the Vatican Gardens.

ALAN COLQUHOUN AND PIA ON ONE OF OUR FIELD TRIPS

ROME—A MODERN CITY WITHOUT MODERN ARCHITECTURE, POWERFULLY HAUNTED BY A DEEP TIME PRESENCE

Pyramid of Caio Cestio 18 B.C., one of the pearls along the necklace of the Aurelian Wall

MY SKETCHES WERE COLLECTED AND PUBLISHED AS *ITALIAN SKETCHBOOKS* IN 1985

At the center is the Galvin Playhouse with the Dance Studio Theater. The curving arcade/aqueduct delivers water to three fountain locations, one of which is at the theater entry. The theater is reached through the trellised foreground arcade. Gradations of color lead from light to dark, ending with purple-black acoustic side walls of the theater itself.

The poetry of Garcia Lorca describes the desert dualities "sol y sombra." This building acknowledges those aspects of the terrain, both spiritually and physically. Necessary respites from the sun are created by zones of lacy shade, like the patterns palo verde leaves cast on the desert floor. Spiky trellis elements help to cool spaces both cavernous and labyrinthine.

Other trajectories extend to the sky—via terraces, balconies, and towers that define the west campus entry as a gateway. There is both an ascent and a descent from the middle ground, where the theaters and the theater arts spaces are located. The descent to the shadowy, water-associated, much cooler museum entrance yields immediate respite from the ground level. These multidirectional itineraries become personal trails as each visitor experiences the Center.

Progressive Architecture

JUNE 1989

THE NELSON FINE ARTS CENTER DEMONSTRATES A SPECIAL ATTITUDE TOWARD THE DESERT, ACKNOWLEDGING ITS HARSH AND RELENTLESS PRESENCE, RATHER THAN TRYING TO TAME IT.

The design of the Nelson Fine Arts Center—containing a museum, theater, and the theater arts and dance departments—involved a special attitude toward the desert—much more than simply imposing the building program on the quasi-urban university site. The harsh and relentless desert presence in Arizona is often denied; the prevailing tendency (in terms of development and attitudes toward public architecture) is to convert the desert into an oasis, to tame the desert.

The building defines an episodic procession; it defines options and potentials rather than particular paths. It is an open matrix of possibilities for engagement both vertically and horizontally. Art galleries extend the procession. They are anchored by exterior terraces for sculpture installations. These terraces are partly shaded by steel-plate trellises. The gallery sequence is open ended; visitors can use the sculpture terraces to explore inside and out, or they can proceed indoors to the large upper gallery, which has the highest ceilings and straddles the main entry.

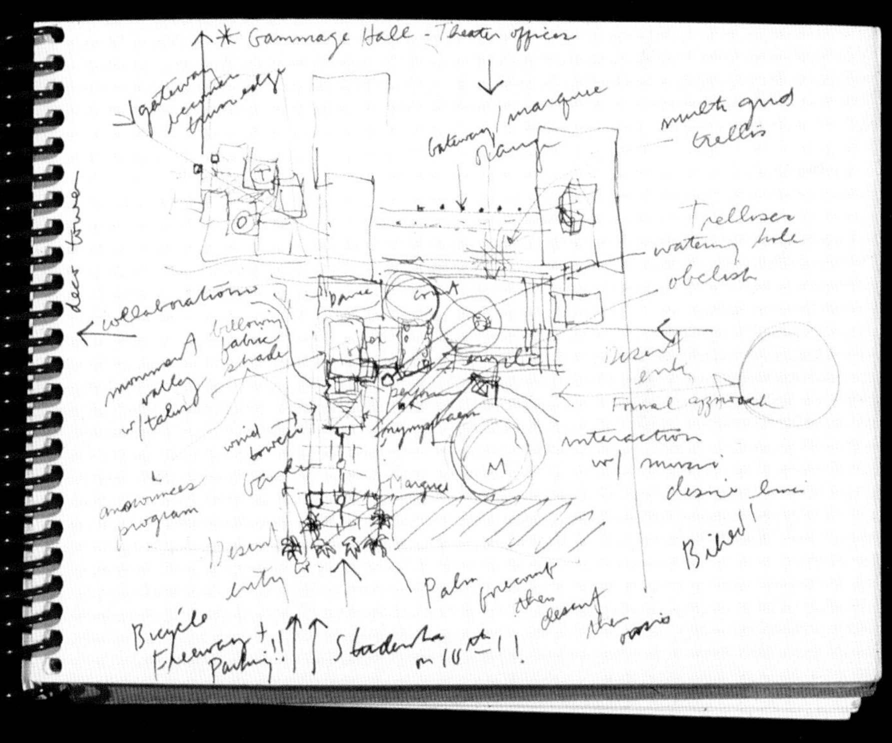

"This is architecture parlante, Southwestern style. And yet, the Fine Arts Center is not a simple building, nor is it one readily understood. It escapes documentation in two dimensions—via plan, photographs, or the simple and generally inaccurate diagrams attempted by the students. This 3D design calls upon all the senses, extending the palette of architecture to encompass sound, smell, and touch. In the process of choreographing a "sensurround" experience, Predock has sacrificed some legibility for imagery, but that too may be considered part of his plan."

Daralice D. Boles, "Magic Mountain," *Progressive Architecture*, June 1989

NELSON FINE ARTS CENTER

ARIZONA STATE UNIVERSITY
TEMPE, ARIZONA 1985/89

"It tells us ... how it is possible for a piece of architecture to be deeply ingrained in the traditions and spirit of a place—yet unlike anything we have seen before."

Paul Goldberger, "Speaking the Language of the Desert and Mountain," *New York Times*, January 28, 1990

-"sol y sombra." This building acknowledges those aspects of the terrain, both spiritually and physically.

RIGHT AWAY, EVEN DURING CONSTRUCTION, STUDENTS FROM THE MUSIC SCHOOL, WHICH IS IMMEDIATELY ADJACENT TO THE SITE, WOULD INVADE AND FIND THE PERFECT PRACTICE REALM... MYSTERIOUS PRACTICE SOUNDS COMING FROM UNKNOWN PLACES—IMAGINE SOUNDS OF THE TROMBONE OR THE OBOE FLOATING THROUGH THE AIR.

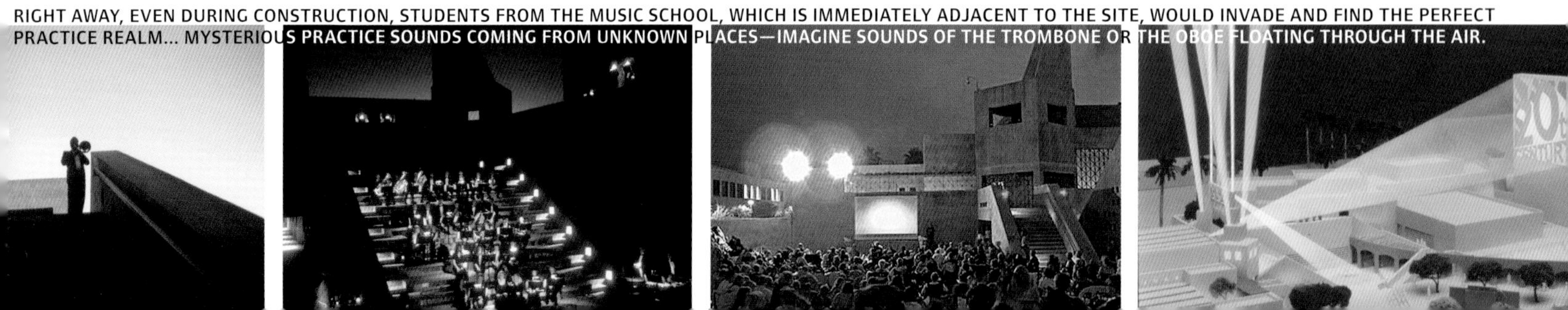

The poetry of Garcia Lorca describes the desert dualities –

"... his work has not lost its fundamental quality, which is the ability to express, in terms that seem one part modernist, one part mystical, the spirit of a place. Mr. Predock's real gift is his ability to deal in emotion without being sentimental. He is a theatrical architect who has the discipline to control his theater, and he is a traditional architect who has the inventiveness to reinterpret those traditions that inspire him. His southwestern buildings are not cute little adobe structures, cloying stage sets of a tourist's Santa Fe: they are tough, hard-edged and self-assured, and they would strike most people as being modernist more than traditional. Yet unlike most modernism which is pathetically indifferent to its surroundings, Predock buildings belong where they are."

Paul Goldberger, "Speaking the Language of the Desert and Mountain," *New York Times*, January 28, 1990

"This is a building of episodes, a building of pieces that fit together to make a complex whole but are intended to be experienced separately, over time, and not necessarily in any sequence ..."

Paul Goldberger, "Speaking the Language of the Desert and Mountain," *New York Times*, January 28, 1990

"The roof does not mark the end of the building, but transforms itself into an outdoor auditorium from which viewers can watch films projected onto the adjacent indoor theater's fly tower. The whole building has the sense of being somewhere between the massiveness of a mesa and the fragmented, specific massing of a functional structure. Predock has made an artificial mountain, hollowed it out to contain a cave, and then fissured and occupied the building so that the analogy begins to break down as the building breaks open."

Aaron Betsky, *Landscrapers, Building with the Land,* 2002

r derived from a rock I discovered in the nearby foothills.

s adobe color with silly fences around the fountains—aping the steel trellis.

The rugged silhouette—a landscape abstraction of the surrounding mountains and ridges—with the col

Now stuccoed a ridiculou

"And then, finally, there is the color which Mr. Predock took from a rock found on a nearby mountain: it is exactly right, neither too much like concrete, which would have made the building brutal, nor too strong in its color, which would have made the building too soft and sentimental. It Is not so much that this beautiful purplish gray is of the desert, though it very much is, as that it is so perfectly poised between being color and not being color. It evokes a timelessness and a depth, as if it had not been added to the stucco but had risen through its very being."

Paul Goldberger, "Speaking the Language of the Desert and Mountain," *New York Times*, January 28, 1990

"... place making of an allusive sort, like Ronchamp, an enigmatic building with no special interpretation that unlocks its secret, but many different keys that work on parts."

Charles Jencks

LOOKING NORTH TO THE FOOTHILLS BEYOND, WHERE I FOUND A ROCK THAT BECAME THE BASIS FOR THE BUILDING STUCCO COLOR.

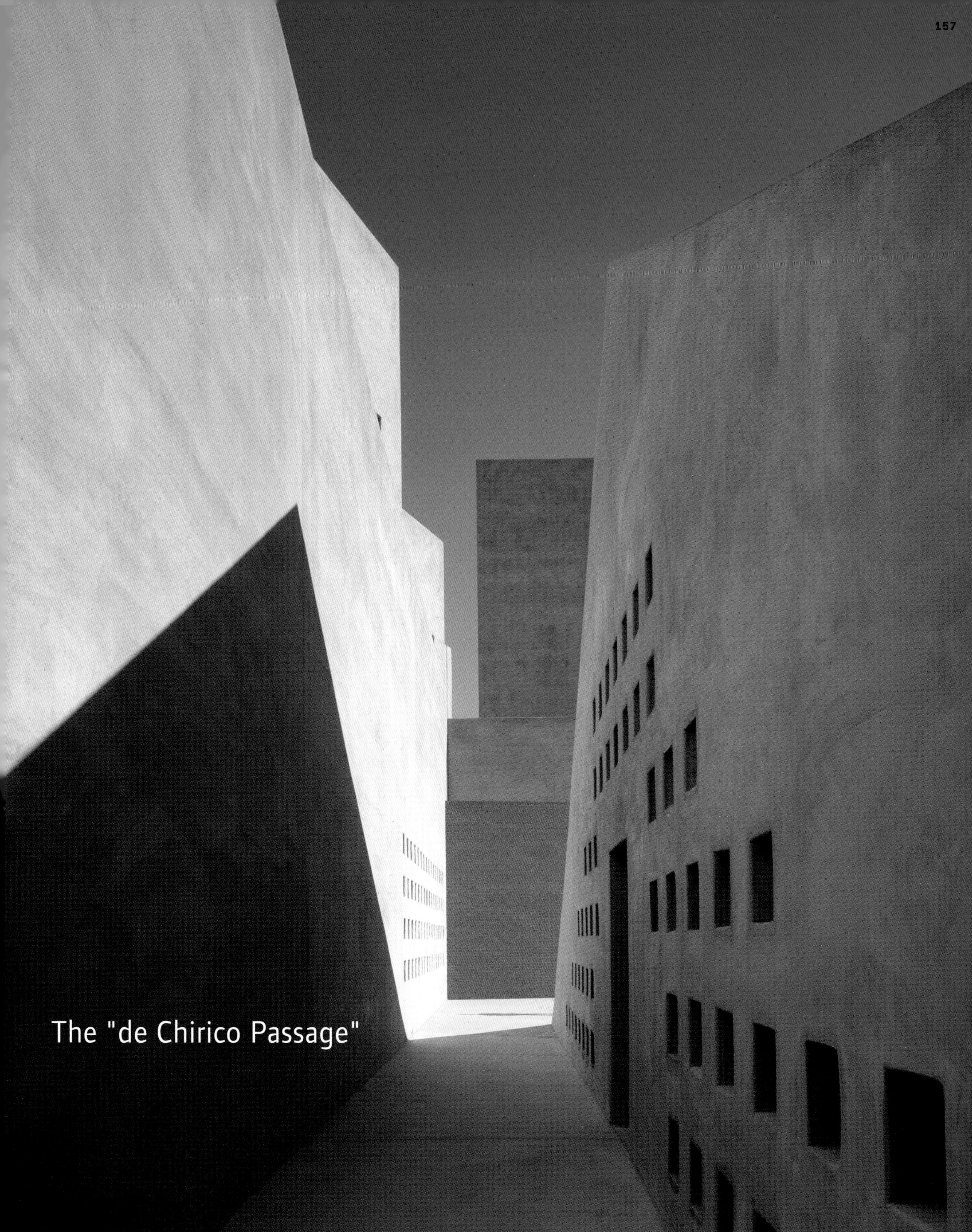

The "de Chirico Passage"

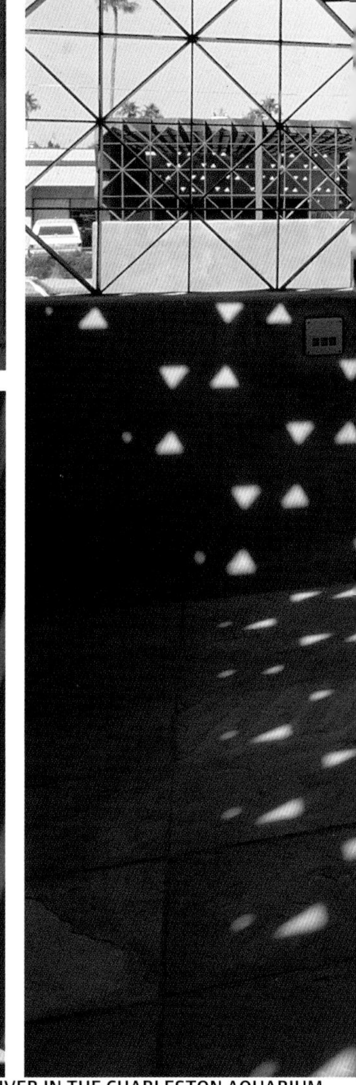

POLITE, ORGANIZED CHARLESTON MEETS THE COOPER RIVER IN THE CHARLESTON AQUARIUM.

CHARLESTON AQUARIUM
COMPETITION CHARRETTE
CHARLESTON, SC 1986

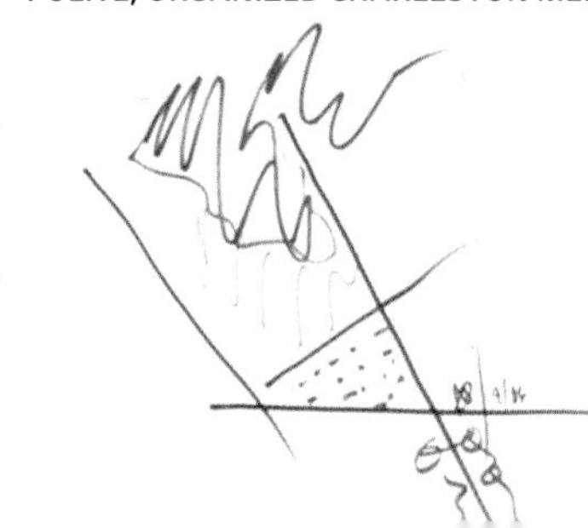

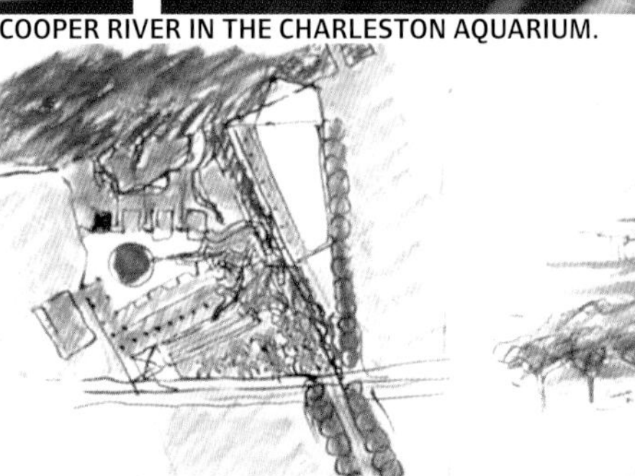

THE COOLER, SUBTERRANEAN, MUSEUM ENTRY LEVEL, ASSOCIATED WITH WATER AND PATTERNS OF LIGHT FROM THE SLOTS IN THE GAPPED BLEACHERS ABOVE.

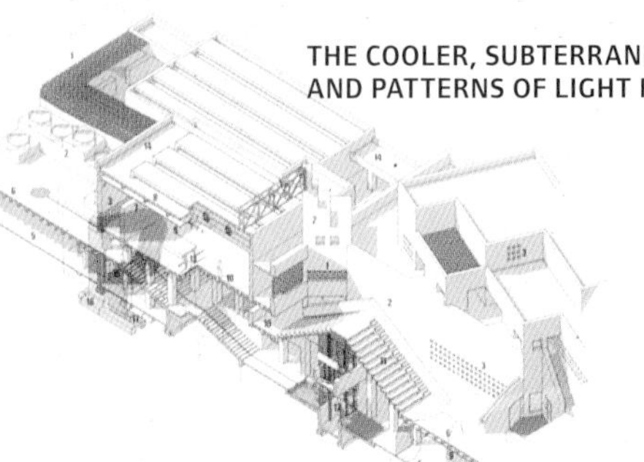

"Just as spectators climb the mountain to watch the stars, both heavenly and human, so visitors to the museum descend into the mountain to find its buried treasures."

Daralice D. Boles, "Magic Mountain," *Progressive Architecture*, June, 1989

EACH "LIGHT BOUNCE" FROM THE GALLERY SKYLIGHTS DILUTES THE EFFECT OF UV ON THE ARTWORK.

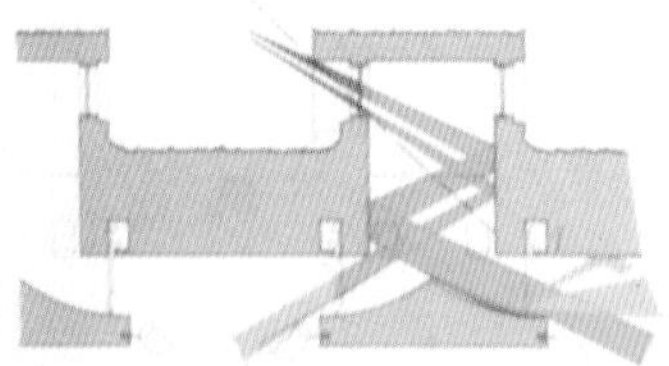

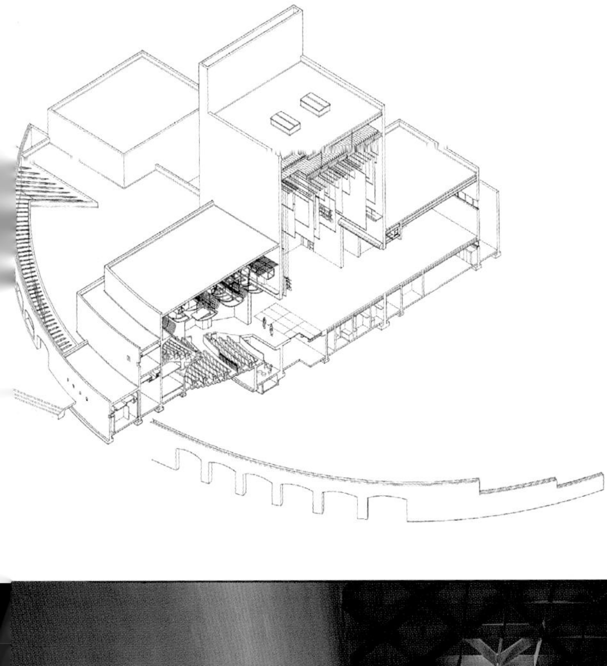

Galvin Playhouse entry court/"Aqueduct."

DANCE STUDIO/THEATER—OPENED BY MERCE CUNNINGHAM WITH SCORE BY MORTON SUBOTNICK, ACCOMPANIED BY ANDY WARHOL'S HELIUM PILLOWS.

"In a splendid gesture the flytower of the theater in the rear or the complex has been placed right on axis with the front of the museum, so this highest of the elements of the casual rear section or the project becomes the ultimate anchor to the classical symmetry of the front."

Paul Goldberger, "Speaking the Language of the Desert and Mountain," *New York Times*, January 28, 1990

UCLA NORTHWEST SECTOR—DELTA HOUSING AND ASSOCIATED CONFERENCE/LECTURE FACILITY

Nelson Fine Arts Center was awarded the Gran Premio Internacional of the Bienal Internacional de Arquitectura de Buenos Aires in 1989.

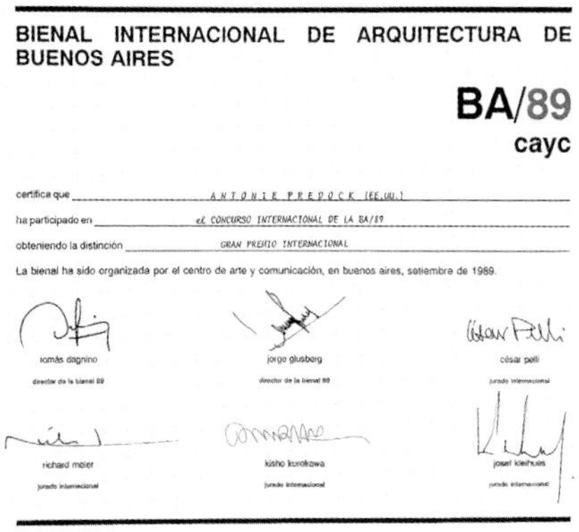

BIENAL INTERNACIONAL DE ARQUITECTURA DE BUENOS AIRES

BA/89
cayc

certifica que ANTONIE PREDOCK (EE.UU.)
ha participado en el CONCURSO INTERNACIONAL DE LA BA/89
obteniendo la distinción GRAN PREMIO INTERNACIONAL

La bienal ha sido organizada por el centro de arte y comunicación, en buenos aires, setiembre de 1989.

tomás dagnino, director de la bienal 89
jorge glusberg, director de la bienal 89
césar pelli, jurado internacional
richard meier, jurado internacional
kisho kurokawa, jurado internacional
josef kleihues, jurado internacional

ZUBER HOUSE

PARADISE VALLEY, ARIZONA 1986/89

Poised on the face of a mountain in Paradise Valley, the Zuber House attains a dynamic equilibrium through the studied juxtaposition of its two "houses." The north-south house, an outcrop of split-faced block, anchors the building to the hillside. The counterbalancing east-west house, forms the major building façade and contains the entertainment/art display spaces.

"Drawing equally on tangible and intangible sources of inspiration, Predock fashioned a well-protected structure that emerges like a bunker out of a rocky outcropping and expands into a stately Wrightian horizontal bar punctuated by vertical observation posts and, more dramatically, an eggplant-colored steel balcony/bridge."

Karen D. Stein, "Raising Arizona," *Architectural Record,* Mid-April 1990

EARLY '80s PARIS TRIP WITH HADRIAN AND JASON

LAS VEGAS CENTRAL LIBRARY AND CHILDREN'S MUSEUM

LAS VEGAS, NEVADA 1986/90

Fragments of mountain, desert, casinos, neighborhoods, and technology come into focus from perimeter openings and atop the Mad Scientist Tower. This visual confluence of nature, fantasy, urbanization, and science underscores the complexities of the desert environment and the task of making architecture responsive to its many faces.

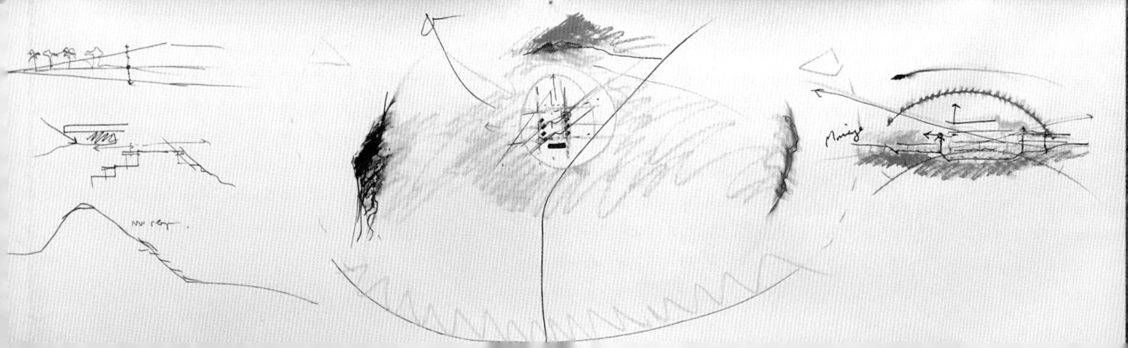

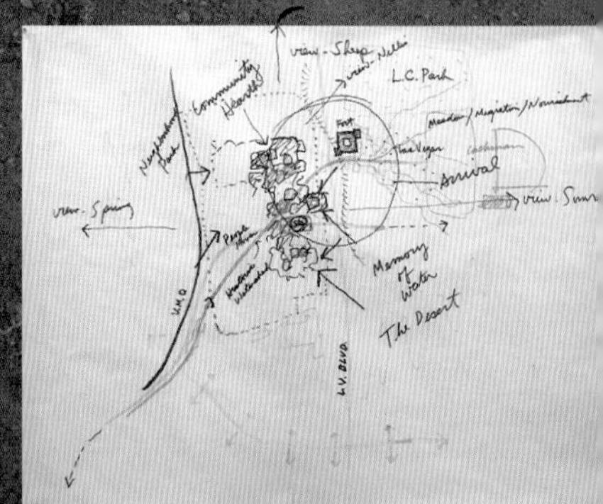

The fragility of desert and the communities that colonize it—apparent when one views Las Vegas from the air—the Strip, Glitter Gulch, and the city form a thin, permeable membrane that keeps the desert marginally at bay.

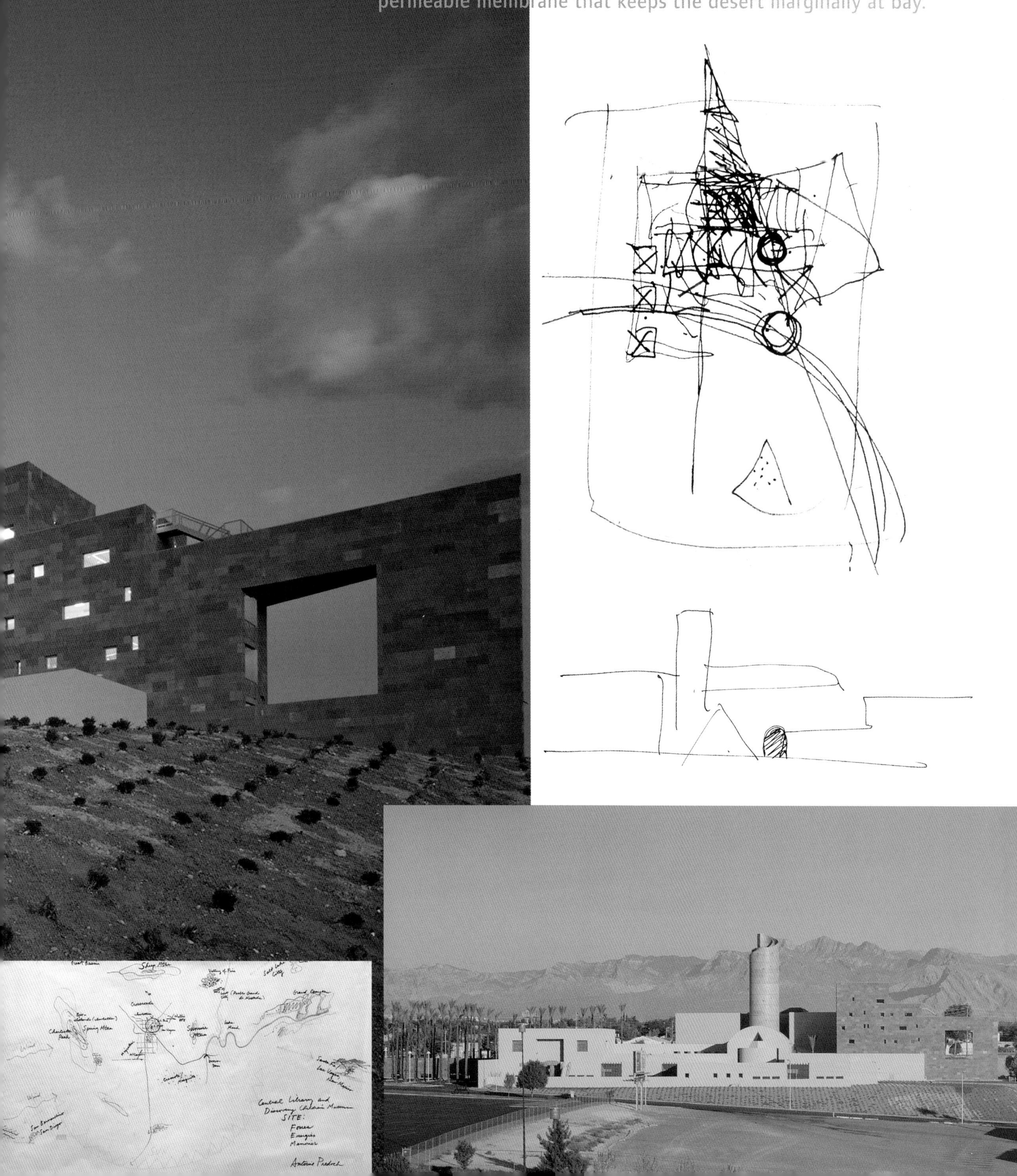

The Las Vegas Central Library and Children's Museum are built at the cultural heart of the city where a spring, nomadic Paiute shelters, and later, Anglo-American settlements were sited. Visitors experience the library and children's museum as desert building and civic monument. These overlays surface immediately in the Palm Court which signals shelter amid parking. From here the water course and sandstone wall lead to the entry.

I was teaching at Harvard in '87 and I had a budget for the students to travel with me. So I gave them the project called "Learning from the other Las Vegas"—from the Valley of Fire, to Michael Heizer's *Double Negative*, to the Hoover Dam, where we descended through a time warp into the '30s, with its genuine, original, art deco detailing. I thought it would be good to drop these East Coast students into that soup of Vegas surrealism/raw landscape.

THE LANDSHARK IS A TAPERED BLADE RISING OUT OF THE SAND, EVOKING THE POWER AND MYSTERY OF THE OCEAN. IT IS LEGEND ENGAGING TECHNOLOGY. IT IS A BEDOUIN

LANDSHARK
SANTA MONICA, CA 1988

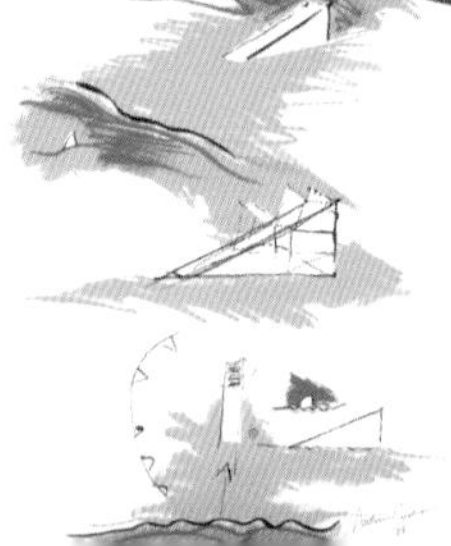

I talked them into doing a tower.
There was no tower in the program,
or anything for gravity experiments.
I called it the Mad Scientist Tower.

The conical "birthday party" room resembles a party hat punctured by irregular light apertures. These Coke bottle holes are located on a spiral defined by the Fibonacci series.

TENT TRANSPLANTED FROM THE SAHARA—A BLACK EPHEMERA THAT WASHES UP ON THE SHORE. IT IS THE MYTH OF THE OCEAN INVERTED.

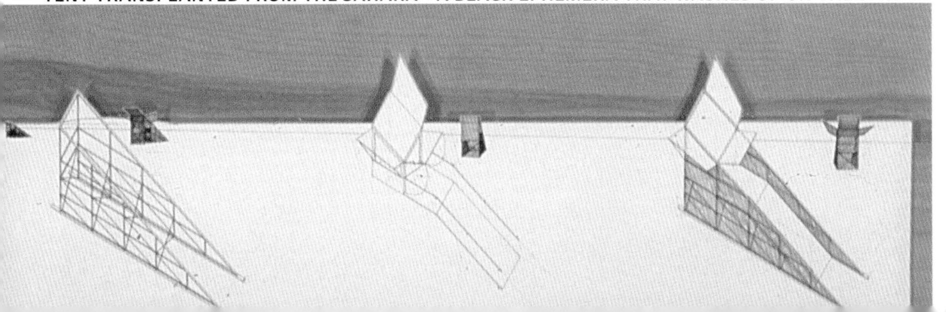

"The stark sandstone and concrete shapes of Antoine Predock's Las Vegas Library/ Discovery Museum seem far removed from the neon-encrusted hotels and casinos that dominate The Strip."

Karen D. Stein, "Down The Strip," *Architectural Record*, Oct. 1990

"Behind us, something—a cloud, a mountain-occluded the setting sun, and the landscape ahead seemed suddenly darker, and that was fine because just after the next or next-but-one turn of the Interstate, the lights of Las Vegas would come into view—more like a dream city dissolving in its own ecstasy.

It didn't dissolve, of course. It became more solid and profane as we approached and the sun came out again to confuse the issue further. But for maybe half a minute it had been an incredible image of an architecture of light drowning in light more beautiful than its own. The great terminal oasis had become the ultimate optical illusion."

Reyner Banham, *Scenes in American Deserta*, 1982

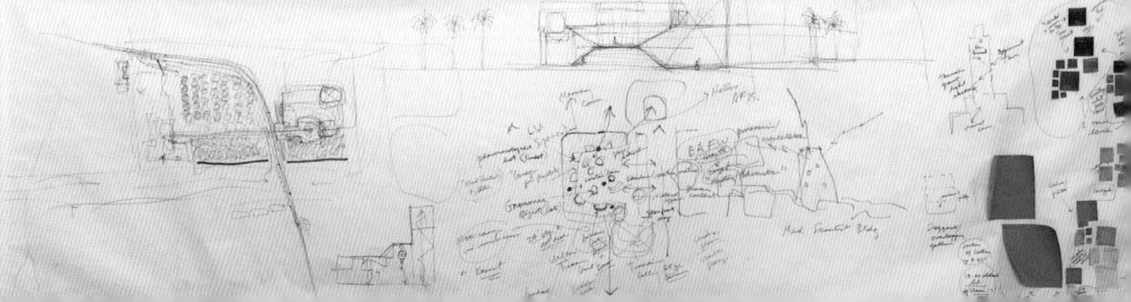

At the end of the Children's Library, toward the east, is a walk-in kaleidoscope.

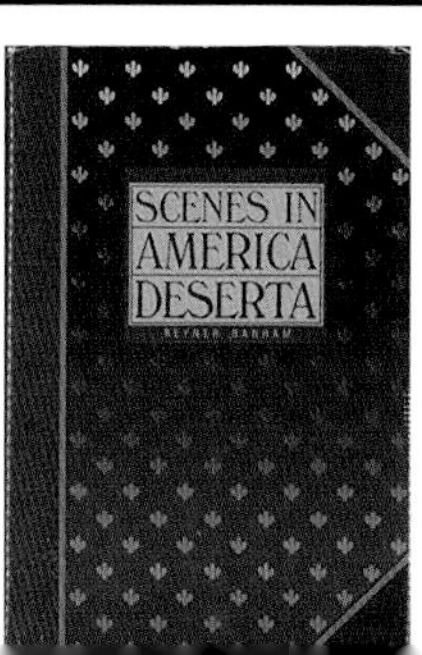

AMERICAN HERITAGE CENTER AND ART MUSEUM

UNIVERSITY OF WYOMING
LARAMIE, WYOMING 1986/93

Throughout Wyoming there is a sense of landscape in formation, of landscape in transition. The appearance of this "archival" mountain can be thought of as parallel to the slow but certain upheaval of the Laramide geologic deformation.

The building axis that links the two distant mountains, the "rendezvous axis," recalls the gathering of Native Americans, French trappers, and early European settlers. Now it is a place of intellectual and social rendezvous.

At the core of the mountain is a hearth with a timber armature that guides the flue up through the mountain to the sky. Upper floor levels wind around the hearth, each level rotating, creating a spiraling ascent to the sky-lit aerie.

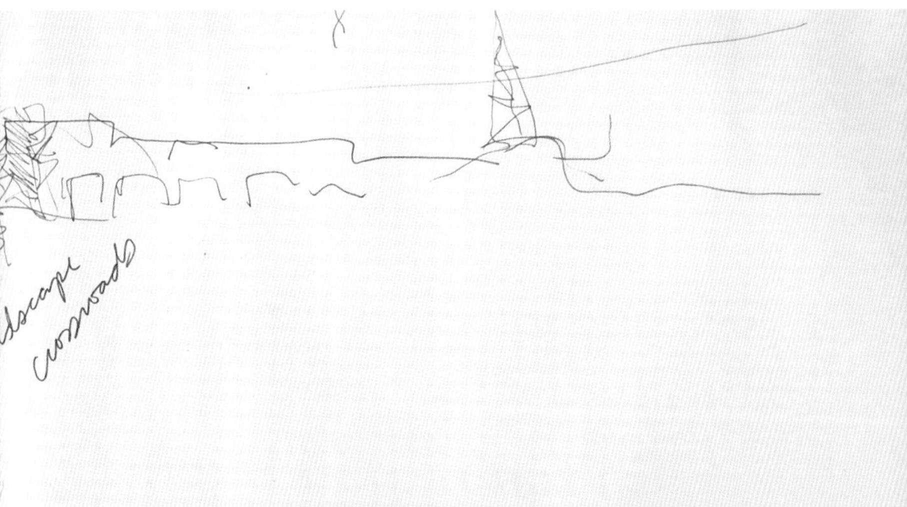

Throughout Wyoming there is a sense of landscape in formation, of landscape in transition. The appearance of this "archival" mountain can be thought of as parallel to the slow but certain geologic deformation upheaval. This new mountain is detailed like an airplane wing and is aerodynamically positioned with respect to Wyoming's omnipresent winds. Openings in the cone are abrupt and limited.

The asymmetry of the mountainous stretched cone guides visitors to a common ground between the American Heritage Center and University Art Museum, the two halves of the building. The entire structure is set on a man-made mesa, a surrogate landform that absorbs archival and curatorial spaces below the public realm.

This archival mountain is axially linked to Medicine Bow Peak to the west and Pilot's Knob to the east. A web of site-specific alignments anchors the building into the campus and landscape.

The art museum is reminiscent of a village at the foot of a mountain. It is poised on the mesa, with spruce trees on a bermed embankment establishing the foreground.

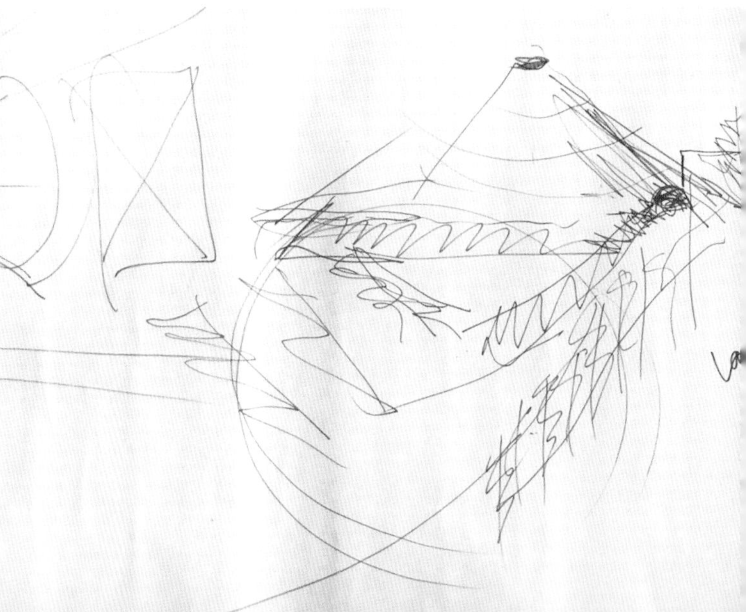

At that time, in the '80s, we had no software to describe the stretched conical form, so we had to use trigonometry, and constructed a three-foot-long "topographic model" of the cone ... handmade!

RALPH LAUREN, THE FASHION DESIGNER, INVITED ME TO DESIGN A "MOUNTAIN CABIN" THAT WASN'T BUILT

RRL RANCH HOUSE
WESTERN SLOPE, CO 1986

JOHN MCPHEE'S STORIES WERE REALLY INSPIRATIONAL FOR THIS PROJECT

AN EFFORT TO POETICALLY DECENTRALIZE THE PAUL ALLEN ESTATE...

ALLEN ESTATE
MERCER ISLAND, WA 1988

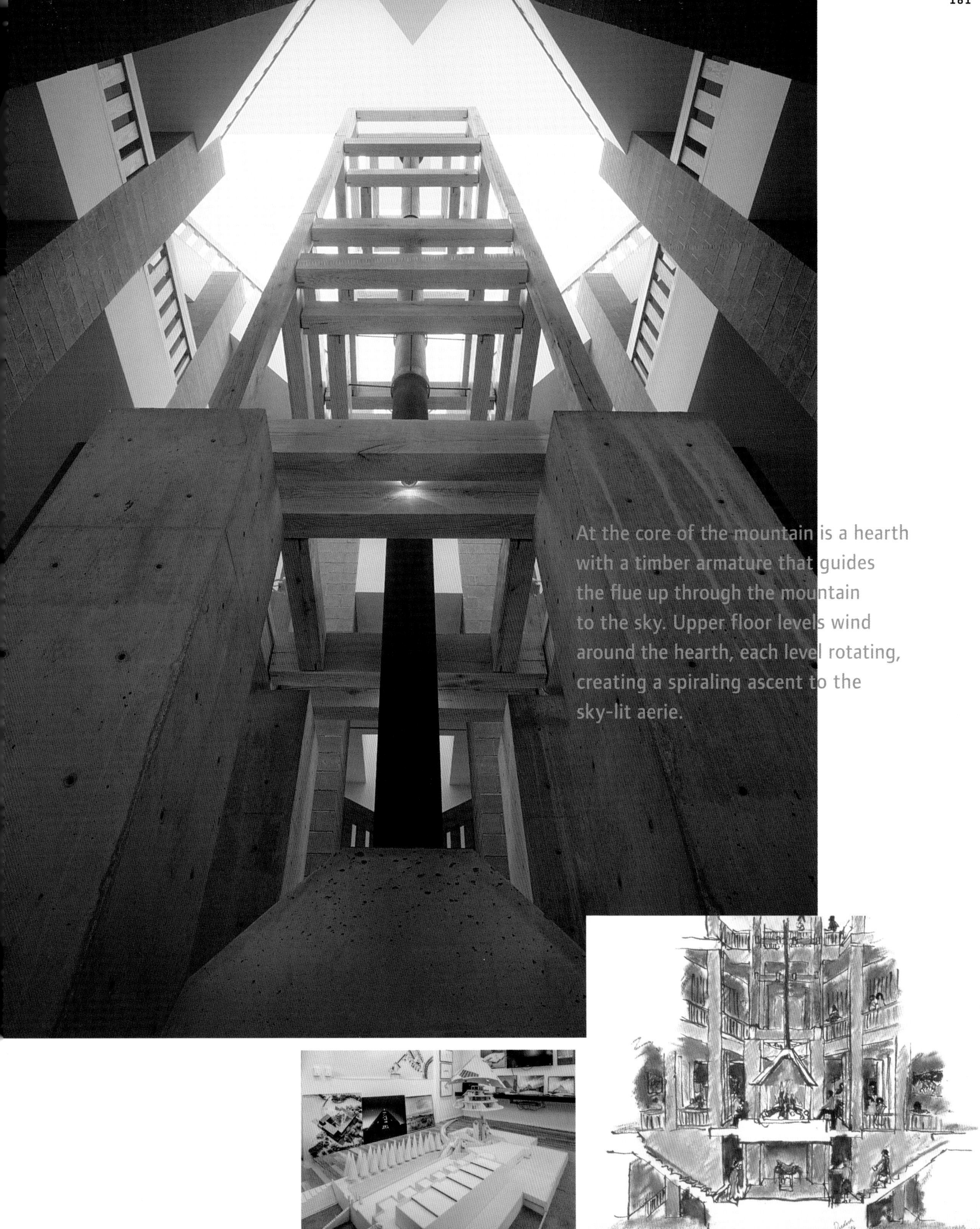

At the core of the mountain is a hearth with a timber armature that guides the flue up through the mountain to the sky. Upper floor levels wind around the hearth, each level rotating, creating a spiraling ascent to the sky-lit aerie.

"He [Predock] was determined that the American Heritage Center and Art Museum should go 'one-to-one' with those big man-made shapes and also merge with the landscape and the urban context. 'But the design was not meant to be merely a formal exercise,' he explains. 'It was meant to be an exercise in feeling.'"

Ellen Posner, *Landscape Architecture*, August 1996

IN 1989, A ONE-PERSON SHOW ORGANIZED BY FRIEND/COLLEAGUE STEVEN HOLL AT THE NICHOLS GALLERY IN SOHO, NEW YORK CITY.

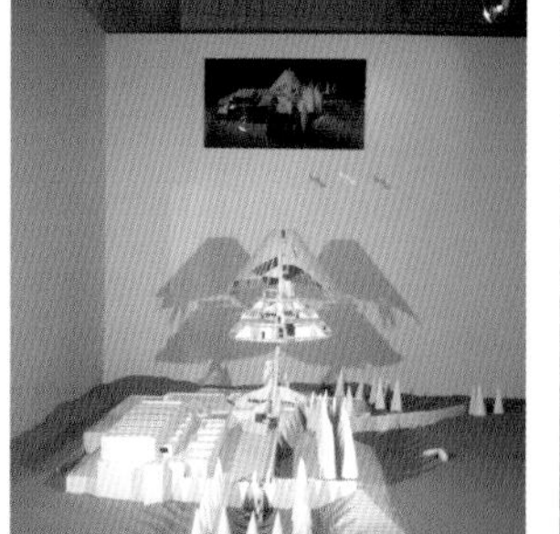

"The circularity of the shape calls out in all directions, gathering the distant plains and ranges within its orbit. Predock creates another attachment to its surroundings by aligning the building between Medicine and Pilot's Knob peaks—what he calls the 'rendezvous axis,' after the ancient gatherings of Indian tribes. The building, finally, is sited on a cross-axis of the stadium and the landscape, at an intersection of the works of man and nature."

Joseph Giovannini, *Architecture*, December 1993

An archival mountain with an art museum "village" at its base.

"'LANDSCAPE APPARITIONS,' drawings, sketches and photographs by Antoine Predock, an architect in Albuquerque, N.M., is at the John Nichols Gallery through Nov. 26. Above is a model of the American Heritage Center in Laramie, Wyo., conceived by Mr. Predock as an 'archival mountain in Marlboro Country.' The works show Mr. Predock's interest in geological and Southwestern architectural forms, and gives clues to the germination of his ideas."

Patricia Leigh Brown, "Mountain Apparitions By New Mexico Architect," *New York Times*, Oct. 13, 1988

TRIP TO SOUTH AMERICA AT THIS TIME—FLYING OUT OF QUITO—COTOPAXI & CHIMBORAZO WINDOW VIEW...

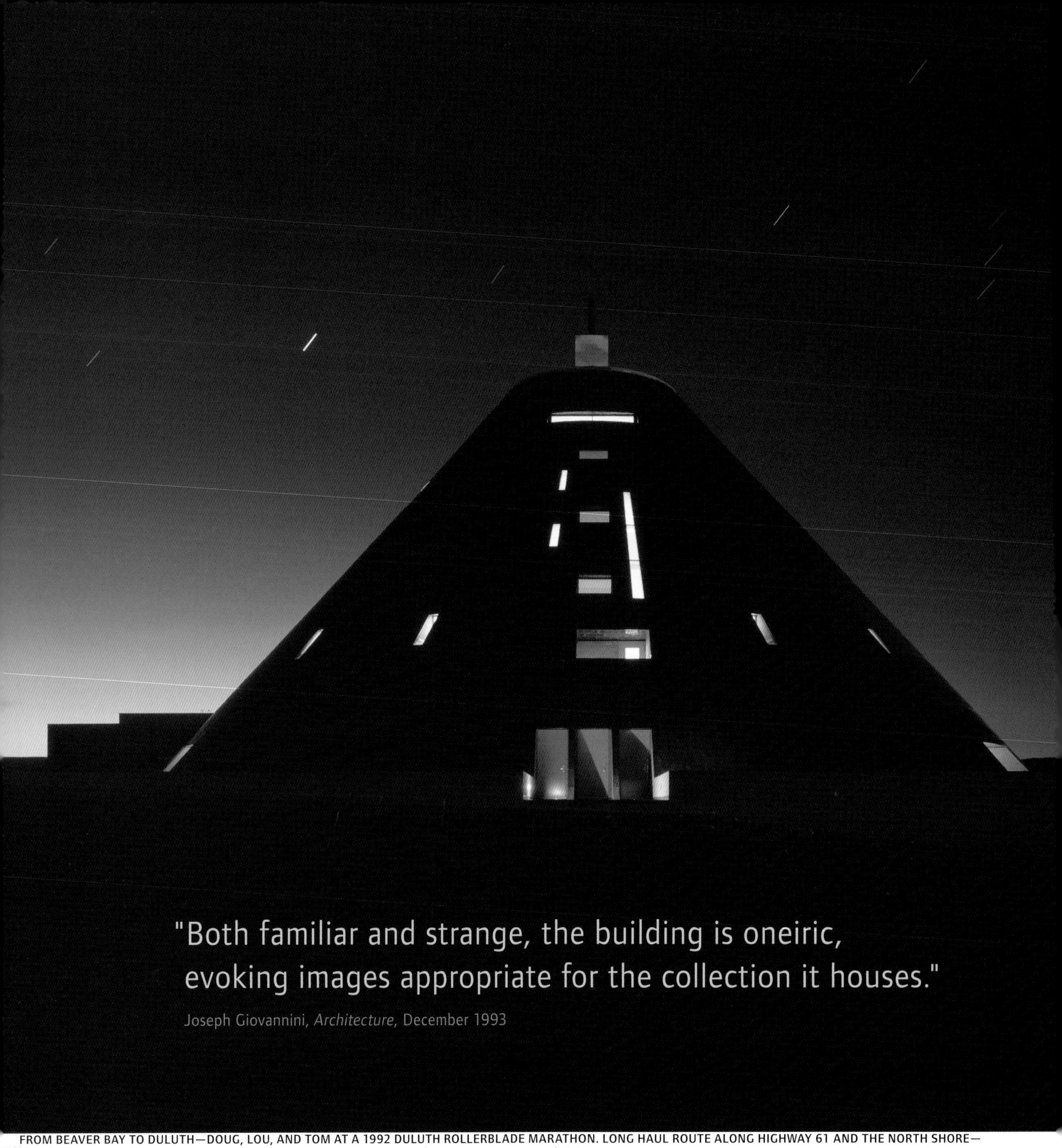

"Both familiar and strange, the building is oneiric, evoking images appropriate for the collection it houses."

Joseph Giovannini, *Architecture*, December 1993

FROM BEAVER BAY TO DULUTH—DOUG, LOU, AND TOM AT A 1992 DULUTH ROLLERBLADE MARATHON. LONG HAUL ROUTE ALONG HIGHWAY 61 AND THE NORTH SHORE—THINKING OF BOB DYLAN ON THE WAY—TO CENTRAL SQUARE IN DULUTH—MOSTLY PAYING ATTENTION TO BREATHING AND MY BODY.

"Predock's design ... focuses on a gigantic abstract cone that rises from a mesa of books and artifacts the way real mountains in Wyoming continue to rise from the plain. This primal shape ... part earth mound—is intended to make a direct visceral connection to the experience of the real Western landscape, where there is no middle distance, or middle scale, only near and far, little and big. Such a relationship is what 'fitting in' means in the West."

David Dillon, "Border Crossings," *Architecture*, August 1991

STUDIO HOLIDAY CARD—2001

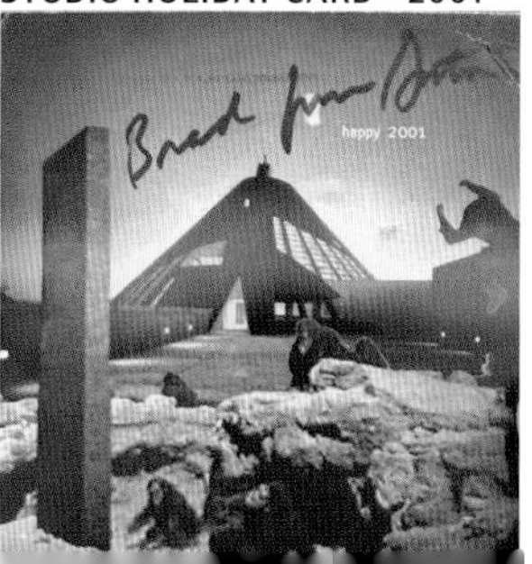

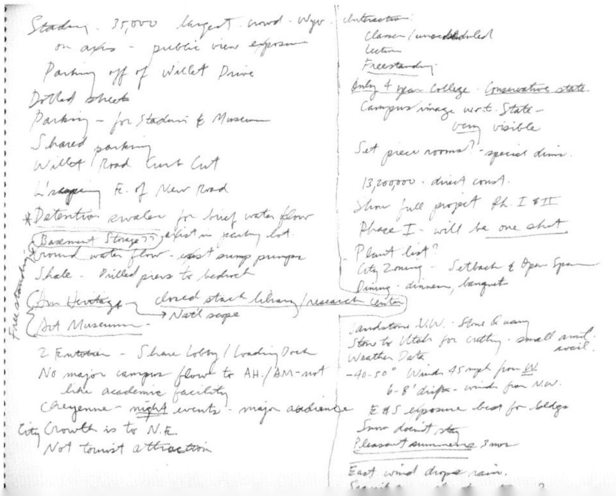

ROSENTHAL HOUSE

MANHATTAN BEACH, CALIFORNIA 1986/93

I IMAGINED THE SHIP OF THE DESERT SETTLING IN ACROSS A DRY WASH...

SHIP OF THE DESERT
NEVADA 1987

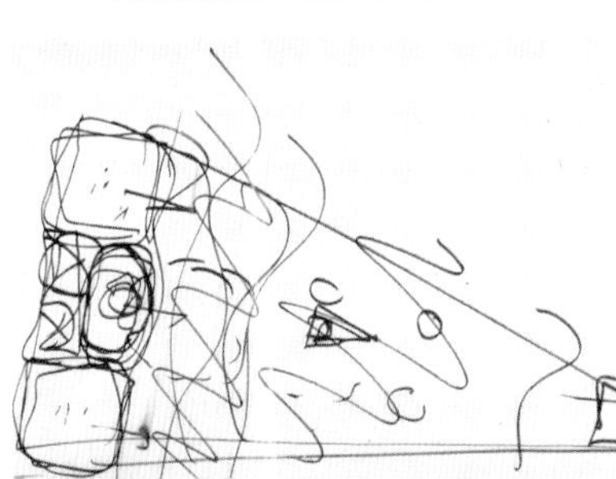

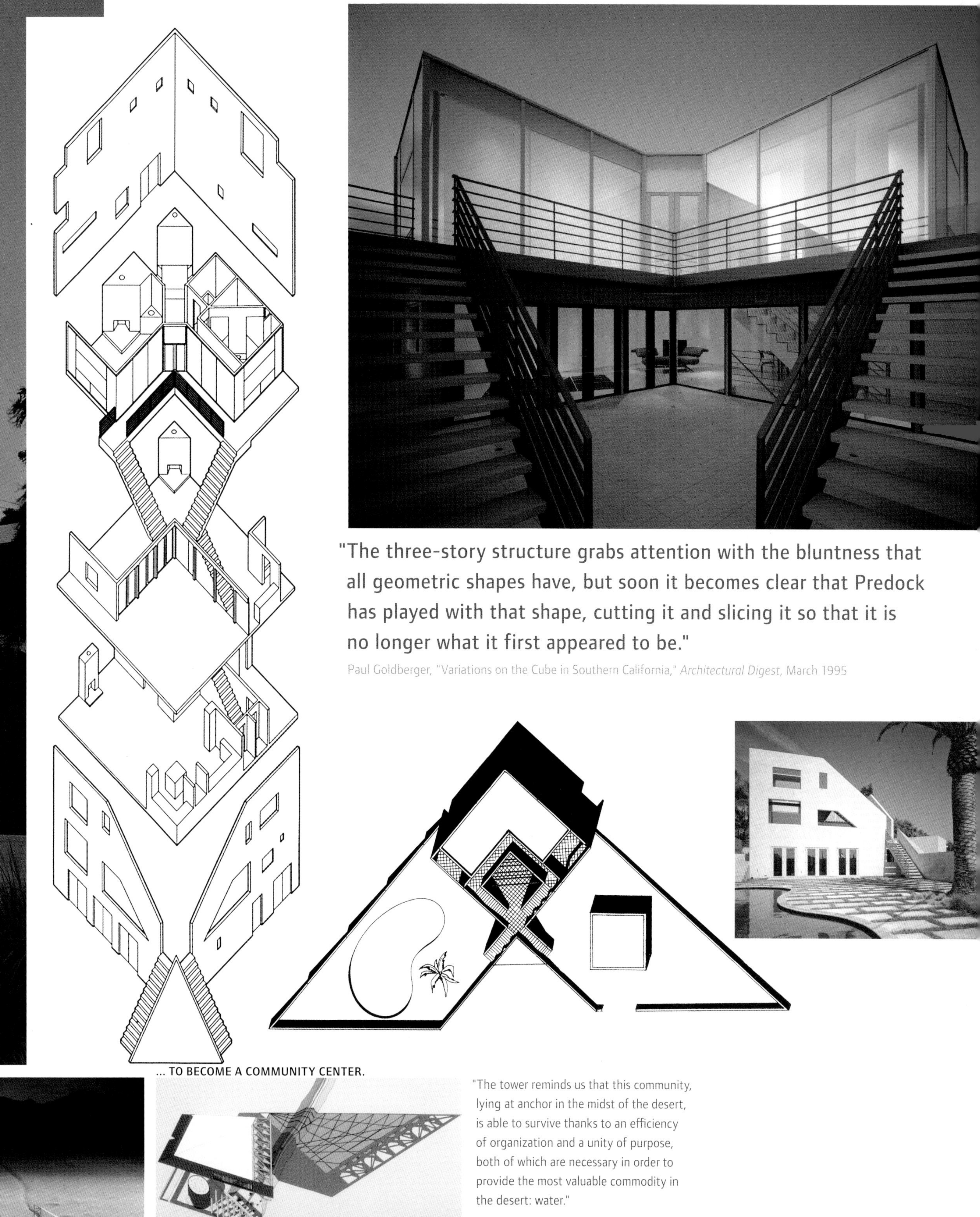

"The three-story structure grabs attention with the bluntness that all geometric shapes have, but soon it becomes clear that Predock has played with that shape, cutting it and slicing it so that it is no longer what it first appeared to be."

Paul Goldberger, "Variations on the Cube in Southern California," *Architectural Digest*, March 1995

... TO BECOME A COMMUNITY CENTER.

"The tower reminds us that this community, lying at anchor in the midst of the desert, is able to survive thanks to an efficiency of organization and a unity of purpose, both of which are necessary in order to provide the most valuable commodity in the desert: water."

Luigi Moiraghi, *l'ARCA*, August 1992

THE WINANDY HOUSE—PROGRESSION THROUGH A DARK WATER COURT TOWARD LIGHT

WINANDY HOUSE
PHOENIX, AZ 1988/91

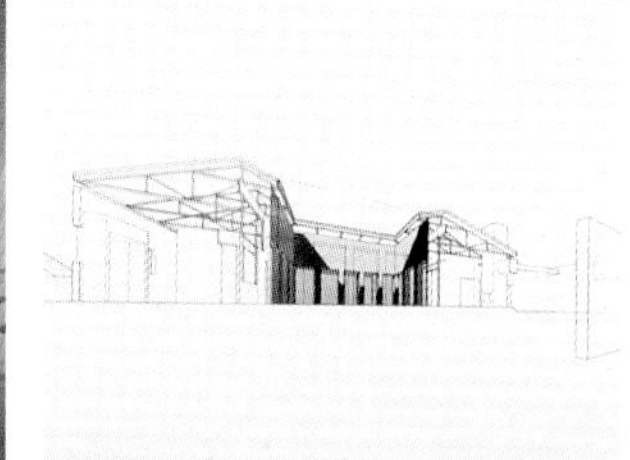

Jacket of light

The fog, the clouds, and the color of the ocean all conspire to create a greenish, *Twilight Zone* light. The intensity of the sun beating down on the window walls facing the courtyard is tempered by a series of sliding panels of translucent, tempered glass that, depending on the layering, vary from translucent to dense bottle green.

"The stucco exterior shapes the light, creates ventilation and also, through openings in the wall, captures remnants of the landscape, almost like snapshots. The exterior wall is like a babushka, a Russian nesting doll. One building stacks inside another, a room inside another room."

Encarna Castillo, *Maximalist Houses*

CLASSROOM, LIBRARY, ADMINISTRATIVE BUILDING

CALIFORNIA POLYTECHNIC UNIVERSITY
POMONA, CALIFORNIA 1987/92
IN MEMORIAM: BORN 1987—DIED 2022

"Seen from across the campus or the valley, the tower rises up like a machined canyon wall set against the spiraling stack of classrooms. Up close, it's a progression of geometrically posed blocks that dance around you as you find your way through the building. It is monumental, purposely complicated, and hard to ignore."

Aaron Betsky, "Magic Marker," *Architectural Record*, February 1993

Altered landscapes result inevitably from human settlement and successive transformations. The scenery shifts—the dry Rancho San Jose, the romantic and verdant ranch of W.K. Kellogg, the superscale freeway interchange—producing a panorama of cultural depth and visual intensity.

EXHIBITED—NICHOLS GALLERY, NEW YORK, 1989

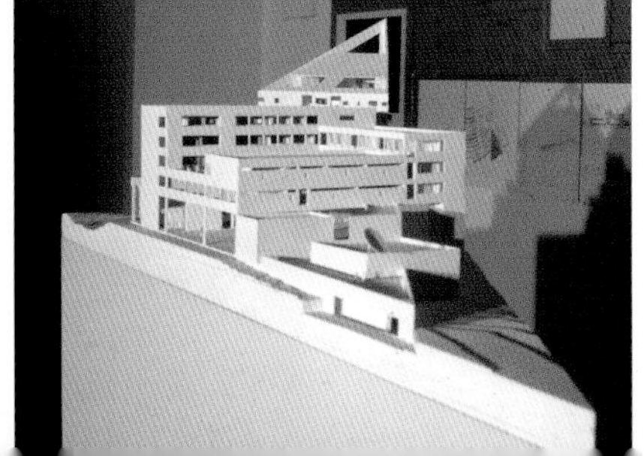

Unscathed by the powerful Northridge earthquake of 1994, thanks to the brilliant structural engineering of Robin Parke.

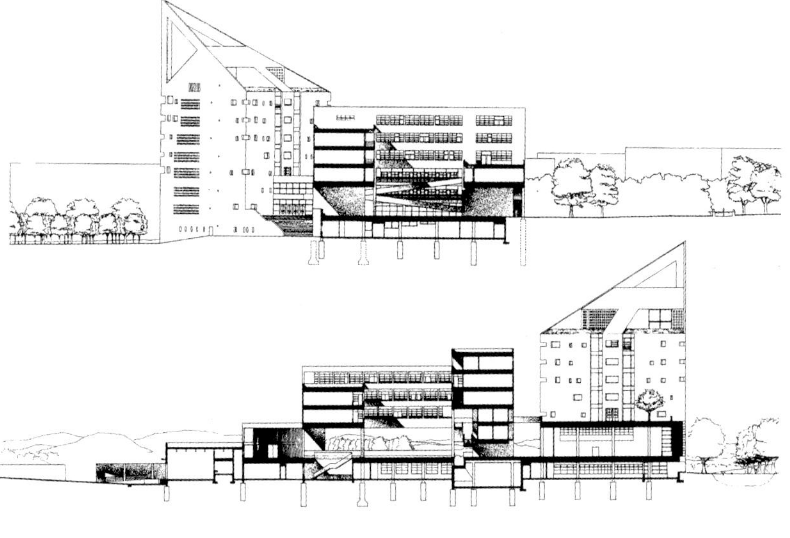

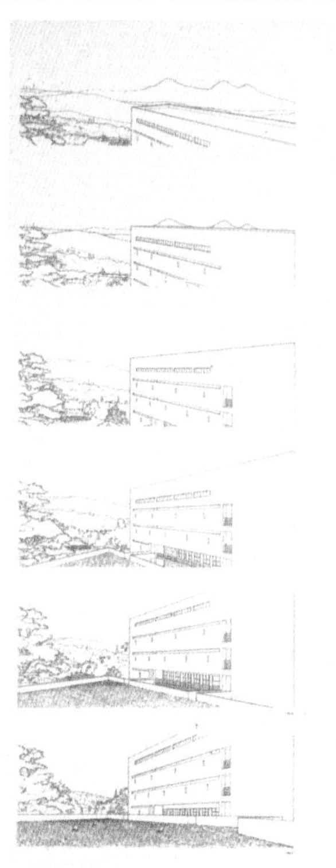

BECOMING A PART OF OUR CULTURE, HOLLYWOOD DISCOVERS CAL POLY POMONA—*GATTICA* (1998) AND *IMPOSTOR* (2001)

Each vertex aims a view toward a special place/event. From the prow terrace one views LAX flight patterns—with wide-body jets lumbering across the sky at low altitude, spaced at one-mile intervals—and imagines the exotic associated places of origin.

FORAY INTO SUN VALLEY FOR THE CLARENDON BATHS

CLARENDON BATHS
KETCHAM, ID 1988

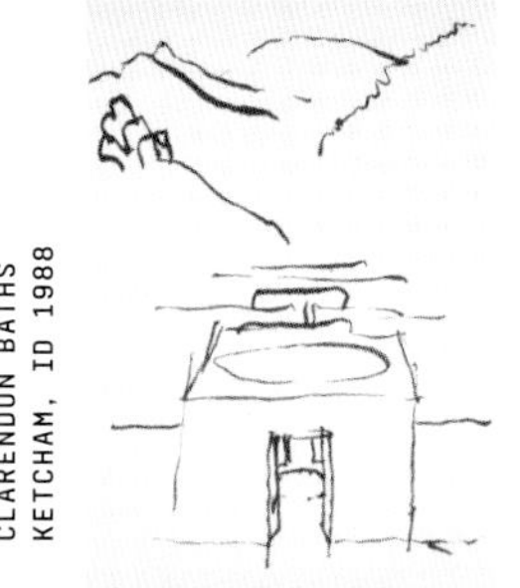

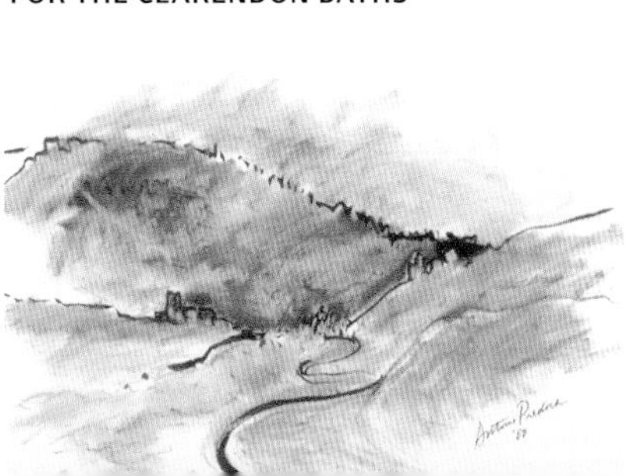

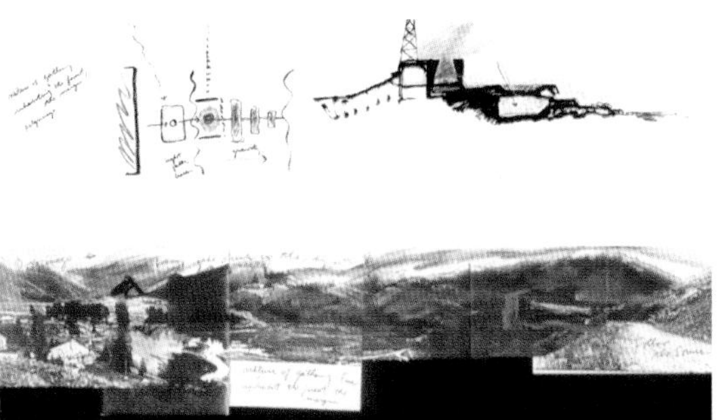

"What Antoine Predock hath wrought in the Southern California desert is the most transcendent piece of academic architecture since Louis I. Kahn's library at Exeter."

Eve M. Kahn, "Antoine Predock on Campus," *The Wall Street Journal,* October 23, 1992

THE BUILDING APPEARS AS A GEOLOGIC FORM IN ABSTRACTION, A PUNCTUATION ALONG INTERSTATE 10.

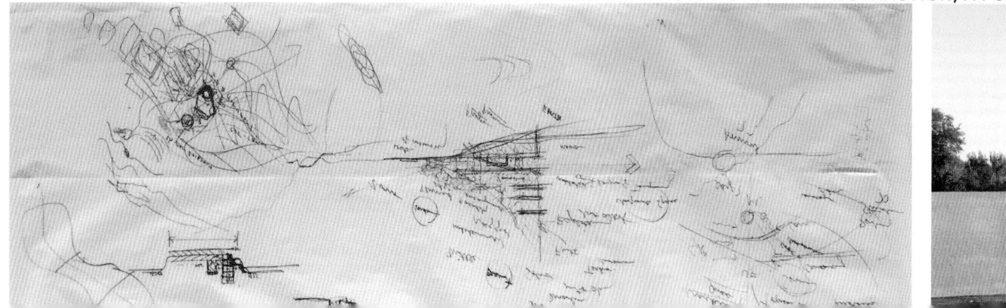

"We wanted a building that was a symbol of our transformation from an 'Ag school' into a true polytechnic—and we got it. This building stands for a new age."

Dean Marvin Malecha, School of Environmental Design Cal Poly, "Magic Marker," *Architectural Record*, February 1993

TURTLE CREEK HOUSE

DALLAS, TEXAS 1987/93

"The rusticated limestone (six-foot-long half-ton chunks slid into place on ice rollers) gives a benign Pleistocene face to the twenty-first-century concrete structure behind, sweetening and humanizing the all-but-windowless façade of the house ..."

Kurt Andersen, "Sensuous Modernism in Dallas," *Architectural Digest*, March 1994

"... the new house is a not-quite-severe collage of limestone, concrete and black steel, simultaneously grave and jazzy. Nor is it simply a multimillion-dollar one-liner. ... With its impeccable detailing and rich, complex plan, the building reinvigorates the idea of the modernist villa."

"The Best Design of 1993," *Time Magazine*, January 3, 1994

SEVILLE EXPO 92—USA PAVILION DESIGN COMPETITION, WHICH WE WON. *AMERICA THE BEAUTIFUL* WAS PHYSICALLY/DIAGRAMATICALLY PRESENT—"AMBER WAVES OF GRAIN"... "FRUITED PLAIN"... "SEA TO SHINING SEA"... PROJECTED "SPACIOUS SKIES" AND OF COURSE "PURPLE MOUNTAIN MAJESTY," POSING AS A ROCKET NOSE CONE RISING AND SINKING ON HYDRAULIC LEGS. THINK *CLOSE ENCOUNTERS OF THE THIRD KIND* BRILLIANT LIGHT STREAMING FROM WITHIN.

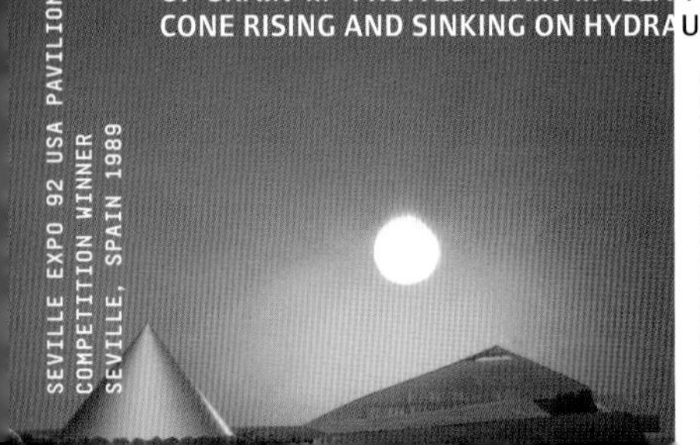

SEVILLE EXPO 92 USA PAVILION
COMPETITION WINNER
SEVILLE, SPAIN 1989

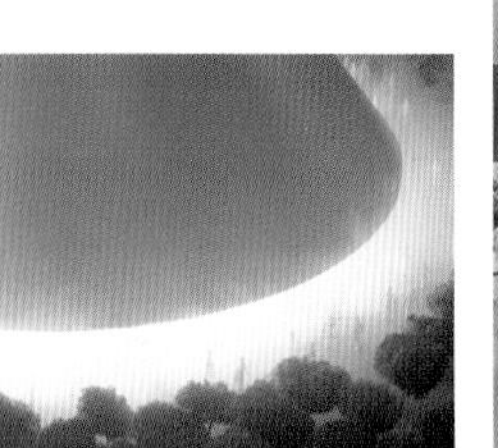

Sited along a prehistoric trail that follows the Austin limestone formation in a landscape where woodlands, prairie, and stream overlap. Anchoring limestone ledges forming the entry extend geologic strata and ancient memories. The stone ledges hold native flora with "plants birds love."

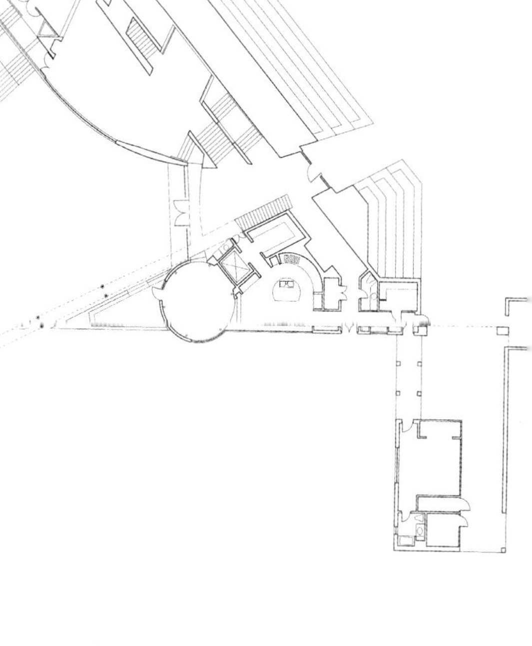

"The shell of the house is poured concrete suggestive of Louis Kahn's nearby Kimbell Art Museum (built, in fact, by the same contractor)."

Kurt Andersen, "Sensuous Modernism in Dallas," *Architectural Digest*, March 1994

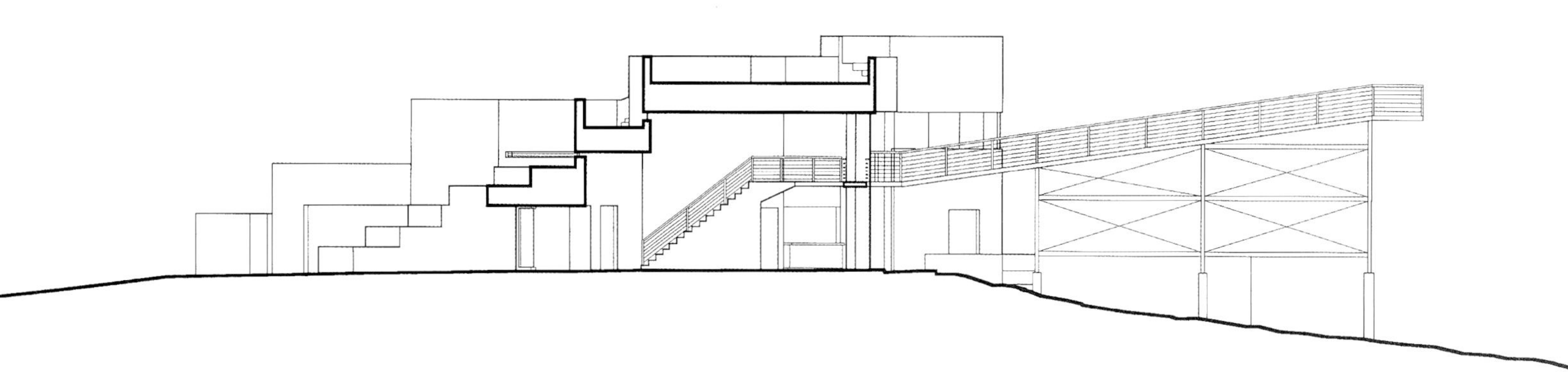

ON THE HEELS OF THE SEVILLE EXPO COMPETITION CAME THE HOTEL SANTA FE AT EURO DISNEY... DISNEY CEO MICHAEL EISNER INVITED ME TO HIS BEL AIR HOUSE AND IN A MOMENT-OF-TRUTH KIND OF ENCOUNTER I PITCHED THE IDEA OF A HIGHWAY 66/*PARIS, TEXAS* EVOCATION THAT WOULD BE TIED TO ITS SITE AT MARNE-LA-VALLÉ, FRANCE—"HAPPY TRAILS."

HOTEL SANTA FE, EURO DISNEY
MARNE-LA-VALLÉE, FRANCE
1988/92

"... the Rose house is a striking abstraction, at once sleek, sensuous and minimal. ... This is not a design that makes any pretense of relating to neighbors; indeed, on a street of banal suburban houses its blunt geometries hit you like a ton of, well, limestone. Once through the door, however, the house breaks wide open and creates its own universe: the interior is a set of bright, sharply angled spaces, with huge walls of glass facing a stunning site overlooking Turtle Creek ...

Rose's earnestness led her, at first, to put almost too much trust in Predock. 'We described to him what we wanted from the house—a sense of mystery, a place that would unfold gradually, architecture that would delight,' she says. 'But I never told him how I wanted it to look. After all, he is the architect, and he came up with something that never in 1,000 years could I have dreamed up.'"

Paul Goldberger, "Houses as Art," *New York Times Magazine*, March 12, 1995

IN HOTEL SANTA FE DISNEY, CEO MICHAEL EISNER SOUGHT A THEMATIC OVERLAY. FOR ME, THAT MEANT A DISTILLED, EPISODIC, EXPERIENTIAL COLLAGE OF "WESTERN" ARCHETYPES AND MYTHS—NATURAL, CINEMATIC, EXTRATERRESTRIAL. PARKING EVOKES A DRIVE-IN MOVIE, AND A "YELLOW LINE ON THE HIGHWAY" BLASTING THROUGH IT... WITH A BEAUTIFUL STAINLESS STEEL UFO CULMINATION.

"The high road north from the living room is the way to the most spectacular parts of the house. A zigzag stairway leads to a short black steel bridge spanning the central entrance hall. Once again, like a plot-your-own-adventure branching novel, there is a set of intriguing choices. Straight ahead is the twenty-two-foot-wide circular dining room-cum-observation tower, which itself opens onto a rooftop set of several concrete terraces, including a compact amphitheater. Turn away from the dining room instead, and you are immediately outside, heading up a rather steeply inclined steel walkway toward Turtle Creek, the treetops and the sky."

Kurt Andersen, "Sensuous Modernism in Dallas," *Architectural Digest*, March 1994

FLANKING CIRCUITOUS PATHS MOVE THROUGH THE SEQUENCE OF INTIMATE COURTYARDS DEFINED BY THE LOW-RISE, MOTEL-LIKE HOTEL.

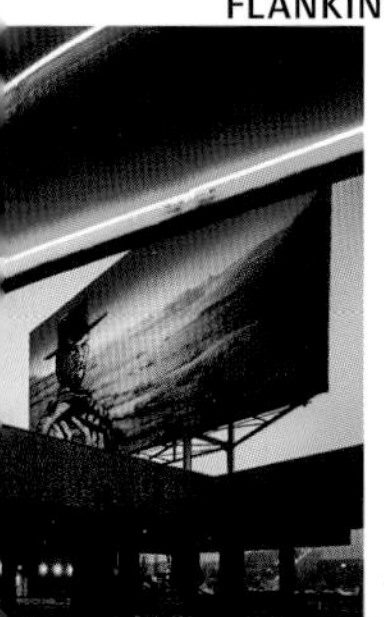

"What Predock calls the Skyramp extends out sixty feet and rises thirty-five feet off the ground. Standing at the end, you experience the house in apotheosis. Looking back, you get a splendid postcard view, a suddenly lucid one-shot revelation of its complex interconnections; look out and you are inserted radically and a little vertiginously into nature."

Kurt Andersen, "Sensuous Modernism in Dallas," *Architectural Digest*, March 1994

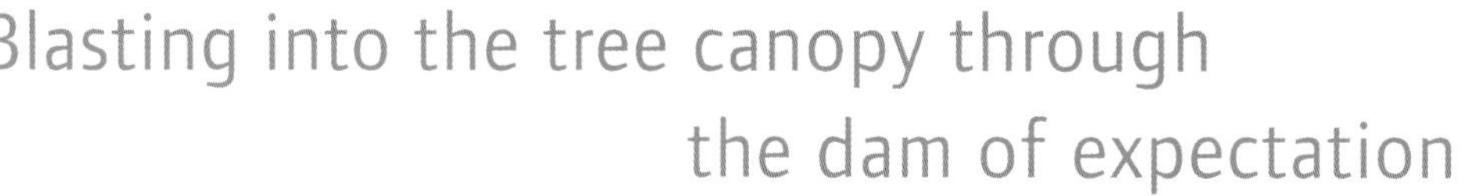

Blasting into the tree canopy through the dam of expectation

INTERNAL COURTYARDS FRAMED BY THE 1,000 ROOMS THAT GRADATE IN COLOR FROM EARTH TO SKY—DISSOLVING INTO SKY AT TIMES... WITH A CAPTIVE "FAKE" SAGUARO, A VOLCANO, JUNKED CARS, AND A RUIN—ALLUDING TO WILD WEST ICONOGRAPHY, ROOMS OF SILVER, ROOMS OF GOLD, A CONCRETE JAIL, AND A RED BORDELLO... WITH THE WHITE HAT AND BLACK HAT, REMINDING US OF THE WILD WEST DUALITY OF GOOD AND EVIL...

"... Predock cooled his heels in Eisner's dining room. Looking around at the walls hung with paintings, he realized there was no place to put his twenty-five-foot-long Hotel Santa Fe collage. Like its creator, it would fit no conventional frame.

He carried the collage into Eisner's backyard and pinned it up on the patio wall. Lawn chairs were hauled out onto the grass, and the group settled in to hear Predock's explanation, 'The West is about trails,' he said. Vapor trails in the sky, Interstate 40, dirt roads leading to nowhere—all are trails of the imagination.' He showed them the yellow line cutting right up the center of the collage. 'This is the trail of infinite space, one of those trails that makes you want to follow it, wherever it goes. And here, at the end of it, is a spaceship, a U.F.O.' Eisner, his whole body leaning forward in his chair, listened intently as Predock talked."

Miriam Horn, "The Rise of the Desert Rat," *Vanity Fair*, March 1992

A SIDE TRIP TO LE CORBUSIER'S VILLA SAVOYE

"The topographic roofscape bridges the earthbound arrival experience and the dance of the ephemeral Skyramp and reflective arc. This house has very different personalities—from earthbound to flying on the end of a string. The roofscape puts a "lid" on it all; and the succession of levels provides varied view aspects between those extremes—sometimes the connection to the natural realm is close and intimate, and other times, from far away."

Antoine Predock, "Introduction," *Turtle Creek House*, 1998

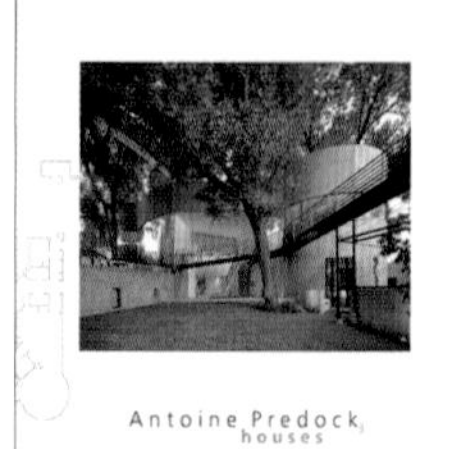

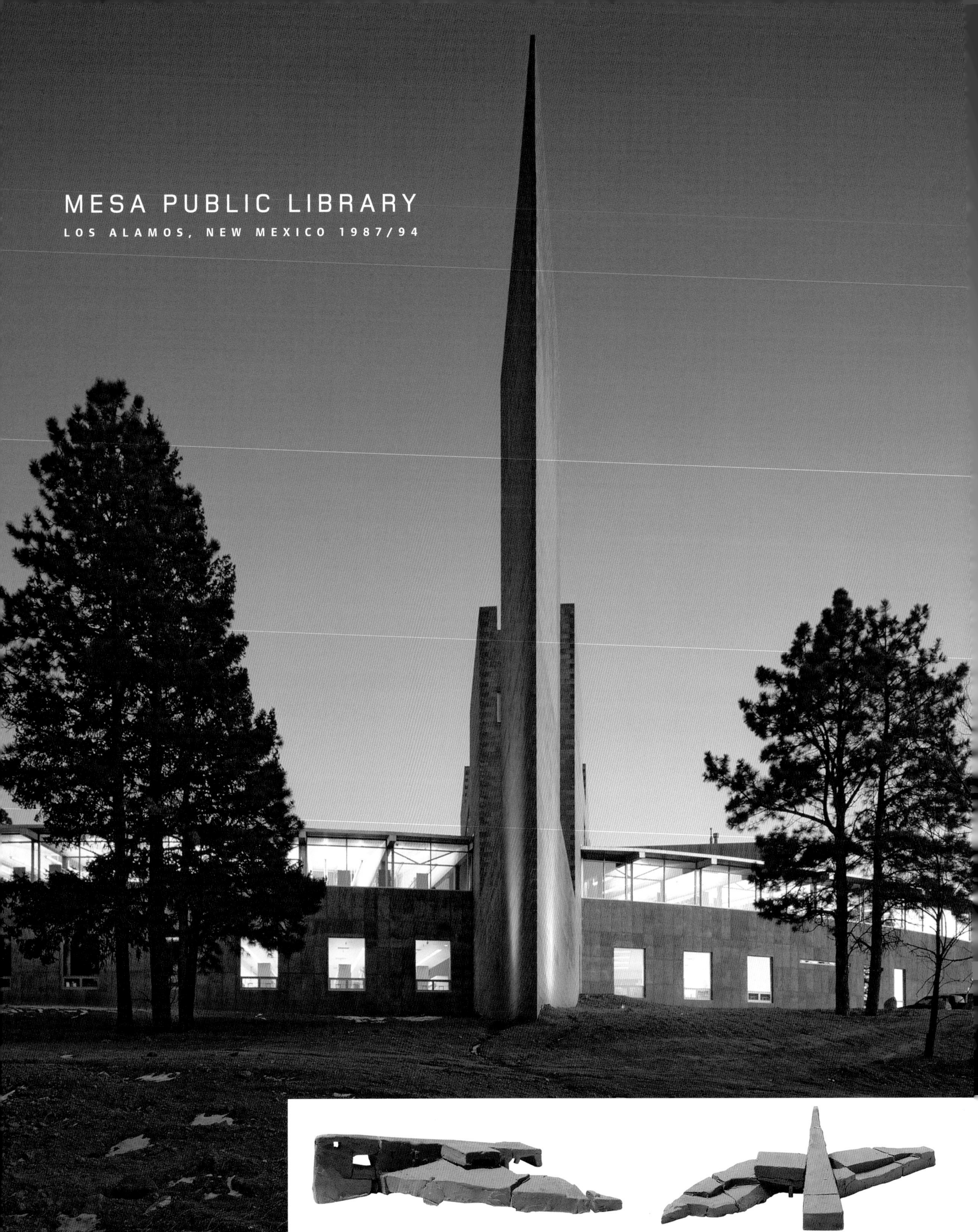
MESA PUBLIC LIBRARY
LOS ALAMOS, NEW MEXICO 1987/94

In the eroded tufa landscape, a north arrow emerges, aiming at the Pajarito Peak. At ground level an episodic approach ensues, leading multidimensionally through exhibitions, meeting areas, and kids realms, all focused on the Jemez Mountain drama.

The Library is characterized by two types of spaces: the cellular organization of the "wedge" houses lobby, meeting room, bookstore, and private reading areas; the sweeping arc wraps a large, open plan with the circulation desk, various stacks, reference area, and special collections. South-facing clerestory windows bring natural light into the stack areas.

"The openness also transformed movement through the building into a kind of theater, with many different sets, entrances, and exits."

David Dillon, "Reading Circle," *Architecture*, March 1995

AT THE TIME OF THE LIBRARY PROJECT, SPECTRAL SLUG WAS COMMISSIONED BY THE DES MOINES ART CENTER, ABSTRACTING A METAPHORICAL ADVENTURE FOR KIDS—CRAWL THROUGH TUNNEL UP A RAMP, UNDER RAINBOW COLORS, THEN OVER AN INVERTED BUBBLE SKYLIGHT "LAKE" COMPLETE WITH GOLDFISH, FINALLY EXITING DOWN A SLIDE TO FLOOR LEVEL.

SPECTRAL SLUG
DES MOINES, IA 1989

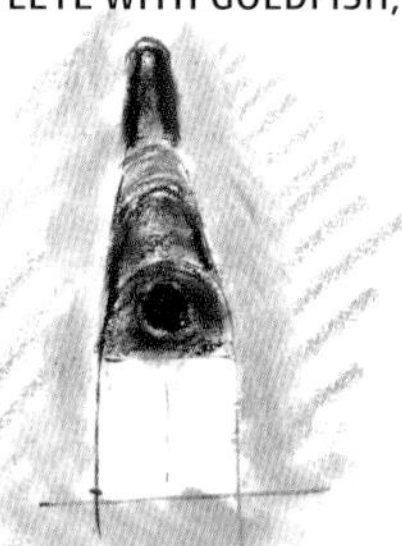

"From above, the library resembles a bird in flight while from the ground level, it displays some of the intricate cellular quality of an Indian pueblo, beckoning people in from the windy mesa. By joining natural, cultural, and technological associations, Predock has thoroughly rooted the library in its place."

David Dillon, "Reading Circle," *Architecture*, March 1995

TASKED WITH CREATING A MEDITERRANEAN HOTEL "CITY," I TURNED TO MYTHS OF THE MEDITERRANEAN CULTURES. IT WAS A WAY OF TRICKING MYSELF TO AVOID CLICHÉ THEMES, AND TO AVOID OVERT NOSTALGIC REFERENCES.

MEDITERRANEAN HOTEL, DISNEY WORLD
ORLANDO, FL 1988/91

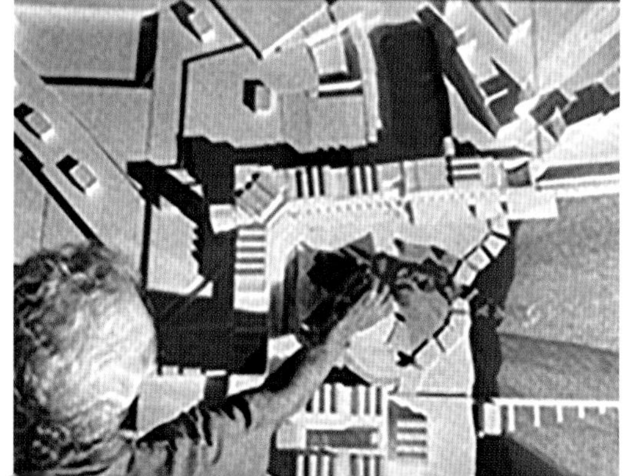

BEFORE PLUNGING INTO THE FINAL "MEDITERRANEAN" REFERENCED HOTEL, I GOT INTERESTED IN *DARK LABYRINTH* BY LAWRENCE DURRELL—THE NOTION OF LABYRINTH—DREAMING OF THE MINOTAUR—MY TEAM READ *THE HOUSE OF ASTERION* BY BORGES. WE DIAGRAMMED IT, LIFTING THE PHYSICAL DESCRIPTIONS IN THE STORY, AND BEGAN TO EXTRAPOLATE PROJECT SPACES.

A polished black monolith as a base covered with a film of water.

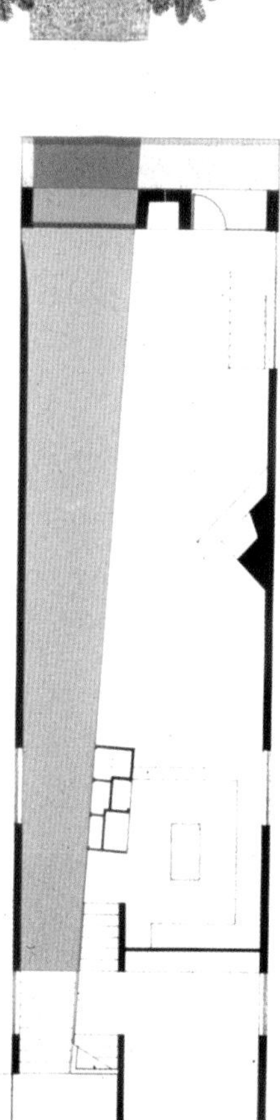

FLIGHTS BACK AND FORTH TO SOUTH AMERICA IN THE LATE '80s OVER THE ATACAMA DESERT AND THE SPINE OF THE ANDES.

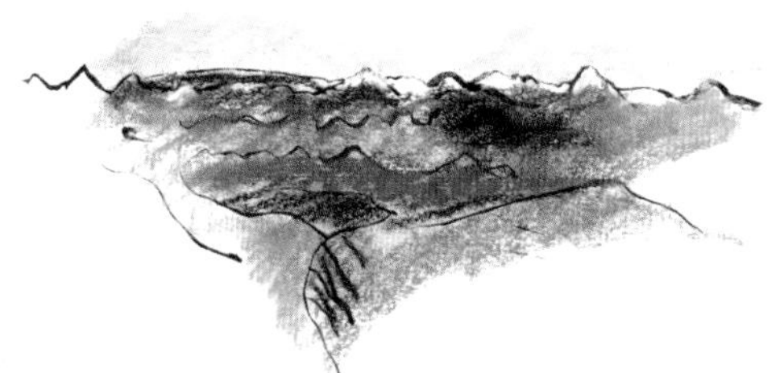

A seismic armature—
concrete evoking bleached bones along the shore.

GETTING STINK EYE FROM A VENICE SQUIRREL OUTSIDE AT OUR BRANCH STUDIO.

VENICE BEACH HOUSE

VENICE, CALIFORNIA 1988/1991

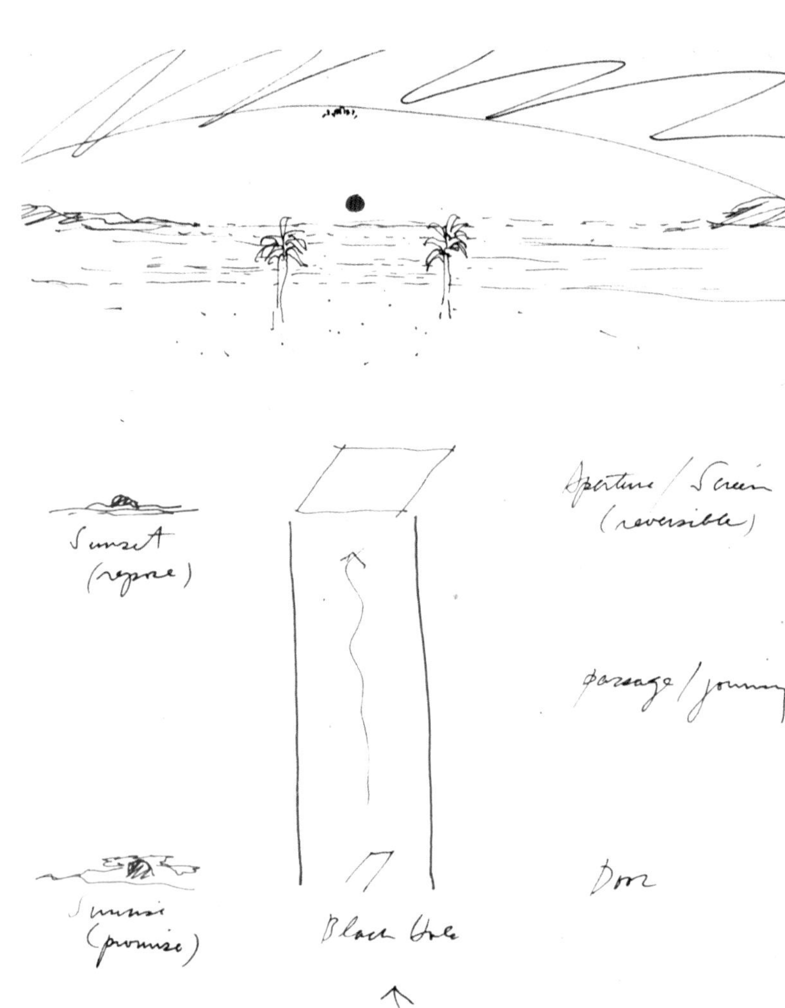

As construction was wrapping up, I spent one night in the house. Going downstairs the next morning, I opened the giant pivot. A group of people outside on the boardwalk began applauding—architecture as performance?

"The main vista is through a nine-by-fourteen-foot glass panel enclosed in a red steel border; this crystalline expanse pivots at the touch of a hand, actually disintegrating the boxy barrier between inside and out. Adjacent to this exploration of transparency, a concrete niche shelters a vertical slash of glass. The narrow pane has been inserted sideways, and it sends a laserlike beam of sea-green light slicing through the interior. Peering through its one-foot thickness, one sees the ocean fragment and refract in an endless collage."

Sylvia Lavin, "Dynamics of Venice Beach," *Architectural Digest*, Dec. 1990

Honoring the power and deep time of the LA basin as opposed to the LA "bling"—a tapering polished black granite runway and sloping ceiling set up a "Mantegna-ish" reverse perspective—drawing the viewer closer to the ocean visually. A conceptual compression of space between urban Los Angeles and the rising sun of Japan. The pivot piece, red, as in the Japanese flag.

A stairway ascends from the main level through the bedrooms to a roof-top sky amphitheater with views in all directions: beach, ocean, city lights, LAX flight paths...

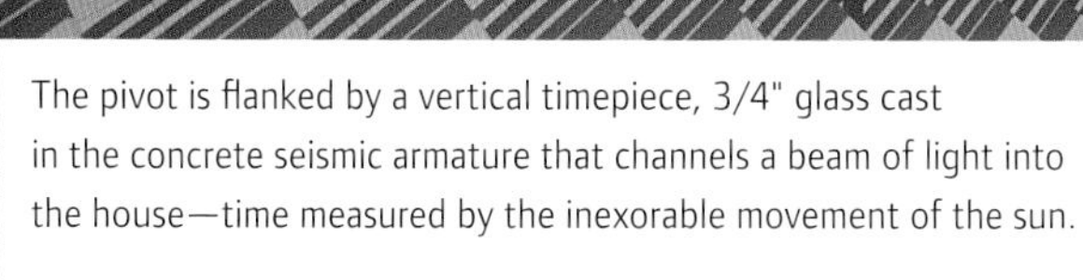
The pivot is flanked by a vertical timepiece, 3/4" glass cast in the concrete seismic armature that channels a beam of light into the house—time measured by the inexorable movement of the sun.

"A house Predock just completed on Venice Beach ... indicates that the extremes of glitzy ephemera and organic permanence are far from polar opposites. His almost anthropological approach to architecture has led to a powerfully serene and understated design that both stands out in and embraces the crowd.... He revels in the city's fanciful and flavorful mix and uses these ephemeral facts of modern life as a springboard to making timeless and permanent architecture."

Sylvia Lavin, "Dynamics of Venice Beach," *Architectural Digest*, Dec. 1990

WITH HADRIAN AND JASON ON VENICE BEACH—AND LATER, YELLOWSTONE WITH JASON

"Predock renders the aesthetic exclusiveness of Modern Movement abstraction accessible by reference to the familiar, whether this be modern 'trivia' as in his narcissistic mirror to the garage of the Venice House on the Venice boardwalk at Los Angeles ..."

Geoffery Baker, *Antoine Predock*, 1997

In the realm of the San Andreas fault, the seismic frame that is required is usually made of steel and hidden in the walls. I decided to celebrate that element by revealing it to become the frontispiece of the house ... thinking about the post-apocalyptic *Planet of the Apes* scene when Charlton Heston sees the torch of the Statue of Liberty emerging from the sand. I hope as the sea-level rises these seismic concrete bones will be a reminder to future architects to "build good ruins."

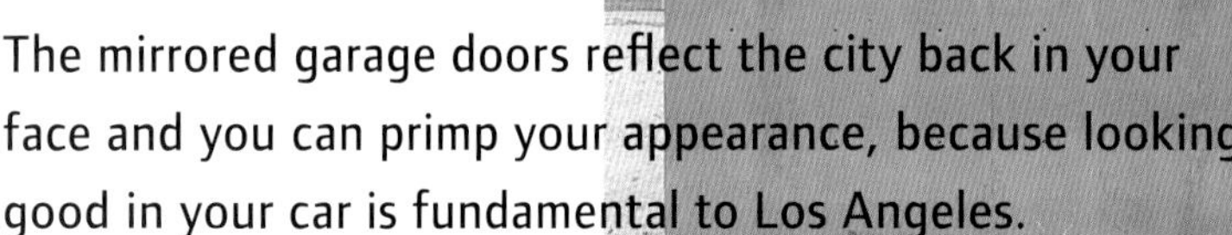

The mirrored garage doors reflect the city back in your face and you can primp your appearance, because looking good in your car is fundamental to Los Angeles.

1990 BMW K1 TURBO SHOWN BOTH CLOTHED AND NAKED, DEPARTING FOR MY COMMUTE TO ALBUQUERQUE FROM OUR VENICE STUDIO. (GOT THE WORST SPEEDING TICKET OF MY LIFE IN ARIZONA ON IT.)

A QUASI-FERAL CAT WANDERED INTO THE STUDIO ONE DAY AND ADOPTED US, THAT WAS BARNEY.

OPENING ANNOUNCEMENT—VENICE STUDIO

A N T O I N E   P R E D O C K
A R C H I T E C T   F A I A
3 0 0   1 2   S T .   N W .
A L B U Q U E R Q U E
N . M .   8 7 1 0 2
5 0 5   8 4 3   7 3 9 0

A N T O I N E   P R E D O C K
A R C H I T E C T   F A I A
1 1 3 6   W E S T
W A S H I N G T O N   B L V D .
V E N I C E ,   C A .
9 0 2 9 1
2 1 3   3 9 2   5 9 0 6

OPEN

"90% west, 10% east façade"

TWO EXTREMES IN ARGENTINA, THE HAPPY URBANISM OF SAN TELMO IN BUENOS AIRES AND THE MAJESTY OF THE QUEBRADA DE HUMAHUACA NEAR THE BOLIVIAN BORDER IN THE EXTREME NORTH.

IN PATAGONIA, FARTHER SOUTH IN ARGENTINA, THE BREEDING REALM OF THE SOUTHERN RIGHT WHALES OF PUERTO MADRYN.

MANDELL WEISS FORUM/LA JOLLA PLAYHOUSE

UNIVERSITY OF CALIFORNIA SAN DIEGO
SAN DIEGO, CALIFORNIA 1988/91

The approach to the theater is through an aromatic eucalyptus grove and then an unexpected 276-foot-long mirror foreground to the building itself.

Moving through the grove, the amplified reflection gives way to a personal mirror (a collective checking oneself out). Passing through the aperture/threshold, reality gives way to the dream of the stage.

From that threshold, a long slow black steel ramp ascends to a landing point with a balcony viewing over the shoulder to the grove and the Pacific beyond. The ramp switches back and ascends to an arrival lobby with the arcing seating bowl flowing down to the stage platform.

... Predock turned the commission into a multi-layered complex of reflective and opaque forms, shifting levels and perspectives. It offers a mediation on the interplay of illusion and reality, and on the experience of theater-going; a response to the site and the changing seasons. Within, he created a performance space that has delighted audience and players. Des McAnuff, for ten years Artistic Director of the Playhouse, calls it, 'a Rolls Royce in comparison to the Warren ... a perfect combination of a classical Greek amphitheater and the most high-tech, flexible thrust stage I've ever worked on. I could produce here for ten years without exhausting its possibilities.'"

Michael Webb, "Criticism: Mandell Weiss Forum," *a+u*, no 268, January 1993

1987-89 ALL HELL BROKE LOOSE FOR A SMALL STUDIO—AND WE WELCOMED IT!

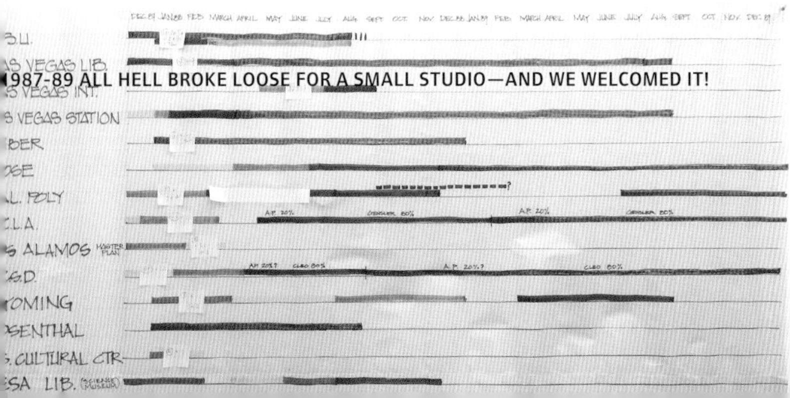

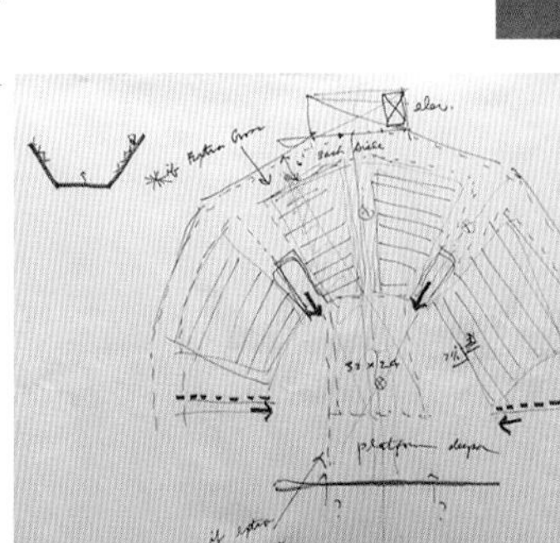

N

The theater is a fusion of a classical Greek amphitheater configuration incorporating a walk-on tech grid above the stage.

APART FROM DEEP TIME UNDERSTANDING AND RESEARCH INTO OUR PROJECT SITES, MY 12'x4' COLLAGES BECAME VEHICLES FOR USE IN INTERVIEWS FOR POTENTIAL PROJECTS—UNSUCCESSFUL AT TIMES, LIKE THIS 1991 PIECE FOR A PROJECT AT THE UNIVERSITY OF UTAH.

UNIVERSITY OF UTAH
COLLAGE 1991

"The Mandell Weiss Forum is resonant of theater itself. Mute during the day, much like an empty stage, its courtyards, second-story terrace, and lookout points are bare; the mirrored glass of the wall shifts between translucence and opacity with the changing light, and offers subtle ambiguities of spatial depth. On the night of a performance, uplights among the trees and runway lights along the path make the images reflected in the wall—now including those of the audience—sharp and dramatic."

Ellen Posner, "Supporting Role," *Architecture*, September 1991

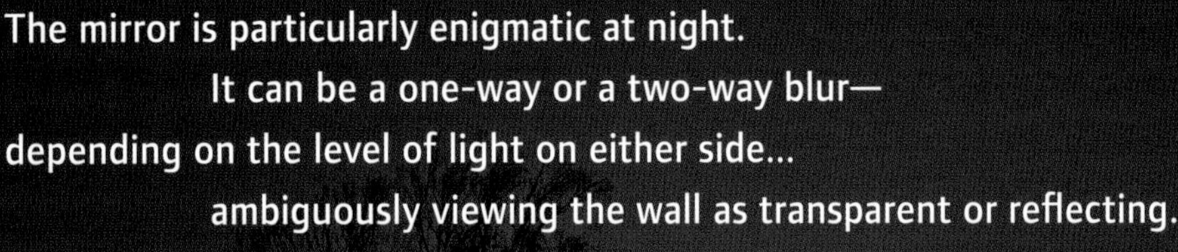

The mirror is particularly enigmatic at night. It can be a one-way or a two-way blur— depending on the level of light on either side... ambiguously viewing the wall as transparent or reflecting.

DE YOUNG MUSEUM COLLAGE
SAN FRANCISCO, CA 1991

THOUSAND OAKS CIVIC ARTS PLAZA

THOUSAND OAKS, CALIFORNIA 1989/94

INSTITUTE OF AMERICAN
INDIAN ARTS MUSEUM
SANTA FE, NM 1989/92

A MUSEUM IN A RENOVATION OF THE OLD SANTA FE POST OFFICE

MY FIRST DRAWING OF THE CIVIC ARTS PLAZA—WHAT'S CONSPICUOUSLY MISSING ON THE FINISHED BUILDING ARE THE STAGE HOUSE RABBIT EARS. "CONEJO" MEANS RABBIT. CONEJO VALLEY—RABBIT EARS. BUDGET-IMPOSED AMPUTATIONS HURT—EVEN WHEN IT'S NOT PART OF YOUR BODY.

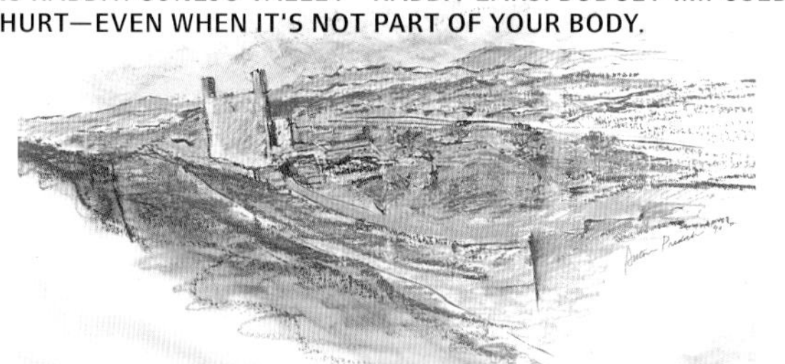

The site, in the Conejo Valley, previously a preserve for retired movie industry animal performers, was a strange, protected island of pure live oak natural landscape.

Visitors first encounter the building and the live oak trees that define the site while blasting along on the 101, a freeway that never sleeps. The complex turns its back to that, while presenting a wind-activated kinetic copper "curtain" on the fly tower of the theater.

"The monumental scale and head-on orientation of the auditorium to the freeway make the Civic Arts Plaza impossible to miss at 70 miles per hour: The rear of the auditorium's fly tower faces east toward oncoming traffic like a giant billboard."

M. Lindsay Bierman, "Freeway Acropolis," *Architecture*, March 1995

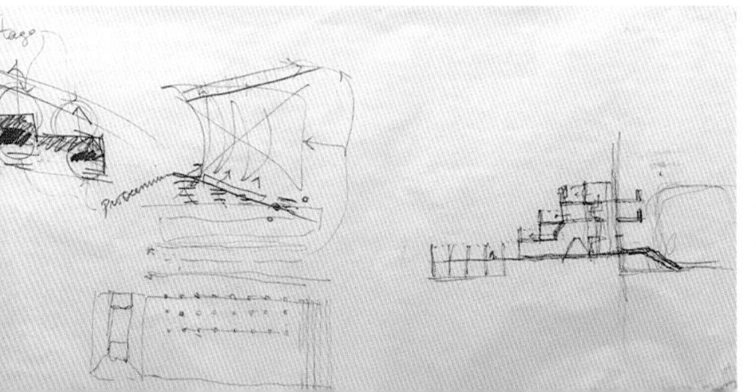

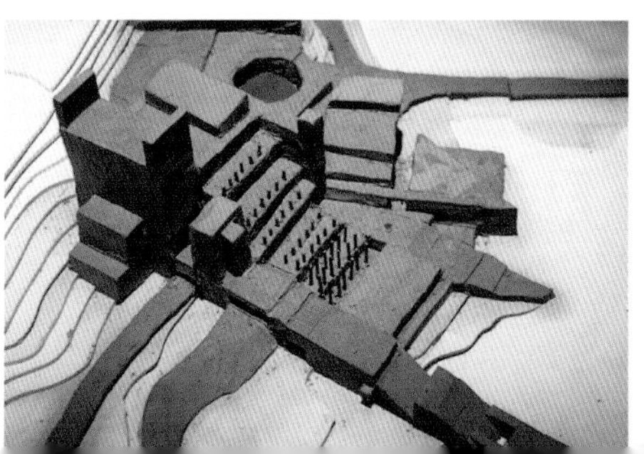

The building turns its back on the highway, fronting a seven-acre community park with the massive programmatic elements, siting the various chunks—a 2,000 seat theater, a blàck box, and another 500-seat performance hall—atop the "mesa" of Thousand Oaks City Hall.

US OLYMPIC HALL OF FAME
COLORADO SPRINGS, CO 1990/91

US OLYMPIC HALL OF FAME SITE VISIT—OUR TEAM AND OLYMPIC ADMINISTRATORS

PIKES PEAK—

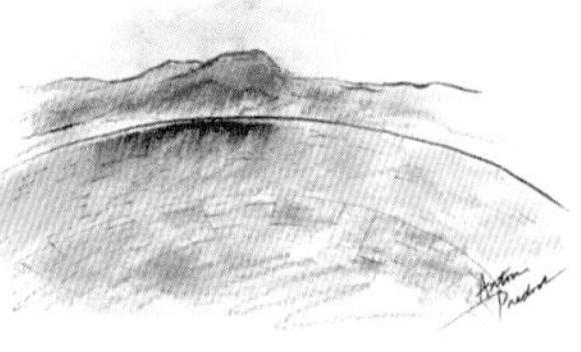

The acoustic "seismically" disturbed side wall of the 2,000 seat theater.

"The architects have played on the binary oppositions of concentration and dispersal, closure and transparency, mass and lightness, geometrical precision and freedom of spatial layout ... carefully avoiding the kind of rhetoric often associated with either planning work or the vacuous populist projects still in vogue in the United States (and elsewhere), the cold functionalism of the International Style or even new versions of Sixties Brutalism. Predock has used carefully gauged measure and architectural sensibility to satisfy the demands of the various site users ... who were expecting the Civic Arts Plaza to provide a congregation area with which the entire community could identify."

Aldo Castellano, *L 'Arca*, October 1995

THE CULMINATING VIEW, AND DIAGRAMMING THE CIRCUITOUS OLYMPIC PATH

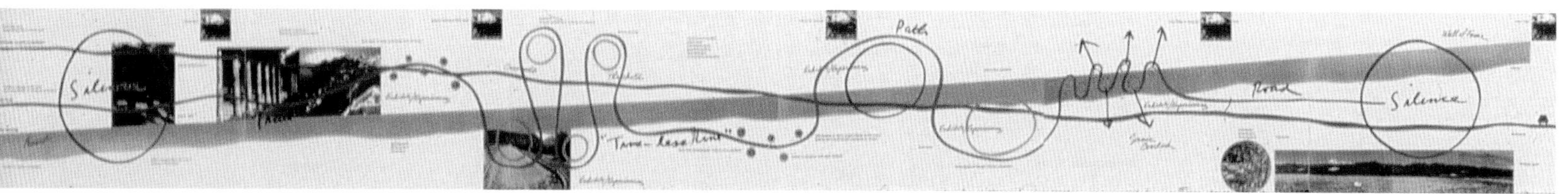

The Civic Arts Plaza serves as a datum for the 2,000-seat Auditorium above, and the governmental functions set below the energy-conserving reflecting pool.

"It's clever how the plaza's pool prevents us from approaching the outer edge of the terrace, blocking the view of the street two stories below. Predock thereby ensures that no matter how many awful buildings sprout from the surrounding fields, none will obstruct our view of Nature, naked and enthroned on the horizon."

M. Lindsay Bierman, "Freeway Acropolis," *Architecture*, March 1995

The pictograph wall, legible on the exterior and interior of the building, is an abstract reference to the sacred cosmology of the Chumash people, the original inhabitants of the valley—the condor wing, the serpent—and the starry sky, and the diminishing horizon.

MUSIC FACILITY

UNIVERSITY OF CALIFORNIA SANTA CRUZ
SANTA CRUZ, CALIFORNIA 1989/97

This UCSC "maverick" branch campus, with the Music Facility commanding the view over Monterey Bay from one of the most extraordinary sites in the University of California system.

The multiple personalities of the site above Monterey Bay: the bright blue sky/water, the fog layer, sunset, and the night sky over deep blue/black water.

RANGERS HILL, A BALLPARK FOR THE TEXAS RANGERS. AN ASCENT UP A BLUE BONNET-COVERED HILLSIDE THROUGH THIS FAMILIAR TEXAS BIOME TO THE MAIN CONCOURSE ARRIVAL LEVEL.

FROM THAT DATUM, RAMPS LEAD UP TO THE HIGHER GRAND STANDS OR DOWN INTO THE FIELD LEVEL... THE "MOTHERSHIP" HAS A LITTLE LEAGUE "BABY" BY ITS SIDE.

TEXAS RANGERS BALLPARK
ARLINGTON, TX 1992

To the north and east, bermed walls visually wrap the meadow over the Music Center. An open-to-the-sky sunken garden leads to practice rooms and other academic facilities. The Music Center maintains a low profile, respecting the view corridors of the buildings to the north, with a sweeping view of Monterey Bay from south facing spaces and deck areas. A separate Gamelan pavilion honors the University's special collection of those instruments and the Javanese culture of Indonesia.

THE COLLAGE EXPLORES THE DEEP CONNECTIONS OF THE BALLPARK TO THIS TEXAS SITE... AND TO BASEBALL

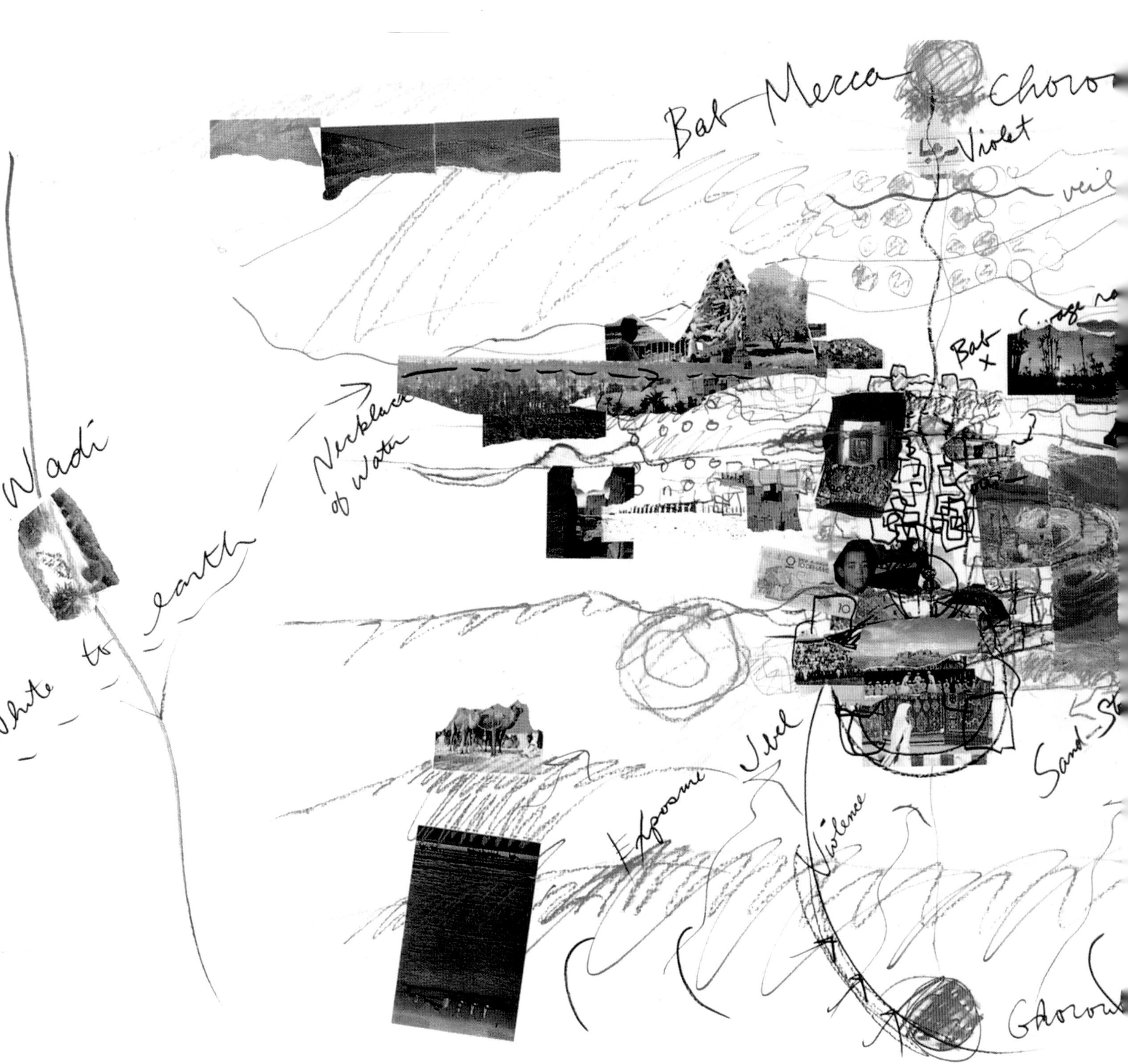

Shems, the sun; kamar, the moon; choroub, the sunrise; ghorub, the sunset; jebel, the mountain; l'maa, water; and the all-pervasive ramla, sand.

Each site we work on is only surficially representative of different strata—the vast geologic time that we honor and, of course, the thin layer of human occupation. While some levels may be visible, others lie beneath the surface and need to be uncovered to understand a site in its totality. This exploration yields an architecture that truly evokes a place rather than merely representing it. Clarifying what is present and amplifying it suggests what it might become. It is this investigation of site—physical, environmental, cultural, programmatic—that is explored here at the edge of Palm Bay and the twenty-first century. This project responds to the intersection of a mythic, timeless Morocco and the promise of its future with a catalytic architectural district plan.

The site is rooted in the region's varied landscape by its location at the end of a great descent from the Atlas Mountains, across a desert plateau and then the Souss Valley to the sea. Behind the line of sand dunes a weaving line of black eucalyptus trees occupies a depression with an underlying freshwater aquifer next to the bay. The image of an oasis is evoked—respite from the Sahara.

The spirit of Morocco resonates in the labyrinthine passages of the souk, the presence of water in fragrant courtyards, in its complex geometries, and in the haunting strain of repetitive Berber melodies. These things, among many others, give testament to a timeless, tenacious culture. The project seeks to reinforce and nurture this spirit, while overlaying program elements that look far to the future.

This project attempts to reveal the Palm Bay site in all of its complexities by grounding it in its geographical and historical context. Such an expansive view of its location enhances the original brief for the complex and reaffirms the existing presences on site, allowing them to posit a pattern toward the future. It is a specific site response avoiding stylistic cliché in favor of a global reach for Agadir Bay and its surroundings.

PALM BAY RESORT

AGADIR, MOROCCO 1990

This 12'x4' collage embeds the iconography of the Moroccan Maghreb, with dune preserving strategies, a breakwater protection from the northwest wave direction on this Atlantic coastline, the repetitive patterning of Zélige, a water necklace of Riyadh courtyards—collectively establishing a multi-use resort base for interpreting the richness of Moroccan culture in a web of ecological responses.

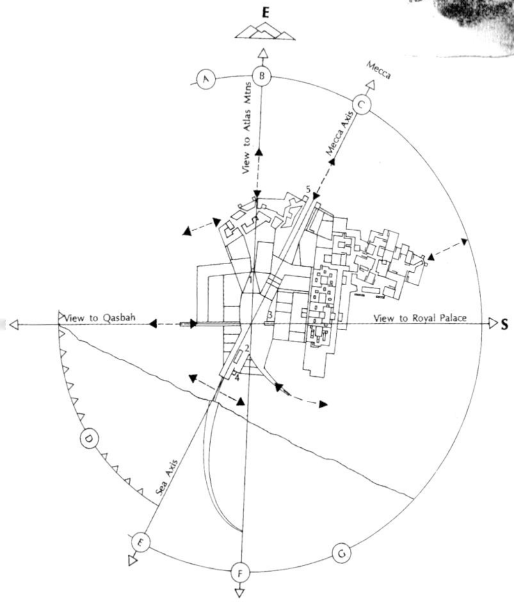

Orange

(Violence)

Sahara

Magreb

Berber Woman

(Yellow)

E

Mecca

View to Atlas Mtns

Mecca Axis

View to Qasbah

View to Royal Palace

S

Sea Axis

W

SITE DETERMINANTS

A. Summer Solstice Sunrise
B. Equinox
C. Winter Solstice Sunrise
D. Prevailing Winds
E. Summer Solstice Sunset
F. Equinox
G. Winter Solstice Sunset

1. Sunrise Gateway
2. Sunset Tower
3. Sun Dial
4. Moon Tower
5. Medina Gates

◀- -▶ Pedestrian Access

SEAFRONT ELEVATION

Protection—a critical theme in the assault from the East of the Sahara Desert and from the West, the power and unpredictability of the Atlantic Ocean.

The Islamic notion of relentlessly repetitive patterns, Zélige—surficial, yet profound—as in the Alhambra, the "binder" that gathers all together in a calligraphic-like expression.

MASTER SITE PLAN

1. Gateway Hotel A with Underground Parking
2. Gateway Hotel B with Underground Parking
3. Medina Gates
4. Club C with Underground Parking
5. Hotel D with Underground Parking
6. Hotel E with Underground Parking
7. Hotel F with Underground Parking
8. Hotel G with Underground Parking
9. Club H with Underground Parking
10. Club I with Underground Parking
11. Conference Center
12. Dunes
13. Corniche Pedestrian Route
14. Commercial Activities
15. Pedestrian Path
16. Underground Service Route
17. Entry Ramp to Underground Parking
18. Grand Axis
19. Luxury Apartments
20. Conference Center/Hotel Auto Court
21. Royal Chamber Auto Court
22. Palmerie
23. Water/Ryadh (Typical)
24. Hotel Arrival
25. Club Arrival
26. Pier/Breakwater
27. Hotel/Club Access Road
28. Sahat
29. View Terraces
30. Souk
31. Protected Sunning Area
32. 100 Room Luxury Hotel - Sea View Suites
33. 100 Room Luxury Hotel - Valley Suites
34. Conference Center Reception
35. Hotel Reception
36. Royal Chamber Reception
37. Beach Level Terraces
38. Ramp up to Sahat
39. Shaded Vehicular Zone

HOTEL WITH PARKING BELOW
HOTEL WITH PARKING BELOW
RESTAURANT
HOTELS
HOTELS
CONVENTION CENTER
RESTAURANT
NIGHTCLUB
PARKING BELOW
HOTELS

Largest clay model I ever made, 4'x6'.

Bab Mecca — Mecca gateway

Antoine Predock '90

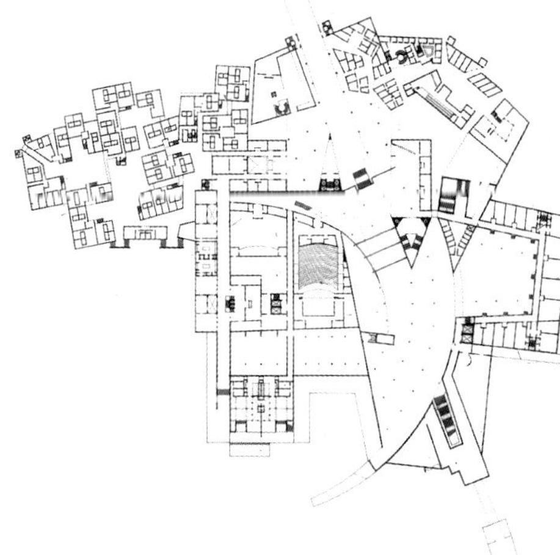

North and south wings—sequential linked riyadh townhouse water courts drawn together—frame a central mass of theater, convention facilities, hotel, mixed-use retail, and an elevated prayer chamber located on the Mecca axis.

"Is it any surprise that the controversial American architect Antoine Predock (whose sobriquet is Desert Rat) should place as a finalist (and winner) in the worldwide competition held by his Royal Highness the King of Morocco for the commission of the proposed Palm Bay Convention Center and Resort Hotel in Agadir? Predock has exploited every natural asset of the site which is on the Atlantic Ocean side of the country. He has exaggerated the sand dunes for their privacy from the highway, introduced breakwaters to calm the action of the waves and strengthened a natural eucalyptus forest whose minty scent is hypnotic and whose density suggests a lush, green valley hugging the protected shoreline. Clearings in the forest have been planned to embrace the man-made shelters which house the activities of the resort. In response to strong desert winds and the shimmering heat the buildings have been arranged in cellular configurations which take advantage of cooling breezeways and softly tented courtyards." Paula Rice Jackson, "Desert Drama," *LYS, vol 12*, 1992

熱砂のドラマ

陽炎の大地

The public facilities are grouped around a Sahat, a grand plaza, with extensive upper terraces providing expansive views of the Atlantic Ocean; a vertical triangular titanium blade is the gnomon for a sundial, whose shadow travels around marks on the Sahat. The arcing breakwater shelters a marina from the northwest wave action, and the preservation of the black eucalyptus grove along the dune line ensures ongoing stability of the dunes. We were the winners of this international design competition, but because of political upheaval the project was never completed.

MUSEUM OF SCIENCE AND INDUSTRY

TAMPA, FLORIDA 1990/95

"Bold geometric forms that rise out of the land itself characterize the architecture of Antoine Predock. Set on the edge of the Florida wetlands, the Museum of Science and Industry in Tampa easily fits this description—its main organizing element is a shimmering blue sphere that seems to clutch the earth and reflect the water and sky around it."

James Grayson Trulove, *Designing the New Museum: Building a Destination,* 2000

WITH SAM STERLING, HADRIAN PREDOCK, AND KIRA SOWONICK AS WE BEGIN TO COLLECT IMAGERY FOR THIS COLLAGE.

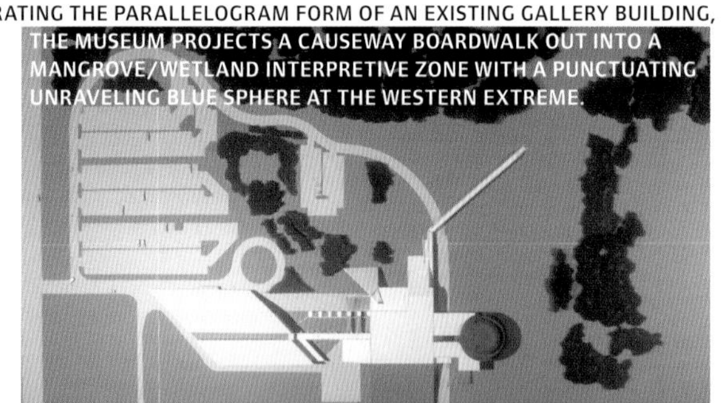

INCORPORATING THE PARALLELOGRAM FORM OF AN EXISTING GALLERY BUILDING, THE MUSEUM PROJECTS A CAUSEWAY BOARDWALK OUT INTO A MANGROVE/WETLAND INTERPRETIVE ZONE WITH A PUNCTUATING UNRAVELING BLUE SPHERE AT THE WESTERN EXTREME.

The mirror-finish blue stainless steel unraveling sphere of the Omnimax Theater evokes the waters and sky of Tampa Bay. The glass blade as an entry marker guides the visitor to the midpoint of the Museum and doubles as a vertical circulation element,visually eavesdropping on the four-story lobby and exhibition spaces to the east.

"After an extensive review of qualifications, involving such distinguished offices as Richard Meier, Frank Gehry and Cambridge Seven, Antoine Predock Architect, in association with Tampa-based Robbins, Bell & Kreher Architects, was selected to complete an addition of 135,000 square feet."
Reed Kroloff, "Sculptural Sequence," *Architecture*, November 1995

TRAVELING TO EGYPT AROUND THIS TIME WITH ITS OVERWHELMING ARRAY OF PHARAONIC MONUMENTS AS IN THE FUNERARY TEMPLE OF QUEEN HATSHEPSUT IN DEIR EL-BAHARI.

To the rear of the Museum, "Florida Biomes" footpath is an experiential journey through several protected Florida biomes—from the low marshlands to the higher and drier, live-oak hummock and an oblique view of the detached Butterfly Pavilion.

APART FROM CREATING A BUTTERFLY HABITAT, THE BUTTERFLY PAVILION HAD A NUMBER OF UNDERLYING EDUCATIONAL AND SUSTAINABILITY RESPONSES—MOST NOTABLY THE CYLINDRICAL PROCESSING TANKS THAT CONVERTED SEWAGE INTO GREYWATER FOR LANDSCAPE IRRIGATION.

BIOWORKS BUTTERFLY EXHIBIT
1994/1996

The Blue Sphere becomes an ascending walkway wrapper around the precast-concrete inner sphere that houses the Omnimax Theater. Internal to the theater is a 360-degree projection scrim that, when not activated by projection, ambiguously reveals support scaffolding behind.

"Predock's chopping, colliding, sculptural vistas often seem as if they are taking form before our eyes, yet have somehow always been there—an enigmatic duality that provides a satisfying architectural analogue to the processes of natural science and industry."

Reed Kroloff, "Sculptural Sequence," *Architecture*, Nov. 1995

The blue sphere rises on concrete piers surrounding an open-air assembly area. The unraveling, ascending, blue stainless steel skin creates spiraling circulation ramps leading to the apex of the sphere where the internal concrete mass of the theater surfaces as a vantage point for views across the wetlands to Tampa Bay.

PANTHEON "SLICE" FROM PIAZZA CAMPITELLI IN ROME–1994

"... the Museum of Science and Industry was conceived as an outstanding structure in an absolute sense, as an alien body, as something which, for the very reason that it was so different with respect to its surroundings, might arouse one's curiosity and induce the public to go inside to observe the scientific-technological marvels contained in the body of this "good master" made of cement, metal and glass ..."

Carlo Paganelli, *L'Arca, no 103*, April 1996

SOCIAL SCIENCES AND HUMANITIES BUILDING

UNIVERSITY OF CALIFORNIA, DAVIS
DAVIS, CALIFORNIA 1990/94

THIS PROJECT THAT STUDENTS REFER TO AS "THE DEATH STAR," WAS A KIND OF WILDCARD. I HAD DONE A NUMBER OF UNIVERSITY OF CALIFORNIA PROJECTS, FROM SAN DIEGO TO UCLA, UC SANTA BARBARA, UC SANTA CRUZ, AND THEN UP THE CENTRAL VALLEY TO DAVIS. I WAS ONLY ABLE TO REALIZE THIS PROJECT BECAUSE CHANCELLOR TED HULLAR TRUSTED ME.

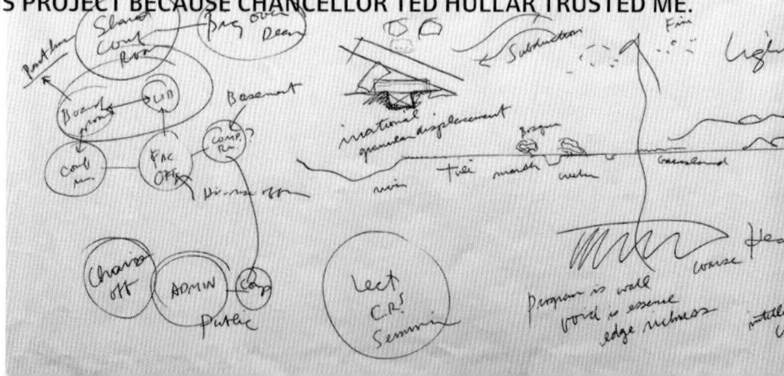

Flying across the San Joaquin Valley and over the Sacramento River watershed, with the upthrust tectonic displacement of the Sierras in the distance, I was struck by the collision of sinuous natural water courses with the man-made agricultural grid of the San Joaquin Valley. That juxtaposition of curvilinear movement through the grid was the inspiration for the baseline circulation in the organization of Social Sciences and Humanities components—the recycled aluminum-clad office blades that are suggestive of the Sierras. These interwoven geometries yield courtyards and carve-outs for collegial encounters—circumstantial exchanges of information or evening romance.

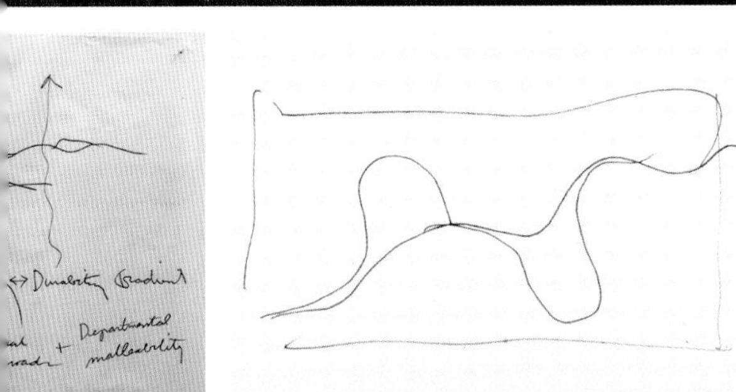

"The design defines a world within itself, rich enough to be a kind of architectural exploratorium.... The UC Davis building works like an optical instrument on its site, and anyone who sees with this building is delivered to a larger geographical and cultural context."

Joseph Giovannini, "Planting Knowledge," *Architecture*, March 1995

The sunken courtyard circulation trajectory defines a curvilinear path from one corner of the site, arriving diagonally at the assembly hall, and then becomes a grand stairway gateway receiving this circulation from the student union and campus core. This episodic lower-level pathway is punctuated by a series of ornamental vegetable gardens honoring both the "Ag School" heritage of Davis and the cornucopia of the agricultural "Breadbasket of America."

The "valley floor" of the Social Sciences and Humanities building is fragmented by lines perpendicular to tangents along the serpentine path. These forms further define the courtyards below and create a pattern reminiscent of the deformation of the Valley's agricultural grid by natural waterways.

The upper strata of the project, rising from the site in two linear metallic blocks that bridge the courtyards below, contains academic offices, departmental libraries, conference rooms, and research areas. Suggesting the subductive forces that formed the Sierra Nevada and Coast Range, these forms erupt from the site at key intersections, taking advantage of views, natural light, and the cooling Sacramento Delta breezes.

IN OUR SECTION OF THE 1991 MASTER PLAN OF IBM SOLANA, NEAR THE DFW AIRPORT, WE IMAGINED A CURVILINEAR FLOW WITH A FORESTED BACKDROP—LINKED VERTEBRAE-LIKE

IBM SOLANA
FORT WORTH, TX 1991

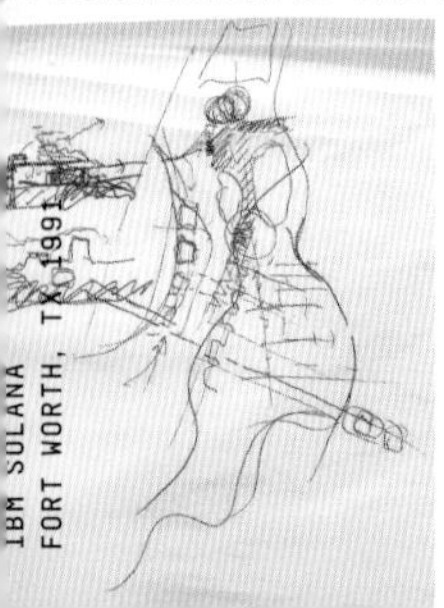

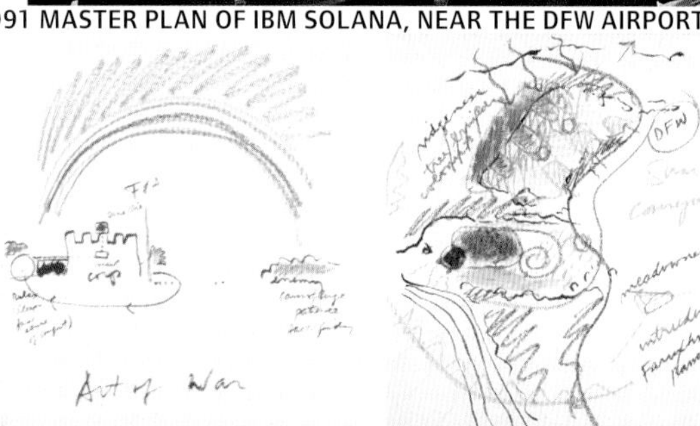

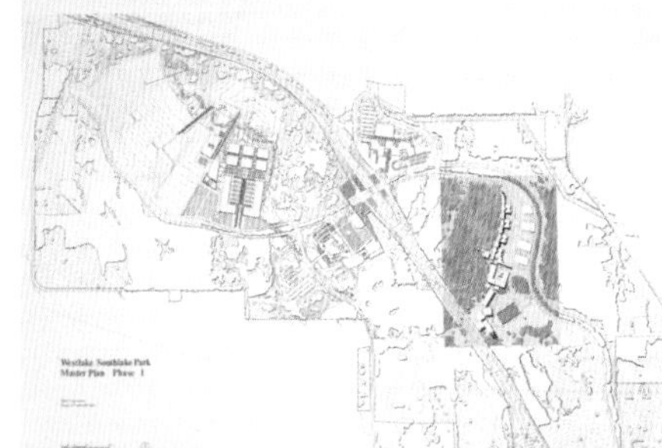

"Predock ... designed this building ... to encourage social interaction.... Ingenious. The Death Star perplexes most people, but it's something that makes UC Davis more interesting and unique. This unusually stimulating building houses an array of activities and serves a great communal purpose."

Savannah Holmes, "Trying to understand: Doomed in the 'Death Star'," *The Aggie*, 2013

OFFICE COMPONENTS TIED TO THE MOTHERSHIP OF SHARED CORPORATE FACILITIES AS A BASTION IN THE MESQUITE COUNTRY PRAIRIE.

The collage diagrams topographic and phenomenological essences of north-central Arizona—peaks, boulder-strewn talus slopes, the yellow line in the highway, the scarcity and power of rain when it finally comes, the theater of the sky...

ARIZONA SCIENCE CENTER

PHOENIX, ARIZONA 1990/97

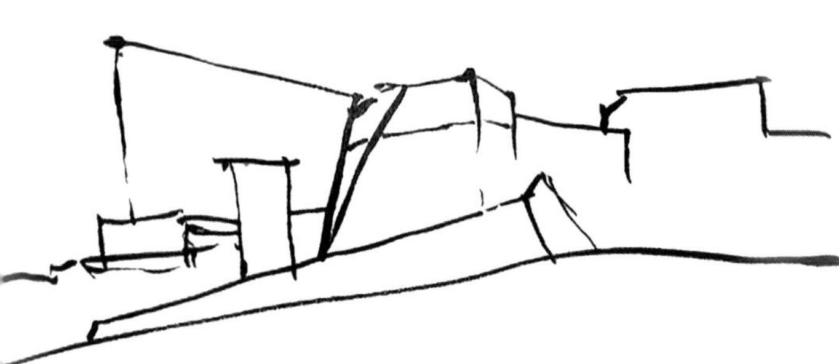

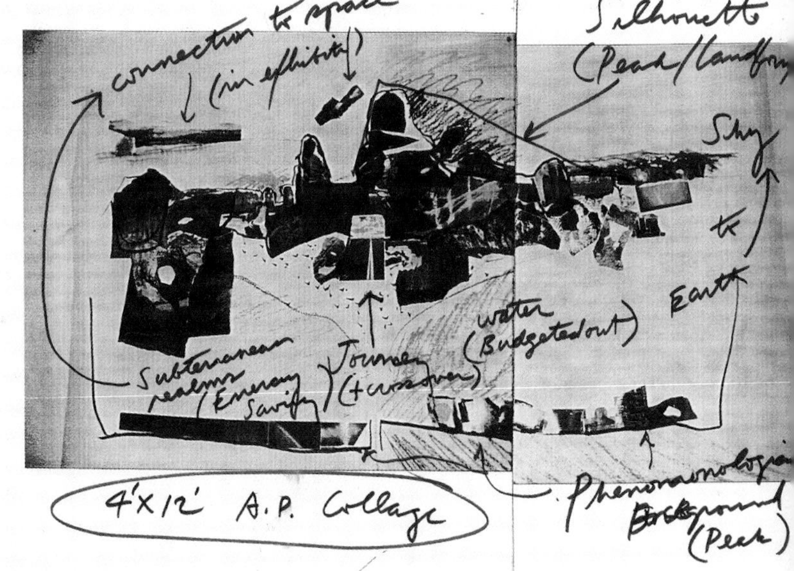

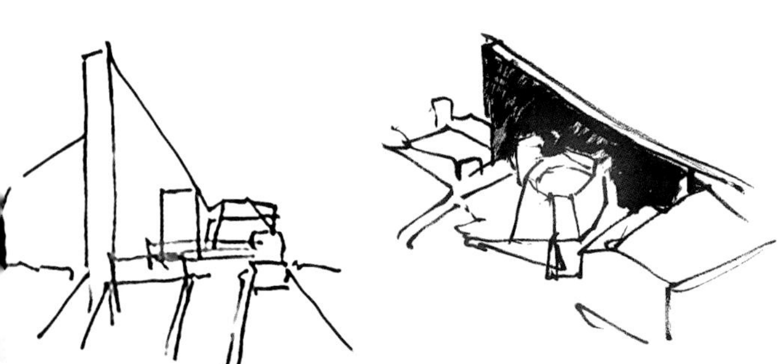

MY CLAY MODEL, CLINICALLY DIAGRAMMING PROGRAMMATIC AREAS BUT MOST IMPORTANTLY

In the Sonoran Desert, phenomena act on architecture—the metallic blade is a kind of stelae, a sacred marker, that can merge with or vanish into the sky when the annual monsoon roars through Arizona... ascending from Earth to Sky.

TRANSLATING THE COLLAGE IMAGERY INTO DISCRETE 3D FORMS.

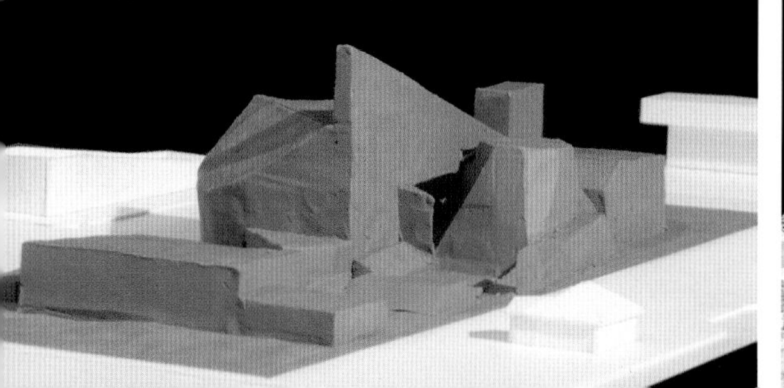

ON A 1991 SCI-ARC PANEL WITH COA.

The Sky Terrace aperture atop the Dynamax Planetarium—sometimes a hawk or Southwest Airlines passing overhead—night sky viewing for school kid campouts.

"For each of his buildings, he returns to architecture's first principles: the bony structure, the massive stripped masonry wall, the ritual of procession and arrival, the retreat into the dark, cool cave. There are archaic, sacred forms in his work, stepped pyramids and soaring obelisks, ceremonial stairways and circular pools. But there is also titanium and neon, Wim Wenders and James Bond, Stealth bombers and even Bart Simpson's hair."

Miriam Horn, "The Rise of the Desert Rat," *Vanity Fair*, March 1992

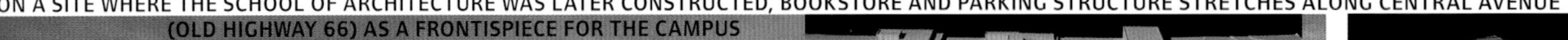

ON A SITE WHERE THE SCHOOL OF ARCHITECTURE WAS LATER CONSTRUCTED, BOOKSTORE AND PARKING STRUCTURE STRETCHES ALONG CENTRAL AVENUE (OLD HIGHWAY 66) AS A FRONTISPIECE FOR THE CAMPUS

BOOKSTORE AND PARKING STRUCTURE.
UNIVERSITY OF NEW MEXICO
ALBUQUERQUE, NM 1992/93

"Beyond the drama of its grand, mysterious shapes (already a site for fashion shoots), the great success of the Science Center is that visitors clamber around the building ... The visitor is not merely a passive user but a participant: The way the design draws in the elements heightens the physical dimension of the visit."

Joseph Giovannini, "Arizona Science Center," *Architecture,* July 1997

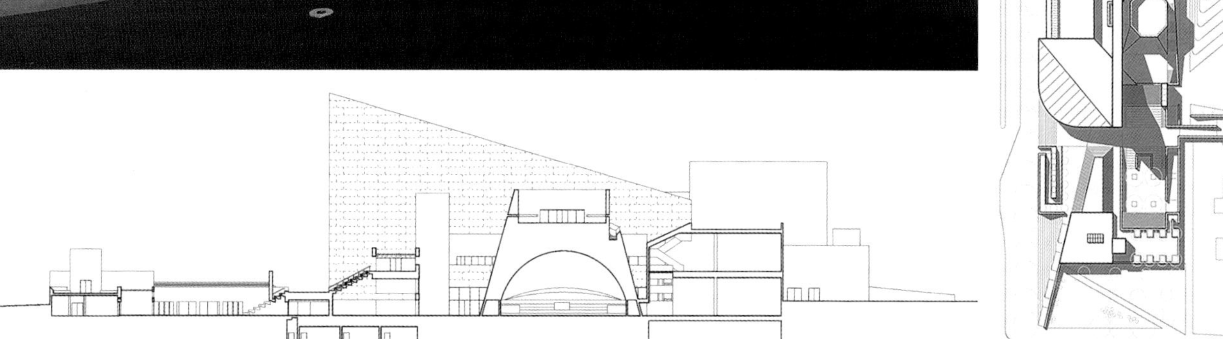

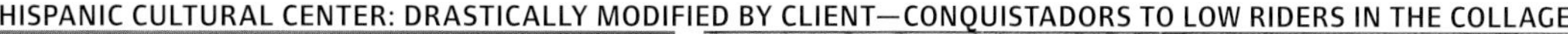

HISPANIC CULTURAL CENTER: DRASTICALLY MODIFIED BY CLIENT—CONQUISTADORS TO LOW RIDERS IN THE COLLAGE

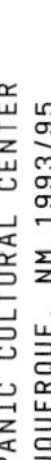

HISPANIC CULTURAL CENTER
ALBUQUERQUE, NM 1993/95

ERUPTING FROM THE SLOPING SHORELINE, THE HOUSE BECOMES A VIEWING PLATFORM—TO THE SOUTH OF THE SITE, MARBLEHEAD ON THE DISTANT SHORE.
ON-SITE CHARRETTE WITH MY COLLEAGUE JOHN BRITTINGHAM.

MASSACHUSETTS BAY HOUSE
BEVERLY, MA 1993

"In a country noted for energy wastage, ecological insensitivity, constant renewal, standardized formulae and artificial environments, Predock mounts a corrective attack on the consumerist tidal wave that has created a placeless wilderness of strips and shopping malls. He confronts all this head-on with the most diligent research into the genius loci, producing an architecture as responsive to the local culture as it is to the regional variations in climate and landscape."

Geoffrey Baker, *Antoine Predock*, Academy Editions, 1997

/ly rollerblade wheel got stuck in an obscured grating nd I was hurled to the ground, dislocating my right lbow. Of course it was my right arm, my drawing arm, hat was injured and incapacitated for a few weeks. 'his drawing, exploring an exploded stone monolith, vas done with my left hand...

ectionally, the spatial development starts from the rooted bedrock which, metamorphoses ito the stone of the building. Given the numerological proportioning, the heaviest blocks all to the bottom while the lightest blocks at the top form the more open part of the iatrix, allowing the light to enter and filter down, creating a dreamlike and sequestered ense in the lower level, musty—with the smell of censers, like a Gothic cathedral.

ut into the bedrock at the very base of the transept is a new baptistry that utilizes spring, which is currently capped, under the crossing of the cathedral. The water is eleased and flows along the strata of the Manhattan schist to fill the baptistry and o introduce a groundwater source into the building's passive energy system.

he south transept allows the ascent into the light from the crossing of the cathedral. /loving toward the light along the carved spiral ramp, chapels and gardens illuminated y translucent sheets of marble lodged in the stone matrix throughout the ascent give piritual and liturgical intention to the procession. Spaces magnify and reflect the roperties of the real world while providing the traveler a quiet sensory experience: grape arbor floats above the Wedding Chapel; an herb garden stimulates olfactory senses vhile recharging oxygen for the Cathedral; the Chapel of the Reflecting Fish harbors koi wimming slowly but effortlessly in a shallow pool, the light reflecting from their scales nto the limestone. Near the baptistry, the flame of the Chapel of Fire burns, invoking ohn the Baptist's prophesy of one who would baptize "with the holy ghost and with fire."

SO MANY ADVENTURES WITH

A limited, invited design competition with Ando, Calatrava, and others for the new south transept of the Cathedral Church of Saint John the Divine in New York (where my graduation ceremony from Columbia University was held).

When traveling to New York in the '90s, I always stayed as close to Central Park as possible since my transport system in New York was Rollerblades and I would do laps around the Park enjoying the wonder of Frederick Law Olmstead. During the design competition for the South Transept I rollerbladed from the Park to Amsterdam Avenue to meet the competition advisor and the fellow competitors including Tadao Ando and Santiago Calaltrava. After the briefing, returning through the Park to my hotel, my rollerblade wheel got stuck in an obscured grating and I was hurled to the ground, dislocating my right elbow. Of course it was my right arm, my drawing arm, that was injured and incapacitated for a few weeks—the drawing, exploring an exploded stone monolith, was done with my left hand...

Our Rene Dubois Bioshelter proposes an environmental "Lung" for the cathedral—a protected realm for flora and fauna, and a refuge for city dwellers.

The observation of nature yields the DNA for making an architecture of divine presence. The intersection of organic geometries with the sacred numbers of the Christian tradition creates a spatial matrix from which to construct the new south transept, an inhabitable kaleidoscope of solid and void, light and shadow.

The sacred numbers determine the size and shapes of the blocks of the new stone mountain. Conceived as a solid with myriad divisions with the envelope of the transept these numerological blocks were then exploded, creating an interstitial realm. A spiral is then carved through this matrix along a tilted axis that aligns with the high noon summer solstice in Manhattan.

CONSTANCE DE JONG, ARTIST, IN HER STUDIO, AND THE GALLERY

CATHEDRAL OF SAINT JOHN THE DIVINE SOUTH TRANSEPT

NEW YORK, NEW YORK 1991

502
CONSTANCE DE JONG
MAY 2, 1991—FOREVER

The new South Transept embraces an ascent toward light—with chapels and gardens illuminated by translucent sheets of marble lodged in the stone matrix.

This spiral, serving liturgical purpose, passes stone chapels along the ascent/roadway to the sky, waystations along the route. The axis of the spiral is calibrated to the summer solstice high noon sun angle in Manhattan.

The spiral reaches its conclusion, its omega point (in math, the point where the spiral just vanishes) at a cosmic meeting point—an imagined rendezvous point above Manhattan.

CONSTANCE BEGIN TO UNFOLD—INTERNATIONAL TRAVEL, SOMETIMES IN CONNECTION WITH ACTIVE PROJECTS.

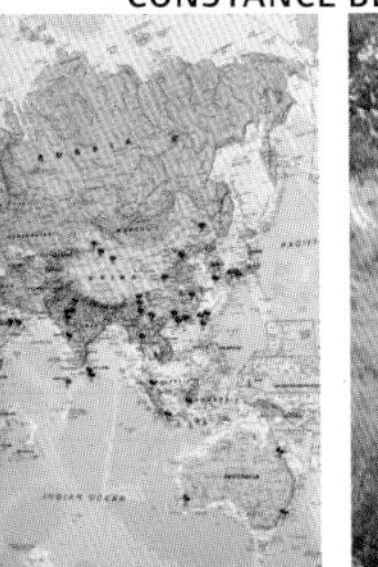

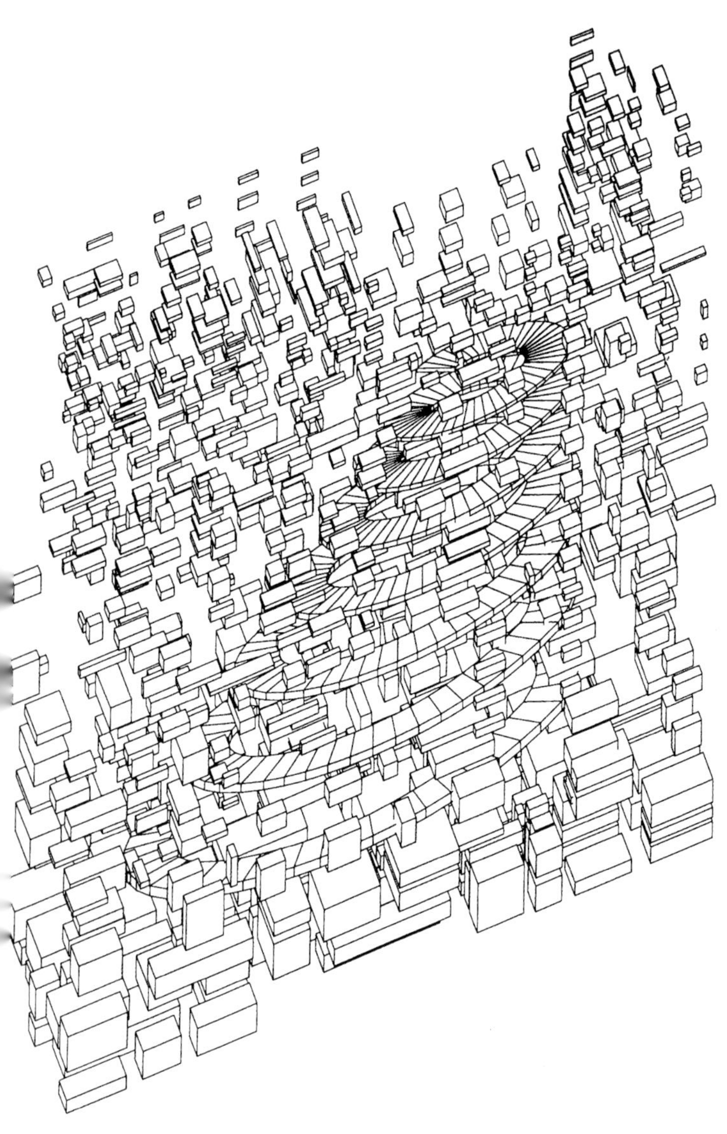

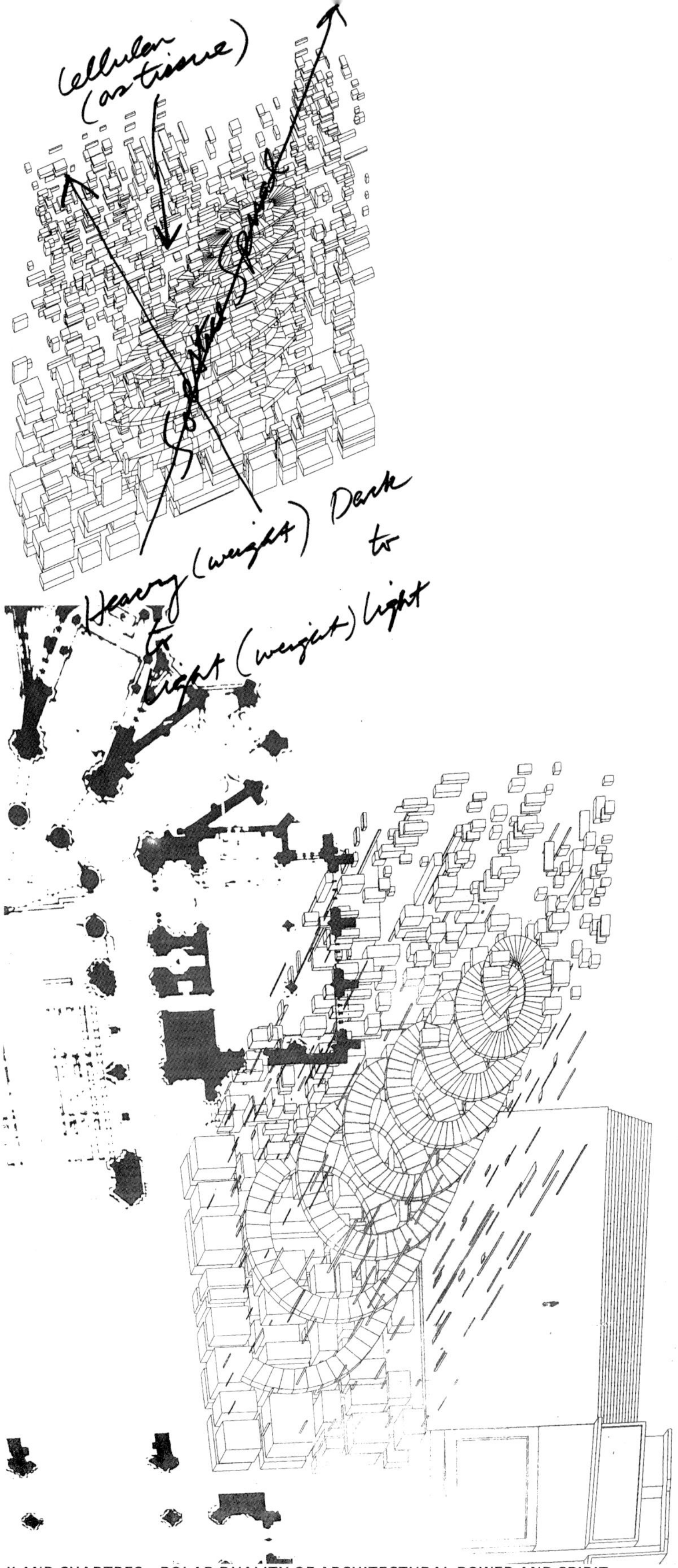

Cellular (as tissue)

Heavy (weight) Dark to Light (weight) light

Sacred numbers determine the size and proportions of the blocks of this new stone mountain.

Conceived as a solid with myriad subdivisions within the envelope of the transept, these numerologically proportioned blocks are then "exploded," creating an interstitial realm with the block sizes diminishing—darkness to light.

THE PANTHEON IN ROME AND RYOAN-JI IN KYOTO, A SPIRITUAL GUIDEPOST. RYOAN-JI AND CHARTRES—POLAR DUALITY OF ARCHITECTURAL POWER AND SPIRIT.

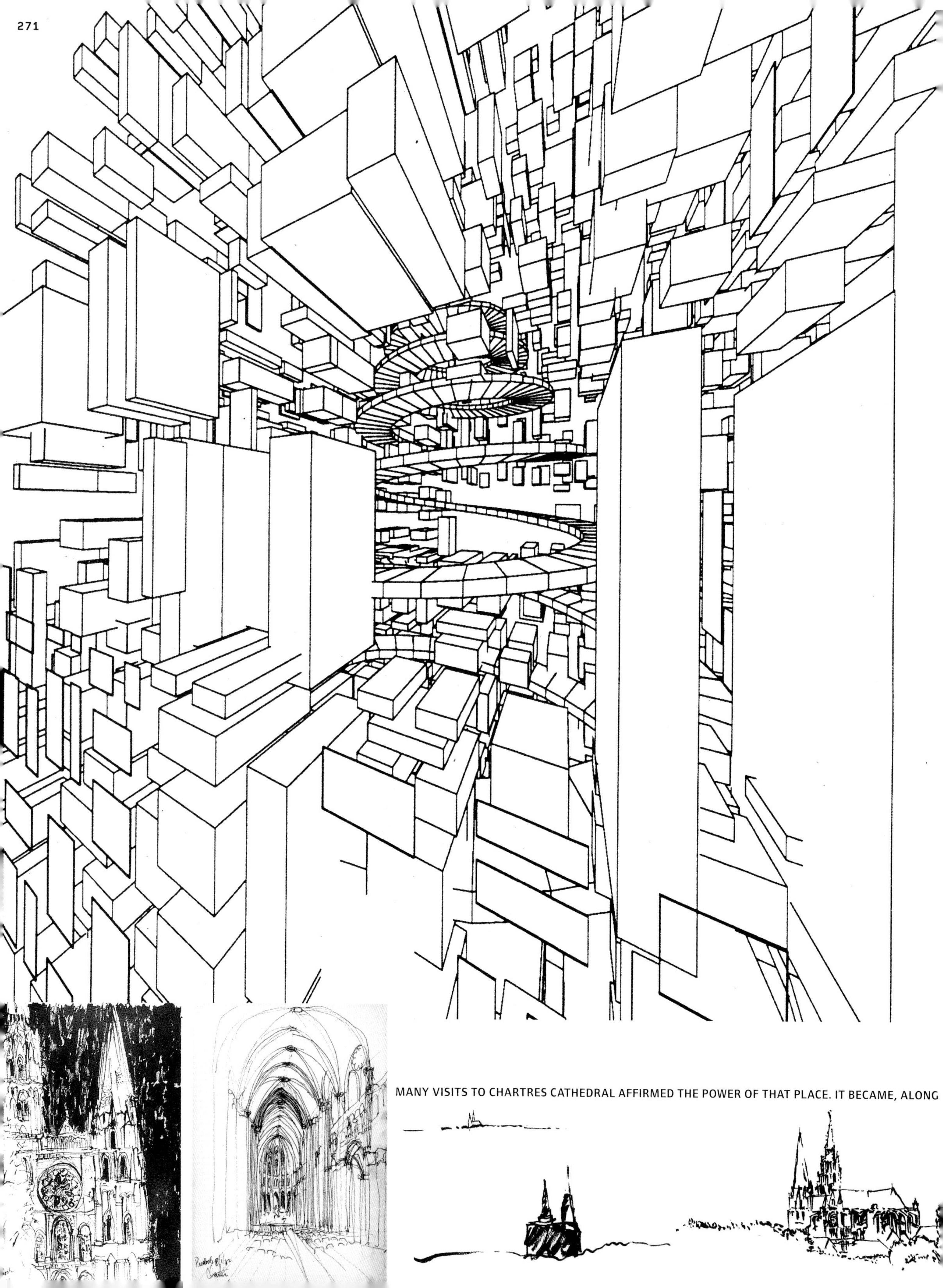

MANY VISITS TO CHARTRES CATHEDRAL AFFIRMED THE POWER OF THAT PLACE. IT BECAME, ALONG

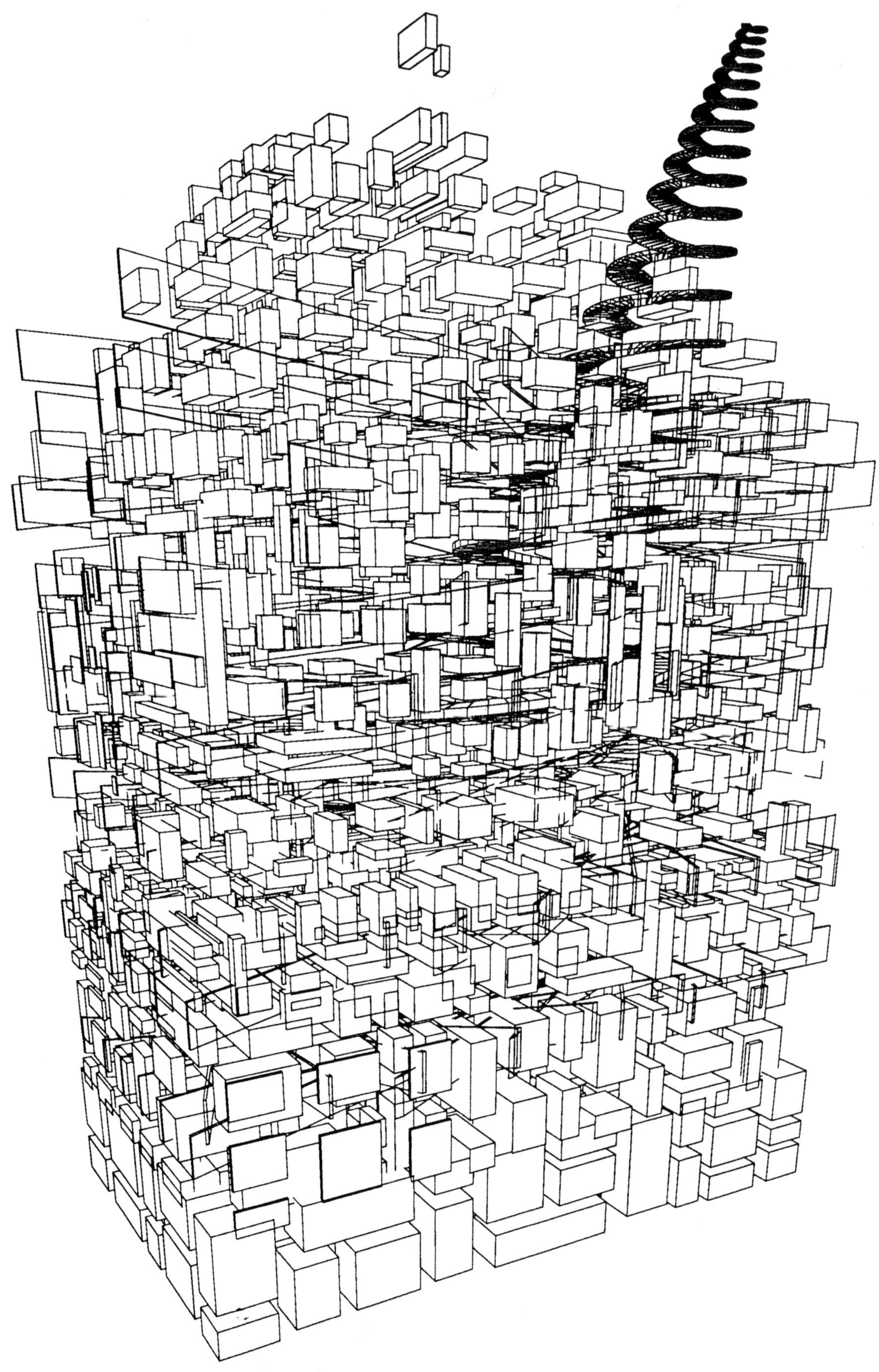

"Constance DeJong ... has responded to the suppressed, often denied, and ever-present poetry of minimalist practice by creating a body of work that not only carries on the rigor of the practice but forces us to re-consider the stated intentions of her predecessors. This is a job worth doing and, even if it weren't, DeJong has created work worth seeing and thinking about under any circumstances."

Dave Hickey, *Constance DeJong: Metal*, 2003

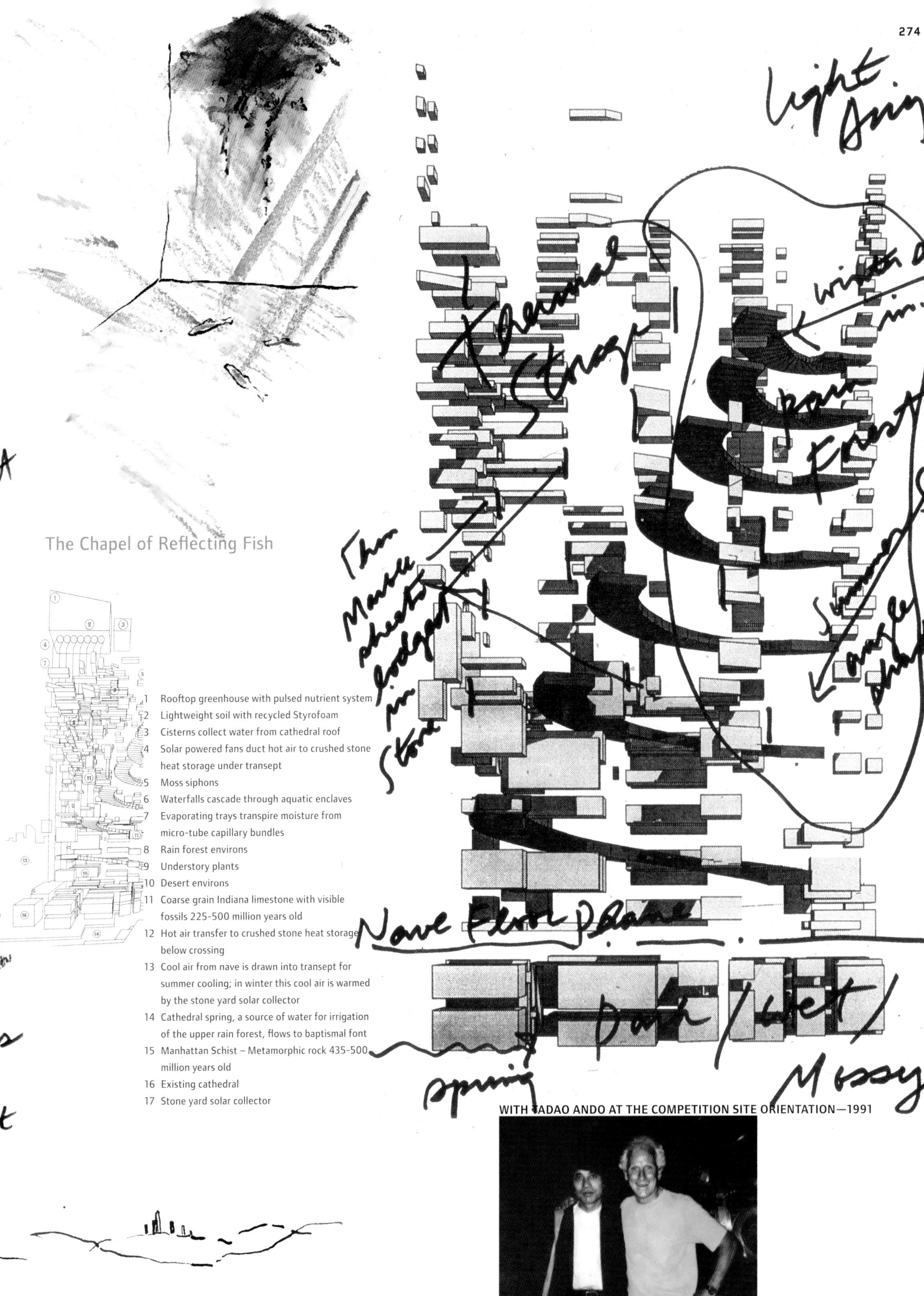

The Chapel of Reflecting Fish

1 Rooftop greenhouse with pulsed nutrient system
2 Lightweight soil with recycled Styrofoam
3 Cisterns collect water from cathedral roof
4 Solar powered fans duct hot air to crushed stone heat storage under transept
5 Moss siphons
6 Waterfalls cascade through aquatic enclaves
7 Evaporating trays transpire moisture from micro-tube capillary bundles
8 Rain forest environs
9 Understory plants
10 Desert environs
11 Coarse grain Indiana limestone with visible fossils 225-500 million years old
12 Hot air transfer to crushed stone heat storage below crossing
13 Cool air from nave is drawn into transept for summer cooling; in winter this cool air is warmed by the stone yard solar collector
14 Cathedral spring, a source of water for irrigation of the upper rain forest, flows to baptismal font
15 Manhattan Schist – Metamorphic rock 435-500 million years old
16 Existing cathedral
17 Stone yard solar collector

WITH TADAO ANDO AT THE COMPETITION SITE ORIENTATION—1991

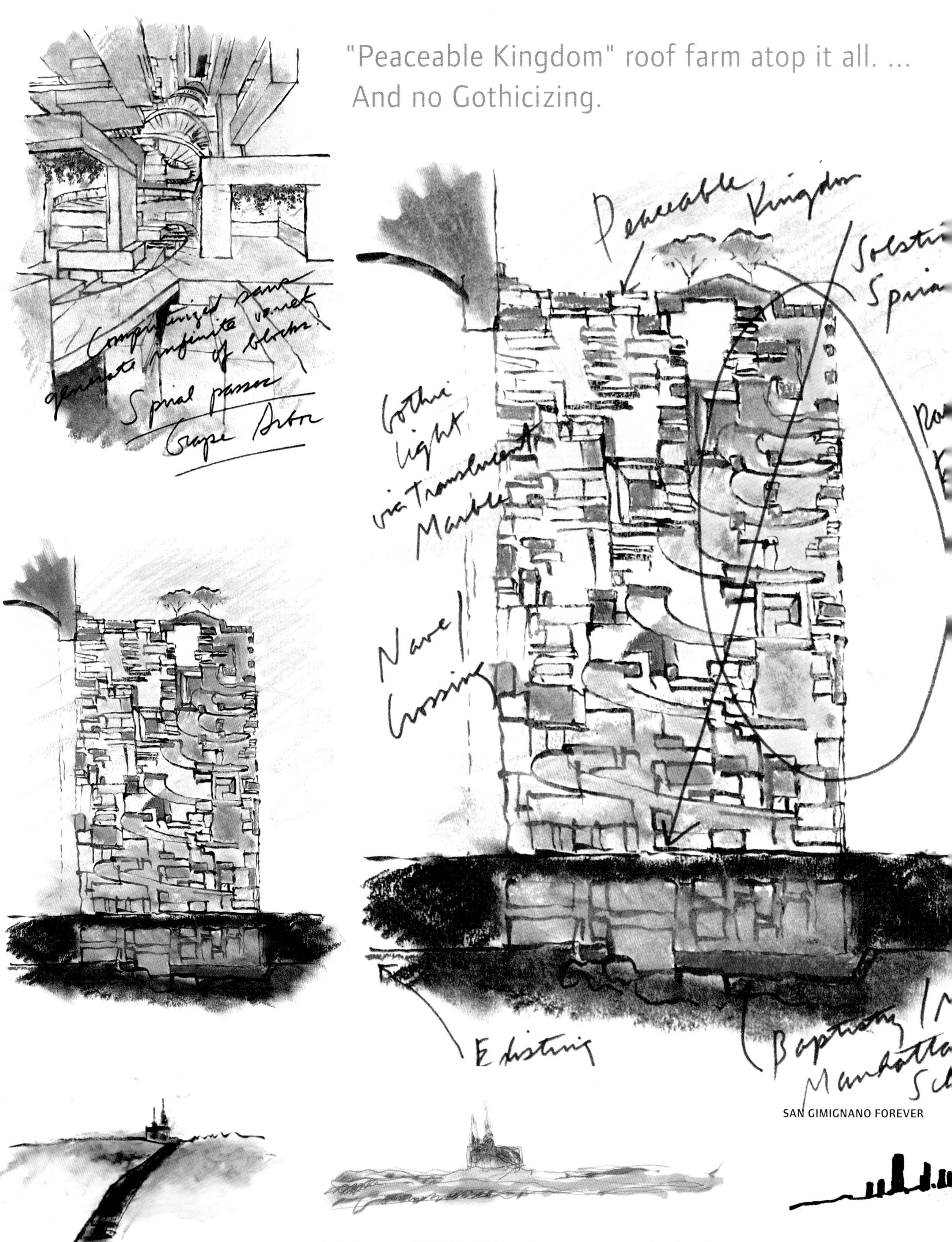

SAN GIMIGNANO FOREVER

Sectionally, the spatial development starts from the rooted bedrock, which metamorphoses into the stone of the building. Given the numerological proportioning, the heaviest blocks fall to the bottom while the lightest blocks at the top form the more open part of the matrix, allowing the light to enter and filter down, creating a dreamlike and sequestered sense in the lower level, musty, with the smell of censers, like a Gothic cathedral.

TWO-NIGHT CAMPING TRIP HIKING THROUGH THE OTHERWORLDLY HALEAKALA CRATER IN MAUI WITH CONSTANCE AND MY SON JASON—SCI-FI SUNRISES AND TECHNICOLOR CLOUDS CURLED OVER THE RIM OF THE CRATER, WILD GOATS... THE WHOLE PACKAGE.

RAFTING THE CHAMA WITH THE KAMINSKYS

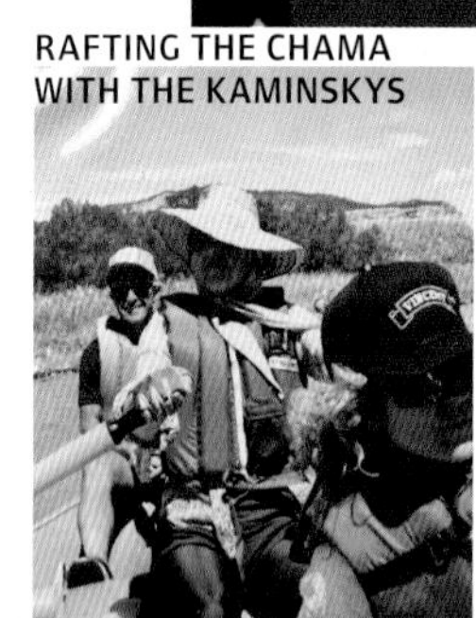

CLARK COUNTY GOVERNMENT CENTER LAS VEGAS, NV 1992

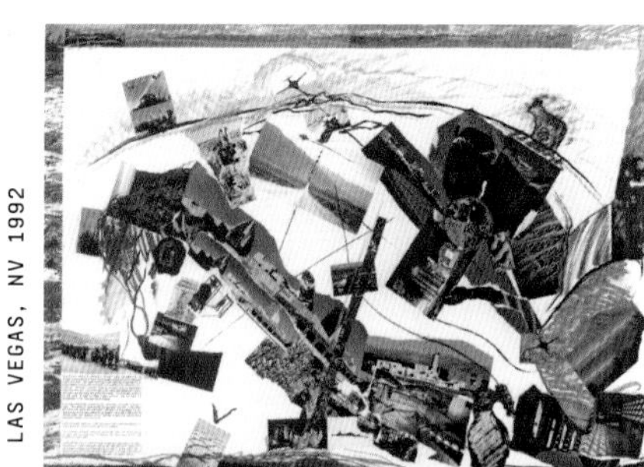

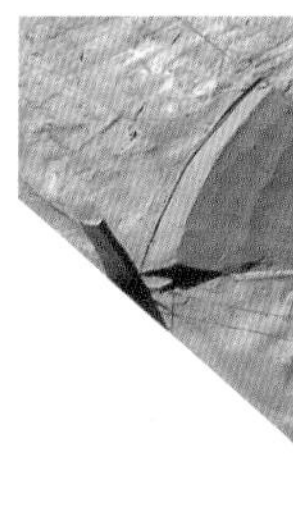

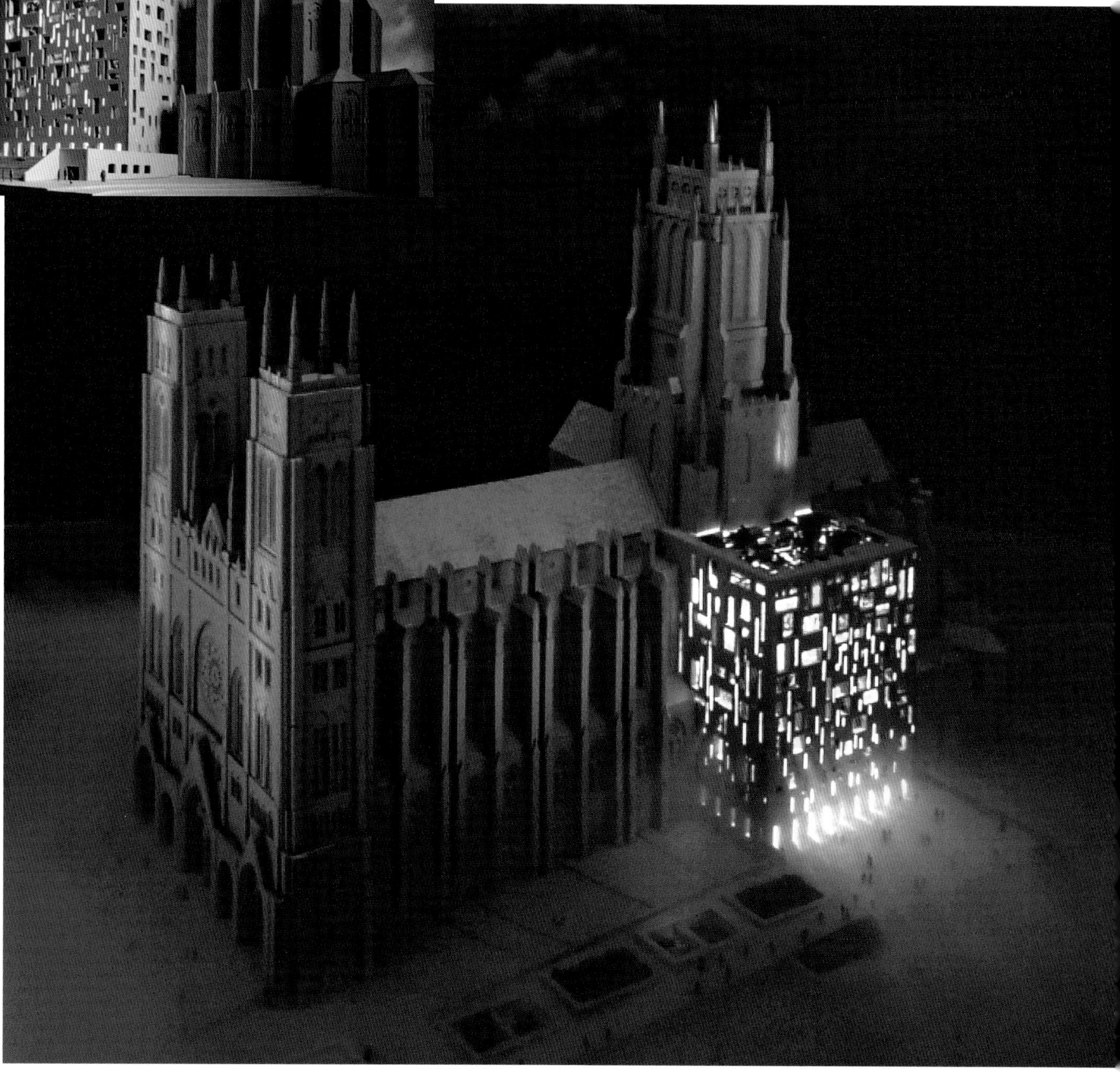

DESERT SITE ON THE EDGES OF LAS VEGAS—GEOLOGIC FORMATIONS, RED SANDSTONE IN THE VALLEY OF FIRE, THE PRESSURES OF ARTESIAN WATER.
COPPER, STAINLESS STEEL, GLASS, AND THE SPARING PRESENCE OF WATER.

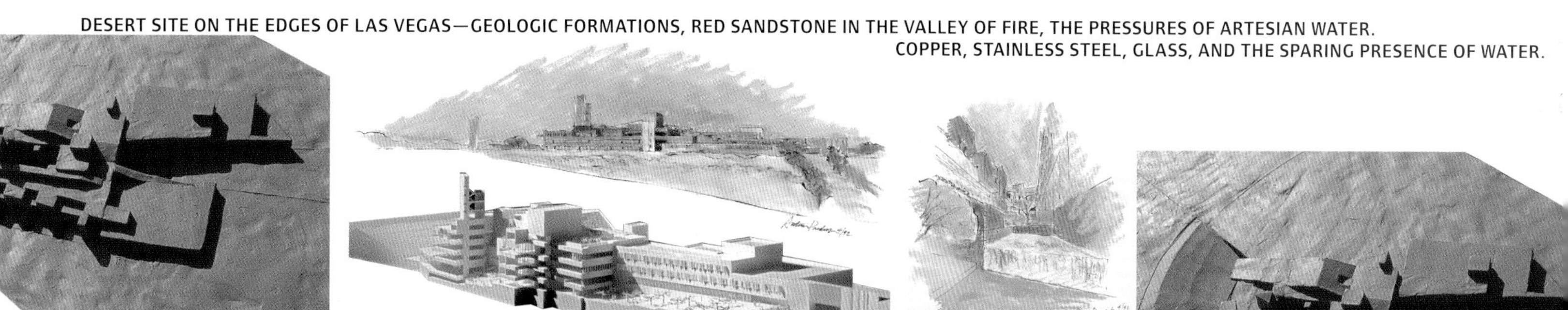

VENTANA VISTA ELEMENTARY SCHOOL

TUSCON, ARIZONA 1992/95

Like an ancient ruin, a desert embedded "city for children"
with a tent/sunshade as crossroads—
a reminder of the nomadic nature of desert occupation.

FRAGMENTING WHAT TYPICALLY WOULD BE AN "ADMIN BUILDING" INTO A SERIES OF UNEXPECTED PROGRESSIONS THROUGH VOLUMETRIC CHUNKS.

STUDENT AFFAIRS AND ADMINISTRATIVE SERVICES BUILDING, UNIVERSITY OF CALIFORNIA SANTA BARBARA
SANTA BARBARA, CA 1992/96

FORMER SENIOR ASSOCIATE DOUG FRIEND WAS AN ANCHOR IN THE STUDIO ALL THROUGH THE '90s—A BRILLIANT UCLA GRADUATE, INSTRUMENTAL IN ESTABLISHING OUR LA STUDIO. HE WAS A KEY DESIGNER/MANAGER ON CAL POLY, MINNESOTA GATEWAY, UCSB, SPENCER THEATER, AND MANY OTHER PROJECTS CULMINATING IN THE PADRES BALLPARK—A TRUE BROTHER IN ARCHITECTURE, SKI BUDDY, AND ENERGY MACHINE!

"The message from Predock's impressive variety of architectural interventions is that the discovery process of education include the physical environment where it takes place—from recess courtyards to the impressions of the desert itself."

Reed Kroloff, "Desert Education," *Architecture*, March 1995

Passages through the village-like scattered components of the school are strewn with locational markers like this chalkboard in one of the exterior courtyards. Kindergartners and first graders have spy holes interconnecting their classrooms with an intimate reading cubbyhole suggestive of a subterranean turtle with its shell of porthole skylights. Containing desert fragments, it foregrounds the Solstice Wall.

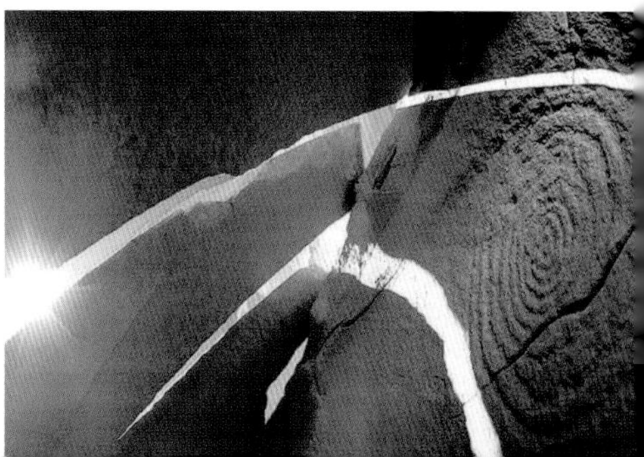

The entire desert site is a laboratory for studying and engagement. Within the circuitous circulation realm of the school, gathering areas link together, celebrating the desert with focused intention.

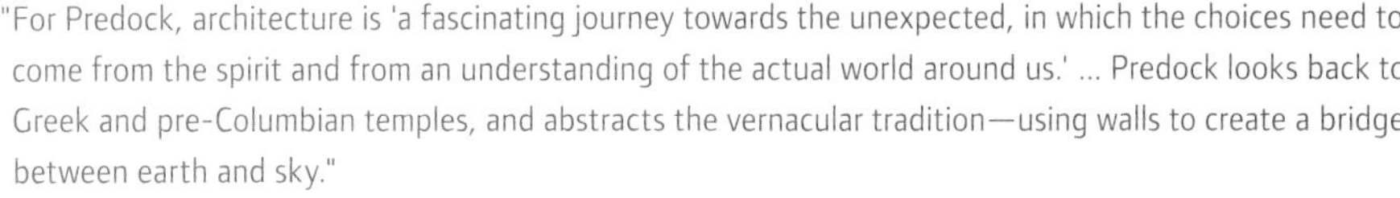

"For Predock, architecture is 'a fascinating journey towards the unexpected, in which the choices need to come from the spirit and from an understanding of the actual world around us.' ... Predock looks back to Greek and pre-Columbian temples, and abstracts the vernacular tradition—using walls to create a bridge between earth and sky."

Michael Webb, *Antoine Predock*, Korean Architect, 1998

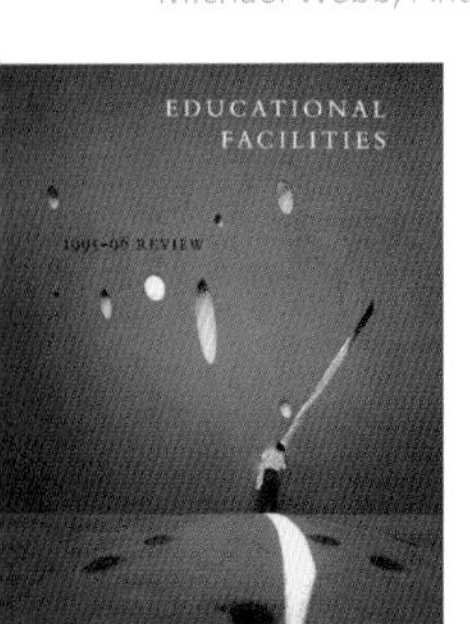

HAVING HELD THE KEA CHAIR AT UNIVERSITY MARYLAND IN COLLEGE PARK, A COMPETITION FOR THE PERFORMING ARTS CENTER WAS FAMILIAR TURF FOR ME. THIS PERFORMING ARTS CENTER AND MUSIC SCHOOL FINALLY MORPHED INTO A GUITAR.

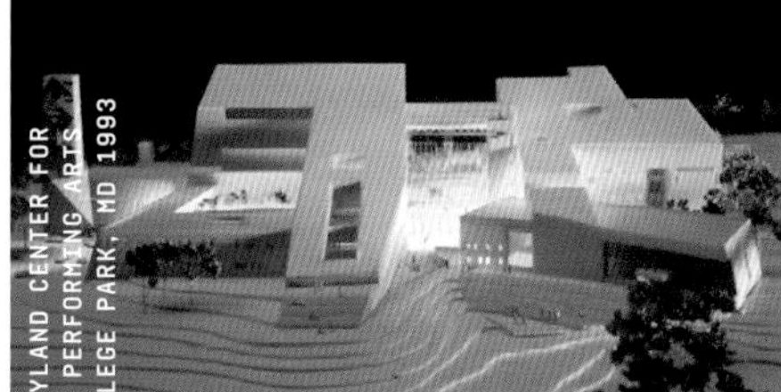

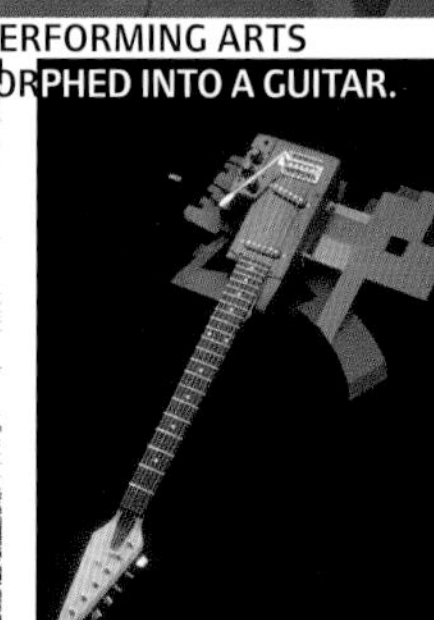

SIMILARLY, BALTIMORE WAS ALSO ON MY RADAR FOR THE BALTIMORE PERFORMING ARTS CENTER—A CRYSTALLINE MONOLITH SET IN LOCALLY SOURCED STON

BALTIMORE PERFORMING ARTS CENTER
BALTIMORE, MD 1993

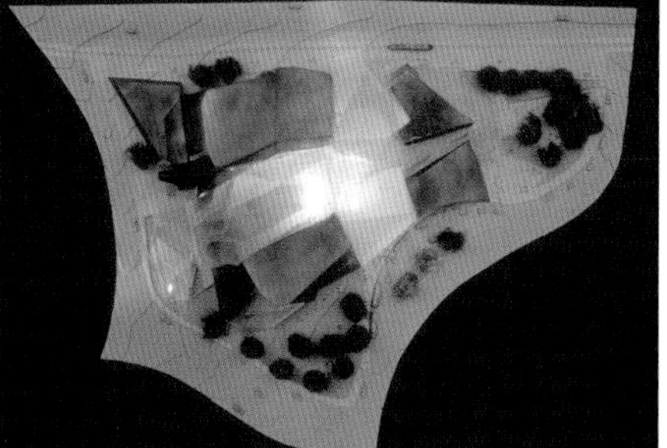

ATLANTIS

LAS VEGAS, NEVADA 1993/94

AS A BMW DISTANCE RIDER DURING THE '60s, I WOULD HEAR RUMORS OF A LEGENDARY BIKE CALLED THE VINCENT. IT BECAME A MYTHIC UNATTAINABLE DREAM FOR ME TO EVER IMAGINE EVEN SEEING, MUCH LESS OWNING ONE. IN 1992 I SPOTTED ONE AT AN AUCTION IN FLORIDA AND I HAD TO HAVE IT. SO OFTEN THEY LAND IN MUSEUM COLLECTIONS OR COLLECTORS' LIVING ROOMS—BUT I WAS DETERMINED TO RIDE ONE. THIS VINCENT BLACK SHADOW WAS MY DREAM COME TRUE AND I WON THE AUCTION. I HAVE RIDDEN IT IN CALIFORNIA AND NEW MEXICO; AND IT WAS EXHIBITED BRIEFLY IN THE TANG MUSEUM.

"IF YOU RODE THE BLACK SHADOW AT TOP SPEED FOR ANY LENGTH OF TIME, YOU WOULD ALMOST CERTAINLY DIE. THAT IS WHY THERE ARE NOT MANY LIFE

I shattered some glass panes we had in the model shop to see how those fragments looked. Those shapes formed the fractured Atlantean Plateau.

Then, using the finer shards of glass, Doug Friend constructed a tiny model that landed on the Vegas Strip.

I imagined that through some plate tectonic anomaly, Atlantis, sunken off the north coast of Spain, mysteriously migrated westward to emerge on the Strip in Las Vegas.

MEMBERS OF THE VINCENT BLACK SHADOW SOCIETY." HUNTER S. THOMPSON

FOLLOWING THE '50s VINCENT SPORT/RACE BIKE, THE 1990 HONDA RC30 WAS ANOTHER HOLY GRAIL MOTORCYCLE. THE RC30 GRAN PRIX RACER APPEARED AS A STREET-LEGAL MOTORCYCLE IN 1990 AND BECAME MY FIRST TRUE RACE BIKE. IT HAD SENSATIONALLY ADVANCED FEATURES LIKE TITANIUM CONNECTING RODS AND A DIGITAL TACHOMETER; AND ALTHOUGH STREET LEGAL, IT WAS REALLY THE SAME WORLD CHAMPIONSHIP MOTOGP PERFORMER RIDDEN BY THE LIKES OF FREDDIE SPENCER.

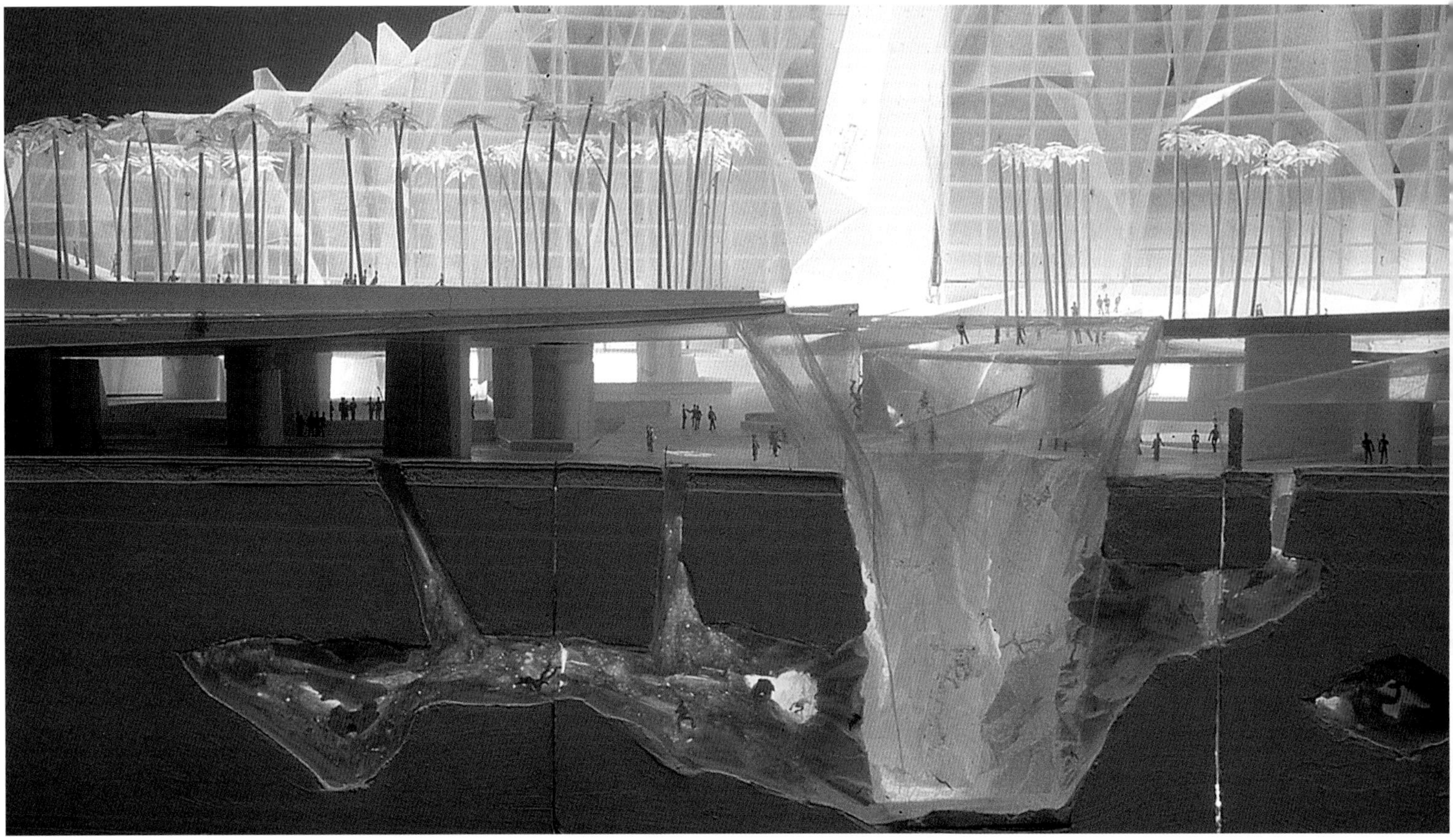

The 60'-deep salt water vortex is available to card-carrying scuba divers. Tunnel branches lead off laterally, terminating in glass-covered apertures in the casino floor above. Gamblers pulling slot machine handles might look down and see a masked diver gazing up at them.

Objects suggesting future technologies define the entry path from the Strip. We went to a hobby store and collected all the weirdest models to use for those. The transparency of sections of the floor plane suggest a deeper mysterious realm.

RC30 WAS THEN FOLLOWED BY THE LIMITED PRODUCTION 1992 HONDA NR (RC40) OVAL PISTON RACE TRACK/SHOWPIECE, ONE OF THE ICONS OF MOTORCYCLE HISTORY, WITH EARLY EXPERIMENTATION IN COMBINING CARBON FIBER, MAGNESIUM, AND TITANIUM COMPONENTS—TOO SPECIAL TO RIDE MUCH, SO IT JOINED ME IN THE LIVING ROOM.

IN THE MID-2000s THE DUCATI DESMO DUCATI PRODUCED A LIMITED-EDITION

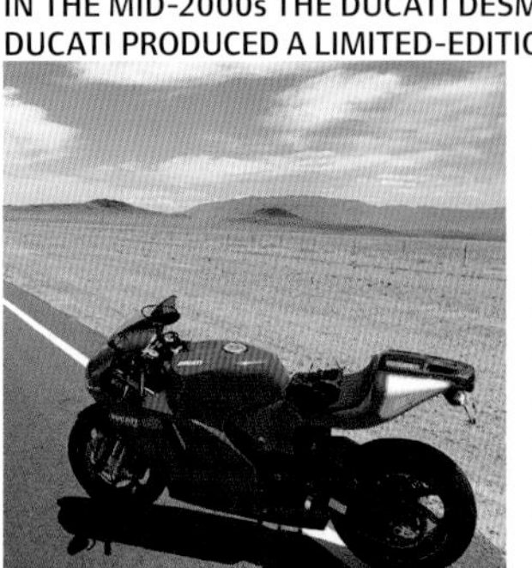

"Designers such as Antoine Predock ... create buildings that assimilate the complexities of our urban environment into shapes that somehow seem appropriate and alien at the same time."

Aaron Betsky, *Icons: Magnets of Meaning*, 1997

SEIDICI BEGAN TO DOMINATE MOTOGP AND STREET-LEGAL VERSION IN TWO COLOR SCHEMES.

THE EXTREMELY RARE DUCATI SUPERMONO, MAYBE THE APOGEE OF DUCATI PRODUCTION, APPEARED IN THE EARLY '90s. THIS #10 BIKE CAME FROM THE DUCATI MUSEUM IN BOLOGNA AND LANDED IN MY LIVING ROOM.

THE DISTINGUISHED GENTLEMAN MEETS THE SUPERMODEL

The reference to Plato's Atlantis is evident in the fragments of a subterranean culture that configure the scheme. Light emanates from a realm below, from which the culture erupts. The 4,000-room hotel with casino ascends from the tectonically fractured Atlantean plateau—inspired by the patterns of shattered glass—metamorphosing from stone and concrete into crystal. Water carves its way through the plateau at the base of the hotel. The water course leads to a ramp, from there one can climb the building's nautilus spiral with a sky spike announcing the High Roller's Suite. A 60'-deep vortex of salt water drills into the earth: divers can explore hidden grottoes and a reef. The light that shimmers from the depths of the vortex implies a connection to an otherworldly power source below.

THE ARCHITECTURE OF THE CENTRAL STANFORD CAMPUS IS RICHARDSONIAN—ROUGH STONE ARCHES, RED TILED ROOFS, ETC. SINCE I DON'T DO THAT IN A TWENTIETH-CENTURY BUILDING, THIS PROJECT HAS A KNIFE EDGE PATINATED-COPPER ROOF WITH A PARALLEL COPPER- WRAPPED VAULTED ENTRY AND FINELY WROUGHT STONE FACING.

STANFORD UNIVERSITY
PALO ALTO, CA, 1993/96

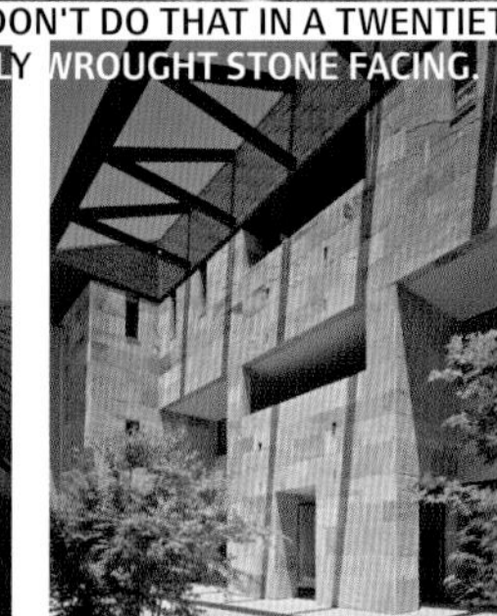

THIS HUGE MODEL WAS LOADED ONTO A U-HAUL FOR A PRESENTATION IN NYC WITH THE SHERATON GROUP. I WAS TOLD TO "PULL OUT ALL THE STOPS." THE DESIGN COMPETITION INCLUDED MICHAEL GRAVES AND OTHERS. WHEN THE CLIENT SAW THE RESULT OF "PULLING OUT ALL THE STOPS" THERE WAS A CORPORATE FREAK OUT—THEY THOUGHT I HAD BEEN EATING TOO MANY DESERT PLANTS. THEY ABANDONED THE PROJECT AND INSTEAD RENOVATED AND RE-BRANDED THE DESERT INN.

CONSTANCE AND I DO AS THE ROMANS DO—GRAB A SCOOTER AND GO.

SPENCER THEATER FOR THE PERFORMING ARTS

RUIDOSO, NEW MEXICO 1994/97

CONVERGENCE OF THE THEATER OF LANDSCAPE AND THE THEATER OF PERFORMANCE...
DEAD CENTER BETWEEN CAPITAN MOUNTAIN, ON THE EAST HORIZON, AND SIERRA BLANCA PEAK

The opening night performers were Dave Brubeck and Nadja Salerno-Sonnenberg.

"This is about the best place that I have ever played. The acoustics remind me of some of the small opera houses we played in Italy. They knew what they were doing in old times, and the Spencer Theater has the same feeling of closeness."

Dave Brubeck, "New NM Arts Center Impressed Jazz Legend," *El Paso Times*, Oct. 4, 1997

My copy of *Time Out*, from decades earlier, signed by Dave Brubeck on opening night.

Erupting from a fissure on the north flank, is a crystalline, chandelier-like shell of laminated glass—a faceted glass entry lobby and gathering space that consciously contrasts and subverts the stone mass of the body of the building.

RIZZOLI 2 COMES ALONG...

AUTUMN ARRIVES—A CLOUD BANK CURLS OVER THE SANDIAS

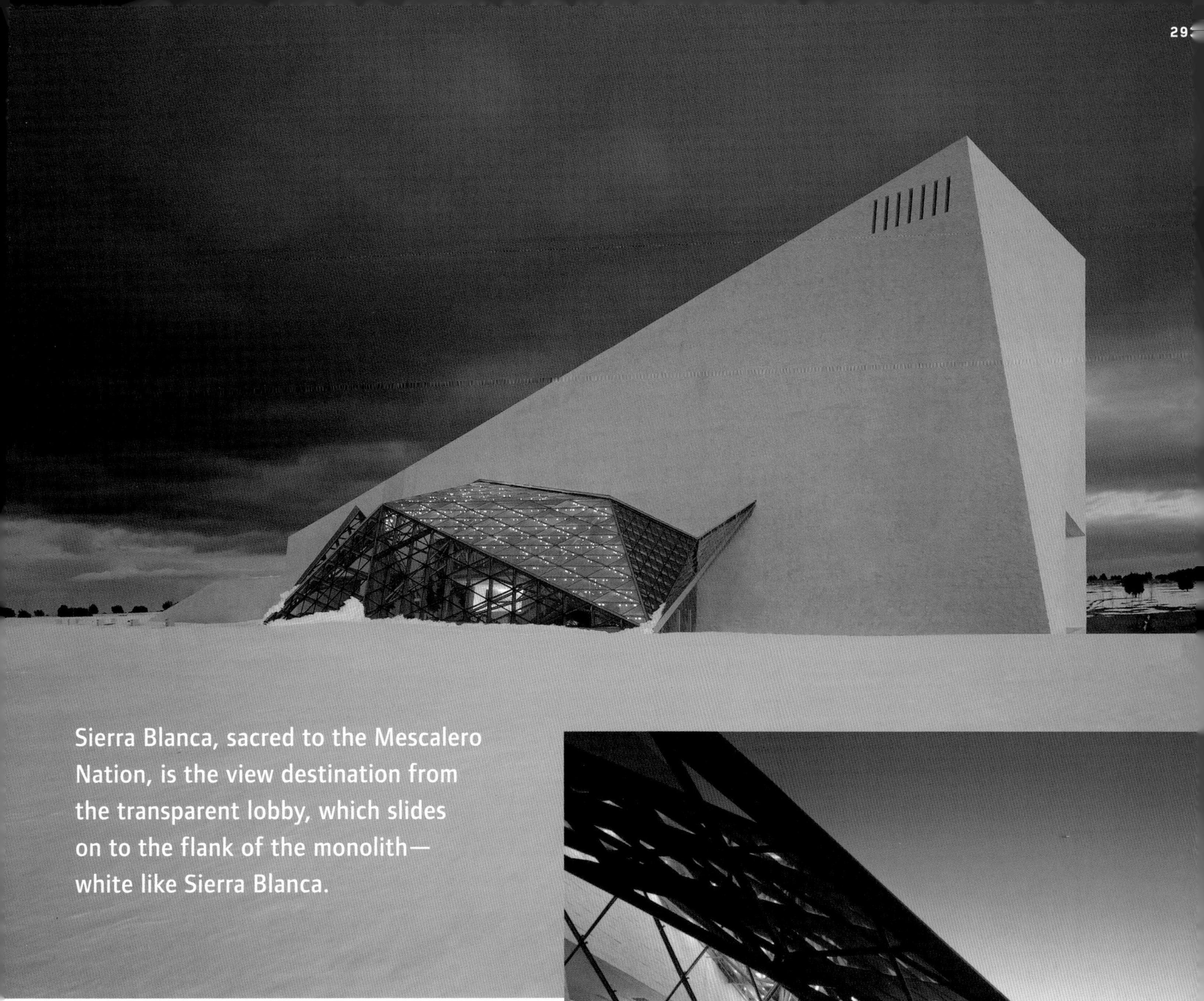

Sierra Blanca, sacred to the Mescalero Nation, is the view destination from the transparent lobby, which slides on to the flank of the monolith—white like Sierra Blanca.

"To create a dramatic entrance for this man-made mountain, Predock affixed a crystalline lobby to the exterior, resulting in a form he likens to a fragment of a Stealth bomber that has crashed into the building."

Karen D. Stein, *Architectural Record*, May 1998

THE CRYSTALLINE CHANDELIER IS A HALLMARK FOR MANY THEATER LOBBIES. THIS FACETED EXTRAPOLATION WITH TINY POINTS OF LIGHT ESTABLISHES A CELEBRATORY VIBE.

IN THE CHANDELIER WHILE UNDER CONSTRUCTION

1995 BOOK OF COLLECTED DRAWINGS PUBLISHED BY RIZZOLI

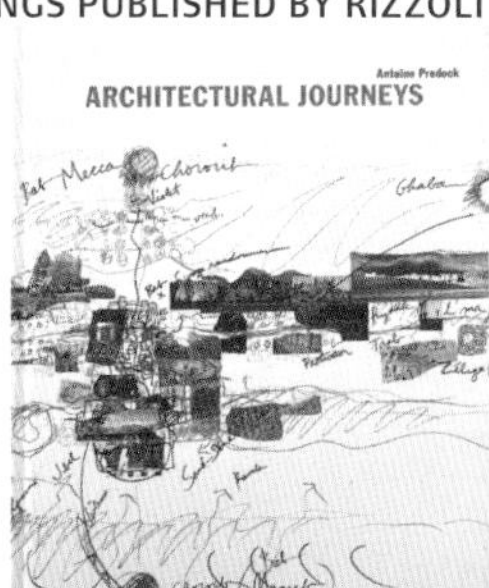

Ceremonial stair with fractured-glass rail to the upper lobby/playhouse entry.

WITH HADRIAN AND JASON AND DOUG FRIEND AT THE SPENCER THEATER OPENING NIGHT.

CENTER FOR NANOSCALE SCIENCE
AND TECHNOLOGY, RICE UNIVERSITY
HOUSTON, TX 1994/1997

NANOSCALE STUDIES WRAPPED IN THE STYLISTICALLY-ALLUDING ENVELOPE OF THE RICE UNIVERSITY CAMPUS—

"The relatively small blocks of Spanish limestone cladding reinforce the explicit geological reference of the structure, as the stacked, split-faced blocks stratify the expressive forms. The crystalline fissure of laminated glass inserted in its flank announces a crystalline interior, which is strongly illuminated to reveal its presence to the vast horizons of the New Mexico desert."

David Dernie, *New Stone Architecture*, 2003

WITH NOBEL LAUREATE RICK SMALLEY AS MY CLIENT.

STUDENT FAN

DANCE STUDIO

UNIVERSITY OF CALIFORNIA SAN DIEGO
LA JOLLA, CALIFORNIA 1995/97

The massive arcing wall invites in central campus circulation and deep apertures become stage sets for dancers.

WHILE HOLDING THE CLEMSON SCHOOL OF ARCHITECTURE ROBERT MILLS CHAIR IN 1995, SPEAKING TO AN ELEMENTARY SCHOOL CLASS

AFTER FINISHING THE SEMESTER AT CLEMSON, LECTURING AT THEIR EUROPEAN

Lodged in the eucalyptus grove, rather than reflecting it
as the adjacent Mandell Weiss Forum does—
mystery vs. celebration
PROGRAM IN GENOA, WITH ITS FABLED LIGHTHOUSE AND CIMITERO STAGLIENO—THEN MEETING UP WITH CONSTANCE ON THE AMALFI COAST
ON A BIMOTA YB9 THAT I RODE DOWN FROM RIMINI

"They use virtually every inch of the building, gathering along the curved wall to stretch and bend, wedging their legs into its slots. They dance in the small courtyard and run up the walls. They respond to the freedom of the loftlike spaces, their resilient sprung-rubber floors, flexible lighting grids, and natural ventilation."

Aaron Betsky, "Second Position," *Architecture*, August 1998

PAUSING FOR A FERRY TO CAPRI, THE MOTORCYCLE TRIP CONTINUES PAST POMPEII AND ON TO FLORENCE, WITH MANY STOPS IN BETWEEN.

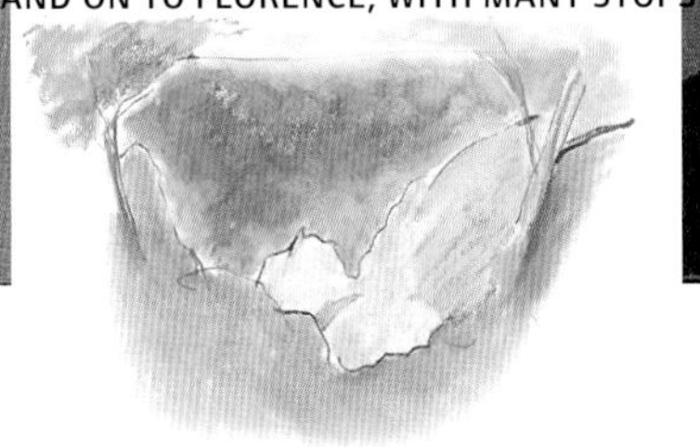

"Next to this wry vantage point, the Dance Studio fans out, Aaltolike from the mesa, posing its choreography of simple certainty against the ticky-tacky confusion of the suburban miasma below."

Aaron Betsky, "Second Position," *Architecture*, August 1998

The Danish National Archive was conceived as a fortress of memory—an accessible fortress guarding against the loss of the past. Cleaving the enormous storage volume of strong rooms into giant runestones, great masses or towers diagram the monumental weight of Danish history.

DANISH NATIONAL ARCHIVES

COPENHAGEN, DENMARK 1996

MONOGRAPH FROM ITALY BY PIERLUIGI FLORENTINI

GIANT RUNESTONES CLOAK A BUZZING DIGITAL REALM WITHIN—THE MONUMENTAL WEIGHT OF THIS NATION'S HISTORY. DEEP TIME RESEARCH—DOLMEN, MENHIR—ANCIENT HISTORY SHAPING THE CLAY MODEL.

IN 1996 A YOUNG GRADUATE STUDENT NAMED PAUL FEHLAU BEGAN WORKING WITH US—HAND PICKED BECAUSE OF HIS TALENTS. LITTLE DID I KNOW HE WOULD GO ON TO BECOME MY RIGHT-HAND MAN AND FUTURE LEADER OF THE STUDIO. THROUGH THE YEARS HE SHOWED SUCH DIVERSE DESIGN AND MANAGEMENT SKILLS THAT HE BECAME THE NATURAL CHOICE. WITH A POLYMATH SENSIBILITY THAT COULD TACKLE ANYTHING THAT CAME ALONG, HE TRANSFORMED FROM SKI BUM TO BRUCE WILLIS.

Beyond the foreground rapid transit connection to central Copenhagen from Amager, the entry—a photovoltaic "sail" leading to a garden atrium orientation point.

ON MY HONDA VFR, CONNECTING WITH FRIEND BILL EASTER IN ENGLAND PRIOR TO CONSTANCE'S ARRIVAL—THEN ON TO THE COTSWOLDS, WEST SUSSEX, THE SALISBURY PLAIN,

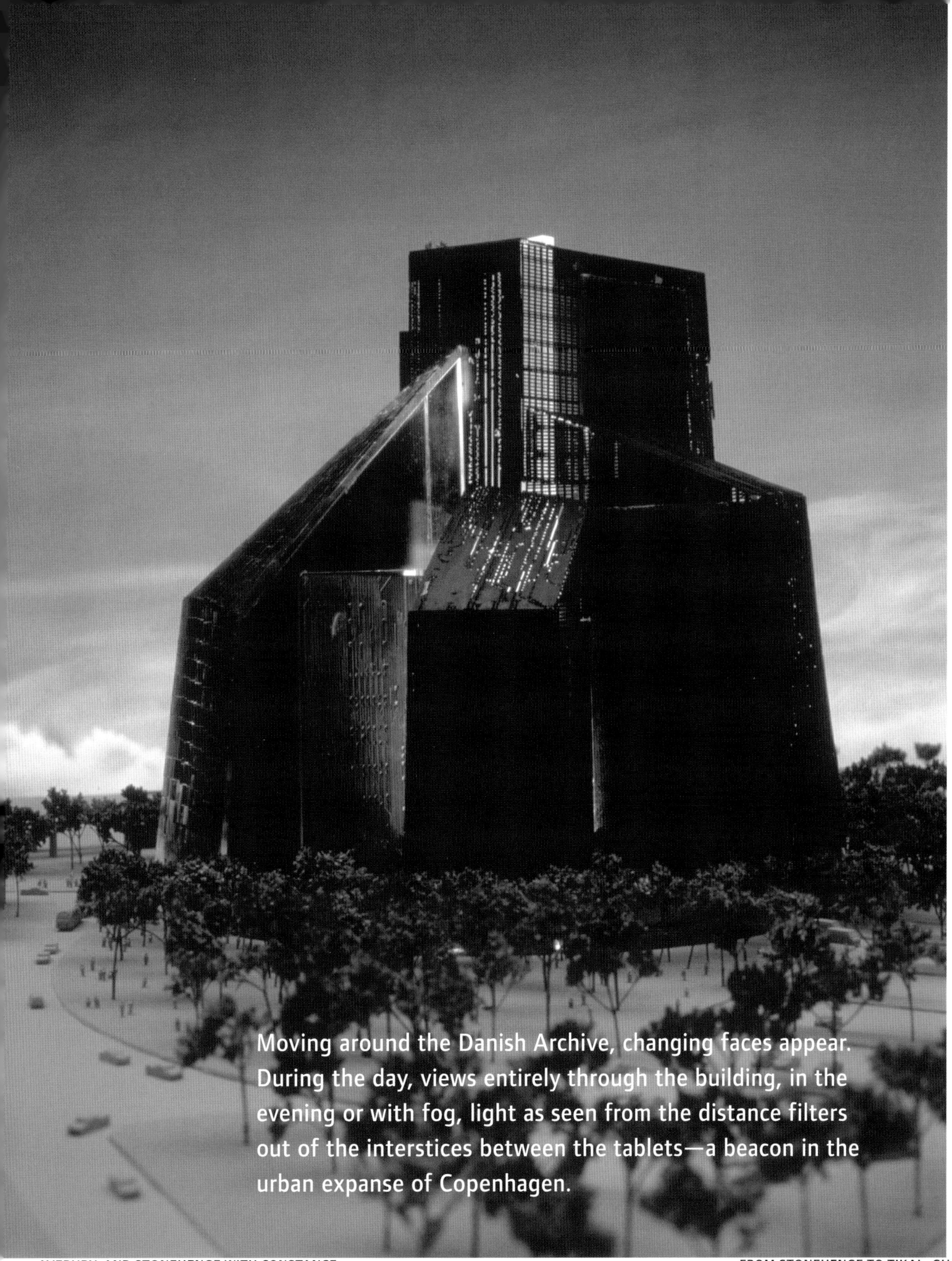

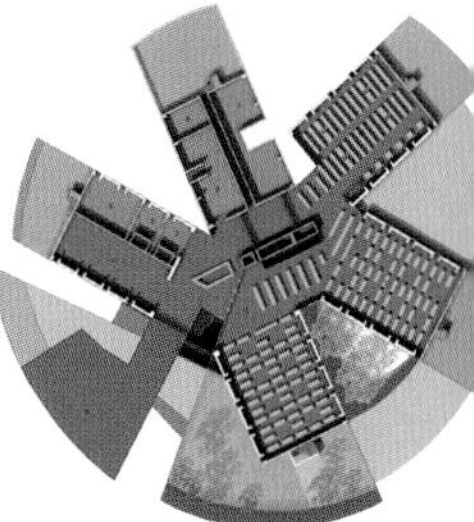

Moving around the Danish Archive, changing faces appear. During the day, views entirely through the building, in the evening or with fog, light as seen from the distance filters out of the interstices between the tablets—a beacon in the urban expanse of Copenhagen.

2. Etage MÅL 1:500

1. Etage MÅL 1:500

Stueetage MÅL 1:500

AVEBURY, AND STONEHENGE WITH CONSTANCE.

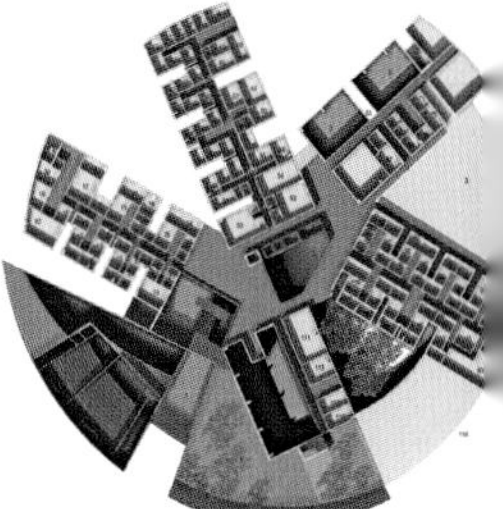

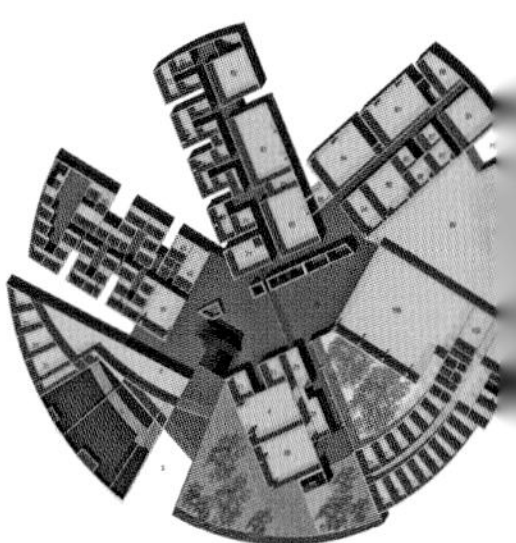

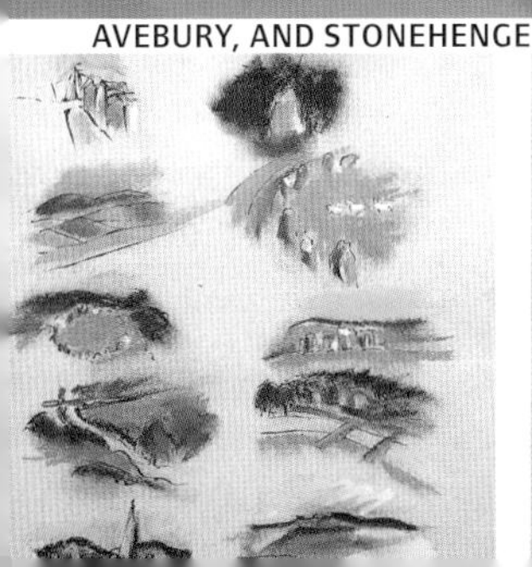

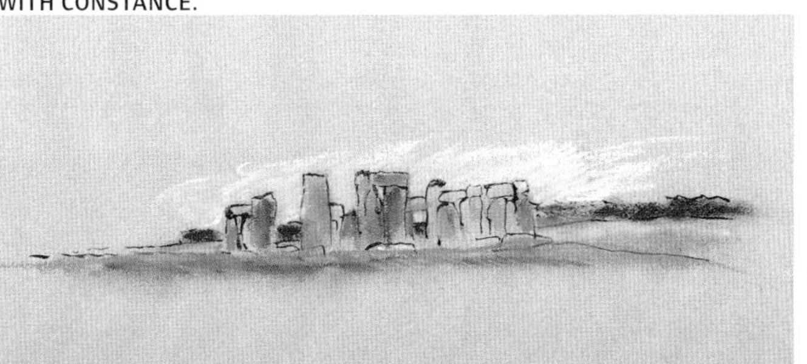

FROM STONEHENGE TO TIKAL, GUATEMALA, WITH CONSTANCE

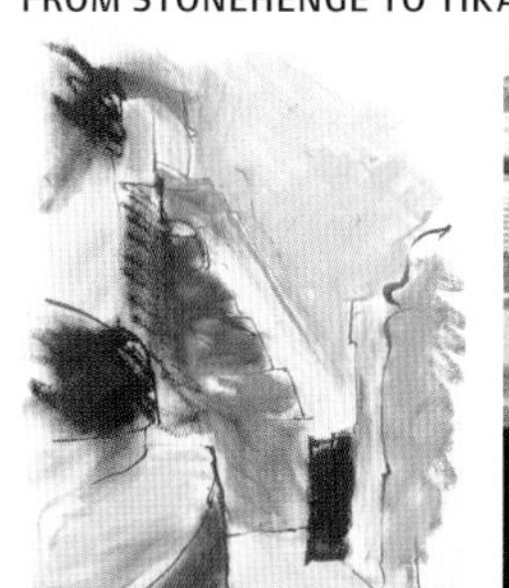

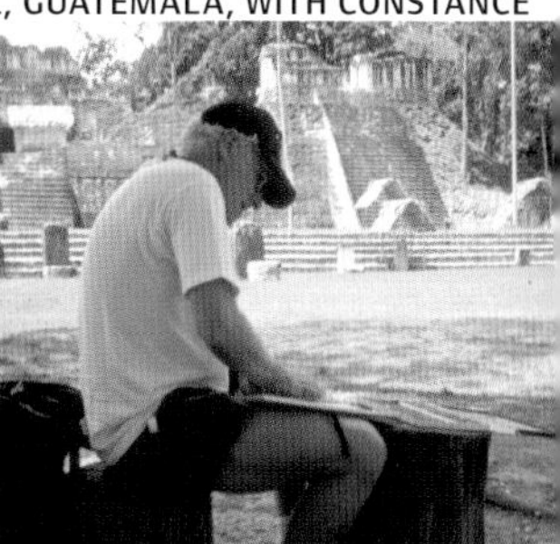

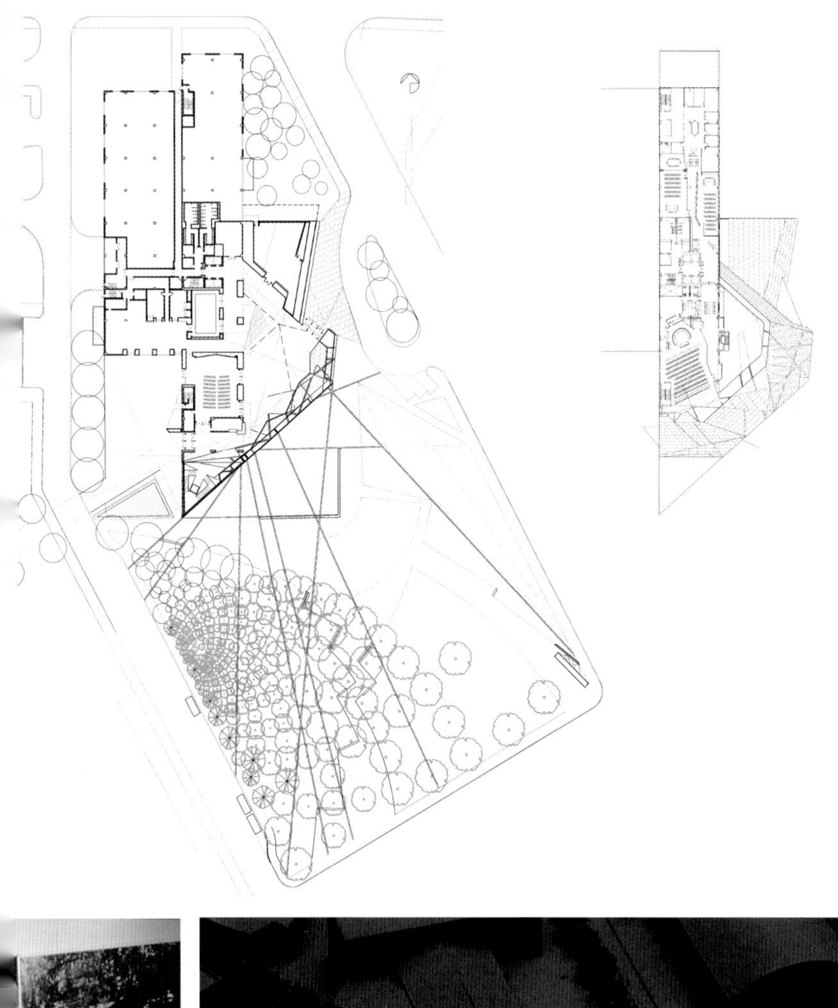

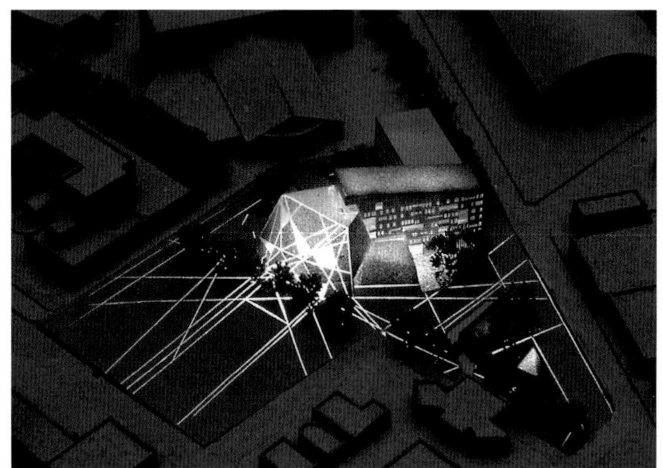

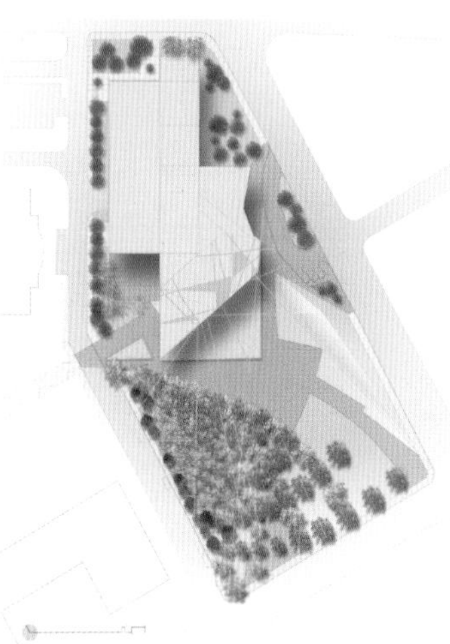

AMERICAN INSTITUTE OF ARCHITECTS
Western Mountain Region Conference

2002
Design Awards

MERIT AWARD
presented to
ANTOINE PREDOCK ARCHITECT
for
GATEWAY CENTER

The New Mexico Chapter
of
The American Institute of Architects
is proud to present an Honor Award to

Antoine Predock Architect

for the Gateway Center
at the University of Minnesota

constructed by M.A. Mortensen, Contractor

So often with project interviews, as was the case with the Gateway Center, potential clients are confronted by white men in suits and ties and somewhat dry presentations. When my time came, since I hadn't worn a tie in years, I just walked in with a huge roll of paper. When I unrolled it, and with my colleagues attached it to the wall, it revealed a panorama starting with deep time in Minnesota, traveling through the cultural layers of native people finally landing on locals Judy Garland and Bob Dylan. It seemed to really touch the University's interview team so I guess the suit and tie weren't necessary. Many University community meetings unfolded with my super associate Doug Friend.

MCNAMARA ALUMNI CENTER (GATEWAY CENTER)

UNIVERSITY OF MINNESOTA
MINNEAPOLIS, MINNESOTA 1996/2000

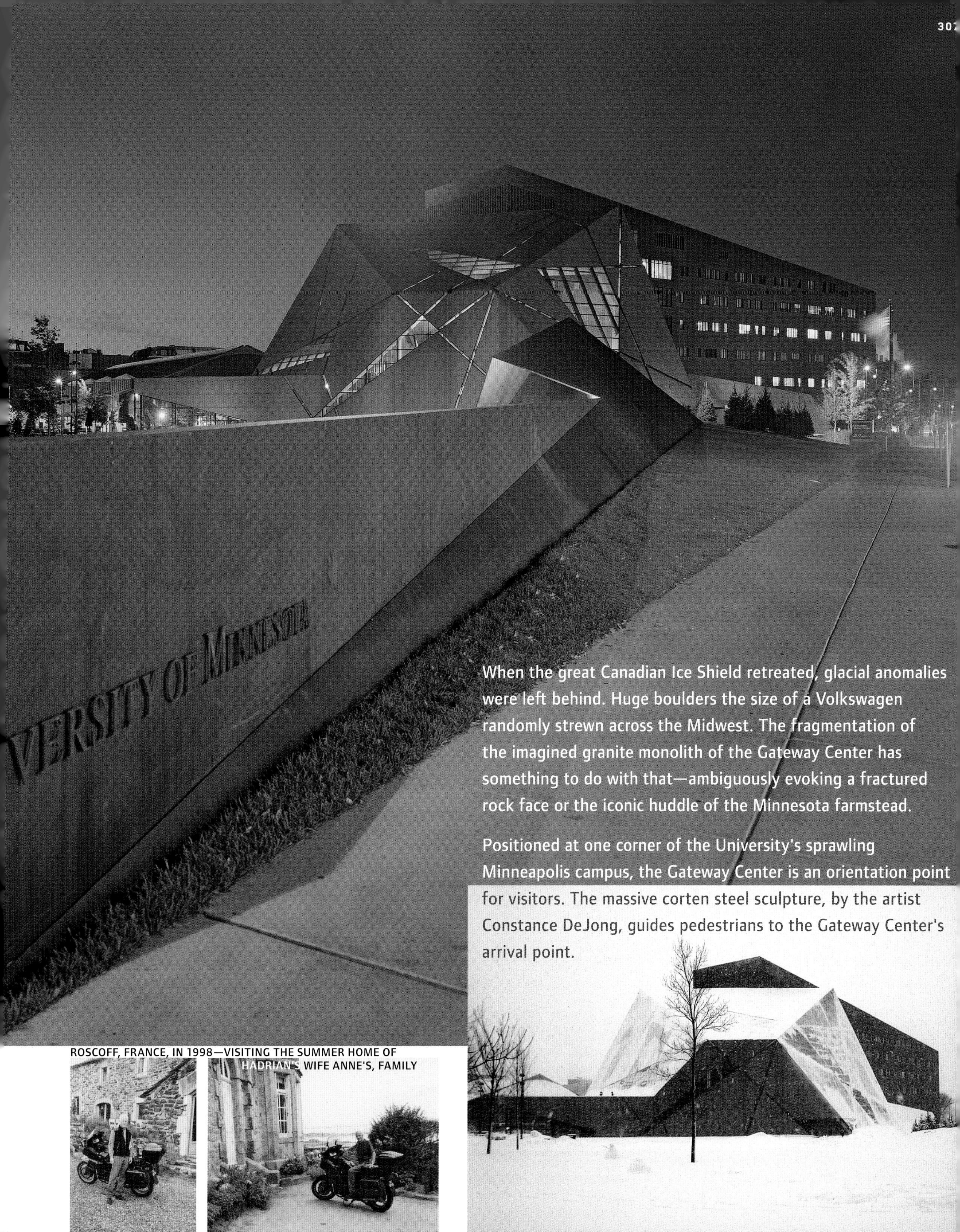

When the great Canadian Ice Shield retreated, glacial anomalies were left behind. Huge boulders the size of a Volkswagen randomly strewn across the Midwest. The fragmentation of the imagined granite monolith of the Gateway Center has something to do with that—ambiguously evoking a fractured rock face or the iconic huddle of the Minnesota farmstead.

Positioned at one corner of the University's sprawling Minneapolis campus, the Gateway Center is an orientation point for visitors. The massive corten steel sculpture, by the artist Constance DeJong, guides pedestrians to the Gateway Center's arrival point.

ROSCOFF, FRANCE, IN 1998—VISITING THE SUMMER HOME OF HADRIAN'S WIFE ANNE'S, FAMILY

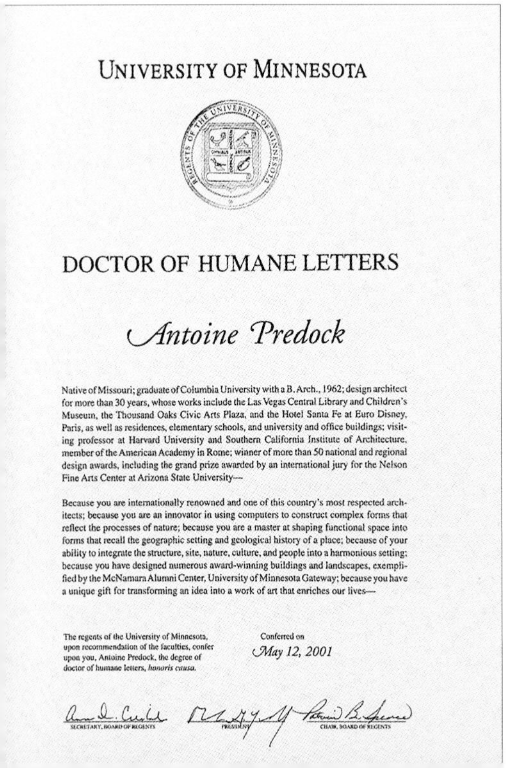

UNIVERSITY OF MINNESOTA

DOCTOR OF HUMANE LETTERS

Antoine Predock

Native of Missouri; graduate of Columbia University with a B. Arch., 1962; design architect for more than 30 years, whose works include the Las Vegas Central Library and Children's Museum, the Thousand Oaks Civic Arts Plaza, and the Hotel Santa Fe at Euro Disney, Paris, as well as residences, elementary schools, and university and office buildings; visiting professor at Harvard University and Southern California Institute of Architecture, member of the American Academy in Rome; winner of more than 50 national and regional design awards, including the grand prize awarded by an international jury for the Nelson Fine Arts Center at Arizona State University—

Because you are internationally renowned and one of this country's most respected architects; because you are an innovator in using computers to construct complex forms that reflect the processes of nature; because you are a master at shaping functional space into forms that recall the geographic setting and geological history of a place; because of your ability to integrate the structure, site, nature, culture, and people into a harmonious setting; because you have designed numerous award-winning buildings and landscapes, exemplified by the McNamara Alumni Center, University of Minnesota Gateway; because you have a unique gift for transforming an idea into a work of art that enriches our lives—

The regents of the University of Minnesota, upon recommendation of the faculties, confer upon you, Antoine Predock, the degree of doctor of humane letters, *honoris causa.*

Conferred on *May 12, 2001*

SECRETARY, BOARD OF REGENTS — PRESIDENT — CHAIR, BOARD OF REGENTS

QUITE AN HONOR TO RECEIVE MY HONORARY DOCTORATE THERE, BUT THE SPACE IS ALSO USED FOR HOCKEY GAME TAILGATING, WEDDINGS, AND MOST IMPORTANTLY AN ARRIVAL RECEPTION AREA FOR CAMPUS VISITORS AND PROSPECTIVE STUDENTS. AUTOMOBILE ADS AND VIDEO PERFORMANCES, LIKE THE INCUBUS MUSIC VIDEO, ARE ALSO SHOT THERE. THE PRESENCE OF WATER, THE SCENT OF THE WOOD, COPPER, THE GRANITE FLOORING—ALL EVOCATIVE OF MINNESOTA...

STRATA HOUSE FROM THE LATE '90s NEAR PHOENIX

MACKAY (STRATA) HOUSE
PARADISE VALLEY, AZ 1999

SAM STERLING, DEVENDRA CONTRACTOR, AND HADRIAN PREDOCK DURING RESEARCH PHASE OF PROJECT.

MEDIATING GLASS BRIDGES LINK TO A NEW ADDITION, CONSTRUCTED TO EXPAND THE OFFICE SPACE OF THE CENTER.

"You dash for the door through blinding snow, and—wham!—the building explodes into a six-story cavity framed in a glassy waterfall, a surreal Anasazi cliff palace, and the ghost of football seasons past."

Lawrence W. Cheek, *Architecture*, November 2000

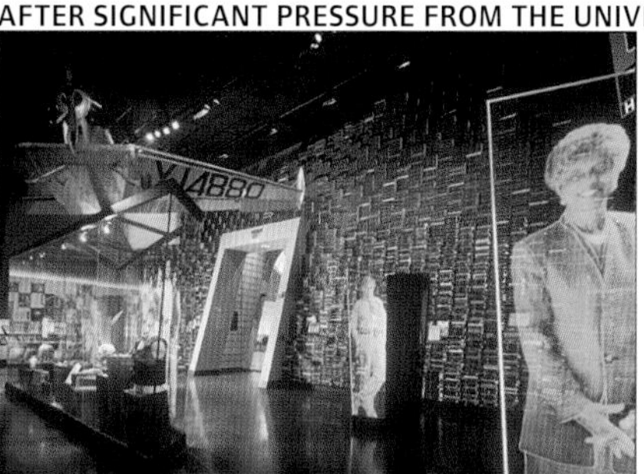

AFTER SIGNIFICANT PRESSURE FROM THE UNIVERSITY TO FEATURE IT ON THE EXTERIOR OF THE GATEWAY CENTER, THE MEMORIAL ARCH, A FRAGMENT FROM THE STADIUM FORMERLY ON THIS SITE, WAS "INVITED" INSIDE TO BECOME THE FRONTISPIECE OF THE UNIVERSITY HISTORY GALLERY—I THOUGHT THAT WAS A WIN-WIN.

Seen both as the casual and formal heart of the building, Memorial Hall is an irregular polyhedron of colliding granit planes and glazed fissures that guide sunlight into this large open gathering space. Abstracting the granite strata of Minnesota, with the admixture of water, Memorial Hall rises out of the ground as an upheaval, emerging from deep time.

The granite skin of the fractured monolith gives way to ar acoustically gapped and fissured wood lining. The copper clad offices plow into the monolith like the hull of a ship.

The copper office and conference face fronting the Hall act as theater balconies while doubling as points of attachment for theatrical lighting instruments in support of events in the space.

AROUND THIS TIME, VERY SPECIAL DUCATI MOTORCYCLES TURNED UP IN MY LIFE—THE TWIN SISTERS, 750 F1 MONTJUICH AND THE F1 LAGUNA SECA ON THE HEELS OF MY 851 KIT, WITH ITS SIREN CALL OF THE VORTEXING OF THE RACING AIRBOX VERGING ON EAR DAMAGE.

THE BLOCK-LONG CORTEN STEEL GATEWAY PIECE BY ARTIST CONSTANCE DEJONG ABSTRACTS THE NIGHT SKY AT THE TIME OF THE UNIVERSITY'S FOUNDING IN 1851.

SHUTTLING BIKES BETWEEN ALBUQUERQUE AND LA, THE (1929 INDIAN 101 SCOUT) WOULD BE THE STARS, WHEN

"Up close, approaching the entrance ... the composition works wonderfully. The building reads as an abstract cliff of sloping, intersecting planes and wedges, all slashing into the sky with equal bravado. And inside, Memorial Hall pulses with Architecture Power, and not in the predictable manner of a beaux-arts train station or cathedral nave of comparable volume. It's not size that matters; it's heart and intelligence. In a perfect world, all university buildings would have as much to say."

Lawrence W. Cheek, *Architecture*, November 2000

1970 EL CAMINO SS 396 WITH CONSTANCE AS DRIVER AND MOTORCYCLES WE PULLED INTO TRUCK STOPS.

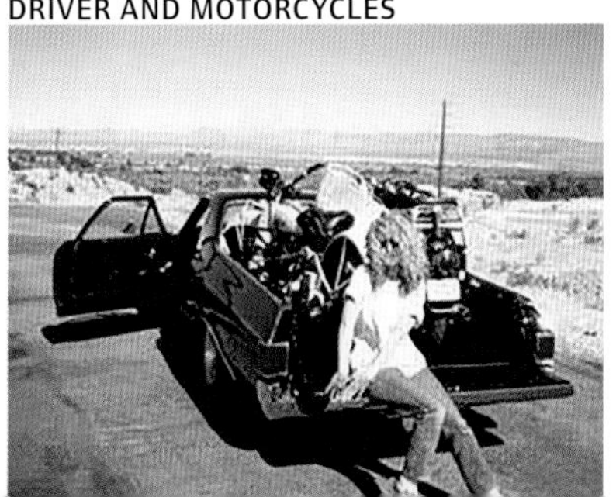

TANG TEACHING MUSEUM AND ART GALLERY

SKIDMORE COLLEGE
SARATOGA SPRINGS, NEW YORK 1996/2000

BILLED ALONG WITH BARENAKED LADIES FOR A KEYNOTE LECTURE DELIVERED IN SPOKANE, WASHINGTON IN 1997 AT THE MET THEATER.

THE SKIDMORE COLLAGE PROCESS AND MANY CONSENSUS MEETINGS WITH CAMPUS GROUPS.

This "open collection" art/teaching museum marks a confluence of pedestrian access alignments—one from the housing section, another from central campus, another reaching toward a contemplative pond. In its geologic realm, the Tang Museum erupts with the colors of the deeper limestone strata, suggesting a kind of glacial erratic. The building fragments are climbable and participatory.

"Students are all over the Tang Teaching Museum and Art Gallery at Skidmore College. They hang out on the rooftop terrace and often cross through, over, and around the museum, located at a major pedestrian crossroads of the campus. Tracks in the snow atop the sloping roof indicate attempts to literally sled off the building in winter. Architect Antoine Predock, FAIA, intended the museum, his first public building in the Northeast, to be open to manipulation and full of life and energy. His building is a radical departure from the rest of the well-planned but architecturally dull campus and quaint Victorian vernacular of the nearby town of Saratoga Springs, N.Y."

John E. Czarnecki, *Architectural Record,* May 2001

"The resulting building is as asymmetrical and angular as a structure can be, erupting out of the ground and striving toward the sky. Even some of the roofs and ceilings slope, like giant slides you yearn to try out."

Christine Temin, "Startling Tang Museum takes center stage at Skidmore College," The Boston Globe, November 12, 2000

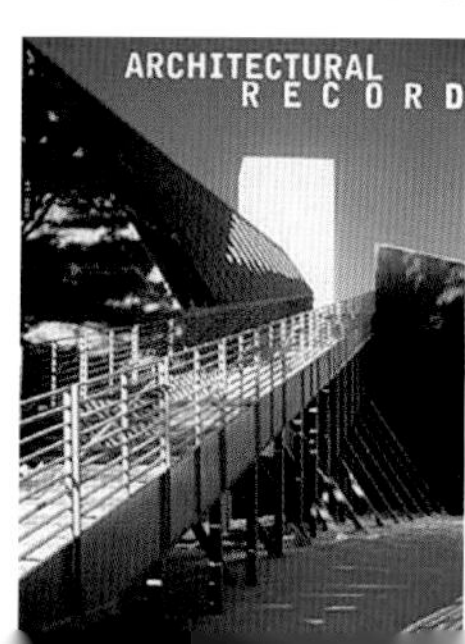

"Its two-story design ... suggests (to these eyes at least; Mr. Predock may have had other things in mind) a cross between adobe cubes and the sloping, weather-darkened lines of the barn roofs that dot the horse-country landscape: an abstract, newfangled version of American monumental."

Holland Cotter, "Party Time: Inside and Out, Playful Wit Reigns at Skidmore's New Museum," *New York Times*, December 22, 2000

THE UNIVERSITY CENTER STRADDLES A STRONG PEDESTRIAN DESIRE LINE—GUIDING DESCENDING CIRCULATION FROM THE CAMPUS CAMPANILE.

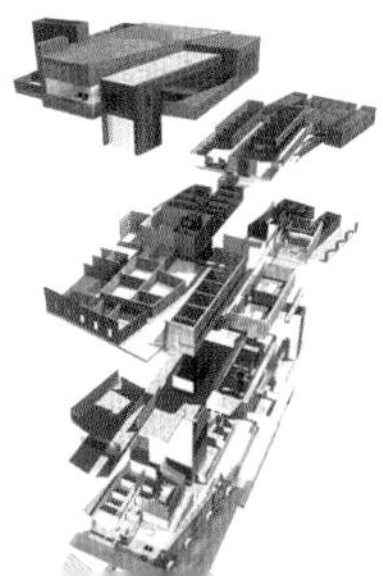

"Designed to foster cross-disciplinary experiments in the arts, the Tang is finished in stone, metal and concrete, and is surrounded by a circle of white pines. Two giant staircases converge to form a symbolic crossroads of culture and nature. Not since the glory days of the Beaux-Arts have we seen such an extravagant representation of the ascent to Parnassus."

Herbert Muschamp, "Design That Coaxes Buildings Out of Themselves," *New York Times*, September 10, 2000

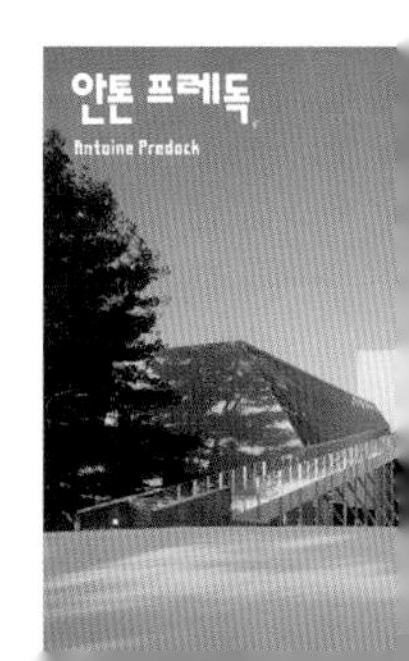

Traditional hierarchical and programmatic separations merge as spaces visually eavesdrop and the distinctions between display and archive, subject and object dissolve—inviting one to pause, reflect, perform, explore.

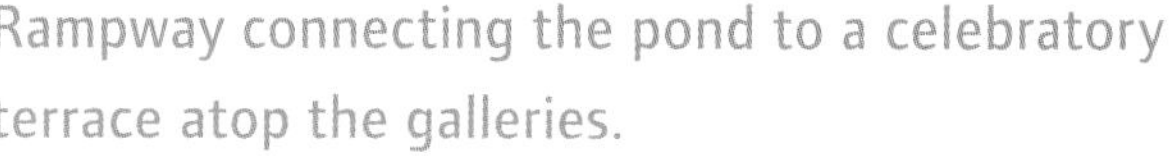

Rampway connecting the pond to a celebratory terrace atop the galleries.

/ARIOUS LECTURES AROUND THE COUNTRY IN THE MID 90s, INCLUDING THIS ONE IN LOS ANGELES, DELIVERED FROM A CHERRY PICKER SCAFFOLD USING THE SCI-ARC TEMPORARY TENT AS A SCREEN WHILE THE DEPOT WAS BEING REMODELED.

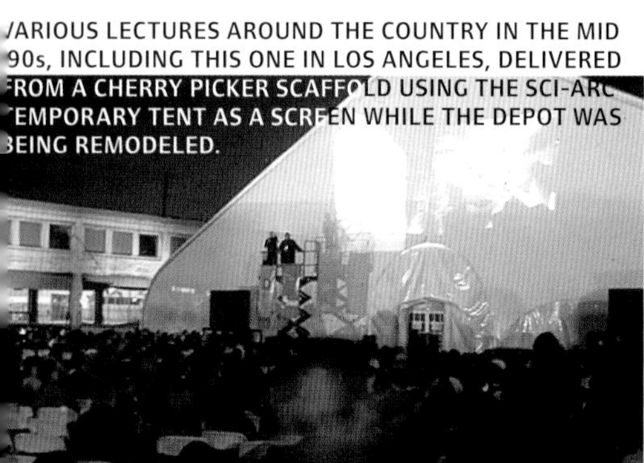

MY 1950 VINCENT BLACK SHADOW INSTALLED IN A TANG MUSEUM EXHIBITION.

AN ARCHITECT'S DREAM COME TRUE—
YOUR BUILDING IN A SNOW GLOBE.

GREEN VALLEY PERFORMING ARTS AND LEARNING CENTER

PIMA COMMUNITY COLLEGE
GREEN VALLEY, ARIZONA 1998/2004

THE AUTHOR, AN ETHNOLOGIST, WAS TALKING TO A YOUNG O'ODHAM (PAPAGO) BOY ASKING HOW HE WOULD DESCRIBE THE DESERT. THE BOY RESPONDED, THE DESERT SMELLS LIKE RAIN."

LIVING IN THE HIGH DESERT OF NEW MEXICO FOR 70 YEARS, I UNDERSTAND WHAT THE BOY MEANT. AFTER THE RAIN IN THE SONORAN DESERT, THE PUNGENT AROMA OF THE CREOSOTE BUSH OVERWHELMS THE ATMOSPHERE.

A SIMILAR PHENOMENA OCCURS WITH THE SAGE OF THE NEW MEXICO ALTIPLANO. AND WORKING IN DUBAI, I KNOW THE ARABIAN DESERT VERY SUBTLY RESPONDS TO THE LEAST PRESENCE OF MOISTURE WITH TINY FLOWERING PLANTS UNEXPECTEDLY APPEARING IN THE DUNES.

BACK AND FORTH TO LA WITH CONSTANCE IN THE BADASS 1990 PORSCHE C4... MONUMENT VALLEY ON THE WAY

Shaded exterior activity spaces with apertures toward the mountain.

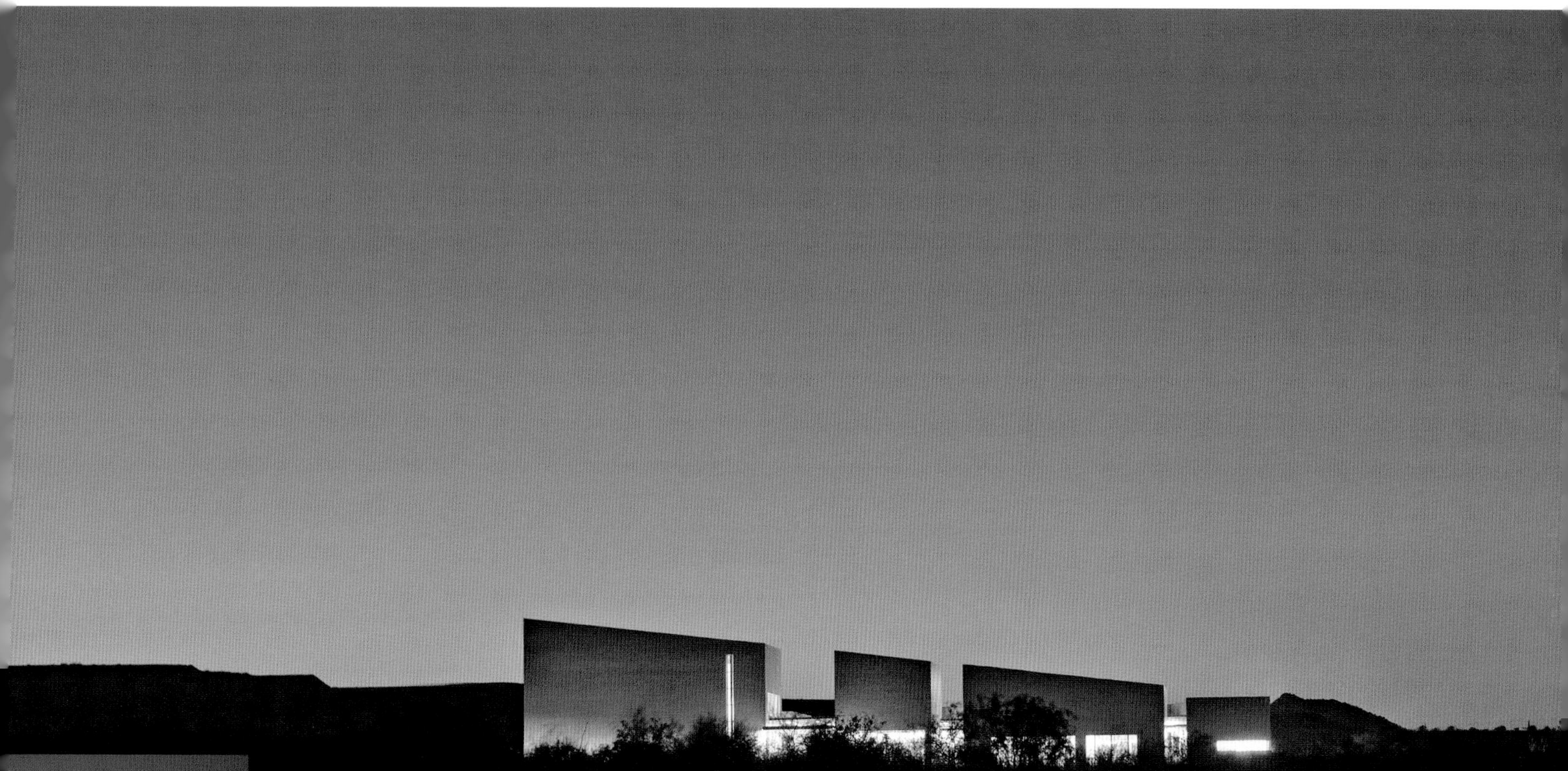

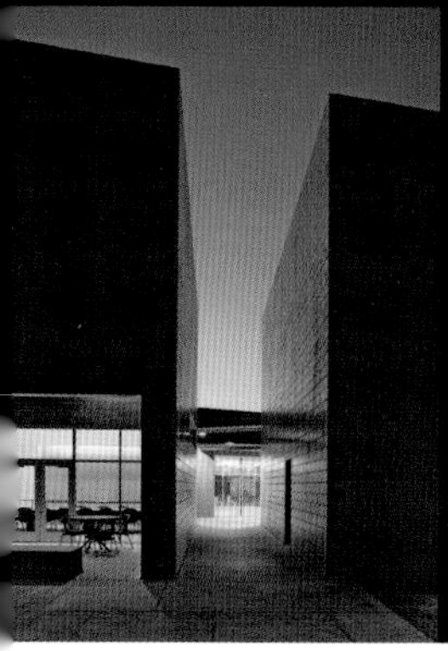

The massive, mute, windowless walls of the performance and rehearsal spaces—inspired by the resonance and power of the walls of places like Canyon de Chelly—float above the glowing, mountain-view-oriented classrooms and meeting spaces.

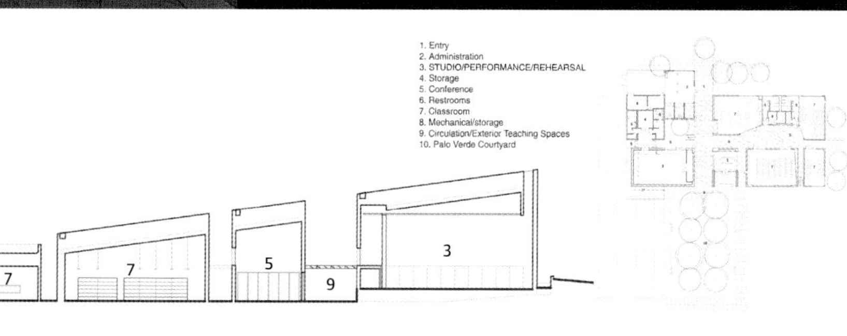

FUTURE 500-SEAT PLAYHOUSE

AIA Arizona

A Component of The American Institute of Architects

Design Awards
2004 Citation Award

Project *Pima County/Pima Community College Community Performing Arts and Learning Center*

Architect *Burns and Wald-Hopkins Architects Antoine Predock Architect*

Owner *Pima County/Pima Community College*

Contractor *Corona Sierra, Inc.*

8.22.04 Date · Design Awards Chair · Jury Chair

COLLAGE PROCESS

The collage is our lead-in to grasping the site—capturing first impulses. It is not a design exercise. It's research—our version of site analysis, but less boring. It's ALIVE—an exploration of the deep time of the place through its literature and culture.

"Consequently, Predock sites buildings like an archaeologist, going deeper and deeper until he strikes cultural bedrock. The first step in the investigation is usually a collage, created by Predock and his team with photographs, postcards, rocks, animal skeletons—anything that helps to assemble a mosaic of ideas about a place. This unique tool enables them to discover the rhythms and the tempo of a site."

David Dillon, "Antoine Predock American Visionary," *Architecture*, March 1995

"I want to have my hand in every step of the process of making a building—from design to occupancy. Since our work involves far-flung sites throughout the world, I need to have an immediate immersion in the spirit of the place."

"American architect Antoine Predock on discovering the spirit of each place," *Stirworld.com*, July 2, 2020

MIRA WOODSON WAS IN CHARGE OF GRAPHICS IN THE STUDIO AND WAS MY RIGHT ARM WHEN IT CAME TO MAKING THE COLLAGES WITH OUR TEAM.

FLINT RIVERQUARIUM

ALBANY, GEORGIA 1998/2004

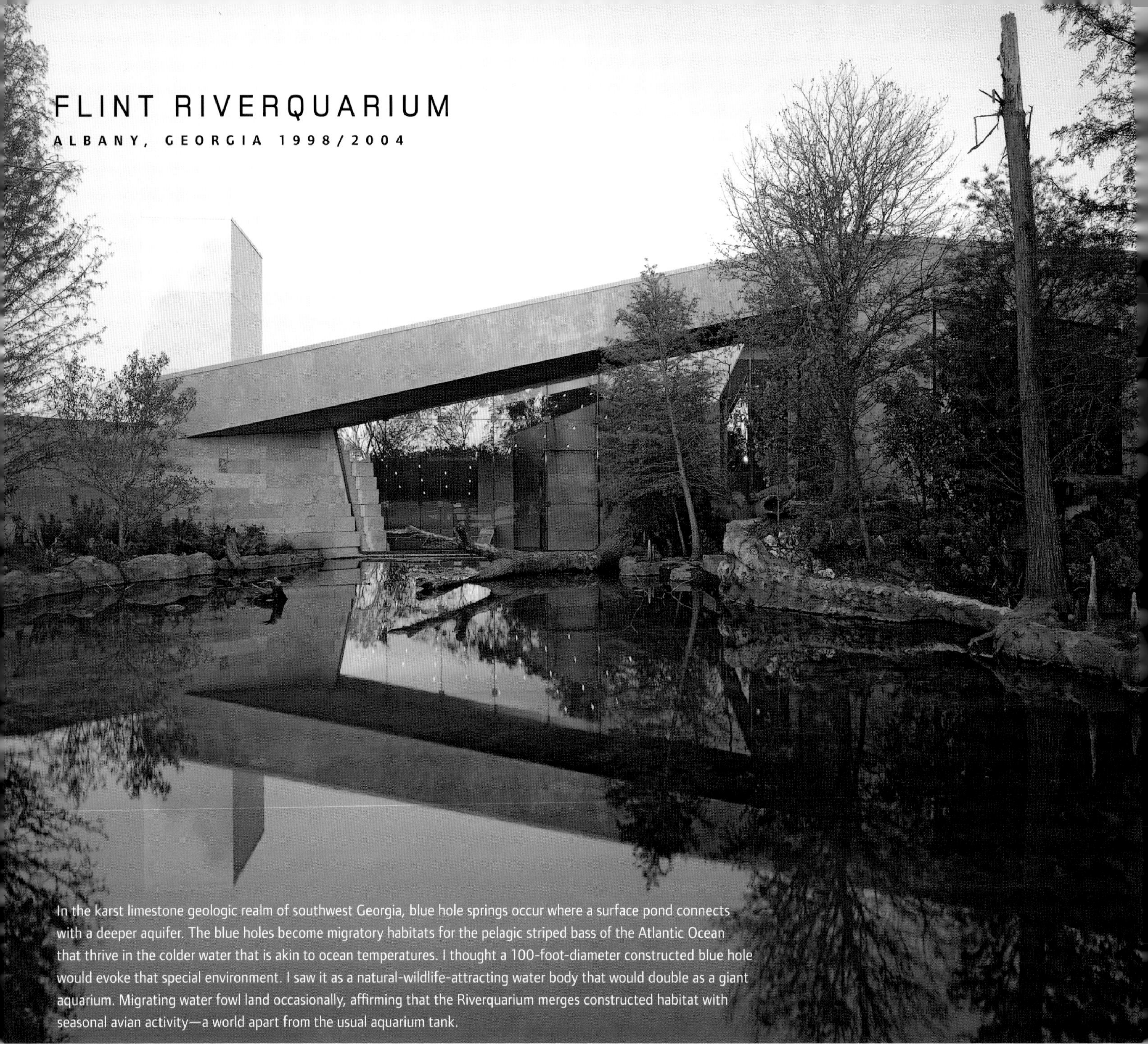

In the karst limestone geologic realm of southwest Georgia, blue hole springs occur where a surface pond connects with a deeper aquifer. The blue holes become migratory habitats for the pelagic striped bass of the Atlantic Ocean that thrive in the colder water that is akin to ocean temperatures. I thought a 100-foot-diameter constructed blue hole would evoke that special environment. I saw it as a natural-wildlife-attracting water body that would double as a giant aquarium. Migrating water fowl land occasionally, affirming that the Riverquarium merges constructed habitat with seasonal avian activity—a world apart from the usual aquarium tank.

Massive cliff-like perimeter walls containing gallery spaces surround the constructed blue hole spring. On the arrival, side sloping walls and bleachers define the public entry.

A SKIFF RIDE UP FLINT RIVER TO VIEW A RIPARIAN BLUE HOLE SPRING WITH SAM STERLING. OTHER REGIONAL RESEARCH TRIPS— INCLUDING SOUTH TO THE PRE-COLUMBIAN KOLOMOKI MOUND.

Kolomoki Mound

ONGOING COMMITTEE/COMMUNITY MEETINGS WITH THE CATALYTIC TOMMY CHATMON, HELEN YOUNG, AND OTHERS.

HURRICANE HUGO DEVASTATED THE AREA, SO RIVERQUARIUM IS SITED WELL ABOVE THE FLINT RIVER FLOODPLAIN WITH A FORESTED CATWALK DESCENT TO THE RIVER'S EDGE.

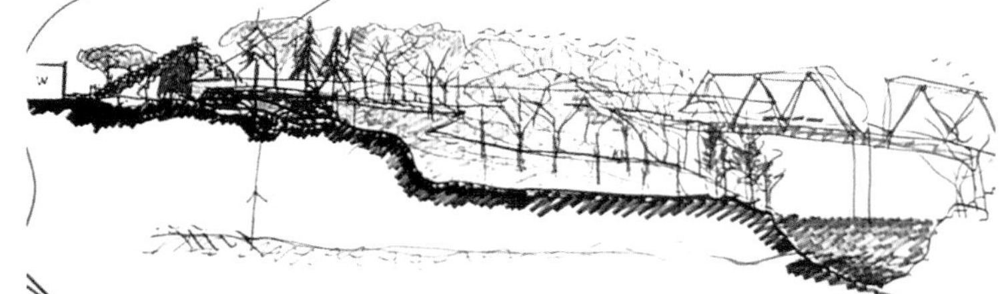

The Corps of Engineers dammed the river, landlocking a population of migratory striped bass, deep ocean nomads. Because of the cool water blue holes, they survived. The natural realm takes over after human desecration—up to a point.

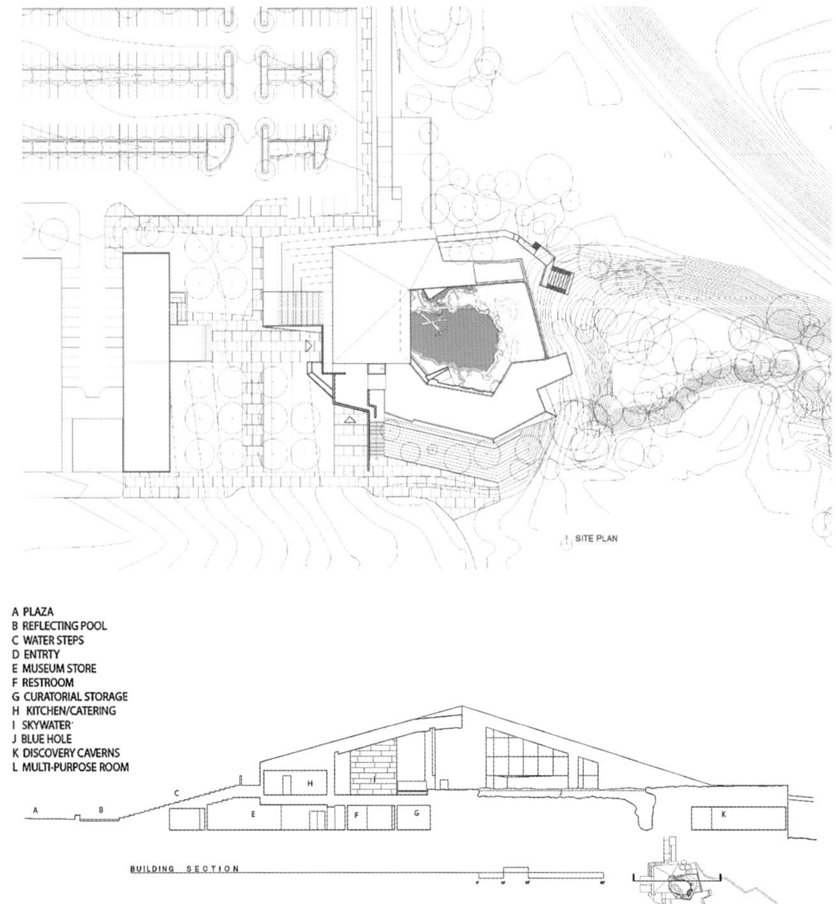

WITH THE FORCE OF NATURE TOMMY CHATMON.

The fortress-like perimeter wraps a 100' diameter "aquarium tank" with ramped descending views into this literally natural aquatic habitat—and finally at the bottom, a view upward through this giant lens to the sky.

TAOS SKI TRIPS WITH THE STUDIO TEAM, AND A SPECIAL ONE WITH MY SON JASON.

LATE '90s, PREPARATION FOR A UNIVERSITY OF CINCINNATI PROJECT INTERVIEW, A 12 X4' RESEARCH COLLAGE WAS ASSEMBLED.

EGYPT WITH CONSTANCE, 1999—GIZA AND THE BENT PYRAMID OF DASHUR, THEN SOUTH TO LUXOR AND THE KARNAK TEMPLE.
A SMALL SCULPTURE OF THE GOD HORUS IN THE EGYPTIAN MUSEUM HIT ME JUST AS DEEPLY.

"After seeing the blue hole from above, visitors continue down the interior's main path, a circle with ramps descending below the water level. Here, through glazing, the water appears as a lens to the sky, visually merging aquatic and heavenly realms."

Sarah Amelar, *Architectural Record*, May 2005

FALL BEGINS AT THE 12TH STREET STUDIO—WITH PAUL, REGINA, MIRA, DOUG, AND OTHERS.

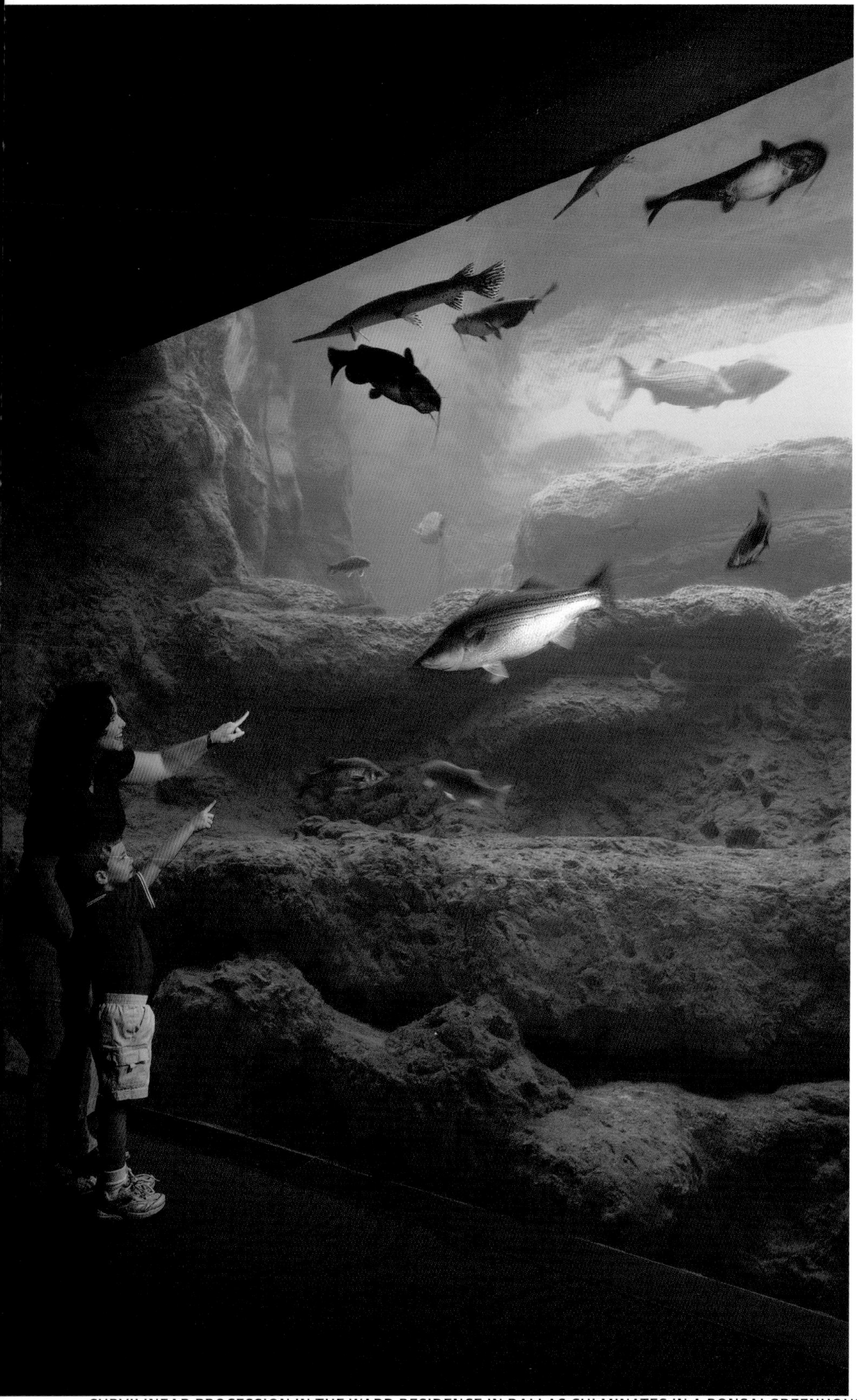

I wanted it to be a hybrid of an educational display and natural place—not another typical aquarium. Following the rampway descent to the lowest level, one gazes up through an aquatic window to the sky.

Viewing from the upper arrival level across the blue hole to the edge of the Flint River beyond.

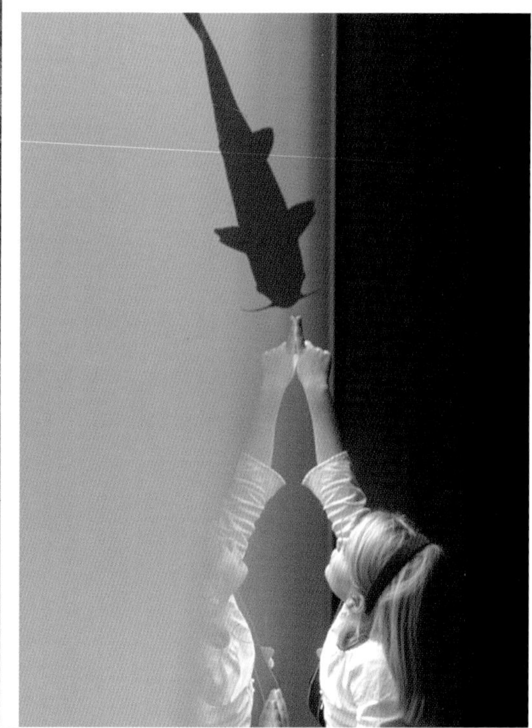

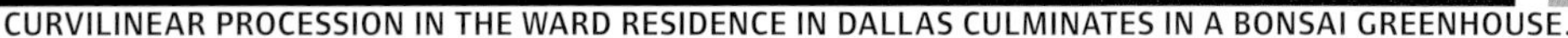

CURVILINEAR PROCESSION IN THE WARD RESIDENCE IN DALLAS CULMINATES IN A BONSAI GREENHOUSE.

WARD RESIDENCE
DALLAS, TX 1999

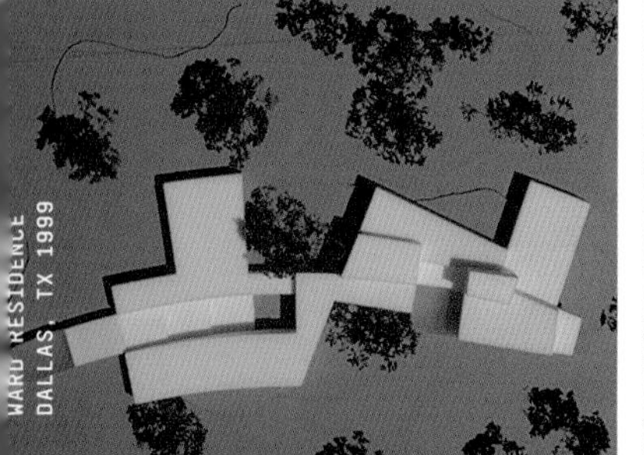

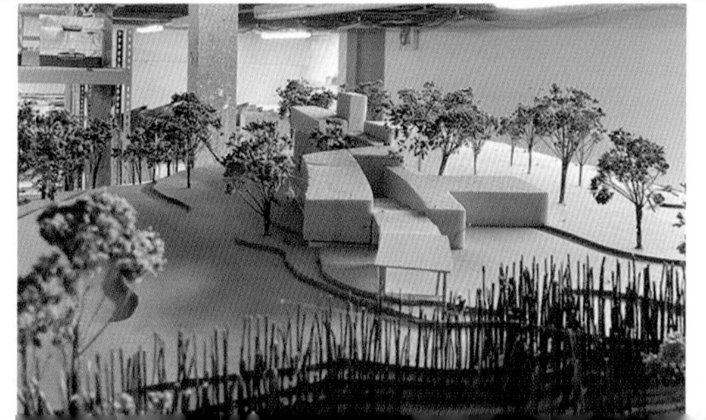

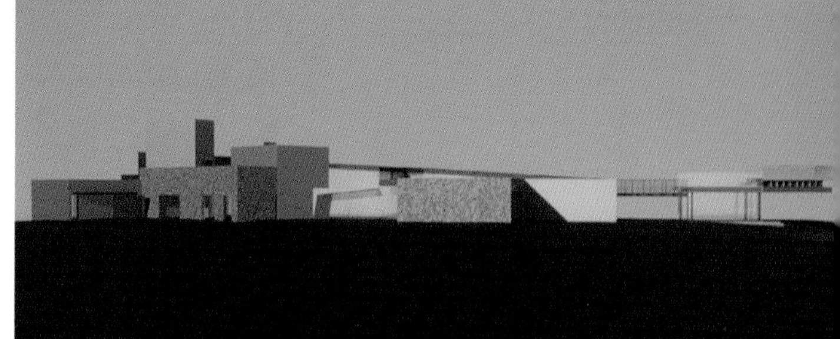

This 12'x4' collage was my fundamental piece in the architect interviews for the project—exploring the deep geologic/cultural past of San Diego and the history, poetry and meaning of Baseball in America.

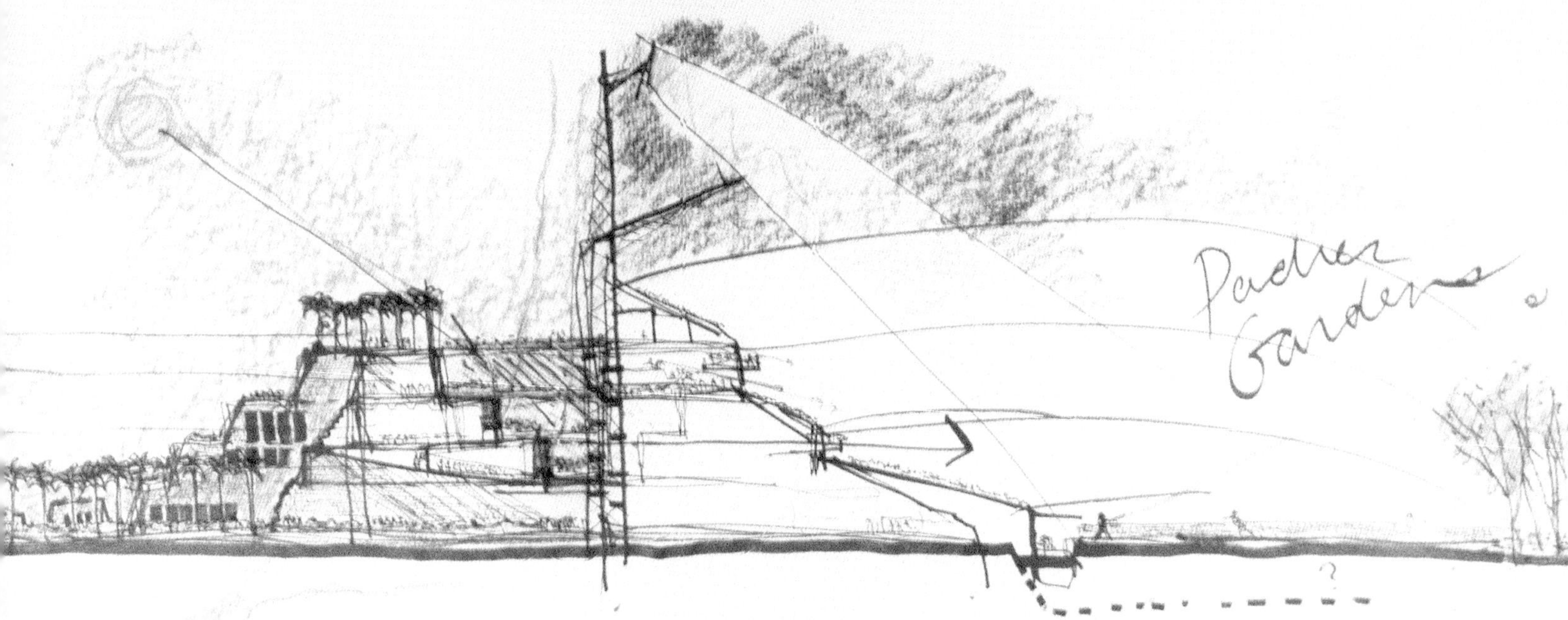

EARLY SITE-POSITIONING STUDY WITH OUR URBAN DESIGN TEAM

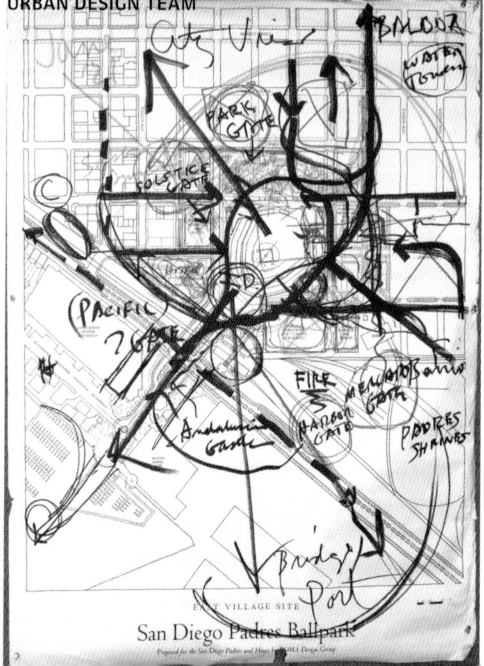

ANTOINE PREDOCK

A BALLPARK FOR SAN DIEGO

Antoine Predock puts the park back in "ballpark" with his design for a new home for the Padres in downtown San Diego by introducing terraces, gardens, and fountains throughout the 40,500-seat, open-air facility. While most stadium architects crowd offices, concessions, and lounges into the residual spaces beneath seats, Predock and associate architect HOK Sport leave the skeletal, white-painted steel structure of the seating free. Steel bridges connect to surrounding, free-standing blocks that house the ancillary functions and retail, and provide entrances to the ballpark. The landscaped terraces between the outer and inner structures serve as a concourse.

Predock punctuates the sandstoneclad outbuildings with punched openings, parapets, and trellises draped in bougainvillea and jasmine. A series of towers contains field lighting, luxury suites, and vertical circulation. A citywide referendum, scheduled to be held this month, will determine public funding for the $267.5 million ballpark. *N.C.*

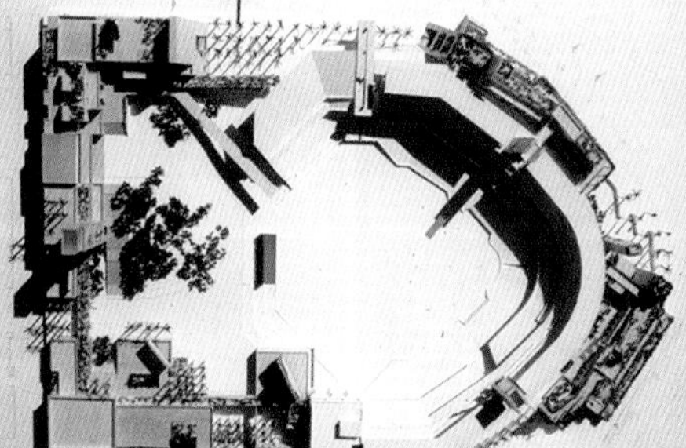

architecture: November 1998/ 129

IAJOR LEAGUE STADIUMS WITH A LOT OF PRESSURE AS GARDEN IN THIS CITY OF GARDENS—A TERRACED ENSE WITH BOUGAINVILLEA, FLOWERING FLORA OF ALL THE SEASON'S OPENING DAY.

"IF SAN DIEGO CONTINUES TO 'TACO BELL MISSION STYLE' EVERYTHING IN SIGHT, INCLUDING LAMPOSTS IN SHOPPING CENTERS, WHAT DO THE REAL MISSIONS MEAN ANY MORE?"
Antoine Predock in a public forum

Before

After

As the multilevel grandstands and bleachers wrap the playing field views splay, sweeping from northeast to northwest over the Gaslamp District to central San Diego skyline ... and the developer feeding frenzy of view-oriented condos/office buildings spawned by the presence of the Ballpark.

The palm arrival/ticketing court at street level is gateway to the grand stairway/escalator bank that ascends along the waterwall to the sky garden concourse. The mission of this concourse is to open mid-level views down to the playing field—framed by the stepping grandstands. Instead of concessions, restrooms, team offices, etc. blocking the view to the field, they are positioned across the concourse on the Ballpark perimeter. The seating levels above connect decentralized hanging garden bridges to suite-level lounges with dining terraces that have views of the harbor and over Coronado Island to the Pacific Ocean, locking the Ballpark into the spectacular San Diego realm. The movement of the sun defines the home plate location and the batter's optimum focus away from the sun. This resulted in placement of the left field yellow foul pole right at the corner of the historically important Western Metals building, now integral to the Ballpark—the one keeper of all the nearby existing buildings. Respecting the sun angles, the main seating bowl turns away from the harbor and ocean views and toward the skyline. Terraces and view alignments from the club lounges and concessions dramatically connect with the port and the Pacific Ocean.

We got past the dangerous and controversial "mission style" nostalgia debate—enduring plenty of "architorture" along the way—to deliver PADRES GARDENS... in collaboration with Andy Spurlock, fantastic landscape architect colleague.

Padres owner, John Moores, and Larry Lucchino, the CEO, suffered their own version of "architorture," fending off 27 lawsuits and major project delays, but they never gave up.

EVIL POSTMODERNISM, PROMULGATED IN THE 1980 VENICE BIENNIAL, COURSED ITS WAY THROUG
IN SAN DIEGO FOR THE BALLPARK TO BE "MISSION STYLE." TO ESCAPE THAT I IMAGINED A BALLPA
STONE PERIMETER/BASE WRAPPING AROUND AN OPEN-TO-THE-SKY VERDANT MAIN CONCOURSE-
SORTS, AN ARCADE OF JACARANDA TREES, BLOSSOMING PURPLE IN EARLY SPRING, JUST IN TIME

SAN DIEGO PADRES BALLPARK

SAN DIEGO, CALIFORNIA 1998/2004

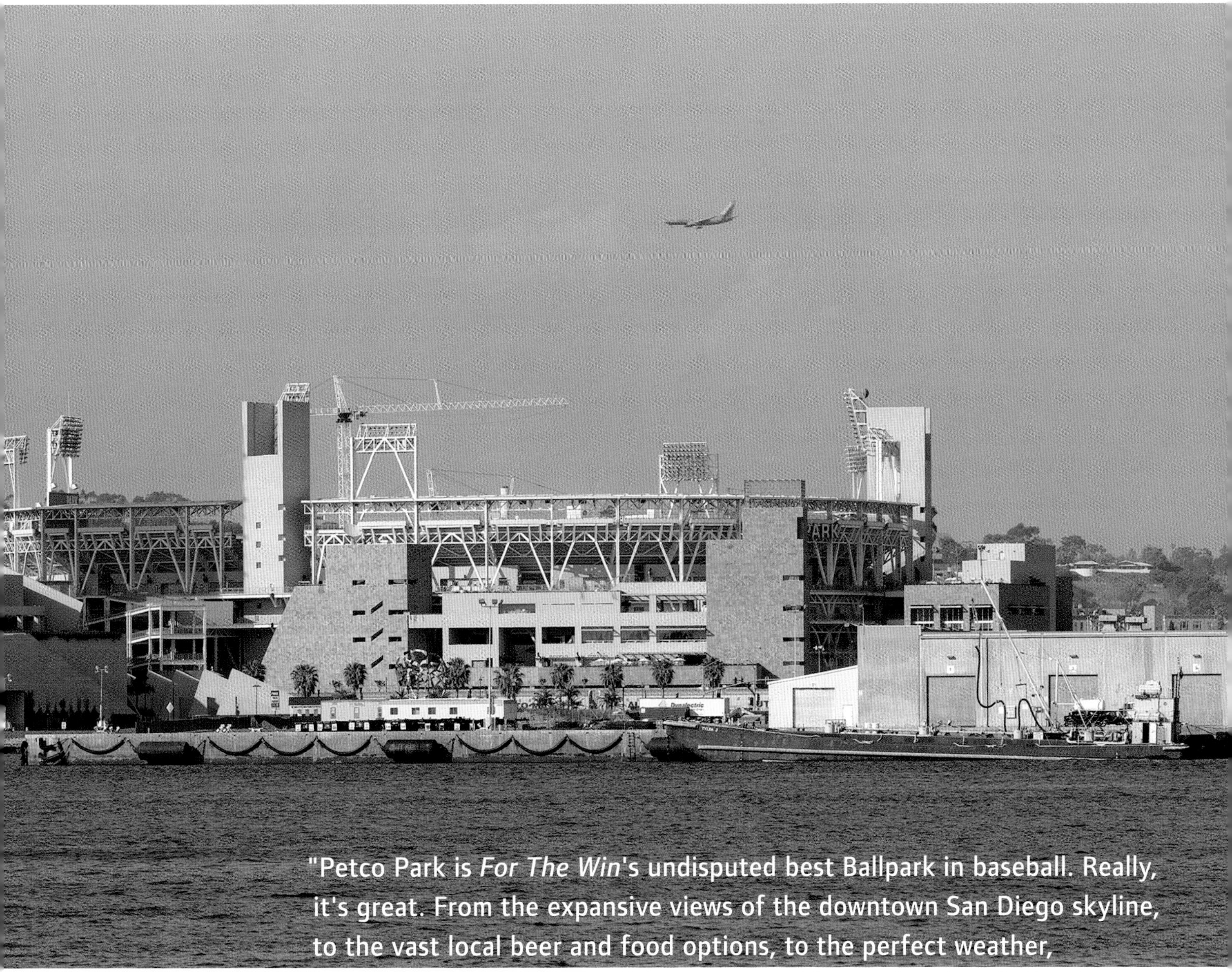

"Petco Park is *For The Win*'s undisputed best Ballpark in baseball. Really, it's great. From the expansive views of the downtown San Diego skyline, to the vast local beer and food options, to the perfect weather, Petco Park is everything MLB teams should want for their Ballparks."

Andrew Joseph, "Best Ballparks in America," *USA TODAY SPORTS*, August 3, 2016

"STILL THE STADIUM CHAMPS.

Petco Park is simply the best place to watch a baseball game. The location (embedded in downtown San Diego), the weather, the food, the beer and, of course, the stadium itself—it's all phenomenal. Petco Park often doesn't get the credit it deserves when compared to the Fenways and Wrigleys of the baseball world. But don't listen to those people. Petco Park is the best stadium in baseball."

Andrew Joseph, "All 30 MLB stadiums, ranked: 2022 edition," *USA TODAY SPORTS*, April 2, 2022

OPENING DAY 2004 VIEWING THE FIELD WITH HADRIAN, THEN LATER AT THE GAME WITH CONSTANCE, PAUL, NEIL KAMINSKY, KAROLE, TOM, AND LOU.

AMERICAN ARCHITECTURE AWARD

2002

BALL PARK FOR THE SAN DIEGO PADRES

ANTOINE PREDOCK ARCHITECT
ARCHITECTS

SAN DIEGO PADRES
CLIENTS

THE CHICAGO ATHENAEUM
MUSEUM OF ARCHITECTURE AND DESIGN

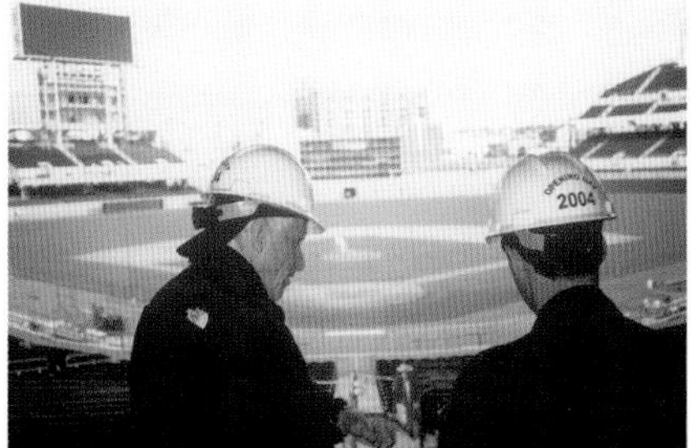

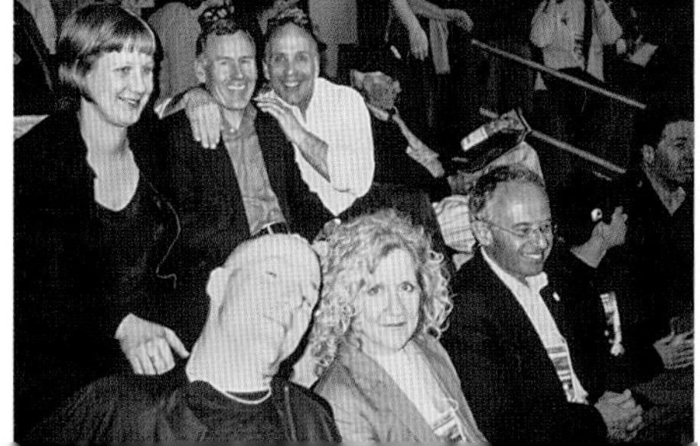

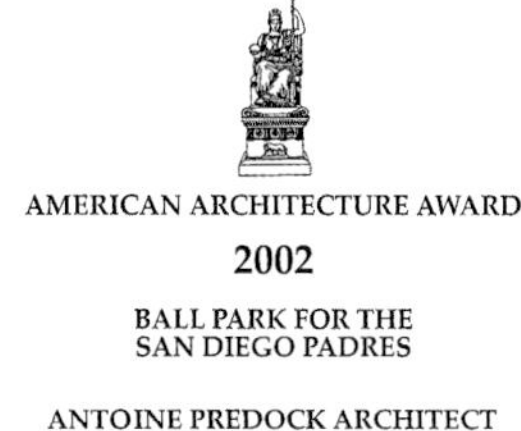

to cardboard

to lasercut media

"Sports fans and everybody else, hear this: architecture is not a spectator sport. To really "get" architecture's sweeping effects, its fine points and everything in between, you gotta get into the game.

Padres fans already know this about Petco Park, the new downtown ballpark that is so intriguingly designed that it demands exploration."

Ann Jarmusch, "Petco Packs in Energy, Excitement, and Essence of San Diego", *San Diego Union Tribune*, April 10, 2004

TIONS. THE KEY MODEL THAT TRIGGERED DESIGN DEVELOPMENT...
HEN IT SEEMED AS THOUGH THE ICONIC MEXICAN BREWERY

UP ON ONE OF THE FIELD LIGHT STANCHIONS WITH ERIK JUDSON, MY PADRES GUIDING LIGHT FOR THE PROJECT; JOE SPEAR, THE GENIUS OF HOK SPORT, WHO HELPED US MAKE THE DREAM REAL, FINESSING THE UNPRECEDENTED OPEN-TO-THE-SKY GRAND CONCOURSE AND ALL THE MYRIAD DETAILS OF SEATING GEOMETRIES, SIGHTLINES, AND ALL THE BASICS OF A MAJOR LEAGUE BALLPARK; AND RICK VOGEL ON THE RIGHT, MASTERMIND OF DEVELOPMENT STRATEGIES. (WHEN WE WOULD TALK TO LARRY LUCCHINO ABOUT UPPER-LEVEL MOUNTAIN VIEWS HE WOULD RESPOND "WHAT MOUNTAINS?" SO WE HAD TO DOCUMENT THAT REALITY.)

From clay

That glorious moment in a late afternoon game when the field lights snap on

"Looking to create an identity for the district, the Padres turned to Antoine Predock to design a bold structure and provide an anchor for continued development. Using the striking geometrical formations he is known for, Predock created a stadium with a strong presence."

"Business Week/Architectural Record Awards 2007," *Architectural Record*, November 2007

OUR VICTORIA STREET STUDIO IN VENICE WAS A HUB FOR MEETINGS AND MODEL WORK ON THE BALLPARK.

MY ASSOCIATE DOUG FRIEND, AT ONE OF THE EARLIEST PRESE
ND I'M WEARING THE "TECATE GARDENS" CAP THAT WE MAD
OULD NAME THE BALLPARK... BUT THEY WERE OUTBID BY PE

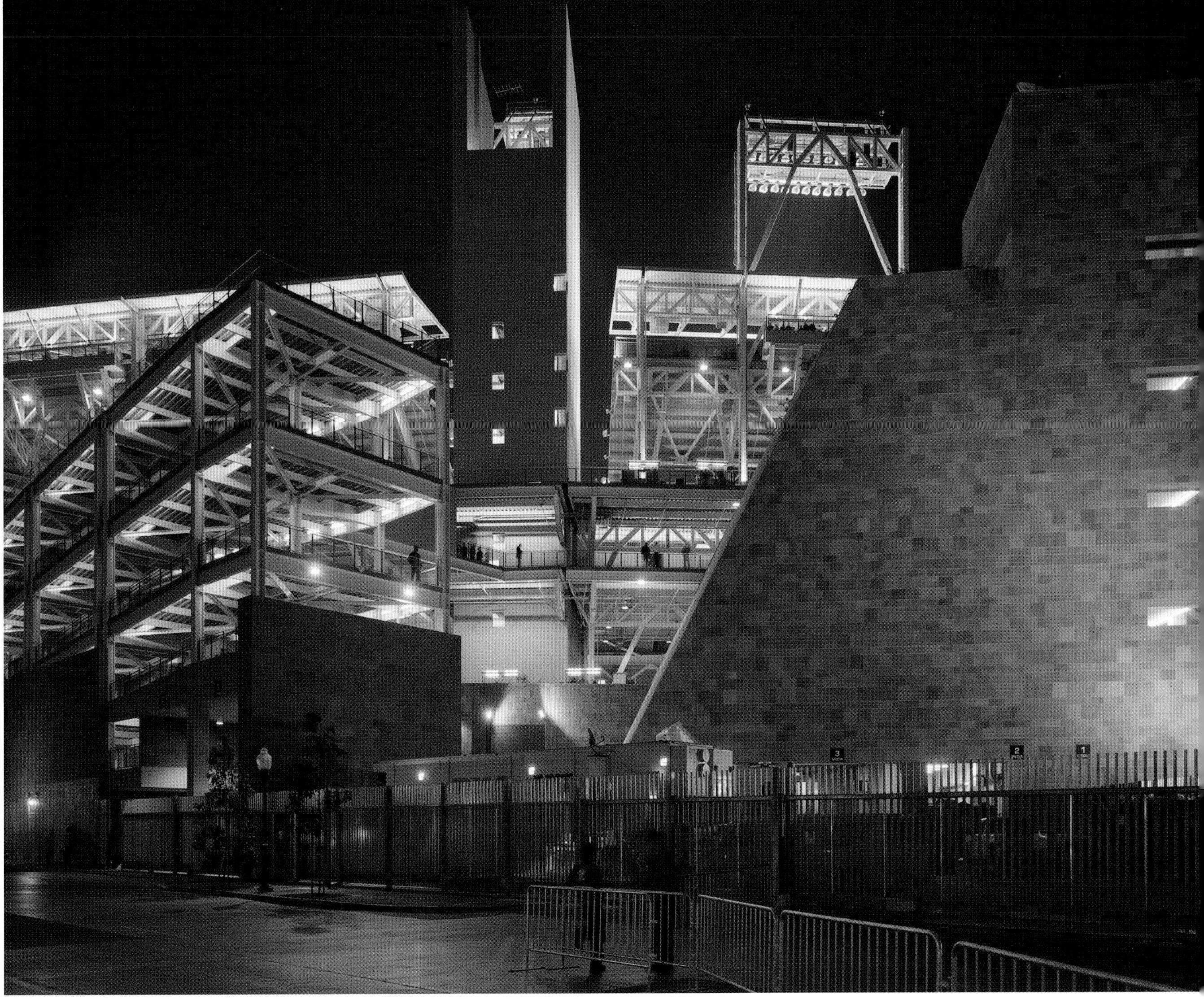

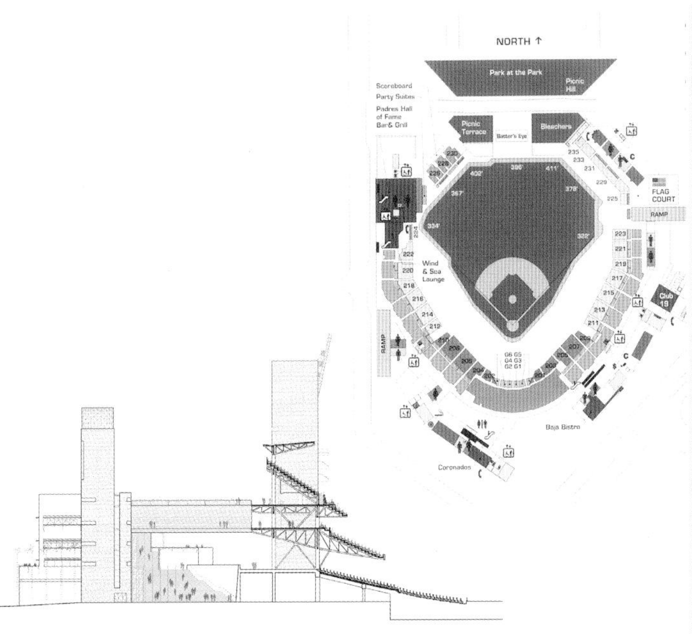

MY BASEBALL GLOVE AND OTHER MEMORABILIA FROM THE TIME OF THE OF THE OPENING

"It's not any one thing about Petco that makes it so enjoyable; it's everything. Aesthetically, it's spectacular, one of few contemporary parks that opted for a contemporary look over the nostalgic nonsense typical of too many stadiums. The spread-out concourses sort of weave their way around the seating sections, up and down levels and even under some hanging plant life. And the relative newness of the park means modern amenities, and plenty of bathrooms and beer stands."

Ted Berg, "San Diego's Petco Park is the best ballpark in baseball," *USA TODAY SPORTS*, July 12, 2016

MY HERO, SAMUEL L. JACKSON'S STAMP OF APPROVAL

PADRES MANAGEMENT ASKED ME TO HELP CUSTOMIZE THE SIGNAGE FOR THE MYRIAD CONCESSION STANDS OF THE BALLPARK, SO I DREW THESE.

AT THE TENTH ANNIVERSARY ON MARCH 30, 2014, I WAS INVITED TO RING THE TRADITIONAL GAME OPENING BELL.

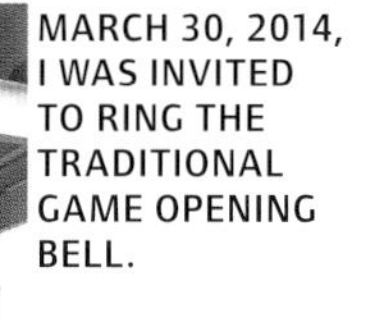

POSING WITH ERIK JUDSON AND THE USUAL SUSPECTS

WORKED WITH REALLY GREAT LANDSCAPE ARCHITECTS SPURLOCK POIRIER

"Antoine Predock put the park back in 'Ballpark' with his design for a new home for the Padres in downtown San Diego ..."

Ned Cramer, *Architecture*

"More Americans have probably seen Petco Park, the San Diego Padres ballpark that Predock designed with HOK Sport, than any other of his projects. Predock sought to recast the traditional sports complex as an expansive Southern California garden. He delights in explaining that the park skirted the popular retro revival and imitation Mission styles in favor of an 'authentic statement' of outdoor life, water views, the color of local cliffs and the natural dynamic of the game, which is movement."

Linda Hales, "Architecture's Natural Winner," *The Washington Post*, December 9, 2005

"Most people don't appreciate the effort, expertise and professionalism that went into this place. I saw it, and it was unbelievable. It was mind-boggling, almost overwhelming, how meticulous the planning was, and the workers were just as precise. In baseball, we'd say they executed perfectly. We can all take pride in Petco Park. And so I would like to tip my cap and say 'Thank you' to all the people who built this Ballpark."

Tony Gwynn, Baseball Hall of Famer, and 15-time All Star

Serving as the "catcher's mitt" terminus of the connection from Balboa Park to the Bay, the Ballpark, aside from baseball, is a civic meeting/ performance base and a focus as Downtown extends eastward, further animating the Gaslamp District.

Interview and an Intervention

"Although there were so many highlights of the project during our 8-year journey to develop the ballpark, two events stand out to me. These include the Interview and an Intervention.

To say that Antoine and his team shocked the room during the interview is an understatement. The highlight, his team unveiling a 30' collage depicting the evolution of baseball with primates holding clubs through to the current Padres in 1997. After we picked our jaws up off the ground, Antoine dazzled us with an inspiration for a ballpark like no other. Some in the room believed we should be taking a more traditional approach with our design architect selection. Thankfully, we did not.

Antoine almost left the project one night after unveiling design concepts to the Padres faithful before a game at the old stadium. The meeting did not go well. Our fans did not like the initial concepts and provided pointed criticism and a desire for a mission style building. As I drove Antoine back to his hotel, we sat in the front of my truck for almost 2 hours as he expressed his frustration and felt he was compromising his esthetic and ethic with the work to date. Suggesting that it might be best if he resigned, I channeled my inner Antoine, challenging him to use the opportunity to present the solution that he believed achieved the inspired vision we all desired. He went off to Albuquerque—and the rest is history."

Erik Judson, Former San Diego Padres VP, 2022

ROLLING STONES AT THE BALLPARK

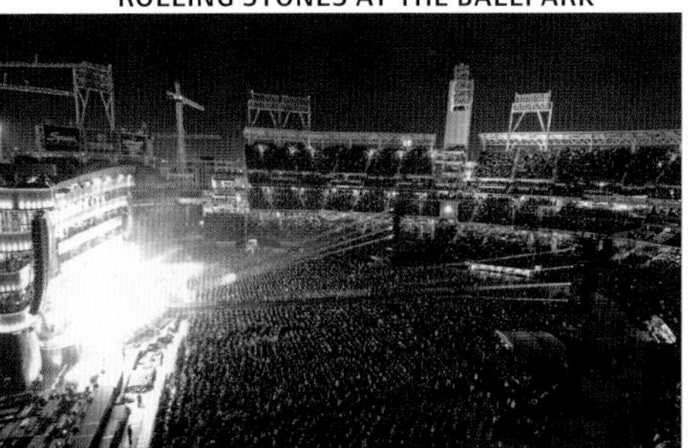

ERIK JUDSON OF THE PADRES (CENTER), MY "SPIRITUAL GUIDE" FOR THE PROJECT AND NOW A FRIEND FOR MORE THAN TWO DECADES, WITH OTHER MEMBERS OF THE DEVELOPMENT/ CONSTRUCTION TEAM—SPECIAL THANKS TO BADASS ALAN PETRACEK.

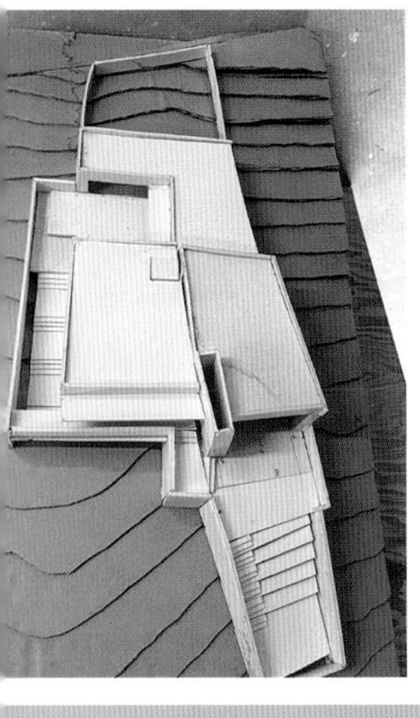

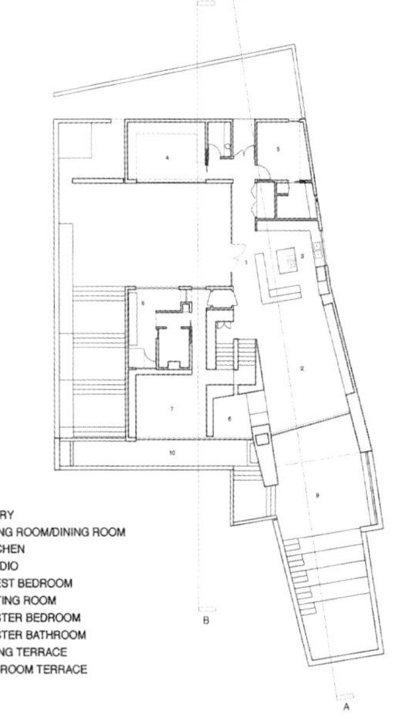

KAMINSKY II

ALBUQUERQUE, NEW MEXICO 1999/2001

Neil Kaminsky, my doctor and friend since the late '60s, and his wife Dorothy Gohdes, also a doctor, left the house I designed for them in the '70s and moved farther up the river. Positioned high on the site to optimize 180-degree views below and across the Rio Grande to the Sandia Mountains, the house extends into the landscape. Visitors ascend a stepped passageway to the arrival court. Earth-pigmented poured concrete masses, perfectly executed by Paul Kenderdine, juxtapose with sage stucco.

WITH MY CREW CALIBRATING VIEW ALIGNMENTS.

VISITING THE YUCATAN, WITH THE PALPABLE POWER OF THE MAYAN CULTURE, IN 2001—CHICHEN ITZA WITH ITS MINIMALIST BALL COURT,

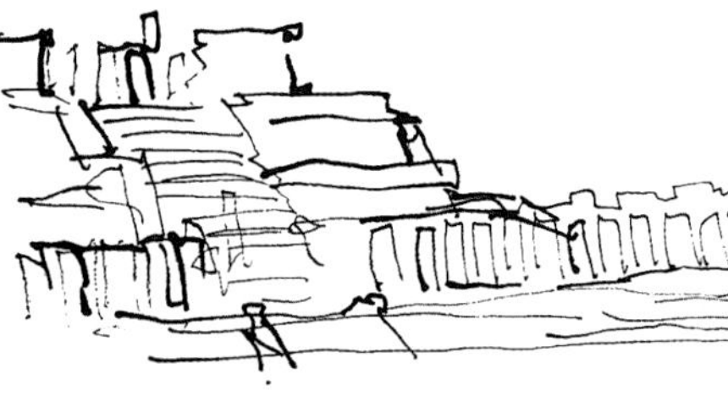

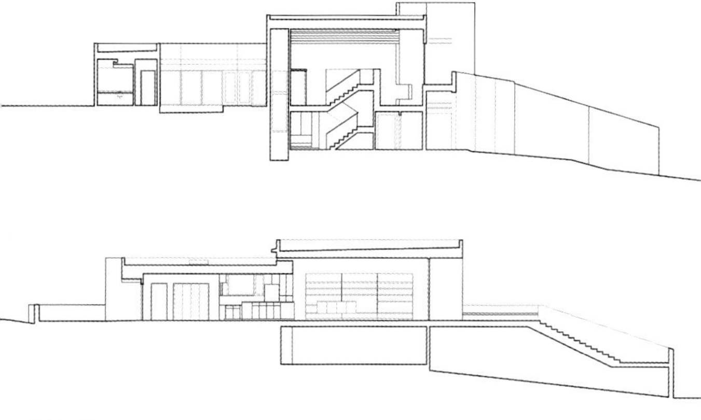

CARACOL, MIL COLUMNAS, THEN TO THE COAST—TO TULUM AND THE GRAN CENOTE.

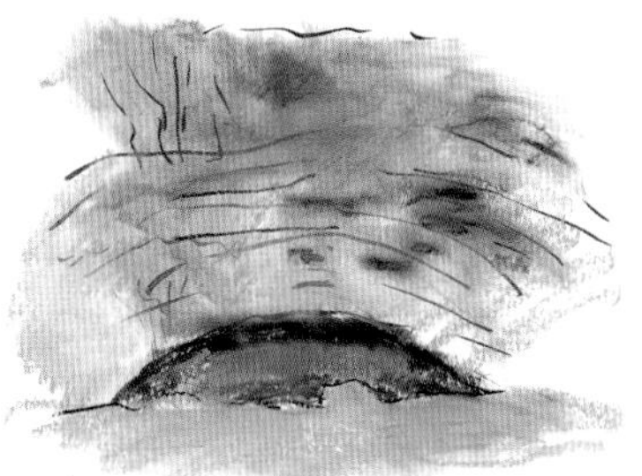

The New Mexico Chapter o
The American Institute of Archi
is proud to present the 2002
Merit Award for Architecture
to
Antoine Predock Archite
for the
Gohdes Kaminsky
Residence

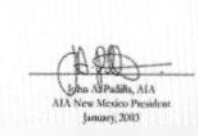

John A. Padilla, AIA
AIA New Mexico President
January, 2003

STUDENT ATHLETIC AND RECREATION CENTER

THE OHIO STATE UNIVERSITY
COLUMBUS, OHIO 1999/2006

ON A COCKTAIL NAPKIN OF A VANISHED AIRLINE, A DIAGRAM OF THE CONNECTIONS FROM THE FAMED OHIO STATE OVAL TO THE OTHER MULTI-DIRECTIONAL APPROACHES TO THE CENTER

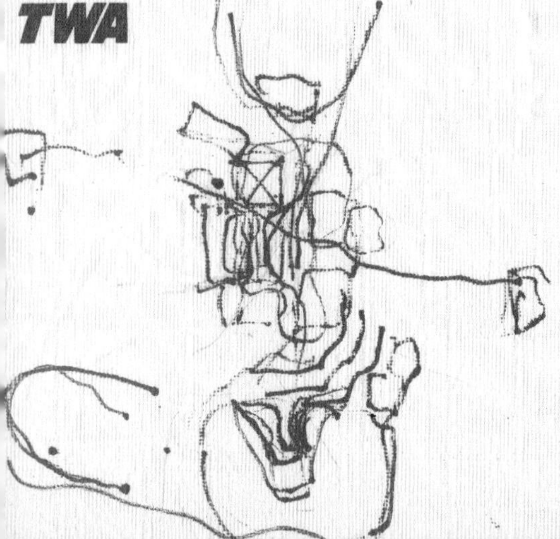

KEEPING UP WITH THE CLAY MODEL PROCESS WHILE FLYING TO OSU—BACK WHEN I COULD FLY WITH MY CLAY KNIFE

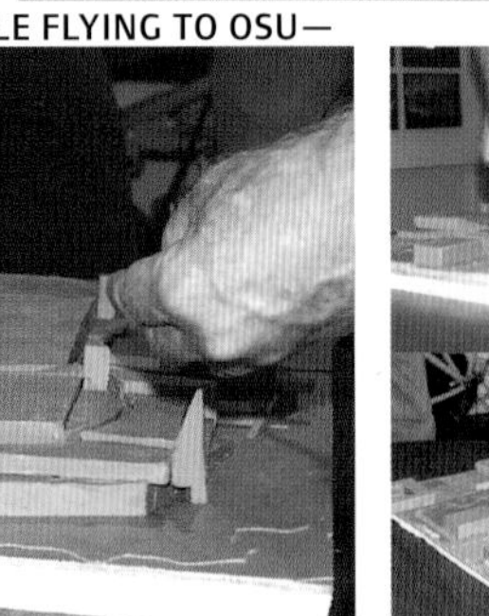

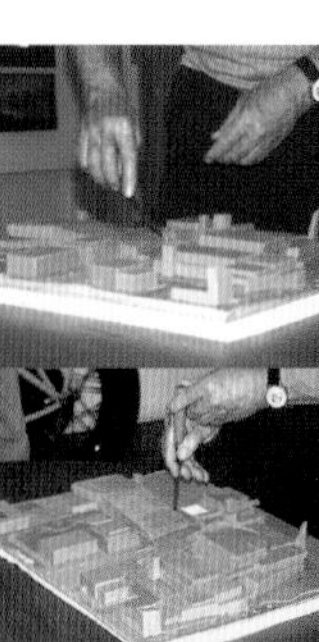

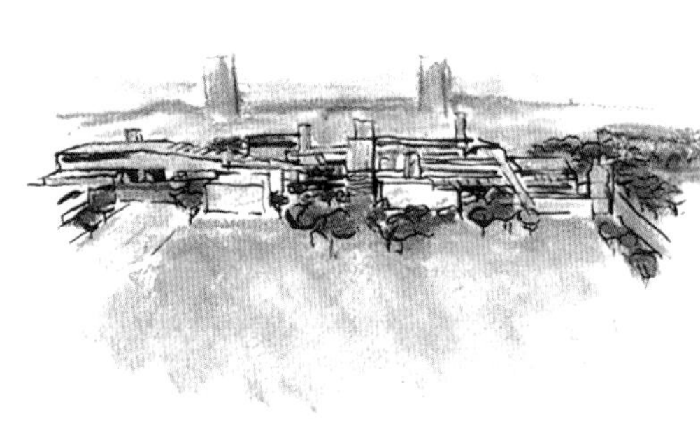

A one-half-million-square-foot "City of Sport," the world's largest student facility of its kind: running track passes into sport science and testing facilities, multilevel gym, multistory five court basketball, handball/squash courts, and world-class Olympic pool facilities.

WORKING WITH PROJECT MANAGER/SENIOR ASSOCIATE SAM STERLING, WITH CORY GREENFIELD TAKING OVER LATER

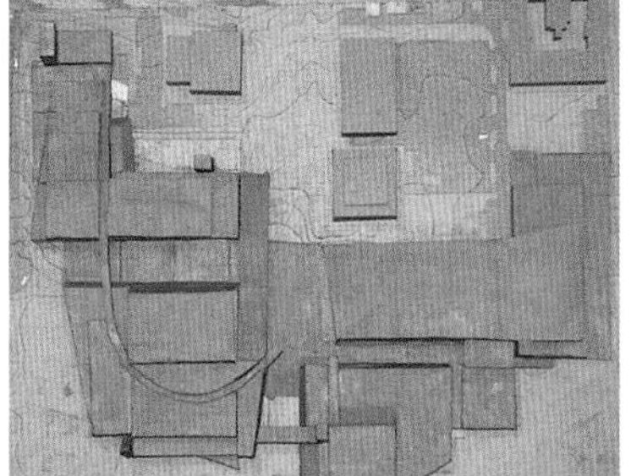

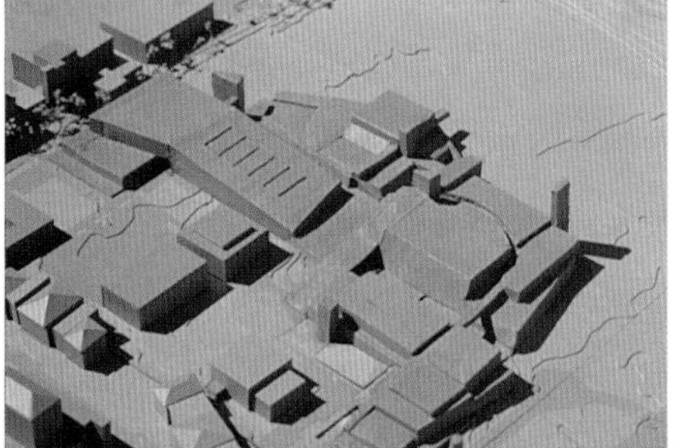

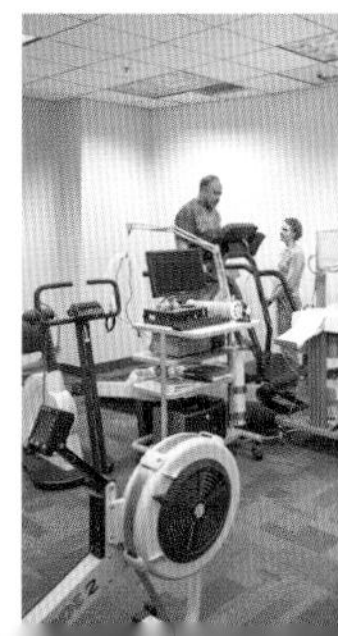

The northwest entry, coded with the OSU color, episodically engages various sections of this sport village, becoming a running track and visual eavesdropping trajectory for crossfire views of the different activities as one passes through. The iconic Buckeyes Stadium is linked to the athletic center across courts and playing fields.

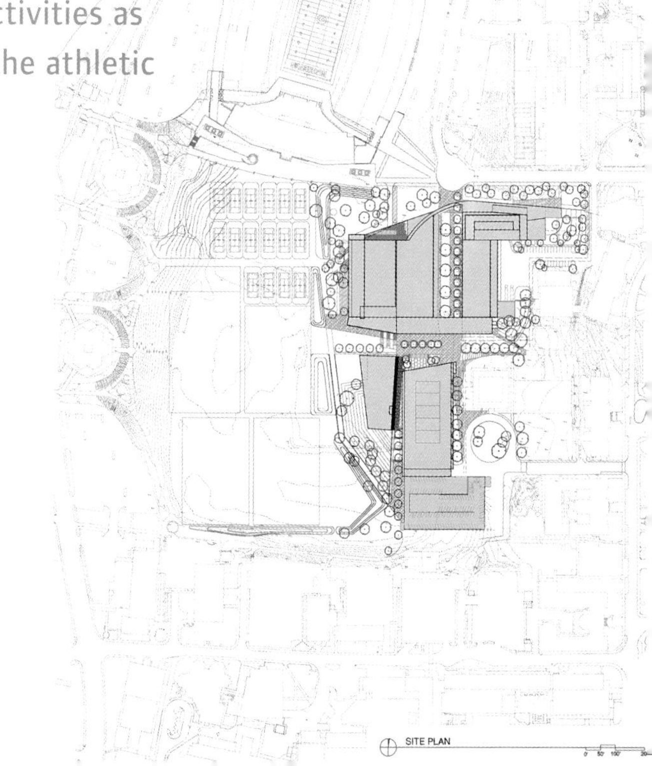

A "City of Sport"

STEALTH DOG HOUSE, SUCCESSFULLY BID ON IN CHARITY AUCTION BY VIDAL SASSOON AND SUGGESTED GROOMING FOR A STEALTH POODLE DWELLER.

In the central amenity hub, views extend across the plaza toward the Aquatic Center with its five water bodies. This hub has food service and administrative functions and other amenities, and steps down from the plaza main level to a dining court.

The running track/main circulation route has circumstantial pauses widening occasionally for views of the full athletic menu, yielding a variety of spatial/view episodes.

This project cemented the strong relationship I had with Curt Moody and his team, which led later to our collaboration on the National Museum of African American History and Culture in Washington, D.C.

THE AMPHITHEATER-LIKE TERRACED STEPS SET UP VIEWS TOWARD A PRESENTATION ZONE WHERE BARACK OBAMA SPOKE.

WITH CORY AND CURT AND HIS TEAM

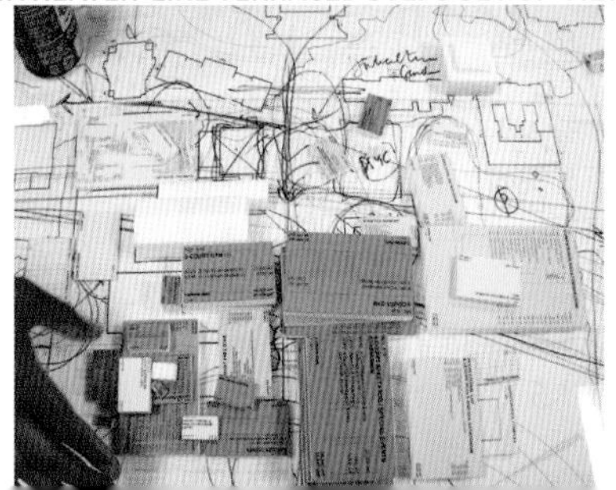

Four other water bodies—for training, pure recreation, and therapeutic treatments—are adjunct to the central Olympic-scaled competition pool.

KAROLE MAZEIKA JOINED US IN 1999 THROUGH A DESTINED SERIES OF EVENTS—STARTING WITH HER STUDIES AT UC DAVIS IN STRUCTURAL ENGINEERING. AS A STUDENT SHE WAS STRUCK BY THE SOCIAL SCIENCES AND HUMANITIES BUILDING THAT WE RECENTLY HAD COMPLETED ON THE CAMPUS. SHE DECIDED TO MOVE TO ALBUQUERQUE WITH THE INTENTION OF SWITCHING HER MAJOR TO ARCHITECTURE FROM ENGINEERING... AND SHE WAS DETERMINED TO WORK IN OUR STUDIO BECAUSE OF THE WAY THAT THE UC DAVIS BUILDING MOVED HER. SHE IMMEDIATELY DEVELOPED SOLID EMPATHY WITH EVERYONE IN THE STUDIO AND, WORKING AS A GRAD STUDENT, WAS SOON EQUIPPED WITH EXTRAORDINARY GRAPHIC SKILLS, COLLABORATING WITH ME TO INSTILL ATMOSPHERIC/STORYBOARD MAGIC IN OUR DIGITAL PROJECT IMAGES. SHE BECAME A SENIOR ASSOCIATE, BRINGING HER MAGIC TO THE STUDIO ON MANY PROJECTS—MOST NOTABLY THE TAIWAN NATIONAL PALACE MUSEUM SOUTHERN BRANCH.

HELICOPTER SKIING IN THE IDAHO SAWTOOTHS, WITH HADRIAN AND JASON—1999

The vast gym is reflective of the "Mighty Buckeye" Big 10 Conference powerhouse legacy.

SHADOW HOUSE

SANTA FE, NEW MEXICO 2000/02

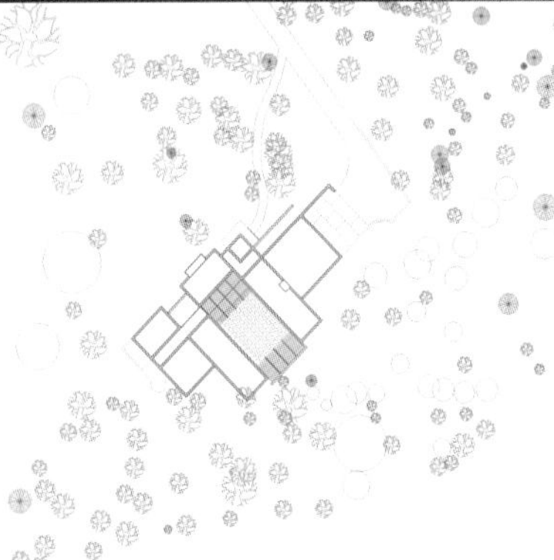

The house is organized around a sloping water courtyard. Recirculating water flows over ancient Chinese granite slabs salvaged from the Three Gorges Dam project—charging the living spaces of the house with dynamic reflected and refracted light phenomena and sound.

THE INN AT THE FRENCH LAUNDRY FOR THE LEGENDARY CHEF THOMAS KELLER, ACROSS THE ROAD FROM HIS FAMED RESTAURANT, IS AN AGGREGATION OF BUNGALOWS THAT ORIENT TO SEQUENTIAL COURTYARDS, WATER EVENTS, SPA TREATMENT AREAS, AND A MAJOR KITCHEN GARDEN FOR THE RESTAURANT.

INN AT THE FRENCH LAUNDRY, YOUNTVILLE, CA 2001

AN IMAGINED COMPOUND CURVATURE NET CLIPS THE TOPS OF THE SINGLE- AND TWO-STORY BUNGALOWS, SUGGESTING THAT THE ENTIRE COMPLEX IS SUBTRACTIVELY CARVED OUT OF ONE MONOLITH.

THE RESEARCH COLLAGE HADRIAN PREDOCK AND MY COLLABORATORS ON

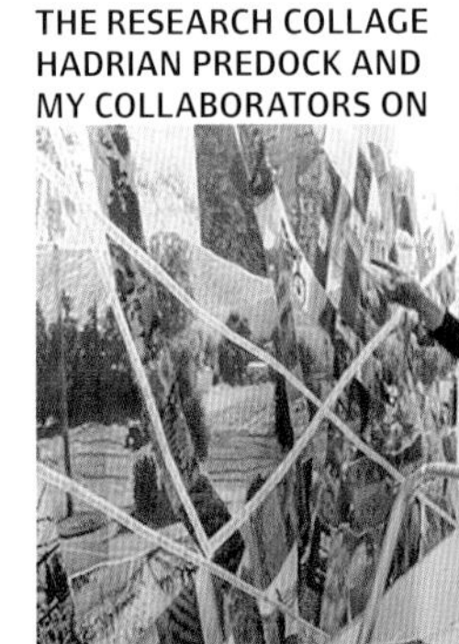

"Antoine Predock designs buildings that convey a sense of the primordial. Low-lying and earth-toned, glimpsed only partially durin a long approach through the enveloping pines [Predock] recognizes both the horizontality of the surrounding mesas and the local architectural vernacular. But instead of a quaint carved wood door hung with dried peppers, the entrance path leads to a tall, box-shaped tower clad in cast concrete."

Peter Haldeman, "The House of Shadows," *Architectural Digest*, May 200

PHASE WITH JOHN FRANE, THIS PROJECT.

THE COLLAGE MAPS AND SCORES THE JUXTAPOSITIONS OF FOOD CULTIVATION AND PREPARATION AMIDST NAPA VALLEY IMAGERY AND DWELLING POSSIBILITIES, EVOKING THE DEEP GEOLOGIC TIME AND CULTURAL STRATA OF THE SITE. THE LINEAR TEXT TRAJECTORIES QUOTE PASSAGES FROM NOTABLE AUTHORS AND POETS THAT RELATE TO THE PLACE.

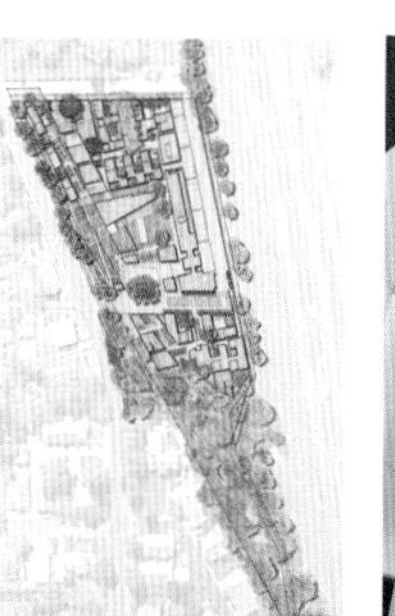

The copper "chainmail" mesh window covering—in dialogue with the copper wall across the courtyard.

Entry chamber of light—a giant glass prism mediating light from the sky.

OUR 2000 CHRISTMAS CARD WITH CLOSE TO 40 COLLEAGUES ABOVE—AND ASSOCIATES JOSE, PAUL, GRAHAM, GEOFF, REGGIE, CHRISTINE, KAROLE, KENJI, CORY, AND STUART BELOW. "IT TAKES A TEAM!"

MOTORHEAD SKOSHI ON MY PARIS-TO-ISTANBUL LAMBRETTA

Jewel-box office lined in natural wood and the jewels contained.

Tatami alcove with view slot to the garden—an homage to Ryoan-ji in Kyoto.

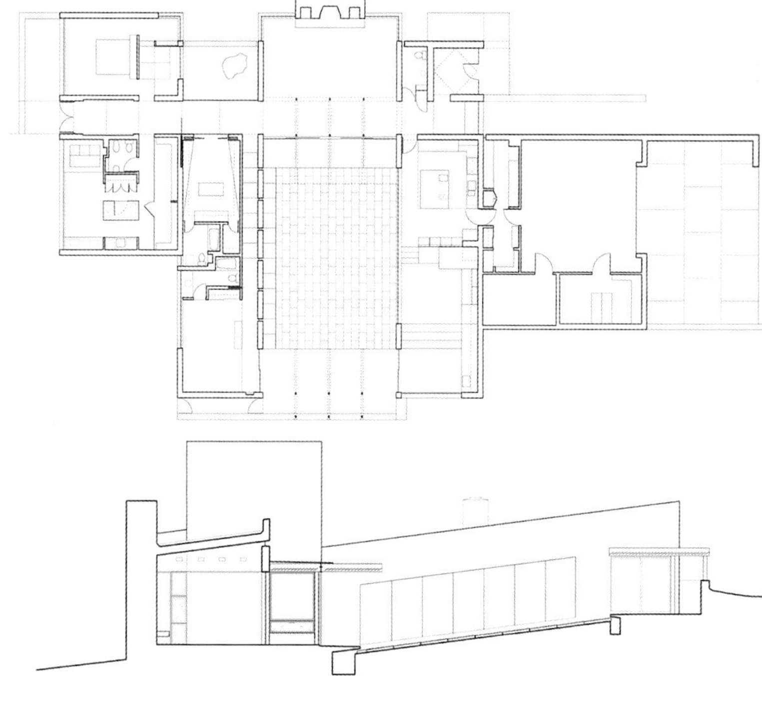

THE NEW WORLD OF SPORTBIKES IN THE 12TH STREET STUDIO DRIVEWAY.

SANDIA MOUNTAIN MULTIPLE PERSONALITIES FROM OUR WESTSIDE STUDIO.

2004 ARCHITECTURAL DESIGN AWARDS

THE AMERICAN INSTITUTE OF ARCHITECTS

HONOR AWARD

SHADOW HOUSE

ANTOINE PREDOCK ARCHITECT

The New Mexico Chapter of
The American Institute of Architects
is proud to present the 2003
Honor Award
to

Antoine Predock Architect
for the
Shadow House

HONOR AWARD

SHADOW HOUSE

Glass box shower, and soapstone tub with reclining profile matching Le Corbusier's chaise lounge beyond.

DIVING IN BORA BORA WITH CONSTANCE IN 2002. SCHOOLS OF MANTAS AND WHITE TIPPED SHARK FEEDING FRENZIES.

Hunkered into the rolling hillside with views toward the Jemez Mountains.

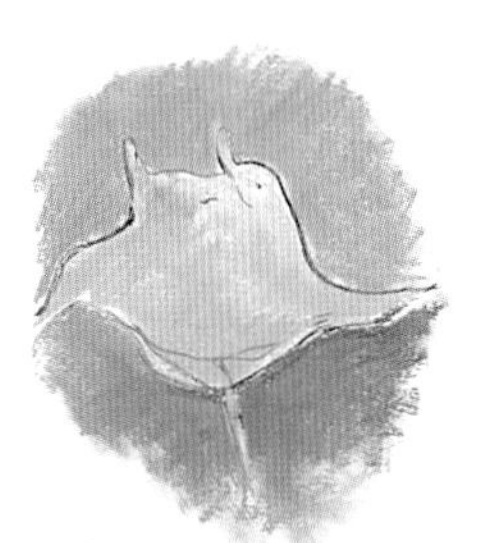

THEN FAKARAVA IN THE TUAMOTO ARCHIPELAGO.

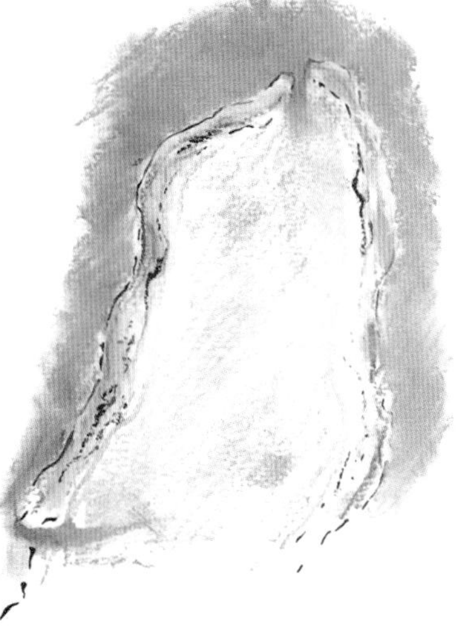

TACOMA ART MUSEUM

TACOMA, WASHINGTON 2000/03

The arrival plaza extending to the left of the overall view was intended to be protected by a carbon-fiber-reinforced triangular canopy to create a major gathering area, out of the omnipresent rain. The overall material stratification of the museum moves from the massive concrete supporting legs; to mill-finish stainless steel skin, in the spirit of the rugged vernacular of the Port of Tacoma; to the glass of the two-story lobby, with its panoramic views toward Mt. Rainier, the waterway, and the Port of Tacoma.

"... Predock, who best captures the region's mutable light in the connections he offers to the outdoors and in his choreography of movement. Like a director working with an actor, he captures and amplifies the Northwest's changeable oyster sky."

Sheri Olson, AIA, *Architectural Record*, August 2003

Upper level public spaces open to views of Mt. Rainier

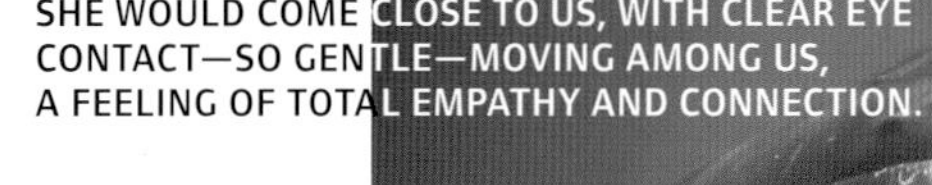

A FEMALE ATLANTIC HUMPBACK IN THE SILVER BANK OFF THE DOMINICAN REPUBLIC—SHE WOULD COME CLOSE TO US, WITH CLEAR EYE CONTACT—SO GENTLE—MOVING AMONG US, A FEELING OF TOTAL EMPATHY AND CONNECTION.

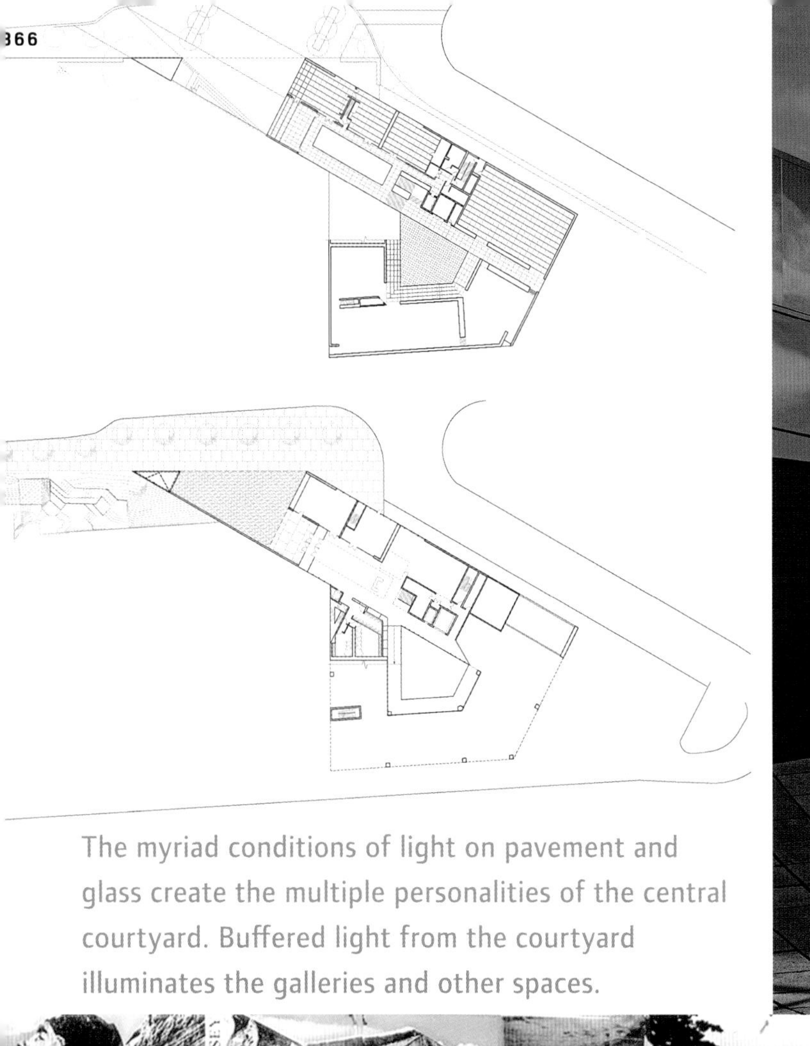

The myriad conditions of light on pavement and glass create the multiple personalities of the central courtyard. Buffered light from the courtyard illuminates the galleries and other spaces.

STARTING WITH A RESEARCH COLLAGE, ASSISTED BY SAM AND KIRA, THEN A CLAY MODEL, AND ON TO LARGER, MORE-DETAILED MODELS, AND A STUDY MODEL OF

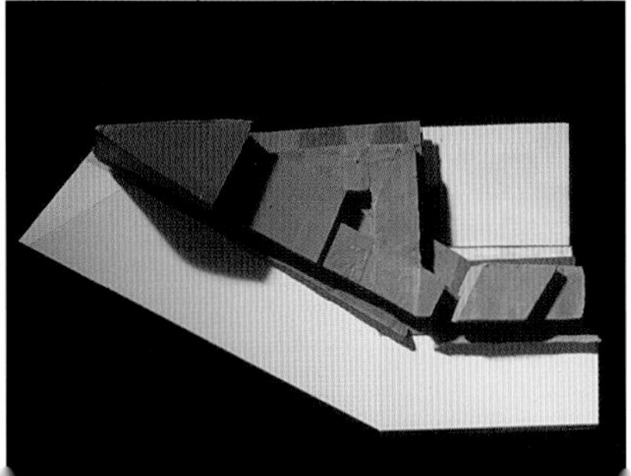

PROJECT TEAM—PAUL, MAIA PARIKH, DERRICK BALLARD, ROSS TISDALE, JARROD ARELLANO, STUART BLAKLEY, DEVENDRA CONTRACTOR, AND DEAN COWDREY.

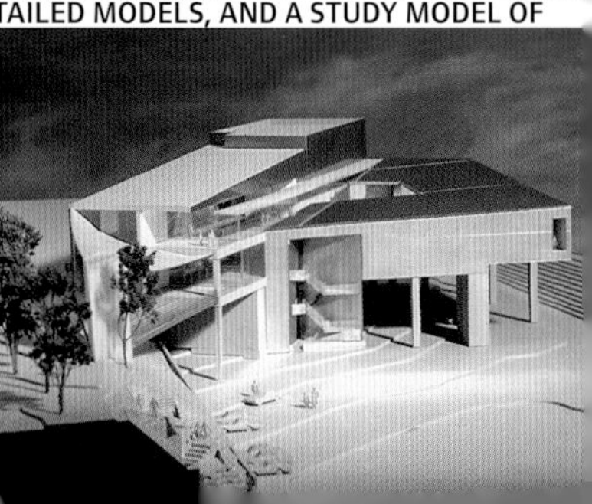

THE CENTRAL COURTYARD.

"Predock conceived of a space that centered on a stone garden, allowing light and air to fill the core of the building. Mirrored glass would be positioned around the stone garden at the end of a central hallway that joined the lobby and museum entrance with the galleries. The mirrored glass would reflect both the stone garden and the natural panoramas, including Mt. Rainier, creating an infinite reflecting vista in the core of the building."

Caitlin Condell, "An Infinite Reflecting Vista," *CooperHewitt.org*, October 10, 2020

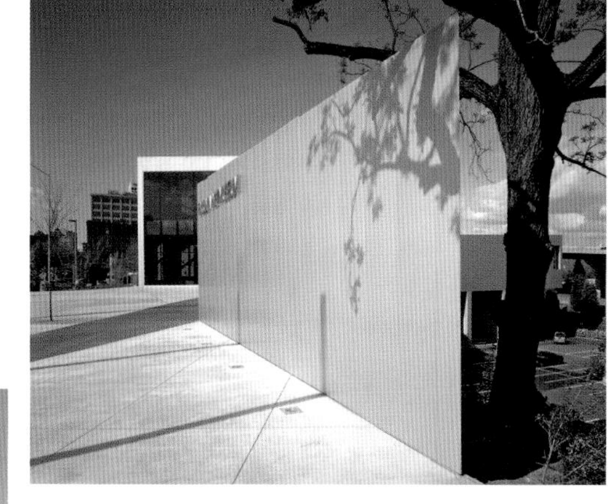

FLYING FROM LA TO SEATTLE, THE MOUNTAIN IS IN YOUR FACE.

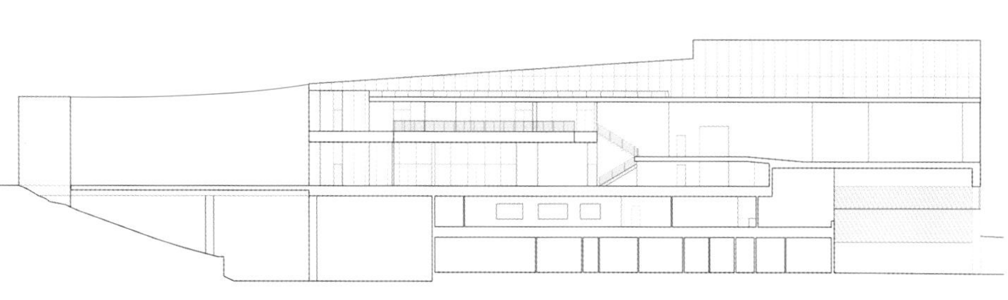

Mt. Rainier, Tahoma in the language of the indigenous Puyallup People, anchors Tacoma and select views from within the museum.

THE WONDERFUL ENERGY MACHINE, REGINA HARRIS, OUR OFFICE MANAGER FOR DECADES, GRAHAM HOGAN, A SUPER TALENTED YOUNG INTERN WHO EVOLVED INTO A MAJOR DESIGN/PROJECT MANAGEMENT ROLE... AND THE EVER-PRESENT PAUL FEHLAU.

REGINA HARRIS BEGAN WORKING FOR THE STUDIO AS A BOOKKEEPER IN 1990 AND THROUGH HER 17-YEAR TENURE SHE GREW TO BECOME THE MANAGING ASSOCIATE. REGGIE'S JOB TITLES NEVER DID JUSTICE TO THE MANY JOBS AND ROLES SHE FULFILLED DURING HER TENURE. SHE WORKED TIRELESSLY BEHIND THE SCENES TO MAKE SURE THE TEAM AND I HAD EVERYTHING WE NEEDED DURING THE BUSIEST TWO DECADES IN THE STUDIO'S HISTORY. EVERYTHING FROM MAKING SURE PAYROLL AND BILLING MOVED ALONG LIKE CLOCKWORK TO MAKING SURE THE TEAM WAS WELL FED DURING COMPETITION CHARRETTES TO ARRANGING TRAVEL FOR THE STAFF TO ORGANIZING THE ANNUAL HOLIDAY PARTY—NO TASK WAS TOO BIG OR SMALL.

ROBERT HOAG RAWLINGS PUBLIC LIBRARY

PUEBLO, COLORADO 2000/03

Sited on the higher ground to the west in Pueblo, the views from reading areas are omni-directional—Pike's Peak, the Arkansas River Valley, the Spanish Peaks, the early industrial structures, and the old historic center. At the fork of two streets, one reading area spans the road with a trellised deck at the end. The propeller-like plan defines different zones—kids library, primary reading areas, administration, and a "Newseum" Gallery on top. The dark copper patination relates to the now-defunct steel mills in the distance.

TRIP TO THAILAND IN 2000—SKETCHING THE ROYAL PALACE IN BANGKOK, THE RECLINING BUDDHA IN AYUTTHAYA, THEN CHIANG MAI AND PHUKET.

FROM THAILAND TO CAMBODIA... ANGKOR WAT SKETCHING WITH AN AUDIENCE.

Pueblo Colorado's history translated to collage—tracking geologic, indigenous, and cultural deep time paralleling the recording of history: cave paintings, Assyrian tablets, Rosetta Stone... infinite memory.

AYON

BICYCLING IN SIEM REAP, AND THE FLOATING VILLAGE ON TONLE SAP, CAMBODIA

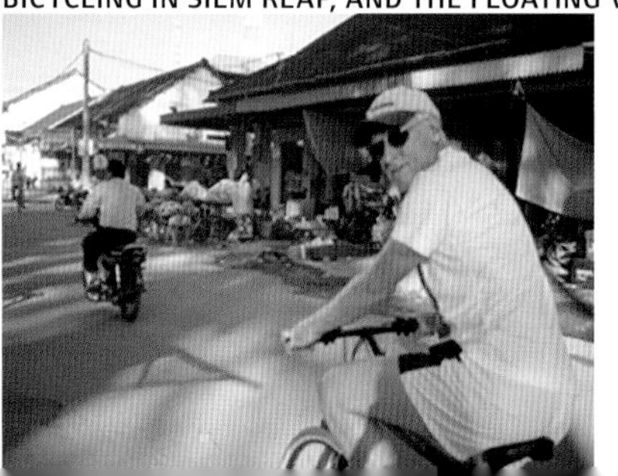

The entry approach into the courtyard with a grid of fruit trees—a trellised arcade and linear pool leads to the main entry just below the stair tower.

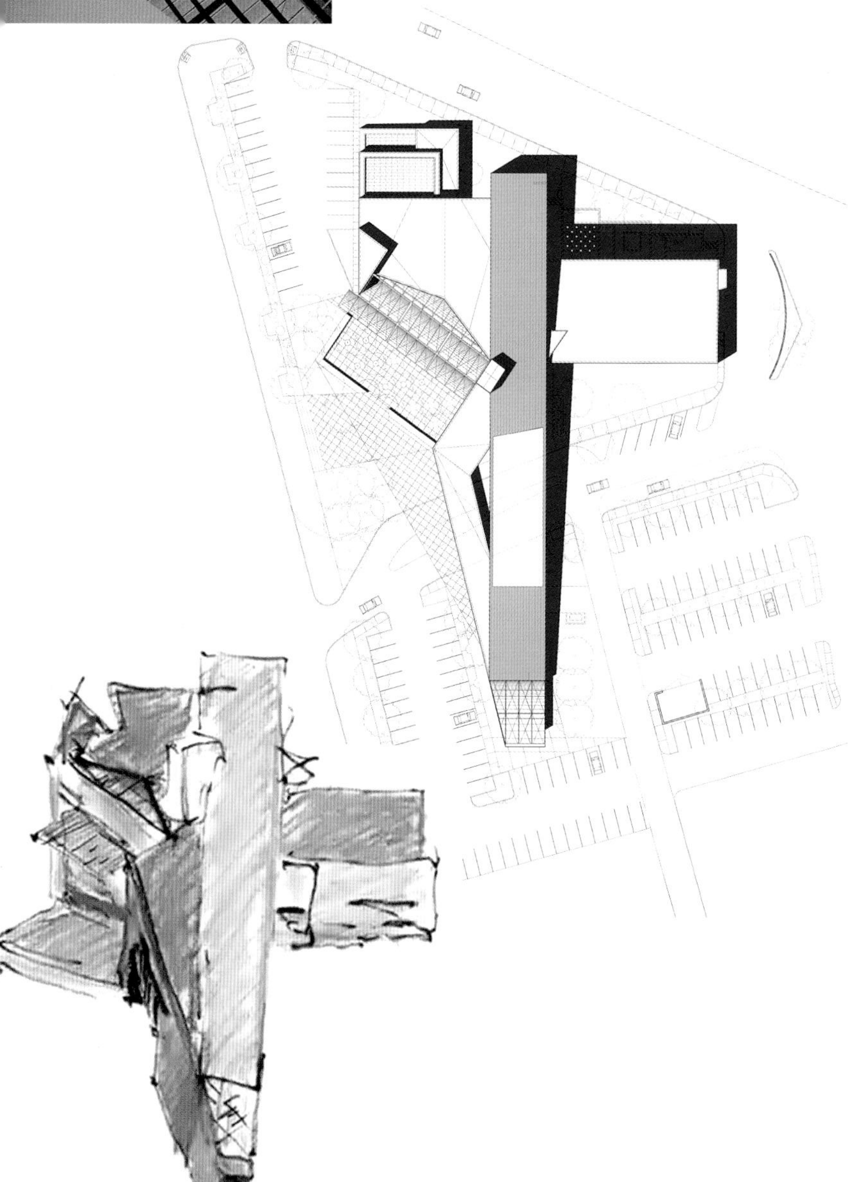

WITH THE INSPIRING CLIENT GLENN BALLANTYNE

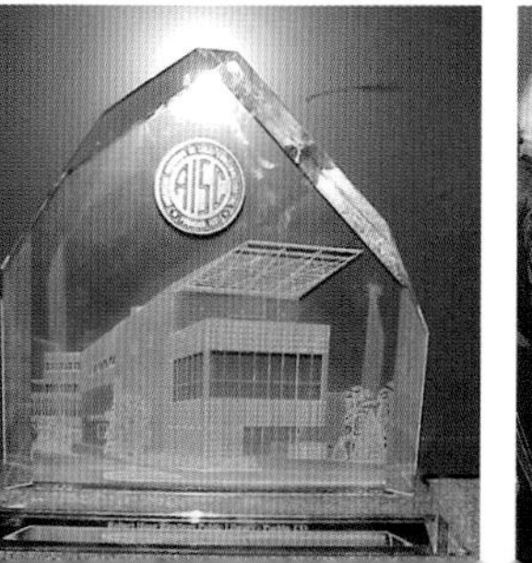

RAWLINGS NEWSEUM ON THE UPPER LEVEL

BRANDENBURG GATE, BERLIN TRIP 2000

AUSTIN CITY HALL AND PUBLIC PLAZA

AUSTIN, TEXAS 2000/04

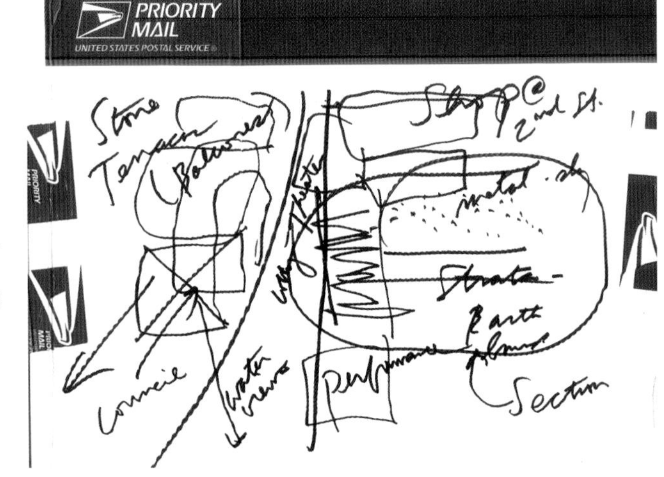

Radically different geographically from other parts of Texas, the Hill Country around Austin is laced with water courses with terraced limestone embankments. The Spanish referred to those river edge conditions as "balcones." They became an inspiration for the stratified local limestone base of City Hall, stepping down toward the shore of Lady Bird Lake, and capped by a folding copper roof that follows the sectional profile of the building.

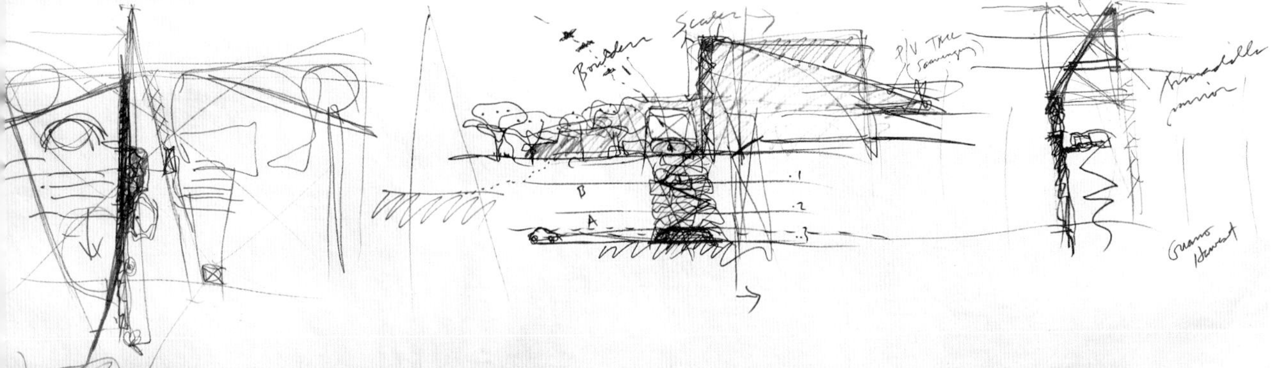

WITH PAUL AND OUR AUSTIN COLLEAGUE JUAN COTERA

On the Second Street side, a copper tail blasts out, continuing the converging geometry of the interior copper lining of the lobby. A local comment is often "What the hell is that thing?" My retort, with a strong Texas accent, is, "*It's a armadillo tail.*" Pulling that off is one of the great achievements of my career, second only to having an image of one of my buildings featured on the Canadian $10 note.

Austin, the city of music, is acknowledged by a performance platform with bleacher-like seating beneath a photovoltaic-embedded glass trellis, harnessing energy to match the performances.

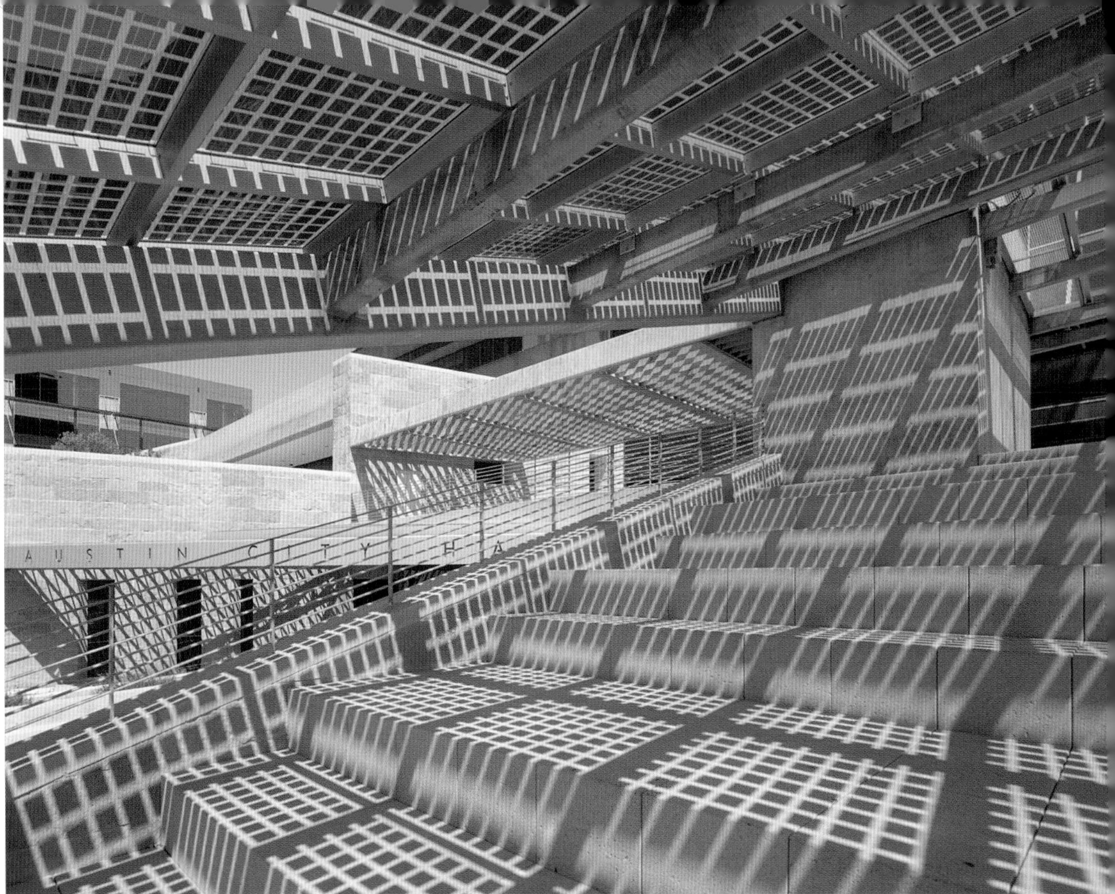

Across the shaded main entry from the stepped bleacher seating on the lake side and the Public Plaza are the stepping executive offices with the council chamber below.

Multilevel parking below is accessed by a grand staircase passing a water-coated rugged limestone wall, affirming the connection to the "balcones" and watersheds of the "Silicon Hills."

RESEARCH FIELD TRIP TO THE HILL COUNTRY "SILICON HILLS"—RIVER, LIMESTONE STRATA, WATERFALLS—IN THE BUS WITH KIRA, LIZ, NATHAN, AND ELEANOR.

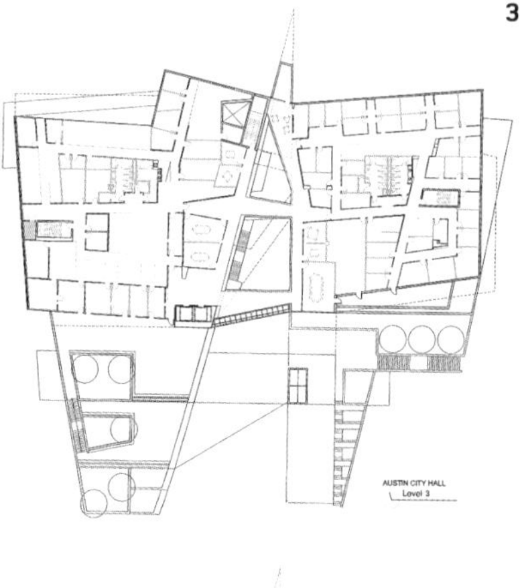

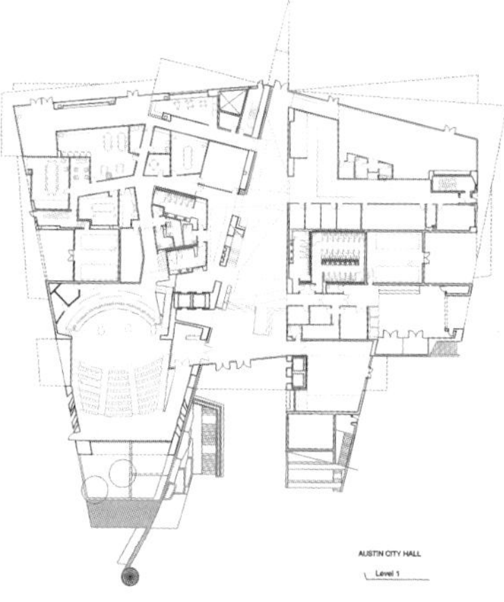

Concrete bridges span the tapering lobby fissure. The copper ceiling wraps down to land on the "balcones" limestone base.

"His architecture bonds our modern world of science and technology with a mythic past revealing dimensions of existence man does not even know he has lost. A search for truth pervades his work, so that tradition is both honored and reinvented. Modern life is celebrated in steel, glass and concrete, these being combined with natural materials in an expressive palette, that like his research, knows no boundaries. Avoiding the egocentricity of signature architecture, his buildings use signs and symbols to communicate at every level, embracing human concerns with candor and generosity. In an architecture of subtle power and undoubted grandeur, Predock's gift to the world is to invest his buildings with a poetry born of their purpose and place in the landscape."

Geoffrey Baker, *Antoine Predock*, Academy Editions, 1997

IN 2003 A YOUNG GRADUATE STUDENT, VEREE PARKER (NOW VEREE SIMONS), CAME TO WORK WITH US ON A FLOW OF PROJECTS—WITH A CRITICAL ROLE ON THE CANADIAN MUSEUM FOR HUMAN RIGHTS. THROUGH THE YEARS AS SHE MATURED AS AN ARCHITECT IT BECAME CLEAR THAT SHE WILL JOIN PAUL AS A FUTURE LEADER OF THE STUDIO. SHE IS RELENTLESS IN HER PROBLEM SOLVING ABILITIES IN DESIGN PHASES AS WELL AS BOOTS ON THE GROUND CONSTRUCTION OBSERVATION. I'M PROUD THAT PRINCIPALS VEREE SIMONS AND PAUL FEHLAU WILL VENTURE FORTH DEEP INTO THE 21ST CENTURY.

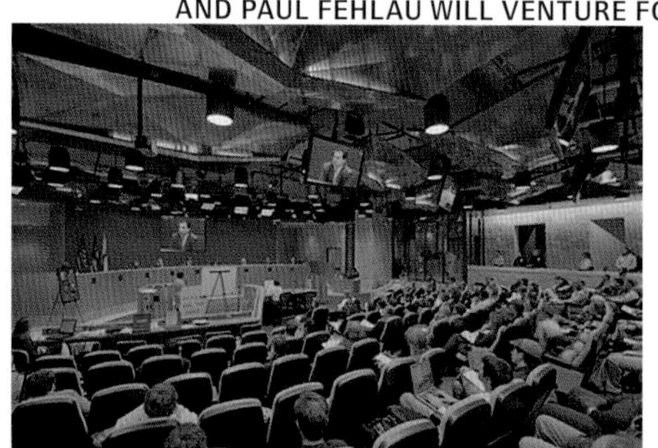

"Predock's body of work and his inventive use of materials seem to owe allegiance to European antecedents. However, his architecture is like America—expansive, inclusive, and characterized by bold invention."

Bill Lacy, Director Architecture and Design program of the National Endowment for the Arts and president of the State University of New York at Purchase

FOUR-FOOT-TALL PRESENTATION MODEL TO THE CITY COUNCIL WITH INNER LINING OF COPPER CONTINUING TO A PRECISE SHARP POINT OVER THE STREET. IN MY ENTHUSIASM DURING THE PRESENTATION, I WAS BENDING DOWN TO ILLUSTRATE A POINT ABOUT THE MODEL AND WAS SPEARED IN THE CHEEK BY THE COPPER POINT. AS WITH ALL SHAVING CUTS, THE FACE BLEEDS PROFUSELY, SO AS I MOPPED UP THE BLOOD WITH A KLEENEX, KEEPING MY COMPOSURE I SAID, "SEE, YOUR ARCHITECT WILL BLEED FOR YOU." IT WORKED, THE PROJECT RECEIVED UNANIMOUS COUNCIL APPROVAL, THAT BEING A RARITY IN AUSTIN'S "TERMINAL DEMOCRACY."

The City Hall fronts the lake and the South 1st Street Bridge. Just upstream is the Congress Street Bridge, home to the legendary Austin summer Bat Flight.

The U.S. Green Building Council

hereby certifies that

Austin City Hall and Public Plaza

Austin, Texas

has successfully met the sustainable building design and performance standards required for the following level of certification under the Leadership in Energy and Environmental Design (LEED®) Green Building Rating System

LEED®-NC v2 Gold

LEED

2006

Kevin Hydes, Chairman

S. Richard Fedrizzi, President, CEO and Founding Chairman

DOUDNA FINE ARTS CENTER

EASTERN ILLINOIS UNIVERSITY
CHARLESTON, ILLINOIS 2000/07

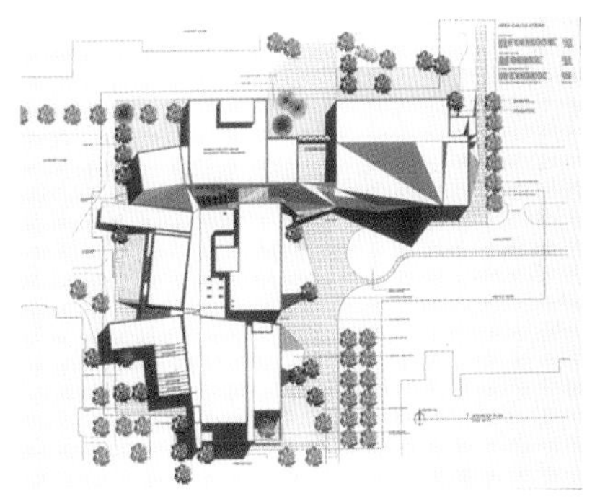

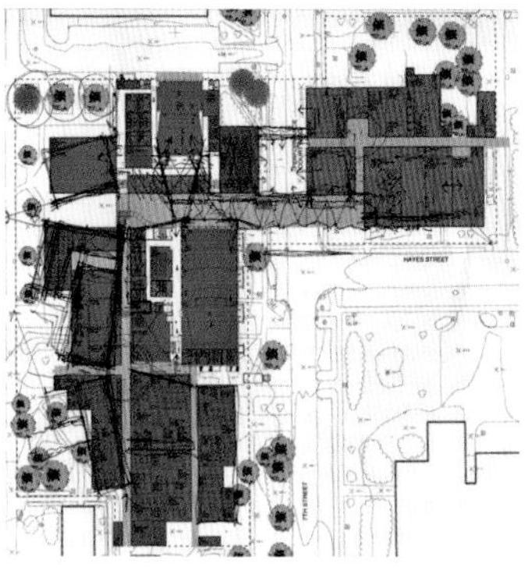

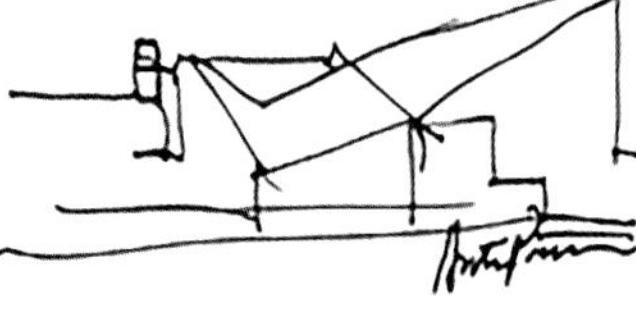

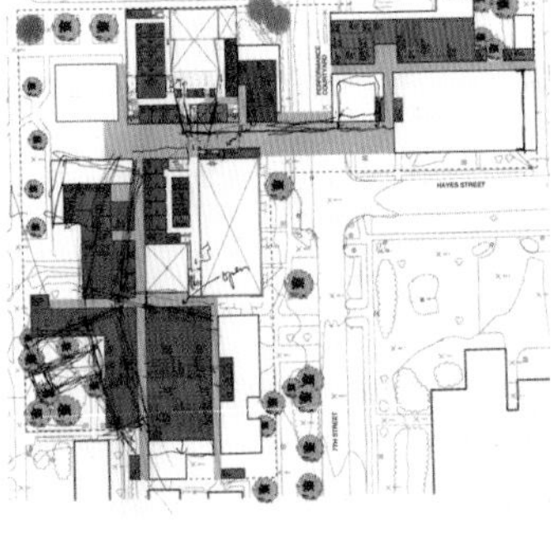

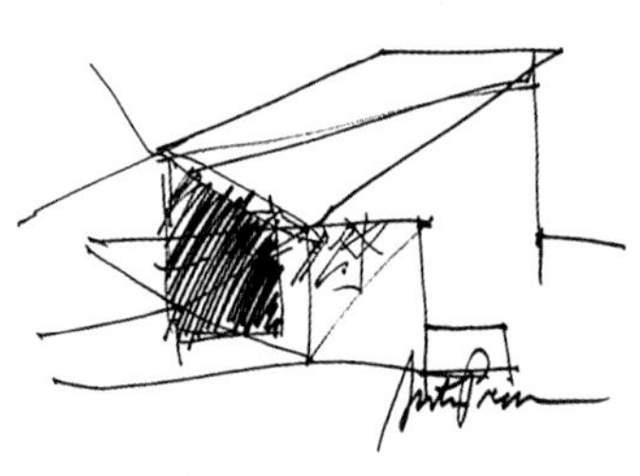

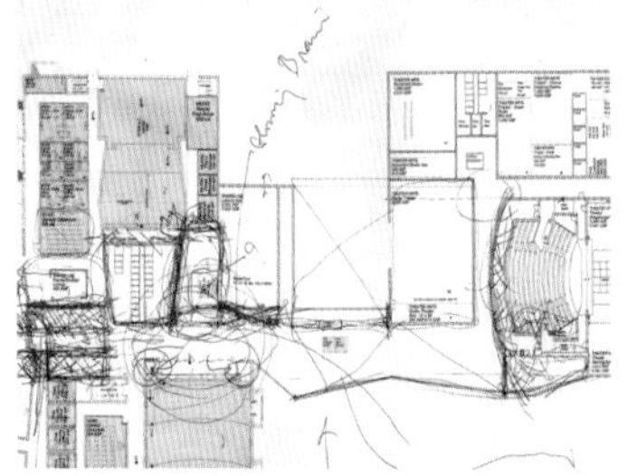

9/11/2001 WAS ON TUESDAY AND ON THE FRIDAY OF THAT WEEK, A MAJOR PROJECT PRESENTATION TO THE UNIVERSITY HAD LONG SINCE BEEN SCHEDULED. THE MODEL, IN ITS CRATE, HAD ALREADY BEEN SHIPPED TO CHARLESTON, ILLINOIS. I HAD TO MAKE THE PRESENTATION, TAKING FLIGHTS FROM ALBUQUERQUE THROUGH NEAR-DESERTED AIRPORTS (I REMEMBER WOODY HARRELSON KEEPING US DISTRACTED IN A SECURITY LINE AT DFW). THE PRESENTATION HAPPENED AND I BEGAN BY PLACING A TINY AMERICAN FLAG ON A TOOTHPICK ON THE APEX OF THE MODEL.

From the apex of the Proscenium Theater stage house, a volumetrically varied linear Concourse, copper-clad on the exterior, guides off-campus arrival on one end to the Quad on the other—and along the way, an episodic ride past and through the varied fine arts components. This crystalline sequence at the intersection of 7th and Hayes Street forms a new Campus arrival point/gateway that unifies the arts while connecting to the community—a Concourse of celebration and encounter that sequentially evolves, folds, and merges one moment to the next, interweaving exhibits, critiques, rehearsals, performances, and concerts.

The concourse procession begins with the copper fronted Proscenium Theater entry, then past the translucent glowing Studio Theater and Sculpture Garden, the "Hall of Mirrors" foreground to the Concert Hall, Recital Hall, Lecture Hall, upper-level Faculty Offices, Art and Music School entries, the "Red House," and then the Campus Quad.

Enveloped in facets of clear, translucent, mirrored, and pigmented glass... passing through a kaleidoscope.

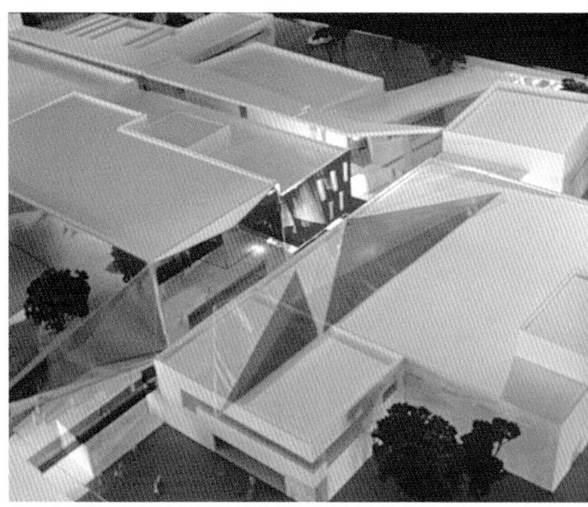

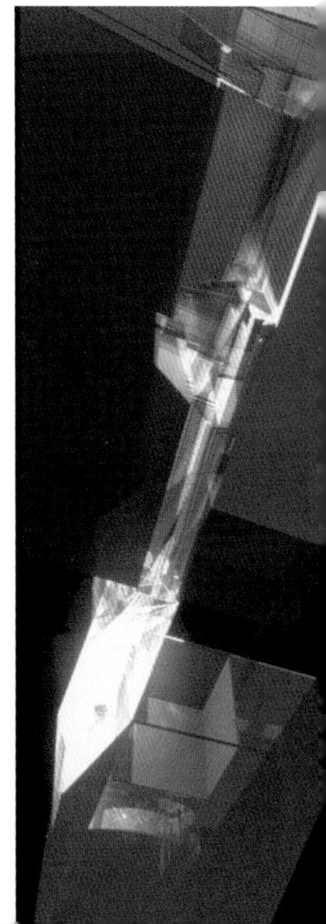

DEAN JEFFERY LYNCH WAS AN INSPIRATIONAL COLLABORATOR THROUGHOUT THE PROJECT.

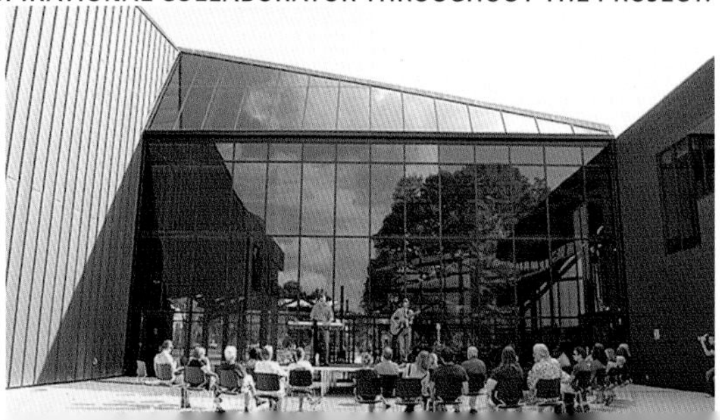

The Recital Hall and Rehearsal Hall in action, the Concert Hall, and the Studio Theater with its catwalk grid and movable seating creating many theatrical and improvisational possibilities—these spaces surround the Hall of Mirrors. The lightwell/Gallery of the Art Department flows laterally off the concourse.

Mavis Staples, American icon of R&B and Gospel, delivering the first performance in the new Center. Such a warm, approachable superstar, she honored me with my name in one of her lyrics.

THE EARLY POST-9/11 YEARS WERE WHEN ASIAN PROJECTS BEGAN TO BE A POSSIBILITY FOR US, AND THAT TRAVEL MADE POSSIBLE SCUBA DIVING TRIPS TO THE GREAT BARRIER REEF WITH CONSTANCE, AND LECTURES IN SYDNEY AND PERTH. BRUCE CHATWIN'S *THE SONGLINES* WAS REVELATORY IN TRYING TO UNDERSTAND AND APPRECIATE AUSTRALIAN ABORIGINAL COSMOLOGY.

THE COLLAGE EXCAVATES THE SITE OF IMAGINATION—MERGING DEEP TIME WITH REGIONAL AND CAMPUS CULTURE. STAR ALUMNI LIKE JOHN MALKOVICH AND JOAN ALLEN JOIN IMAGES OF THEATER/PERFORMANCE HISTORY.

Foreground to the music school entry off the Concourse celebrates Jimi Hendrix, a favorite of Dean Lynch. This glowing "Red House" with floor and ceiling of integrally colored reflective glass punctuates the campus Quad end of the Concourse progression.

PARTY TIME IN THE "RED HOUSE" ON THE OPENING NIGHT OF THE DOUDNA FINE ARTS CENTER! DEAN LYNCH, WITH THE RED SNEAKERS, CONSTANCE AND STACIA, AND MY STUDIO PROJECT ARCHITECT/MANAGER JOSÉ SANCHEZ. BESIDES BEING AN OBVIOUS SPECIAL OCCASION CELEBRATORY SPACE, IT IS A GREAT PLACE FOR LOUNGING AND SELFIES.

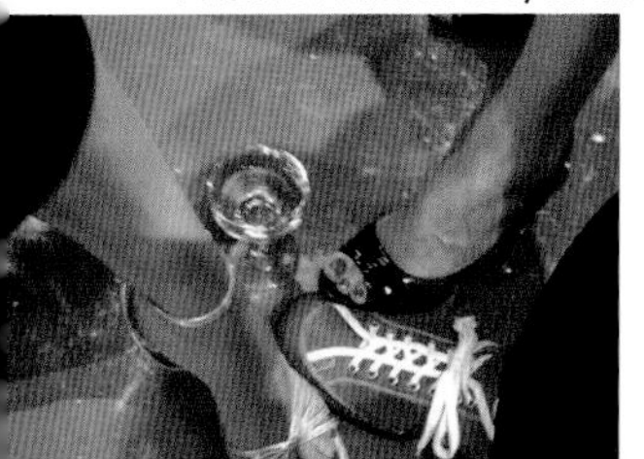

On the campus Quad side of the Fine Arts Center—to the right of the Concourse entry passage, bleacher seating descends from the music school with its classrooms, practice rooms, and administrative offices.

A GSA DESIGN COMPETITION THAT WE WON—CLOSE TO THE MEXICO BORDER. THE PUBLIC SPACE BETWEEN THE SPLIT SECTIONS OF THE COURTHOUSE AIMS VIEWS TOWARD

UNITED STATES FEDERAL COURTHOUSE
LAS CRUCES, NM 2002/09

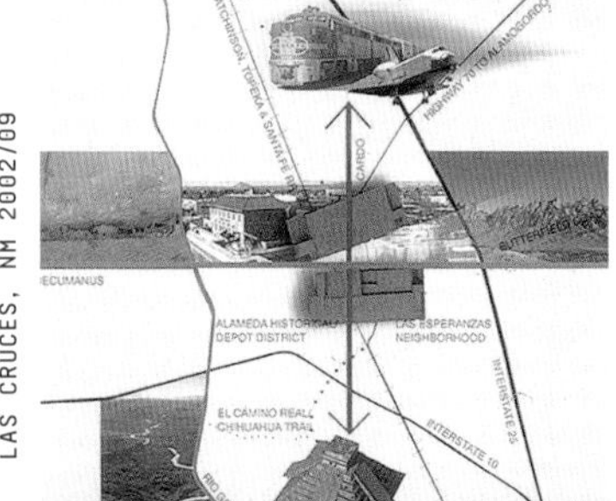

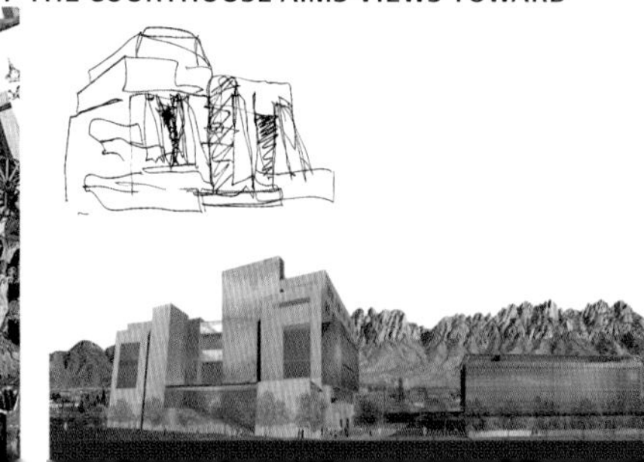

THE ORGAN MOUNTAINS. DIAGRAM OF THIS IMPORTANT CROSSROADS SITE, THEN THE COLLAGE, SKETCHES, CLAY MODEL, DRAWINGS, THEN CONSTRUCTION.

SCHOOL OF ARCHITECTURE GEORGE PEARL HALL

UNIVERSITY OF NEW MEXICO ALBUQUERQUE, NEW MEXICO 2000/08

In 1954 I drove my 1940 Plymouth from Missouri, following Highway 66, to Albuquerque to study engineering. Then, in 2000, I won the design competition for the new School of Architecture, sited on Highway 66 (a.k.a. Central Avenue). The Architecture School is the only building on Campus where the lights are on all night.

MAPPING THE DAILY LIFE OF THE STUDENTS.

GIANT PROJECTION SURFACE FLANKS THE ENTRY WITH A SLIDE OF ME ON MY VINCENT BLACK SHADOW—*BEYOND THUNDERDOME* WAS THE OPENING FILM PROJECTED FROM THE BLEACHER TERRACE.

"Instead of a monotonous outer façade facing both parking lot and street, the five-story façade consists of alternating volumes of earth-tone concrete and glazing, the indentations creating ever different perspectives for passerby. The earth-tone coloring of the concrete façade does refer to the adobe architecture of the rest of the campus; however that is where similarities cease. The hard edges and generous glazing of the surfaces have more in common with Louis Kahn than with Navajo dwellings."

Stanley Collyer, "A New Front," *Competitions*, Fall 2008

DURING A PHOTOSHOOT FOR *META MAGAZINE* I POSED ON MY ZERO FXS ELECTRIC MOTORCYCLE IN FRONT OF THE GREAT WALL AND THEN POPPED IN TO CONGRATULATE NEW GRADUATES—PASSING PROFESSOR NORA WENDL ON THE WAY.

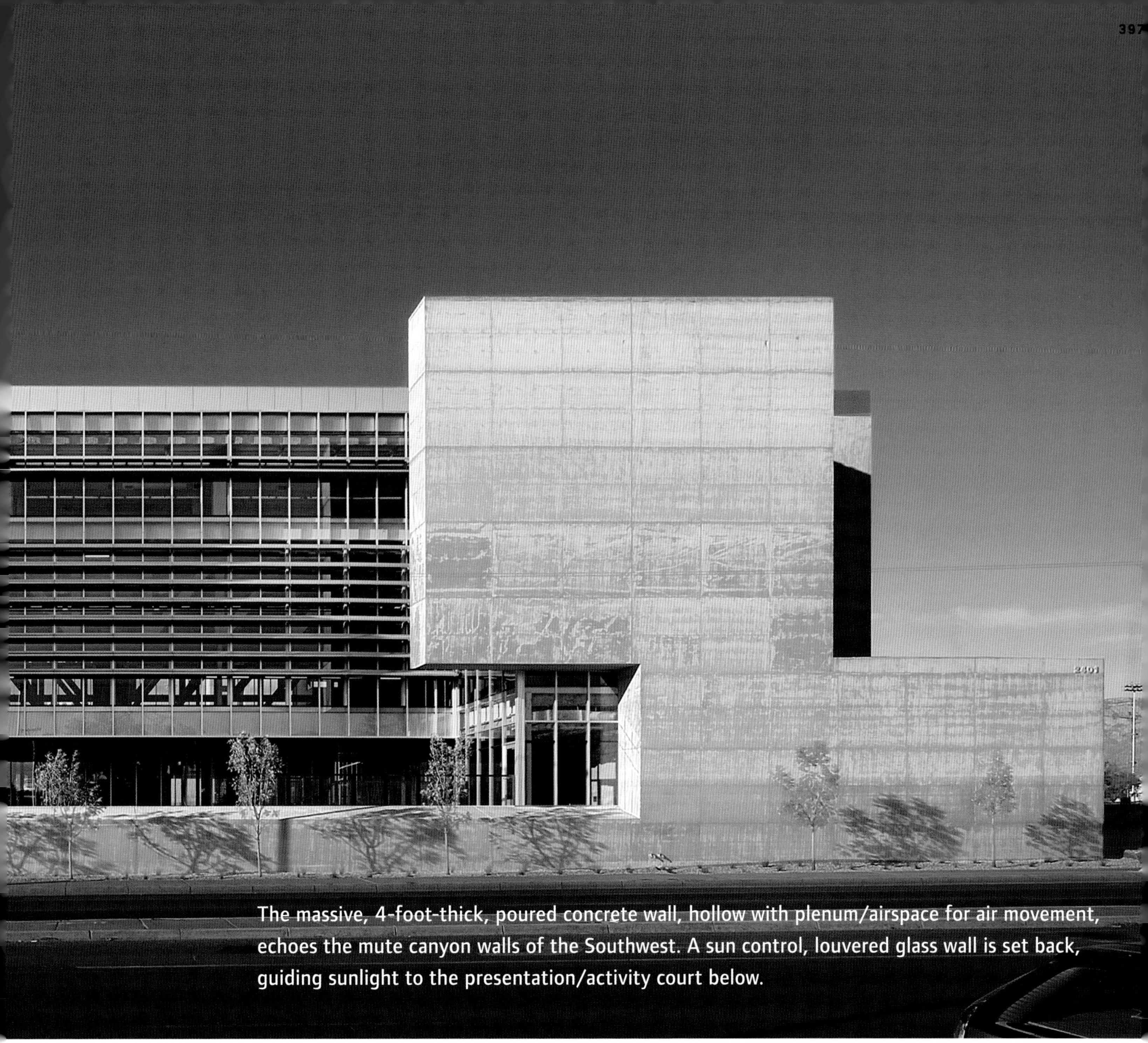

The massive, 4-foot-thick, poured concrete wall, hollow with plenum/airspace for air movement, echoes the mute canyon walls of the Southwest. A sun control, louvered glass wall is set back, guiding sunlight to the presentation/activity court below.

"Unlike the neighborhood's tarted-up restaurants and motels, it does nothing to call attention to itself. It's as big, as timeless, and as self-assured as a geological feature, like the impressive La Bajada escarpment between here and Santa Fe."

Lawrence Biemiller, "At the U. of New Mexico, A Predock Building Worth the Wait," *The Chronicle of Higher Education*, October 1, 2008

2001 LECTURE IN JAKARTA, INDONESIA, THEN JAVA, VISITING PRAMBANAN TEMPLE AND THE PHENOMENAL BOROBURDUR. THEN ON TO ULUWATU TEMPLE IN BALI WITH THIEVING MONKEYS AND A LEGENDARY SURF BREAK BELOW THE CLIFF.

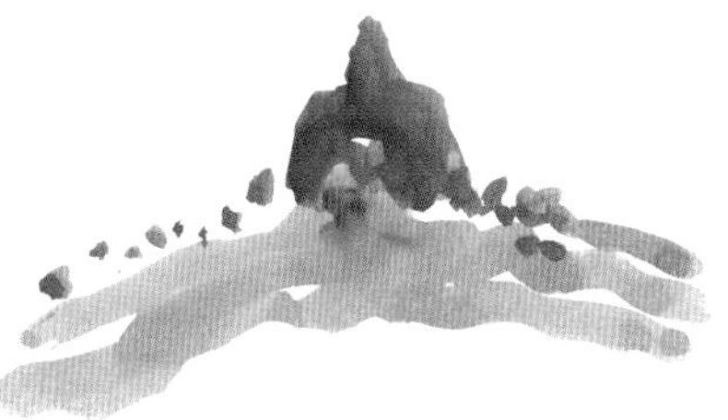

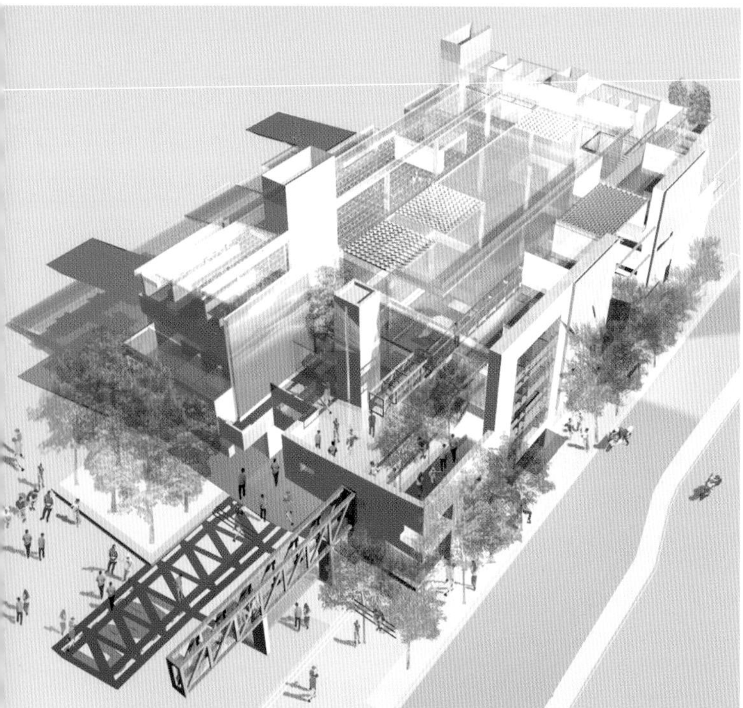

The vertical layering of the building goes from the sunken presentation court level up to administration: the Larry and Dorothy Rainosek Gallery, Critique Bridge, and Garcia Family Lecture Hall; undergraduate classrooms and studios; then graduate and landscape architecture studios; and at the highest level, the Fine Arts Library. Classrooms and seminar rooms are scattered throughout.

With structural, mechanical, and electrical systems exposed, it becomes a teaching machine—a pedagogical three-ring circus with multidirectional views of the School's activities. The Crit Bridge as the central focus is the presentation/review heartbeat. Below the Crit Bridge is a protected presentation courtyard for models of all scales, major installation pieces, and post-charrette partying.

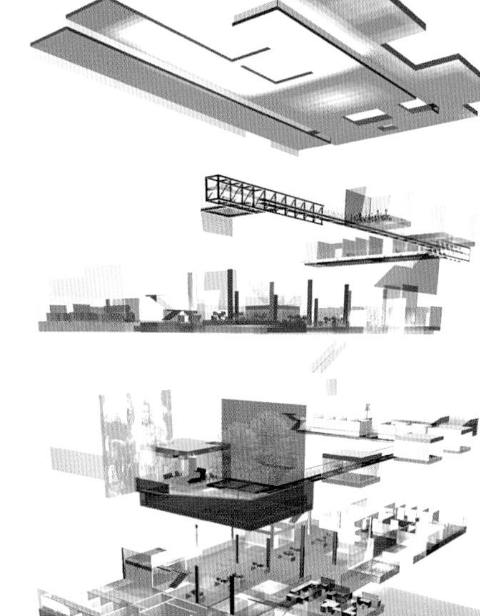

"Predock has crafted an open, unified space, with studios and critique space organized around a three-story well. Balconies, stairs, and a bridge encourage what Predock calls 'visual eavesdropping' fostering social interaction and an environment in which students can learn from instructors and each other."

Katie Gerfen, *Architect*, November 2008

Transparency from studio levels into Crit Bridge below ... showing the late Prof. Kramer Woodard—a much missed design conscience of the School

SPYING ON STUDENTS AND PROFESSOR GEOFF ADAMS, ONE OF MY STUDIO'S MANY ALUMNI THAT HAVE TAUGHT AT UNM.

THE INAUGURAL RAINOSEK GALLERY EXHIBITION SHOWED OUR WORK, MY SKETCHES, AND THE COLLAGES SUSPENDED VERTICALLY.

OCCUPIED IN THE FALL OF 2008 JUST AT THE TIME OF THE PRESIDENTIAL ELECTION. I TOOK STUDENTS TO VOTE IN MY HONDA VAN. IT HAPPENED EVERY TWO YEARS, INCLUDING THE MIDTERMS, UNTIL COVID HELL DESCENDED.

"In fact, the building is a kind of monument to openness. You can see it in the way the concrete walls on the main façade pull apart to reveal the glass within, and in the way the staircase and elevator lobbies at the west end of the building overlook both its gallery space and the Frontier Restaurant across the street. On the campus side, another glass wall shows off the truss system. Roger L. Schluntz, the dean of architecture and planning, says the aim of the design was to let everyone see what everyone else is doing—and he says the quality of students' work has improved markedly since the school moved in."

Lawrence Biemiller, *The Chronicle of Higher Education*, October 1, 2008

SAVAGE JUNGLE
ISLA MAGDELENA, CHILE
2008

2006 SOUTH AMERICA TRIP WITH JOSÉ FOR A SITE VISIT TO SAVAGE JUNGLE, A NEW RESORT PROJECT IN THE FAR SOUTH OF CHILE. AIRPLANE CHARTER FROM SANTIAGO, THEN A BOAT TRIP TO THE ISLAND, AND HUDDLING WITH COLLEAGUE JOSÉ AND DWAYNE, MY CLIENT, ATOP THE WATERFALL.

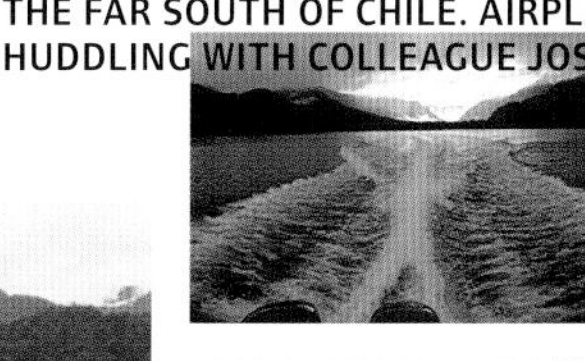

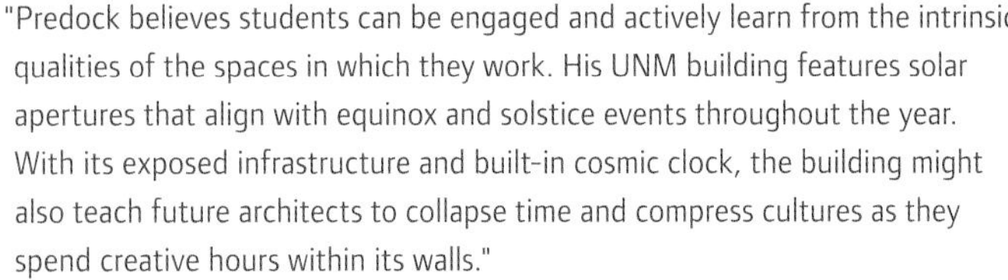

"Predock believes students can be engaged and actively learn from the intrinsic qualities of the spaces in which they work. His UNM building features solar apertures that align with equinox and solstice events throughout the year. With its exposed infrastructure and built-in cosmic clock, the building might also teach future architects to collapse time and compress cultures as they spend creative hours within its walls."

"The Architect at Full Throttle," *Trend*, Fall 2009/Winter 2010

BEFORE DEPARTING CHILE, SUMMER SKIING (THE SOUTH AMERICAN WINTER) AT VALLE NEVADO.

THEN TO PERU—CUZCO WITH THE POWERFUL SACSAYHUAMAN, THEN A TRAIN UP THE VALLEY PAST TAMBOMACHAY AND OLLANTAYTAMBO, ARRIVING BELOW MACHU PICCHU.

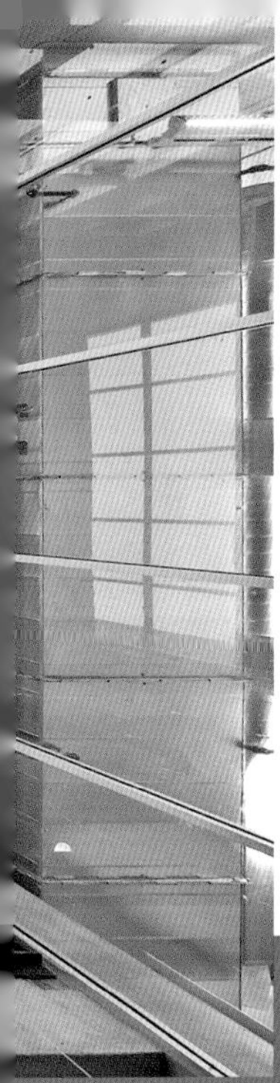

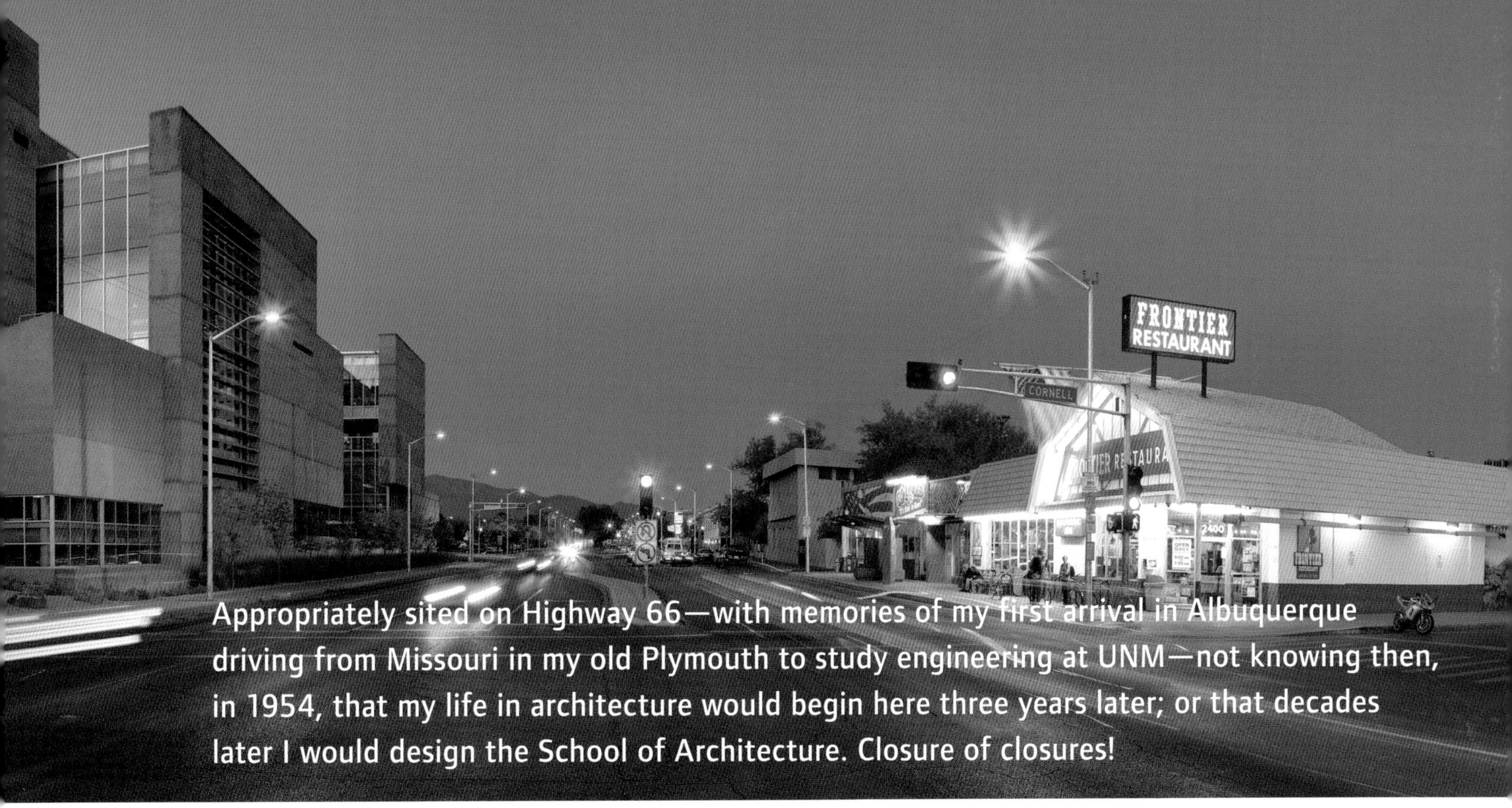

Appropriately sited on Highway 66—with memories of my first arrival in Albuquerque driving from Missouri in my old Plymouth to study engineering at UNM—not knowing then, in 1954, that my life in architecture would begin here three years later; or that decades later I would design the School of Architecture. Closure of closures!

WAYNA PICCHU IS THE ICONIC PEAK LOOMING ABOVE THE RUIN WITH A VERY CHALLENGING CLIMB TO THE TOP.

CORNELL PARKING STRUCTURE AND VISITORS CENTER

UNIVERSITY OF NEW MEXICO
ALBUQUERQUE, NEW MEXICO 2001/03

ON AN ACTION-PACKED BORDER, THE FEDERAL COURTHOUSE IN EL PASO, A GSA DESIGN EXCELLENCE INVITED COMPETITION THAT WE WON, SPLITS TO CHANNEL VIEWS CITY-VIEW-ORIENTED WAITING AREAS FOREGROUND THE COURTROOMS. THE COPPER-CLAD OFFICES AND JUDGES' CHAMBERS ORIENT TO THE NORTH. A GLAZED BRIDGE

UNITED STATES FEDERAL COURTHOUSE
EL PASO, TX 2001/09

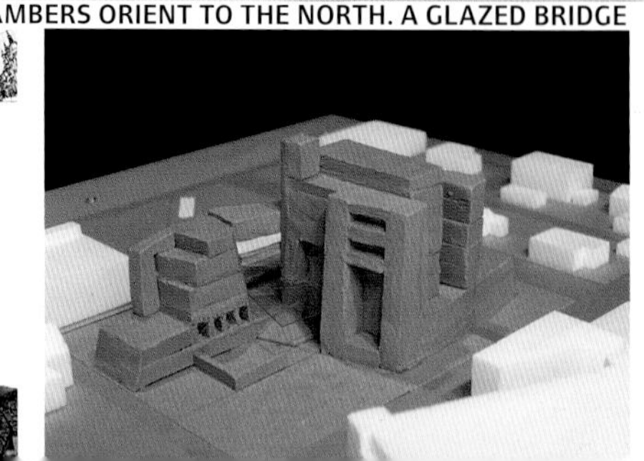

A parking structure in drag, immediately opposite the School of Architecture—swallowing the parking function to appear as a "building" from primary campus circulation vantage points, with stepped bleachers for socializing and shaded, upper-level terraces above office spaces facing the Fine Arts Center across the campus pedestrian mall.

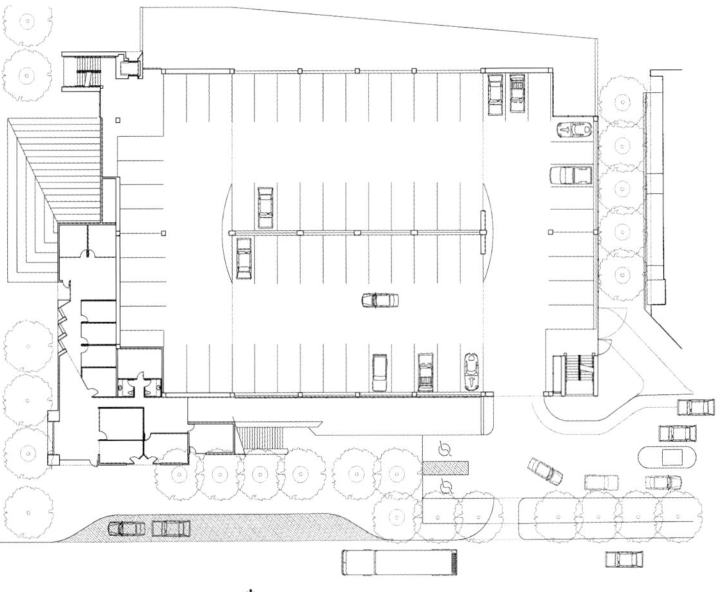

TO FRANKLIN MOUNTAIN. IT IS ORGANIZED AROUND VERY COMPLEX VERTICAL CIRCULATION SEPARATING PUBLIC, JUDGES, LAW ENFORCEMENT OFFICIALS, AND PRISONERS.
LINKING THE LIBRARY TO THE SOUTH, SHOWN IN THE ORIGINAL COMPETITION VERSION OF THE COURT HOUSE BUT ELIMINATED BY THE GSA.

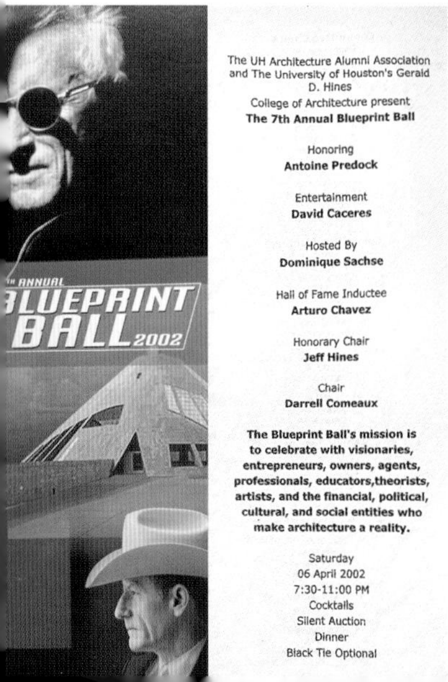

The UH Architecture Alumni Association and The University of Houston's Gerald D. Hines College of Architecture present
The 7th Annual Blueprint Ball

Honoring
Antoine Predock

Entertainment
David Caceres

Hosted By
Dominique Sachse

Hall of Fame Inductee
Arturo Chavez

Honorary Chair
Jeff Hines

Chair
Darrell Comeaux

The Blueprint Ball's mission is to celebrate with visionaries, entrepreneurs, owners, agents, professionals, educators,theorists, artists, and the financial, political, cultural, and social entities who make architecture a reality.

Saturday
06 April 2002
7:30-11:00 PM
Cocktails
Silent Auction
Dinner
Black Tie Optional

BILLED ALONGSIDE LYLE LOVETT, A FELLOW DUCATI RIDER.

MY TWO RACE TRACK MOTORCYCLES IMPROBABLY AT 10400'— DUCATI DESMOSEIDICI AND HONDA RC30

"While Predock's buildings remain consistently sparse, planar and primal, they are richly inflected by ideas and images from a plethora of sources ranging from folklore to cyberspace.... As architectural practice becomes more narrowly focused, Predock's intensely personal vision offers the possibility of a genuinely timeless architecture, unencumbered by the transience of fashionable theories. His kaleidoscopic readings of the work tap into a deep reservoir of human emotions, yet his work maintains a fundamental simplicity and directness."

Catherine Slessor, *Concrete Regionalism*, 2000

TRAVELS TO ITALY DURING TIME OF CONSTRUCTION.
SAN GIMIGNANO—FAVORITE TOWN FOR ARCHITECTS.

UNITY CHURCH OF CHRISTIANITY
HOUSTON, TX 2002

A "SNOW STORM" OF ILLUMINATED GLASS FRAGMENTS FILL THE BELL TOWER.

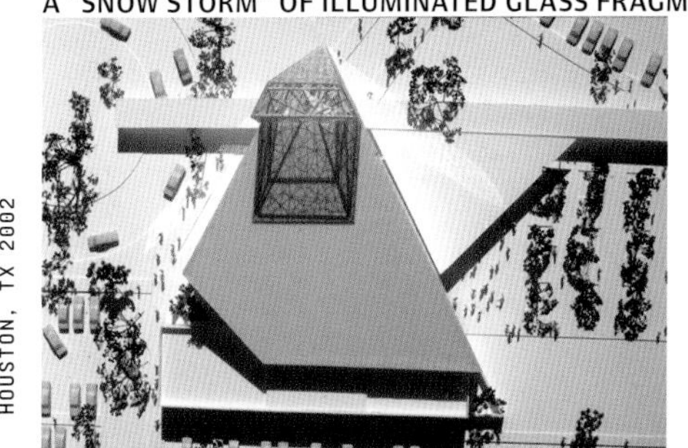

CASA MALAPARTE WORKSHOPS

CAPRI, ITALY 1999, 2000, 2008

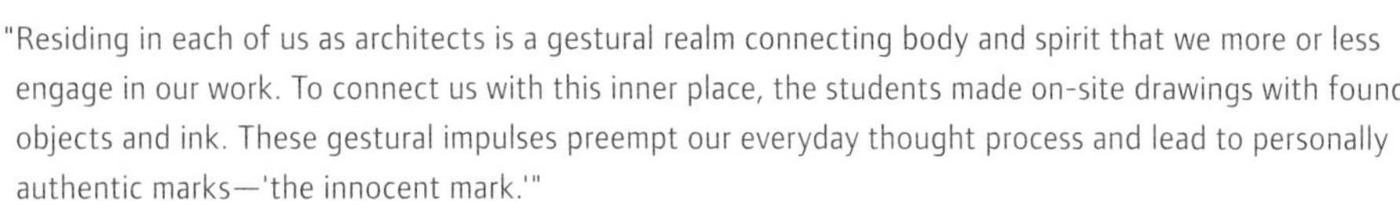

"Residing in each of us as architects is a gestural realm connecting body and spirit that we more or less engage in our work. To connect us with this inner place, the students made on-site drawings with found objects and ink. These gestural impulses preempt our everyday thought process and lead to personally authentic marks—'the innocent mark.'"

Antoine Predock, *The Casa Malaparte Workshop*

OLLECTIVELY ASSEMBLED COLLAGE WITH EACH STUDENT CONTRIBUTING A SECTION—AN EXPLORATION INTO MALAPARTE'S MEDITERRANEAN SURREALISM.

Teaching successive workshops for international students at the magical Casa Malaparte, the legendary home and gathering space of the writer/philosopher Curzio Malaparte. Collage assembly and individual drawing assignments played out over several days with field trips to the evil Tiberius' Villa and around the Isle of Capri.

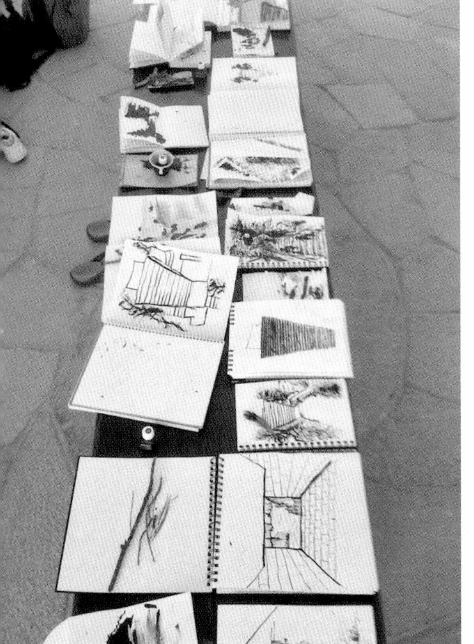

Organized by architect colleague/professor Ann Cederna (fellow Ducati rider) with Alessia Rositani of the Foundation Eredi Malaparte, our fabulous host for the workshop.

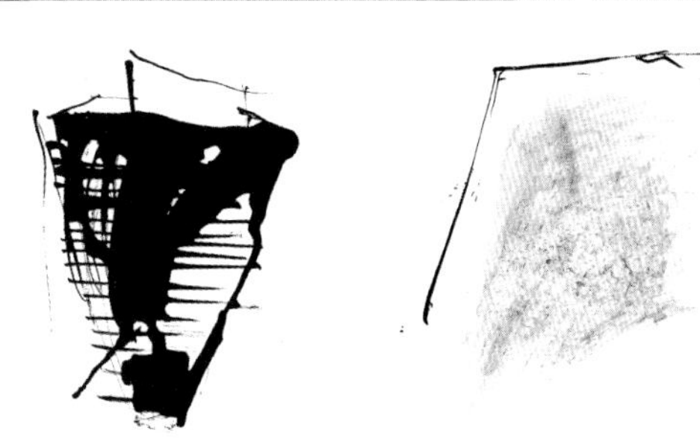

The Casa Malaparte Workshop

The School of Architecture and Planning, The Catholic University of America

Photography by Stanley Ira Hallet

Additional images and text by Antoine Predock, Ann Cederna and David Shove-Brown

Hello sky, its nice to meet you.

Chacoans needed ponderosa logs for their building at home and built a colony here to oversee the importation of logs.

Colors scotch-taped to the sky

strewn with the tiny skeletons of turtles and fish, all as white and dry as if they had been expert

scribble like a postcard to a friend

That's funny, I dropped it on the other side, and it came out of this side, and it came out of this side!

And that was the beginning of a game called Poohsticks.

movements of the sun, moon, and stars in the heavens, just as the same movements and changes of seasons determined their lives.

A house pressed close to the earth and sky

new bit of world, beautifully ridged with ripple marks.

The research collage intersects the family's urban homebase with a site-specific Rio Blanco, Colorado, response. I consulted with Franny, Miriam's three-year-old daughter. She and I were in full agreement that we would have trees fall down and make the house. I started dropping sticks on the block model randomly, her parents were kind of bystanders. When we built it using deadfall trees collected from the site, positioning the house in the Ponderosa clearing, doing very little rearrangement.

"'Trees have a life span, and I thought about what would happen if the trees fell down,' says Predock. 'Just the gesture of dropping a clutch of dowels on the model felt, and looked, right.' He was seriously proposing logs landing on the house.

From his student days as a painter, when he was influenced by Abstract Expressionists, Predock knew that making a mark on canvas constituted a special event. "Inside all of us, we have that innocent mark, the gesture of painting, and I honor the idea of that gesture even off the canvas," he says. For him the scatter of logs and blocks represented gesture. It was also a sophisticated transformation of the sentimental log cabin.

'Antoine was holding something behind his back in his right hand,' recalls Miriam, 'and then he threw these sticks on the model in an uncontrolled way that couldn't produce a predictable geometry. It was a dramatic moment—and sheer fun—as though he was making some Jackson Pollock effect.'"

Joseph Giovannini, "A Not So Log Cabin," *Architectural Digest*, January 2008

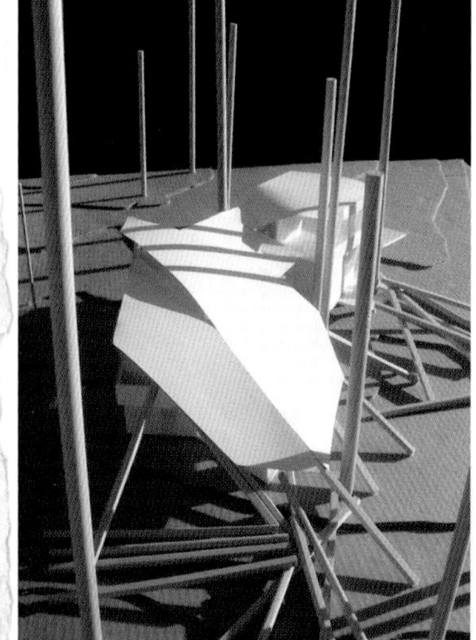

Located at the remote northeastern end of the Rio Blanco River Basin, a high mountain area of farms and ranches, the site is defined by high peaks and alpine vegetation. The location of the house on the site was chosen for its spectacular grove of mature Ponderosa Pine trees. The straight, thick trunks form a sheltered space and provided the impetus for the design of the house. Three-year-old Franny and I envisioned the grove as fallen—an intertwining, sheltering accumulation of logs lodged in the house—thus diagramming a symbolic warping of time in which the decomposed grove produces new life. (In the construction of the house, the Ponderosa grove was untouched, the deadfall logs collected from the multi-acre site.)

Intended as a retreat for the family, the house manifests the shelter of the grove in the realm of the senses. The texture of the ground cover, sunshine, the sound of the Rio Blanco, and the vanilla scent of the pine trees weave through the house. Large glass areas offer a constantly changing view of pines and aspen groves as one moves through the house. The trees of the grove frame the grander, distant views of mountain peaks, creating targeted vignettes of the alpine surroundings. Recessed glazing in bedrooms, join the rooms with floating decks. Defined outdoor spaces for activities that follow the sun along its path skirt the southern and eastern sides of the house. The kitchen, dining, and living spaces are one contiguous double-height space overlooked by guest bedroom and workroom. The upper-level prime bedroom is a "tree house" close to the Ponderosas. Downstairs, Franny's room is full of light and open, with a play/camping deck adjacent to one of the largest trees in the grove.

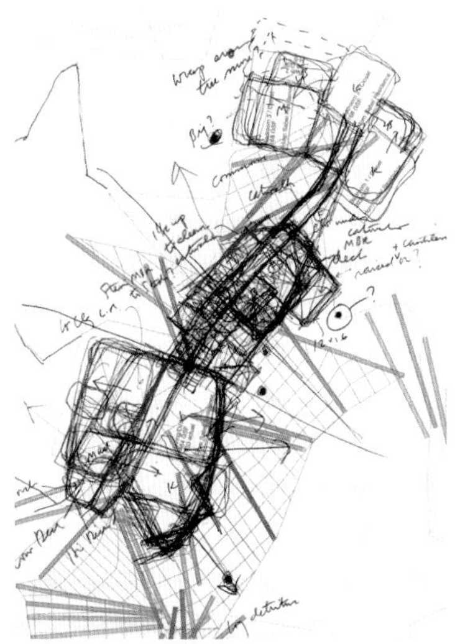

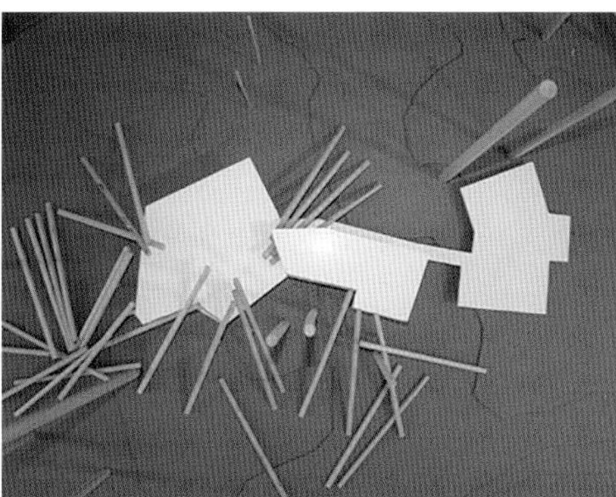

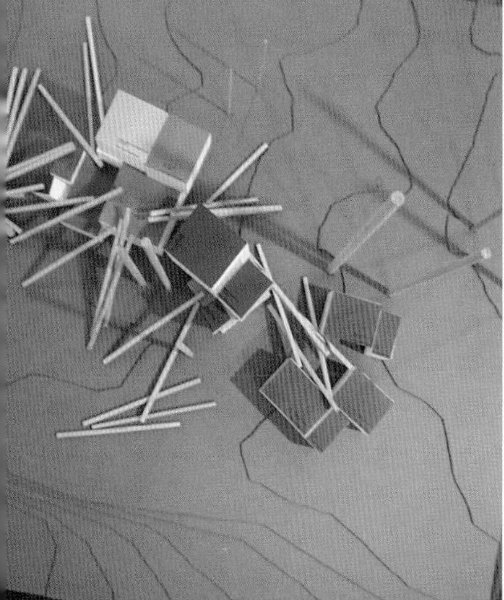

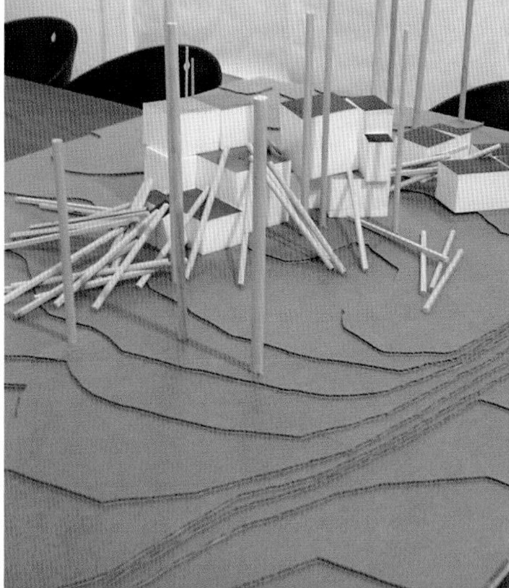

LOGJAM HOUSE

(FOR MIRIAM AND FRANNY)

RIO BLANCO, COLORADO 2001/06

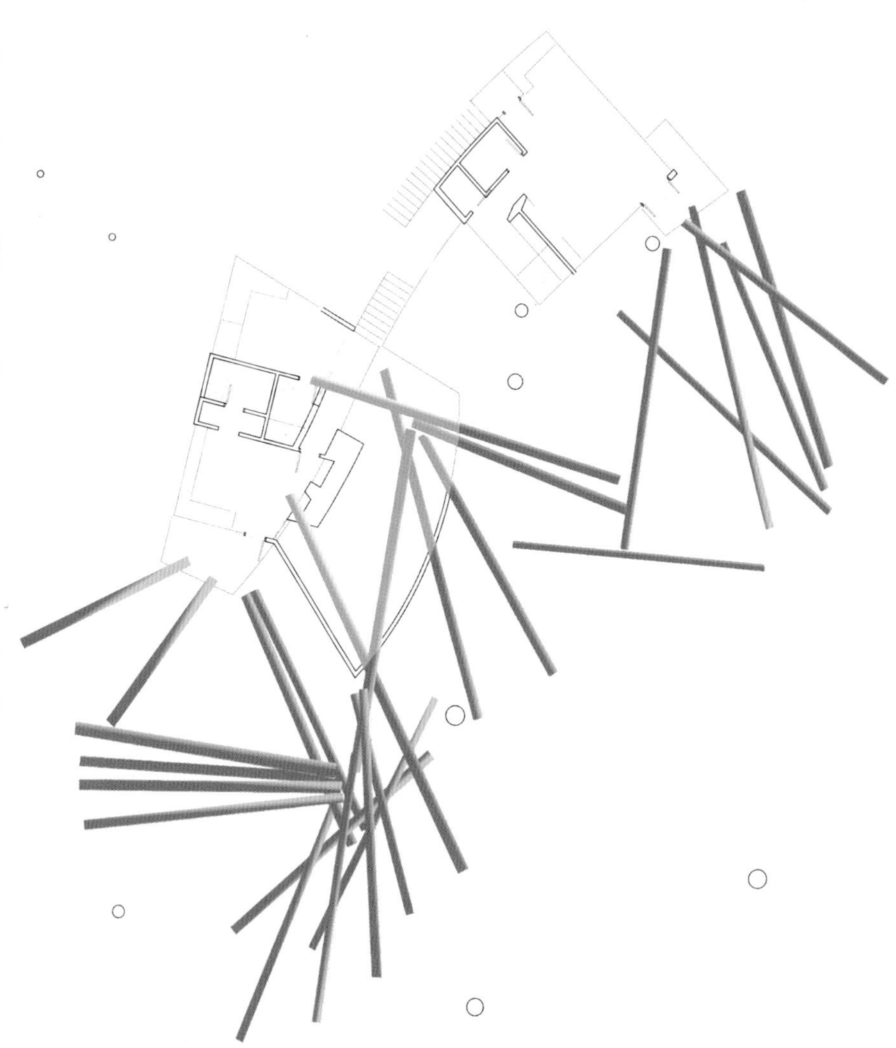

"Now as you drive across a bridge over the river and approach the house on a long switchback, glimpses of the house shimmer through the woods. In the winter, the luminous metal takes to the snow like a duck to water, with light reflecting off the snow onto the metal and back. At the last turn toward the house, the metal siding evokes the most prominent feature of the valley, the glaciated walls of a cliff whose face is composed of a polished, silvery-gray granite."

Joseph Giovannini, "A Not So Log Cabin," *Architectural Digest*, January 2008

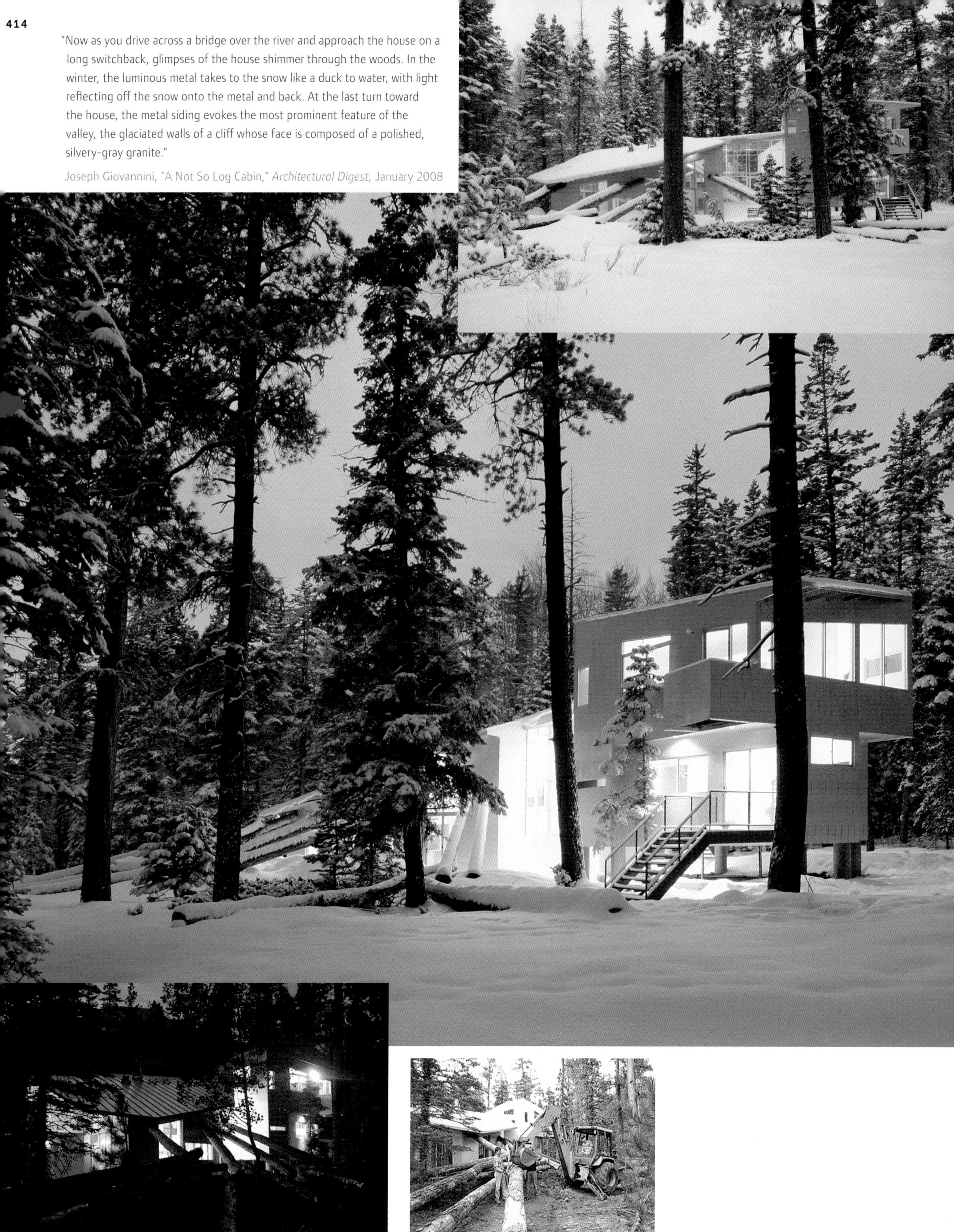

With the remoteness and almost supernatural beauty of the location, a glowing aura arose. So in a sense, it's a haunted house—haunted by the aura of the collapsed forest becoming the bones of the house—straight, thick fallen Ponderosa Pines forming an entwined sheltering exoskeleton of logs.

"The essence of Predock's architecture can be simply stated: He has found original ways to connect dramatic, abstract forms with both the natural and cultural conditions of a particular place. Predock's best buildings tell stories in memorable forms and spaces, and this makes him different from most other modern architects."

Benjamin Forgey, "In the High Desert, An Oasis of Design," *The Washington Post*, September 30, 2001

"His approaches to architectural design, such as listening to the land, building with environmental sensitivity, and embracing all facets of a site's culture, influence and inspire the profession."

"Antoine Predock: Abstract Landscape," *Urban Environment Design*, June 2012

THE HOUSE ON THE COVER OF *WORLD ARCHITECTURE* MONOGRAPH PUBLISHED IN CHINA.

Logjam, in the shelter of the grove, dwells in the realm of the senses—the resilient ground plane, filtered sunlight, the sound of the Rio Blanco, and the vanilla scent of the Ponderosas that weaves through the house (the aromatic invasion of the logs).

HOUSE OF BLUES IN SAN JOSE, BRINGING THE AMPHITHEATER INSIDE.

HOUSE OF BLUES
SAN JOSE, CA 2002

"The spare simplicity becomes a sculpturally articulate house of fine bones and crisp volumes. The couple purposely hang nothing on the walls."

Joseph Giovannini, "A Not So Log Cabin," *Architectural Digest*, January 2008

SCIENTIST HOUSING ADJACENT TO BIOSPHERE 2 IN ORACLE, ARIZONA—SHIPPING CONTAINERS AND OFF-THE-SHELF MATERIALS.

COLUMBIA UNIVERSITY
SCIENTIST HOUSING AT
BIOSPHERE 2
ORACLE, AZ 2003

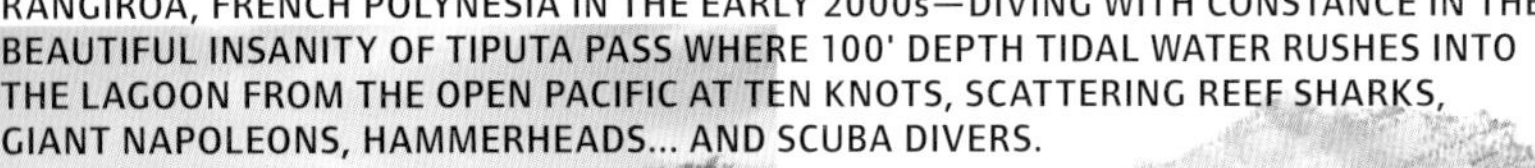

RANGIROA, FRENCH POLYNESIA IN THE EARLY 2000s—DIVING WITH CONSTANCE IN THE BEAUTIFUL INSANITY OF TIPUTA PASS WHERE 100' DEPTH TIDAL WATER RUSHES INTO THE LAGOON FROM THE OPEN PACIFIC AT TEN KNOTS, SCATTERING REEF SHARKS, GIANT NAPOLEONS, HAMMERHEADS... AND SCUBA DIVERS.

BETWEEN THAT, THE TUAMOTO ARCHIPELAGO, AND HAWAI'I ARE THE VOLCANIC

MARQUESAS ISLANDS ASTRIDE THE MID-PACIFIC RIFT.

DRAWING THE PAEKE RUIN WITH AN AUDIENCE ON NUKU HIVA.

2006—SERVING AS UNIVERSITY OF OKLAHOMA BRUCE GOFF CHAIR OF CREATIVE ARCHITECTURE.

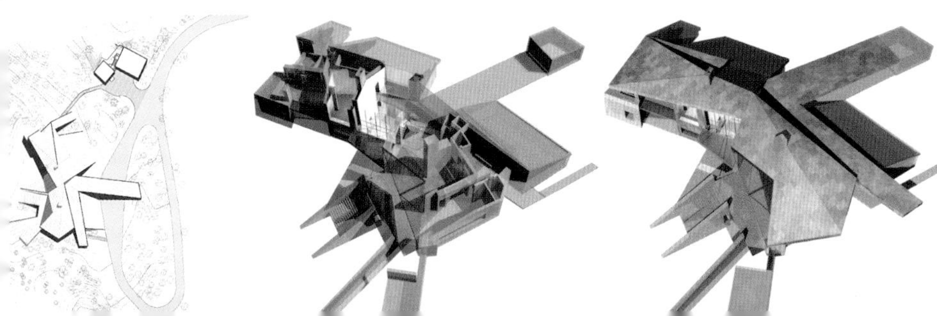

As a landscape abstraction, it has no expression of façade; rather, it's a series of slope extensions, with its entrance under the titanium porte cochere, bookended by granite berms.

HIGHLANDS POND HOUSE

ASPEN, COLORADO 2002/06

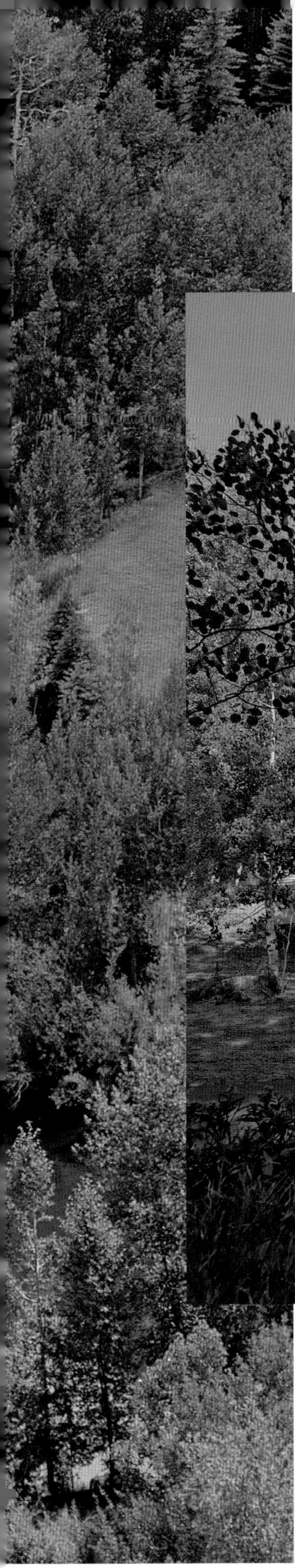

Analogous to the tectonic upheaval of the Rockies, Highlands Pond House emerges from the site with angular references in profile to the surrounding ridges—a fusion of stone, concrete, glass, and titanium. The arrival plaza/porte cochère and the mute sloping stone planes reverse on the pond side with panoramic mountain view glazing and terraces that reach toward the water.

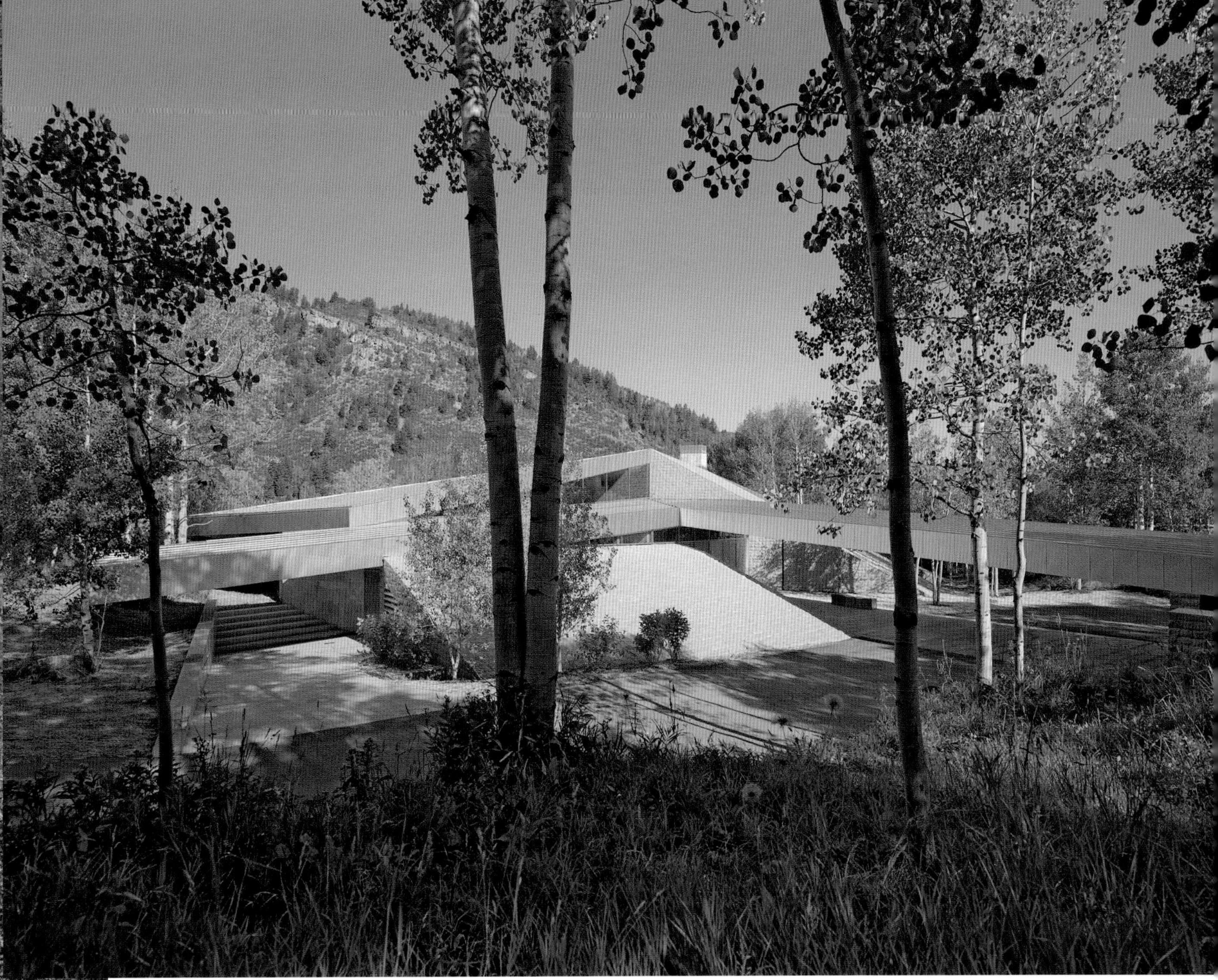

"The expansive residence is as inscrutable from the approach as it is revealing of the interior at the more transparent rear. The bermed front elevation appears as a single level; it is in fact a series of slopes that mimic the nearby exposed ridges ..."

Therese Bissell, "Where Earth Meets Sky," *Architectural Digest*, October 2007

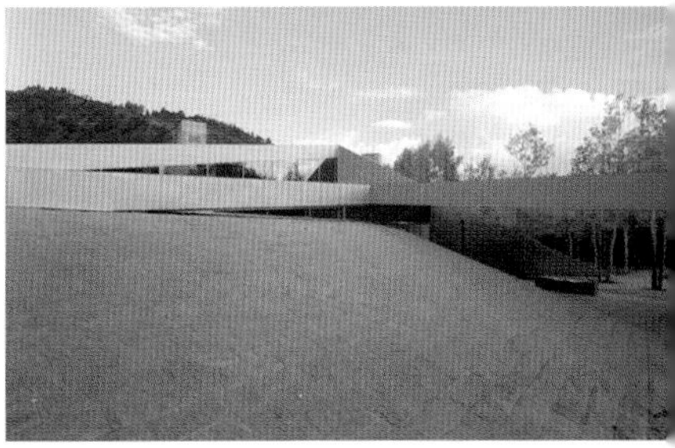

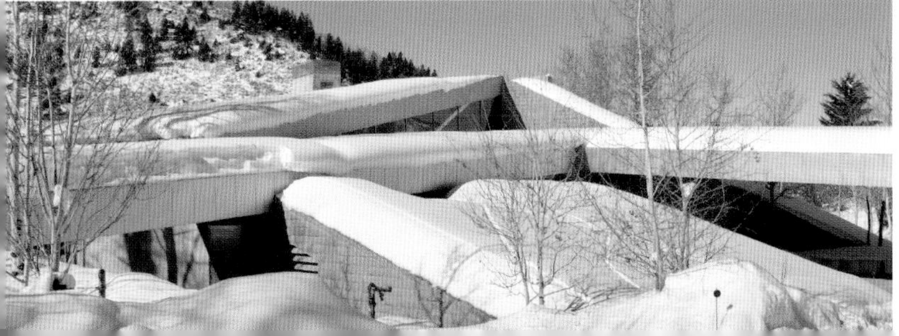

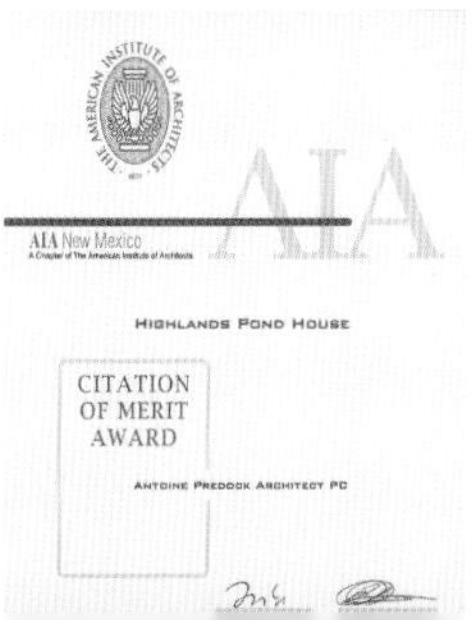

AIA

AIA New Mexico

A Chapter of The American Institute of Architects

HIGHLANDS POND HOUSE

CITATION OF MERIT AWARD

ANTOINE PREDOCK ARCHITECT PC

rom the stone here and the abyss here. Where it goes--who knows? One hardly remembers from where one came."
n melting snows, joining together to make streams, joining together to make the river that flows past their little village.
"If you want to stand out from the pack, you have to stand outside the pack.
of their land...to gather around the agency on Smoking Earth River, their carniva growing up along the river like a grove

Every space on the pond side of the house views across trellised terraces toward the distant Maroon Bells peaks.

"The house settles into the site as if becoming displaced strata, delimited by its adjacent origins from the land. The underlying faults and its outcroppings are heightened as hidden copper planes refract light, suggesting the landscape's dynamism by transforming the interior space throughout the passage of the day."

GA Houses, 2003

With the rugged accumulation of exterior materials appropriate to the site, I wanted the ceiling to be a continuous refined wood surface—the beauty of a butcher block counter came to mind and I imagined a "butcher block" lining that would spawn other components of the house—railings, stairs, banquettes. The exterior glass detailing invades the house to become railings—bridges with an arcing cast glass partition wall slices through the house like a curved blade.

Steve Hansen's construction team was brilliant at every level especially the refinement of the poured-in-place concrete that has the feeling of a fine porcelain glaze—and those concrete forming skills had counterparts in the extraordinary finish carpentry and metal and glass detailing.

SURROUNDING RIDGE ANALOGOUS STONE

THE PORTE COCHÈRE BECOMES A SNOW FIELD

HIKING WITH OUR CLIENTS

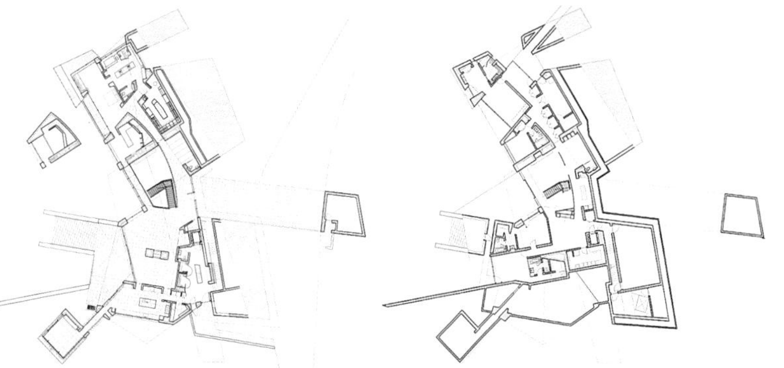

THE OMNIPRESENT MAROON BELLS FROM THE GROUND AND FROM THE AIR.

"In continuous fluctuation, Aspen's seasonal changes vary widely in hues and tonality and it is this communion of reflection that allows the house to dissolve inside its own landscape."

GA Houses, 2004

HIGHLANDS POND
CARETAKER RESIDENCE
ASPEN, CO 2002/06

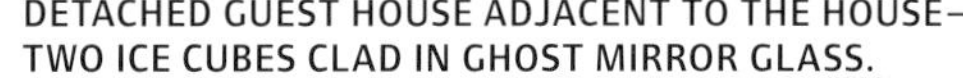

DETACHED GUEST HOUSE ADJACENT TO THE HOUSE—TWO ICE CUBES CLAD IN GHOST MIRROR GLASS.

MOLTEN GLASS BECOMES WALL—POLISHED CONCRETE—STAINLESS STEEL

Link to the study

"Social stratifications form a home with flexible and overlapping public and private realms, while geological layering weave in and out of the house to provide grounding between family and landscape."

GA Houses, 2003

UNIVERSITY CENTER, GRADUATE SCHOOL OF MANAGEMENT, UNIVERSITY OF DALLAS, DALLAS, TX 2004

IMAGINING THE BUILDING AS A MULTI-FINGERED CREATURE GRASPING THE HILLTOP IN DALLAS.

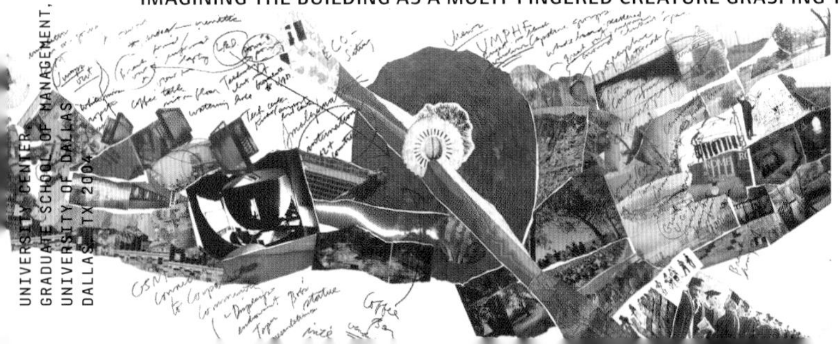

"An abstract voluptuousness defines each of the levels, with rooms tumbling and flowing into each other and linked by devices such as the visually aerobic glass catwalk."

Therese Bissell, "Where Earth Meets Sky," *Architectural Digest,* October 2007

TRAVEL TO ISTANBUL WITH THE MAGNIFICENT HAGIA SOPHIA, AND MARRAKESH WITH THE CRAZY ENERGY OF JEMAA EL-FNA SQUARE—THE MINARET PUNCTUATED SKYLINE AND THE ARRAY OF KILIM RUGS IN THE SOUK. ALTHOUGH I AM NOT A MUSLIM, RAMADAN WAS IN PROGRESS AND I JOINED THE MONTH-LONG TRADITION WITH MY HOST, BREAKING FAST AT SUNSET DAILY WITH FRESHLY HARVESTED POMEGRANATE SEEDS AND MOROCCAN TEA. THE RAMADAN EXPERIENCE WAS POWERFUL AND I HAVE GREAT RESPECT FOR THOSE THAT OBSERVE IT AS AN ANNUAL SPIRITUAL RECHARGE.

The 58-foot-long cast-glass wall has a fantastic presence as a material chunk and not just a translucent material.

The mountain view prime suite and its accompanying study with grade-B horror movie rotating bookcase that conceals a stair to the loft above.

SKIING THE HIGHLANDS POND HOUSE

"Antoine Predock has captured the soul of our land like no other architect."

Deborah Dietsch, "Predock's Example," *Architecture,* March 1996

Sustainably harvested teak, soapstone tub, mirror blades, stainless steel columns— showering in an aspen glade.

BRAD COLLINS, FOUNDER OF GROUP C, AND I DEVELOPED AN EMPATHETIC CONNECTION THAT ROLLED INTO SIX DIFFERENT MONOGRAPHS—FIVE WITH RIZZOLI, THANKS TO DAVID MORTON WHO BECAME RIZZOLI'S ARCHITECTURE EDITOR AFTER A LONG STINT AT *PROGRESSIVE ARCHITECTURE* WHERE HE HAD CHAMPIONED MY WORK GOING BACK TO 1973; AND ONE FOR MONACELLI PRESS. THOSE WERE FOLLOWED BY A MONOGRAPH FOR UNM PRESS ON THE WORK OF CONSTANCE DE JONG, ARTIST AND MY LIFE PARTNER. AFTER A HIATUS OF MORE THAN A DECADE, THE GODS OF INEVITABILITY REJOINED US TO CREATE THIS BOOK. BRAD, AND TAD KIMBALL, ANOTHER PRINCIPAL AT GROUP C, GUIDED ME THROUGH A PROCESS VERY SIMILAR TO MINE WHEN ENCOUNTERING A SITE—UNEARTHING, MINING, SIFTING, TESTING, INTEGRATING THE VARIED STRATA OF MY LIFE TO CONSTRUCT THIS "MEMOIR-OGRAPH." TAD ESPECIALLY WAS MY OFTEN DAILY PARTNER FOR MORE THAN A YEAR—ABSORBING, EDITING, AND DESIGNING WITH GREAT AGILITY, TRANSFORMING TENS OF THOUSANDS OF IMAGES AND HUNDREDS OF HOURS OF CONVERSATION INTO THIS BOOK. TO BOTH OF THEM, AND EVERYONE AT GROUP C—THANK YOU.

TRINITY RIVER AUDUBON CENTER

DALLAS, TEXAS 2002/08

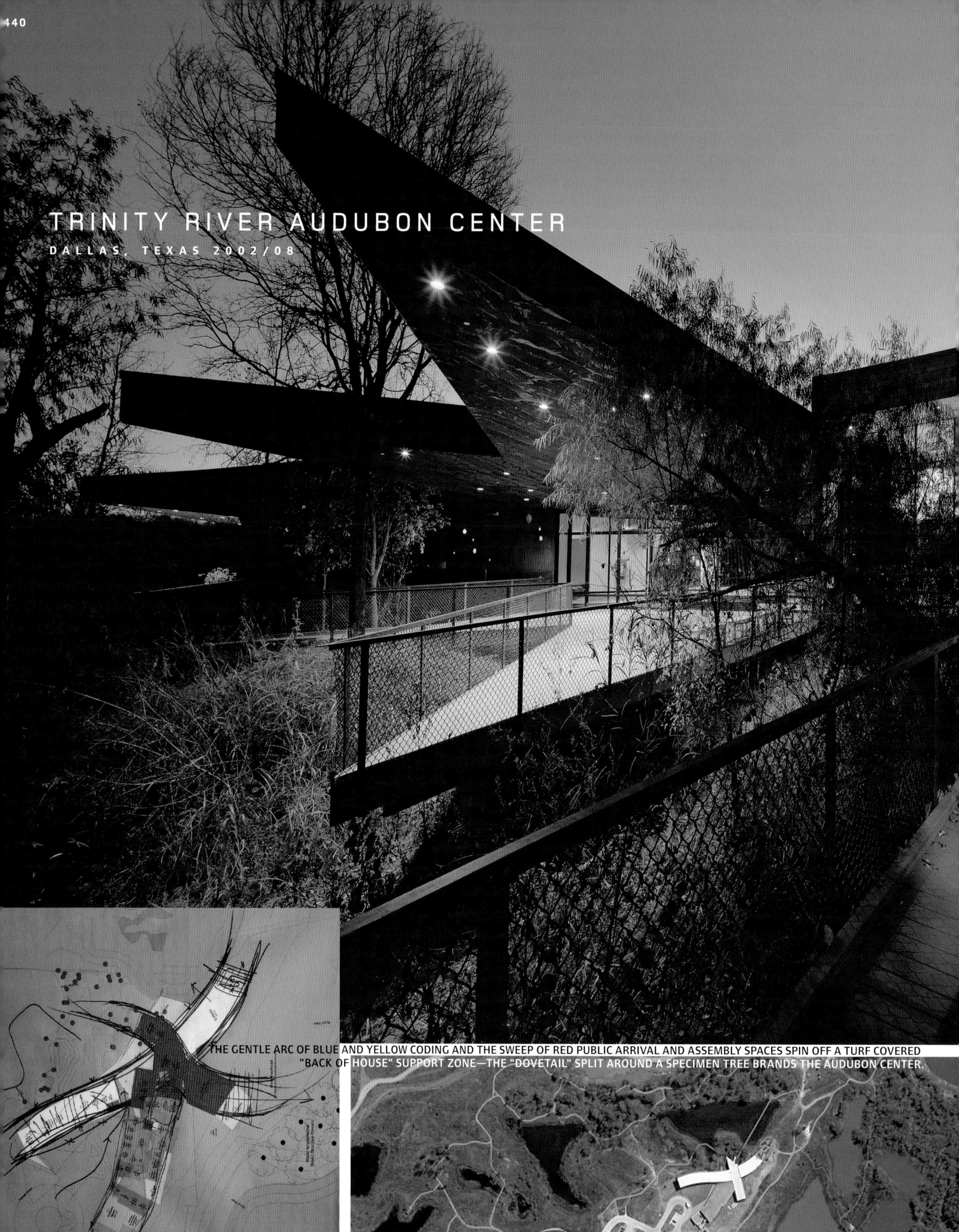

THE GENTLE ARC OF BLUE AND YELLOW CODING AND THE SWEEP OF RED PUBLIC ARRIVAL AND ASSEMBLY SPACES SPIN OFF A TURF COVERED "BACK OF HOUSE" SUPPORT ZONE—THE "DOVETAIL" SPLIT AROUND A SPECIMEN TREE BRANDS THE AUDUBON CENTER.

The Trinity River weaves through the Great Trinity Forest, the largest urban forest in the United States, and crosses through an area described by naturalists as the biological "crossroads of North America"—the meeting point between the Blackland Prairie and Cross Timbers regions in southwestern Dallas.

We started with a site containing a massive city solid waste operation with large areas having been used for illegal dumping—so the project began with a master plan for that Trinity River sector. It included cleanup, restoration, and flood mitigation work—the mountains of trash became fields of wildflowers and native grasses.

Preventing bird crashes, the angled glass wall defines the classroom wing and leads to the public areas with the work of exhibit designer Frank Zaremba.

The corten steel aperture wall highlights interpretative moments of landscape and avian activity.

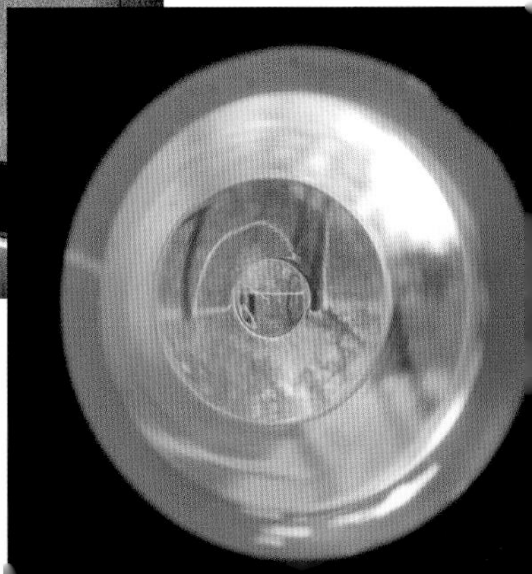

STATE OF NEW MEXICO—FEBRUARY 13, 2006 "ANTOINE PREDOCK DAY"

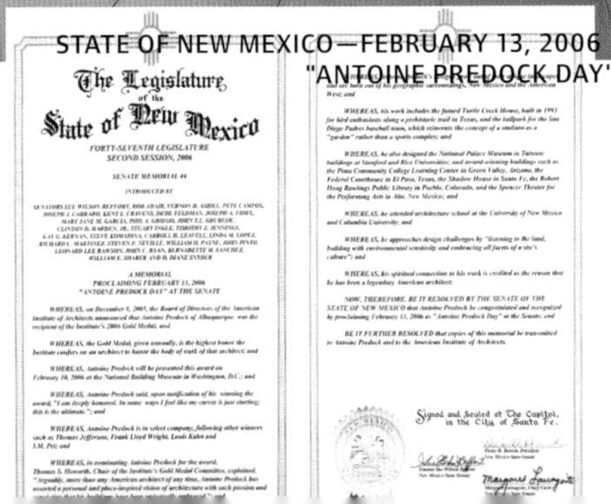

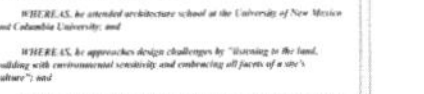

The Legislature of the State of New Mexico

FORTY-SEVENTH LEGISLATURE
SECOND SESSION, 2006

SENATE MEMORIAL 44

INTRODUCED BY

SENATORS SUE WILSON BEFFORT, ROD ADAIR, VERNON D. ASBILL, PETE CAMPOS, JOSEPH J. CARRARO, KENT L. CRAVENS, DEDE FELDMAN, JOSEPH A. FIDEL, MARY JANE M. GARCIA, PHIL A. GRIEGO, JOHN T.L. GRUBESIC, CLINTON D. HARDEN, JR., STUART INGLE, TIMOTHY Z. JENNINGS, GAY G. KERNAN, STEVE KOMADINA, CARROLL H. LEAVELL, LINDA M. LOPEZ, RICHARD C. MARTINEZ, STEVEN P. NEVILLE, WILLIAM H. PAYNE, JOHN PINTO, LEONARD LEE RAWSON, JOHN C. RYAN, BERNADETTE M. SANCHEZ, WILLIAM E. SHARER AND H. DIANE SNYDER

A MEMORIAL
PROCLAIMING FEBRUARY 13, 2006
"ANTOINE PREDOCK DAY" AT THE SENATE

WHEREAS, on December 8, 2005, the Board of Directors of the American Institute of Architects announced that Antoine Predock of Albuquerque was the recipient of the Institute's 2006 Gold Medal; and

WHEREAS, the Gold Medal, given annually, is the highest honor the Institute confers on an architect to honor the body of work of that architect; and

WHEREAS, Antoine Predock will be presented this award on February 10, 2006 at the National Building Museum in Washington, D.C.; and

WHEREAS, Antoine Predock said, upon notification of his winning the award, "I am deeply honored. In some ways I feel like my career is just starting; this is the ultimate."; and

WHEREAS, Antoine Predock is in select company, following other winners such as Thomas Jefferson, Frank Lloyd Wright, Louis Kahn and I.M. Pei; and

WHEREAS, in nominating Antoine Predock for the award, Thomas S. Howorth, Chair of the Institute's Gold Medal Committee, explained, "Arguably, more than any American architect of any time, Antoine Predock has asserted a personal and place-inspired vision of architecture with such passion and ...

... and are born out of his geographic surroundings, New Mexico and the American West; and

WHEREAS, his work includes the famed Turtle Creek House, built in 1993 for bird enthusiasts along a prehistoric trail in Texas, and the ballpark for the San Diego Padres baseball team, which reinvents the concept of a stadium as a "garden" rather than a sports complex; and

WHEREAS, he also designed the National Palace Museum in Taiwan; buildings at Stanford and Rice Universities; and award-winning buildings such as the Pima Community College Learning Center in Green Valley, Arizona, the Federal Courthouse in El Paso, Texas, the Shadow House in Santa Fe, the Robert Hoag Rawlings Public Library in Pueblo, Colorado, and the Spencer Theater for the Performing Arts in Alto, New Mexico; and

WHEREAS, he attended architecture school at the University of New Mexico and Columbia University; and

WHEREAS, he approaches design challenges by "listening to the land, building with environmental sensitivity and embracing all facets of a site's culture"; and

WHEREAS, his spiritual connection to his work is credited as the reason that he has been a legendary American architect;

NOW, THEREFORE, BE IT RESOLVED BY THE SENATE OF THE STATE OF NEW MEXICO that Antoine Predock be congratulated and recognized by proclaiming February 13, 2006 as "Antoine Predock Day" at the Senate; and

BE IT FURTHER RESOLVED that copies of this memorial be transmitted to Antoine Predock and to the American Institute of Architects.

Signed and Sealed at The Capitol, in the City of Santa Fe.

DETAIL SKETCH OF SWALE FOR THE DALLAS ARBORETUM PROJECT

Bird-feather acoustic ceiling of main school group assembly space

"Design architect Antoine Predock ... celebrates this flourishing riparian world with a building that simultaneously appears to dissolve into the bottomland while also emerging from the alluvial muck. In plan, Predock's concept metaphorically takes flight, with the literal expression of a bird spreading its wings. But seen from the ground, his elemental abstractions tie the tripartite building to its context with trajectories toward land and water.

Predock intuits these connections through surface textures that simulate both nature and humankind's precarious attempts for domination over it. He juxtaposes industrial materials with earthy elements, wielding mottled steel panels as homage to 'Corps of Engineers vernacular' and cypress siding to evoke the woodland's essence."

Stephen Sharpe, "Audubon Takes Flight," *Texas Architect*, November 2008

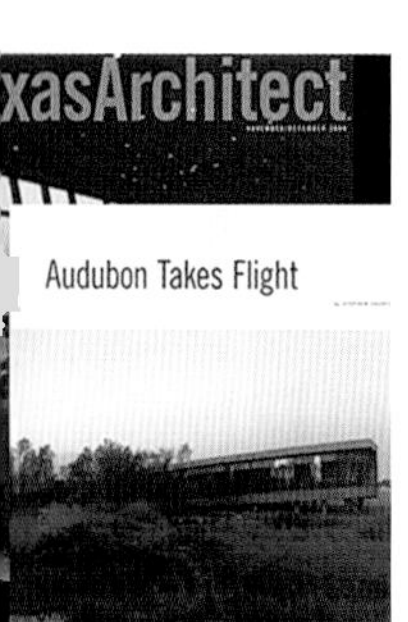

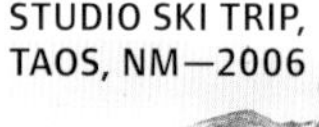

STUDIO SKI TRIP,
TAOS, NM—2006

MY SKI-KNEES FINALLY GAVE UP IN 2006 AND BECAME TITANIUM WITH TIDY ROUND TEFLON KNEECAPS.

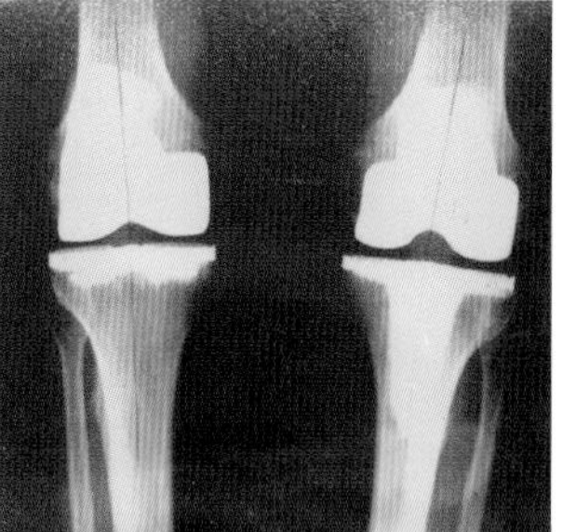

DOCTOR: "NO MORE SKIING FOR YOU."—SKIING FULL BLAST SIX MONTHS AFTER SURGERY THANKS TO DR. RICHARD WHITE.

The site has a tangible connection to Trinity River, providing a secluded counterpoint to urban Dallas. Visitors approach the new center on a boardwalk that weaves though reconstituted prairie, wetlands, and slivers of forest. The building's program focuses on environmental education—giving an introduction to the riparian habitats along the Trinity River, and the species that make it their home.

DRAWING GIFT FROM TADAO ANDO

For Antoine Predock,

ON AN EARLY 2000s TRIP TO MEXICO, FROM TLAXCALA—THE TWO LOVERS, POPOCATÉPETL AND IZTACCIHUATL, DEFINING THE EASTERN RIM OF THE VALLEY THAT IS MEXICO CITY.

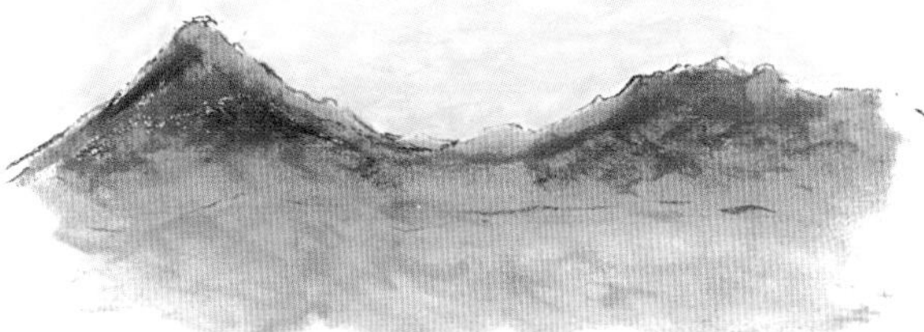

AND TO THE SOUTHEAST THE GIGANTIC PRE-COLUMBIAN PYRAMID OF CHOLULA WITH AN INSULTING COLONIAL CHURCH ATOP, TRYING UNSUCCESSFULLY TO DRAIN ITS POWER.

INDIAN COMMUNITY SCHOOL

MILWAUKEE, WISCONSIN 2003/07

Unfolding elements of the Indian Community School flow through the site, focusing specific planned narrow/wide angle views toward a landscape so similar to the Tribal territories of Wisconsin. Indigenous children of urban Milwaukee are connected to those ancestral lands that many of them have never seen, making the profound heritage of the Chippewa, Ho-Chunk Nation, Menominee Tribe of Wisconsin, Ojibwe, Oneida Nation, Potawatomi, Stockbridge-Munsee, and others, available on a daily basis.

Frustrated with Milwaukee's public school system, discrimination against Native students, and a lack of cultural direction, three Oneida mothers—Marj Stevens, Marge Funmaker, and Darlene Funmaker Neconish—pulled their children out of the public school system and began home schooling them in the basement of one of their homes. Teaching a curriculum that included Native histories, cultures, and communities, what started as seven students quickly grew into thirty-six. Needing a facility, the homeschooling operation moved to the basement of the Church of All People.

In 1971 they moved their growing school to an abandoned Coast Guard station along the Milwaukee lakefront, which they were soon granted control of, and the school was officially incorporated as a nonprofit institution known as the Indian Community School of Milwaukee.

LIKE AN INQUISITIVE SERPENT, MY CLAY MODEL EXPLORES THE SITE. PROGRAMMATIC CUT OUT BLOCKS REFERENTIALLY KEEP IT REAL.

The school flourished in the late '70s under the leadership of Dorothy LePage (Menominee), but it closed in 1983 due to Reagan-era budget cuts. Undeterred, the indigenous leadership raised the money to reopen. They formed partnerships with other local indigenous groups and in 1999 acquired the land where the new school ultimately opened in 2007.

The school provides tuition-free education to students from over fifty different tribal Nations, and offers instruction in four Native languages. Through its Our Ways Teaching and Learning Framework™ it seeks to cultivate in students tribal cultural identity and critical thinking by combining indigenous teachings with a distinguished learning environment.

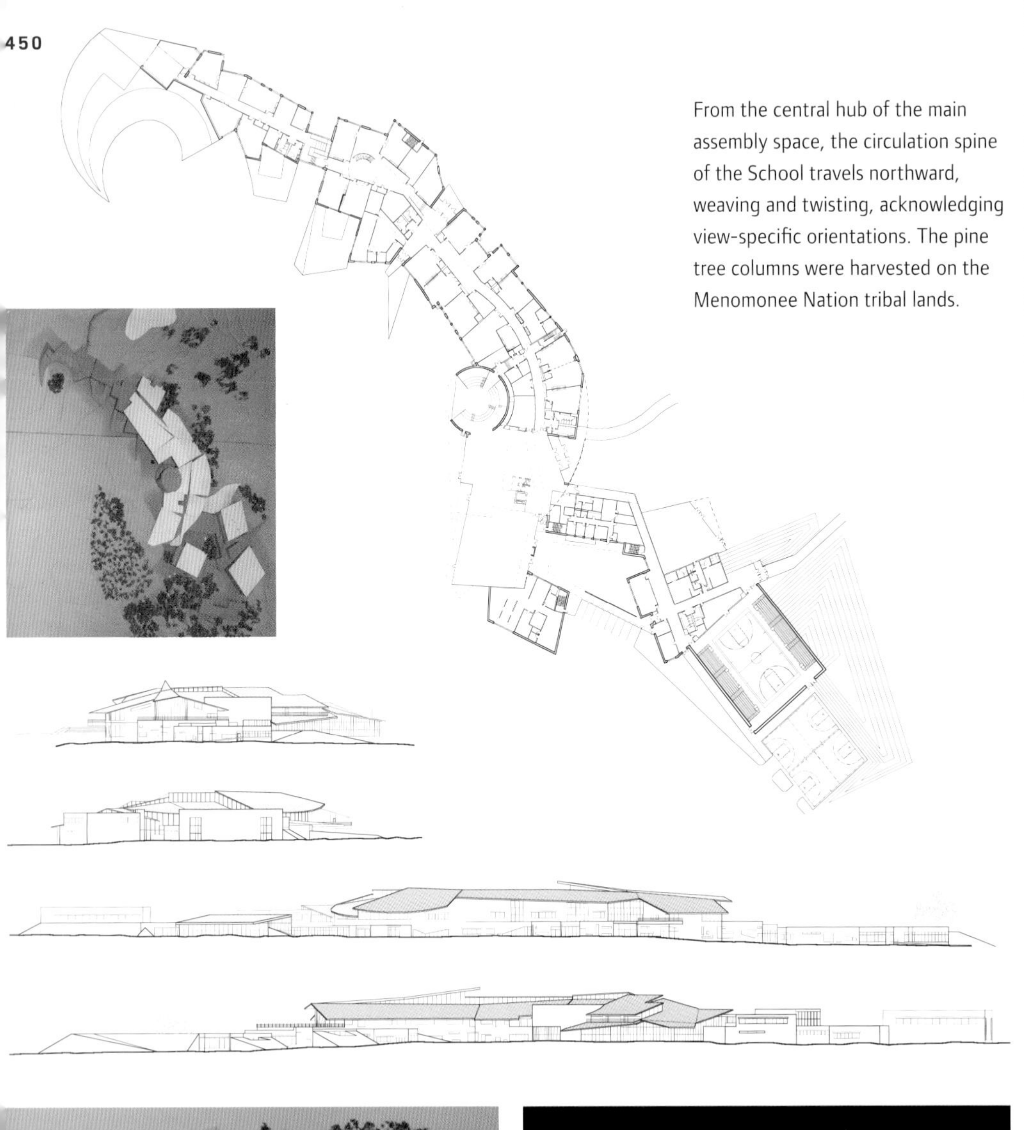

From the central hub of the main assembly space, the circulation spine of the School travels northward, weaving and twisting, acknowledging view-specific orientations. The pine tree columns were harvested on the Menomonee Nation tribal lands.

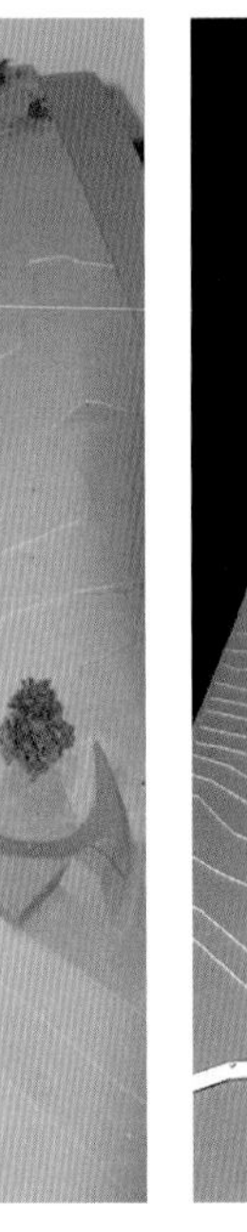

JUDGE JACQUELINE D. SCHELLENGER, A MEMBER OF THE STOCKBRIDGE-MUNSEE BAND OF THE MOHICANS, ICS BOARD MEMBER, AND THEN GENERAL COUNSEL, WAS FOUNDATIONAL TO THE PROJECT'S DEVELOPMENT AND SUCCESS; THE FUNDING OF THE SCHOOL; LOCATING THE SITE; AND PROVIDING INDIGENOUS PEOPLES' CULTURAL INSIGHTS—AND COLLABORATING ON DESIGN DETAILS. PAUL FEHLAU DEVELOPED A CLOSE WORKING RELATIONSHIP WITH JACKIE, AND OF ALL THE MYRIAD PROJECTS HE WAS IN CHARGE OF IN THE STUDIO, THIS IS CLEARLY ONE OF HIS FAVORITES.

ON SITE WITH JACKIE AND EXPLORING WITH THE KIDS WHO WOULD SOON INHABIT THE SCHOOL.

THE DEDICATION CEREMONY OF THE SCHOOL INTRODUCED VISITORS AND DIGNITARIES TO A BUILDING THAT QUITE LITERALLY EXPLORES AND HONORS THE SITE AND THE EASTERN WOODLANDS TRIBAL CULTURES.

A matrix of regionally quarried Mankato limestone elements brings the School exterior expression inside, joining the native timber columns and wood framing. This central ceremonial space is the focus of the curvilinear spine. Other major spaces on the upper level—the library, the classroom progression, and the circular contemplation space that reaches toward the sky—intersect spatially and visually to create activity transparency, reinforcing the unity of the Eastern Woodlands Tribes.

Limestone blocks—communal gathering/instructional spaces, classrooms, gymnasium, and office spaces—anchor the building to the site, captured by prairie grass berms. A flying origami copper roof shelters. Large, glass-enclosed gathering spaces integrate interior and exterior spaces with the surrounding environment. This cross-pollination transparency and connection of learning spaces with the natural environment allows external elements and phenomena to become didactic influences within.

AUTRY NATIONAL CENTER

LOS ANGELES, CALIFORNIA 2005

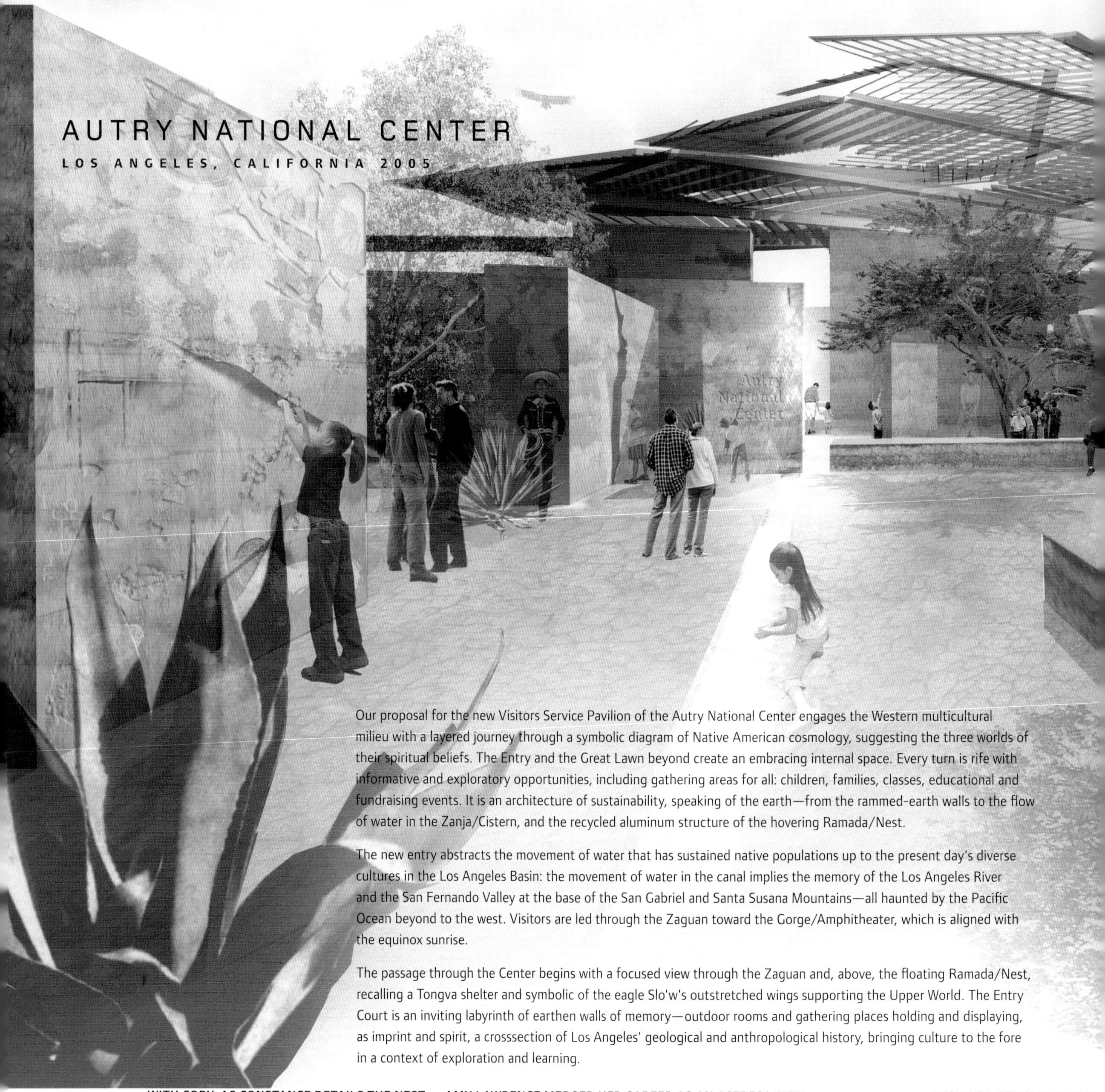

Our proposal for the new Visitors Service Pavilion of the Autry National Center engages the Western multicultural milieu with a layered journey through a symbolic diagram of Native American cosmology, suggesting the three worlds of their spiritual beliefs. The Entry and the Great Lawn beyond create an embracing internal space. Every turn is rife with informative and exploratory opportunities, including gathering areas for all: children, families, classes, educational and fundraising events. It is an architecture of sustainability, speaking of the earth—from the rammed-earth walls to the flow of water in the Zanja/Cistern, and the recycled aluminum structure of the hovering Ramada/Nest.

The new entry abstracts the movement of water that has sustained native populations up to the present day's diverse cultures in the Los Angeles Basin: the movement of water in the canal implies the memory of the Los Angeles River and the San Fernando Valley at the base of the San Gabriel and Santa Susana Mountains—all haunted by the Pacific Ocean beyond to the west. Visitors are led through the Zaguan toward the Gorge/Amphitheater, which is aligned with the equinox sunrise.

The passage through the Center begins with a focused view through the Zaguan and, above, the floating Ramada/Nest, recalling a Tongva shelter and symbolic of the eagle Slo'w's outstretched wings supporting the Upper World. The Entry Court is an inviting labyrinth of earthen walls of memory—outdoor rooms and gathering places holding and displaying, as imprint and spirit, a crosssection of Los Angeles' geological and anthropological history, bringing culture to the fore in a context of exploration and learning.

WITH CORY, AS CONSTANCE DETAILS THE NEST

AMY LAWRENCE MERGED HER CAREER AS AN ACTRESS WITH DOING SUPPORT ADMINISTRATIVE WORK FOR US IN 2005. I COULD IMMEDIATELY SEE THAT SHE WAS SUPREMELY TALENTED, EASILY HANDLING ANY TASK THAT CAME ALONG. WORKING DEEPLY INTO OUR BOOKKEEPING WORLD, AND LATER BECOMING STUDIO MANAGER ON THE ADMINISTRATIVE SIDE—MY EXECUTIVE ASSISTANT WHO IS A JOY TO WORK WITH ON EVERY LEVEL.

MENLO-ATHERTON PERFORMING ARTS CENTER MENLO, CA 2005

DESIGNED CONCURRENTLY
THE UPPER LEVEL BALCONY

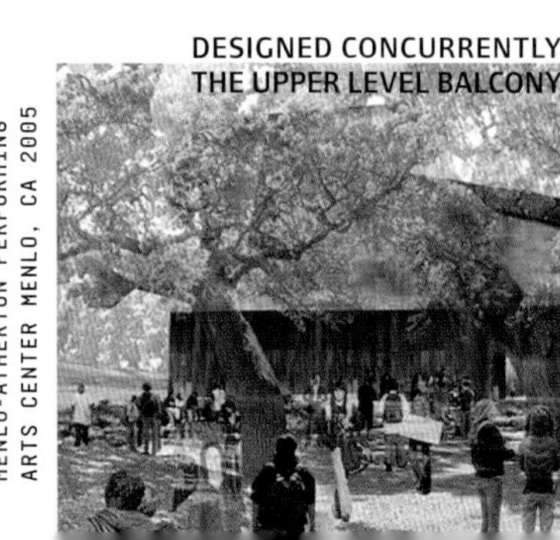

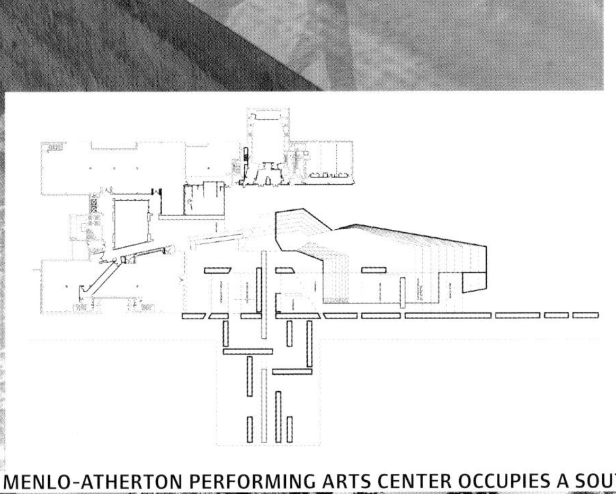

WITH THE AUTRY CENTER, THE MENLO-ATHERTON PERFORMING ARTS CENTER OCCUPIES A SOUTH BAY SAN FRANCISCO SETTING, NESTLING INTO THE LIVE OAK TREES SO
OF THE THEATRE IS TREEHOUSE-LIKE.

RAY AND JOAN KROC COMMUNITY CENTER

CHICAGO, ILLINOIS 2005

IN SOUTH AFRICA DURING THE EARLY 2000s WITH CONSTANCE — CAGE DIVING WITH GREAT WHITE SHARKS, THEN KRUGER NATIONAL PARK "ON SAFARI."

The South Side Chicago project suggests an ascending village overlooking the lobby/interior plaza—a generous sheltered and vibrant communal space with the sociability of a mall. Contemporary culture admixtures make the Community Center accessible to youth, from the Trail of Murals to exterior waystations. Partnerships with "The University of Hip Hop," "Gallery 37," and "After School Matters" build on successful existing Chicago youth mentoring programs. Technology extends the mission in an educational and interactive manner that parallels the neighborhood immersion ethic. Internal and external video projections link the neighborhood to the dynamic life of the Community Center, broadcasting a mini-panorama of events. We won this invited design competition but were denied the commission by the client.

Fully sustainable, and adding nearly 130,000 sf of green roofs and many acres of greenspace to the city landscape, the Kroc Community Center embraces Chicago's remarkable green mandate.

AIR

Ventilation

The open central volume acts as solar plasma naturally ventilating the facility. Air movement is controlled through a series of motorized dampers that open in the summer encouraging natural ventilation and close in the winter. The central concourse provides inductive airflow and functions as a purifying environmental lung. The high central space interconnects the various volumes and will create an environment in which heat rises in a self-purging natural buoyancy effect pushing unwanted heat from the building through motorized louvers. The air distribution systems are designed to accept this natural occurring air movement by using low level, low velocity cooling air ducted through the wall cavities and released into spaces at the floor for unobtrusive and quote supply.

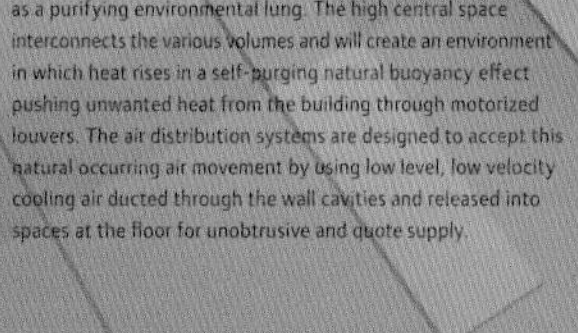

SCIENCE CANYON
COLORADO SPRINGS, CO
2003/07

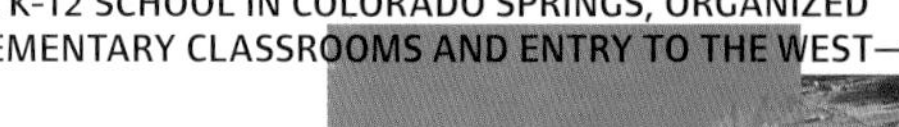

SCIENCE CANYON, A K-12 SCHOOL IN COLORADO SPRINGS, ORGANIZED DESCENDING TO ELEMENTARY CLASSROOMS AND ENTRY TO THE WEST—

From the major approach street, the Kroc Center emerges out of the earth with tilting turf roofs continuing a ground plane of bermed embankments, the backdrop for activities: neighborhood gardening, rooftop receptions, and social gatherings. These strategies of topological displacement define hierarchies of public space ranging from the very intimate to the very large. The animated section creates an integrated plan that utilizes the land to create both enclosed space and open gathering spaces. The external impression is of a building that, although urban, connects to the agricultural areas around Chicago and to an embedded ethos of sustainability.

ENVIRONMENTAL RESPONSIBILITY

Embracing Chicago's commitment to environmental responsibility the RJKCCC is rooted in an environmental response. The RJKCCC incorporates environmental agenda strategies and technologies to enhance occupants' health and well-being, yielding a structure that costs less to operate and requires fewer resources to build and maintain. The re-establishment of prairie grass and native tree groupings alluded to pre-existing natural realms. Entry and public spaces are protected against prevailing winds by RJKCCC massing and are oriented toward the southeast to optimize solar gain. Materials such as quarried limestone and brick are locally sourced to reduce embodies energy. The glazed concourse is ventilated, creating an inductive airflow that is controlled for seasonal heating and cooling, Photovoltaic cells are layered within glazing systems responding to optimal solar collection, desired sun control, and view calibration. Rainwater is collected, controlled and filtered through the green roofs, cistern and constructed wetlands. Vegetation within the sites acts as a bioclimatic "respirator system," constantly purifying the RJKCCC's internal environment. A major goal for the RJKCCC is to be a model for sustainability.

SUN

Solar

Arrays of glazed laminated photovoltaic panels cover the central concourse generating electricity for the RJKCCC while providing filtered sunlight into the interior. This shading reduces mechanical cooling loads.

Natural Light

All areas of the facility are naturally illuminated. High-level windows allow natural light to penetrate deeply into the large sport venues and into the central volume, thereby reducing electrical energy consumption. Louvers are used for sun and glare control. On cloudy days it is anticipated that diffuse sunlight will provide ambient lighting throughout the facility. The artificial lighting system will be installed with a daylight harvesting controller and luminance sensor to reduce electrical use.

Mass

Local quarried limestone embodies qualities of timelessness and thermal stability. The stone and brick finishes clad the facilities yielding thermal stability and a steady stable environment. The durable finishes give the facility not only an aesthetic gravity, but also a thermal stability during the summer months. The cool nighttime summer air is circulated in the space to subsoil the internal thermal mass so that less cooling compressor energy is required the following day. This thermal charging of the mass will created a normal level of radiant cooling. In the winter, the internal thermal mass assists the containment of heat within the insulated wall construction.

WATER

Grass Roofs

Contributing to Mayor Daley's commitment to green roofs the RJKCCC adds 125,000 sf of green for to the city, which in turn improves air quality, conserves energy and reduces storm runoff. Through shading, insulation, and evaporative cooling the facility's green roof will conserve energy use and lower life cycle costs. In addition to energy conservation the green roofs will control storm water runoff by slowly saturating the soil and reducing and releasing runoff in a controlled manner.

Wetland

Storm water that is collected on the roofs and the site will be directed into a constructed wetland to the west with native plants that absorb water and filter pollutants. Rainwater that falls onto paved areas is directed by bivalves to the wetland and is filtered through the native plants. Porous pavement will also be utilized to allow water to seep into the soil rather than runoff. The landscape irrigation system will be connected to this storage system.

Water source heat pump

The RJKCCC will utilize a heat pump system for heating and cooling taking advantage of the free cooling and tempered heating that comes monopolizing on the earth's 54°F temperature in a ground-coupled heat exchanger loop. Using the thermal mass of the wetlands pond as a heat sink, heat is either extracted from or rejected into the water depending on the building cooling or heating cycle. This system uses plastic piping loops in the pond that circulate to the heat exchanger in the central mechanical plant.

Cistern

Water is collected off of the glazed roofs and is funneled to an interior pool near the worship space elevator. This cistern coupled with plants to provide a level of low cost humidification for public gathering spaces.

AROUND A SUNKEN AND PROTECTED EXTERIOR CIRCULATION CORE STRETCHING FROM THE AMPHITHEATER AT THE UPPER GRADES TO THE EAST—AIMING VIEWS TOWARD THE MASSIVE PIKES PEAK.

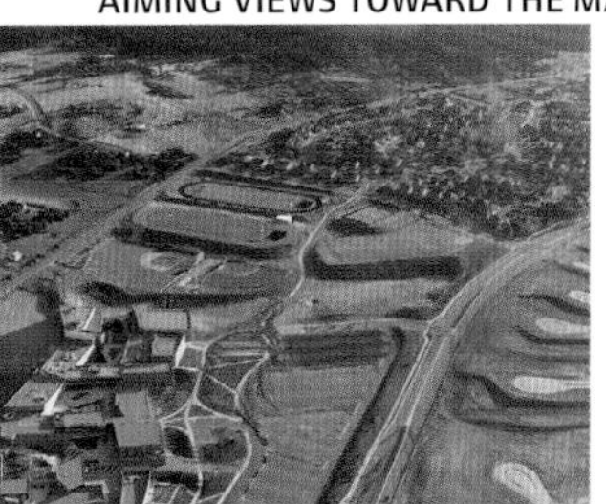

Buddha in the Mogao caves

Drawing at the Jiaohe ruins, Turfan

Sam Sterling

Drawing critique from Uyghur friend

Dunhuang

Turfan adobe mosque and minaret

With my colleague Sam Sterling in Turfan

Temple spires, Dali, Yunnan

Dali

Connected with Italian bikers riding the Silk Road

FORBIDDEN CITY, BEIJING

WINTER PALACE, BEIJING

TEMPLE OF HEAVEN, BEIJING

NOMADIC STUDIO

Competitions—won and lost—are critical exercises. They have a catalytic effect on the studio. There is an intense compression to our process. They affirm, in a most profound way, the shared belief system we, in the studio, have about architecture. Other projects do the same thing, only in slow motion compared to the competition charrette.

The rhythms of the studio are ever changing—with high-stakes competitions played against large projects that are years in the making. There is always a cross-pollination between the two. In fact, the boundaries between concurrent projects often blur. There is an all-pervasive energy that ricochets around the studio, that moves as my teams move.

The terrain of the studio is malleable when all this parallel work is going on—especially the model work, often starting with clay and moving to mixed media of every sort. The collages that are often constructed as part of the competition process are embedded in a studio-wide engagement that is itself collage-like. The cacophony of images on computer monitors is part of an overall atmosphere that merges random research and physical results in a collective aura.

Amid the charrette energy is the travel and the drawing, the capturing of the spirit and the critical information of a specific place. The studio is part of an ongoing creative diaspora, with teams scattering to unknown lands. The studio is decentralized and nomadic. **I am always in my studio, no matter where I am.** The wonderful dislocation of travel intersects the process alignments of all projects—the longer-term and the short-lived.

On the Silk Road in China, I may be doing pastel drawings while colleagues who accompany me may be documenting and decoding cultural strata, all of which is transmitted back to Albuquerque, or Taipei, or wherever the focus of activity may be.

Filtering all of the information we gather, merging it, infusing and informing our other efforts with it, the results of the competition charrette process are intensely molded and distilled. How we present the result, like the scroll created for the National Palace Museum competition, drawing on the memory of the hand scrolls of the Northern Song Dynasty, may be as competition and place specific as the result itself.

All of the competitions we do, all of my projects, become deeply personal—the process of cultural and geographic immersion being so intense. But some, in the context of competitions that are programmatically eclectic and widely scattered geographically, have the admixture of being personal from the very inception. The competition for the University of New Mexico School of Architecture was one of those.

In the 1950s I drove an old Plymouth across the country on Highway 66 to enter the engineering program at the University of New Mexico. The drama of the transition from the Great Plains to the first mountains on the horizon, and the procession through the notch in the great wall of the Sandia Mountains suddenly revealing the sweep of the Rio Grande valley and the nascent and sprawling city of Albuquerque were unforgettable. As I got closer to Albuquerque, the highway took on a more quasi-urban character with a succession of motels, tourist courts, and neon cafés. The site for the competition, amazingly, was on Highway 66, across the street from what I remember as the campus soda fountain.

I could never have imagined, arriving on the UNM campus fifty years ago as an engineering student, that I would have the opportunity to design a building with the intention of providing the same inspiration that I had received. Winning that competition, bringing to it (and the building) the deeper continuities of my accumulated experience provides an extraordinary kind of closure for me.

You never know, even if you think you do, where you're going. That cross-country trip I took 70 years ago has led somewhere I could never have imagined. Every project is like that too. Every competition, even if we don't get the commission, is a win—what we have made, what we've experienced, goes into a spiritual savings account from which we can withdraw forever.

Great Wall at Mutianyu

SILK ROAD AND ASIA TRAVEL

2005/PRESENT

Bezeklik Caves, Taklamakan Desert

Mogao Caves

Reclining Buddha Mogao Caves

My drawing of the vast array of ceramic warriors signed by the Star of the Visitor Center, Yang Zhifa

2005 TRIP WITH SAM—CERAMIC WARRIORS, HORSES, AND THE CELEBRITY OF THE VISITOR'S CENTER, YANG ZHIFA, WHO DISCOVERED THEM, XI'AN, CHINA.

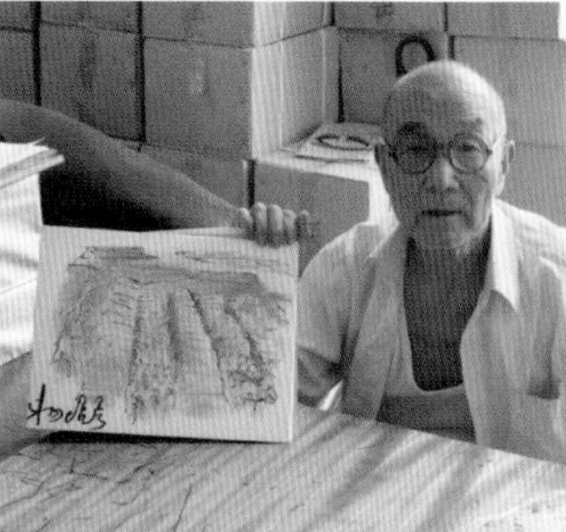

Jiaohe ruins, Turfan

Tourist Architects Sam and Cory with me in Lijang

Thinker/Designer Sam Sterling preceded Paul Fehlau as my Executive Senior Associate and was ground floor on so many projects, most notably the launch of the National Palace Museum competition—and Cory Greenfield picked up the reins on OSU when Sam left, having major design/management responsibilities on many projects with Aperture Center standing out along with the OSU Student Athletic Center.

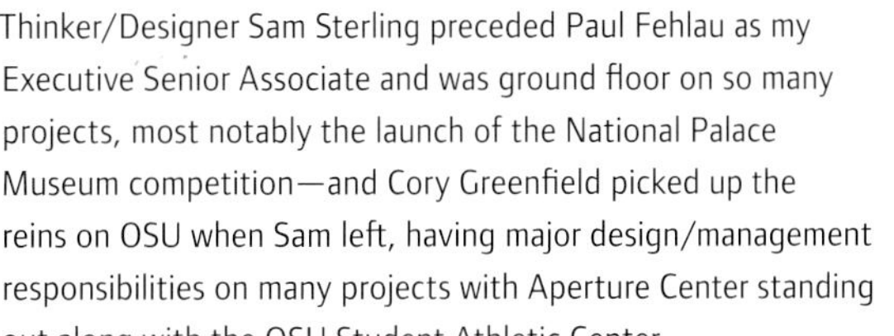

Gualthang, Tibetan Monastery

Lakeside temples, Lijang

Wild Goose Pavilion, Xi'an

MODERN TOWERS, BY KPF AND SOM,
PUDONG, SHANGHAI

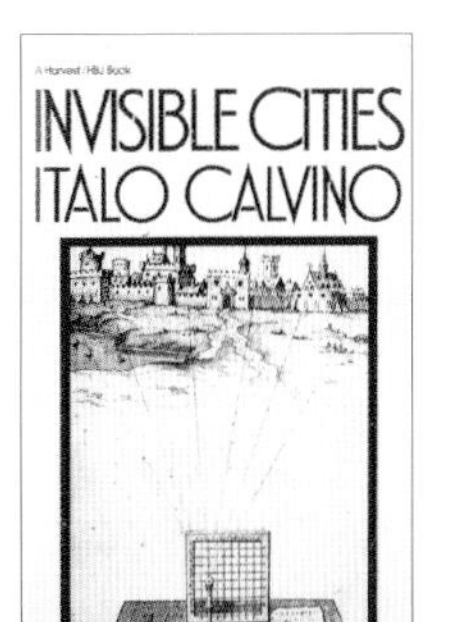

"ARRIVING AT EACH NEW CITY, THE TRAVELER FINDS AGAIN A PAST OF HIS THAT HE DID NOT KNOW HE HAD: THE FOREIGNNESS OF WHAT YOU NO LONGER ARE OR NO LONGER POSSESS LIES IN WAIT FOR YOU IN FOREIGN, UNPOSSESSED PLACES."

Italo Calvino, *Invisible Cities*, 1972

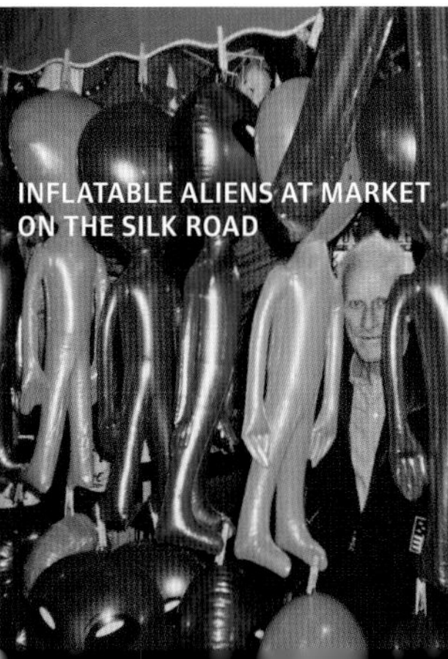

INFLATABLE ALIENS AT MARKET ON THE SILK ROAD

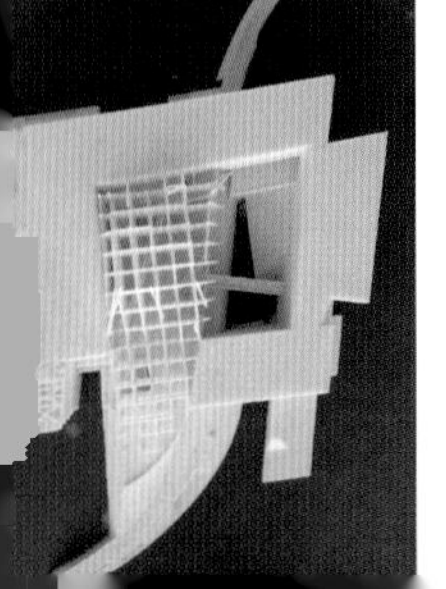

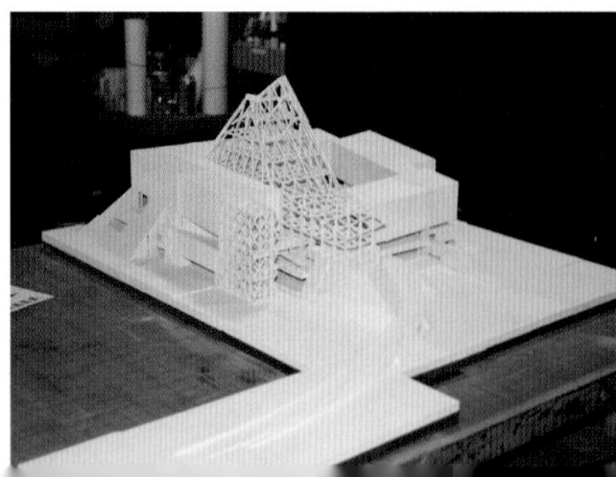

Through natural biomes, evoking diverse pan-Asian landscapes, the Museum comes into view: a base of ancient stream-washed Taroko marble rising low and long out of watery mists; a slow ascending gallery spiral, an artifact of inscripted, weathered bronze embracing a mythic garden as the glass and cypress Jade Mountain dissolves into the clouds. The Mountain of Longevity and the Sea of Happiness inextricably and symbiotically linked by an internal journey—an episodic scroll—that travels through Asian space and time.

The conceptual armature of the Museum is both literal and abstract—an inhabited mythic Asian space embedded with auspicious content, symbolic of Asian reverence for nature and man's position between heaven and earth. The literal Chinese definition of landscape—Shan shui—is "mountains" and "water." Like a calligraphic radical (the visual component set that forms the basis of Chinese characters), the Museum is a landscape, it is mountain and water. A faceted, jade-tinted glass and cypress structure—Jade Mountain—rises from the Museum courtyard, aiming toward the tallest peak in Taiwan, Yu Shan. In Taiwanese aboriginal cosmology, Yu Shan is known as Pattonkan, "Glowing Mountain" or "Quartz Mountain." Water flows from our Jade Mountain to the quarry-like Lotus Pond amphitheater. The "Three Friends of Winter"—Bamboo, Plum, and Pine—extend the courtyard garden landscape with fortuitous symbolism.

The Taroko marble base recalls Taiwan's geologic origins. Slowly rising, the galleries are sheathed in protective bronze skin, patinated to the color of Shang dynasty bronze. Digital projections activate the glass skin of the Jade Mountain and paint the inside of the Media Lantern, reinforcing cultural fusion and programmatic intention. Red-lacquered ramps weave through the wood structure as this subliminal procession through Asian heritage culminates in a rarified mountaintop refuge, affording magnificent views over the Museum, lake, and Yu Shan beyond.

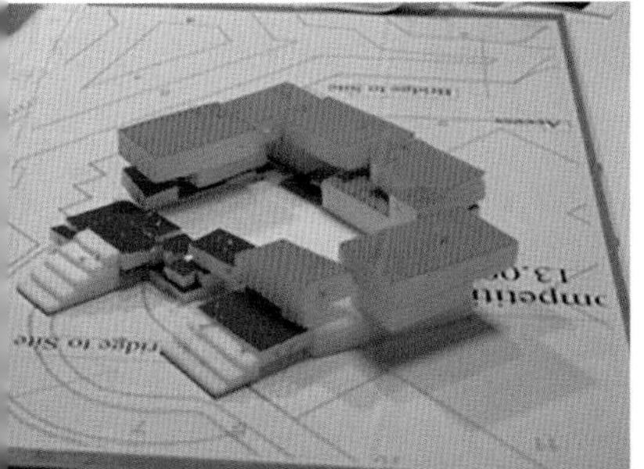

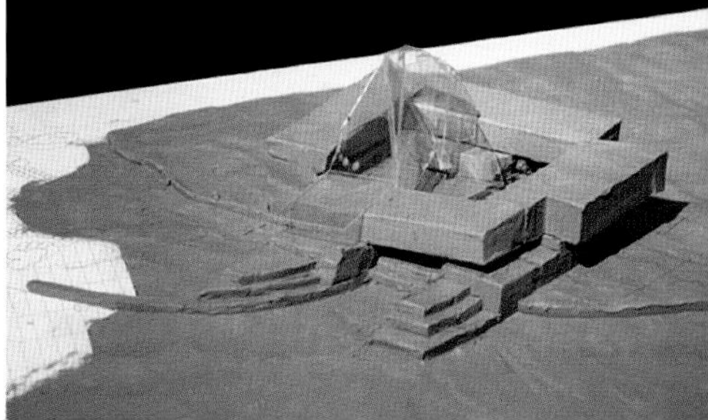

NATIONAL PALACE MUSEUM SOUTHERN BRANCH

CHIAYI, TAIWAN 2004/08

FROM CLAY TO GROUNDBREAKING

"You can go into a deep, mysterious gulley, dredge out a spring and dig out a watercourse at the bottom; then excavate the hollows and the foot of the hill, banking up earth on which to build rooms and walkways. All kinds of trees will reach up to the sky, and the tops of towers will appear and disappear among the clouds. Flowers in profusion will cover the ground, and terraces will rise at varying heights above the surface of the water.

The misty water spreads into the distance, cloudy mountains shimmer on the horizon … water birds soar through the air. The rooftops are hidden in the drifting layers of mist; terraces rise to meet the new moon."

Ji Cheng, *Yuan Ye (The Craft of Gardens)*, 1634

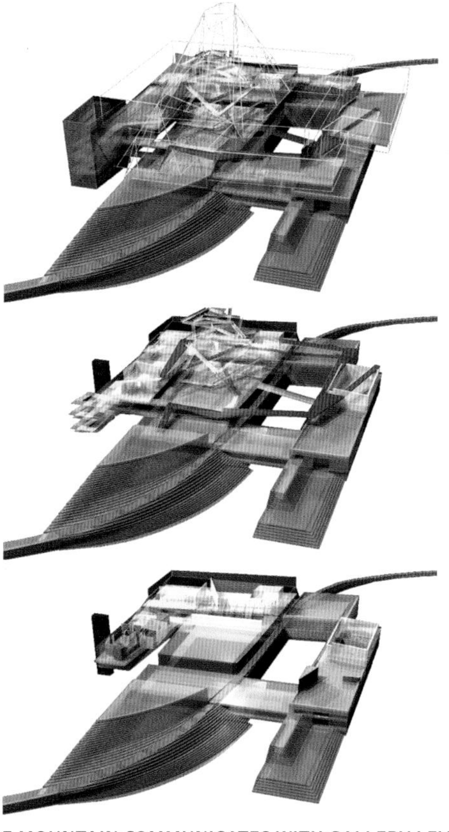

Circulation diagrams show the open public-access route through the museum and beyond to the Pan-Asian gardens, independent of Museum hours.

Cooler air strata over the lake surface rises inductively to ventilate and naturally cool Jade Mountain.

SECTIONALLY, JADE MOUNTAIN COMMUNICATES WITH GALLERY LEVELS

PLAN REVIEW WITH MUSEUM CURATORIAL STAFF

The Museum experience is offered as a cinematographic unfolding of space. Similar to a viewer visually traveling through a Northern Song Dynasty Shan Shui hand scroll, museum visitors accumulate experiences as spatial episodes, accruing an ebbing and flowing Pan-Asian experience, aided and abetted by digital media.

FOR THE JURIED COMPETITION PRESENTATION, WE MADE A HAND SCROLL AND THE PROJECT TEAM ACCOMPANIED ME TO TAIWAN. HIGHLY RESPECTED COMPETITORS WERE THERE,

INCLUDING KENGO KUMA, MVRDV AND OTHERS. PREPARING WITH CHRISTINE AND BRIAN FOR THE PRESENTATION IN OUR HOTEL ROOM.

IN FRONT OF THE PRESENTATION VENUE

OUR PRESENTATION BOARDS AND MODEL INSTALLED

"Especially impressive is the way in which Predock developed public spaces that will wind their way through the building, providing highly dramatic and shaded outdoor areas in which the natural setting and the cultural fortress will become entwined.

Predock understood better than any of the other finalists that the NPMSB is a symbolic structure that must make its own place, becoming a built argument for the necessity of displaying Chinese art on this site."

Aaron Betsky, "Towards a Magic Mountain," *Competitions*, Spring 2005

Museum Internet café

AT THE NATIONAL SCIENCE EDUCATION CENTER PRESENTATION VENUE WITH MY TEAM.

HUDDLING WITH THE MUSEUM DIRECTOR AND MINISTER LIN.

JURY MEMBERS, INCLUDING AARON BETSKY, VIEWING OUR MODEL.

24/7 public circulation route flows through the Museum base, passing the lotus pond, irrespective of Museum hours.

WITH TEAM MEMBERS JOSÉ AND CHRISTINE

DIGNITARIES ANNOUNCING OUR WINNING COMPETITION ENTRY

主體建築以太魯閣大理石、檜木建材象徵台灣山水

故宮南院設計案 黑馬普列多克出線

Scroll Gallery

Buddhist Gallery

17th-Century Gallery... the time when awareness of Western culture permeated Asia... deployment of controlling perspective in Chinese art supplants the freedom of circumstantial spatial organization as was in hand scrolls depicting villages.

Quentin Tarantino's *Kill Bill* was a reversal, co-opting Japanese Manga and folklore and, in doing so, becoming another kind of Western intruder—just as Western architects designing a museum for Asian art, so the circle closes...

AFTER RECEIVING COMPETITION RESULTS OUR WINNING TEAM HEADED OUT FOR R&R IN TAIPEI AND SOUTHERN TAIWAN. PARTY TIME!

KENJI AND JOSÉ

And surely you have seen, in the darkness of the innermost rooms of these huge buildings, to which the sunlight never penetrates, how the gold leaf of a sliding door or screen will pick up a distant glimmer from the garden, then suddenly send forth an ethereal glow, a faint golden light cast into the enveloping darkness, like the glow upon the horizon at sunset.

Jun'ichiro Tanizaki, *In Praise of Shadows*, 1933

Tapestry Gallery

The viewer experiences spatial episodes, accruing a Pan-Asian perspective that continually branches, ebbs, and flows. A wireless digital overlay throughout the site and all galleries, interweaves pan-Asian subtexts—culminating in the glowing stone Media Lantern, a digitally painted Mogao cave. Like a colophon on a scroll, the Museum accumulates memory and experience from digital iterations.

Digital Gallery

KAOHSIUNG AND POINTS SOUTH—

BEACH PENT-UP ENERGY RELEASE.

AND THEN BACK TO TAIPEI

PROJECT DEDICATION EVENT, WITH TAIWAN'S PRESIDENT CHEN SHUI-BIAN

MEETING THE 2ND DIRECTOR

MUSEUM TEAM AND OUR TEAM

WITH MY HEAVY HITTERS SAM, PAUL, CORY, MING, AND OUR COLLEAGUE HSINGPING

Jade Mountain, the fortress-like repository of the National Palace Museum's Pan-Asian collection, in dialogue with Yu Shan, highest peak in Taiwan

TAIWAN TEAM WITH PAUL—FUYUAN SU, HSINPING LIN, CHI-CHENG LEE, MING CHEN

PROJECT SITE— FILLING THE LAKE

The procession through the sequenced museum galleries culminates in an ascent of the Tower of Hope with panoramic views of sky, city, and the natural realm. With glacial timelessness, the Tower of Hope is a peaceful beacon for humanity. Symbolic of changes in the physical state—ice, water, and vapor—the tower speaks to the life-affirming hope for positive change. The crystalline glass Cloud wrapping the Garden of Contemplation illuminates the layered, open trays of administrative and curatorial support of the Museum. The light-filled and buoyant Cloud rises in marked contrast to the gravity of the Roots and Stone Galleries. The emerging Tower a visible reminder of the Power of Hope.

Along with exhibition spaces, the Museum program includes office areas, classrooms, museum store, and café. Local Tyndall limestone, a high-performance glazing system, and cast-in-place concrete comprise the perimeter shell of the Museum. Major interior materials include limestone wall cladding, basalt paving, alabaster, cast-in-place concrete, plaster walls and ceilings, and ground-and-polished concrete floors. The Canadian Museum for Human Rights is LEED® certified. The Auditorium, Great Hall, and Garden of Contemplation are all equipped with services and rigging systems and can be deployed for Museum and off-hour private events. The Museum's education wing has flexible classroom space that can be divided into three classrooms, used as a single studio, or for community workshops.

The Canadian Museum for Human Rights—one of Canada's now five National Museums, and the first outside the nation's capital of Ottawa—makes visible the fundamental commonality of humankind. Joined to the earth, and dissolving into the Winnipeg horizon, the abstract ephemeral wings of a white dove embrace a mythic stone mountain of 450 million-year-old Tyndall limestone. The structure is a timeless landmark for all nations and cultures—a symbolic apparition of ice, clouds, and stone set in a field of sweet grass—appropriately sited at the Forks—the historic location where First Nations leaders peacefully negotiated treaties and territorial disputes.

The Visitor's entrance, between protective stone arms/roots suggestive of an ancient geological event, symbolically recognizes the earth as the spiritual center for many indigenous cultures. Clutching the earth, the Roots are positioned to block northern and northwestern winds, and celebrate the sun with apertures marking paths for the sun at the equinox and solstice.

The arrival heart of the building, the Great Hall, is carved from the earth—evoking the memory of ancient gatherings at the Forks of First Nations peoples, and later, settlers and immigrants. Poised above the great hall is the basalt mass of the Garden of Contemplation, becoming a Winter Garden for Winnipeg. A columnar basalt matrix defines pools with medicinal plants within the Garden, commingling with an assembly/event space. The Garden functions as a purifying "lung," reinforcing the fundamental environmental ethic that grounds the building.

CANADIAN MUSEUM FOR HUMAN RIGHTS

WINNIPEG, MANITOBA 2004/14

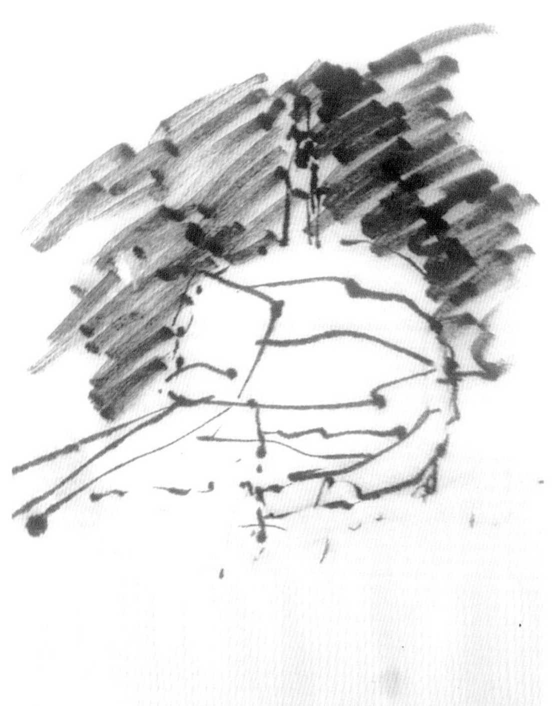

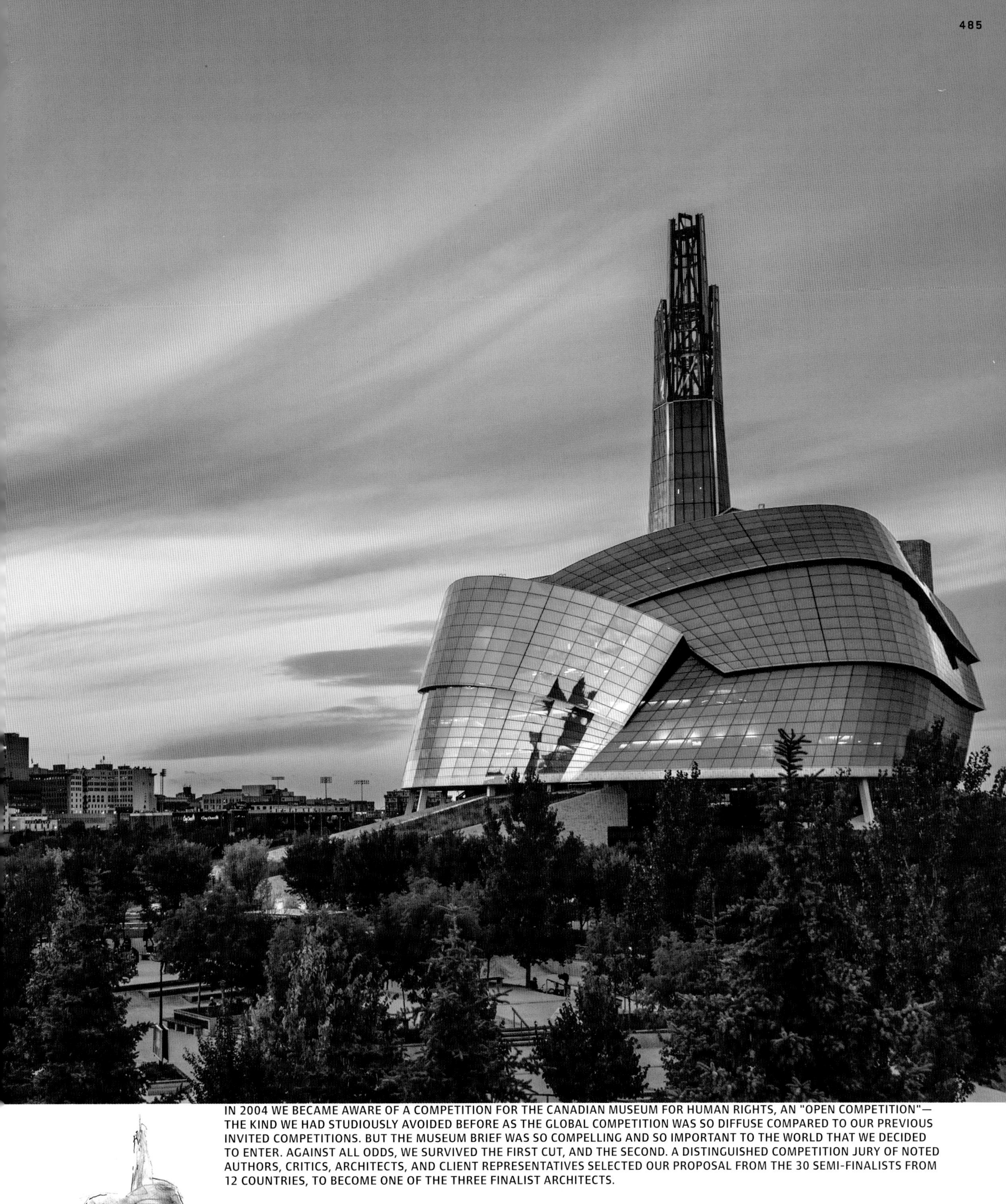

IN 2004 WE BECAME AWARE OF A COMPETITION FOR THE CANADIAN MUSEUM FOR HUMAN RIGHTS, AN "OPEN COMPETITION"—THE KIND WE HAD STUDIOUSLY AVOIDED BEFORE AS THE GLOBAL COMPETITION WAS SO DIFFUSE COMPARED TO OUR PREVIOUS INVITED COMPETITIONS. BUT THE MUSEUM BRIEF WAS SO COMPELLING AND SO IMPORTANT TO THE WORLD THAT WE DECIDED TO ENTER. AGAINST ALL ODDS, WE SURVIVED THE FIRST CUT, AND THE SECOND. A DISTINGUISHED COMPETITION JURY OF NOTED AUTHORS, CRITICS, ARCHITECTS, AND CLIENT REPRESENTATIVES SELECTED OUR PROPOSAL FROM THE 30 SEMI-FINALISTS FROM 12 COUNTRIES, TO BECOME ONE OF THE THREE FINALIST ARCHITECTS.

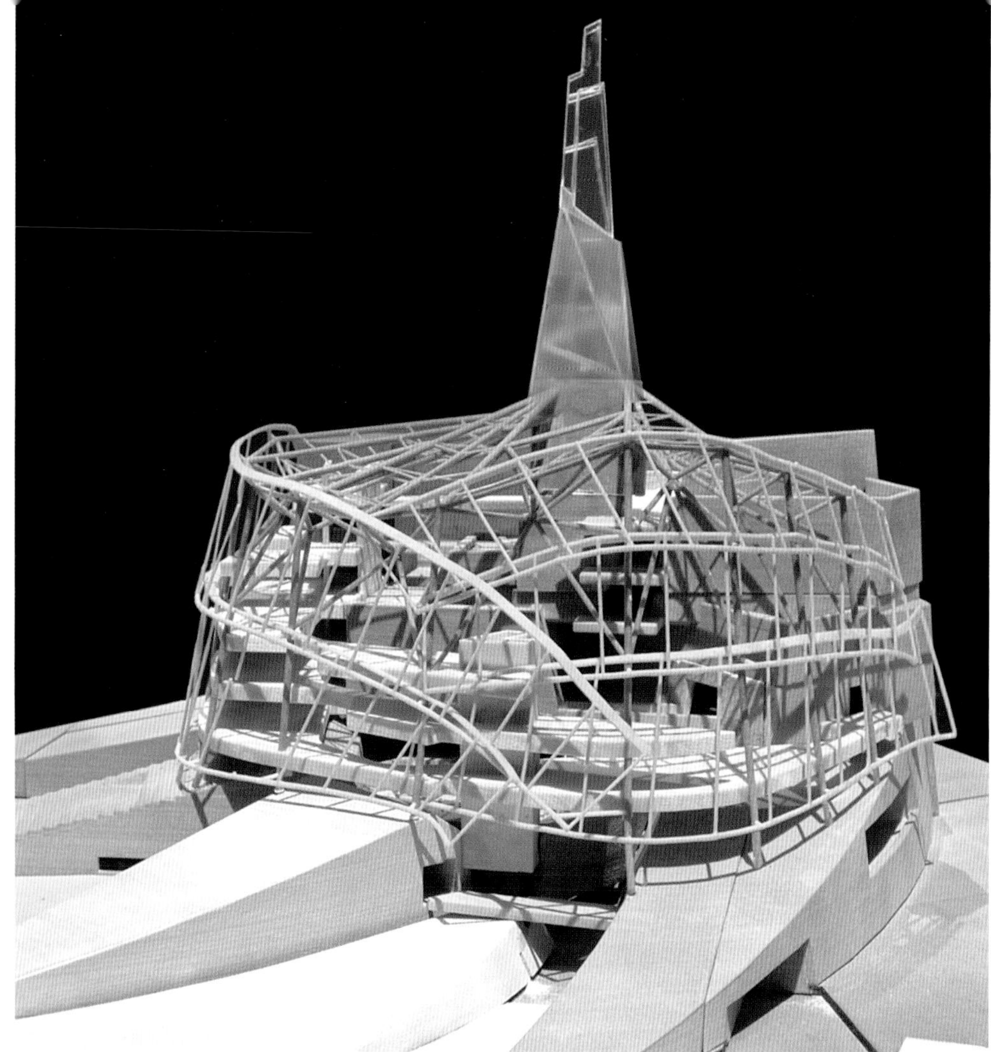

"... the Museum for Human Rights appears to have been designed from the inside-out—driven less by photogenic form than by a cinematically and psychologically immersive experience over time. 'It isn't a museum of objects,' Predock says. 'It's a museum about ideas. It's a process building. It's a procession building.'"

Thomas de Monchaux, *Architect Magazine*, Jan. 19, 2015

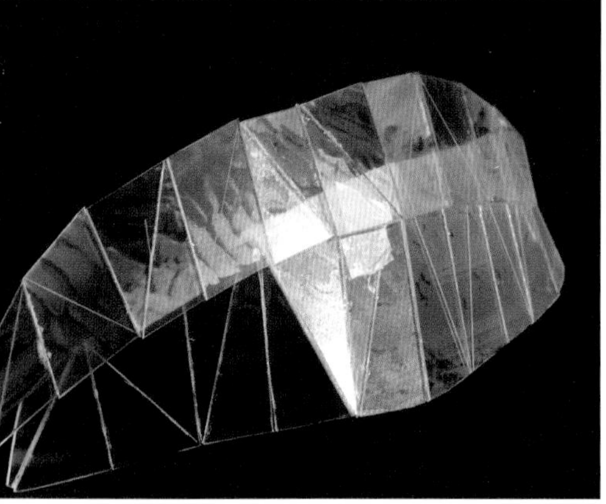

Friends of The Canadian Museum for Human Rights Inc. announced the 30 architectural firms selected by the Architectural Review Sub-Committee in Stage 1 of the International Architectural Design Competition for The Canadian Museum for Human Rights. They were chosen from almost 500 architectural firms internationally that indicated their interest and 63 who answered a Call for Expression of Interest in Stage 1 of the competition. The Sub-Committee members were Ms. Gail Asper, Mr. David Covo, Mr. Gustavo Da Roza, Mr. Robert Fulford, Mr. Moe Levy, and Dr. Raymond Moriyama. The 30 firms, spanning 12 countries (Canada, U.S.A., South Africa, Germany, India, Spain, El Salvador, Norway, Australia, Denmark, Austria, and the U.K.) from five continents (North America, Europe, Africa, Asia, and Australia), are:

Antoine Predock Architect, USA
Architects for Human Rights, El Salvador
Ashton Ragatt McDougall Pty Ltd (ARM), Australia
Behnish, Behnish & Partner Architekten, Germany
Charles Correa Associates, India
Coop Himmelb(l)au, Austria
Cote y Terradas, Arquitectos, Spain/Canada
Dan Hanganu & The Arcop Group, Canada
Diamond and Schmitt Architects Incorporated, Canada
Douglas J. Cardinal Architect, Ltd, Canada
Gehry Partners, LLP, USA
Marosi + Troy/Jodoin Lamarre Pratte/Architects, Canada
Mashabane Rose Architects, South Africa
MEDIUM/Tomizo Yamamoto Architect, Canada
Michael Fieldman, Architect, USA
Michael Maltzan Architecture, Inc., USA
Moshe Safdie and Associates Inc., USA
Saia Barbarese Topouzanov/Tetreault Parent Languredoc Architectes, Canada
Saucier + Perrotte Architects, Canada
Schmidt Hammer & Lassen, Denmark
Schwartz Architects and EHDD Architecture, USA
SITE, USA
Skidmore, Owings & Merrill LLP, USA
SNOHETTA, Norway
Studio Daniel Libeskind, USA
Sturgess Architecture with IBI Group/Stecheson Katz Architects, Canada
TEN Arquitectos and Kuwabara Payne McKenna Blumberg Architects, USA/Canada
VanTine/Guthrie Studio of Architecture and Neumann/Smith & Associates USA
Zaha Hadid Architects, UK
Zeidler Partnership Architects, Canada

CMHR GUITAR HAPPENED ALONG THE WAY...

The mother and her babies.

My initial clay model and sectional sketch, established the intention: roots engaging the Earth, then a progression—from darkness to light.

Former Senior Associate José Sanchez, CMHR project architect, worked closely with me to keep my clay model accurate with respect to programmatic space planning as we went along. Then José, phase-by-phase, directed technical and engineering coordination through construction, assisted by Graham Hogan.

Many, many model iterations flowed through the competition design process—chipboard, foamcore, rapid-prototyping 3D printing. My colleague for more than ten years now, Senior Associate Veree Simons; as seen with Associate Kenji Kondo and so many others, delivered brilliantly throughout the charrette.

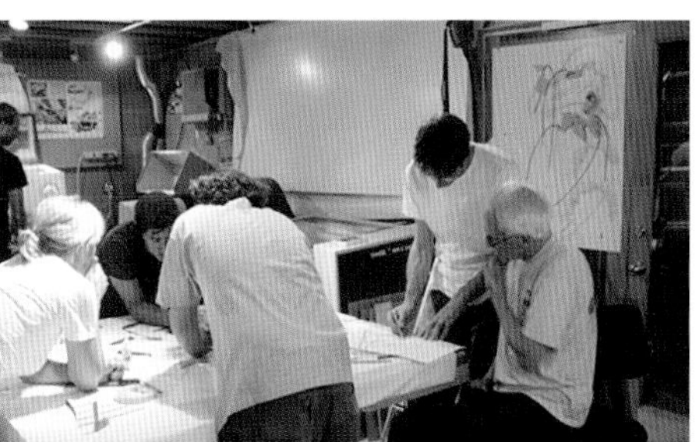

"Something about Predock's Canadian Museum for Human Rights serves as a reminder that, even as you seek to live out humane values far from the follies and fortunes that architecture requires, sometimes—however secularly, however awkwardly, however ambitiously—you also need a Cathedral."

Thomas de Monchaux, *Architect Magazine*, Jan. 19, 2015

FROM OUR MULTI-BUILDING STUDIO HUDDLE EMERGED WHAT WE CALLED "THE CANADA HOUSE" WHERE THE EARLY PROCESS WORK UNFOLDED.

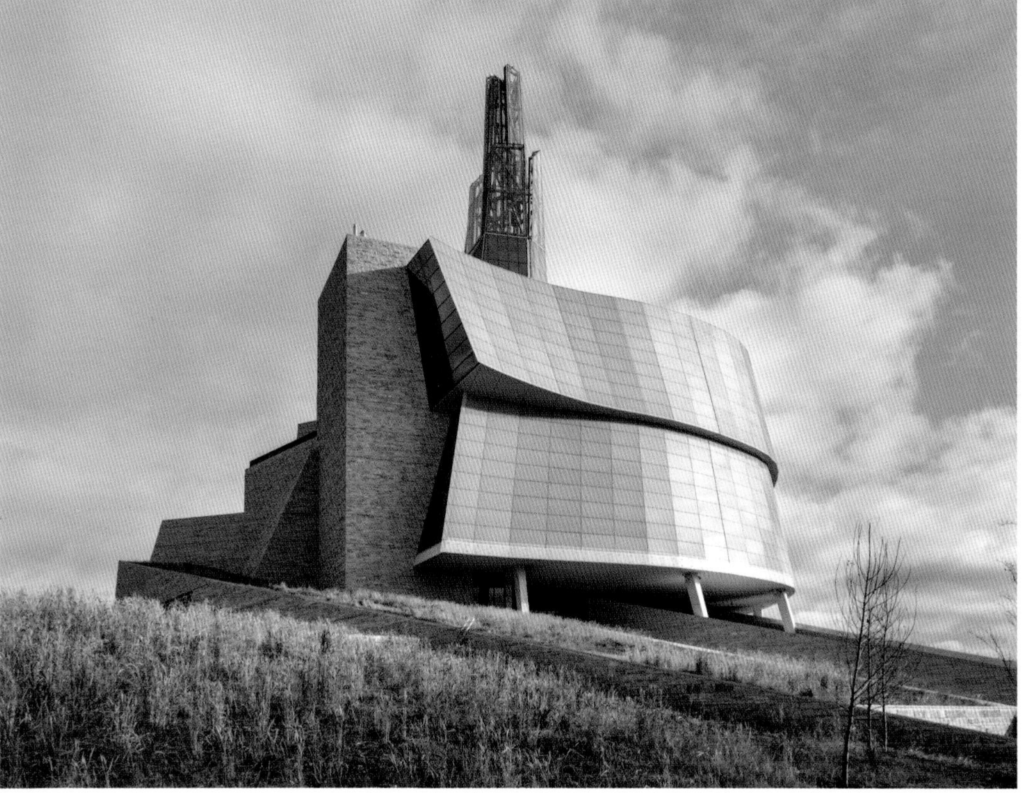

"Let's remember what we're trying to do here. Look out at this Winnipeg landscape! What have we got? Grey square box after grey box and another grey square box! When you look out at Jerusalem, for example, what catches your eye? The Dome of the Rock. It's round. It's bright. It's different. It's beautiful. We just can't have more of the same here."

Gail Asper, *Miracle at the Forks*, 2014

VISITING WINNIPEG, QUEEN ELIZABETH GAVE HER BLESSING TO THE PROJECT. HER ROYAL HIGHNESS BROUGHT WITH HER A STONE FROM RUNNYMEDE WHERE THE MAGNA CARTA WAS SIGNED, WHICH WAS INCORPORATED INTO THE STONEWORK OF THE MUSEUM.

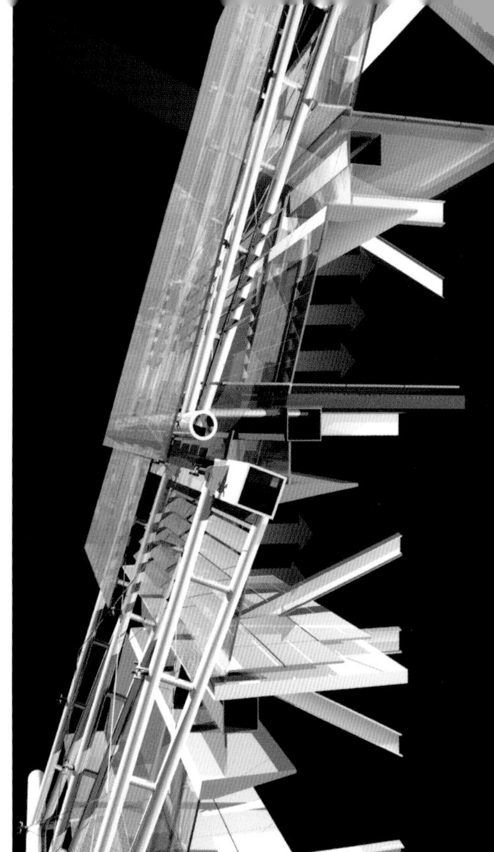

"His architecture is more art than science, an outgrowth of his considerations of how Mother Earth connects with humanity—and by extension, with the organic elements of his unusual designs. Debate and criticism doesn't rile this master architect—not one bit. It only encourages him. In assessing his work, Canadian visitors must never forget that Predock knew exactly what he intended doing: to build a museum that would be like no other, in that it would take its visitors' breaths away. He has achieved precisely that."

Peter C. Newman, Allan Levine, *Miracle at the Forks*, 2014

:TITION MODEL FOR SHIPMENT AND THEN OUT THE T THROUGH DENVER TO RENDEZVOUS WITH THE VSTORM CAUSED ME TO MISS THE CONNECTION TO T DAY SO MY ONLY ALTERNATIVE WAS TO CHARTER A N OF A LIFETIME." MY HATRED FOR UNITED AIRLINES E HAD WON THE COMPETITION.

VEREE—A KEY PLAYER IN THE DESIGN PROCESS

CLOUD

The crystalline Cloud structure that wraps the south façade is a double-glazed cavity that captures natural light, solar radiation, and induces gravity ventilation. The vented cavity is an active buffer between the external and internal environments. In the heat of the summer the cavity produces a solar chimney providing natural ventilation. Louvers between the different planes are located at the base and the top of each plane. These louvers are opened on the cooling cycle, drawing cool air in low and then out through an exhaust slot at the top. In the winter months the louvers are closed, creating an insulative buffer in the cavity to temper sub-freezing outdoor air temperatures.

CLOUD SKIN

The Cloud is composed of a series of overlapping arcing steel "wing" structures that support the outer skin of glass. Each individual "wing" has a curved primary support tube at the top, from which tapered tubular trusses drop vertically to support the glass at approximately 4 meters on center. The ends of these glazed trusses are tied together by 400 mm diameter pipes. The 600-750 mm primary tubes are the main spanning members, and are connected back to the columns through thermally isolated joints. At the top wings, and in areas where the wings extend out beyond the columns, the tube's torsional stiffness resists movement. The bottom tube provides another degree of bending stiffness to the overall system, and cable cross-bracing is provided between the top and bottom chords to provide unified truss action and rigidity.

CLOUD FLOORS

The primary structure for the Cloud floor trays that wrap the central volume and overlook the Garden, consists of arched trusses that anchor to the Roots at their base. Inclined exterior columns spring from the foundation level, extend through the roots, and continue up through to the Tower of Hope. Column spacing is approximately 10-12 meters on center to limit the structural depth of the floors. At floor levels, steel braces connect to inner columns. At specific bays, the inner and outer columns are braced together for rigidity. For space planning flexibility, floor diaphragms can be used to distribute forces back to the trussed bays. Rotation of the inclined columns is resisted by the U-shaped floor plates, which are braced in plan and act as horizontal arches, transferring inward forces back to the Stone Gallery structures.

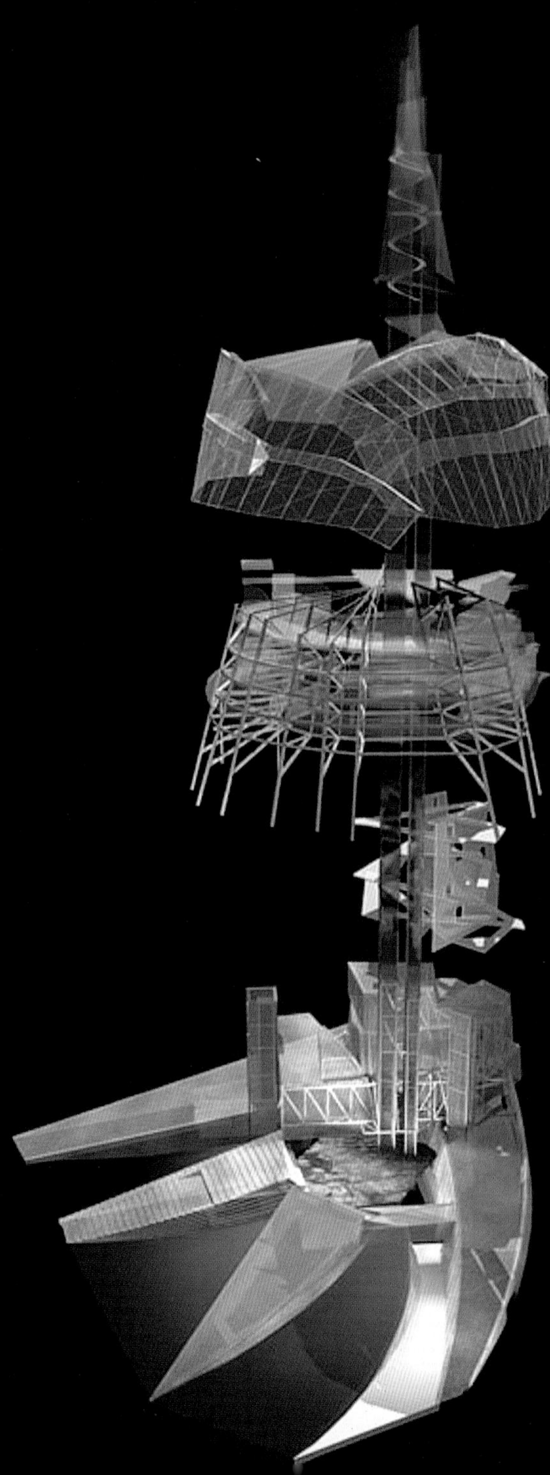

WITH VEREE AND TEAM PREPPING THE COMP
DOOR INTO THE TRUCK. ON MY WINTER FLIG
MODEL FOR THE JURY PRESENTATION, A SNO
WINNIPEG. I HAD TO BE IN WINNIPEG THE NE
JET ($$$$) TO MAKE IT TO THE "PRESENTATI
DISSIPATED WHEN WE WERE NOTIFIED THAT

KAROLE MAZEIKA, JARED WINCHESTER, AND JOSÉ SANCHEZ

REVIEWING THE COMPETITION PRESENTATION WITH GRAHAM AND EXECUTIVE SENIOR ASSOCIATE PAUL.

"Predock's buildings are marked by the burden and possibility of history, the beauty and beastliness of nature—and by the signs of a search for shared experience that can transcend the vagaries of time and place."

Sylvia Lavin, Professor of History and Theory of Architecture, Princeton University

AFTER AN EXTENSIVE ARCHAEOLOGICAL INVESTIGATION, CONSTRUCTION BEGAN...

FROM THE BARE SITE STAIR TOWERS WERE THE FIRST TO SPROUT—ALONG WITH THE BLACK CONCRETE ARMATURES THAT ANTICIPATE THE ALABASTER LABYRINTH

THEN THE SKELETAL "RIB CAGE" OF THE CLOUD.

WITH MOE LEVY AND GAIL ASPER, WHO WAS THE FORCE BEHIND THE MUSEUM AFTER IZZY ASPER, HER FATHER, PASSED AWAY. GAIL LEAD THE CHARGE SPIRITUALLY AND IN FUNDRAISING. MOE WAS THE OMNIPRESENT EXPEDITER OF THE PROJECT FROM CONCEPTION TO DEDICATION, AND BECAME A FRIEND, ALONG WITH GAIL AND HER MOTHER, BABS.

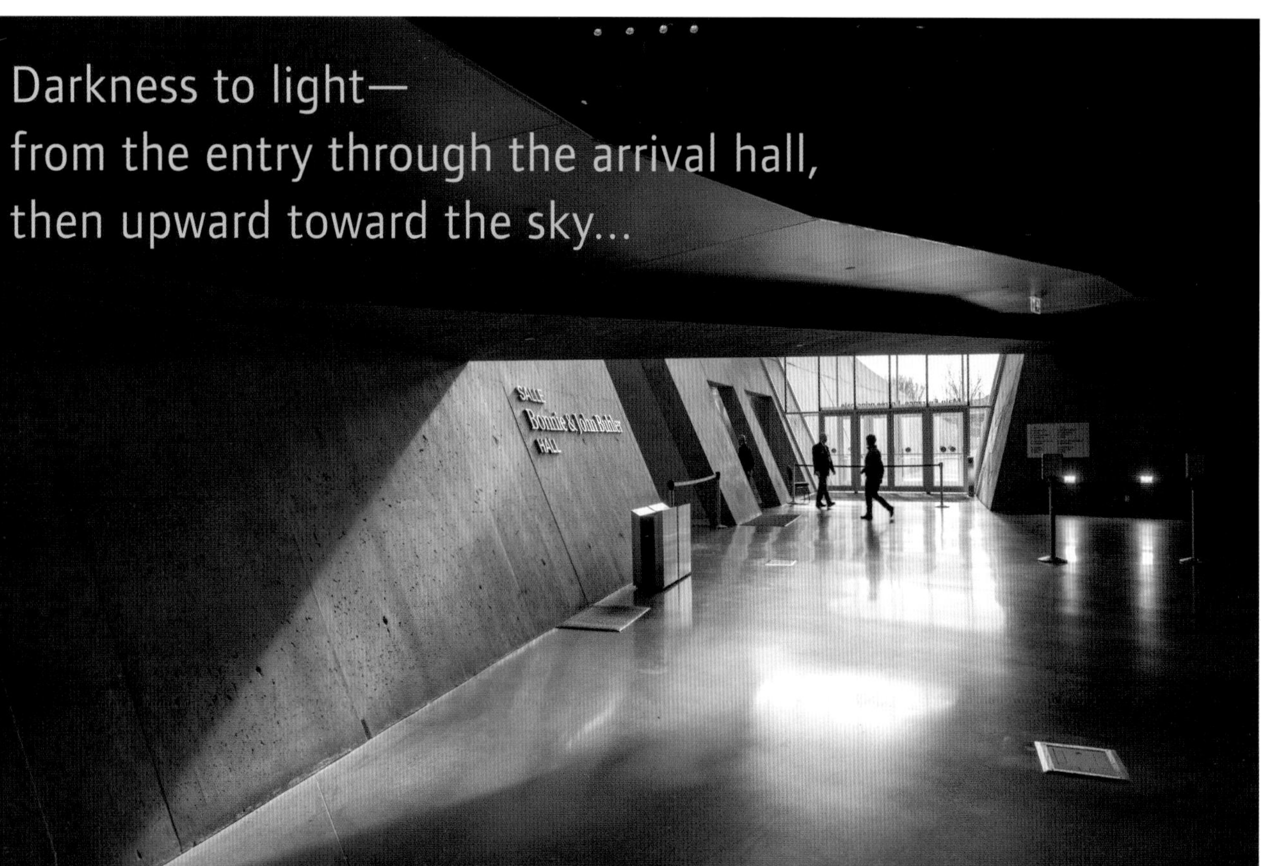

Darkness to light—
from the entry through the arrival hall,
then upward toward the sky...

QUARRIES IN ARAGON, SPAIN TO CONFIRM THE SELECTION FOR THE ALABASTER RAMPWAYS.

WITH COLLEAGUES JOSÉ AND GRANT VAN IDERSTEIN MEETING WITH REPRESENTATIVES OF THE QUARRIES.

THE ALABASTER READY FOR DEPARTURE TO CANADA.

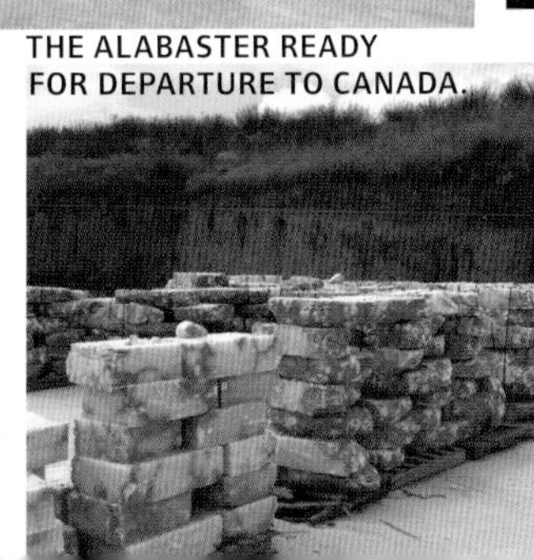

A FEW SAMPLES ARRIVING AT OUR ALBUQUERQUE STUDIO.

Alabaster is a sacred material to me—evoking ancient times, as a container for potions and unguents. The Canadian Museum for Human Rights is also a vessel—transporting/containing an investigation into horror and humanity. There is a freshness, a cleansing aspect intrinsic to the alabaster. The glowing bridges provide a pause for personal reflection in the black void between galleries. There's about a kilometer of circulation in this Museum. In those pauses, visitors can process what they've experienced and prepare for the next gallery.

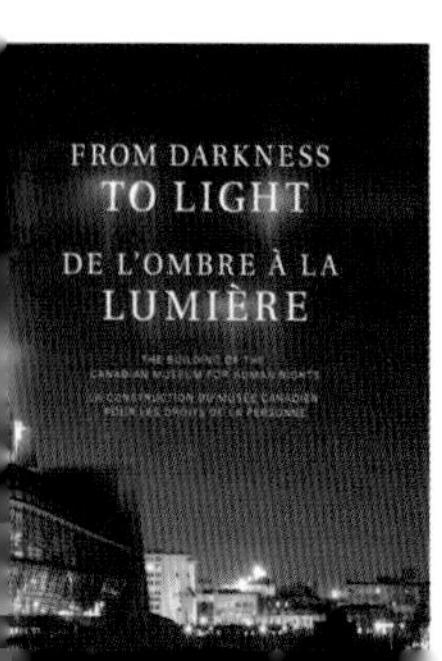

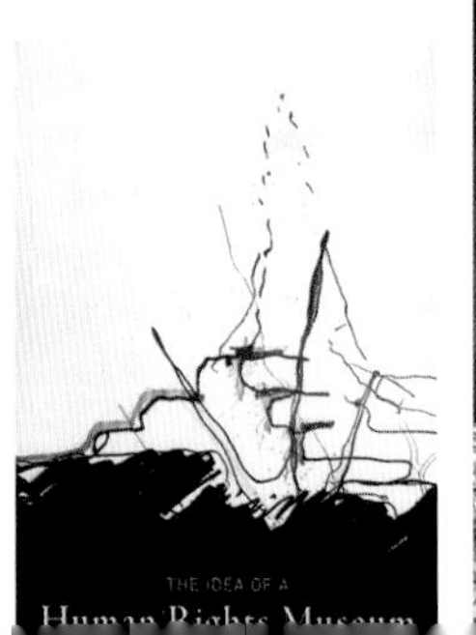

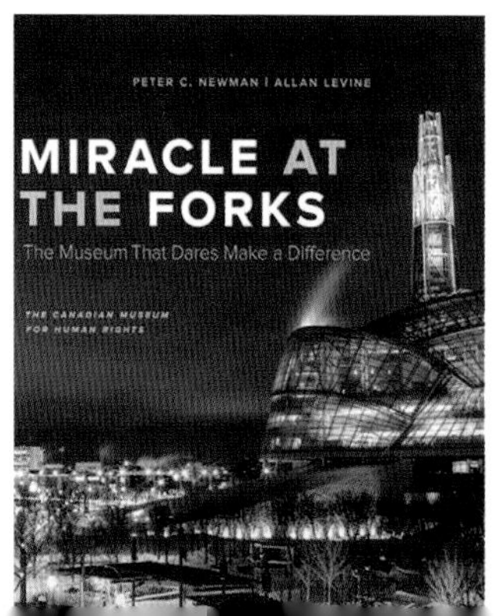

"Competition aside, the new museum is a glorious structure, meant to impress not only by what it is but also by the positive influence its staff and visitors are expected to yield. This is not another public service boondoggle or a political football. It is, for once, an altruistic and urgently required facility to improve the vital arena of how we treat one another. It will mean nothing if it doesn't make the people whose actions deserve it become furious and frantic when, following due process, they are forbidden to continue doing unto others what they don't want done to themselves. And that applies to anybody, anywhere, who is abusing human rights."

Peter C. Newman and Allan Levine, *Miracle at the Forks*, 2014

You ascend toward the light from darkness—from the semi-darkness of the arrival, into the ground with muted light in the great hall arrival point, then ascend the glowing alabaster rampways to the light of the Tower of Hope, and then descend via the ramps or elevator to land at the Garden of Contemplation to process what you've seen.

"The procession is choreographed and kinetic. Recalling the switchback canyon roads where he rides his motorcycles, Predock describes the path through the museum as a 'back and forth duality of light and of dark. It's a big-picture duality, dark where you begin, light where you ascend.' At the entrance, 'you're in a chamber with fissures of light coming in under dark above,' he says. Then 'you ascend, like in a John Cage concert when he would just sit at the piano and not play.' The ascent leads, 'to a narrow space that starts out as a black void. It's lined in integrally colored black concrete, not paint or plaster,' and spanned by ramped bridges clad in luminous alabaster. A full kilometer of shallow switchback ramps crisscross that void, leading in and out of all the galleries. ... 'It's episodic,' Predock says. 'Along the way, the bridges are waystations. When you are on them, one after the next, you are in this safe zone, and you can look up at the sky and down to the earth. You think about what you've seen and get ready for the next gallery. There's a lot of bad stuff you learn about. But a lot of good stuff too. You look up and you think: 'Oh man, I've got a long way to go,' and 'I wonder if I'll make it to that tower.'"

Thomas de Monchaux, *Architect Magazine*, Jan. 19, 2015

The black-walled void—the silence, no exhibitry, no sound. It's a pause between courses of a sometimes hard-to-handle meal.

Visitors may need the pauses the ramps provide.

THE DRIVE TO THE ZARAGOZA TRAIN STATION PAST THE GIANT VETERANO BRANDY BULLS—
THEN SKETCH VIEWS OUT THE WINDOW ON THE TRAIN TO BARCELONA TO FLY HOME.

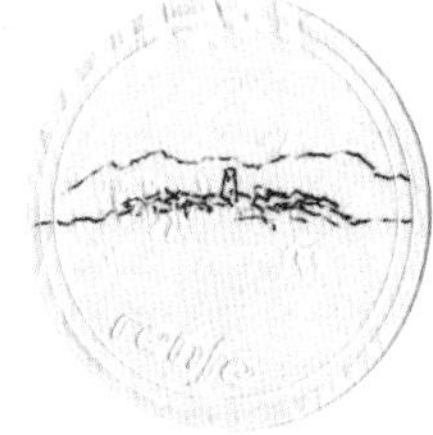

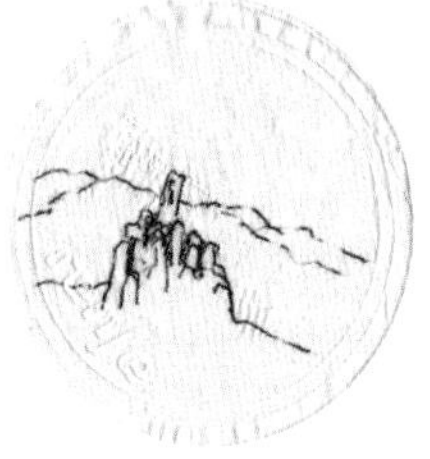

QUARRYING THE MANITOBA TYNDALL LIMESTONE, WITH ITS ENDLESS SEABED FOSSIL STRATA. INSPECTING THE EARLY POURED CONCRETE WALLS.

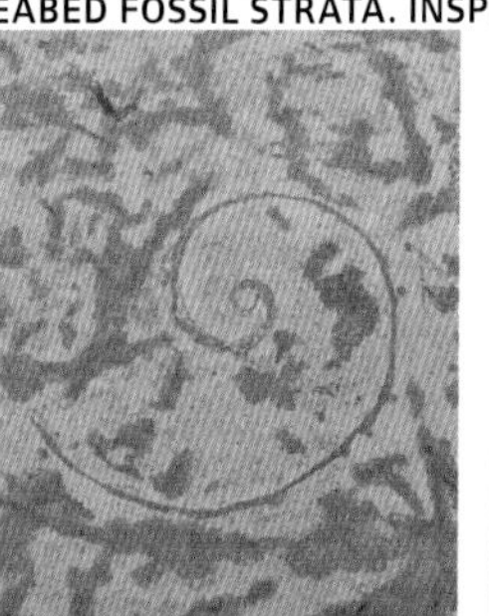

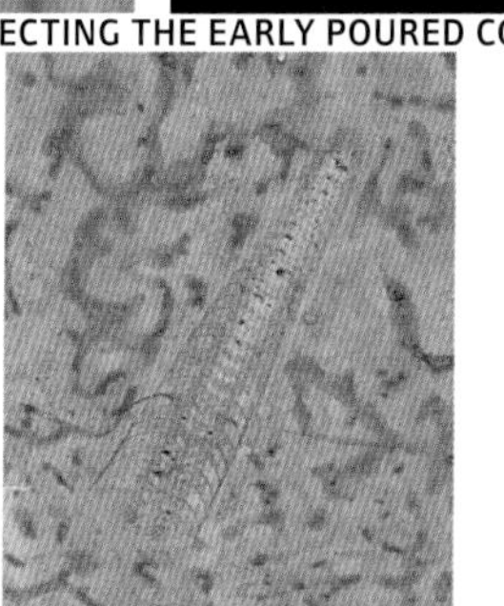

"This building is itself, perhaps, more about action than seamless completion—more open to personal experience and individual interpretation than the totalizingly hermetic self-reference to which many contemporary would-be monuments are prone. There is something of the deliberate awkwardness of a modern dancer who eschews the pretty gesture in order to tell you something else: Here, the seams show—massive nodes of raw structural steel push past the stone and glass to let you know that for all its volcanic and glacial geomancy, the building is the work of human industry and intention."

Thomas de Monchaux,
Architect Magazine, Jan. 19, 2015

"Utzon and Saarinen, and now perhaps Predock, have long served as an irritating conscience to an architectural profession that has, steadily and calculatedly, settled for less and less in the aspirational mission of the built environment."

Thomas de Monchaux, *Architect Magazine*, Jan. 19, 2015

A globally active administrative/research "village" arrays within the Cloud—an international participant with "its finger on the pulse" of conflict and resolution. Those successive trays of human rights workers, in full view of Museum visitors, are an exhibit—it's not just a museum of objects.

HILLARY CLINTON AND COUNTLESS OTHERS HAVE LEFT NOTICE OF THEIR EXPERIENCE IN THE MUSEUM AT THE CONCLUSION OF THE GALLERY SEQUENCE.

The overarching transparent Cloud has at its base the Garden of Contemplation—a place of respite and reflection amidst exhibitions of Human Rights tragedy and hope.

As the Museum use has played out, it is clear that the Garden has become a special place for non-museum-based gatherings of all sorts—public, corporate, and private: receptions, musical events, weddings... It has also become a Winter Garden for a city that is bitterly cold for considerable lengths of time.

THE INNER MONGOLIA BASALT QUARRIES

TORONTO LECTURE

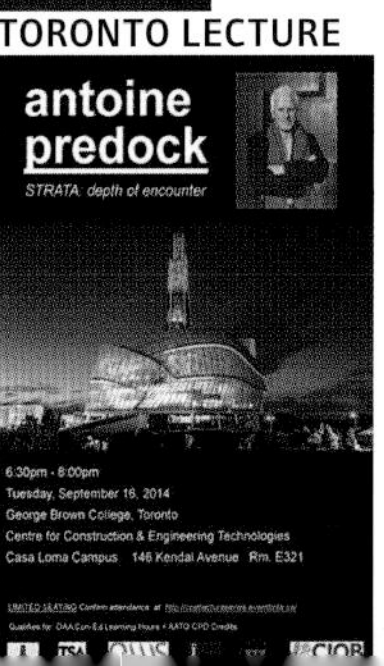

CLARENCE NEPINAK SPEAKING FOR FIRST NATIONS PEOPLES AT THE DEDICATION

BARB AND CLARENCE NEPINAK, FIRST NATIONS COLLABORATORS

DANCE, MUSIC, AND A SPECIAL PERFORMANCE BY BUFFY ST. MARIE AT THE OPENING CEREMONY

"Something about Predock's Canadian Museum for Human Rights serves as a reminder that, even as you seek to live out humane values far from the follies and fortunes that architecture requires, sometimes—however secularly, however awkwardly, however ambitiously—you also need a Cathedral."

Thomas de Monchaux, *Architect Magazine*, Jan. 19, 2015

LIGHTING OF THE TOWER CELEBRATES CANADA DAY AND OTHER AUSPICIOUS EVENTS

10 CANADA

THIS NOTE IS LEGAL TENDER
CE BILLET A COURS LÉGAL
ÉMISSION / ISSUE 2018 • OTTAWA

SPECIMEN

VIOLA DESMOND

BANK OF CANADA • BANQUE DU CANADA
DIX • TEN DOLLARS

SOUS-GOUVERNEURE DEPUTY GOVERNOR GOVERNOR GOUVERNEUR

10

10

JHS2912607

La loi ne fait acception de personne et s'applique également à tous, et tous ont droit à la même protection et au même bénéfice de la loi, indépendamment de toute discrimination [...]
Charte canadienne des droits et libertés, article 15

Every individual is equal before and under the law and has the right to the equal protection and equal benefit of the law without discrimination...
Canadian Charter of Rights and Freedoms, section 15

JHS2912607

SPECIMEN

CANADIAN MUSEUM FOR HUMAN RIGHTS
MUSÉE CANADIEN POUR LES DROITS DE LA PERSONNE

10 CANADA

A new Canadian $10 note honors Civil Rights icon Viola Desmond, with the Canadian Museum for Human Rights on the reverse side.

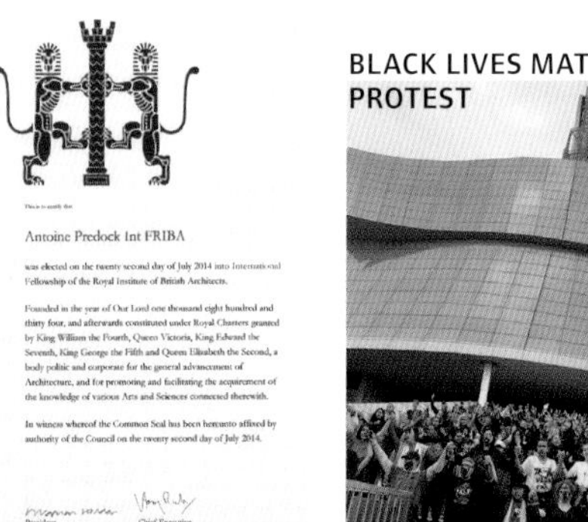

This is to certify that

Antoine Predock Int FRIBA

was elected on the twenty second day of July 2014 into International Fellowship of the Royal Institute of British Architects.

Founded in the year of Our Lord one thousand eight hundred and thirty four, and afterwards constituted under Royal Charters granted by King William the Fourth, Queen Victoria, King Edward the Seventh, King George the Fifth and Queen Elizabeth the Second, a body politic and corporate for the general advancement of Architecture, and for promoting and facilitating the acquirement of the knowledge of various Arts and Sciences connected therewith.

In witness whereof the Common Seal has been hereunto affixed by authority of the Council on the twenty second day of July 2014.

President Chief Executive

BLACK LIVES MATTER PROTEST

WITH WANDA DESMOND, SISTER OF VIOLA DESMOND, AT THE DEDICATION CEREMONY FOR THE NEW $10 NOTE, ALONG WITH CANADIAN LEADERS

GAIL ASPER PROUDLY DISPLAYING THE $10 NOTE

Canada Post postage stamp and mail cancellation stamp

The anchoring of the Museum as a major Canadian landmark...

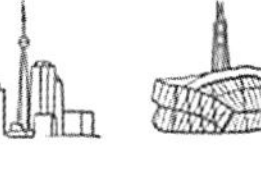

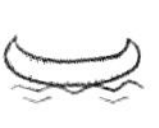

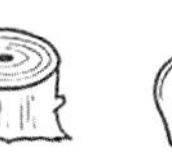
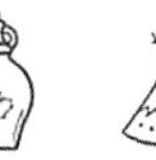

Included in a set of quintessential Canadian symbols

With my Associate Architect leaders Grant Van Iderstine and Jim Weselake of Architecture49, who delivered the project along with the great contractor team of PCL Construction

This Is To Certify That

Antoine Predock

was admitted on the 29th day of May 2014 as an

HONORARY FELLOW

of the

ROYAL ARCHITECTURAL INSTITUTE OF CANADA

Founded in the year of our Lord, One thousand nine hundred and seven, and afterwards constituted under Royal Charters granted by King Edward the Seventh, King George the Fifth, and Queen Elizabeth the Second, a body politic and corporate, to establish and maintain a bond between the Royal Institute and component or allied societies, to promote architectural appreciation and the interchange of knowledge pertaining to the practice of architecture, and to encourage and recognize worthy aspirants to the profession.

IN WITNESS whereof Officers of the College of Fellows have hereto set their hands, and the Common Seal of the Institute has been hereto affixed under authority of the Board of Directors dated the 28th day of May 2014.

Registered Serial No. 1231

Chancellor

Registrar

President of Architecture Canada / RAIC

RAIC Fellowship induction ceremony at the Museum

Drawn for pleasure by Canadian Prime Minister Justin Trudeau, later auctioned on eBay in support of the Museum

Canadian Architect magazine

Thank you PCL Construction!

Honorific Tattoo

The first building on a Canadian note

Grandstand array for the Opening Ceremony

CHOCOLATE SCULPTURE BY CANADIAN CHOCOLATIER CONSTANCE POPP (ON HER BIKE AT -10°F)

MUSEUM POSTER SIGNING

"To enter his new museum, visitors must find their way through four gigantic stone arms extending out from the center of the building, calibrated to block northern and northwestern winds, and descend below ground level into Mother Earth, where everyone's journey begins. This connection is a dramatic curtain raiser for a riveting climb that climaxes, many impressions later, in the Tower of Hope."

Peter C. Newman and Allan Levine,
Miracle at the Forks, 2014

ANTOINE PREDOCK

AIA GOLD MEDAL, SMITHSONIAN COOPER-HEWITT MUSEUM LIFETIME ACHIEVEMENT AWARD, NATIONAL ACADEMY ACADEMICIAN

2006, 2007, 2014

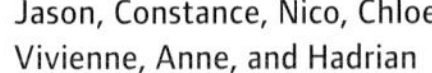
Jason, Constance, Nico, Chloe, Vivienne, Anne, and Hadrian

THE AMERICAN INSTITUTE OF ARCHITECTS
IS PRIVILEGED TO CONFER THE

GOLD MEDAL

ON

ANTOINE PREDOCK, FAIA

MIND, HEART; BODY, SOUL;
TIMELESS YET OF THE MOMENT,
HIS ARCHITECTURE RESOLVES DICHOTOMIES,
ORCHESTRATING HARMONIES OUT OF
THE DISPARATE VOICES OF MATERIAL AND SPIRIT,
TEASING THE MOST ARTICULATE CRAFTSMANSHIP
FROM THE GRASP OF THE EARTH'S ELEMENTAL GEOMETRY,
GIVING A SHAPE TO DUST.
OF HIS PASSION, OF HIS GENIUS
IN LISTENING TO HOW A SITE SPEAKS TO HIM,
IT MAY BE SAID THAT THE SPIRIT OF THE LAND
RISES UP TO MEET HIM
AND THE VERY ROCKS THEMSELVES REJOICE IN
THE COMPANY OF HIS ART.

10 FEBRUARY 2006

KATHERINE L. SCHWENNSEN, FAIA
PRESIDENT

JOHN C. SENHAUSER, FAIA
SECRETARY

Honoring Don Schlegel at the ceremony

"I know that architecture is a ride—an intellectual/spiritual and physical ride, a ride with the adrenalin of a rollercoaster, a fascinating journey towards the unexpected."

Antoine Predock, Gold Medal Remarks

COOPER-HEWITT LIFETIME ACHIEVEMENT AWARD—2007

COOPER-HEWITT

NATIONAL DESIGN AWARDS

07

LIFETIME ACHIEVEMENT AWARD

Antoine Predock

October 18, 2007

Paul Warwick Thompson
Director, Cooper-Hewitt, National Design Museum

Dr. Cristián Samper
Acting Secretary, Smithsonian Institution

Smithsonian
Cooper-Hewitt, National Design Museum

NATIONAL ACADEMY—2014

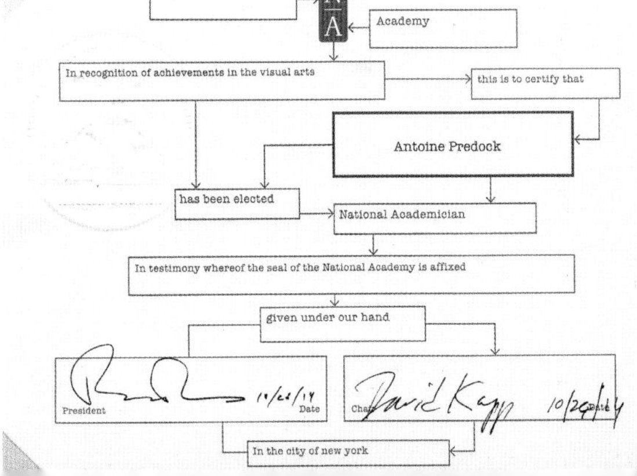

National

N A

Academy

In recognition of achievements in the visual arts

this is to certify that

Antoine Predock

has been elected

National Academician

In testimony whereof the seal of the National Academy is affixed

given under our hand

President 10/24/14 Date

Chair 10/24/14

In the city of new york

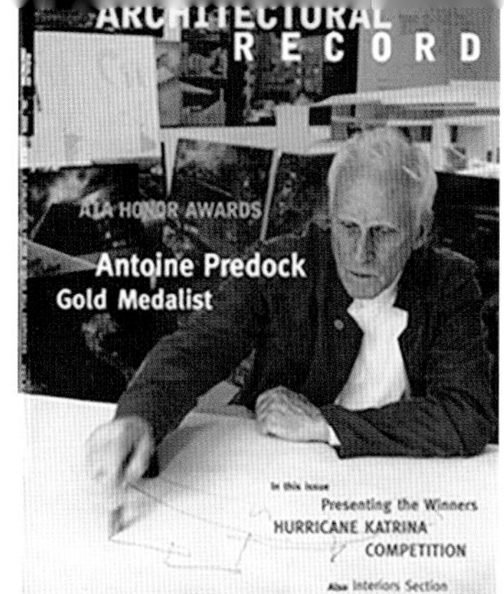

"No matter what he's doing—whether it's designing or diving Antoine Predock makes visceral connections. To fully appreciate his buildings you must touch them, kick them, walk through them, sit on them. Years ago, he told this writer, 'Before you start designing, you have to get your bony ass on the ground and feel the site with your body.'

The best of his buildings ... emerge from their rugged sites as if they had been pushed up by geological forces. They do not sit lightly on the land, but engage it in a strenuous embrace. Eventually, they become part of the landscape itself ..."

Clifford A. Pearson, "Antoine Predock Rides High With the Gold Medal," *Architectural Record*, June 2006

"Antoine Predock, architecture's poet of sky and earth, has won the 2006 Gold Medal of the American Institutes of Architects ... 'Arguably, more than any American architect of any time, Antoine Predock has asserted a personal and place-inspired vision of architecture with such passion and conviction that his buildings have been universally embraced,' Thomas S. Howorth, chairman of the AIA medal committee, said in a statement."

Linda Hales, "Architecture's Natural Winner", *Washington Post*, Dec. 9, 2005

"'Life,' Predock believes, 'is a series of linked destinies.' It was one such destiny that brought him his first commission and went a long way toward establishing him in his practice. As the architect tells the story, 'A guy I hung around with who was a painter knew a guy with some money. They were both looking for a piece of land to do a new project on, and I was invited in. I quit a job, a really good job I had where I was a principal designer on major projects like the UNM law school. I just dropped everything and took a flier with these guys.'

The architect describes the La Luz community on the Rio Grande in Albuquerque as a 'modern town house project that would link the buildings to preserve open space. I called it ecological design—it's what you needed to do in the desert. You needed to respond to the wind and sun and protect the floodplains. It was a landscape in itself. That project put me on the map.'

Antoine Predock has been on the map ever since, culminating last winter in his being given the 2006 Gold Medal by the American Institute of Architects, the same award presented to Frank Lloyd Wright and Louis Kahn, the two figures in the field he admires most. Like Wright before him, he is no longer a regional architect. 'I work all around the world, so I don't talk about the Southwest that much anymore,' says Predock, who now has an office in Taipei and is even studying Mandarin.

Still, he acknowledges his debt to the Southwest, where, he has written, he learned about 'responding to the forces of a place'—lessons that 'can be implemented anywhere.' Speaking with the appreciation of a landscape architect, which he also is, he adds, 'The prime communities of the Southwest are survival communities. Their sustenance is governed by rainfall and wind direction. You can study little enclaves of plant materials, how they huddle together for protection. Some are nurse crops. The legendary tumbleweed is really a nurse crop that protects the growth of prairie grasses under its shade, and then it sacrifices itself and blows away.'"

Nicholas von Hoffman, "A Fearless Vision, The Evolution of the American Institute of Architects' 2006 Gold Medal Winner," *Architectural Digest*, October 2006

Antoine Predock | The Professionals

A Fearless Vision

The Evolution of the American Institute of Architects' 2006 Gold Medal Winner

By Nicholas von Hoffman

Whether designing a house or a public venue, New Mexico–based Antoine Predock (left) expresses what he calls the "spirit of place." BELOW: His model for Winnipeg's Canadian Museum for Human Rights.

ALTHOUGH HE FIRST achieved prominence in the Southwest, architect Antoine Predock is, Where do the poetic impulses come from?" His answer: From his mother. "She was a liberal arts college graduate. that I would even remember. I think I was three or four. It took me a long time to realize how valuable that was and what matic, a Mr. Fix-It kind of guy."

After high school, Predock says, he wanted to go to college far away from St. Louis,

"There is no more deserving architect and no one who better represents both the profession and the American spirit. In his work, steel, glass and concrete are combined with natural materials to celebrate modern life. A search for truth pervades, so that tradition is both honored and reinvented. ...

Antoine has morphed architecture from 3D built forms to multidimensional spaces that are replete with symbolism, history, culture, myth and a profoundly sensuous tangibility. He has rejoined the 'mind' of architecture with its 'body.' He has fused the mental and the physical and embedded both with the spiritual.

Antoine has revolutionized architecture with his philosophy that the land is the most important client and the building's interaction with its inhabitants is the basis of design. He teaches and runs his office in a similar manner. Always listening, he summons voices—from colleagues, clients and students, and from mythologies, current folklore, and the emotion of a place—that would otherwise remain silent. He then transforms them into a tangible built environment. His talent is to be able to apply a 'stethoscope' to the heart of the matter that forces everyone to abandon the ordinary and to produce unimagined results."

Rob Livesey, Professor & Director Emeritus, Knowlton School, The Ohio State University, AIA Gold Medal Presentation, 2006

THANK YOU ROB LIVESEY!

A chiseled topography of Taroko marble defines the processionally ascending ramped entry to the Opera House

TAICHUNG OPERA HOUSE

TAICHUNG, TAIWAN 2006

Like an island in the city, interpreting Taiwan as metamorphic/metaphoric island, a new marble and crystalline Opera House rises from the urban park setting creating a celebratory, glowing event on the Taichung skyline. Viewed from many vantage points in the surrounding residential towers, a stage is set for dynamic urban events, for theater rituals and the audience arrival procession.

A CONTRAST TO THE TAIWAN SEMI-TROPICAL ENVIRONMENT—ARABIAN DESERT TRAVEL, 2005

WORLD MAMMOTH AND PERMAFROST MUSEUM

YAKUTSK, SIBERIA, RUSSIAN REPUBLIC 2007

Viewed from a distance, the World Mammoth and Permafrost Museum is a geologic projection from the Chochur Muran hillside, an animistic presence in the process of emerging from the permafrost. The museum is a landscape abstraction from myths of Sakha cultures and their spiritual predecessors. The building expresses the seasonal cracking and shifting of the ground plane that continually reawakens the memory of previous epochs beneath. The silhouette of the building suggests the sheer power and bulk of the Mammoth and marks the vast Siberian landscape with an iconic and lasting symbol. An icy assemblage of titanium-clad exposition galleries austerely weathers the extremes of the Siberian climate.

Inside—a crystalline icy realm tunneling into the permafrost

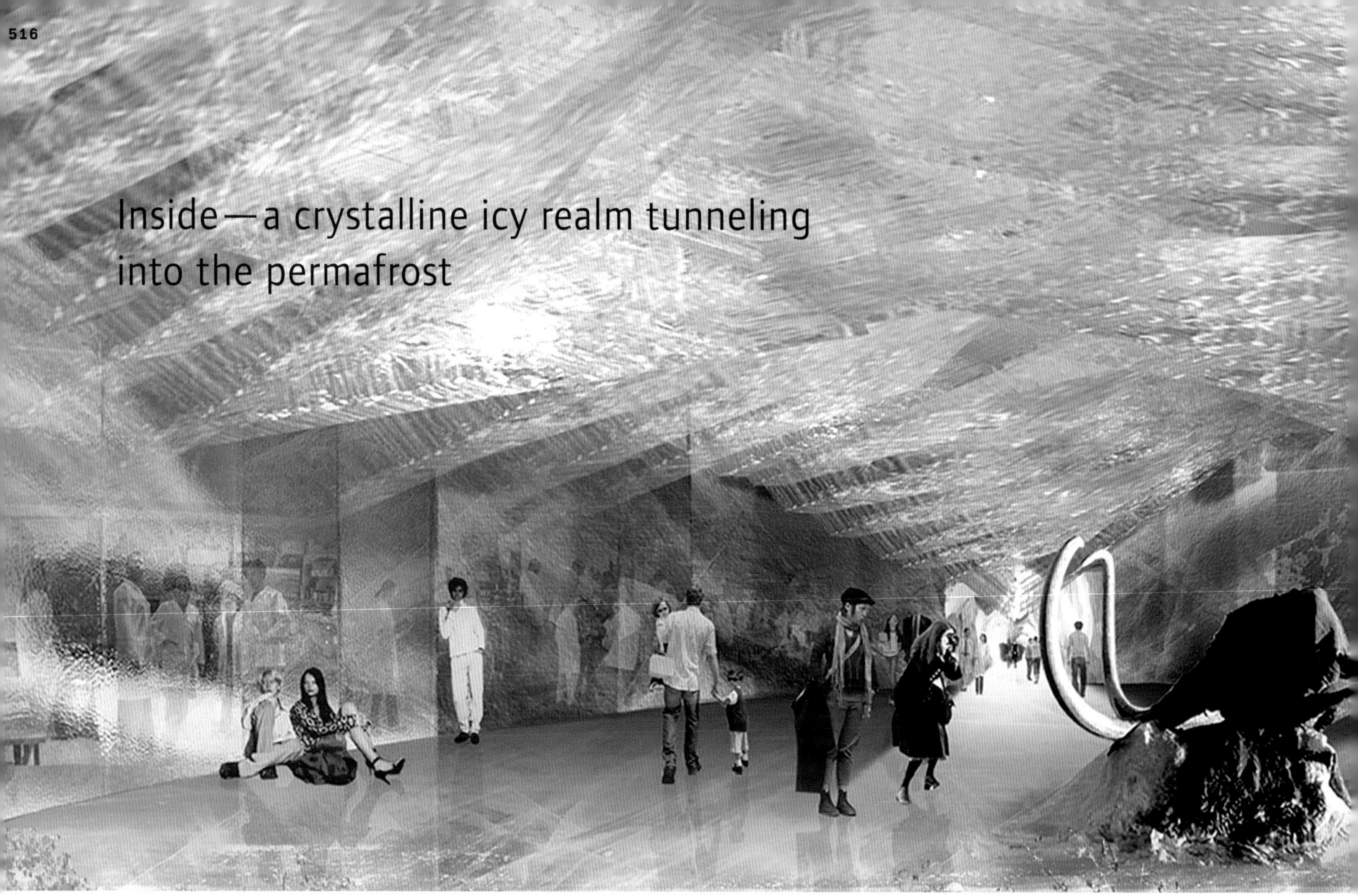

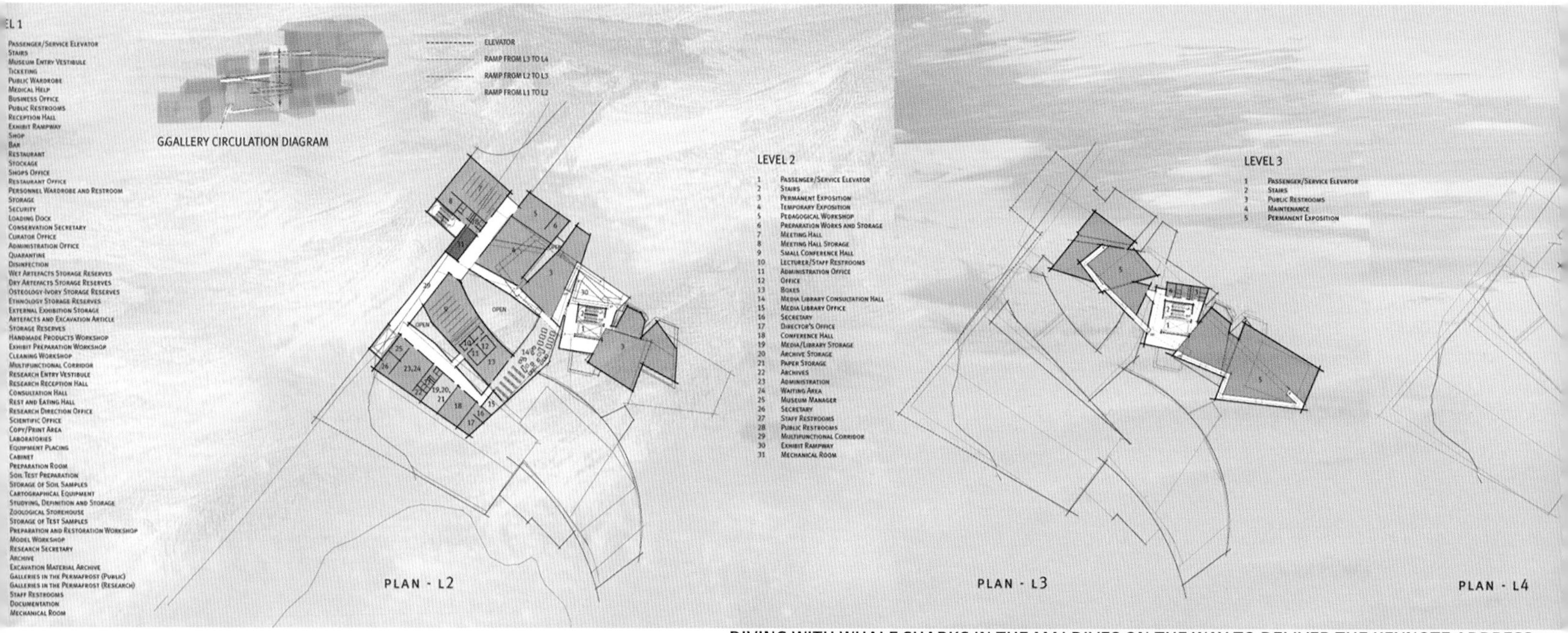

EL 1
Passenger/Service Elevator
Stairs
Museum Entry Vestibule
Ticketing
Public Wardrobe
Medical Help
Business Office
Public Restrooms
Reception Hall
Exhibit Rampway
Shop
Bar
Restaurant
Stockage
Shops Office
Restaurant Office
Personnel Wardrobe and Restroom
Storage
Security
Loading Dock
Conservation Secretary
Curator Office
Administration Office
Quarantine
Disinfection
Wet Artefacts Storage Reserves
Dry Artefacts Storage Reserves
Osteology-Ivory Storage Reserves
Ethnology Storage Reserves
External Exhibition Storage
Artefacts and Excavation Article
Storage Reserves
Handmade Products Workshop
Exhibit Preparation Workshop
Cleaning Workshop
Multifunctional Corridor
Research Entry Vestibule
Research Reception Hall
Consultation Hall
Rest and Eating Hall
Research Direction Office
Scientific Office
Copy/Print Area
Laboratories
Equipment Placing
Cabinet
Preparation Room
Soil Test Preparation
Storage of Soil Samples
Cartographical Equipment
Studying, Definition and Storage
Zoological Storehouse
Storage of Test Samples
Preparation and Restoration Workshop
Model Workshop
Research Secretary
Archive
Excavation Material Archive
Galleries in the Permafrost (Public)
Galleries in the Permafrost (Research)
Staff Restrooms
Documentation
Mechanical Room
G.GALLERY CIRCULATION DIAGRAM
ELEVATOR
RAMP FROM L3 TO L4
RAMP FROM L2 TO L3
RAMP FROM L1 TO L2
LEVEL 2
1 Passenger/Service Elevator
2 Stairs
3 Permanent Exposition
4 Temporary Exposition
5 Pedagogical Workshop
6 Preparation Works and Storage
7 Meeting Hall
8 Meeting Hall Storage
9 Small Conference Hall
10 Lecturer/Staff Restrooms
11 Administration Office
12 Office
13 Boxes
14 Media Library Consultation Hall
15 Media Library Office
16 Secretary
17 Director's Office
18 Conference Hall
19 Media/Library Storage
20 Archive Storage
21 Paper Storage
22 Archives
23 Administration
24 Waiting Area
25 Museum Manager
26 Secretary
27 Staff Restrooms
28 Public Restrooms
29 Multifunctional Corridor
30 Exhibit Rampway
31 Mechanical Room
LEVEL 3
1 Passenger/Service Elevator
2 Stairs
3 Public Restrooms
4 Maintenance
5 Permanent Exposition
OPEN
PLAN - L2
PLAN - L3
PLAN - L4

10/2007
wettbewerbe aktuell

CONCEPT
vol. 101
World Mammoth & Permafrost Museum

COMPETITIONS

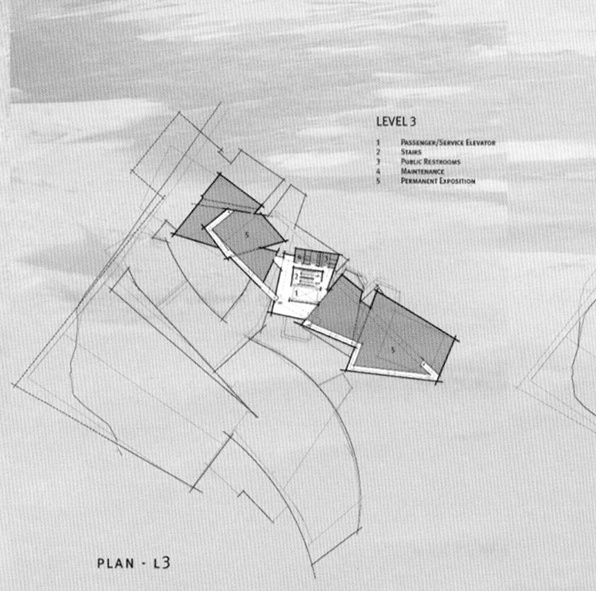

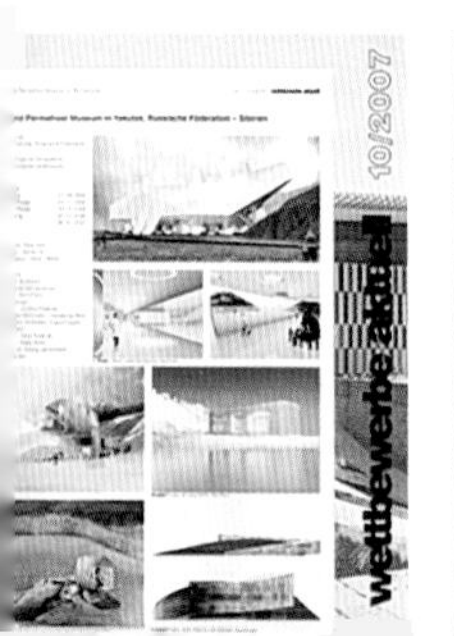

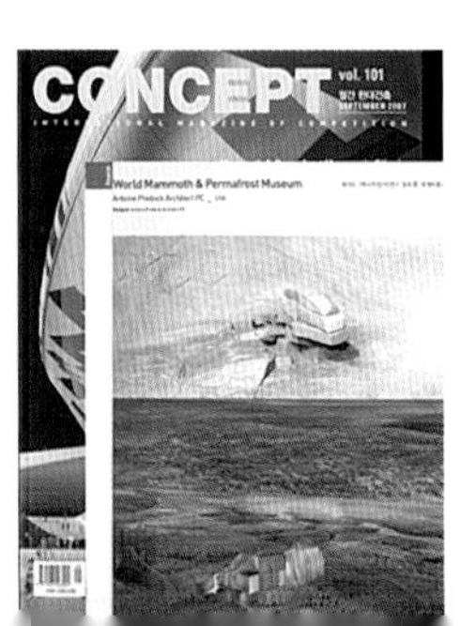

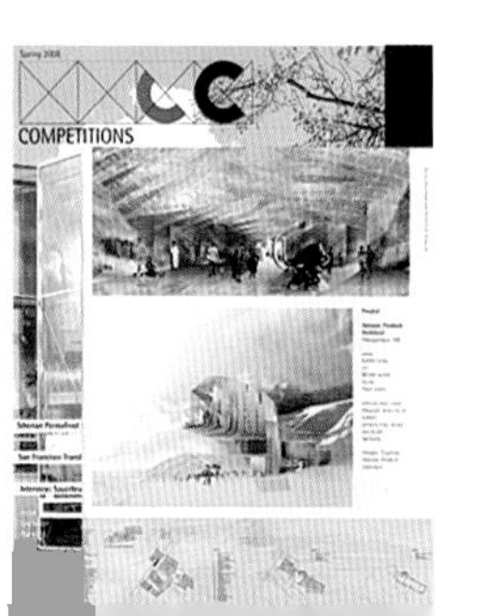

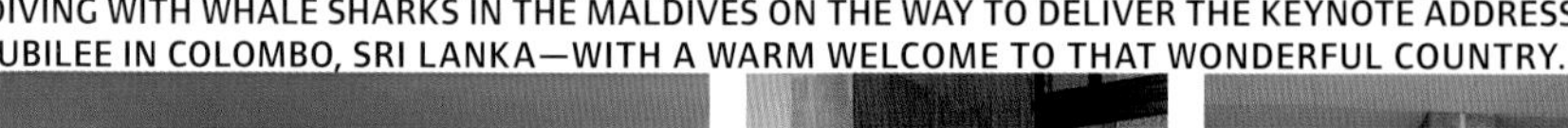

DIVING WITH WHALE SHARKS IN THE MALDIVES ON THE WAY TO DELIVER THE KEYNOTE ADDRESS JUBILEE IN COLOMBO, SRI LANKA—WITH A WARM WELCOME TO THAT WONDERFUL COUNTRY...

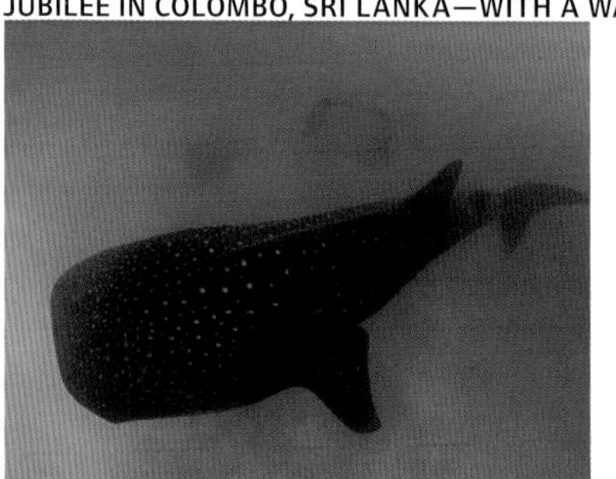

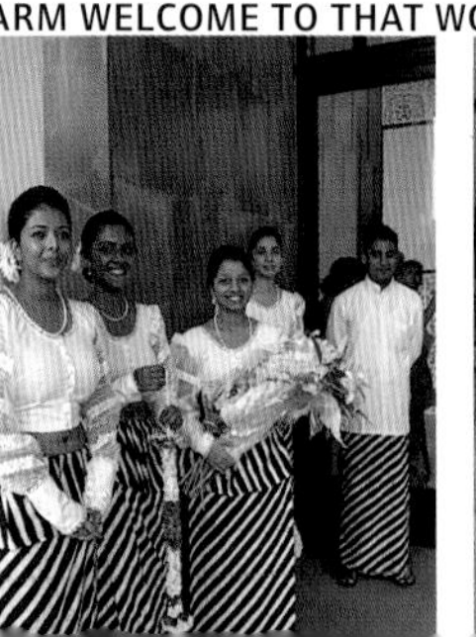

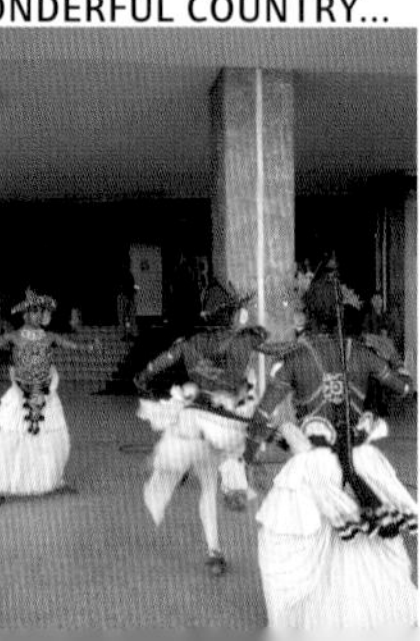

The building adopts its environmental responses from the Mammoth's characteristic hardy resistance to the Siberian climate. Massive concrete and earth-sheltered enclosures insulate from the extreme conditions. In winter, the titanium wrapping around the stacked gallery boxes traps air close to the "body" of the building, allowing the sun's rays to warm the perimeter thermal mass. A low-maintenance paradigm is tendered across the entire facility—in the same sense that the Mammoth was in harmony with its setting. Traditional Sakha habitation patterns and cultural rituals extrapolate into the architecture and experience of the building. The inviting Arrival Plaza and Entry Terrace offer space for community celebrations such as the Sakha traditions of Ysyakh. The building is oriented toward the Southeast in anticipation of the rising winter sun, a Sakha object of worship. The central axis is aligned to the Winter Solstice sunrise maximizing the morning sunlight penetration to the building entry. The stacked galleries inflect toward the sunrise angle corresponding to the Farewell to Winter celebration.

My hulking clay model

"Predock's museum design includes transparent walls and ceilings that appear to be made of ice, referring both interior and exterior to the environment of the mammoths, the permafrost that preserves their remains, and the crystalline glaciers that led to their demise."

Wesley Pulkka, "Antoine Predock: Architecture and Time," *Trend*, Fall 2009/Winter 2010

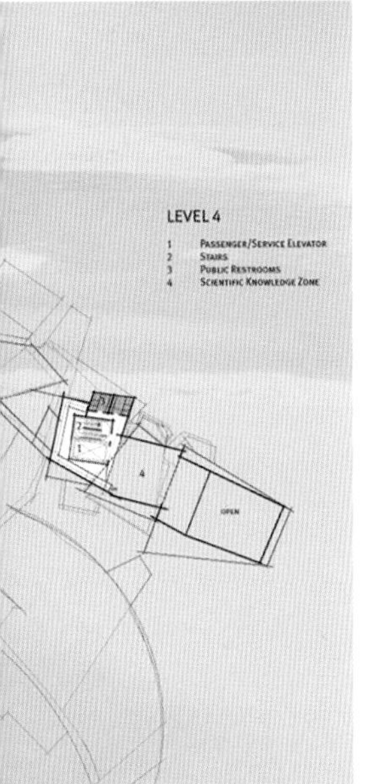

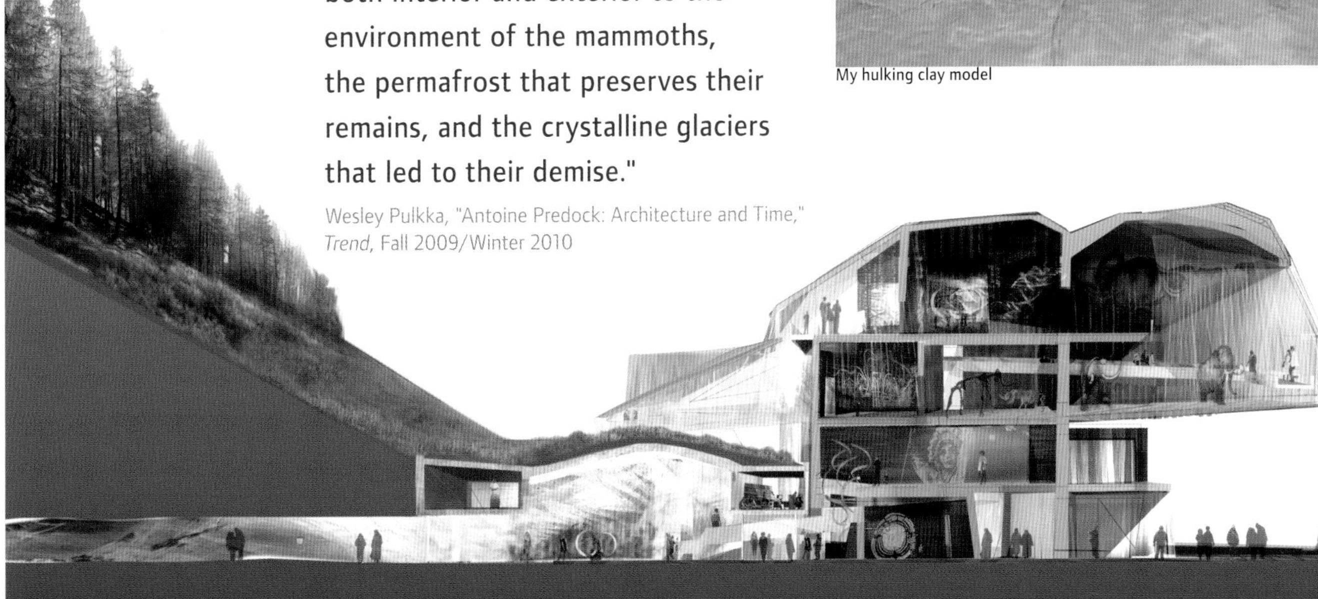

AT THE 2007 SRI LANKA INSTITUTE OF ARCHITECTS 50-YEAR GOLDEN COMPLETE WITH TRADITIONAL DANCE AND THE GIFT OF FLOWERS.

DRIVING SOUTH PAST CARNAGE FROM THE RECENT TSUNAMI EVENT TO THE BEAUTIFUL ESTATE OF THE GREAT SRI LANKAN ARCHITECT SIR GEOFFREY BAWA.

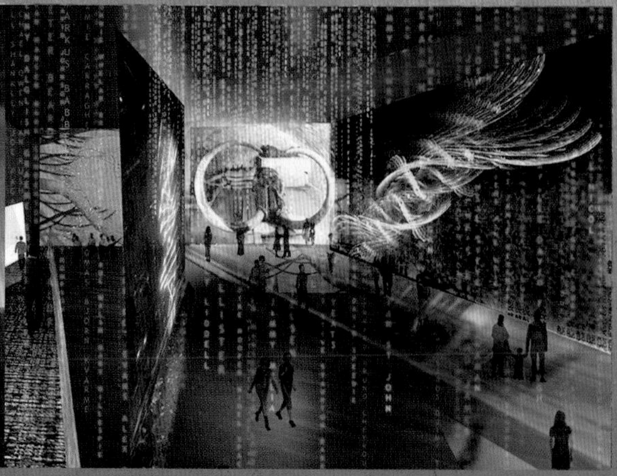

Evoking local Shamanistic traditions, the building combines its physical presence with implied mythic and spiritual crossovers. Embedded in its overwhelming physical presence and the content within is the Spirit of the Mammoth—understood through the wisdom of Sakha cultures. Voids between the galleries resemble fissures beneath the constantly shifting permafrost. During the long winter days and months with scarce daylight, the building is a glowing mysterious presence visible across the Lena River floodplain, inviting exploration and participation.

OUR COMPETITION ENTRY FOR THE NEW NATIONAL LIBRARY OF THE CZECH REPUBLIC

CZECH NATIONAL LIBRARY,
PRAGUE, CZECH REPUBLIC 2007

KINDERGARTEN TOUR OF OUR STUDIO IN 2009

TWO SPECIAL BIKES DISPLAYED IN THE STUDIO—1974 LAVERDA SFC AND NORTON MANX TRITON

SAGE HOUSE

TAOS, NEW MEXICO 2007/08

Rooted within an unobstructed panorama that stretches from the Sangre de Cristo Mountains to the east across a gray green blanket of sage toward distant peaks to the west, the Sage House is organized along a circular sweep, focusing on Vallecito Peak. A courtyard/orchard, sheltered from prevailing southwestern winds by house walls and an embracing earthen berm, completes the inscribing circle.

IN JERUSALEM WITH BABS ASPER AND MOE LEVY IN 2011. SKETCHED FROM A DISTANCE, ALONG WITH THE TEMPLE MOUNT AND THE WESTERN WALL. THEN MASADA AND THE DEAD SEA.

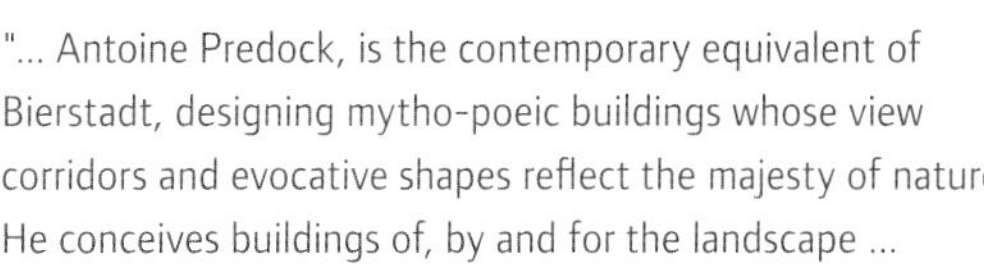

"... Antoine Predock, is the contemporary equivalent of Bierstadt, designing mytho-poeic buildings whose view corridors and evocative shapes reflect the majesty of nature He conceives buildings of, by and for the landscape ...

The sage that carpets the whole valley rolls right up to terraces and walls, and the many windows invite the intoxicating scent in. The east-west axis may point to Vallecito Peak, the entrance may align with the winter solstice sunrise, and the roof terrace may situate the couple and their frequent guests under the panoply of bright desert stars, but Predock doesn't forget simple olfactory pleasures.

Joseph Giovannini, "Natural Wonder," *Architectural Digest*, July 2010

Dave Mattison, pilot friend and ex F-4 fighter pilot, shuttled me to Taos ski trips in his aerobatic, handmade jewel—with Sage House flyovers.

THEN CONTINUING TO QATAR AFTER STOPPING IN JORDAN—THE ROMAN TOWN OF JERASH, NORTH OF AMMAN; THEN WADI RUM AND PETRA.

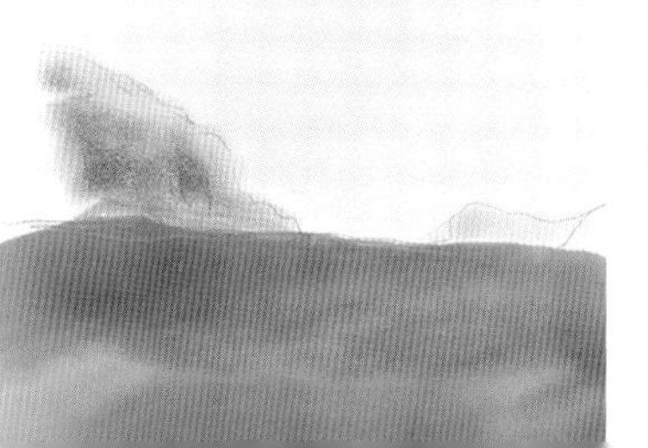

THE NEW SILK ROAD ARABIC CULTURAL AREA

XI'AN, CHINA 2007

This competition-winning project that we call Arabic Memory is presented as a cinematographic compression of time and space within which unfolds a panorama of stories. Arabic cultural shadows appear episodically within the cinematic digital score.

"'And yet I have constructed in my mind a model city from which all possible cities can be deduced,' Kublai said. 'It contains I need only foresee the exceptions to the norm and calculate the most probable combinations.'" Italo Calvino, *Invisible Cities*

OVERLAPPING WITH THE NEW SILK ROAD PROJECT, BOHIOS IS A BEACHFRONT VACATION VILLAGE IN THE DOMINICAN REPUBLIC FOR FRENCH TOURISTS. FROM THE BEACH, CABAÑAS CLIMB A GENTLY SLOPING HILLSIDE WITH A COMMONS AND RECREATION FACILITIES AS A HUB AT THE TOP.

BOHIOS EN EL MAR CARIBE
RIO SAN JUAN, DOMINICAN
REPUBLIC 2005/08

The visitor experience is informally guided along three north-south routes. Traversing the Desert Transit Route, Village Transit Route, and Sea Transit Route with the aid of digital media, visitors accumulate experience. The routes are spatial episodes, accruing a continually branching pan-Arabic perspective. A digital overlay throughout the site interweaves pan-Arabic subtexts amplified in the Silk Web Cafés and media enhanced Archive and Exhibit realms.

everything corresponding to the norm. Since the cities that exist diverge in varying degree from the norm,

MARIPOSA COMMUNITY CENTER
RIO RANCHO, NM 2007

MARIPOSA COMMUNITY NEAR ALBUQUERQUE, SITED ON THE EDGE OF A DRAMATIC ESCARPMENT, IS SUPPORTED BY OUR COMMUNITY CENTER.

ACCOMPANYING ME OR ON HIS OWN, PERIPATETIC PAUL, BACK AND FORTH SO MANY TIMES... ABQ/LAX/HKG/CTU WITH SHANGHAI AND TAIPEI IN THE MIX... DEFINITELY AN IRON MAN.

CONCEPT vol. 102

CORNERSTONE ARTS CENTER

COLORADO COLLEGE
COLORADO SPRINGS, COLORADO 2007/08

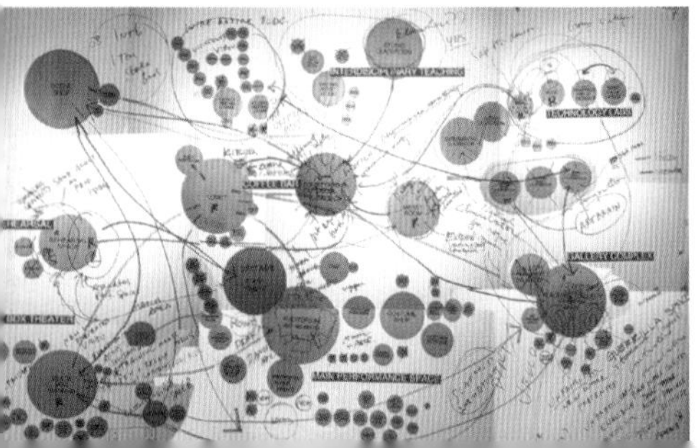

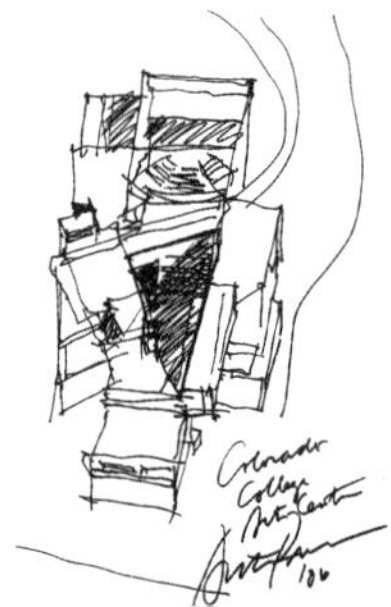

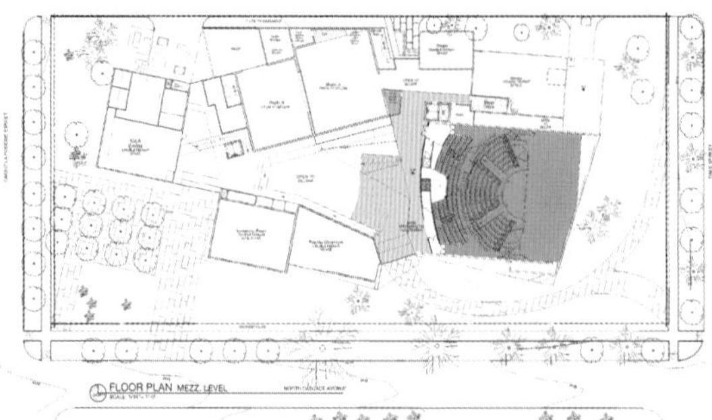

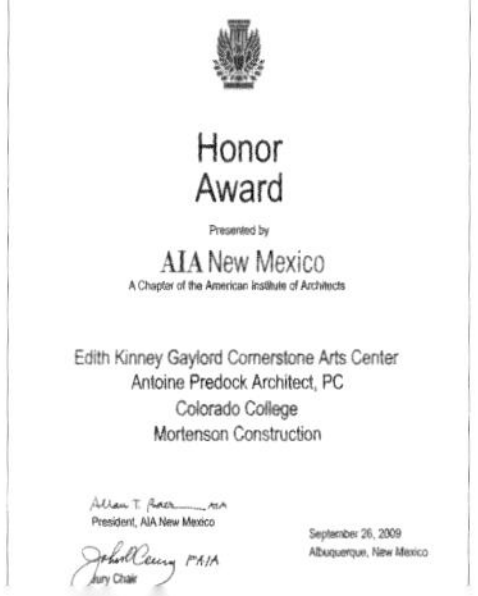

Honor
Award

Presented by

AIA New Mexico

A Chapter of the American Institute of Architects

Edith Kinney Gaylord Cornerstone Arts Center
Antoine Predock Architect, PC
Colorado College
Mortenson Construction

President, AIA New Mexico

Jury Chair

September 26, 2009
Albuquerque, New Mexico

MANY PREDOCK STUDIO SKI TRIPS TO TAOS

REGINA HARRIS, OUR TASK MASTER FOR DECADES, DEPARTURE FROM STUDIO CELEBRATION AT TAOS

"A biologist, a musician, and a playwright enter a classroom; this isn't the setup for a joke, but rather the pedagogy of Colorado College, a liberal arts school in Colorado Springs. Classes are taught by a team of professors from different departments and culminate in a project that weaves all subjects together. Cornerstone Arts Center, the first building to unify all arts programs under one roof, manifests this teaching philosophy in flexible architecture ..."

David Sokol, *Architectural Record*, February 2008

The Cornerstone Center contains a variety of spaces to encourage scheduled and impromptu interdisciplinary arts events. Anyone entering the building becomes a potential spectator or performer, where the architecture itself is the stage.

THE LITERAL "CORNERSTONE"

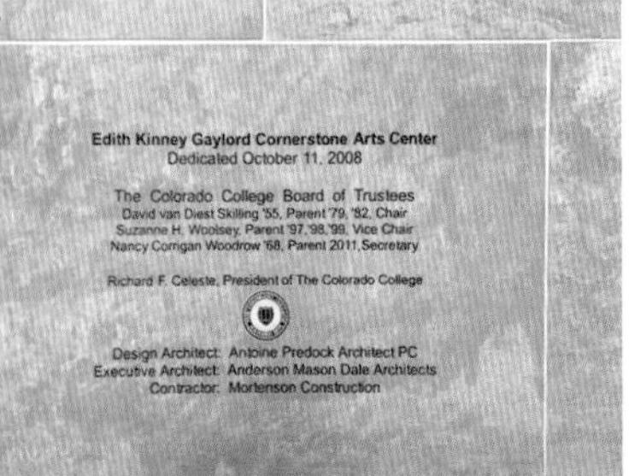

DURING THE OPENING CELEBRATION, PROJECT BANDALOOP DANCERS USE THE BUILDING FAÇADE AS THEIR STAGE

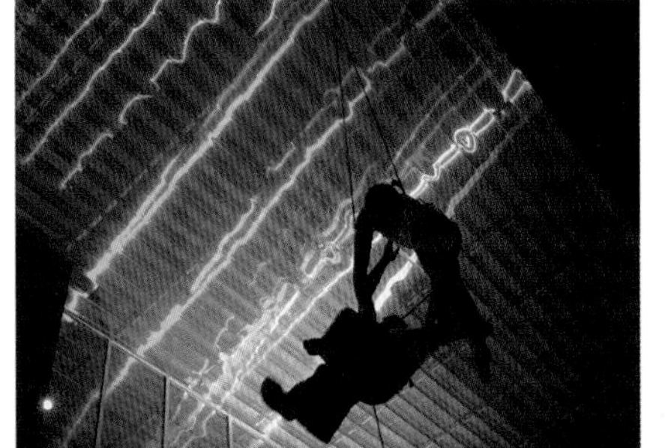

On a major student desire line to downtown Colorado Springs, the Center captures and channels the alignment—linking to an alley that will take you to a street where one can walk downtown most efficiently. It's a shortcut that exposes one to whatever's going on in the central space—at times a three-ring circus, which is reflective of interdisciplinary pedagogy of the college. Some of that might rub off...

"Art House" film theater

Accessed from the central space—the Richard F. Celeste Theatre

The crossroads of the Center where theatrical/musical performances can occur along with major interdisciplinary installation pieces. The surrounding catwalks with structural attachment points and theatrical lighting rails, also serve as participatory balconies over the central space.

WITH HADRIAN AND DAUGHTER-IN-LAW ANNE AT MY GRANDSON NICO'S GRADUATION FROM COLORADO COLLEGE. NICO WITH PRESIDENT TIEFENTHALER.

APERTURE CENTER

WITH THE UNIVERSITY OF NEW MEXICO FILM AND DIGITAL MEDIA CENTER ALBUQUERQUE, NEW MEXICO 2007/08

An artifact of place channeling the ancient weathered presence of the bones we found on this high desert site—an exploration of different aspects of bone—from the interstitial beauty of bone lattice structure to volumetric fragments.

THE MIGHTY COOPER RIVER BRIDGE IN CHARLESTON, SOUTH CAROLINA, WHERE WE WORKED WITH MOODY-NOLAN ON AN AFRICAN AMERICAN MUSEUM, A PRECURSOR

INTERNATIONAL AFRICAN AMERICAN MUSEUM CHARLESTON, SC 2008

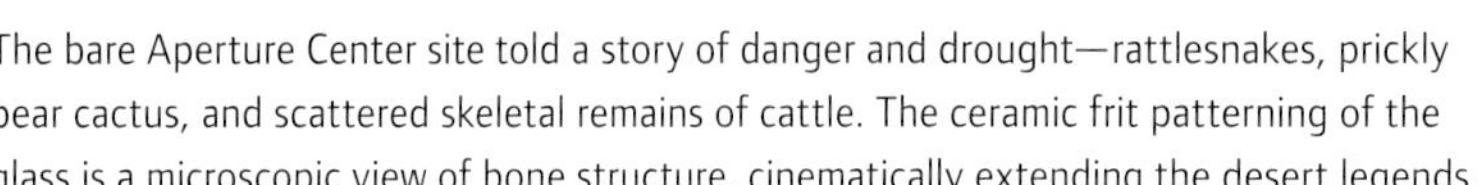

The bare Aperture Center site told a story of danger and drought—rattlesnakes, prickly pear cactus, and scattered skeletal remains of cattle. The ceramic frit patterning of the glass is a microscopic view of bone structure, cinematically extending the desert legends.

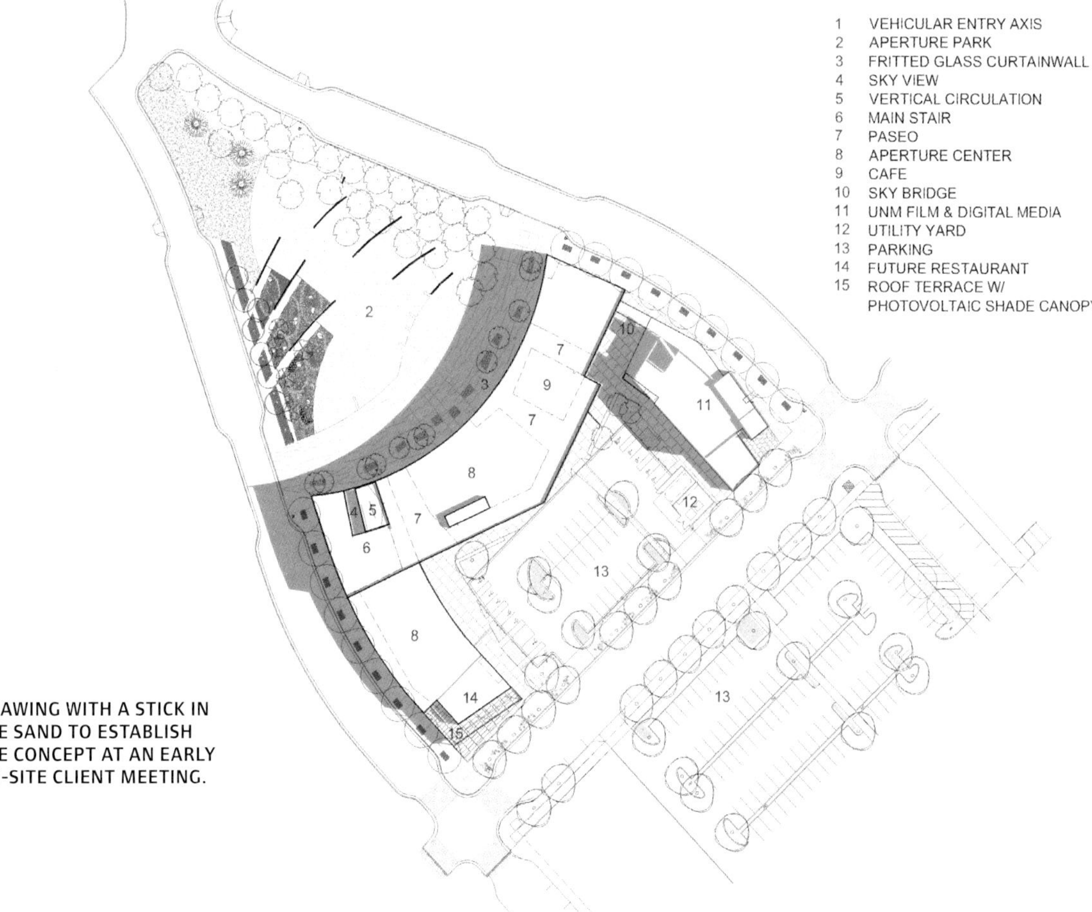

DRAWING WITH A STICK IN THE SAND TO ESTABLISH THE CONCEPT AT AN EARLY ON-SITE CLIENT MEETING.

As the "catcher's mitt" terminus of the miles-long University Boulevard extension, Aperture Center is a glowing magnet at night and a "film park" during the day.

TO OUR MALL IN WASHINGTON COMPETITION COLLABORATION.

The "Red Stair" arrival/entry space with the beautiful Pre-Cambrian Granite boulder that Cory Greenfield tracked down.

MY PADRES CONNECTION ERIK JUDSON AND HIS WIFE ERIN HOSTED ME IN BEIJING FOR THE 2008
THE US AND SPAIN—KOBE BRYANT, AS POPULAR AS YAO MING, WAS CLEARLY A TREAT FOR CHINESE

The internal planning of the Aperture Center anticipates a variety of users. The ground floor is dominated by retail, dining, and a visitor center. Occupying an arm to the main arcing volume, and connected by a glass bridge, the University of New Mexico Film and Digital Media Center is an experimental program with theater, editing suites, studios, all of which are connected internally by an ephemeral black stair.

OLYMPICS—THE OPENING CEREMONY, THE COOL AQUATIC VENUE AND VIEWING, THE GOLD MEDAL GAME BETWEEN FANS—UPSTAGING THE GAME ON THE COURT.

IN FRONT OF BIRD'S NEST WITH FRIENDS

Adjacent to the Netflix Albuquerque Studios soundstages, the University of New Mexico Department of Film and Digital Arts occupies the northeast wing of Aperture Center.

LECTURING IN NEW ZEALAND IN 2008 WITH A STOPOVER AT KAIKOURA PENINSULA ON THE SOUTH ISLAND—BREEDING GROUND OF THE SOUTHERN SPERM WHALE.

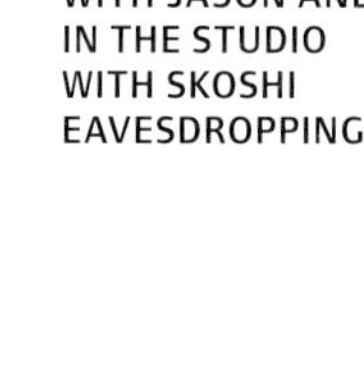

WITH JASON AND CHLOE IN THE STUDIO WITH SKOSHI EAVESDROPPING.

Solar collector—shaded terrace using a system similar to the one we designed at Austin City Hall eight years earlier.

SOME SANTA MONICA MOUNTAINS ADVENTURES WITH FELLOW RIDER, ARCHITECT WILLIAM HOWARD.

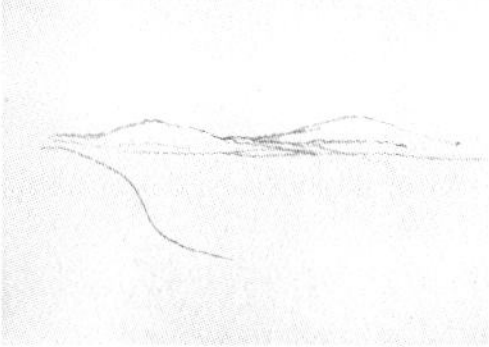

MAUNA KEA/MAUNA LOA FROM MAUI

WITH GRANDSON NICO—HAWAI'I IN 2012 BICYCLE DESCENT FROM HALEAKALA...

FROM BABY TO MAJOR BRO

SOUTH PLANT

RICE UNIVERSITY
HOUSTON, TEXAS 2008

In the context of the Rice University Mediterranean Revival style, the South Plant, with its massive walls of St. Joseph brick, consistent with the campus materiality, drifts away to the edge of campus, foregrounded by the Braes Bayou watershed, a wetland/water retention area that preserves natural habitat.

HONORED TO DO OUR SECOND BUILDING ON THE RICE CAMPUS, MEETING WITH PAUL AND A HIGHLY ENERGIZED AND INSPIRED CLIENT TEAM.

THE FIBONACCI SWEEP OF THE TRANSITION OF BUILDING WALL TO PERIMETER WALL.

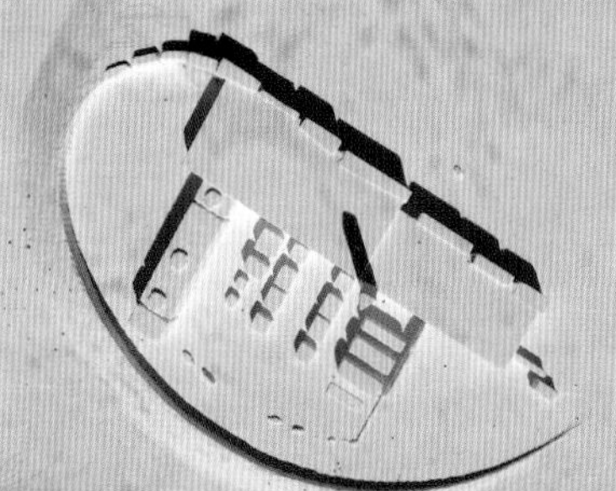

A dichroic glass-clad armature guides tubular exhaust elements. I saw the raw power of the brick masses as a counterpoint to the more decorative campus ornamental language—much like Rome, where Imperial ruins haunt the Renaissance.

CONCURRENT WITH THE SOUTH PLANT PROJECT, A TRIP TO BEIJING AND THE FORBIDDEN CITY, AND THEN ON TO HANGZHOU.

With the dichroic glazed tower floating above, the centrally positioned control room makes the sophisticated control systems visually accessible—an "informational" façade reflecting the projected digital displays back onto the campus. A green roof codifies the hope-for-the-future shifts in energy production.

AFTER CHINA, DUBAI—AND ITS IMPROBABLE INDOOR SKI AREA.

Brick monoliths stand as sentinels—a sweeping, spiral movement of Fibonacci series proportioned building wall "fragments"—transition into the bermed perimeter wall of the equipment yard.

RIDING DUCATIS IN THE SANTA MONICA MOUNTAINS WITH MY SON JASON

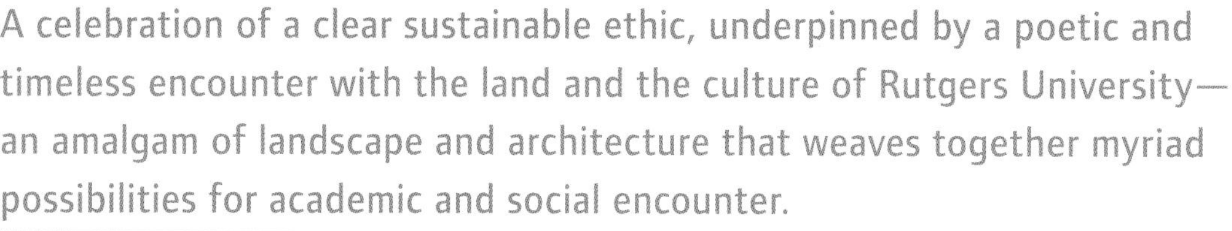

A celebration of a clear sustainable ethic, underpinned by a poetic and timeless encounter with the land and the culture of Rutgers University—an amalgam of landscape and architecture that weaves together myriad possibilities for academic and social encounter.

COLLEGE AVENUE MASTER PLAN

RUTGERS UNIVERSITY
NEW BRUNSWICK, NEW JERSEY 2008
IN COLLABORATION WITH OLIN PARTNERSHIP

"Antoine Predock/Olin Partnership focused on College Avenue, but envisioned an even more startling transportation system. ... Dubbed the "Stealth Bee," these would allow students to socialize as they move along College Avenue. ... Predock charmed his audience with a small remote-controlled model of his invention." *Competitions*, Spring 2007

NAMED AFTER A SYMBOL OF NEW JERSEY—THE HONEY BEE—THE "STEALTH BEE" IS A HYDROGEN-POWERED STUDENT MOVER/MOBILE GATHERING SPACE. MODEL BY STEALTHMEISTER DOUG FRIEND

INTENSE CHARRETTE IN OUR STUDIO, MERGING OUR TEAM WITH THE OLIN PARTNERSHIP CREW.

SPACEPORT AMERICA

JORNADA DEL MUERTO, NEW MEXICO 2008

Mysterious artifact from a distance programmatically appropriate upon approach, Spaceport America leaves a mark in the consciousness, literally connecting earthbound power with celestial adventure. Its physical character reflects the duality of raw New Mexico land meeting technological mastery—simultaneously integral to the desert setting while celebrating and delivering on dreams of space.

WITH CONSTANCE IN THE GALAPAGOS WITH ITS VOLCANIC SURREALISM AND AMAZING CAST OF CHARACTERS...

Sited on what the Spaniards called Jornada del Muerto—"Journey of Death"—but escaping to the sky.

Pantheon, I give up, you win.

BLUE-FOOTED BOOBY, FRIGATEBIRD, AND THE SIGNATURE TORTOISE.

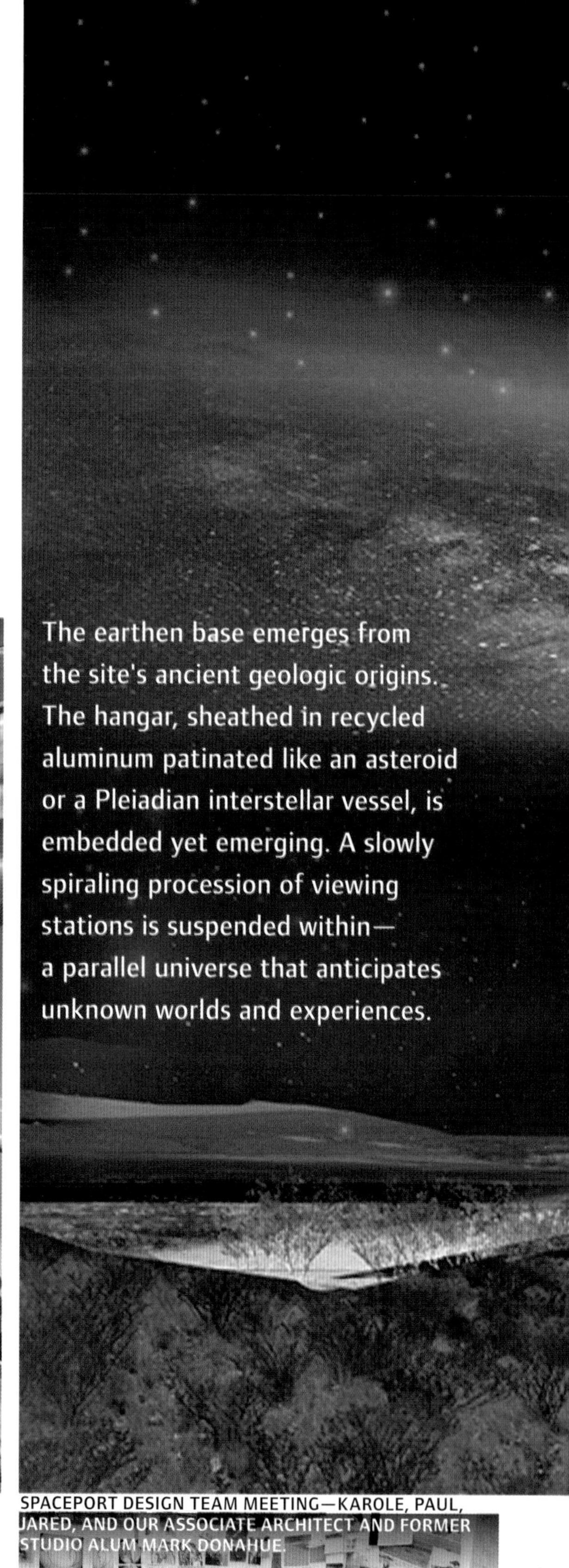

The earthen base emerges from the site's ancient geologic origins. The hangar, sheathed in recycled aluminum patinated like an asteroid or a Pleiadian interstellar vessel, is embedded yet emerging. A slowly spiraling procession of viewing stations is suspended within—a parallel universe that anticipates unknown worlds and experiences.

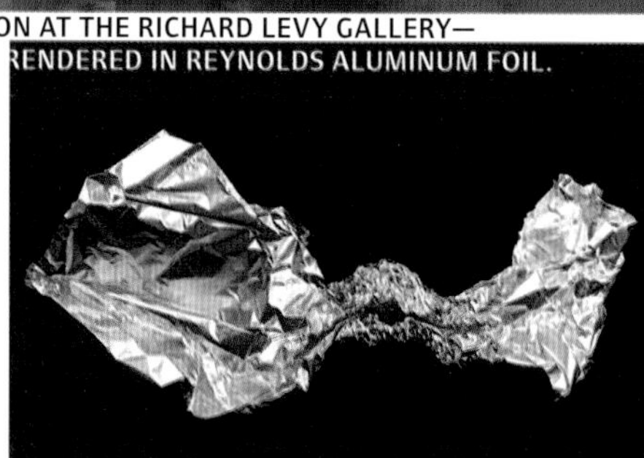

SPACEBAT—BIRDHOUSE FOR AN INSTALLATION AT THE RICHARD LEVY GALLERY—RENDERED IN REYNOLDS ALUMINUM FOIL.

SPACEPORT DESIGN TEAM MEETING—KAROLE, PAUL, JARED, AND OUR ASSOCIATE ARCHITECT AND FORMER STUDIO ALUM MARK DONAHUE.

"I am surrounded by little clouds,
and as I go through the air I change,
becoming spirit only." Geronimo

THE ASTRONAUT'S PASSAGE

"HE HAS OFTEN SAID THAT "MY 'REGIONALISM' IS PORTABLE." EVERY PROJECT IS A RESPONSE TO ITS GEOGRAPHIC SITE AND CULTURAL CONTEXT, AND TO THE PEOPLE WHO WILL INHABIT IT. IN THAT SENSE, EVERYTHING PREDOCK DESIGNS—FROM HIS HOUSES TO HIS INSTITUTIONAL AND CIVIC PROJECTS—IS A FORM OF PUBLIC ARCHITECTURE."

Kristen Richards, *Architecture Celebrating the Past, Designing the Future*, 2008

APPARITION

WINNIPEG, MANITOBA 2009

A haunting, ambiguous object enmeshed within the icy realm—snow drifts on this geologic microcosm while glaciers in miniature advance and recede in the aluminum folds. Solar-powered lighting within the wooden structural armature provides the entry with an inviting, glowing promise of inner respite.

CABINS SPROUT FROM THE EDGE OF AN ESCARPMENT AT THE FOOT OF THE BRAZOS CLIFFS.

BRAZOS CLIFFS (CORKINS LODGE)
BRAZOS, NM 2009

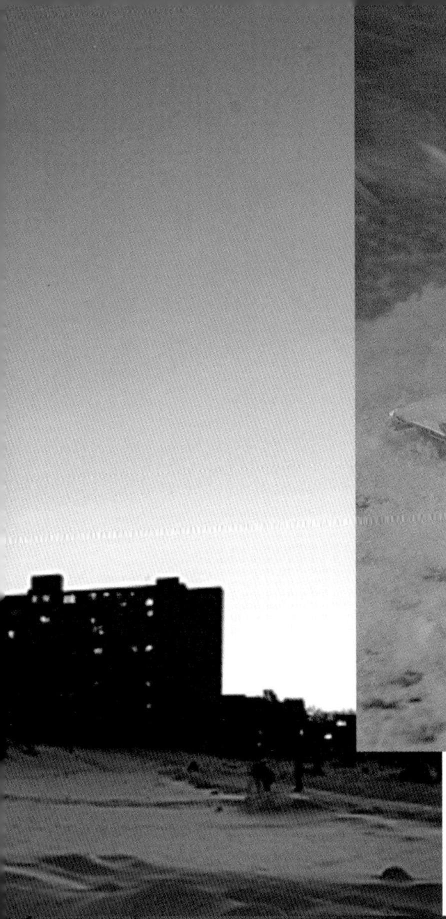

Aluminum foil model translates to heavier gauge aluminum foil object.

Blasting fire extinguisher "snow" with an amused Paul/photographer.

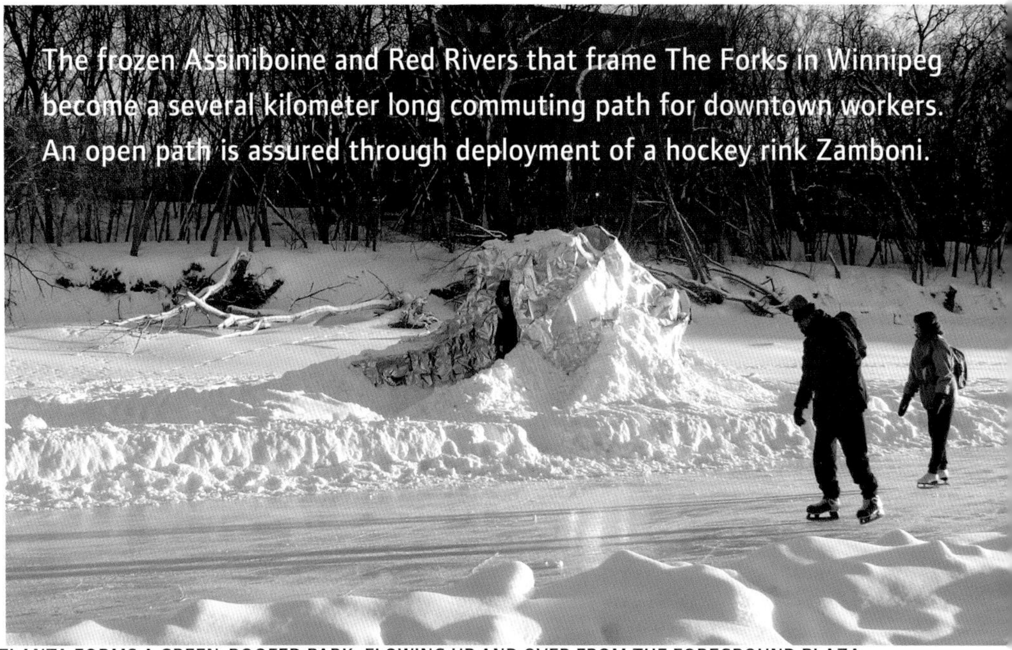

The frozen Assiniboine and Red Rivers that frame The Forks in Winnipeg become a several kilometer long commuting path for downtown workers. An open path is assured through deployment of a hockey rink Zamboni.

THE CENTER FOR CIVIL AND HUMAN RIGHTS PROJECT IN ATLANTA FORMS A GREEN-ROOFED PARK, FLOWING UP AND OVER FROM THE FOREGROUND PLAZA.

IN COLLABORATION WITH PREDOCK_FRANE ARCHITECTS.

CENTER FOR CIVIL AND HUMAN RIGHTS – ATLANTA, GA 2009

LEARNING FROM CURT

"This will not only be a vessel of protection, collection and knowledge, but a space of transformation."

Queen Quet, Gullah/Geechee Nation

Curt Moody of Moody-Nolan, with whom we had recently collaborated on the Student Athletic Center at OSU, approached me about a collaborative effort for the NMAAHC competition. Having worked with Curt for the last few years, it was an obvious fit. The immense responsibility of building on our National Mall, whatever the project may be, was a daunting challenge. Coupled with that was the challenge of expressing the overwhelming power, beauty, and sorrow of African American History and Culture. This demanded guidance by deeply rooted colleagues. Curt, in turn, drew in an impressive admixture of both spiritually and pragmatically attuned advisors—Queen Quet of the Gullah/Geechee Nation; Jack Travis, architect/educator; and other notables such as Rob Livesey, Professor & Director Emeritus, Knowlton School of Architecture, Ohio State University. With our combined teams we began working on a research collage investigating and diagramming African American History and Culture—the horror and terror of the slave ships, the beauty and joy of the culture's arts, and at the center, the Rock of family, church, and the heroes of the struggle for equal rights. Intense programmatic analysis and diagramming ensued; then Curt and I began working with clay...

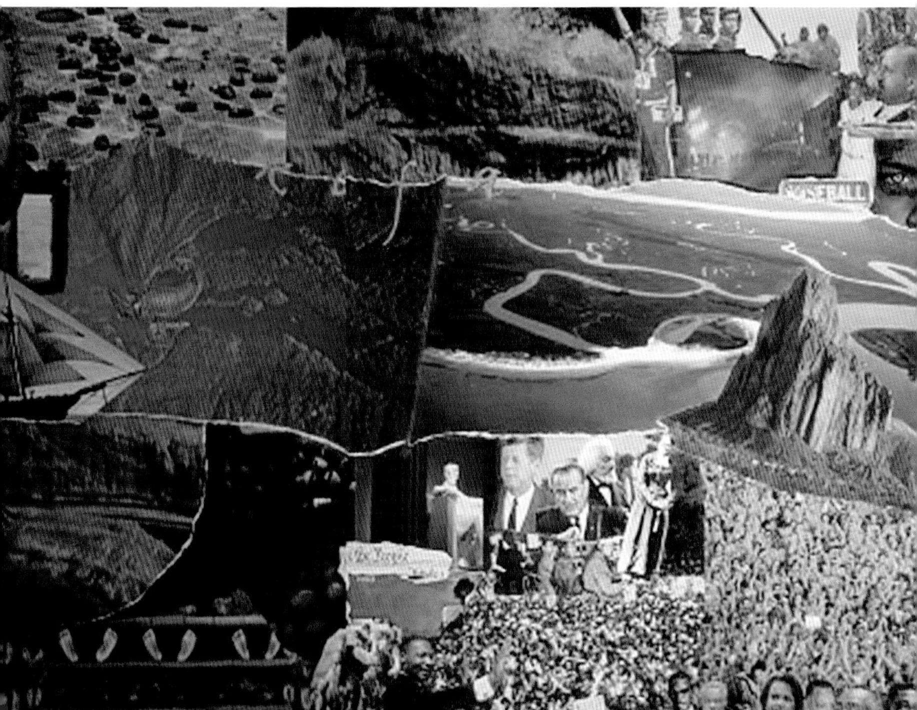

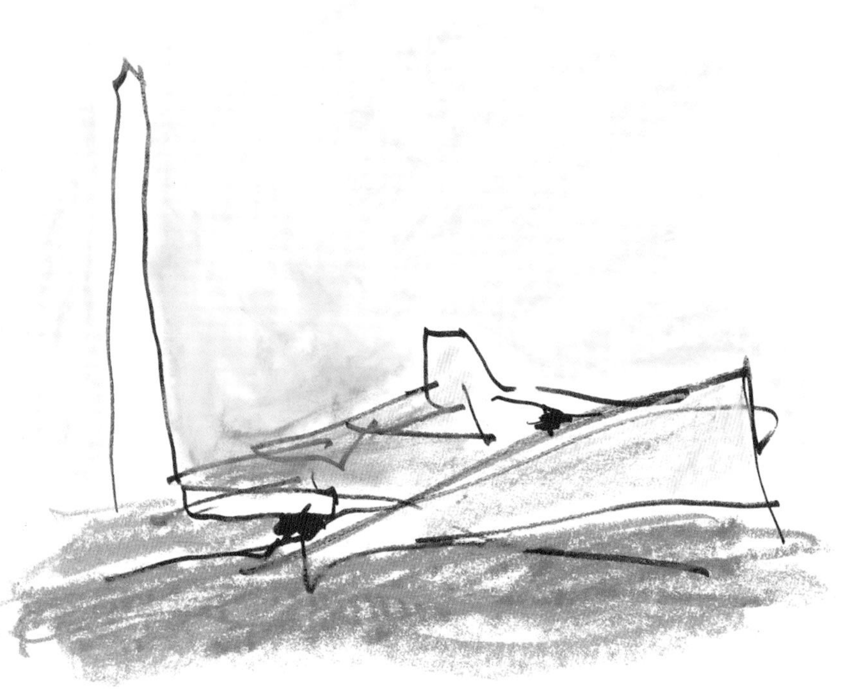

NATIONAL MUSEUM OF AFRICAN AMERICAN HISTORY AND CULTURE

WASHINGTON, D.C. 2009
A COLLABORATION WITH MOODY•NOLAN

"Moody Nolan, in association with Antoine Predock Architect, envisions a building made of natural materials, rising as if out of bedrock. Along one side runs a wetlands scene, a nod to historic Tiber Creek that ran through part of Washington. Its glass roof features etchings echoing Yoruba ancestral arts, and it also has an outdoor amphitheater facing Constitution Avenue."

Jacqueline Trescott, "Architectural Firms Compete to Design African American History Museum," *The Washington Post*, March 28, 2009

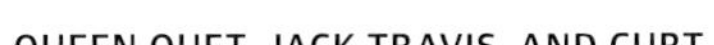

QUEEN QUET, JACK TRAVIS, AND CURT

ROB LIVESEY, DIRECTOR, KNOWLTON SCHOOL OF ARCHITECTURE OSU, REVIEWING OUR DESIGN WITH CURT AND BOB LARIMER AT OUR STUDIO, THEN ON THE SCREEN WITH KAROLE AND CORY.

Flowing from that intensely collaborative research foreground—the project narrative developed experientially, episodically, poetically.

Moving down an allée of American Elms along the National Mall, the Rock, a polyrhythmic mass of stone, ordered as if by tectonic shift, slowly reveals itself rising from the earth amidst the sobriety of the Mall. Beckoning fissures in this stone upheaval reveal an aura within. At the Confluence Entry, the visitor travels along an experience adorned with the haptically transformative qualities of wood and water, light and sound, texture and timbre. The visitor's entire trajectory through the Rock—from the confluence of the entry ramps, down to the quiet reflection of still waters in The Vessel, through the ascent of sequential galleries to the Sankofa Nest, to the culminating brilliance of the Crystal—abstracts critical episodic emotional states of despair and triumph throughout the African American legacy.

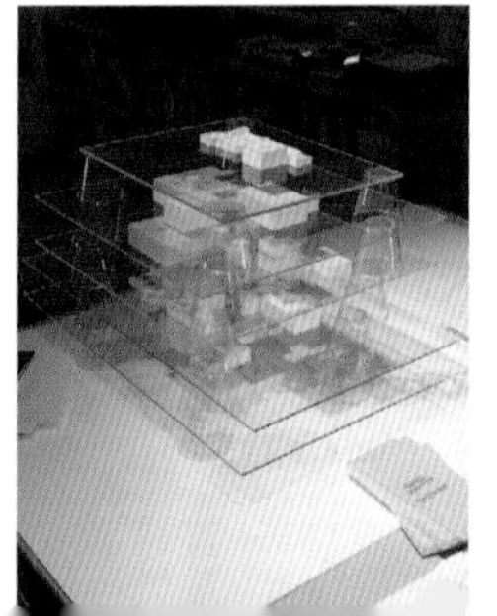

JACK TRAVIS, QUEEN QUET, AND CURT

The Museum is sited adjacent to the Washington Monument—the exclamation point of the Mall. The deep time geologic evocation of the granite administrative slice paralleling 14th Street contrasts the wetland of our proposal as a reminder of the lowcountry Rice Culture context during slavery—and importantly, coupled with the green roof of the western museum spaces, forms a landscape transition to the open space of Constitution Gardens in the northwest quadrant. With the main museum entry to the south, an inviting celebratory amphitheater gestures toward Constitution Avenue.

KATYA AND MIRA

MASTER THINKER/DOER/MODEL BUILDER KENJI KONDO

"Perhaps the most daring concept came from Moody Nolan Inc. in association with Antoine Predock Architect PC. It features natural materials rising from the ground—stone, moss and grasses—with wetlands that extend inside the museum. African woods, harvested from fallen trees and other sustainable means, would adorn the interior. A glass roof at the structure's center depicts a pattern from tribal Africa ..."

Brett Zongker, "National black museum designs break from Smithsonian mold," *The Oklahoman*, April 12, 2009

LEVEL +15
LEVEL +30
LEVEL +50
LEVEL +65
LEVEL +80

Within the Rock we imagine planting a symbolic tree, evoking the power of the historic 1500-year-old Angel Oak on John's Island, South Carolina, a witness to the masses of Africans arriving there. This imagined oak transforms into an ascending network of branches above—the Sankofa Nest.

The spirit of convergence and gathering, historically rooted in the African American Praise House or Church, defines the strength, perseverance, and unity in the cultural symbol of the Rock.

The living atmosphere of our proposal absorbs and illuminates the teachings, struggles, and triumphs of African American culture, which then become lessons—inextricably connected to each visitor. The atmosphere engendered in the Rock highlights the culture's circuitous yet persistent movement toward brighter futures, and translates the trajectory of the horror and terror of the slave ships, the beauty and joy of the arts at the center of African American culture. A fountain of knowledge, diagrammed by the building itself, sprouts from the evolving legacy of the culture's case hardened roots, leaving a powerful imprint on the American landscape, nourishing the branches of the future generations of America.

MANY INFORMATIVE/COLLABORATIVE EXCHANGES WITH PAUL FEHLAU, BOB LARRIMER, AND THE REST OF THE MOODY NOLAN TEAM...

WITH STANDARD CHARRETTE DEBRIS—PIZZA, DONUTS, ETC.

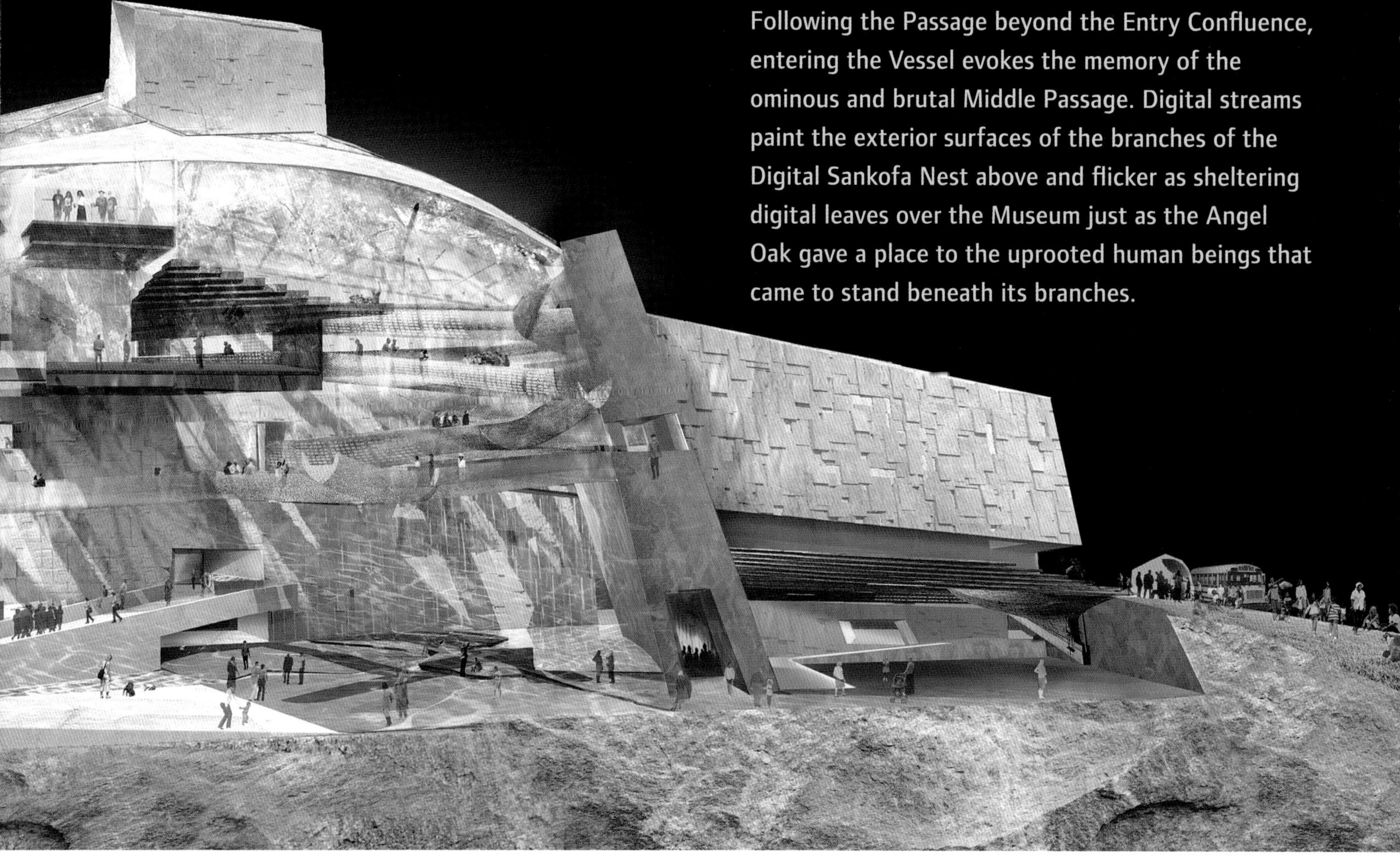

Following the Passage beyond the Entry Confluence, entering the Vessel evokes the memory of the ominous and brutal Middle Passage. Digital streams paint the exterior surfaces of the branches of the Digital Sankofa Nest above and flicker as sheltering digital leaves over the Museum just as the Angel Oak gave a place to the uprooted human beings that came to stand beneath its branches.

The strength and spirit of the Rock—Praise House, Church—have provided a place of restoration, support, and pride for people of African descent in North America since their arrival. The Entry Convergence flows down like the waters that feed the tree that "shall not be moved." The tree, which grew from the branches of Africa stretching to the soil of North America, resonates for not just African Americans, but all Americans. Just as the drums signal the call to return to the past, the rhythms and polyrhythmic textures of the museum sound out an invitation to the passersby, initiating the visitor's journey of Sankofa.

Michael Woods and Julie Cook were instrumental collaborators.

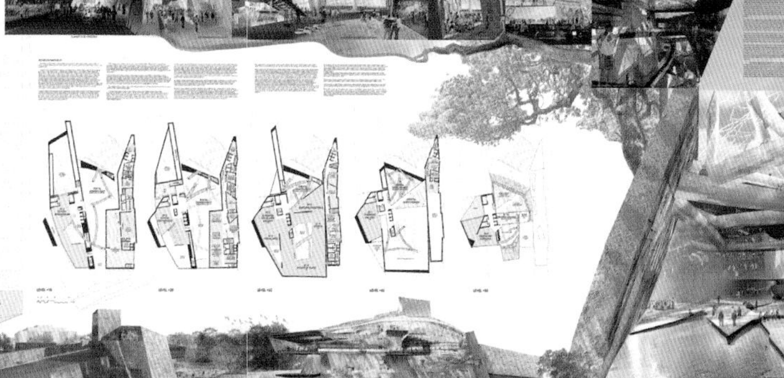

From the Vessel—which synthesizes the Outer hall, Memorial Hall, and the Interior Courtyard—one arrives at the first gallery landing and moves into the sequence of History Galleries that invoke the West African notion of Sankofa, incorporating the practice of carrying the fruits of knowledge from the past for the betterment of our collective futures. This cultural heirloom of Sankofa is a spiritual companion guiding our epic journey that climaxes in an emergent crystalline gem, clearly visible both inside and out, suggestive of the Crystal Mountains of West Africa, inspiring cultural memory.

Continuing forward and upward from the History Galleries, through aperture and shadow, the visitor travels through a series of polyrhythmic gallery sequences whose weaving path of encounter describes a dynamic ascendance along the uphill journey to freedom, equality, and accomplishment. The journey culminates in the Make a Way Somehow Gallery with a window toward the White House, home at the time of Barack Obama and his family—where the pinnacle of American opportunity and citizenship is held up to the light, further emphasizing the cultural ascent built upon hope, independence, and the pursuit of happiness—the quintessential American legacy.

Just as the space beneath the metaphoric great oak within the Rock, the space within the NMAAHC will be a place in which people gather to reconnect themselves to the energy that has brought African Americans through the struggles and triumphs while re-instilling the connection with the earth.

The Bulfinch gatepost at the entry of the wetlands recalls the origins of the land and speaks of enslaved West African contributions made to American technology and prosperity. Africans brought new life and new vitality to the continent by bringing the Rice Culture wetland cultivation practices and water management technologies common to their coastal origins. This West African ingenuity became American tradition in the building of levees, ditches, floodgates, and drains. A boardwalk outlines a path through historical wetlands.

Internally, whether exiting by stair or elevator, or by extending the return journey by retracing the Sankofa Nest, ultimately one's return leads them back to the convergent point of the NMAAHC Central Hall. Where visitors mingle, discuss, and share the power of the Rock with one another, a final exchange under the great tree branches hovering above.

With Curt Moody and our combined teams in Albuquerque and Washington D.C.

HILLSIDE RETREAT

CARMEL, CALIFORNIA 2010

We were approached about a site in Carmel, California, for a community of villas. Clustered around a multiuse Commons Building on a sloping live oak hillside, the villas flow upward from a wildlife preserve, arriving at an Introductory Pavilion. Guests then travel by electric cart throughout the Retreat.

Our vision for the Hillside Retreat emphasizes wellness, the expansion of knowledge, the celebration of an achievement or special event, or simply escaping everyday pressures. The Villas provide guests an extraordinary individualized indoor-outdoor experience. We treat the entire site as a unified architectural and cultural event, responding to the nuances of topography and vegetation, enhancing the site's natural pastoral beauty, and encouraging guests to become completely immersed in this dynamic mix.

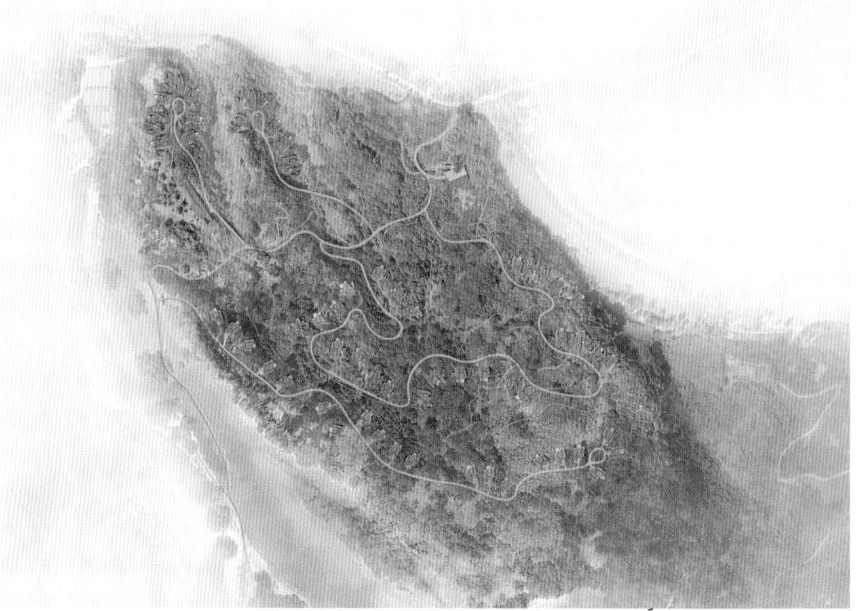

2010 SOUTH AMERICAN TRAVEL—VALPARAÍSO, CHILE, LABYRINTHINE HILLSIDE TOWN ASCENDING FROM THE PORT

The arrival building, "Through the Looking Glass," serves as the resort's "hotel motor court" with a grand porte cochère that protects guests from the sun and weather with a glass photovoltaic trellis as they exit their cars. The trellis spans a fissure in the massive rammed-earth wall that encloses the entry functions and frames the guest's first view of the project.

VECTORWORKS CONFERENCE KEYNOTE LECTURE ALONG WITH WITH PRINCIPAL PAUL FEHLAU IN 2010

AVERY HALL POSTER FOR COLUMBIA UNIVERSITY... WHERE I RECEIVED MY ARCHITECTURE DEGREE IN 1962

2010, DISCOVERING THE APPLE PENCIL—CHARTRES CATHEDRAL, POINT DUME, AND SHIPROCK, NM

DRIVING FROM DUBAI TO OMAN

The heart of the retreat experience is the private refuge of the Villas. The design carefully screens guests from adjacent Villas and opens up to focused views through the landscape.

SKETCHING SULTAN QABOOS GRAND MOSQUE IN MUSCAT...

WITH A DIVE TRIP ON THE SIDE

Commons Building Event Lawn and descent from the Spa

DRAWING WORKSHOP WITH UNM ARCHITECTURE STUDENTS AT THE RIO GRANDE NATURE CENTER WITH PROFESSOR KIMA WAKEFIELD

SHANGHAI SCULPTURE PARK HOTEL

SHANGHAI, CHINA 2011

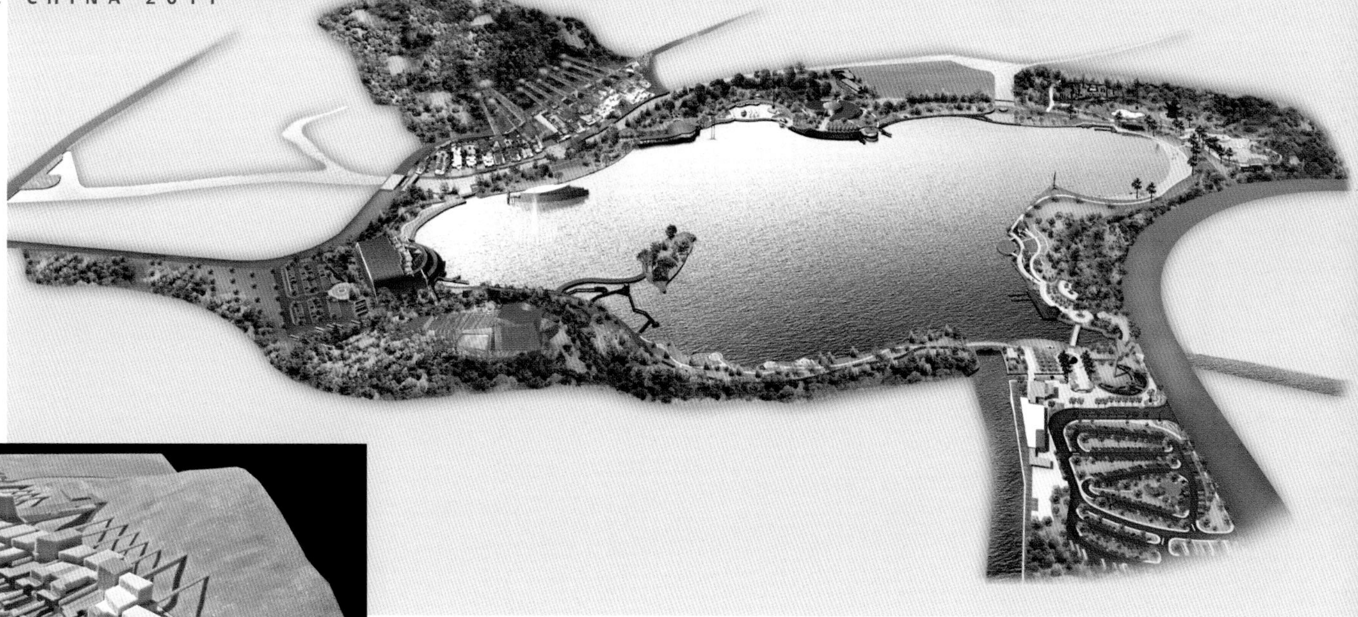

Located west of Shanghai in the Sheshan National Travel and Holiday Area, the Shanghai Sculpture Park Hotel is a figurative waterfall linking Xue Mountain to Moon River. The illusory "waterfall" ceramic frit glazing of the suites suggests a waterfall-to-lake connection. The upper-level suites have rope bridges connecting to private spas in the hillside.

LECTURING AT TONGJI UNIVERSITY OF ARCHITECTURE AND PLANNING IN SHANGHAI, AND THEN ON TO THEIR SISTER CAMPUS IN HARBIN, MANCHURIA. RESTING ON THE STUDENT CHARRETTE COT, BLANKETED BY A POSTER FOR MY LECTURE WHILE RECEIVING A SHOULDER MASSAGE.

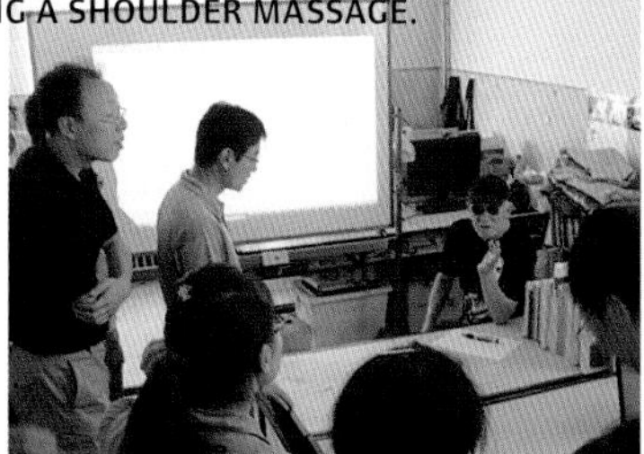

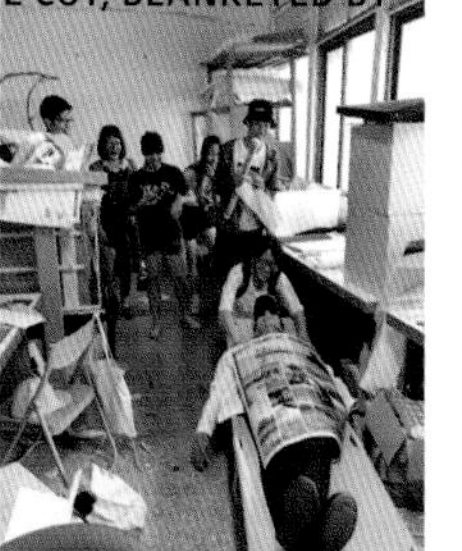

RIVER'S EDGE "BEACH" IN HARBIN WITH MAJOR GEEZER SOCIALIZING AMONGST THEMSELVES.

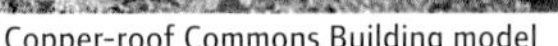

Copper-roof Commons Building model

Campout Treehouse Folly

Bodega Wine Cellar

Celestial Viewing Folly

HANGZHOU, CHINA, CHRISTMAS 2010

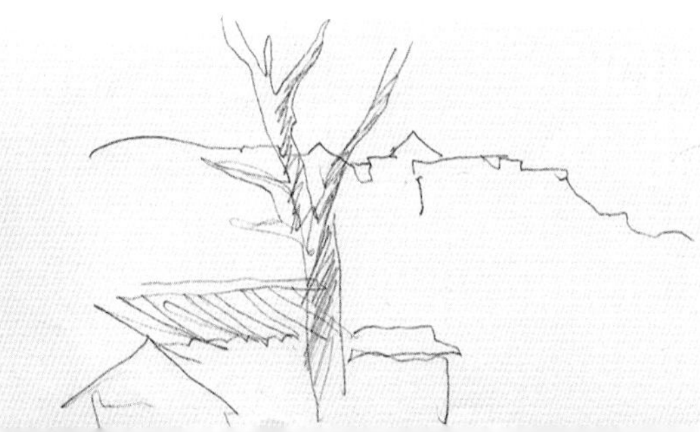

"The morning lake/
drinks up the sky ..." Cat Stevens, *Katmandu*, 1970

The notion of mountain engaging water, channeling Northern Song Dynasty's Shan-Shui hand scrolls—a convergence between near and far, solid and void, light and shadow, blurred in the mist...

The experience begins with entry through a massive stone wall, with the arrival space extending vertically to the upper suites and a common gathering space, passing under the hanging gardens of the rope bridges.

ON FILM SHOOT, RIDING THE VINCENT BLACK SHADOW WITH MY LONG-TIME FRIEND EMILIANO BALLEJOS ON THE MV SENNA

ARCHITECT

THE MAGAZINE OF THE AMERICAN INSTITUTE OF ARCHITECTS

Antoine Predock Architect

THE MASTER OF SOUTHWEST MODERNISM HAS SPENT FOUR DECADES BUILDING A STUDIO CAMPUS IN ALBUQUERQUE. HIS OFFICES DOUBLE AS GARAGES FOR HIS MOTORCYLE COLLECTION: PREDOCK IS ALWAYS READY TO HIT THE ROAD

ROLLERBLADE MISHAP LEAD TO A NEW PART JOINING THE OTHER TITANIUM PIECES IN MY BODY... CHANNELING FLLW WITH A CAPE OVER MY ARM IN A SLING.

ROADCUT AND LIKE A SIGNATURE

SIMULTANEOUS EXHIBITIONS AT THE UNM ART MUSEUM UNIVERSITY OF NEW MEXICO 2011

CURATED AND DESIGNED BY CHRISTOPHER MEAD AND MIRA WOODSON

Noted architectural historian and *Roadcut* author Christopher Mead, in collaboration with Mira Woodson, curated an exhibition that traced our work over forty years: from early work in Albuquerque—La Luz and the Rio Grande Nature Center—to twenty-first-century projects like the Canadian Museum for Human Rights.

"Crucial to the spirit in my work is the enigmatic quality of the desert. You think you've got it, you think you understand; then you turn over a rock or crawl under a larger rock and you discover other worlds, other realms within. In a highway Roadcut, for example, a sectional diagram of the earth is revealed through man's intervention. At the bottom of a Roadcut in the Southwest is pre-Cambrian granite, overlaid by limestone. In geologic time, other sedimentary strata like sandstone and ocean bottom fossils begin to turn up—brachiopods, crinoid stems. Then you begin to see cultural artifacts, in relative scale, just a fraction of an inch compared to the miles of depth of the geologic datum. Prehistoric traces become visible, and then the successive cultural strata. In a New Mexico Roadcut, after Anasazi traces, are later indigenous cultures—then the arrival of the conquistadors, 1930s hubcaps, beer cans, McDonald's wrappers, and the residue of future technologies or whatever else you might imagine out there—the completion of the Roadcut involves a sense of time beyond, that which is unknown but almost palpable here in the Southwest. The Roadcut is a diagram of an investigative process for the making of architecture."

Antoine Predock, *Roadcut* 1994

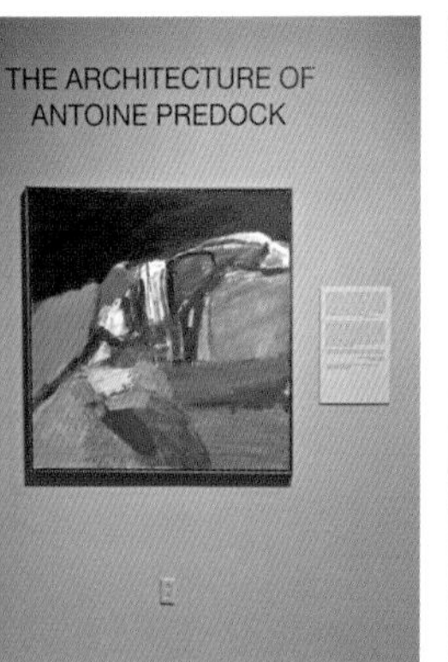

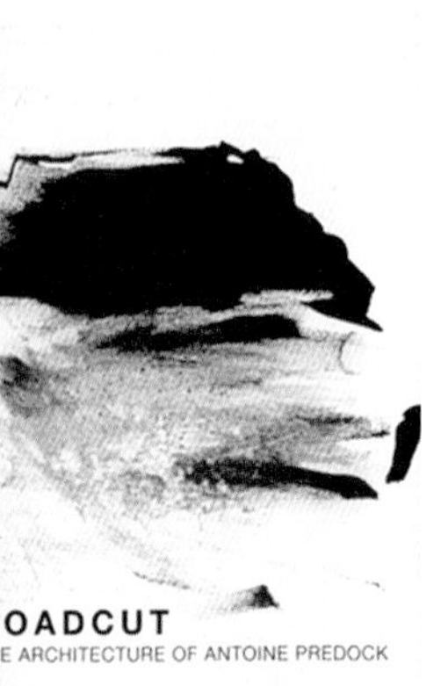

Christopher authored the *Roadcut* monograph, which lead to the later publication of my drawings. As a noted scholar, his view into my work in those books was deep and insightful, articulating a new understanding of my process. Our friendship continued to other special projects.

DISPLAY CASE OF ANTOINE TCHOTCHKES

CHRISTOPHER MEAD, BOOK AUTHOR/CURATOR; MIRA WOODSON, BOOK DESIGNER AND CO-CURATOR—WITH GREGORY WAITS

ON THE VINCENT

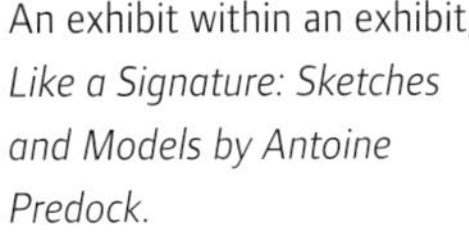

An exhibit within an exhibit, *Like a Signature: Sketches and Models by Antoine Predock.*

FINAL WEEK

EXHIBITIONS CLOSE ON JULY 24TH

ANTOINE PREDOCK
Roadcut: The Architecture of Antoine Predock
and
Like a Signature: Sketches and Models

Two exhibitions about the internationally acclaimed architect, Antoine Predock, will offer a time opportunity to see a retrospective of his extraordinary models, drawings and photog Through ten case studies, *Roadcut* traces Predock's career over forty years. *Like a Sig Sketches and Models* looks beyond individual buildings to visualize architecture's recipro with landscape in an array of works from ca. 1961-2009. Guest Curator, Christopher Cu Mead. On view in the Main and Van Deren Coke Galleries through July 24.

"You never know, even if you think you do, where you're going. That cross-country trip I took, from Missouri to New Mexico, almost eight decades ago has led places I could never have imagined. Every project is like that. Every competition, even if we don't get the commission, is a win—what we have collectively made, what we've experienced, lands in a spiritual savings account from which we can withdraw forever." Antoine Predock, "Nomadic Studio", *Antoine Predock Architect 4*, 2006

FAMILIAR FACES IN ATTENDANCE—DAVE MATTISON, MY TAOS SKI EXPRESS AND FORMER F-4 PILOT, CONSTANCE, CORY, KAROLE, PAUL, AND ACE PHOTOGRAPHER ROBERT RECK—WHO FOR DECADES PHOTOGRAPHED OUR MODELS AND RESIDENTIAL BUILDINGS FOR MANY BOOKS AND PERIODICALS, MOST NOTABLY MANY PROJECTS FOR *ARCHITECTURAL DIGEST.*

BIBLIOTECA PUBLICA DEL ESTADO DE JALISCO "¡AY, JALISCO, NO TE RAJES!"

GUADALAJARA, MEXICO 2011

"The library is inhabited by spirits that come out of the pages at night."

Isabel Allende

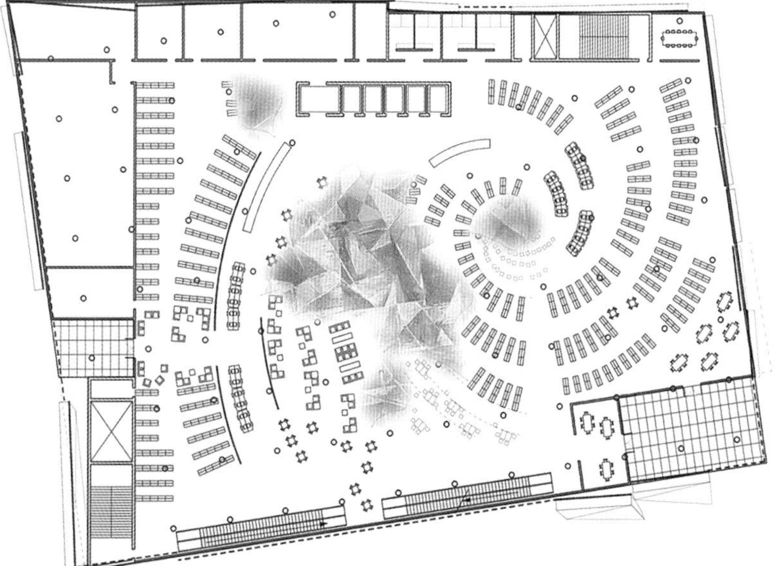

Within the shadows of La Barranca de Oblates, La Nueva Biblioteca Publica del Estado de Jalisco emerges from a limestone plaza, Ixtli Caliza, lined with Zapote trees. A safe box, *caja de tesoros* for books and media sheathed in a copper jacket of light, *manta de luz*, La Biblioteca envelopes an abstract crystalline/digital maguey, *un fuego detenido* (frozen fire) from the past, again awakened. This tree of wonders, *arbol de maravillas*, as it is known to the Otoni people is a source of sweet water '*agua miel*' and symbol of the culture, landscape, and people of Mexico. For the Nahuatl, the maguey was a divine creation representing the goddess Mayahuel. Like Juan Diego's manta enclosing divine roses, or silent walls sheltering a verdant private garden, the copper caja protects La Biblioteca environmentally and spiritually, selectively revealing layers of life, culture, and activity within. A collector of cultures, mixing pueblo and university, casual user and academic, La Biblioteca and its plaza fill with fiesta, quinceañeras, and tiangis, children and jubilados, business people and tourists. Displacements of program elements from below—Theater, Auditorium, and Classrooms—surface on the Plaza, creating a topography for shaded casual gatherings.

From origins within the earth, La Biblioteca grows from a cenote "mythic well touching ancient subterranean waters of Lake Chapala" mirror-like, a reflection of the Azteca calendar stone. A limestone amphitheater, *palenque*, embraces the Cenote. La Pina heart of the abstract maguey, of La Biblioteca and the village of Zapopan, rises through the plaza as a crystalline volume housing the main Library entrances, Mercado, Café, after-hours book return and sorting, Information Desk, Orientation Theater, and Gallery, providing centrality of movement and introduction to the glazed *pencas* (leaves of the maguey). Viscous obsidian ramps, like obsidian deposits found at Cerro Collí, spiral up through La Pina, inviting visitors through the Gallery and the Orientation Theater up to the Biblioteca collections.

From the central open core of the glass maguey, individual pencas reach toward the sky, the sun, views of city, and the land beyond, toward Ixtepete, El Grillo, Cerro el Cuatro, and Cerro Collí. The penca digital surfaces display a deep timeline reflection of Mexican exuberance/fiesta/pachanga from Aztec cosmology to the future, from indigena to mestizaje—charting a kaleidoscope of time. Each penca a magical, fluid realm of memory and pueblo, as in the writings of authors such as Juan Rulfo and Elena Garro emanates from the Pina to carve through La Biblioteca. A Borgesian repository of memory, and conveyor of the intellectual and spiritual flow of La Biblioteca, the pencas reach from the Cenote to the rooftop Cyber Garden, El Jardín Xallí, as sinuous conductors of diffuse light, illuminating and organizing the collections, disseminating embedded digital technology and information, and orienting users.

"... time was not passing ... it was turning in a circle ..."

Gabriel García Márquez,
One Hundred Years of Solitude

PENCAS DEL MAGUEY/NAVEL OF THE MOON

Que me entierren en la sierra, al pie de los magueyales
Y que me cubra la tierra
Que es cuna de hombres cabales.

That they bury me in the mountain range at the foot of the magueyales
and that they cover me with Earth
That is the cradle of man

– México Lindo, Chucho Monge

In Labyrinths, Jorge Borges depicts "The Library of Babel" as a repository for collective memory and a summation of culture. The power of this vision within the context of México's rich cultural and geomorphic layering is seen for La Biblioteca de México José Vasconcelos. The building will evoke the deep time of México and interpret it in form and space.

The Maguey is a symbol of the culture, the landscape, and the peoples of México. This árbol de maravillas (tree of wonders), as it was known to the Otomí, a source of agua miel (sweet water), with its ancient arms, reaches towards light. In the diagram, each penca, or arm, is a programmatic extraction that transforms into La Biblioteca: a penca for knowledge, for creativity, for reflection, for possibility, and a penca of mystery – for poetry yet to be written. For the Náhuatl, Maguey was a divine creation representing the goddess Mayahuél. Mayahuél is the heart of the maguey and it is this heart from which all pencas spring forth. From the Maguey/Mayahuél issue subliminal architectural possibilities – a di Chirico like - public arcade, a mythic vertical stele, a contemplative bridge to the sky and the future, a silhouette where La Biblioteca might suggest landscape abstraction and a towering, weeping copper mountain displaces earth creating plazas linked to the ball courts of ancient times. The Maguey's roots merge with deep time. An Azteca stone calendar reflected in the Mayan cenote (mythic well) of creation is the stage for dancing jaguars and crocodiles, orators and farmers, gods and goddesses. Chichén Itzá, Palenque, Monte Albán, and Teotihuacán occupy the banks of the cenote – the theater of memory. A mighty river moves through the underworld, along the way shards of [illegible] pyrite and Mayan jade reflect a thunderous dance. Lava vaporizes as it merges with a fresh water plaza. In the distance the jungles of Chiapas erupt, splashing the Fridaesque moon with a glyphic cyber[illegible]. Between pencas, a caracara, the memory of the city, and the spirit of [illegible] La Biblioteca [illegible] drenched in Mexican sunlight.

The Architecture of La Biblioteca will be a summation of all these trajectories, fusing elemental spirit with technology. Hacia un país de lectores (towards a nation of readers) is realized in multi-dimensional spaces. The architecture is saturated with history, culture, myth and a sensuous tangibility.

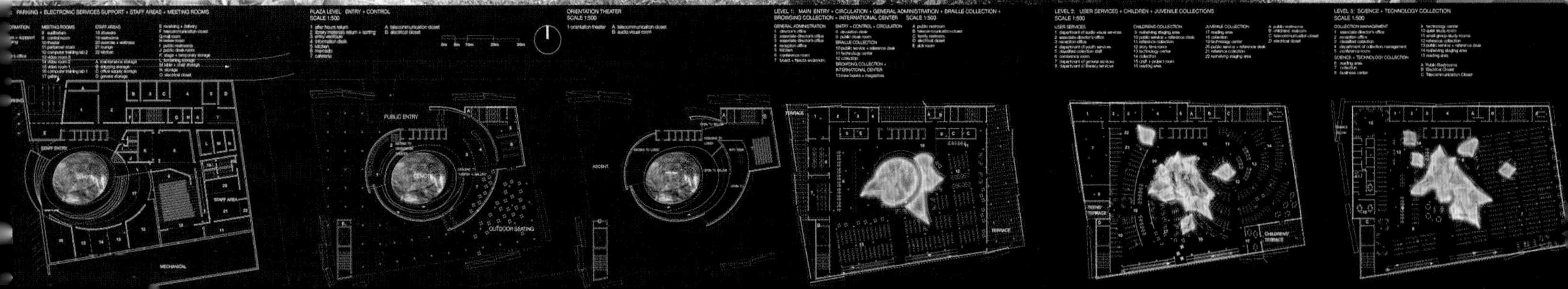

Pencas that escape through the rooftop garden, project beams of light into the night, becoming a beacon for Jalisco. Other pencas imprint the exterior walls of the Biblioteca, deflecting the copper skin. Ventilating cavities along the perimeter also create the manta de luz condition, where light is captured and selectively released to the interior.

Counterpoint to the exuberant glass maguey, rows of regular, precisely ordered stacks are a datum of clear organization, facilitating staff movement and overview, while encouraging immersion in study or social interaction. Although the book as object is finite, an infinity of textual cultural memory intensely emerges in the digital pencas.

> "Methodical writing distracts me from the present condition of men. But the certainty that everything has been already written nullifies or makes phantoms of us all."
>
> Jorge Luis Borges, *The Library of Babel*

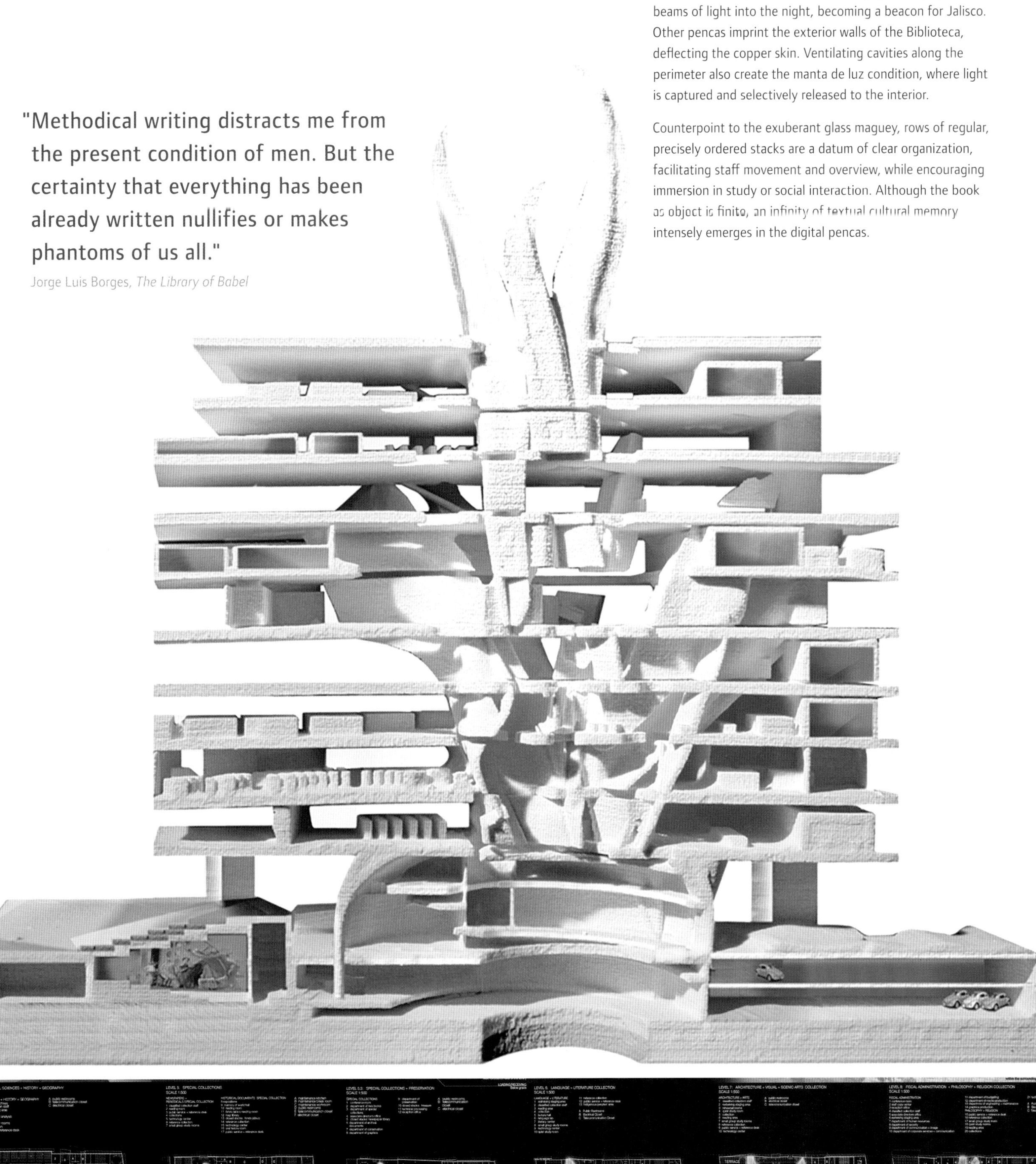

"The library will endure; it is the universe. As for us, everything has not been written; we are not turning into phantoms. We walk the corridors, searching the shelves and rearranging them, looking for lines of meaning amid leagues of cacophony and incoherence, reading the history of the past and our future, collecting our thoughts and collecting the thoughts of others, and every so often glimpsing mirrors, in which we may recognize creatures of the information."
Jorge Luis Borges, *The Library of Babel*
LABYRINTHS
Selected Stories & Other Writings
BY JORGE LUIS BORGES
BAHRAIN FORT

Through journey/procession/pilgrimage, the visitor engages the library toward individual ends, seeking that which inspires and illuminates.

La Biblioteca visually culminates in "el alto grito como la flor amarilla del maguey a la hora de su muerte. Una serenata a la luna."

"I've always imagined that paradise will be a kind of library."

Jorge Luis Borges

VISITING BAHRAIN ON THE WAY TO QATAR WITH STOPOVERS IN ISTANBUL AND ABU DAHBI—2011

ICE MOUNTAIN

JACKSONVILLE, FLORIDA 2012

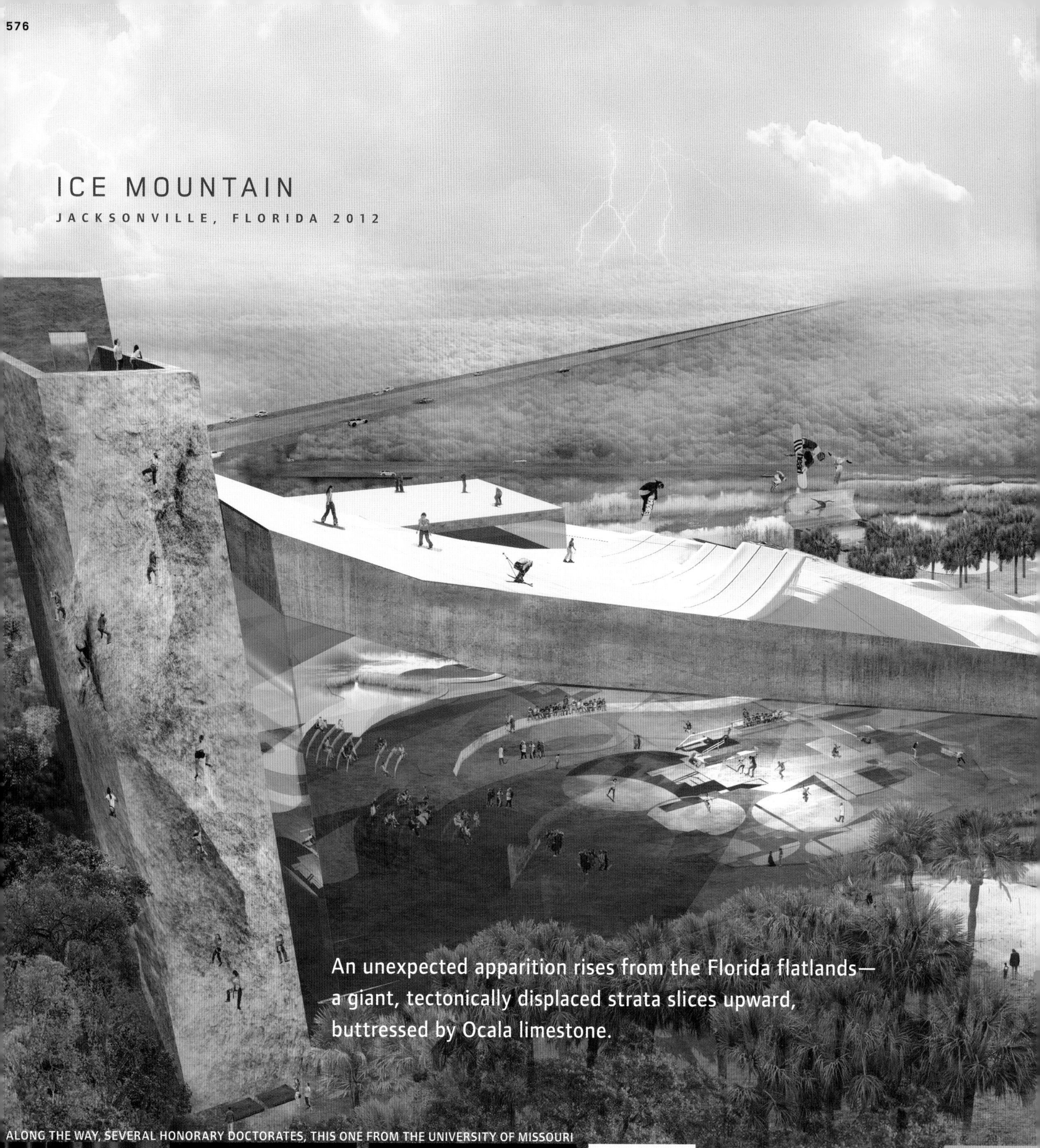

An unexpected apparition rises from the Florida flatlands—a giant, tectonically displaced strata slices upward, buttressed by Ocala limestone.

ALONG THE WAY, SEVERAL HONORARY DOCTORATES, THIS ONE FROM THE UNIVERSITY OF MISSOURI

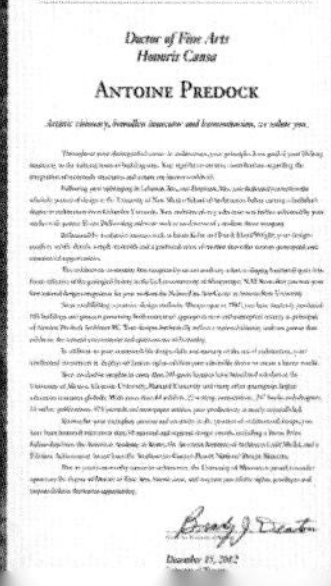

UNIVERSITY OF MISSOURI

Doctor of Fine Arts
Honoris Causa

ANTOINE PREDOCK

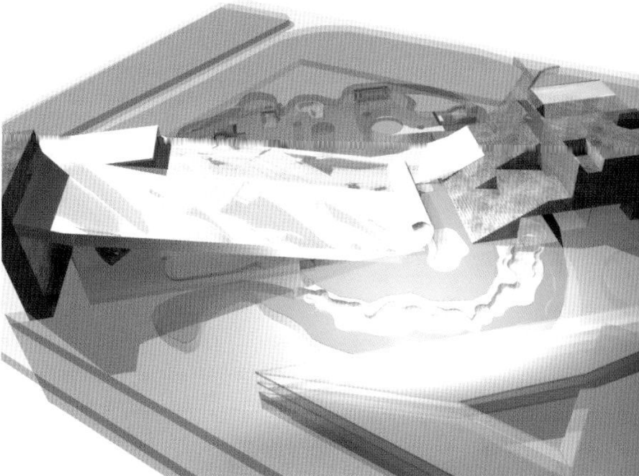

Ice Mountain's dry ski slope ramp descends from an Ocala Limestone wall to wetlands below. An amphitheater/hotel faces the action. Skate, bike, water sport, and media events punctuate the restored Florida wetland landscape.

Ice Mountain faces north to reduce glare for riders and skiers while providing maximum visibility from the freeway approach and adjacent shopping areas. At night, the ramp is lit by a suspended mesh of LEDs that allows nighttime operation and makes the ramp a beacon on Jacksonville's horizon. The ramp culminates in the Banzai Pipeline Snow Tube. Boarders and skiers can ride the tube to the return to the lift, cross the bridge to return to the entry lobby, or drop into the skate and water-sport deck. The Sky Café deck atop Ice Mountain views the action on the ramp and the ocean in the distance.

Directly under the artificial snow ramp is the Media City Skate Plaza. This large indoor area of the park is sized for large skate and BMX events, with space for media and audience. Below the ramp, studio lighting is provided for TV production, and catwalks crisscross the space to allow media to capture the space from any angle. Large-scale monitors under the ramp allow greater audience participation.

PASSING THROUGH THE FAIRYTALE LANDSCAPE OF GUILIN ON THE WAY TO OUR CHENGDU, CHINA PROJECT WITH PAUL AND KAROLE

Surrounding the ramp to the east and west are an array of skate and BMX venues linked together like a golf course. Skate venues are interwoven with water board sport venues. Skaters and water boarders can move from event to event though a palm grove. Each event is separate to allow space for an appropriately scaled observation area with a variety of levels of intimacy. Wave machines, a wake boarding area, a recreational blue hole pool, along with blue hole spas are provided on the deck. The water venues naturally transition into the site's existing wetlands, appearing to grow naturally from the landscape. The water-sports deck has ample space for relaxing in the sun or the shade, as well as a dining terrace, and space for special event tents to be erected.

Hotel guests approach the site from the north and drive directly to the second level porte cochère. After check-in, guests can descend to the podium and the Xero Gravity venues, or ascend to the room levels. Hotel rooms look either north to the ramp or east toward the ocean. The ramp side of the hotel is clad with an LED media mesh that can be used to show live action within the park or provide an additional medium for sponsors and advertisers. The upper deck of the hotel is the "best view in the house" of the action happening within Ice Mountain.

007 AT THE PEARL

DOHA, QATAR 2012

A massive stone island rises from the ocean near Doha, sheltering an inner world of crystalline dichroic glass. Deep time is invoked by Qatari limestone fragments—overlaid with 007 hints.

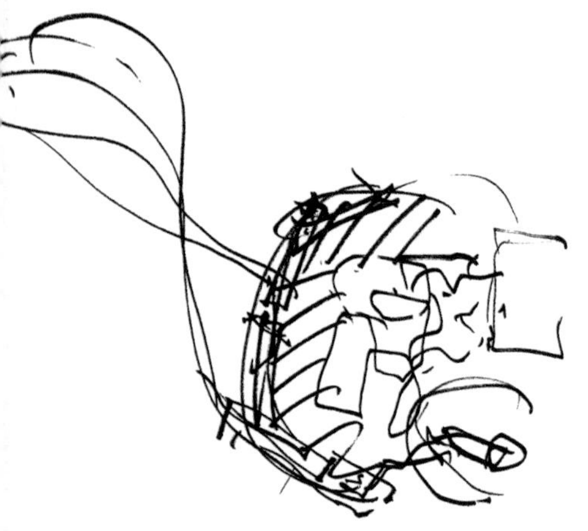

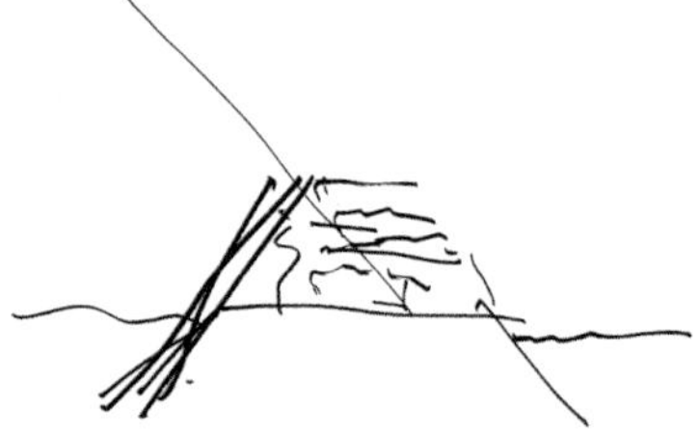

MOTO LIFE CONTINUES TO UNFOLD ON THE HONDA RC30—THEN DISASTER WHEN A BROKEN TIMING GEAR TRIGGERS A DOMINO EFFECT THROUGH ALL THE ENGINE PARTS OF A DUCATI DESMOSEDICI...

CANYON RIDING WITH KEN FRIEDMAN AND HIS FRIEND JAMIE. KEN IS AN IRON MAN ADVENTURER FRIEND WHO "DANCES ON THE PRECIPICE"... HE HAS RIDDEN ON 7 CONTINENTS (WHICH OF COURSE INCLUDES ANTARCTICA!).

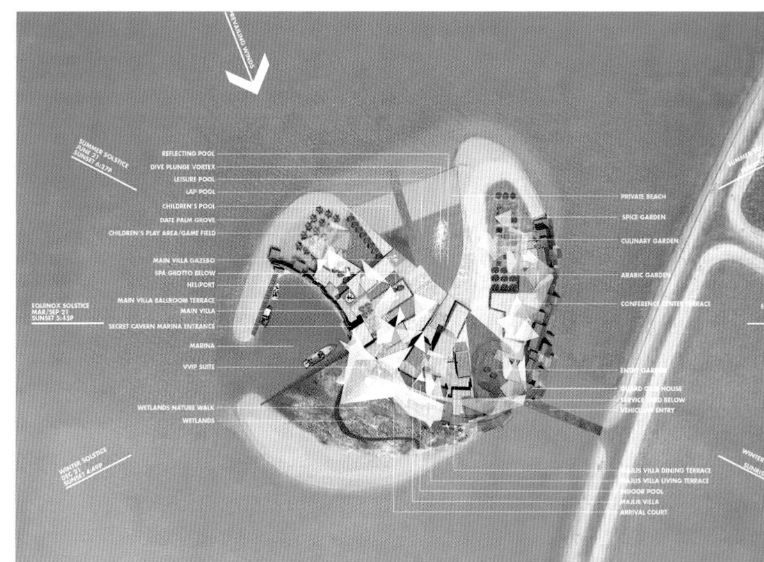

WITH JAY AT THE ROCK STORE MALIBU

RIDING WITH THE DUKE CITY ROCKERS

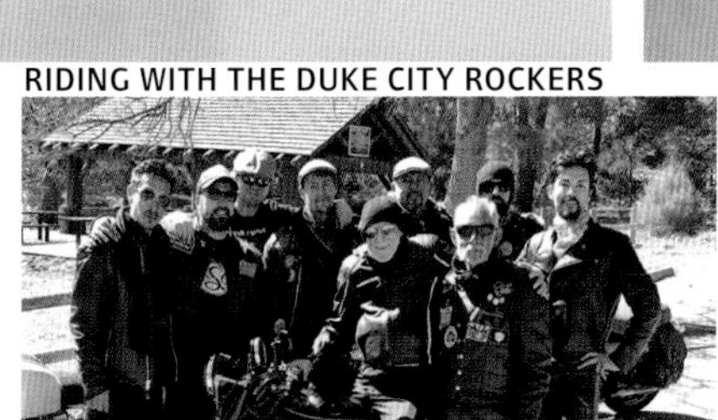

RIDING THE SANTA MONICA MOUNTAINS WITH EMILIANO

ASCENDING SKY PARK

NATIONAL OLYMPIC STADIUM
TOKYO, JAPAN 2012

YEAR OF THE DRAGON NEW YEAR CARD 2012

MEETING WITH COLLEAGUE HIRO IN TOKYO, AND VISITING THE MEIJI SHRINES

SAVANNAH, GA—2013 AIAS FORUM ANNUAL KEYNOTE LECTURE

Ascending Sky Park rises from and extends Shibuya and Shinjuku Ward parks, creating a single year-round green park attraction. The glowing mountain of the grandstands enclosure emerges from the interwoven Ribbon Ramps, creating a participatory, multiple-personality, urban park façade. The sense of anticipation builds as spectators emerge from subway lines and other conveyances to begin the ascent up the sloping park ribbons to the north and south entry plazas at the building podium. Guests enter the luminous tectonic enclosure—a bamboo and concrete clad seating bowl arrays before them. Light issues from the clear, compound-curve tensile structure of entrained air insulative roof panels. The panels above the field pivot open to the sky.

FROM TOKYO AND THE IMPERIAL PALACE, ON TO KYOTO AND THE POWER OF SILENCE IN THE RYOAN-JI TABLEAU. RYOAN-JI GARDEN AND CHARTRES CATHEDRAL—THE TWO MAN-MADE

Elevator and escalator connections allow easy access from the entry plazas to the three general concourses. Every seat in the stands has an unobstructed event view. Movable sections of the first tier stands make it possible to reconfigure from a track and field stadium to a more intimate soccer or rugby venue for ongoing post-Olympic use.

Spectators have a visceral connection to the sky and to the park from within the stadium. Even when closed, the clear entrained air insulative roof does not obstruct the view to the sky. When open, the roof panels create a sensation of raining flower petals or giant dewdrops. Imagery can be projected on the panels' surface during nighttime events and concerts, creating an otherworldly atmosphere.

Throughout the stadium there is a palpable sense of the park rising to enclose the structure. Concourse circulation opens broad views to the Ribbon Parks and the Tokyo skyline beyond, allowing spectators to feel that they are being embraced by one of Tokyo's many garden spaces.

This stadium is an urban garden/park oasis in one of the densest cities in the world.

NAVELS OF THE WORLD.

UT-SAN ANTONIO LECTURE WITH OBI OKOLO AND HIS MOM

2012 IN THE ARABIAN DESERT—DUNES AND FALCONRY

DUBAI SOLAR INNOVATION CENTER

DUBAI, UAE 2012

The earth-engaged Center is partially embedded in arcing dunes and sheltered by a cooling cloud-like "tent." In response to Dubai's climate we have created a light and airy decentralized "village" below a solar-cavity roof structure. The building separates programmatic spaces with riyadh courtyards as part of the building's environmental strategy, and to give visitors the feeling of being enveloped in a cool green oasis. The interactive visitor-walkthrough areas unfurl along gently descending rampways. The low-lying structure takes advantage of the thermal mass of the earth and the dune to maintain a constant temperature. The outer surface of the building's cavity roof is covered with amorphous, cell-thin-film solar collectors, shading the airspace, while the inner surface provides the center's environmental seal. The airspace between insulates the center from the desert heat. A solar chimney, "Burj al Shems," uses the sun's energy to induce cooling air movement though the cavity roof system and the building's riyadh courtyards. At the end of the exhibit sequence visitors ascend the spherical "sun" of the Rising Sun IMAX Theater to experience views in all directions.

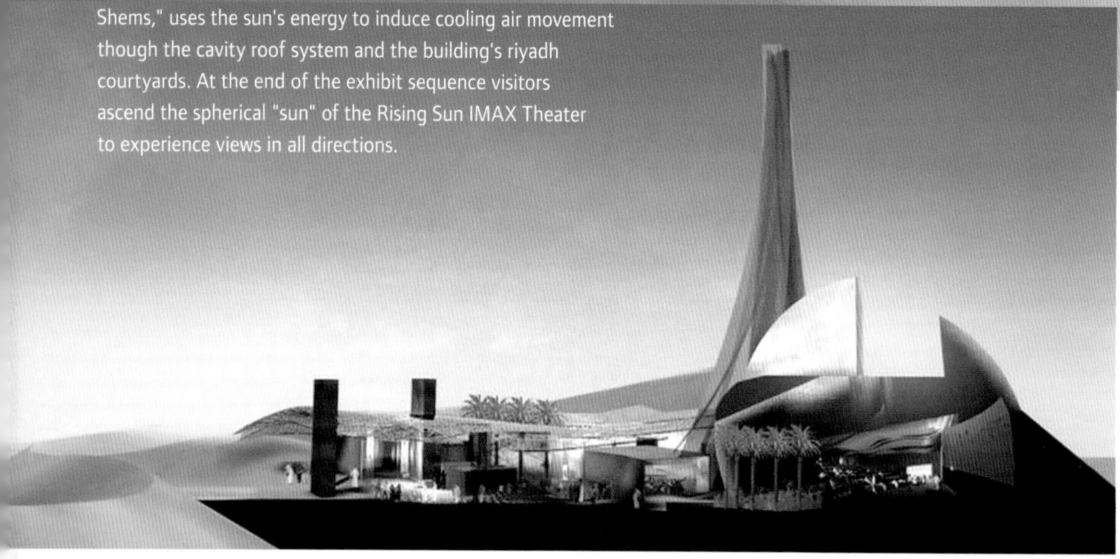

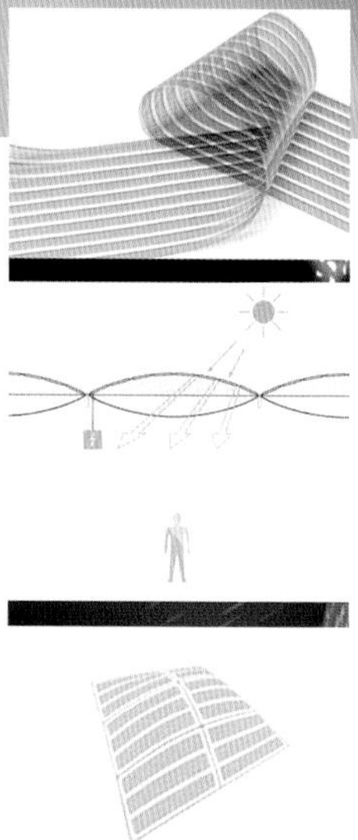

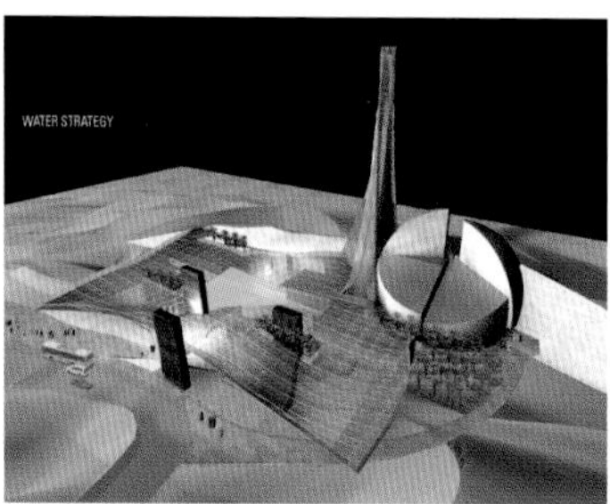

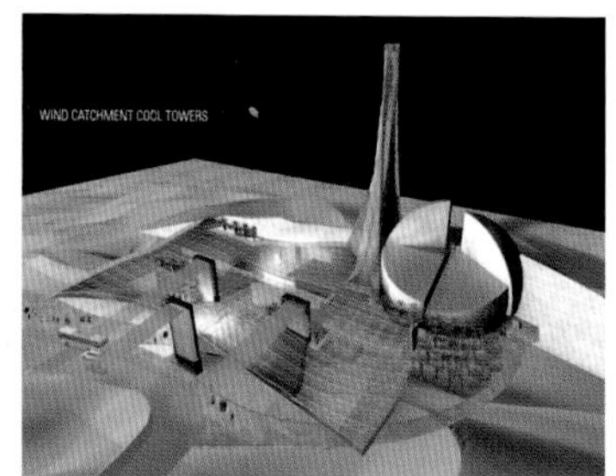

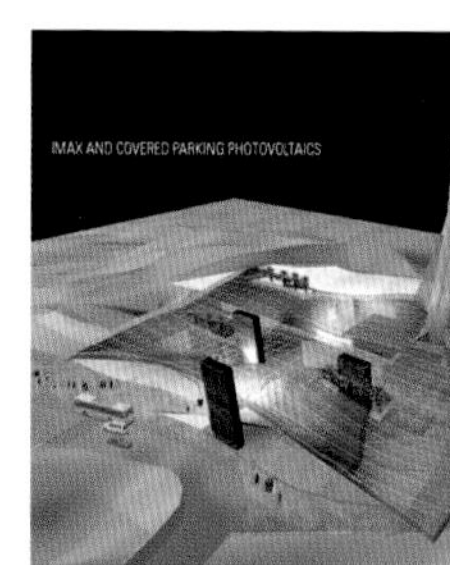

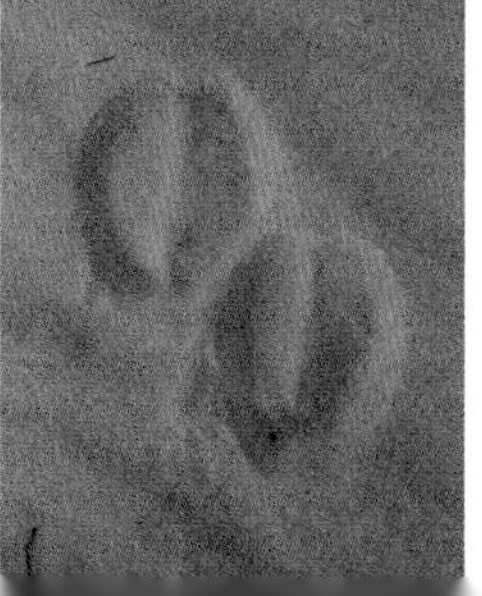

Summer Solstice
Equinox
Winter Solstice
0 20 50 100
1 Solar Innovation Center
2 IMAX Theatre
3 Exhibition Hall
4 Drop Off
5 PV Covered Parking
6 Bus Parking
THIN FILM PHOTOVOLTAICS
VENTED CAVITY ROOF

XIANGFAN CITY MUSEUM

XIANGFAN, CHINA 2014

The Chinese ideogram for landscape—Shan Shui—translates, literally, to mountain/water. This Museum is a mediator as mountain meets water.

DUBAI TO BEIJING, PASSING OVER THE HIMALAYAS

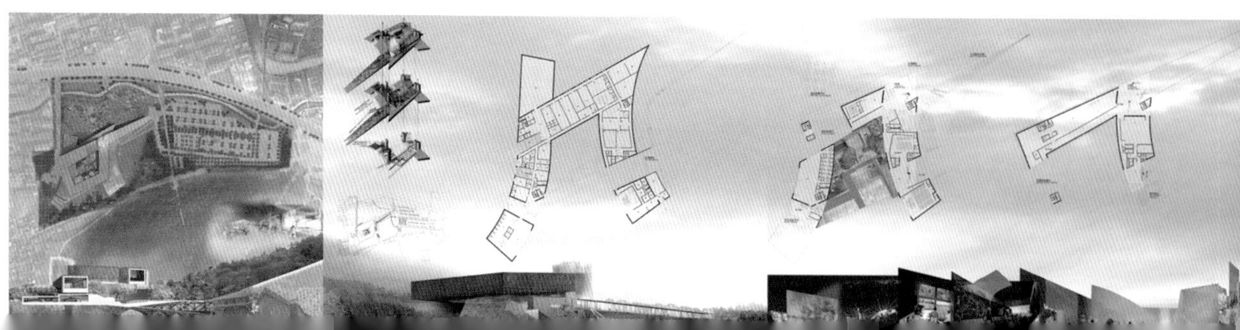

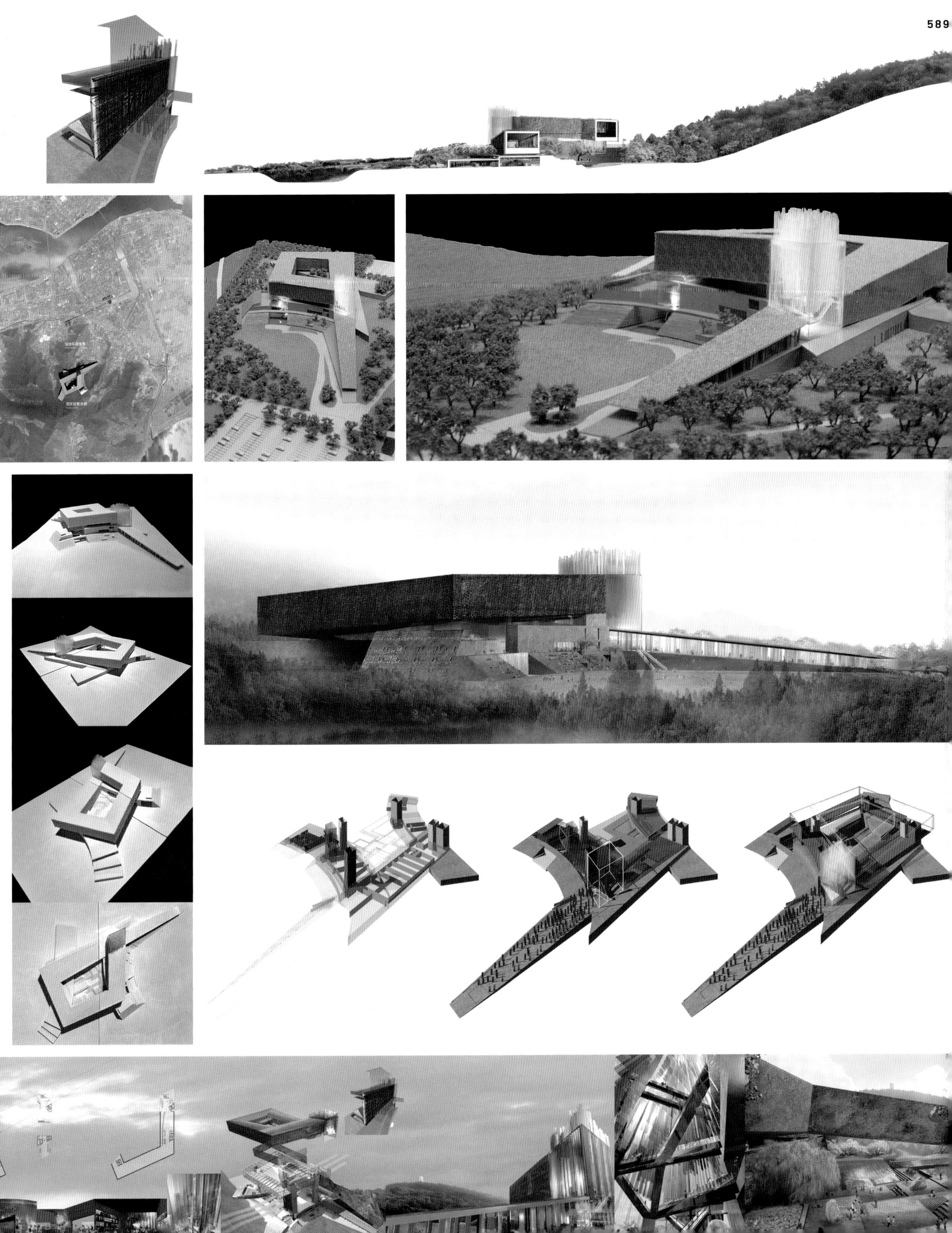

The unraveling segmented rectilinear ascent through the Entry Hall/Glass Rain blades links to themed galleries that hover above the Mountain Gate Court. The inner courtyard walls of this square spiral gallery sequence are covered with flowering vines.

ON THE PROMENADE ATOP THE ANCIENT WALLS OF OLD XIANGFAN.

CONSTANCE AND I HAD TO RENDEZVOUS WITH THE MODEL AT A SHOP IN SHANGHAI, AND THEN TRANSPORT IT TO XIANGFAN. THUMBS UP FOR A SAFE ARRIVAL IN OUR HOTEL ROOM.

GLACIER BAY, ALASKA WITH CONSTANCE

The Entry Hall/Glass Rain absorbs and reflect light through the "highway interchange" of intersecting escalators to begin the exhibition experience.

The east corner of the hall opens to reveal the first view into the central Lotus Terrace Mountain Gate Court. The lushly planted south facing court is positioned to capture heat in the cooler months while the exhibit spiral above and willow trees provide shading in the summer. Water running over a sloping plane of ancient granite delicately fills the space with sound, sacred lotuses float on stepped water terraces with goldfish shimmering below. Views from activity terraces are focused to the mountain. The Lotus Terrace Mountain Gate Court contains spaces for ceremonies, performance, outdoor classroom, and film projection.

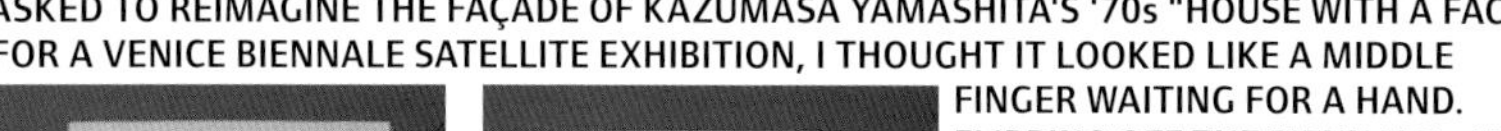

ASKED TO REIMAGINE THE FAÇADE OF KAZUMASA YAMASHITA'S '70s "HOUSE WITH A FACE," FOR A VENICE BIENNALE SATELLITE EXHIBITION, I THOUGHT IT LOOKED LIKE A MIDDLE FINGER WAITING FOR A HAND. FLIPPING OFF THE BIENNALE—IT SEEMED THE PERFECT RESPONSE, GIVEN THE DAMAGE THAT WAS DONE TO ARCHITECTURE BY ITS PROMOTION AND DISSEMINATION OF POSTMODERNISM IN THE '80s. I LIKE SMARTASS YAMASHITA'S WORK AND I KNOW HE WOULD AGREE WITH ME ABOUT FLAGRANT, HISTORICIST POMO.

The Gateway Arrival Building/Art Center serves as the Welcome Center to a new town for 100,000 inhabitants on the outskirts of Chengdu. This Center also serves as a community focus for the new town where visitors and residents can experience art and theatre, as well as dine and conduct varied meeting activities. Embracing the lake with textured concrete masses, the color derived from actual soil from the site, Northern Song Dynasty scroll paintings are evoked—Shan Shui, mountain/water. Drawing from Chinese culture, Sichuan's landscape, and the site's agricultural history, the Center contains an assemblage of programmatic elements edging the lake, which is the matrix linking all components of the new town. Upslope from the lake, merging with the hillside, is the Museum Hill/Expo Center, lodged in the existing topography. The Café Tower, glowing red at night, viewed at a distance, marks the Gateway Center as the arrival hub.

GATEWAY ARRIVAL BUILDING/ARTS CENTER

CHENGDU, CHINA 2008/15

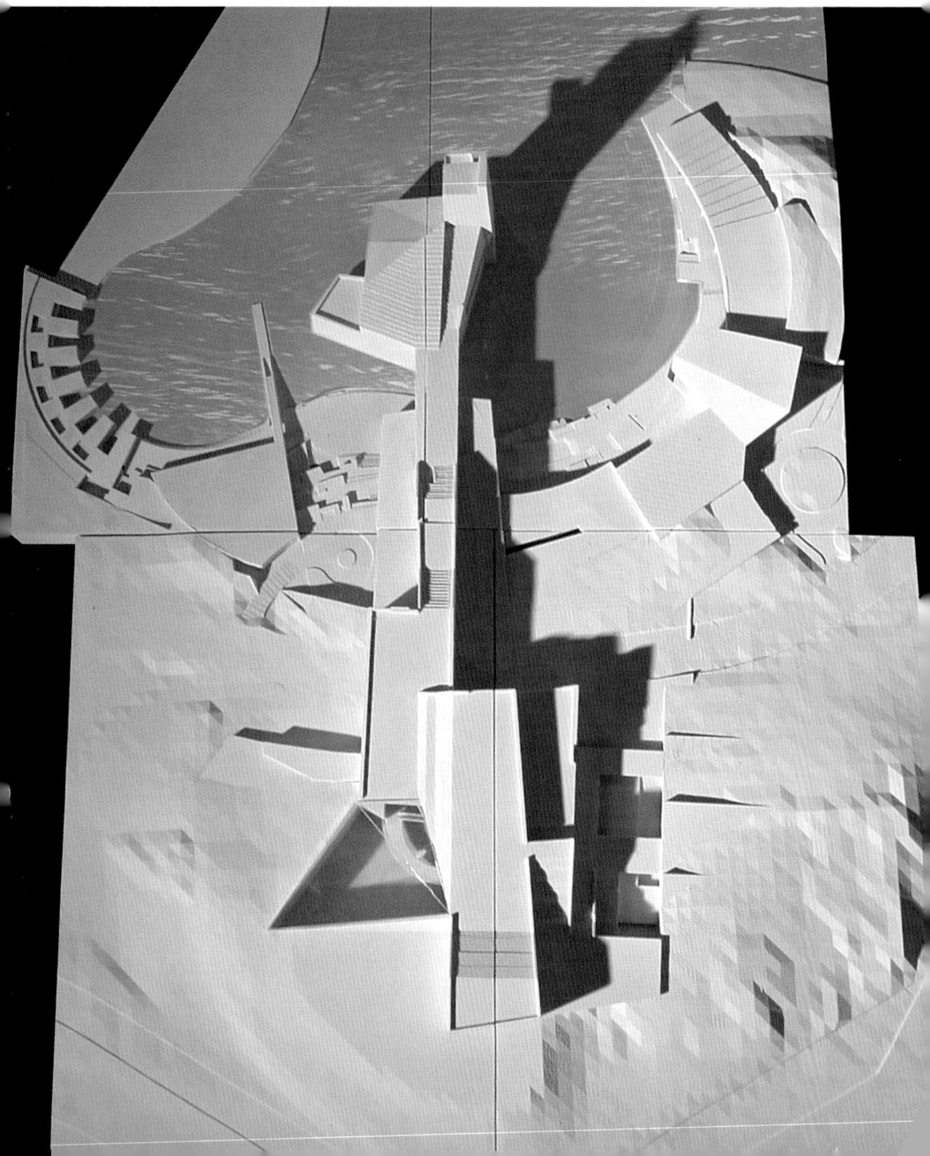

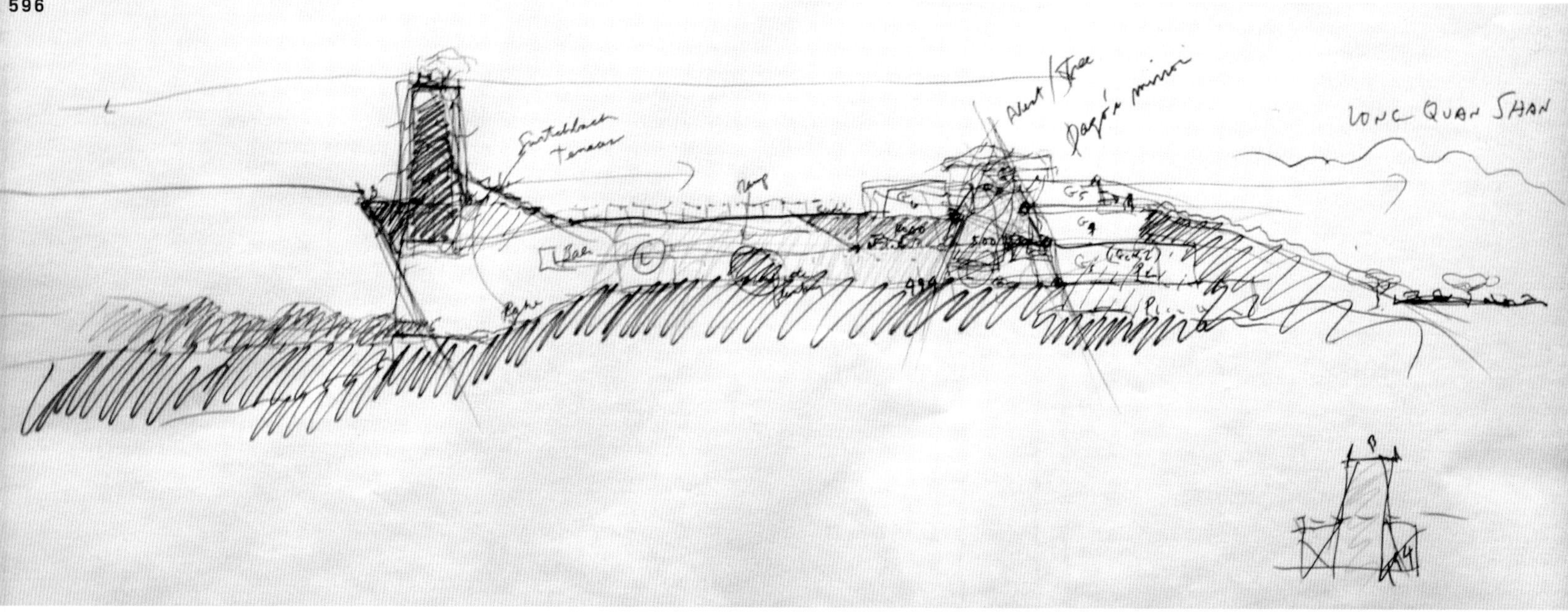

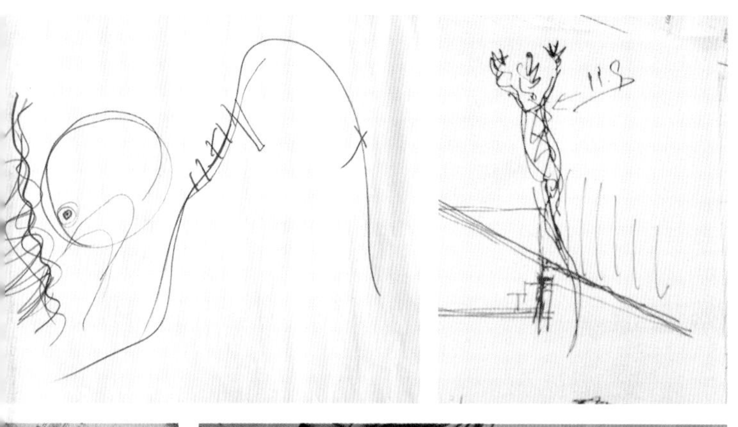

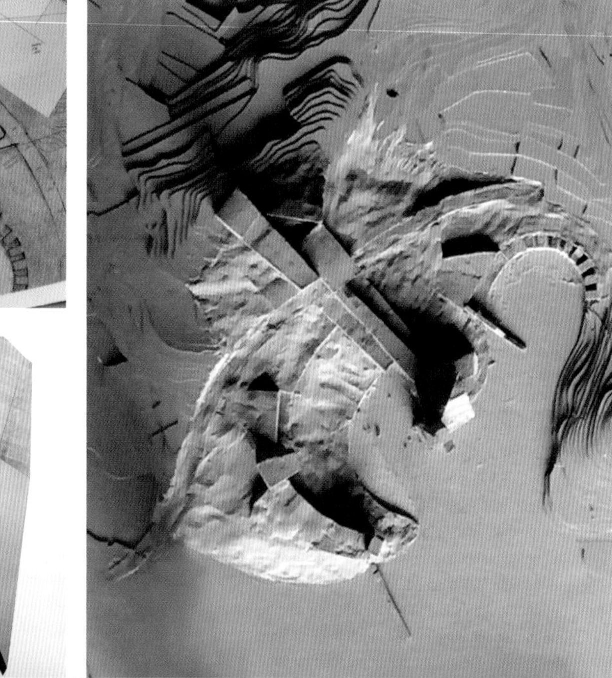

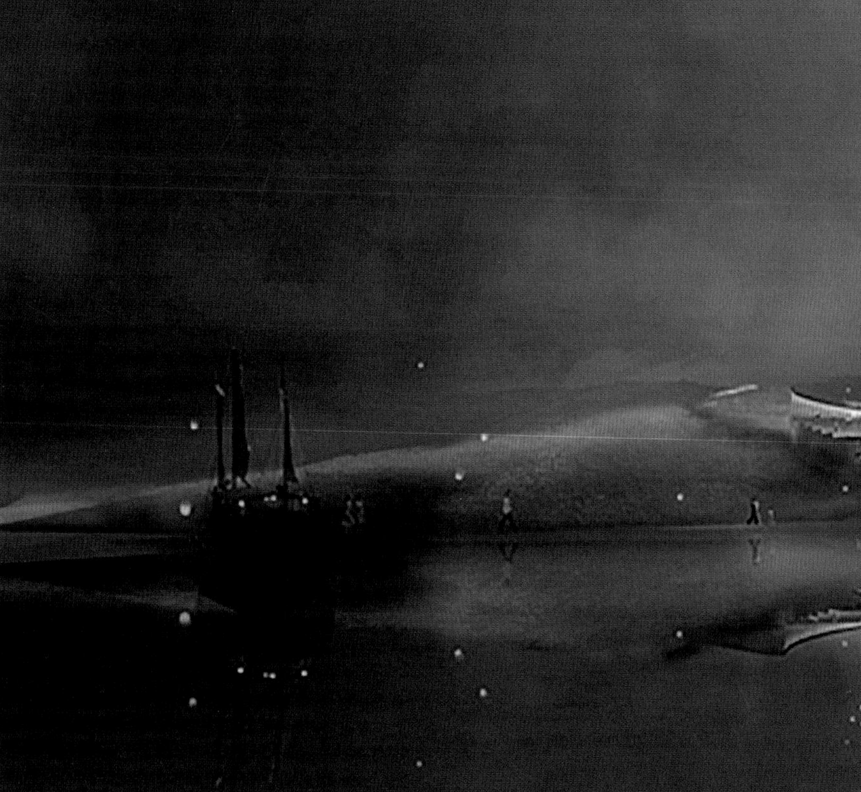

Rugged concrete masses with integral color derived from the red soil of Sichuan engage the Lake. Northern Song Dynasty scroll paintings are evoked—Shan Shui 山水, Mountain/Water.

MEETING AROUND MY CLAY MODEL WITH MR. LUO—ALONG WITH PAUL, KAROLE, XIN YAO, AND THE CLIENT ENTOURAGE.

MEETING WITH JARED, JOSÉ, CHRIS, AND CORY DURING THE DESIGN DEVELOPMENT.

MUSEUM HILL/EXPO CENTER IN THE HILLSIDE.

DETAIL MODEL OF THE CENTRAL CIRCULATION RAMPING CROSSROADS.

"Internationally renowned architect Antoine Predock moves through his life and work like a romantic time traveler, incorporating geology, cultural artifacts, current events, weather patterns, astronomical cycles, personal experiences, and the history of architecture into design."

Wesley Pulkka, "Antoine Predock: Architecture and Time," *Trend*, Fall 2009/Winter 2010

THE WHOLE CREW AT LUNCH IN CHENGDU—KAROLE, XIN YAO, FEI, LUO, AND STEPHEN. CONSTANCE SHOWING CLIENTS HER PUBLIC SCULPTURE IDEA, AND A LATER VISIT WITH HER TO THE BAMBOO ALLÉE AT THE CHENGDU PANDA REFUGE.

LANDSCAPE ARCHITECT COLLEAGUE FEI'S OFFICE WITH HIS PRIZED POCKET BIKE WITH MR. LUO.

Paul astride the upthrust roofscape

With the intense seismic activity of Sichuan, imagining tectonic displacement of the red Earth/Stone.

WITH PAUL, STEPHEN, AND MA LIN ON THE SPRAWLING CONSTRUCTION SITE.

"AT HOME" ON A WORKER'S BIKE.

SICHUAN SKIING CLOSE TO CHENGDU.

MEETING WITH THE RESIDENTS OF THE VILLAGE NEAR THE PROJECT SITE.

MY BUSH-HAMMERED CONCRETE HEROES. VIEWING WITH MA LIN AND OTHERS.

DETAIL INSPECTION WITH MR. LUO. CELEBRATORY EVENT ANNOUNCEMENT.

VIEWING THE ESPLANADE WITH MR. LUO FROM THE CAFÉ TOWER BALCONY...

AND THEN A MOTORCYCLE RIDE.

JADE CASCADE

JUT CONDOMINIUMS
TAIPEI, TAIWAN 2009/16

TAIWAN DELEGATION VISITS OUR STUDIO IN ANTICIPATION OF THE UPCOMING EXHIBITION OF OUR WORK IN TAIPEI.

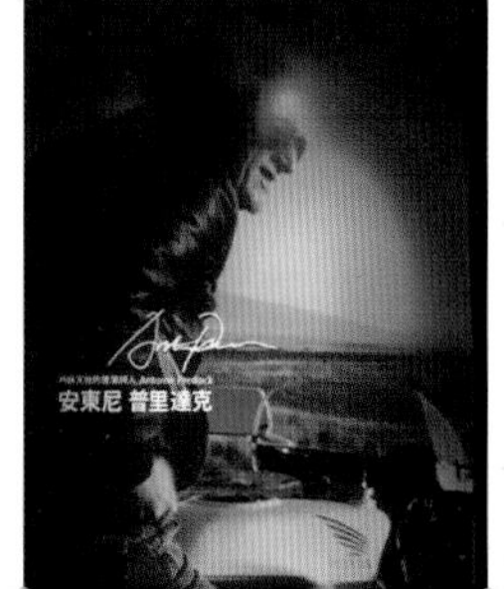

Not far from Taipei, along Taiwan's winding east coast, rocky jungle-encrusted mountains drop precipitously into the Pacific Ocean, talus at their base. Waterfalls surge, creating sheets of mist over the sheer vertical cliffs. Jade Cascade abstracts and extends this rugged landscape into the dense urban Zhongshan district of central Taipei.

MONUMENT FOR THE PEACE CORPS—CELEBRATING THE AMERICAN MISSION TOWARD GLOBAL GOODWILL. ASSEMBLED WITH EMBLEMATIC STONES OF THE COUNTRIES TOUCHED BY PEACE CORPS MISSIONS, ALIGNED TOWARD THE MISSIONS THEY REPRESENT—METAMORPHOSING INTO A CRYSTALLINE QUARTZ APEX.

AMERICAN COMPASS
WASHINGTON, D.C. 2015

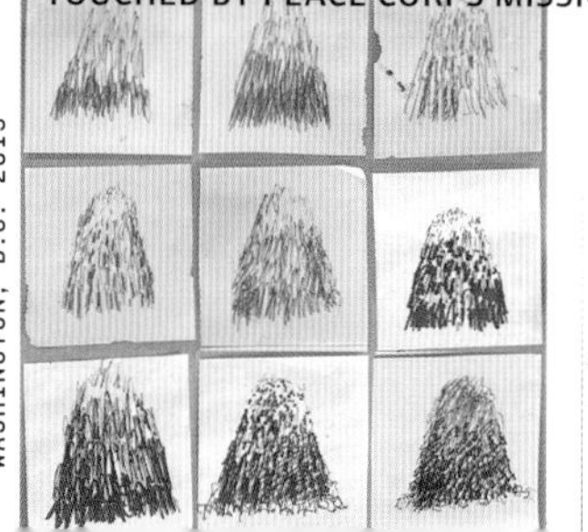

Flame-finished granite of the exterior, quarried in the Taroko Gorge, its rooted sense of gravity gives way to the dancing jade above. The base defines the Jade Cascade entry, encompassing retail along an arcade continuation of the public sidewalk.

PERSONAL PLANET, PLASTIC GRASS COVERED MEDITATION SPACE FOR A CHARITY AUCTION—YOU CLIMB IN, CLOSE THE HATCH AND TAKE IT FROM THERE...

PERSONAL PLANET
ALBUQUERQUE, NM 2016

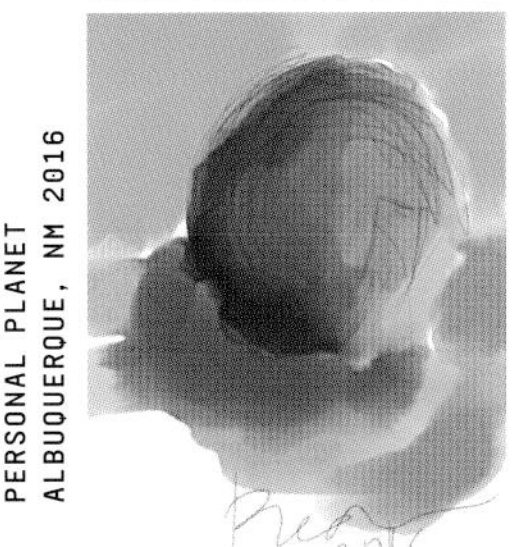

WITH MIRA, CONSTANCE, AND PAUL.

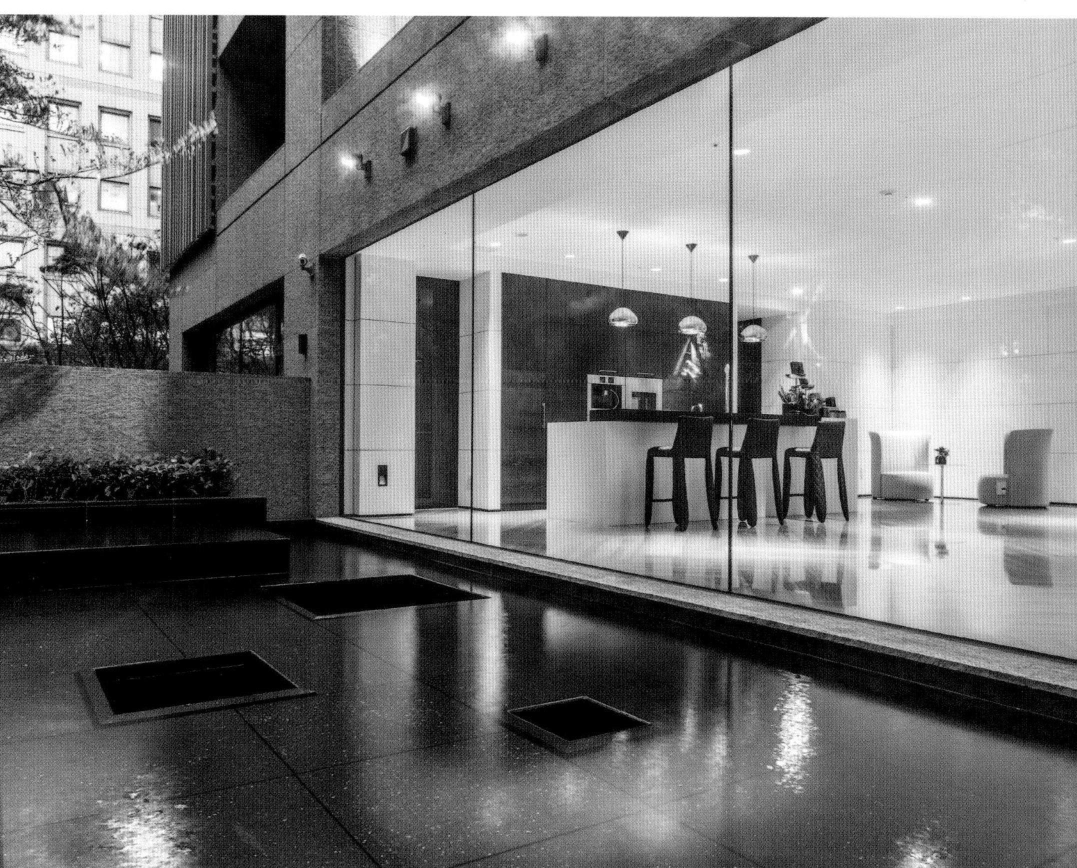

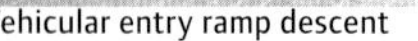
Vehicular entry ramp descent

WITH MY ELECTRIC MOTORCYCLE ENABLER HARLAN FLAGG OF HOLLYWOOD ELECTRICS IN LA. HARLAN, AN ELECTRIC BIKE PIONEER, TOOK A TEAM TO THE PIKES PEAK HILLCLIMB RACE, PLACING HIGH IN THE STANDING AGAINST FOSSIL FUEL BIKES LIKE THE DUCATI MULTISTRADA. I ACQUIRED HIS ZERO FXS #14.

Zero FXS Pikes Peak

2016: AN ELECTRIC MOTORCYCLE EPIPHANY RIDING AT SPEED IN SILENCE WITH BREATHTAKING TORQUE—HOW RIDICULOUSLY COMPLICATED RECIPROCATING ENGINES ARE IN COMPARISON. I DEVELOPED A STRONG ALLERGY TO FOSSIL FUEL.

MY STABLE:

ON A CRITIQUE PANEL WITH HARLAN FLAGG, DUCATI MONSTER DESIGNER MIGUEL GALLUZZI, AND BIKE DESIGNER/ART CENTER CRITIC ALEX EARLE, AFTER LECTURING ON ELECTRIC MOTORCYCLES AT THE ART CENTER COLLEGE OF DESIGN IN PASADENA.

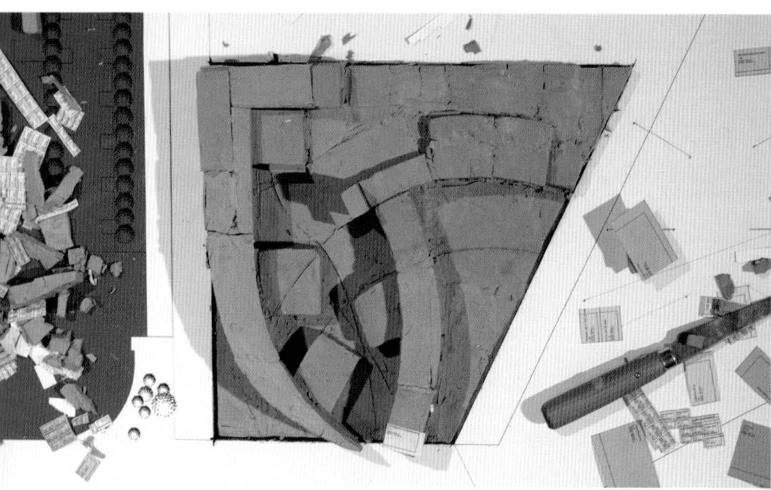

My clay model channeled the wind-shaped arcs of the dunes; Hilal, the crescent sliver of the new moon of Ramadan; and the Saif, the traditional Bedouin scimitar. The geologic ruggedness of sections of Qatar, and the remnants of traditional mud buildings in Doha, accumulate in the research collage imagery and to successive model iterations—all true to the original clay model.

Our building, named The Pressdock Building by the Qatar Foundation—a combination of journalism (press) and Predock—houses Northwestern University's College of Journalism and Communication. Her Highness Sheikha Moza bint Nasser Al-Missned envisioned Education City in Qatar as a campus of campuses bringing together universities from the West to offer degrees in particularized curricula to students predominantly from the region, as well as around the world. The campus is organized around a central "Oxygen Park" greenspace that allows students to circulate between the various campus buildings.

The structure is divided into three sections: a sweeping crescent to the west, an arcing counterpart to the east, and the north bar. The east arc houses student gathering and service functions—lobby, commons, cafeteria, and café, as well as library. The Forum is a reconfigurable space with a media wall, serving as a lounge where students are immersed in real-time global media. It is also a venue for hosting lectures, presentations, and film. The west arc is anchored by a projection theatre and black box theater, accessible via ramp/bridges from the entry lobby, as well as glazed broadcast studios. Administrative and faculty offices are located on the upper floors of the crescent. The tip of the crescent is punctuated by a cantilevered projection clad with media mesh, doubling as a College gateway/media screen—broadcasting a "disc-jockeyed" feed of activities in the College to Oxygen Park and the rest of the campus. Vehicular drop-off and underground parking access on the north has direct access to the conference center, production studios, and dining room. The V-VIP suite is located on the fourth level with a private water terrace with views over the riyadh courtyards and beyond toward Oxygen Park.

DESERT RESEARCH SKETCHES—FROM EGYPT TO BAHRAIN TO JORDAN:
AND THE ARCING DUNES OF THE ARABIAN DESERT

PRESSDOCK BUILDING COLLEGE OF MEDIA AND COMMUNICATION IN QATAR

A COLLABORATION BETWEEN
QATAR FOUNDATION AND
NORTHWESTERN UNIVERSITY

EDUCATION CITY
DOHA, QATAR 2009/19

SECONDARY ARCING BRIDGE LINKS CONNECT PROJECTION THEATER TO RECEPTION/COMMONS AND LARGE EVENT STUDIO WITH ITS ANCILLARY PRODUCTION/EDITING SPACES

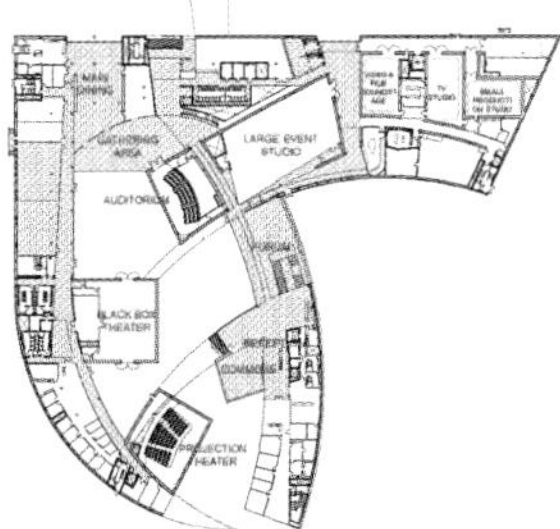

The building expresses a diagram of journalistic ideals while presenting an abstracted expression of the rugged Qatari landscape in silhouette. The fortress-like stone walls shield inner courtyards from the assault of the desert.

When a prototype wall was constructed of the regionally sourced limestone, I thought it was far too regular—lacking the vision of a rugged building perimeter embracing and protecting a more delicate inner series of courtyards. Speaking to the contractor, we decided to "loosen up" the stone mason's ethic of precisely laid stone. "Make the wall seem like a rough sketch of perfection."

FORTRESS OF KNOWLEDGE SHELTERING AN INNER OASIS

CONFERRING WITH THE STONE CONTRACTOR

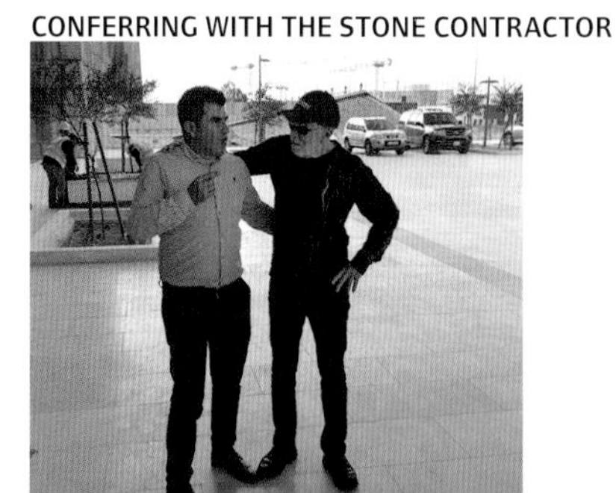

The Crescent is punctuated by the arcing abstracted Saif tip—a cantilevered tensegrity structure that announces the entry gateway. Covered with media mesh, it is a movie screen primarily broadcasting real-time images of Northwestern's media activities to Oxygen Park and the rest of the campus.

FOR THE OPENING CEREMONY EVENT FOR THE COLLEGE—A TIME-LAPSE VIDEO OF THE CONSTRUCTION OF THE BUILDING ON THE MEDIA MESH PROW.

The building gestures calligraphically—a narrative interweaving of courtyards and open atria and a refined materiality in abrupt contrast to the rugged power of the outer shell. The arcing sweeps shape informal gathering spaces and the progression through the interior of the College carries the inner courtyard flow—encouraging visual transparency and creating forums for debate, collaboration, and mentorship.

جامعة نورثويسترن في قطر
Northwestern University in Qatar

TOURING THE COMPLETED BUILDING WITH STUDENTS AND FACULTY.

CELEBRATING DON SCHLEGEL'S 90TH BIRTHDAY AT THE SCHOOL OF ARCHITECTURE GALLERY

WITH ED FAYYAD, OUR LEBANESE MAINLINE CONNECTION TO THE CONSTRUCTION SITE

THE SEQUENCE OF COURTYARDS EVOKE A VERDANT OASIS RESPITE FROM THE ARABIAN DESERT.

FIELD TRIP WITH QATARI FRIENDS TO LOSAIL, THE GLOBALLY RECOGNIZED FORMULA 1 AND MOTOGP RACETRACK...

DREAMING OF RIDING MY TRACK-DERIVED DUCATI DESMOSEDICI MOTOGP BIKE ON THAT TRACK...

MANY LONG FLIGHTS ON BOEING 777ERs BACK AND FORTH FROM ALBUQUERQUE VIA LAX TO DUBAI OR DOHA.

LEED GOLD, OVERSHADOWED BY POETIC IMPULSE. DON'T FETISHIZE SUSTAINABILITY—ARCHITECTURE IS MUCH MORE THAN THAT.

The Forum is a reconfigurable space with a media wall that acts as a lounge where students are immersed with real-time global media and also a "disc-jockeyed" feed of activities in the complex. It is also a venue hosting lectures, presentations, and films.

THEY MADE THE BUILDING HAPPEN

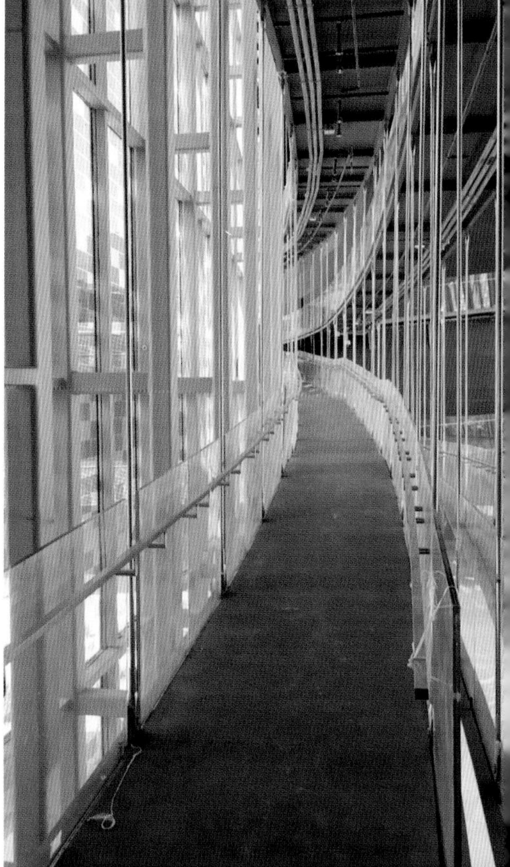

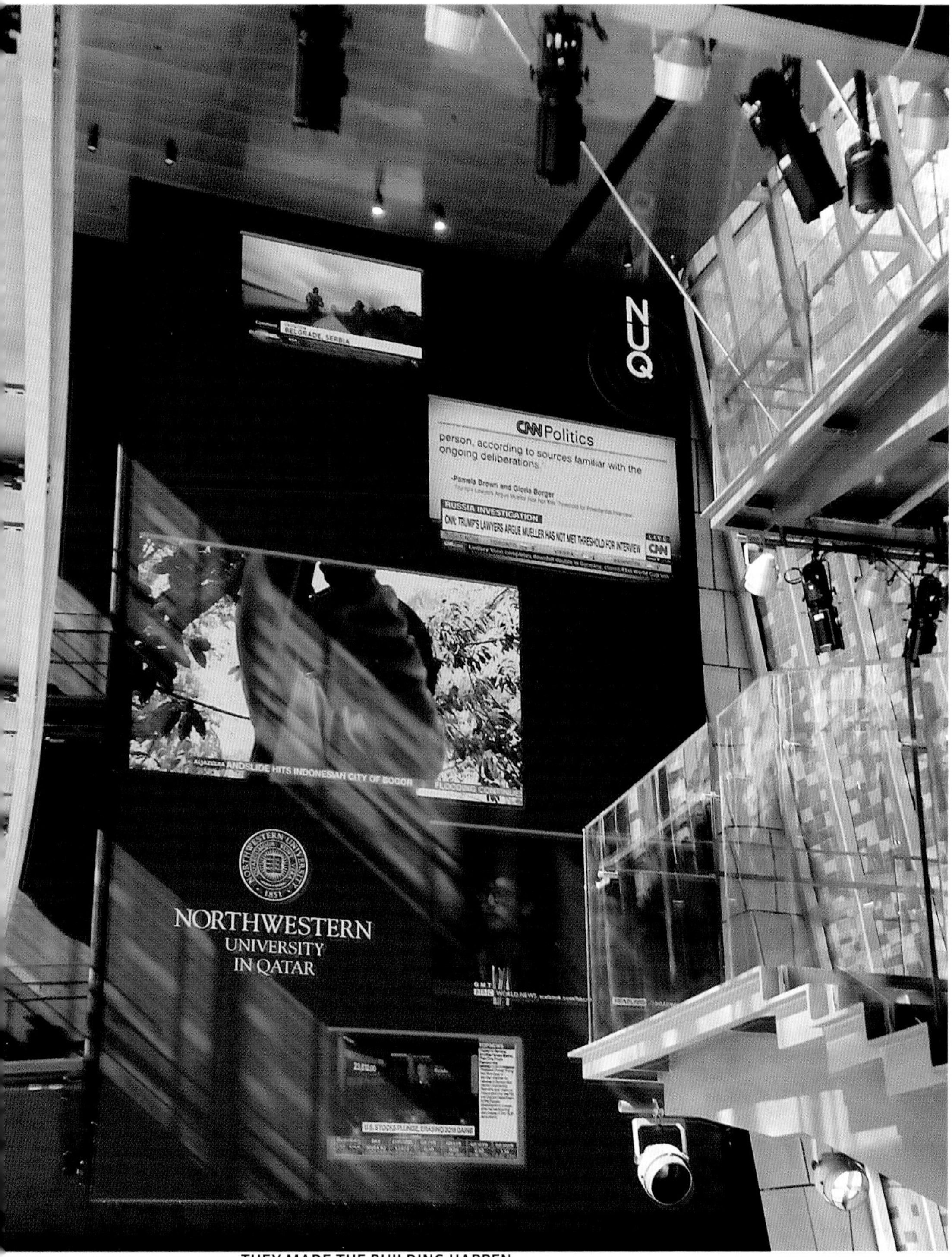

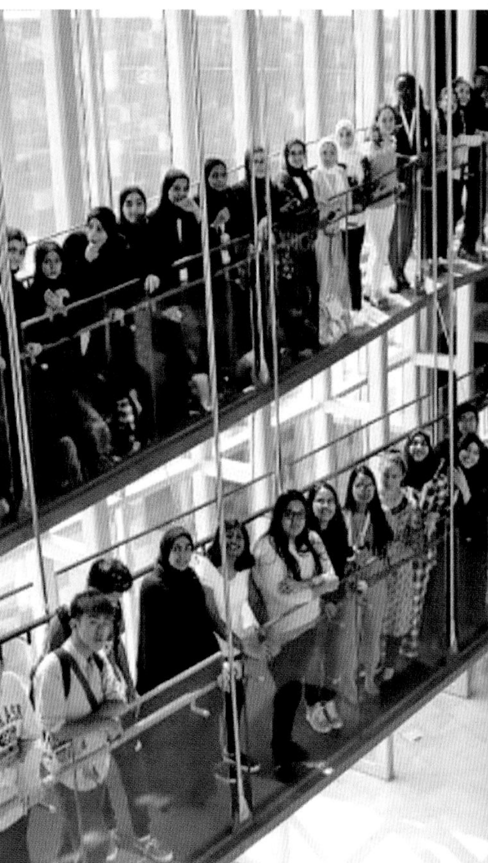

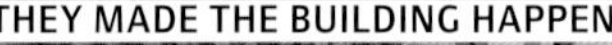

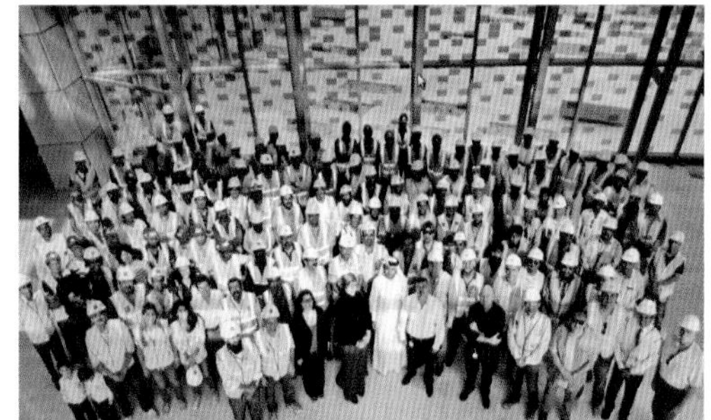

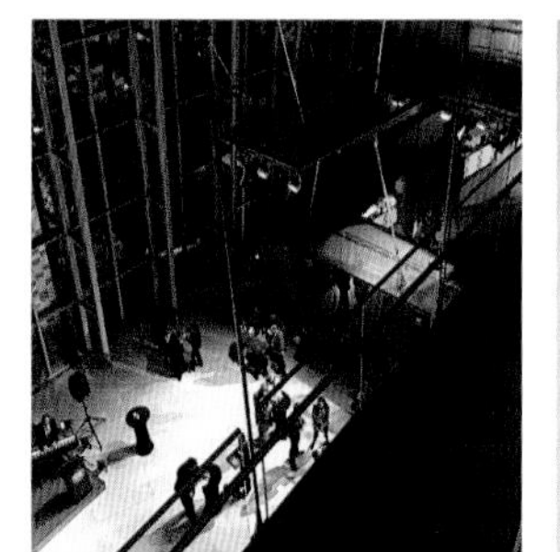

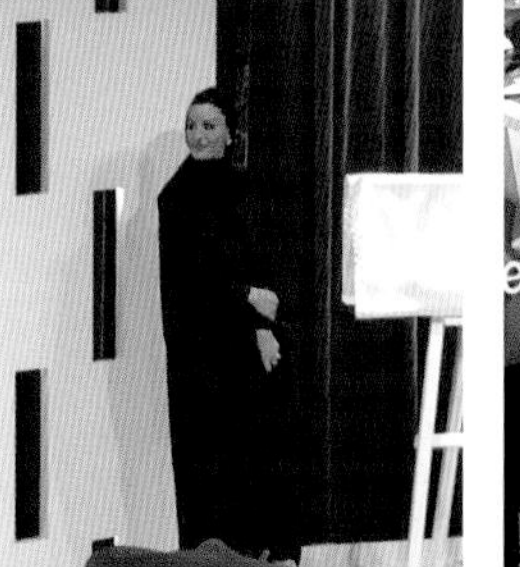

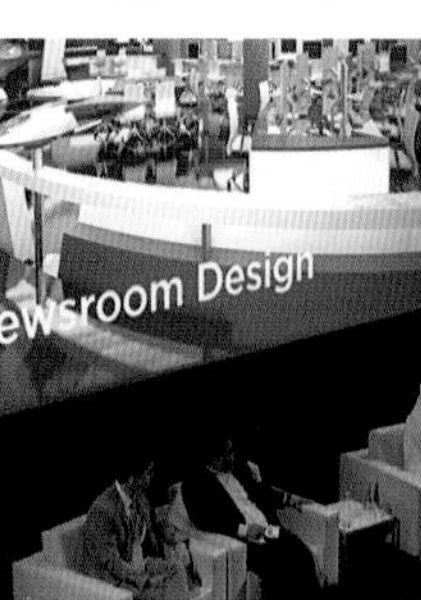

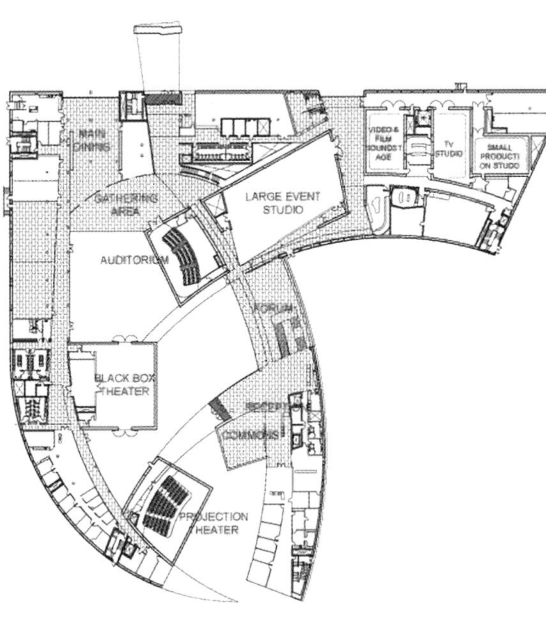

THE DEDICATION CEREMONY/RECEPTION... ALONG WITH NORTHWESTERN'S PRESIDENT MORTON O. SCHAPIRO.

SHEIKHA MOZA BINT NASSER AL-MISSNED'S VISION LEAD TO THE ESTABLISHMENT OF EDUCATION CITY IN DOHA, WITH ITS BRILLIANT PREMISE OF A MULTI-NATIONAL UNIVERSITY PRESENCE YIELDING PEDAGOGIC CROSS-POLLINATION WITH A RICHLY DIVERSE STUDENT BODY.

With Northwestern's famed journalism tradition, of course the physicality of books has to happen, but they are the tip of the iceberg of media and communication studies—I love the smell of books in the morning...

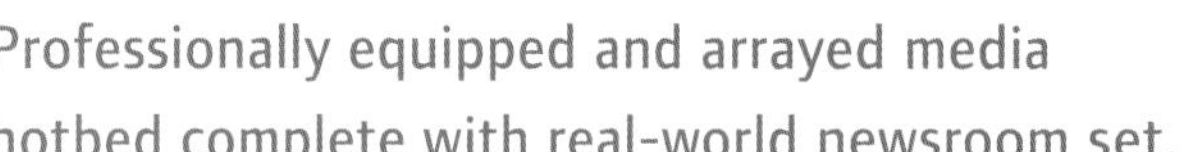

Professionally equipped and arrayed media hotbed complete with real-world newsroom set.

THE LIBRARY STAIR

DEDICATION CEREMONY DINNER WITH CONSTANCE, PAUL, AND OUR INTERIOR DESIGN PROJECT MANAGER MONA HAMAD.

MEDIA MAJLIS - SUB-PROJECT COLLEGE MUSEUM 2019

A "NEWSEUM" WITHIN THE COLLEGE OPENED

The Canyon Stair, central to the structure, links common spaces, media studios, and administrative center.

WITH PREDOMINANTLY DIGITAL MEDIA DISPLAYS RELATING TO ITS COMMUNICATION PEDAGOGY. A STAINLESS STEEL ARMATURE SWEEPS THROUGH THIS SPACE—

MONITOR INSTALLATIONS, DESIGNED TO BE CHANGED FREQUENTLY OVER TIME, ARE ACCOMPANIED BY MORE TRADITIONAL EXHIBITION MODES.

The Canyon Stair circuitously climbs upward and dives down, past the translucent marble walls of the core and the corten steel of the auditorium and large-event studio—providing all levels of the College with socially interactive waystations for impromptu exchange.

"Most of us have lost our connection to the earth. We've forgotten how to improvise, because we work everything, always, all out on paper. We've lived in our heads so long, we need to reintegrate the body and the mind. Antoine is the one architect right now offering us that inspiration." Michael Rotondi

Arcing circulation bridges connect reception/commons and library to the film and black box theaters across the courtyard.

ON THE WAY HOME FROM QATAR WITH CONSTANCE, A STOP IN ROME FOR A QUICK HIT—THE PANTHEON MOTHERSHIP, BADASS BORROMINI, TREVI MORPHING FROM STONE TO LANDSCAP

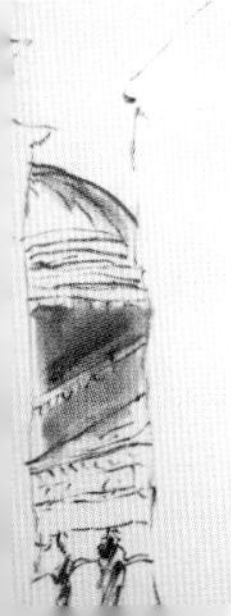

ON THE BORDER— BOX BOOK AND EXHIBITION

HERMOSILLO, MEXICO 2017

Box book of my travel drawings published to accompany this exhibition, designed by curator Arq. Eduardo Delgado Orusco of Madrid, with his accompanying essay and project/travel location map.

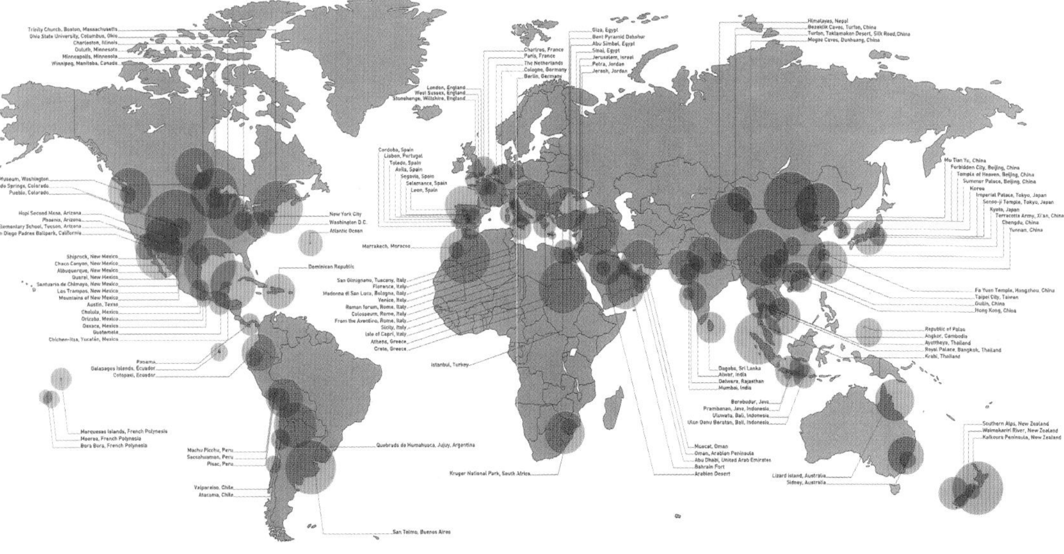

Instituto Tecnológico y de Estudios Superiores de Monterrey at the Sonora Norte Campus invited me to the unveiling of the box book and accompanying exhibition in Hermosillo, Sonora—a wonderful event, lecture, and book signing, with the bonus of a motorcycle ride into the Sonoran Desert with my new friends Fancisco Javier Ibarra and Felizardo Lopez.

DEPARTING ON OUR SONORAN DESERT RIDE WITH A SEND-OFF BY MY HOST DIRECTORA ARQ. ALEJANDRA MARIA MORENO PEÑA AND MY NEW MOTO BUDDIES FRANCISCO AND FELI.

RECEIVING CERTIFICATE FROM ARQ. DIANA URIAS.

MY HOST AND NEW FRIEND, ALEJANDRA MARIA MORENO.

SCHMOOZ-

With Francisco and Feli at the Plaza of the ancient capital of Sonora

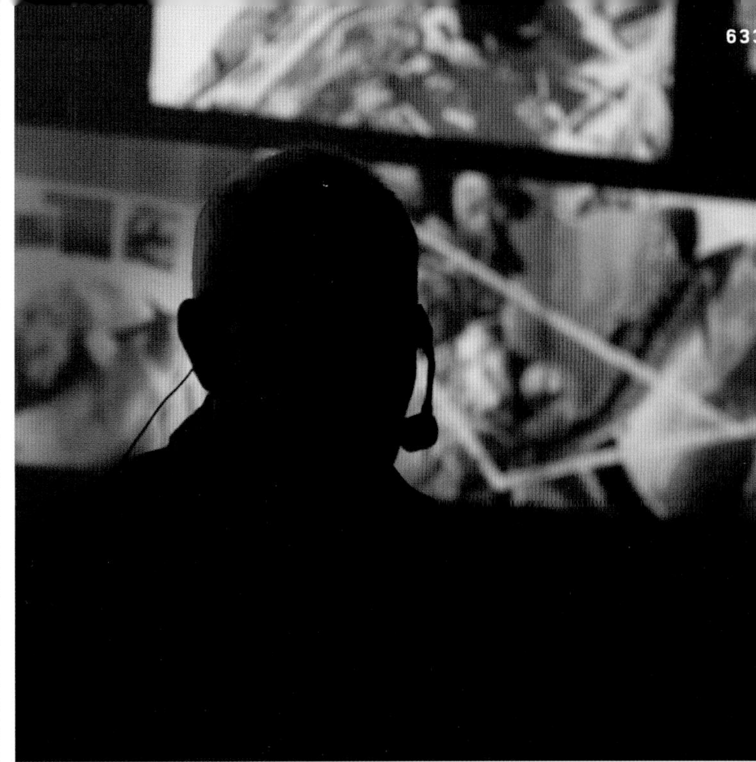
Keynote Lecture

Palacio del Gobierno exhibition venue

O-RAMA

2015 STRATA EXHIBITION—RICHARD LEVY GALLERY WITH SKETCHES, TACOMA ART MUSEUM, ROBINSON/BURNEY HOUSE CLIENTS

AIA LECTURE IN LAFAYETTE, LA—RECONNECTING WITH MY FORMER STUDIO COLLEAGUE MISCHA FARRELL

"Antoine Predock's habit of drawing is incessant and prolific, a continuous outpouring that quickly exceeds the capacity of any one book to contain the resulting torrent. Whether sketching sites seen around the world or designing one of his buildings, Predock has learned through years of experience to condense the multiple sensations and ideas at hand into memorably succinct collations of line and color. His drawings seem inevitable, as if shaping forms on a piece of paper were the easiest thing to do in the world. Hiding the craft involved in their making behind apparently effortless gestures, these drawings trace the telling features of each place visited or imagined and express Predock's understanding of architecture as a form of landscape grounded in the earth."

Christopher Mead, *Drawing into Architecture*, 2017

DRAWING INTO ARCHITECTURE EXHIBITION

ALBUQUERQUE MUSEUM
ALBUQUERQUE, NEW MEXICO 2017

CURATED AND DESIGNED BY
CHRISTOPHER MEAD AND MIRA WOODSON

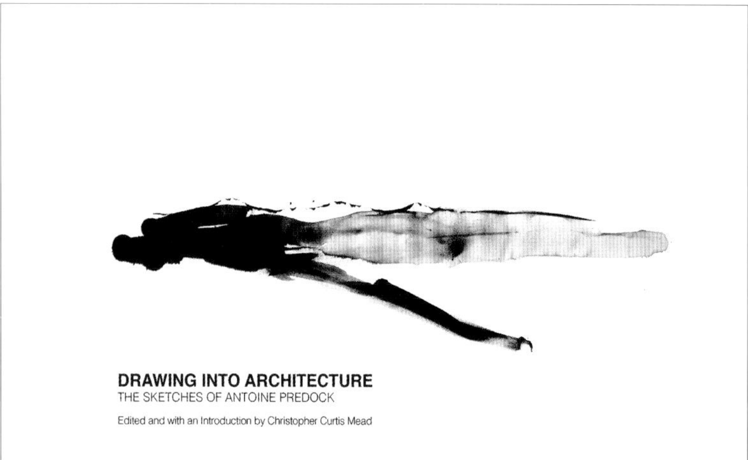

The vintage Lambretta from my Genoa to Paris to Istanbul to Spain ride—many sketches ensued

"His wide-ranging fascination with modern technology and its possibilities—epitomized by his love for precisely engineered motorcycles—extends to every facet of digital rendering, modeling, and fabrication, all of which have been integrated into his architectural practice since the 1990s. Predock continues to draw by hand, not in Luddite opposition to new media and technologies of representation, but for the reason given by Frascari: drawings make 'architectural thinking possible' because 'drawings are instruments of understanding and intuition' that allow architects to form their ideas. If Predock recognizes the usefulness of digital alongside manual drawing, it is because the two techniques are not pitted against each other in a false dialectic of technological progress. Rather, the argument being made is that computer-aided drawing is likely to become better when informed by the necessarily reflective and therefore self-aware and self-critical process of thinking that comes with drawing by hand. When constructing an image by hand, the architect assumes conscious responsibility for directing the pen, pencil, or brush. This awareness can sometimes be neglected when taking advantage of digital technologies whose prepackaged programs allow lines to be produced automatically with keystrokes. The irony here is that the very term used to define these technologies—digital—is rooted etymologically in the fingers of our hands, with our discrete human digits coming to mean discrete (digital) units of information."

Christopher Mead, *Drawing into Architecture*, 2017

FILMING AMC'S *RIDE WITH NORMAN REEDUS* (DARYL OF *THE WALKING DEAD*)— S2 EP. 4, NOV. 20, 2017. ON THE RIDE WITH AIMEE NASH AND NORMAN REEDUS, INCLUDING A BRUSH WITH HIGHWAY PATROL.

With UNM Architecture students—
"You are immersed in the digital, but don't forget the immense pleasure and focus of drawing by hand ... and travel as much as you can, a Lambretta scooter like this one took me from Paris to Istanbul, 'drawing all the way.'"

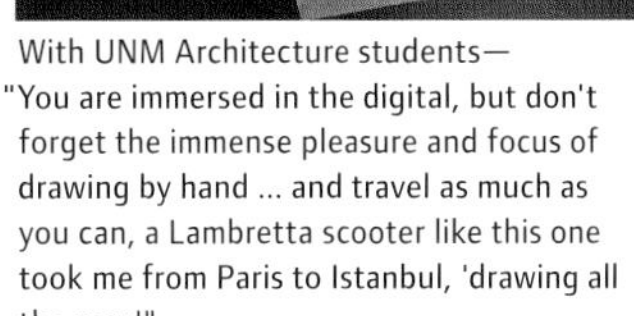

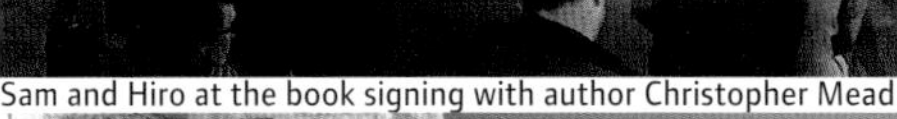

Sam and Hiro at the book signing with author Christopher Mead

Birthday party for me held by author Christopher Mead and partner/photographer Michele Penhall after the Albuquerque Museum exhibition.

2017—I RODE MY ZERO FXS TO LECTURE AT THE ART CENTER COLLEGE OF DESIGN, PASADENA FOR A MOTORCYCLE DESIGN CLASS TAUGHT BY MY FRIEND ALEX EARLE. RETURNING TO MY SANTA MONICA STUDIO, I WAS T-BONED BY A CAR. 17 FRACTURES: R RIB 3-6, R CLAVICLE, T4 SPINOUS PROCESS, T9 VERTEBRAL BODY, L L5 FACET (LOWER SPINE), L SACRAL ALA, L PUBIC TUBERCLE (PELVIS), L PUBIC RAMI (PELVIS), AND RIGHT LOWER LOBE PULMONARY CONTUSION. FANTASTIC UCLA TRAUMA AND ICU TEAM, WITH A SUPRISE VISIT FROM PETE CELONA. RIDING AGAIN A FEW WEEKS LATER. $15K LIABILITY SETTLEMENT. WORTH IT? NOPE! HE'S BACK!

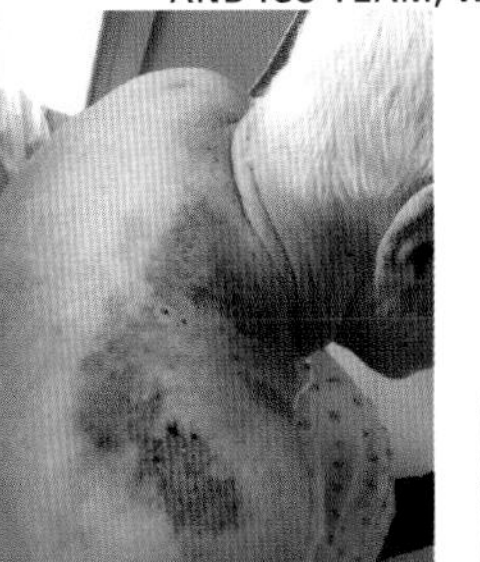

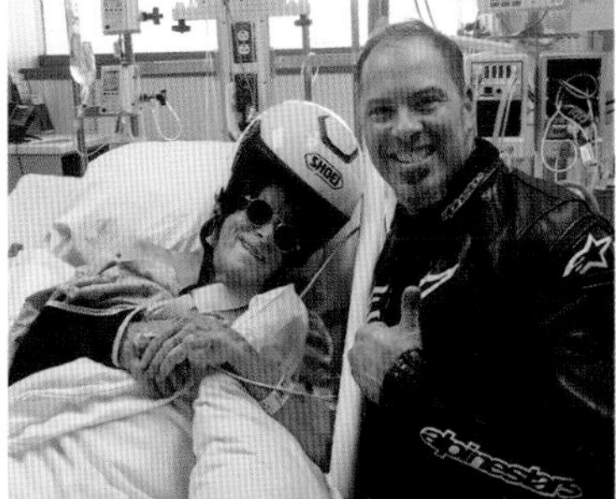

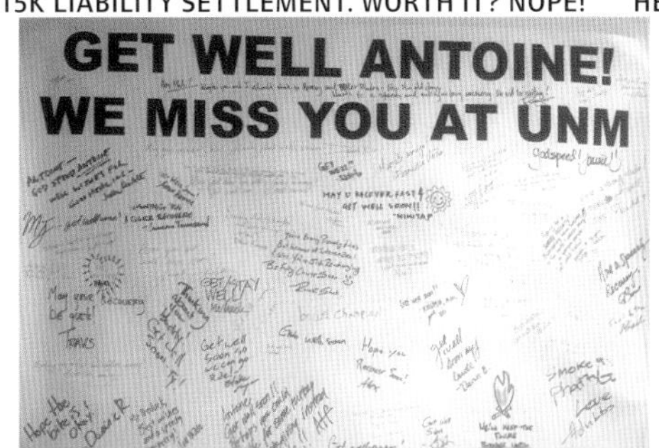

WESTSIDE STUDIO

ALBUQUERQUE, NEW MEXICO 2017/FUTURE

The 2017 gift to the University of New Mexico of the Antoine Predock Studio property on 12th Street displaced on-going Studio activities to a nearby downtown location. The satellite Westside Studio was established at the same time in a traditional New Mexico adobe property. A sampling of the project models that were gifted to UNM as part of the Antoine Predock Archive are displayed there as a gallery, combined with working, special meeting, and administrative spaces—and the motorcycle collection.

The Westside Studio Gallery, displays project models, collages, original drawings, travel sketches, several hundred books, and periodicals featuring our work. It also includes a wall of gift sketches from colleagues including Tadao Ando, Thom Mayne, Robert Venturi, Peter Eisenman, Steven Holl, Jean Nouvel, and Frank Gehry.

OUR WORK IN EVERY BOOK

RAVEN BAKER HOUSE

VAISON-LA-ROMAINE, PROVENCE, FRANCE 2017/21

A walled compound for old friend Didier Raven and his wife Jude Baker wraps a productive olive grove and establishes an internal vantage point below a vine-covered trellis for viewing the majesty of northern Provence.

The joy and sensuality of yellow trace with Jude and Didier.

"The very beginning of this adventure was finding a wildly overgrown small plot of land in the middle of the town of Vaison-la-Romaine in Provence with amazing, far-reaching views of a medieval cathedral, a castle, and the mighty Mont Ventoux."

Judith Baker, 2022

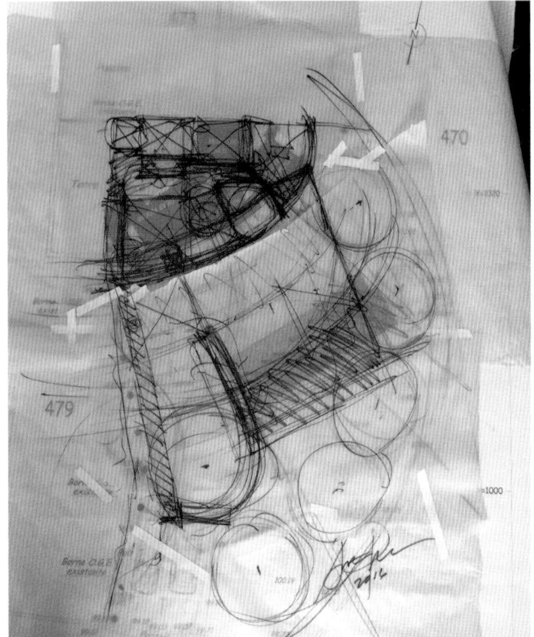

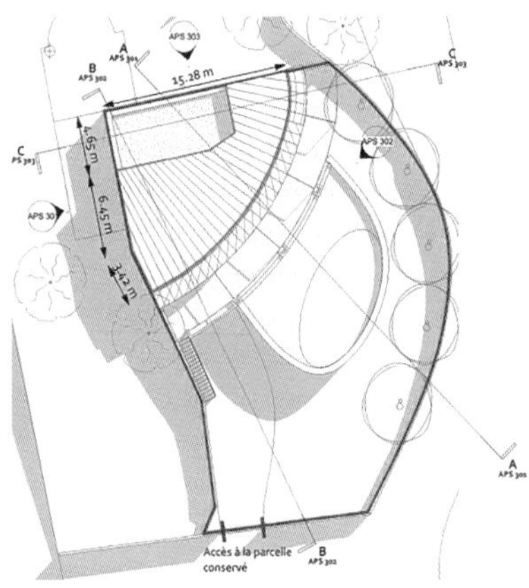

TRAVEL TO INDIA IN 2017—NEW DELHI, JAIPUR, UDAIPUR, AND ALWAR

"Sitting in the Knoll Bastiano couch and chairs in the living room, bought 55 years ago for the house at La Luz, and looking out through the large glass and aluminum windows, crowned by the slatted wood ceiling, similar to the house at La Luz, but at the same time so different, I sometimes close my eyes and imagine being back in New Mexico, picturing the views down the mesa to the Rio Grande, and the spectacular panorama of the Sandia mountains and Albuquerque. What a privilege it has been for me to have lived in two of Antoine's houses."

Didier Raven, 2022

DEVI GARH PALACE—NOW HERITAGE HOTEL, WHERE I STAYED

First olive harvest

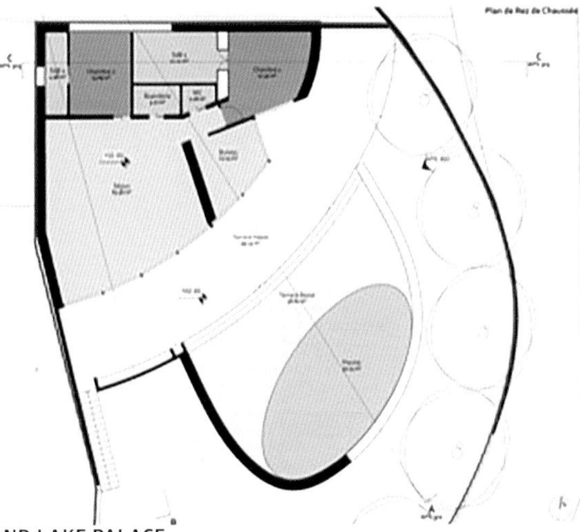

UDAIPUR AND LAKE PALACE

ALWAR DISTRICT IN RAJASTHAN

"Dead center in front of our house—less than 200 meters away—looms the spectacular 12th-century Romanesque cathedral and cloister, Notre-Dame-de-Nazareth, the largest Roman ruins outside of Italy. To the left of the bell tower majestically rises Mont Ventoux, known locally as Le Géant de Provence. To the right of the cathedral and up a hill is the magnificent medieval part of town surmounted by a 12th-century château constructed by Raymond V, Comte de Toulouse."

Didier Raven, 2022

MUMBAI–INDIA GATE, THE HAJI ALI DARGAH, AND THE OVERWHELMING CENTRAL LAUNDRY

ELEPHANTA CAVES

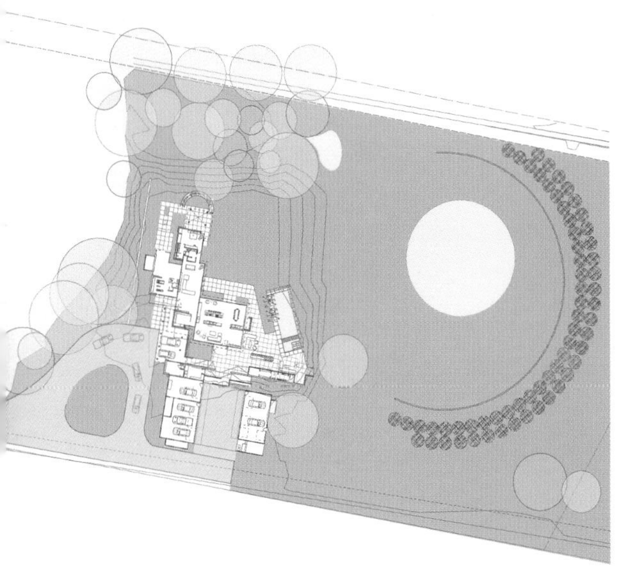

Escarpment, a sweeping angled arc focuses meadow and a contemplative pond... with a passageway to a secret garden

ESCARPMENT VINEYARD

NEW MEXICO 2019/24

The Robb House, designed in the '50s by my mentor Don Schlegel, required massive restoration, expansion, and adaptation for the new owners, including solar upgrades—while totally respecting Don's original intentions.

Bob Gouy, Dawn Nieto-Gouy, and 1.8 sec. 0-60 Tesla in the Garage Plaza

My last photo with Don Schlegel, FAIA, shortly before his passing on February 10, 2019, at the age of 92. He ignited my flame in architecture and it never would have happened without him. Apart from my respect and devotion to Don, he was a widely recognized force in architectural education, while keeping his architectural practice flourishing through decades. Impossible to fully express my debt to him. He gave his blessing to our renovation.

Photo-op mask drop with Superclient Dawn on the construction site... and the mystery passageway through Escarpment from her secret garden

2018 LECTURES IN TAIWAN, SHENZHEN, AND GUANGZHOU—SELFIES, AND SIGNING T-SHIRTS, SHOES, IPHONES, SKETCH BOOKS, ETC...

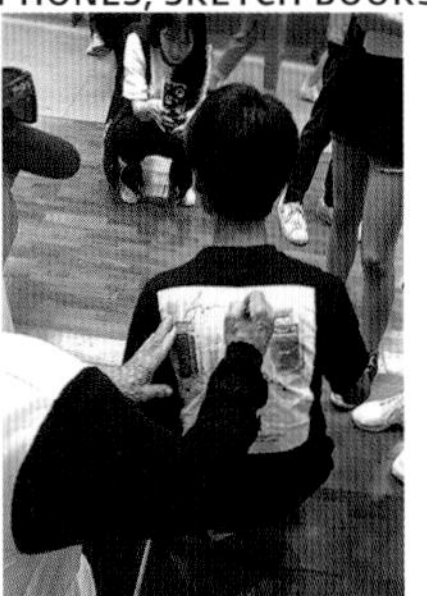

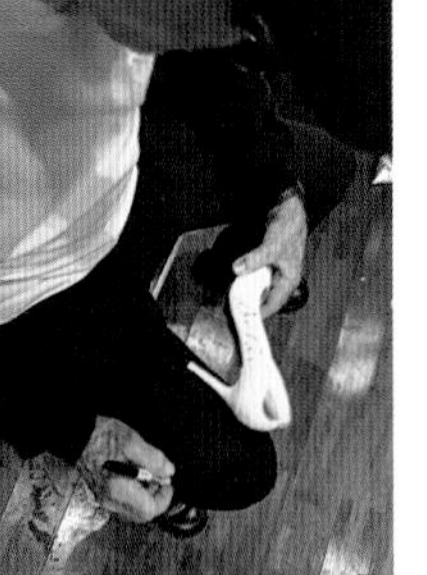

The composite of old and new viewed across the vineyard

DRAWING WORKSHOP WITH STUDENTS OF HUALI COLLEGE

DRAWING A TREE ALONGSIDE
MY HOST PROFESSOR CLAYTON AN

ZOMBIE TOWER—FOUND OBJECT WORKSHOP
WITH ARCHITECTURE STUDENTS

DINODACTYL

NEW MEXICO 2020/23

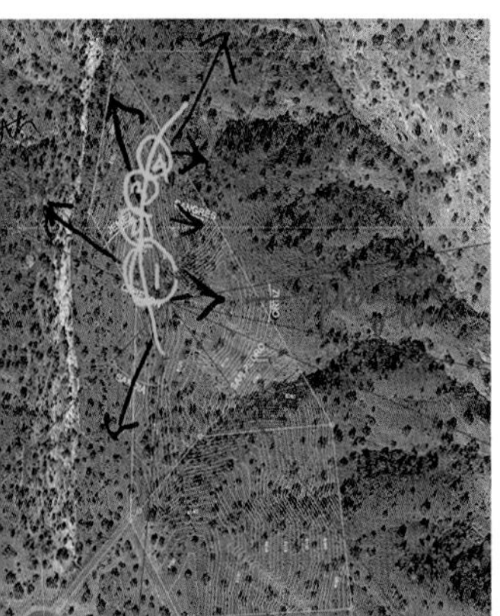

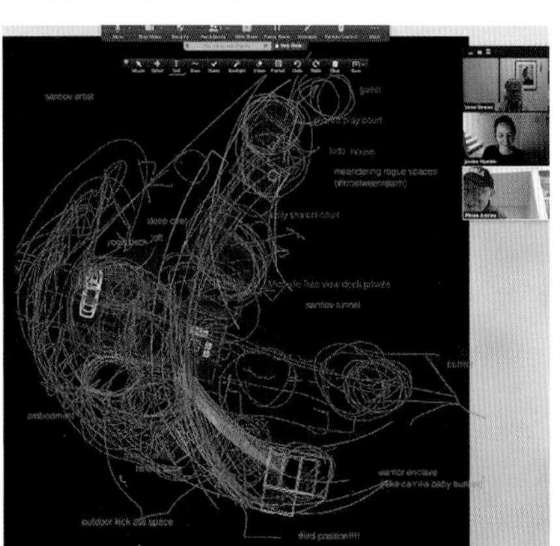

Zoom takes over in the Covid Years

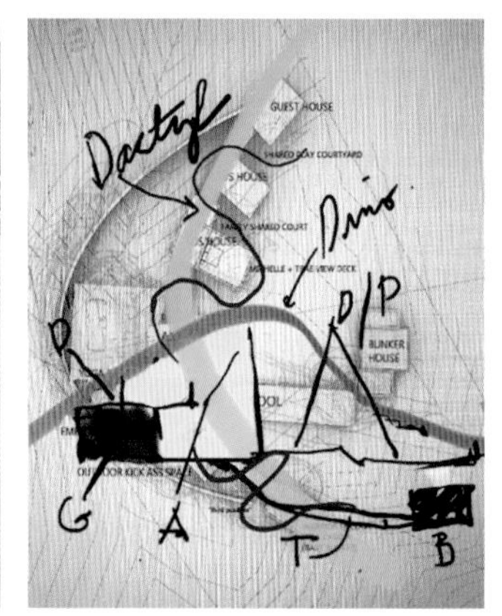

Dinodactyl—a fusion of mythic beasts derived from landforms of the site and view intentions. A village of separate "houses" for a collective of extended family and friends arrayed with sweeping views from each space toward the range that forms the eastern front, where the plains meet the mountains. The weathering steel sheathed centerpiece, "Dino," central to the arcing "Dactyl" array of the individually shaped "houses," aims dead center toward the view. The flanking elements and their roof colors respond to the site color palette and surroundings.

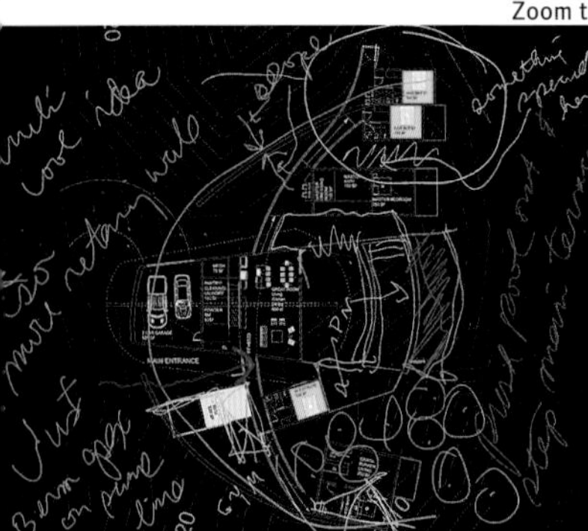

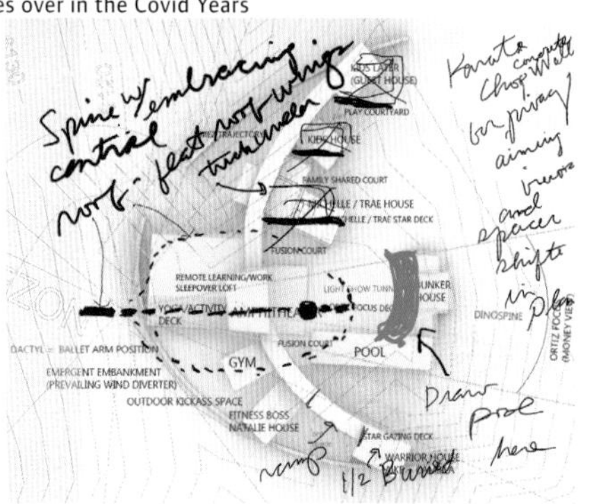

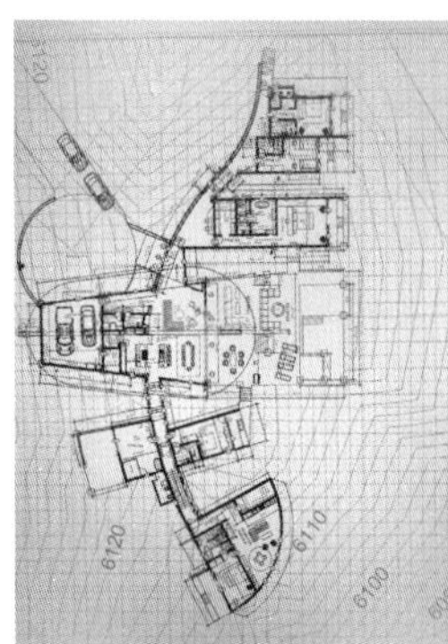

Enigma for archaeologists to come.

NEW MEXICO ERUPTIONS—SPINE OF A BEAST=DINO

JUSTINE PHOTOGRAPHING THE CINEMASCOPE VIEW THAT IS

"It's been so easy to have a universalist vocabulary, but Antoine is a genius at connecting with the place he is working in, and with great artistry. It is that quality, I think, that makes him world-class."

Robert Venturi

The spine of Dino and its analogous landform—Paul Kenderdine masters concrete for us once again.

SHARED BY ALL THE SPACES. DINODACTYL SUMS UP FORMS DERIVED FROM SITE—EMBRACING THE VIEW FROM THE COMPOUND OF COMPONENTS=DACTYL ANALOGOUS TO DANCERS ARCHING FORWARD WITH ARMS IN THE FIRST BALLET POSITION.

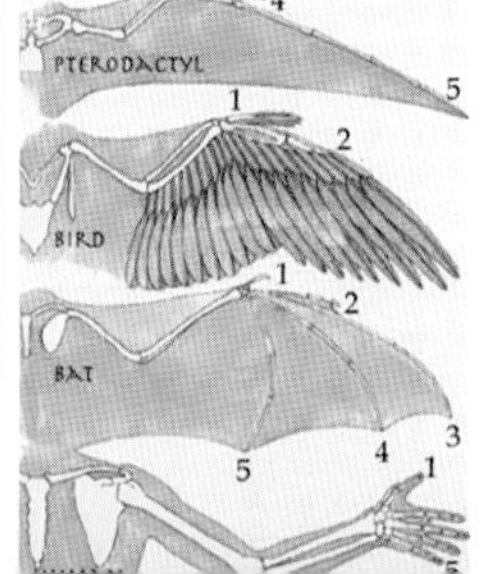

ELLIPSE

NEW MEXICO 2022/24

Ellipse occupies a site in an enclave of cottonwoods toward the western edge of the floodplain. Approached through an orchard, it is an unexpected shimmering object—modulated by the muted, abstract "reflection" of the foreground landscape and sky. A few miles to the east, is a 10,000-foot mountain range. Sweeping elliptical stairways to the left and right of the entry ascend to the main level. The garage, the prime bedroom with its courtyard, and ancillary spaces are tucked below—a silvery apparition emerging in this Bosque landscape.

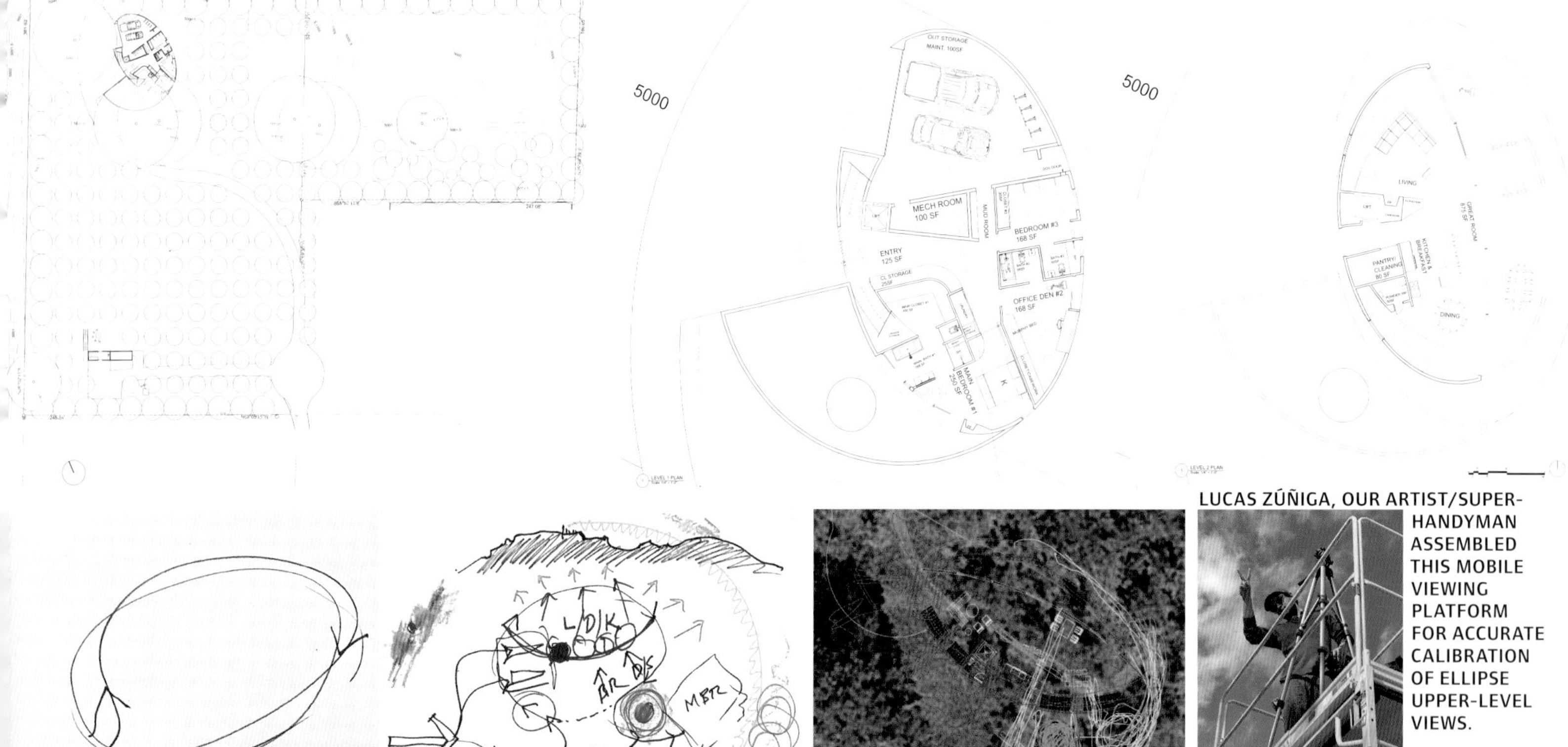

LUCAS ZÚÑIGA, OUR ARTIST/SUPER-HANDYMAN ASSEMBLED THIS MOBILE VIEWING PLATFORM FOR ACCURATE CALIBRATION OF ELLIPSE UPPER-LEVEL VIEWS.

COSTA RICA TOOK US THROUGH THE COVID YEARS, ALONG WITH OUR 4 LB. SPIRITUAL GUIDE WOOKIE.. AND NOW A NEW BABY SISTER... FRØYA!

"It is rare to come across places where architecture, particularly in the case of contemporary buildings, would complement a beautiful natural setting in decidedly positive ways. Most locations are appreciated either because of the landscape, or the architecture, not both. Buildings designed by world-class masters tend to be built in stark contrast to the landscape they are surrounded by, and if we were asked to take a perfect shot of a gorgeous view anywhere, we would most likely make sure that nothing man-made gets in the way. These two contrasting worlds are successfully brought into harmony at Bahías—Antoine Predock's latest masterwork, a community of 13 houses at Costa Rica's famed Peninsula Papagayo."

Vladimir Belogolovsky, "'I Wanted to Dance Here!': a Conversation with Antoine Predock about Bahías, a Community of 13 Houses in Costa Rica," *Archdaily.com*, June 8, 2021

What took me by surprise is that right away, as soon as you enter the site, you are immersed in the jungle. The sheltering tree canopy is overwhelmingly beautiful. You get a feeling of being protected by a hovering umbrella. The area is known for its volcanoes. On a clear day, you can see the iconic Arenal Volcano. There are tufa strata emerging from the slopes, outcroppings of some of the oldest rock formations in the country, and large boulders throughout. We preserved virtually all specimen trees, and no boulders were displaced. The volcanic stone, the tree canopy, the sky, and the Pacific Ocean—fire, earth, air, and water.

I don't see Bahías as 13 houses. They are a continuum bound together by the blue-green patinated copper of all the roofs—a flowing, undulating abstraction of the surrounding jungle canopy. The roofs are distanced from one and other, but appear as a continuous flow. And as the copper canopy hovers above, a necklace of low stepped fieldstone frames the access lane and links all 13 houses along the ridge, like dancers that are twisting and turning. Every wall, space, and terrace becomes a part of that continuity.

Engaging the beauty and power of the Peninsula Papagayo, with its visceral connection to deep geologic time and its extraordinary flora and fauna, is a dream come true. For years I'd envisioned Costa Rica as an exotic, ecologically hyperaware "Switzerland of the Americas." It's true.

ROOF FORMS DANCE THROUGH THE JUNGLE CANOPY

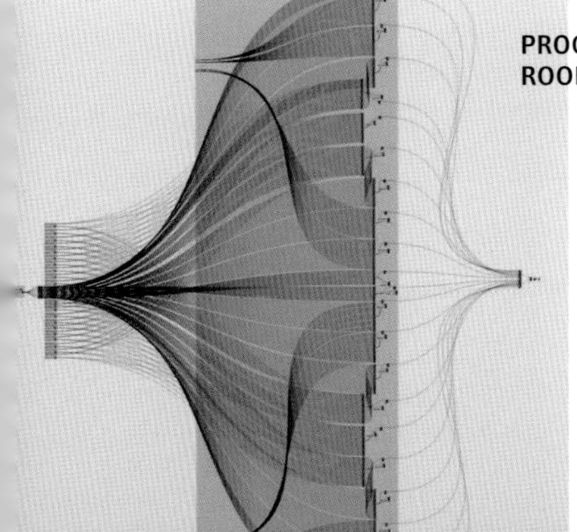

PROGRAMMING SCRIPT WRITTEN FOR SHAPING THE ROOF CURVATURES OF THE 13-HOUSE CONTINUUM

BAHÍAS

PENINSULA PAPAGAYO, COSTA RICA 2017/24

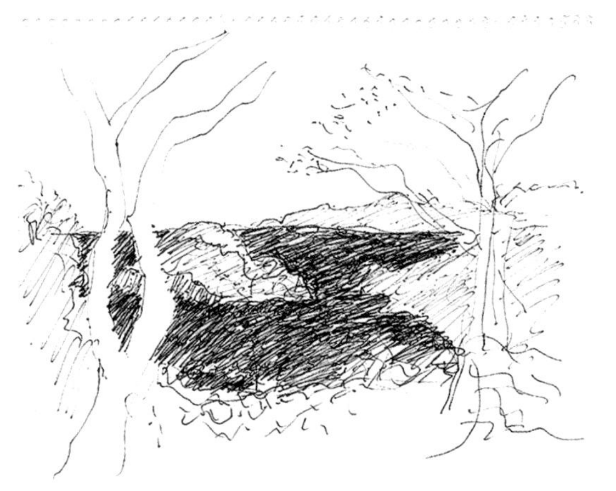

Focused on the islands and Pacific—these secluded jungle compounds, some cascading down the hillside like multi-level tree houses, offer focused but all-encompassing views.

ON OUR FIRST TRIP TO PAPAGAYO, LUNCH IN LIBERIA WITH PAUL, GARY CROCKER, AND ROBERTO FIERRO.

ON SITE WITH CLIENT'S ARCHITECT BOSS GARY CROCKER, AND KEY LOCAL COORDINATING ARCHITECT KEMBLY CESPEDES.

CAUTIOUSLY TREADING THE COVID YEARS—ZOOM HELPED!

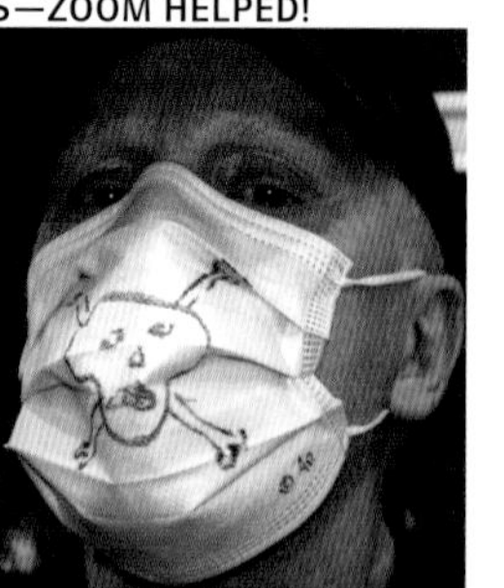

13 houses, 13 sites—each with different topographic conditions. The personality profile for each site analyzed—cliffs, iconic boulders, special trees, variations of view trajectories. It was the topography—flat, climbing, descending—that defined distinct aspects of each house.

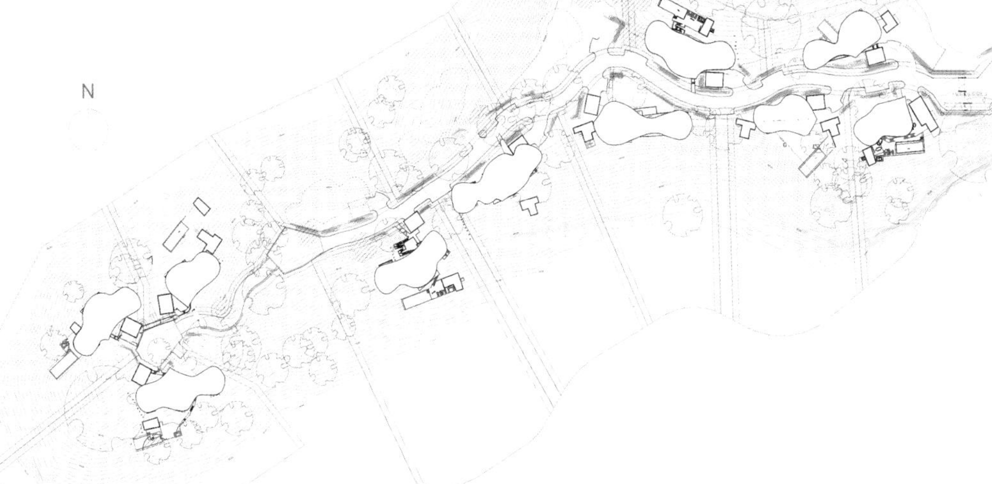

"Control tower" site spread across the largest area of flat terrain on the ridge. Passing through the dichroic glass entry gate, a unifying terraced fieldstone necklace flanks Bahías Lane. The necklace morphs into individual garages and anchors the houses to the volcanic stone ridge. The houses lock into their jungle precinct with precisely aimed views in a 360 degree sweep around the ridge toward bays, islands, and the Pacific Ocean. The hovering green copper roofs shade and shelter terraced pool decks below.

THE FIELDSTONE NECKLACE FOLLOWS THE LANE, FURTHER UNIFYING THE 13-HOUSE CONTINUUM.

WITH PAUL, VEREE AND THE CORE CLIENT TEAM—MARSHALLED BY ARCHITECT/BOSS GARY CROCKER

Just beyond the necklace of stone that weaves along the access lane is an enigmatic glass tower—an elevator that provides a thrilling ride down the cliff face to the house entry. Shaped by the topography, the house inscribes an amphitheater-like arc, with a pool launching one into the landscape.

METAL ROOF FRAMING AWAITING THE COPPER SKIN, MASSIVE EARTH-COLORED CONCRETE WALLS

"His architecture bonds our modern world of science and technology with a mythic past, revealing dimensions of existence man does not even know he has lost. A search for truth pervades his work, so that tradition is both honored and reinvented. Modern life is celebrated in steel, glass and concrete, these being combined with natural materials in an expressive palette, that like his research, knows no boundaries. Avoiding the egocentricity of signature architecture, his buildings use signs and symbols to communicate at every level, embracing human concerns with candor and generosity. In an architecture of subtle power and undoubted grandeur, Predock's gift to the world is to invest his buildings with a poetry born of their purpose and place in the landscape.

Uninhibited by the past and reveling in the present, Predock has exorcised the false gods of Modernism, as science, art and the machine take their place within a greater whole that looks kindly on man's emotional world and indulges the full range of his experiential spectrum."

Geoffrey Baker, *Antoine Predock*, Academy Editions, 1997

RAINBOW

PENINSULA PAPAGAYO, COSTA RICA 2021/24

The beauty of Costa Rica takes on so many guises. In the Bahías project, the jungle canopy was the overarching inspiration for the 13 linked properties. Following Bahías came three much larger houses, all on extraordinary panoramic ocean-view sites. With the sustainability ethos of Costa Rica I searched for a response that would abstractly honor the fauna of this extraordinary country. An iconic symbol of Costa Rica, among many others, is the Rainbow Boa—a non-threatening constrictor famed for its beauty and docility. Looking at the imagery of Rainbow, one might assume that it is literally serpentine—but it is totally topographic—following the contours, with a massive textured concrete anchoring structural wall, from which all the spaces of the house cantilever. The roof surface inspired by the texture and color of the Rainbow Boa and evokes the seasonal flowering of the tree canopy colors—wraps under to become ceiling surface. A suspension "rope bridge" guides circulation while a sweeping cart path crossing the ravine becomes a thrilling ride, serving all components of Rainbow.

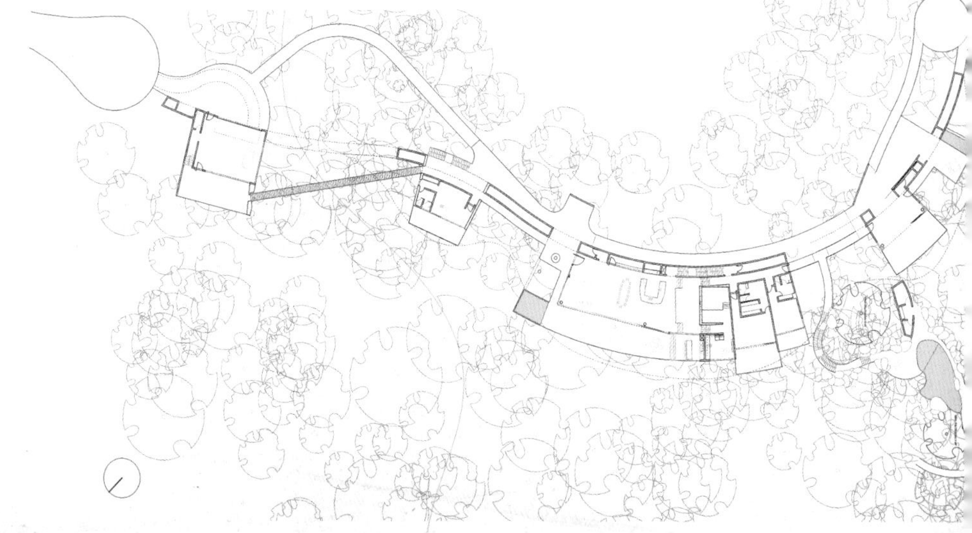

HOJAS

PENINSULA PAPAGAYO, COSTA RICA 2021/24

Hojas (Petals) is organized as the composite of disparate programmatic pieces cascading down the site—each with singular roof expressions and with panoramic views toward the Pacific. Traveling along a narrow lane through dense landscape approaching the house arrival plaza, one encounters what appears to be the verdant leading edge of a giant airplane wing curling downward, framing a panoramic view through an expansive event space that poses as a garage. Entering the house proper, one steps onto a section of the floor that hydraulically lowers into the living spaces like a magic carpet. Off the deck of the main level an undulating path descends to a composite of water bodies. Finally, the lowest two Hojas form the guest house. The surface patination of the Hojas is similar to Bahías, but with the admixture of flecks of color evoking the sometimes florid jungle canopy. On the upper entry level, smaller flanking Hojas contain gym/yoga spaces and prime suites. Like Rainbow, movement through Hojas is episodic, but flowing downward, instead of horizontally—like a breaking wave.

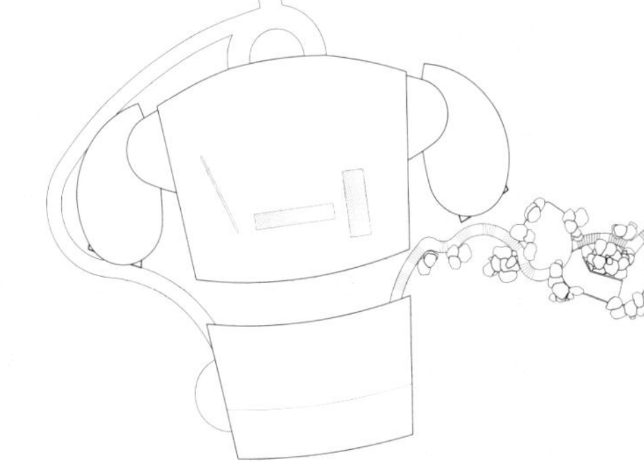

THE BEGINNING OF OUR WORK IN COSTA RICA WAS ROUGHLY CONCURRENT WITH THE COVID PANDEMIC ARRIVAL SO FOR ME, SOCIAL DISTANCING ALONE ON BICYCLES AND MOTORCYCLES DURING THE COVID YEARS WAS MY SPORT LIFE... EMPTY ROADS, EMPTY BEACHES... A KIND OF POETIC ISOLATION

THANKS TO ZERO MOTORCYCLES, HOME GROWN IN CALIFORNIA, I WAS ABLE TO EXPLORE FULLY THE NEW WORLD OF ELECTRIC POWER, DEVELOPING A FOSSIL FUEL ALLERGY.

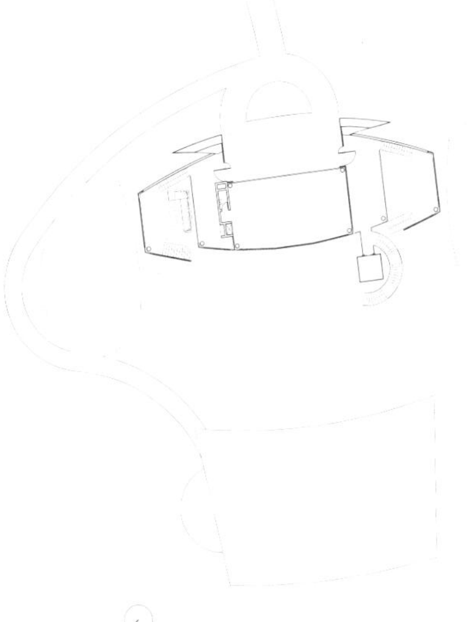

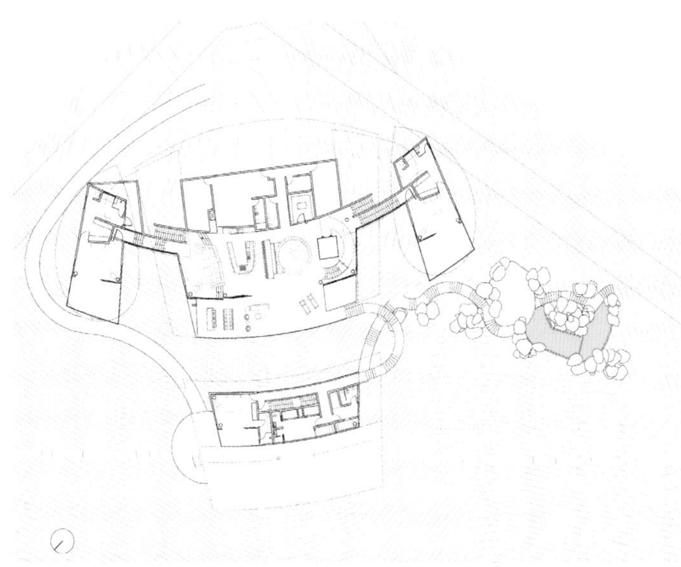

THEN CAUTIOUSLY MAKING A PURCHASE AT HARLEY-DAVIDSON OF GLENDALE—I NEVER IMAGINED OWNING A LOW-PERFORMING HARLEY BAGGER—BUT HD HAD ME WITH THE GAME-CHANGING ELECTRIC LIVEWIRE ROCKETSHIP. IT JOINED MY COVID-19 SOCIAL DISTANCING VEHICLES.

"Riding is a part of me. I have been a rider since high school, and when I ride my experience becomes seamless. My buildings are like those rides; they reveal both topical and timeless. I want them to be experiential, like the Alhambra, one of my favorites of world landmarks, where you realize that architecture is not about linear perspectival order; it is rather about episodic spatial events like a movie storyboard or a pre-17th-century Chinese scroll painting—both can be collage-like, exploring a time/space continuum. That's what my work aspires to. I like it when I succeed in delivering experiential architecture, not simply a one-liner."

Antoine Predock, quoted by Vladimir Belogolovsky, "My Buildings are Rides: In Conversation with Antoine Predock," *Archdaily.com*, June 16, 2020

ESCONDIDA

PENINSULA PAPAGAYO, COSTA RICA 2021/24

Escondida is defined and shaped by towering specimen trees, and the presence of the Pacific ocean—it is the intertwining result of the preservation of those trees and the calibration of particularized views of the ocean from all the spaces of the house. The overlapping house components descend toward the beach, twisting and turning as they adjust to tree position. The raw power of cast-in-place concrete and the massive tree trunks juxtapose to the delicacy of the jungle foliage in an entwining dance. The closer proximity to the water of the Escondida site allows a lower pool terrace to be located just above the beach.

DURING THE COVID YEARS, WHILE UNABLE TO FLY, THIS SOLAR-ENERGIZED AIRSTREAM MERCEDES SPRINTER BECAME MY WINGS BACK AND FORTH FROM NEW MEXICO TO THE LA STUDIO. EMILIANO BALLEJOS, WHO WENT TO ELEMENTARY SCHOOL WITH MY SON JASON AND THROUGH THE YEARS MY MOTO-GURU, BECAME MY PILOT. HE IS ROAD ADDICTED AND WE LOVE THESE NONSTOP 12-HOUR TRIPS TOGETHER... OFTEN ACCOMPANIED BY HIS CO-PILOT SON, JULIAN. THIS TYPE OF RV IS REFERRED TO AS A "COACH" SO ELIZABETH, EMILIANO'S LIFE PARTNER, SUGGESTED WE NAME HER "COACHELLA" AND THAT STUCK. BESIDES LUXE TRANSPORT, COACHELLA IS A GREAT BIKE HAULER—WITNESS THE 1999 DUCATI SPS RACE BIKE IN THE CARRIER.

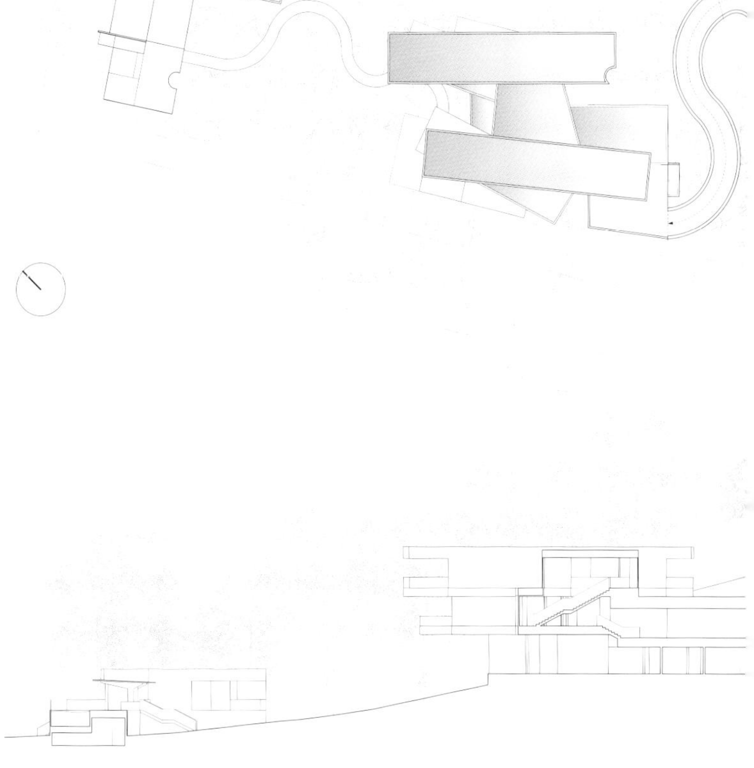

"My connection with Antoine began on a class trip to his studio when I was seven. What struck me most was seeing the models in the studio. I was really into Lego construction, completely addicted to them—making multiple assemblies, creating my own buildings and factories. What blew me away as a kid was the idea that what he was doing was not all that different from what I was doing, just on a grander scale—imagination on a grand and incredible scale. That feeling has never left me. To this day, I can close my eyes and think about that, and once again I am seven years old standing on the spiral stair, looking down at everything in his studio. In my early 20s our paths crossed again and began to intertwine through our shared love of motorcycles and motion. It has been a fantastic journey that has lasted nearly 50 years."

Emiliano Ballejos, 2022

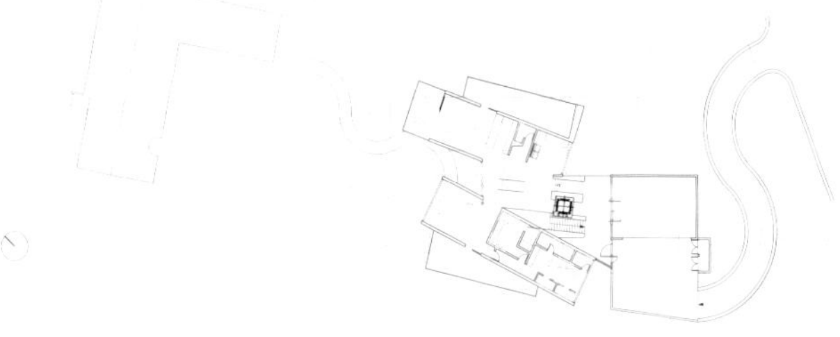

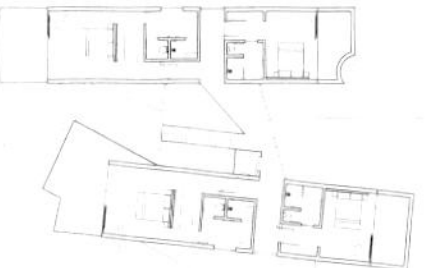

RAIL TRAIL—TRAIL OF ENCHANTMENT

ALBUQUERQUE, NEW MEXICO 2023/26

The Rail Trail, or Trail of Enchantment, is an episodic, 8 mile-urban multi-modal loop circling the heart of Albuquerque. The Trail crosses historic Route 66 and the alignment of El Camino Real. Located along a portion of the existing railroad corridor, it passes through many of the dynamic entities that Albuquerque encompasses.

"Auras" identify and celebrate the dynamic entities and identities intersected by the Trail and Hotspots. Aura is a sweeping cinematic intention from the deepest history to the imagined future. Aura, derived from Latin and Greek meaning wind, breeze or breath, contain the Hotspots where pavement graphics evocatively abstract the mythology and spirit of the Land of Enchantment that makes Albuquerque so special, making us feel grounded in this place. QR codes connect participants to a website featuring deeper historical and visual content.

Electric Tumbleweed, an iconic new landmark for Albuquerque. Blown in this altiplano. Coming to rest at the mythic crossroads of Route 66 and the Santa Fe Railroad. Intersecting trajectories of movement—visible to passing Amtrak and Railrunner passengers, to those coming downhill from UNM or looking east from downtown. A reconfiguration to bring pedestrians up from the skanky dank underpass to greater visibility and safety crossing at grade. Reconnecting the Huning Highlands/EDO neighborhood to Downtown, severed since the construction of the Underpass in 1935. Festive and electrified tentacles of light, reflecting off freshly waxed low riders as they cruise below—Obviously, one of New Mexico's top selfie stops as TOE passes through the Tumbleweed.

This is the epicenter of Southwest myth-making: crossroads of the Santa Fe Railway and Route 66. To the Southwest, today's transit center recreates the 1902, Mission style Alvarado Hotel, largest of the Fred Harvey Houses.

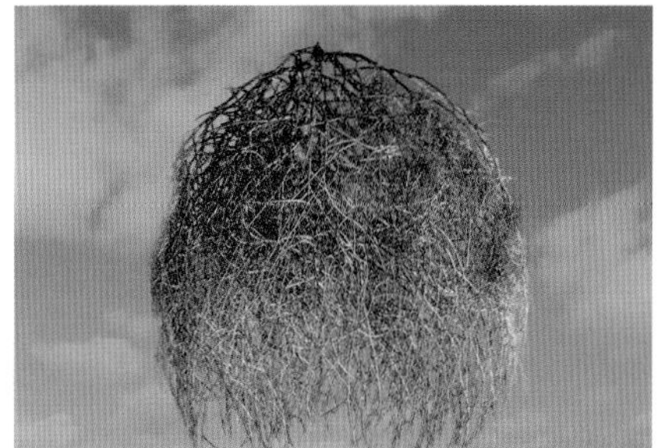

Enchantment Plaza is an elevated platform-bleacher-assembly area attached to the Trail of Enchantment—A visceral connection to the panorama of enchantment. A new gathering place to energize and breathe new life into this rail/warehouse district. An exciting, kinetic experience for cyclists as they ascend the curving path into the cloud like shaded realm to an amphitheater opening out to the Sandia Mountains.

The collage imprinted paving here, as in all the other Auras/ Hotspots, evocatively abstracts the Land of Enchantment. A rendezvous for riders to pause, listen to an intimate musical performance space, or perhaps hear a talk about living in the geological sweep of time before your eyes... from the volcanic Jemez past the upthrust Sandias to Sierra Blanca far to the south.

A notably different interactive zone unfolds as you drop down to the ground plane. A vibrant commercial world of sidewalk cafes, pop ups, retail spaces, beer gardens and the like, inserted into the segmented bays beneath the structural armature proportioned to house reused shipping containers surrounded by generous shaded gathering spaces.

And what will motorists, passing under the Trail, and cyclists above, make of its white lattice amrature? Will it evoke a futuristic ruin of an alien birds wing, fractured feathers frozen in time? Nestled under the enigmatic tree canopy with giant gnarled branches, or a desiccated spinal column of some 1960s sci-fi monster above?

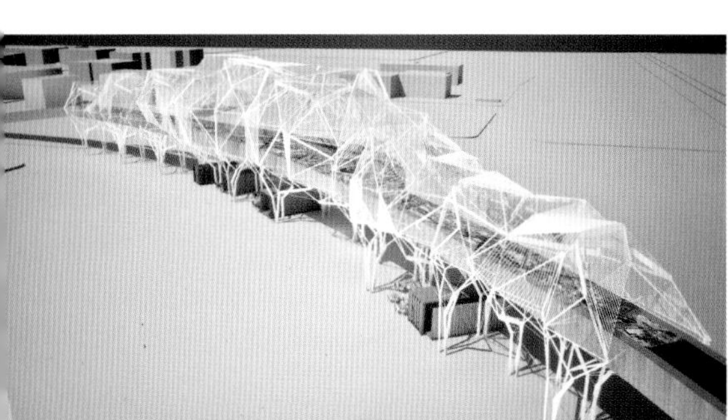

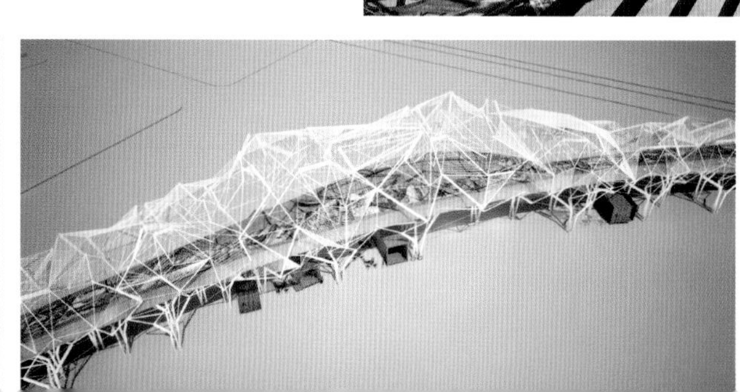

Aura of Umbral Hotspot: Umbral, Spanish for threshold. The threshold of a door. Figuratively, entrada, an entry point. A beginning. A passage between different worlds. A powerful place of contact and cultural exchange.

The place where the Camino Real that connected Mexico City and Santa Fe forded the Rio Grande, and where the later Barelas Bridge carried Route 66 traffic between Chicago and Los Angeles.

Umbral imagines in graphic form the far flung Spanish diaspora and is celebrated on the site of the National Hispainc Cultural Center which was adapted from a plan we designed in 1993.

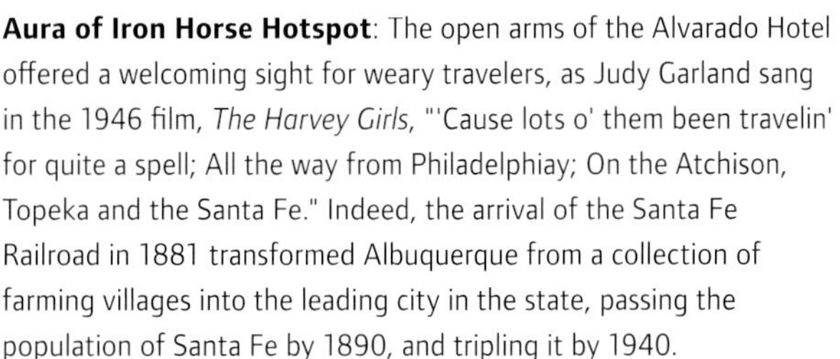

Aura of Iron Horse Hotspot: The open arms of the Alvarado Hotel offered a welcoming sight for weary travelers, as Judy Garland sang in the 1946 film, *The Harvey Girls*, "'Cause lots o' them been travelin' for quite a spell; All the way from Philadelphiay; On the Atchison, Topeka and the Santa Fe." Indeed, the arrival of the Santa Fe Railroad in 1881 transformed Albuquerque from a collection of farming villages into the leading city in the state, passing the population of Santa Fe by 1890, and tripling it by 1940.

The roundhouse, since demolished, and the monumental 1921-23 Locomotive Shops—one of only four on the AT&SF—employed over 1,000 workers, drawn largely from the Barelas neighborhood. The use of a limited number of standardized parts in the construction of the shops, like the integration of its steel I-beam structure, glass curtain walls and overhead traveling cranes into a unified, state-of-the-art industrial design made it the equal of any factory in the world.

The scarred mighty train sheds emerge as an indelible iconic silhouette in the cityscape.

A FOUNDATION FOR THE FUTURE

Inspired Generosity

Luminaries in Architecture and Art Donate Unique Gifts to The University of New Mexico

BY HILARY MAYALL JETTY

NEW MEXICO ENCHANTED Antoine Predock and Constance DeJong long before they met and their lives entwined.
Each vividly recalls traveling along Route 66 and traversing
Canyon's dramatic portal, where mountains flow into a westward
se of land and sky.
never seen mountains like this before," exclaimed Predock. "For me,
ere the West starts." DeJong added, "It was a spectacular gateway."
dock drove his old Plymouth from Missouri in 1954 to begin his freshman
UNM; California native and budding sculptor DeJong arrived to pursue
t of two master's degrees in 1973. Their lives and work have since been
d by the high desert environment and cultural resonance here.
dely renowned, and esteemed by peers and professional organizations
ir many years of creative mastery in architecture and sculpture
ctively, Predock and DeJong are honoring their deep connections to
lexico with two significant gifts to the University.
M's Center for Southwest Research and Special Collections in
erman Library is receiving Predock's archives, a massive compendium
orating sketches and drawings, designs and blueprints, competition
sals, correspondence, photos and
rs. According to Tomas Jaehn, the
's director, this archival collection
preserved for students, faculty,
ects and researchers, and
ed to last for centuries.
is is essentially his life's work, and
are amazing projects here," said
"including the San Diego Padres
rk, the University of Wyoming

Constance DeJong and Antoine Predock

American Heritage Center, the UNM School of Architecture's Pearl Hall, all his international work—projects that have been built, and those that never were. We are honored that he is allowing us to have this collection."

Predock's work also includes many three-dimensional models, ranging in size and complexity. DeJong addressed the conundrum of conserving them, and placing them in a meaningful way, with an exceptional gift to the UNM School of Architecture and Planning (SA+P); Predock's Albuquerque compound near downtown will become The Antoine Predock Center for Design and Research.

"I'm happy that this building, this home, this studio, everything that has been functioning for so many decades will live on," DeJong stated. Architecture can be a 24-hour daily discipline, and the place itself is imbued with the vibrant intensity of its history as a professional center of creation and fabrication. SA+P Dean Geraldine Forbes Isais is excited by the potential for advanced student experiences and instruction, and rotating displays of Predock's work.

"This will honor Antoine Predock's legacy, and the legacy of the School," she noted. "We intend to make the Predock Center the best it can be for our students, the community, and those who believe that architecture, culture and design nurture the soul and elevate society."

DeJong and Predock have been together for more than a quarter century. They share a deep interest in form, structure and light. DeJong's metal sculptures range from monumental to intimate scale. She teaches at the UNM College of Fine Arts, and her work hangs in galleries, museums and private collections.

Predock actually completed his degree at Columbia University in New York and traveled the world to gain insights. Yet New Mexico always beckoned, and he always returned; the atmosphere, geology and antiquity honed his approach to architecture, from Albuquerque to Asia and beyond. His firm now maintains headquarters here, and in California and Taiwan.

Predock uses the term "site specificity" to refer to the way he designs buildings, relentlessly researching history, landforms, climate and culture in the process. His innovative design of the first La Luz residential development on Albuquerque's

A lifelong motorcyle enthusiast, Antoine Predock has acquired a remarkable collection.

A FOUNDATION FOR THE FUTURE

West Side in the 1970s—clustering the units, preserving natural landscape, and providing magnificent views of the Sandia Mountains—was radical at the time, but true to his philosophy.

"New Mexico taught me how to be an architect," he stated. "Architecture has to defend against this place in so many ways. Dust storms, prevailing winds, the assault of the sun from the west—a whole inventory you have to pay attention to and figure out. So I call myself a portable regionalist, because wherever I go, it's in me to think about site that way."

Reflecting on their decisions to entrust the University with their gifts, DeJong remarked, "There were other institutions interested in his archive, but he decided to go with UNM, which I thought was great."

"It's where I started," Predock declared. "New Mexico is my spiritual home. All the clichés, like how it hooks you, apply to me." He smiled. "So where the hell else could the archive go?"

Clockwise from top left: UNM's George Pearl Hall in Albuquerque; Luxe Lake New Town Gateway Art Center in Chengdu, China; Northwestern University Center for Journalism and Communication at Education City in Doha, Qatar; and the Canadian Museum for Human Rights in Winnepeg, Manitoba.

With Dean Robert Alexander Gonzalez

ANTOINE PREDOCK CENTER FOR DESIGN AND RESEARCH

UNIVERSITY OF NEW MEXICO
ALBUQUERQUE, NEW MEXICO 2017/FUTURE

In 2020, Dean Robert Alexander Gonzalez determined that models from the UNM Center for Southwest Research Antoine Predock Archive would be relocated from the Blue Room and Residence of the Compound, to be displayed in perpetuity in the UNM Antoine Predock Center for Design and Research Gallery.

UNM original Proposal to Constance and me for Studio/House Donation

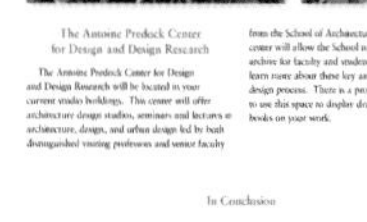

SA·P UNM SCHOOL OF ARCHITECTURE AND PLANNING

In 2021, Dean Gonzalez, held an 85th birthday gathering for me at the Center. I regarded that generous event as the celebratory kick off for the Center. Mayor Tim Keller attended and declared June 24th, 2021 "Antoine Predock Day" for Albuquerque.

With Mayor Tim Keller and Constance

In 2015, the archive of my life's work was gifted to the University of New Mexico Center for Southwest Research. Dr. Audra Bellmore, with her deep knowledge of archival conservation, and her assistant Ryuichi Nakayama became the shepherds of the archive—most importantly in spirit and understanding.

Subsequently, the Predock family compound/studio was donated to the University of New Mexico to create a permanent display of my archive so it would inspire and inform the work of students, faculty, and researches who will use the Center's teaching studios, seminar/meeting spaces, and courtyards.

The compound, now the UNM Antoine Predock Center for Design and Research, functions as a gallery and downtown satellite for the University of New Mexico School of Architecture's George Pearl Hall. While the collection of drawings and documents is principally conserved in a special section of the main campus Zimmerman Library, the models in the collection are displayed in the Gallery at the Center, along with a selection of books, collages, drawings, and other media and objects. Lisa Stewart, Academic Operations Officer, School of Architecture, was instrumental in coordinating with the Southwest Center and the School of Architecture.

STUDIO IN THE EARLY YEARS—TOM, LARRY, STAN, RON, GEOFF, STEPHANIE, BILL, AND JON ANDERSON FAIA (AT RIGHT)—FORMER SENIOR ASSOCIATE WHO MANAGED THE LAS VEGAS LIBRARY AND OTHER MAJOR PROJECTS THROUGH THE EARLY YEARS... JON THEN BEGAN A FLOURISHING DECADES-LONG PRACTICE ON HIS OWN WITH CONSISTENTLY HIGH DESIGN LEVELS, MANY AWARDS, AND SUCCESSIVE ASSOCIATIONS ON SEVERAL OF OUR PROJECTS.

UPPER LEVEL DANCE STUDIO WITH THE MARTHA GRAHAM DANCER, TIM WENGERD

SAME STUDIO, THEN ARCHITECTURE

"'I'm happy that this building, this home, this studio, everything that has been functioning for so many decades will live on,' DeJong stated. Architecture can be a 24-hour daily discipline, and the place itself is imbued with the vibrant intensity of its history as a professional center of creation and fabrication."

Hilary Mayall Jetty, "Foundation For The Future Inspired Generosity: Luminaries in Architecture and Art Donate Unique Gifts to The University of New Mexico"

Antoine Predock Center for Design + Research

UNM School of Architecture + Planning

In November 2017 former Dean Geraldine Forbes Isais held a reception at the AP Center as part of the Crossing Boundaries, ACSA Administrators Conference. Prior to the reception I had presented a keynote lecture at the School of Architecture at the UNM campus. The banner for the Center was signed by all of the participants of the conference.

SEQUENTIAL LINKING COURTYARDS

COLLAGE PROCESS

"Predock drove his old Plymouth from Missouri in 1954 to begin his freshman year at UNM; California native and budding sculptor DeJong arrived to pursue the first of two master's degrees in 1973. Their lives and work have since been inspired by the high desert environment and cultural resonance here.

Widely renowned, and esteemed by peers and professional organizations for their many years of creative mastery in architecture and sculpture respectively, Predock and DeJong are honoring their deep connections to New Mexico with two significant gifts to the University."

Hilary Mayall Jetty, "Foundation For The Future Inspired Generosity: Luminaries in Architecture and Art Donate Unique Gifts to The University of New Mexico"

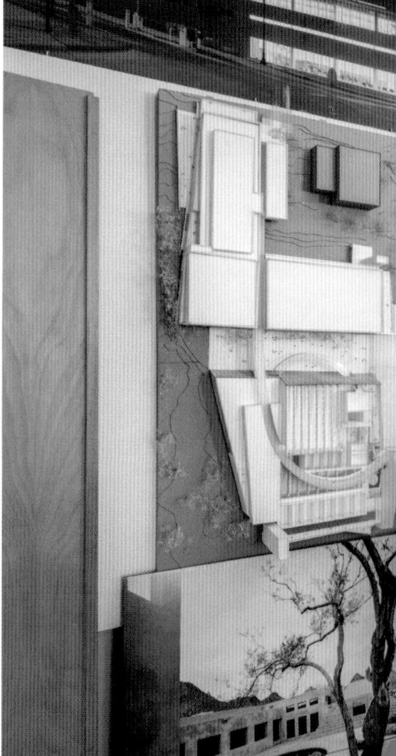

MIRA, PAUL, AND OTHERS ON OMNIPRESENT BIKES IN THE STUDIO

ND WITH CO STANCE + LAVERDA SFC

VIRTUOSO KAROLE MAZEIKA IN HER CONTROL ROOM

MAIN COURTYARD

COURTYARD EVENTS

UPSTAIRS STUDIO

WENDY AND PAUL

BIKES, BIKES, BIKES

WITH PAUL AND GRAHAM REVIEWING COMPETITION BOARDS FOR THE CANADIAN MUSEUM FOR HUMAN RIGHTS

UPSTAIRS STUDIO PERMUTATION

"His house is one piece of a complex of buildings that serve as his primary studio. ... From his kitchen and dining room in Albuquerque, he can look across the courtyard to where his young team, most in shorts or jeans, is trickling in.

The house is open and quiet, but like Predock's studio is filled with the raw material of his inspiration. On a comer table is his collection of kitsch: a plastic Statue of Liberty with a snowstorm pedestal, a tiny sombrero, a Wayne Newton button, a jacked-up toy pickup truck, a plastic pyramid with a coin-operated mummy inside. All of it worms its way into his architecture."

Miriam Horn, "The Rise of the Desert Rat," *Vanity Fair,* March 1992

THE BLUE ROOM MODELS TRANSFERRED TO THE AP CENTER GALLERY WITH DEAN ROBERT ALEXANDER GONZALEZ PRESIDING

"'New Mexico taught me how to be an architect,' he stated. 'Architecture has to defend against this place in so many ways. Dust storms, prevailing winds, the assault of the sun from the west—a whole inventory you have to pay attention to and figure out. So I call myself a portable regionalist, because wherever I go, it's in me to think about site that way.'

Reflecting on their decisions to entrust the University with their gifts, DeJong remarked, 'There were other institutions interested in his archive, but he decided to go with UNM, which I thought was great.'

'It's where I started,' Predock declared. 'New Mexico is my spiritual home. All the clichés, like how it hooks you, apply to me.' He smiled. 'So where else could the archive go?'"

Hilary Mayall Jetty, "Foundation For The Future Inspired Generosity: Luminaries in Architecture and Art Donate Unique Gifts to The University of New Mexico"

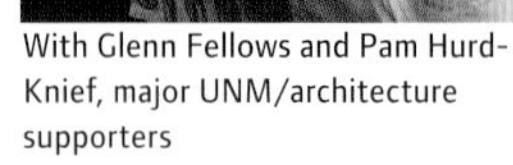

With Glenn Fellows and Pam Hurd-Knief, major UNM/architecture supporters

2017 AP CENTER ESTABLISHED FOR TEACHING SPACE/ARCHIVAL GALLERY WITH PROFESSORS KRAMER WOODARD, KATYA CRAWFORD, AND COLLEAGUE/CRITIC CORY GREENFIELD

11TH STREET STUDIO, OUR NEW HOME, WITH JUSTINE
AND AT THE AP CENTER WITH SIAVASH FROM OUR LA STUDIO

ALUMNI MIRA, KENJI, AND KRISTEN
WITH OUR CREW

STUDIO

1967/2024

Taking it into the future with Principals Paul and Veree—and our team in our newly relocated main Studio.

Hossein (NYC) Justine Paul Charrette Boss Veree Amy Siavash (LA)

Rana K. Abudayyeh
Geoffrey Adams
Lionodes Almaraz
Jon R. Anderson**
Joseph D. Andrade
Anthony A. Anella
Jill J. Annarino
Peter S. Arathoon
Jarrod R. Arellano
Marti A. Arends
Claude Armstrong
Matthew Baird
Sunil R. Bald
Nanci Baldwin
Derrick D. Ballard
Jonathan V. Bandurski
Francisco R. Banogon
Victoria Baran
Joseph K. Barden Jr.
John W. Bass
Genevieve S. Baudoin
Christopher E. Beccone
Geoffrey A. Beebe**
Cole Belmont
Donald C. Bennett
Grant D. Bennett
Leif H. Bennett
Kasha Booraaytee Berry
Kory M. Bieg
Timothy Bicknell
Wendy Bird
Stuart Blakely**
Marcus A. Blasi
Sarah Jane Borch
Kathleen M. Bost
Cynthia A. Bostdorf
Stephen C. Boston
Gail Boyer
John C. Brittingham
Ann Bromberg
Mark L. Bruzan
Luke Bulman
George R. Burbano
Patty Burling
Nathan Burns
Christopher L. Calott
Kathleen Campbell
Leslie A. Campbell
Judith L. Carroll
Michele Marie Caruthers
Phyllis Cece
Kathleen Chambers
Daniel Chavez
Marvin E. Chavez
Ming-Huei Chen
Kameron D. Cheney
Thomas A. Cheney
Sandra L. Cheromiah
Ned Cherry
Justine H. Chibuk
Michael T. Chin
Deanna L. Chino
Linda M. Christensen
Terrance Cisco
April M. Clark
Michele A. Cohen
John-Mark Collins
Devendra Contractor**
Laura Cooper
Arthur Thomas Corsie
Dean P. Cowdrey
Casey Crawmer
Robert J. Cross
Rebecca Davila
Levi Dean
Peter B. DeJong
Shawn J. Delisio
Joy Dennett
Mark T. DePree
Eileen Devereux
Catherine Dimos
Angela E. Dirks
Dan Dixson
Mark K. Donahue**
G. Donald Dudley Jr.
Betty Marie Duffy
Ronald J. Duhamel
Edward Eeds
Raouf El-Beleidy
Joseph K. Ellington
Treveston R. Elliott
Cameron C. Erdmann
W. Anthony Evanko**
Juan P. Fabres
Beth Ann Farley
Mischa L. Farrell
Paul A. Fehlau*
Glenn Fellows
Madonna Fernando
Derek S. Fisher
John D. Fleming
Leandro Flores
Kristin Flurry
Ira Frazin
Alberto I. Frias
Douglas L. Friend**

Malini L. Fuangvuthi
John Van Gaasbeek
Curtis Garcia
Steve R. Gates
Bertrand J. Genoist
Patrick W. Giannini
Allene Gibson
Van H. Gilbert**
Gustavo Giron Sr.
Reyna E. Giron
Westin S. Glass
Paul L. Gonzales**
Susan Gooding
Erica Goranson
Hossein Goudarzi
Aric Grauke
Krystine Graziano**
Cory Greenfield**
Arturo G. Griego
Pantaj Gupta
Lorraine Guthrie
Gabriella Frances Gutierrez
Reginalda Gutierrez
Cathy C. Hahn
Pamela Harling
Sanna M. Harma
Justin J. Harmon
Regina Lynn Harris**
Robert Mark Harris
Darci A. Hazelbaker
John Brian Hearn
Charles W. Hellwig
Maria A. Herrera-Estrada
Susan K. Higdon
Rachel M. Hill
Graham F. Hogan**
J. Craig Holdren
Seth Holt
Nicholas T. Homann
James R. Horn
Katharine E. Howe
David A. Hrabal
Chih-Wei Hsu
Zachary Hulme
Justine G. Humble
C. Aron Idoine
Rebecca A. Ingram
Hiroyuki Isobe
Ronald J. Jacob**
Jennifer Jardine
Irene G. Jimenez
James C. Johnson
Marni L. Johnson
Janet R. Johnston
Karen Justice
Jonathan K. Kahn
Doris C. Kang
Peter F. Karsten
Jocelyn F. Kasero
Kevin Kellogg
Jane Frances King
Karen Jean King
Georgina J. Kish
Marcus P. Koch
Jennifer Kolarik
Kenji Kondo**
William Konopik
Pamela Ku
Peter J. Lagomarsino
Amy Lawrence
Mark B. Lawton
Matthew R. Lawton
Nayah F. Lee
Jennifer M Lein
Franz A. Leitner
Andrea Lenardin-Madden
Karen T. Lente
Lawrence Licht**
Elizabeth Linde
Scott Alan Lindenau
Steven B. Lindsley
Erin Lloyd-Ortigoza
Armando Lopez
Jose G. Lopez
James E. Lucero
Gregory S. Lynn
Daniel G. Macias
Jedediah K. Magee
Juan Marietta
Pedro A. Marquez
Steven R. Maurice
Karole Mazeika**
Steven A. McCaslin
Cara McCulloch-Lieuwen
J. Keith McDonald
Cassandra McDuffie
Robert F. McElheney
Heather J. McGinn
Ann McLaughlin
R. Lawrence Mead
Charles Meade
Romero Ilejay Medina Jr.
C. Courtney Mercer
Quinlin Messenger
Kim Miller
David P. Mishler
Edward George Mitchell
Patricia Montoya
Michael P. Moore
Snow Moore
Stanley G. Moore**
M. E. Morales
Marcia Morris
John J. Morrow
Catherine Mullinax-Jones
Nancy E. Napheys
A. David Nelson
George Newlands
Elizabeth Nicewander
Timothy W. Nichols
Zui Ng
Gary Nolen
Luella Noles
Norman Noonan
Andrew T. Norskog
Darrell Bret Oaks
Lynne Olson
Benjamin Ortega
Thomas R. Ortiz
Kelton E. Osborn
Steven M. Osborn
Albert Otero
Sarah E. Otero
Mala D. Parikh
James T. Parker
Thomas William Parks
Derek Thomas Payne**
Cynthia M. Penn
Jennifer Pepe
Ana R. Petkovik
Theresa Phillips
Thomas Piekenbrock
Dorothy J. Pierson
Angela Pigg
Jean L. Pike
Todd Pilgreen
Patricia J. Pollock
Matthew R. Poncelow
Hadrian Predock
Jason Predock
Denise E. Purley
A. Christopher Purvis
Daniel G. Puzak
Xinyao Qin
Rebecca L. Quigley
Alaa Quraishi
Larry Railey
Carlos A. Ramirez
Ruben Migel Ramirez
Viktor Ramos
Theodore C. Razatos
David Reddy
Matthew J. Reetz
Peter R. Rehn
Ginny Reid
Lucy Reyes
Siavash Rezaei
Daniel P. Richmond
Stephanie M. Rickerman
Rebecca J. Riden
Richard E. Rivera
Elizabeth J. Robbins
Keith D. Robertson
Dennis Rodriguez
Juan Pablo Rodriguez
Timothy J. Rohleder
Christopher Romero
Rob P. Romero
Rachel Leah Rosenthal
Margaret Ross
Sunil S. Sakhalkar
Henry Sanchez
Jose Sanchez**
Rose Sanchez
Kenneth Sandoval
Alcides Santiesteban
Eric S. Santti
Curtis J. Scharfenaker
Michael E. Schissel
Jessica R. Searer
James See
York D. Seiler
Lisa G. Sharp
Kristen J. Shaw
Melanie L. Shelor
Olla M. Shije
Curtis J. Simmons
Veree Parker Simons*
Kimberly J. Smith
Richard V. Smith
David M. Somoza
Kira A. Sowanick**
B. Laine Sparks
Kevin D. Spence
Catherine Spencer
Joanne Spencer
Glade Sperry Jr.
Christopher M. Stachecki
Samuel M. Sterling**
Julie A. Steward
Sara R. Stewart
Douglas W. Strech
Reggie J. Stump
Fuyuan Su
John Scott Taylor
Kristin E. Taylor-Foley
Ross-Alan B. Tisdale
John C. Toomey
Kyle Tsosie
Hajime J. Uesato
Donald H. Vanderpool
Stephanie A. Vencil
Siddhartha R. Verma
James W. Visscher
Leevi Wadzinski
Gregory A. Waits
Deborah Waldrip
Frenando (Eddy) Wauneka
E Suzanne Weisman
Michael E. Wewerka
John White
Brittany Williams
James I. Williams II
Deborah G. Willis
Elizabeth J. Wilson
Ronald A. Wilson
Andrea A. Wilson-Gerber
Jared P. Winchester
Jeffrey Winter
Justin Wiseman
David Witherspoon
Kramer E. Woodard
Mira Woodson
John Woynicki
Jeffrey Wren
Jasmine C. Wu
Zeina A. Yazbeck
Alexia A. Zerbinis
Adam Zientarski
Rachel Kathleen Zollinger

* Principal
** Former Associate

PROJECT ASSOCIATIONS

Hotel Santa Fe Euro-Disney
In association with Fernier and Associates
Marne-le-Vallee, France 1988/92

Institute of American Indian Arts Museum
In association with Louis L. Weller Architects
Santa Fe, New Mexico 1989/92

Thousand Oaks Civic Arts Plaza
In association with Executive Architect Dworsky Associates
Thousand Oaks, California 1989/94

Music Facility, University of California Santa Cruz
In association with Executive Architect BOORA
Santa Cruz, California 1989/97

Museum of Science and Industry
In association with Robbins, Bell, Kreher Architects, Inc.
Tampa, Florida 1990/95

Arizona Science Center
In association with Executive Architect Comoyer-Hedrick Inc., Phoenix, Arizona
Phoenix, Arizona 1990/97

Ventana Vista Elementary School
In association with Executive Architect Burns and Wald-Hopkins Architects
Tucson, Arizona 1992/95

Butterfly Pavilion, Museum of Science and Industry
In association with Robbins, Bell, Kreher Architects, Inc.
Tampa, Florida 1994/96

Center for Nanoscale Science and Technology, Rice University
In association with Brooks·Coronado Associates
Houston, Texas 1994/97

McNamara Alumni Center (Gateway Center), University of Minnesota
In association with Executive Architect KKE Architects, Inc.
Minneapolis, Minnesota 1996/2000

Tang Teaching Museum and Art Gallery, Skidmore College
In association with Executive Architect Einhorn, Yaffe,
Prescott Architecture and Engineering
Saratoga Springs, New York 1996/2000

Green Valley Performing Arts & Learning Center, Pima Community College
In association with Executive Architects Burns and Wald-Hopkins Architects
Green Valley, Arizona 1998/2004

Flint RiverQuarium
In association with Executive Architect Robbins, Bell, Kreher, Architects Inc.
Albany, Georgia 1998/2004

San Diego Padres Ballpark
In association with Executive Architect HOK Sport
San Diego, California 1998/2004

Student Recreation and Activity Center, Ohio State University
In association with Executive Architect Moody·Nolan Inc.
Columbus, Ohio 1999/2006

Tacoma Art Museum
In association with Olson Sundberg Kundig Allen Architects
Tacoma, Washington 2000/03

Robert Hoag Rawlings Public Library
In association with Executive Architect Anderson Mason Dale Architects
Pueblo, Colorado 2000/03

Austin City Hall and Public Plaza
In association with Cotera, Kolar, Negrete, and Reed Architects
Austin, Texas 2000/04

Doudna Fine Arts Center, Eastern Illinois University
In Association with Cannon Design
Charleston, Illinois 2000/07

School of Architecture George Pearl Hall, University of New Mexico
In association with Executive Architect Jon Anderson
Albuquerque, New Mexico 2000/08

Inn at the French Laundry
A collaboration with Predock_Frane Architects
Yountville, California 2001

Parking Structure and Visitor Center, University of New Mexico
In association with Executive Architect Jon Anderson
Albuquerque, New Mexico 2001/03

Logjam House
In association with Executive Architect Jon Anderson
Rio Blanco, Colorado 2001/06

U.S. Federal Courthouse
In association with BPLW Architects & Engineers
El Paso, Texas 2001/09

Trinity River Interpretive Center
In association with Brown Reynolds Watford Architects, Inc.
Dallas, Texas 2002/08

U.S. Federal Courthouse
In association with BPLW Architects & Engineers
Las Cruces, New Mexico 2002/09

Indian Community School
In Association with Eppstein Uhen Architects
Milwaukee, Wisconsin 2003/07

Science Canyon, K-12 School
In association with M.O.A. Architectural Partnership
Colorado Springs, Colorado 2003/07

Ray and Joan Kroc Community Center
In association with Cannon Design and Vernon Williams Architects PC
Chicago, Illinois 2005

Canadian Museum for Human Rights
In association with Architecture 49
Winnipeg, Manitoba 2004/14

Sage House
In association with Executive Architect Jon Anderson
Taos, New Mexico 2006/08

Cornerstone Arts Center, Colorado College
In association with Executive Architect Anderson Mason Dale Architects
Colorado Springs, Colorado 2007/08

Aperture Center
In association with Executive Architect Jon Anderson
Albuquerque, New Mexico 2006/08

South Plant, Rice University
In association with Executive Architect Morris Architects
Houston, Texas 2008

College Avenue Master Plan, Rutgers University
In association with Olin Partnership
New Brunswick, New Jersey 2008

Apparition
In association with Scatliff+Miller+Murray
Winnipeg, Manitoba 2009

National Museum of African American History and Culture
A collaboration with Moody•Nolan
Washington, D.C. 2009

Center for Civil and Human Rights
A collaboration with Predock_Frane Architects
Atlanta, Georgia 2009

Xiangfan City Museum
In association with Executive Architect China Construction (Shenzhen) Design International Co., Ltd Shanghai Branch
Xiangfan, China 2014

Gateway Arts Center
Owner/Developer/Builder
Chengdu Wide Horizon New Town Development Co., Ltd.
Chengdu, China 2008/15

Jade Cascade
JUT Condominium Development
Taipei, Taiwan 2016

Pressdock Building
College of Media and Communication, Northwestern University
In association with Burns & McDonnell
Doha, Qatar 2009/19

Trail of Enchantment
In association with Chris Wilson
Albuquerque, New Mexico 2023/26

TEACHING & LECTURES

EDUCATIONAL POSITIONS

ofessor of Practice, University of New Mexico, School of Architecture and anning, Albuquerque, NM, July 2018–October 2024

siting Professor, Summer Workshop, Huali College, Guangdong University of chnology, Guangzhou, China, 2018

uce Goff Chair of Creative Architecture, University of Oklahoma, orman, OK, 2006

djunct Professor, University of New Mexico, School of Architecture and Planning, buquerque, NM, 2001

siting Professor, Catholic University, Casa Malaparte Workshop, apri, Italy, 2008, 2000, 1999

obert Mills Distinguished Professorship, Clemson University, Clemson, SC, cluding branches in Charleston, SC, and Genoa, Italy, 1995

siting Critic, UCLA, Los Angeles, CA, 1990-91, 1989-90

siting Critic, Centro de Arte Y Communicacion Seminars, uenos Aires, Argentina, 1990

isiting Professor, Southern California Institute of Architecture, os Angeles, CA, 1990, 1984

rchitect in Residence, California State Polytechnic University, Pomona, CA, 1988

stinguished Visiting Professor, Clemson University, Clemson, SC, 1988

siting Professor, Harvard University Graduate School of Design, ambridge, MA, 1987

siting Professor, University of Texas, Design Charrette, Austin, TX, 1985

am Leader, Smithsonian Institution Urban Design Charrette, ashington, D.C., 1984

siting Professor, Arizona State University, School of Architecture, empe, AZ, 1983-84, 1982-83

ea Distinguished Professorship, University of Maryland School of Architecture, pper-Level Design Chair, College Park, MD, 1981-82

udio Critic, University of New Mexico School of Architecture, 1971-72

LECTURES

range County Chapter CSI, Keynote Speaker, Costa Mesa, CA, 2020

niversity of Nevada Las Vegas School of Architecture, Spring 2019 Lecture Series, esert Rat Goes North" Las Vegas, NV, 2019

ectorworks 2018 Summit, Keynote Speaker, "Site Specificity and The Aura of obalization" Phoenix, AZ, 2018

ew Mexico Architectural Foundation, "50 Years of La Luz Community" ith Dr. Christopher Mead, Albuquerque, NM, 2018

niversity of North Carolina Charlotte, Distinguished Convocation Speaker, pirit of Place" Charlotte, NC, 2018

ide Horizons, Luxe Lakes Art Expo Center, "In Time Land Grows" hengdu, China, 2018

uali College, Guangdong University of Technology, Guangzhou, China, 2018

henzhen University, "50 Years in Architecture" Shenzhen, China, 2018

ational United University, Dept. of Architecture, "50 Years of Architecture, rchitect Antoine Predock" Miaoli City, Taiwan, 2018

ing Chuan University, Taoyuan Campus, "50 Years of Architecture, Poetic Architect Who Praises Nature" Taoyuan, Taiwan, 2018

Paso Community College, Spring 2018 Arch Talk, El Paso, TX, 2018

A Orange County Lecture, "Globalization & Its Impact on Architecture" range County, CA, 2018

exas A&M University, Spring Lecture Series 2018, "Landscape Apparitions" ollege Station, TX, 2018

CSA, Administrators Conference, University of New Mexico, Keynote Speaker, buquerque, NM, 2017

ec De Monterrey, Hermosillo, Mexico, 2017

klahoma State University, Stillwater, OK, 2017

A Louisiana Design Conference, Keynote Speaker, "Portable Regionalism" afayette, LA, 2016

Albuquerque Museum, "Drawing into Architecture; Discussion with Dr. Christopher Mead" Albuquerque, NM, 2016

Learning from Education City, Architecture Conference, "Roadcut" Doha, Qatar, 2015

2015 Reinvention Symposium, Keynote Presentation, Detroit, MI, 2015

Dallas Facades, Keynote Address, Dallas, TX, 2014

George Brown College, Toronto, Ontario, Canada, 2014

Light/Site Conference, Rio Rancho, NM, 2014

RAIC Keynote Address, Canadian Museum of Human Rights, Winnipeg, Manitoba, Canada, 2014

University of Texas San Antonio, AIAS Keynote Address, "Motorcycle Reflections" San Antonio, TX, 2013

AIAS Keynote Address, "Motorcycle Diaries," Savannah, GA, 2012

Rio Grande Nature Center 30th Anniversary, Albuquerque, NM, 2012

Harbin Institute of Technology, Harbin, China, 2011

Tongji University, Shanghai, China, 2011

Tsinghua University, Beijing, China, 2011

Beijing University of Civil Engineering and Architecture, Beijing, China, 2011

Texas Tech University, Lubbock, TX, 2011

University of Missouri, Columbia, MO, 2011

University of New Mexico Art Museum, "Roadcut" Albuquerque, NM, 2011

9th Annual International Architectural Roundtable, Toronto, Ontario, Canada, 2010

New Zealand Institute of Architects, Auckland, New Zealand, 2010

AIA Ohio, Cincinnati, OH, 2009

Catholic University, Washington, D.C., 2009

AIA Toledo, Toledo, OH, 2008

AIA Hampton Roads, Norfolk, VA, 2007

University of Oklahoma, Norman, OK, 2007

Sri Lanka Institute of Architects-50-Year Golden Jubilee, Keynote Speaker, Colombo, Sri Lanka, 2007

AIA New Jersey, Ocean Grove, NJ, 2007

AIA London UK, London, England, 2007

New York Institute of Technology, New York, NY, 2007

Montana State University, Bozeman, MT, 2007

University of Philadelphia University, Philadelphia, PA, 2007

CSI, San Francisco, CA, 2007

Art Gallery of Alberta, Edmonton, Alberta, Canada, 2006

New Mexico Young Researchers, Albuquerque, NM, 2006

AIA Colorado Design Conference, Vail, CO, 2006

AIA Omaha, Omaha, NE, 2006

Columbia University-125th Anniversary, Keynote Speaker, "Motorcycle Diaries" New York, NY, 2006

AIA Western Mountain Region, Jackson Hole, WY, 2006

Boise Art Museum, Boise, ID, 2006

AIA National Convention, Los Angeles, CA, 2006

AIAS at AIA National Convention, Los Angeles, CA, 2006

AIA New Mexico, Albuquerque, NM, 2006

Corcoran Museum of Art, Washington, D.C., 2006

Catholic University, Walton Distinguished Critic, Washington D.C., 2006

National Building Museum, Washington, D.C., 2006, 2004, 1998

AIA Baltimore, Baltimore, MD, 2005

Art Institute of Chicago, Chicago, IL, 2005

AIA Columbus, Columbus, OH, 2005

University of Arizona, Tucson, AZ, 2005

New York Institute of Technology, Old Westbury, NY, 2004

GSA at the Center for Architecture, New York, NY, 2004

AIA Atlanta, Atlanta, GA, 2004

AIA San Diego and Museum of Contemporary Art, San Diego, CA, 2004

AIAS National Forum, Austin, TX, 2004

ACE Mentorship Program, San Diego, CA, 2004

ECOSA Institute, Tempe, AZ, 2003, 2000

PINC 4, Zeist, The Netherlands, 2003

AIA Albuquerque, Albuquerque, NM, 2003

AIA Western Mountain Region, Albuquerque, NM, 2002

AIA Arizona, Phoenix, AZ, 2002

University of Houston, Houston, TX, 2002

AIA Palm Beach, West Palm Beach, FL, 2002

Miami University of Ohio, Oxford, OH, 2002

Ball State University, Muncie, IN, 2002

Instituto del Cobre, Sao Paulo, Brazil, 2001

Instituto del Cobre, Buenos Aires, Argentina, 2001

Facultad de Arquitectura, Diseno y Estudios Urbanos, Universidad Mayor, Santiago, Chile, 2001

Pontificia Universidad Catholica de Chile, Santiago, Chile, 2001

AIA Design Conference on Justice, Phoenix, AZ, 2001

Jakarta Arts Festival, Jakarta, Indonesia, 2001

Ohio State University & AIA/Columbus, Columbus, OH, 2001

Philadelphia University, Philadelphia, PA, 2001

University of South Florida, Tampa, FL, 2001

University of New Mexico School of Medicine, Alpha Omega Alpha, Albuquerque, NM, 2001

Arizona State University Desert Cities Lecture, Tempe, AZ, 2001

University of Idaho and Washington State University, Moscow, ID, 2001

World Architecture Congress, Seoul, Korea, 2000

AIA Grand Rapids, Grand Rapids, MI, 2000

AIA and Design Build Institute, San Diego, CA, 2000

University of New Mexico, School of Architecture and Planning, Albuquerque, NM, 2000

Governor's School, Spartanburg, SC, 2000

Clemson University, Clemson, SC, 2000

SCI-Arc Latin American Workshop, Los Angeles, CA, 2000, 1999, 1998, 1997, 1996, 1995, 1994

Drury College, Springfield, MO, 1999

Oklahoma State University, Stillwater, OK, 1999

Pratt Institute-School of Architecture, Brooklyn, NY, 1999

AIA Northwest & Pacific Regional Conference, Yakima, WA, 1999

AIA Jacksonville, Jacksonville, FL, 1999

Rhode Island School of Design, Providence, RI, 1999

AIA National Convention, Dallas, TX, 1999

Portland Products & Services Fair, Portland, OR, 1999

AIA Orange County, Newport Beach, CA, 1999

University of Wisconsin-Milwaukee, Milwaukee, WI, 1999

University of Southern California, Los Angeles, CA, 1999

AIA San Diego and Museum of Contemporary Art, San Diego, CA, 1998

AIA Dayton, Dayton, OH, 1998

University of Washington, Seattle, WA, 1998

Catholic University, Washington, D.C., 1998

Montana State University, Bozeman, MT, 1998

University of New Mexico, JB Jackson Symposium, Albuquerque, NM, 1998

AIA Tennessee, Nashville, TN, 1998

University of Oregon, Eugene, OR, 1998

Stanford University-Board of Trustees Forum, Palo Alto, CA, 1998

University of Texas at Austin, School of Architecture, Austin, TX, 1998

University of California at Berkeley, Berkeley, CA, 1998

La Luz, Albuquerque, NM, 1998

Tulane University School of Architecture, New Orleans, LA, 1997

AIA Student Crossroads Forum, Denver, CO, 1997

AIA Las Vegas, Las Vegas, NV, 1997

SCI-Arc, Los Angeles, CA, 1997

Colorado College, Colorado Springs, CO, 1997

AIA Houston/Rice University, Houston, TX, 1997

AIA Fairbanks, Fairbanks, AK, 1997

AIA Anchorage, Anchorage, AK, 1997

AIA/ACSA-Montana State University, Bozeman, MT, 1997

AIA Spokane, Spokane, WA, 1997

Congresso Internacional de Arquitectura, Mexico City, Mexico, 1997

Bartlett School of Architecture, London, England, 1997

Prince of Wales Institute of Architecture, London, England, 1997

Delft University of Technology, Delft, The Netherlands, 1997

Danish School of Architecture and The Federation of Danish Architects, Copenhagen, Denmark, 1997

AIA National Design Conference, Phoenix, AZ, 1997

Association of Collegiate Schools of Architecture, Dallas, TX, 1997

AIA Central Arizona and AIA Rio Salado, Phoenix, AZ, 1997

AIA Central Pennsylvania, York, PA, 1996

AIA Hampton Roads, Norfolk, VA, 1996

Arizona State University, Tempe, AZ, 1996

AIA Louisiana, Lafayette, LA, 1996

AIA Albuquerque-Architecture Week, Albuquerque, NM, 1996

Penn State, Department of Architecture, University Park, PA, 1996

Baltimore Foundation for Architecture, Baltimore, MD, 1996

SCI-Arc, Los Angeles, CA, 1996

Architectural Institute of British Columbia, Victoria, British Columbia, Canada, 1996

VII Congreso Nacional de Arquitectura, Panama City, Panama, 1996

Desert Design Market & Conference, Phoenix, AZ, 1996

New School of Architecture, San Diego, CA, 1996

School of the Art Institute of Chicago, Chicago, IL, 1996

AIA Orlando, Orlando, FL, 1996

Lawrence Technological University, Southfield, MI, 1996

Woodbury College, Los Angeles, CA, 1996

University of Puerto Rico, San Juan, Puerto Rico, 1995

AIA Memphis/University of Memphis, Memphis, TN, 1995

Drury College, Hammons School of Architecture, Springfield, MO, 1995

University of North Carolina, Charlotte, NC, 1995

San Francisco Museum of Modern Art, San Francisco, CA, 1995

AIA Santa Fe, Santa Fe, NM, 1995

Buro Hamburg, Las Vegas, NV, 1995

Stanford University, Palo Alto, CA, 1995

University of California, Davis, CA, 1995

California Polytechnic State University, San Luis Obispo, CA, 1995

University of Kansas, Lawrence, KS, 1995

Harvard University, Graduate School of Design, Cambridge, MA, 1995

Massachusetts Institute of Technology, Cambridge, MA, 1995

University of Arizona, Tucson, AZ, 1995

Rice University, Houston, TX, 1995

Urban Center, New York, NY, 1995

The Jerusalem Seminar, Jerusalem, Israel, 1994

AIA Denver Design Awards, Keynote Speaker, Denver, CO, 1994

Philadelphia College of Textiles & Science, Philadelphia, PA, 1994

World President's Organization, Dallas, TX, 1994

Manhattan Beach Friends of the Arts, Manhattan Beach, CA, 1994

University of New Mexico, Albuquerque, NM, 1994

Modern Art Museum of Fort Worth, Fort Worth, TX, 1994

Trinity University, San Antonio, TX, 1994

Los Angeles County Museum of Art, "Masters of Modern Architecture" Lecture Series, Los Angeles, CA, 1994

AIA Albuquerque Chapter, Albuquerque, NM, 1993

Lighting Dimensions International, Orlando, FL, 1993

University of Florida, Gainesville, FL, 1993

Florida AIA, Naples, FL, 1993

Iowa State University, Ames, IA, 1993

University of Kentucky, Lexington, KY, 1993

Tucson AIA/University of Arizona, Tucson, AZ, 1993

University of Maryland, College Park, MD, 1993

University of Miami, Coral Gables, FL, 1993

La Frontera Conference/UCSD, Tijuana, Mexico, 1992

VIRTU Design Lecture Series, Montreal, Quebec, Canada, 1992

AIA Mid Central Awards, St. Louis, MO, 1992

AD.AC/Sacramento AIA, Sacramento, CA, 1992

University of California, Davis, CA, 1992

Western Mountain Region Awards, Reno, NV, 1992

University of Minnesota, Minneapolis, MN, 1992

AIA Colorado North Chapter, Boulder, CO, 1992

AIA Albuquerque, Albuquerque, NM, 1992

University of New Mexico, Albuquerque, NM, 1992

NeoCon '92, Chicago, IL, 1992

North Dakota AIA, Grand Forks, ND, 1992

University of Wisconsin, Madison, WI, 1992

University of Illinois, Urbana, IL, 1992

Texas AIA, Austin, TX, 1992

Idaho AIA, Sun Valley, ID, 1992

Phoenix AIA, Phoenix, AZ, 1992

Chicago Art Institute, Chicago, IL, 1992

Alcan Lecture, Montreal, Quebec, Canada, 1992

Kent State University, Kent, OH, 1992

92nd Street Y Series, New York, NY, 1992

University of California, San Diego, CA, 1992

University of Hawaii, Honolulu, HI, 1991

Columbia University, New York, NY, 1991

AIA National Urban Design & Regional Planning Committee, Santa Fe, NM, 1991

Harvard University, Cambridge, MA, 1991

Aspen Design Conference, Aspen, CO, 1991

Banff Session '91, Alberta, Canada, 1991

University of Utah, Salt Lake City, UT, 1991

Princeton University, Princeton, NJ, 1991

Westweek, Los Angeles, CA, 1991

Louis I. Kahn Memorial Award + Talk, Philadelphia, PA, 1991

Architectural League of New York, New York, NY, 1991

SCI-Arc, Los Angeles, CA, 1991

Smithsonian Institution, Washington, D.C., 1991

International Conference of the Royal Australian Institute of Architects, Perth, Australia, 1990

P.A.M.-The Malaysian Institute of Architects, Kuala Lumpur, Malaysia, 1990

Architecture Foundation of Los Angeles, Los Angeles, CA, 1990

Association of Collegiate Schools of Architecture, San Francisco, CA, 1990

Washington University, St. Louis, MO, 1990

1st Congreso IberoAmericano De Architectura Regional, Jujuy, Argentina, 1990

VII Biennal De Quito, Quito, Ecuador, 1990

Cornell University, Ithaca, NY, 1990

Virginia Polytechnic Institute, Blacksburg, VA, 1990

AIA/Smithsonian Institution Seminar "Dilemmas in Design" Washington, D.C., 1990

Binational Conference, Mexicali, "Border Architecture" Baja California Norte, Mexico, 1990

Biennal '89 Architecture, Buenos Aires, Argentina, 1989

Monterey Design Conference, AIA California, Monterey Peninsula, CA, 1989

1988 Seattle Times/AIA, Seattle, WA, 1989

Northwest Regional Conference, AIA Bend, Bend, OR, 1989

Virginia Polytechnic Institute College of Architecture & Urban Studies, Alexandria, VA, 1989

The Graham Foundation, Chicago, IL, 1988

Illinois Arts Festival, Chicago, IL, 1988

University of California, Berkeley, CA, 1988

Sarasota Design Conference, Longboat Key, FL, 1988

AIA Orange County, San Diego, CA, 1988

UCLA School of Architecture and Planning, Los Angeles, CA, 1988

University of Washington, Seattle, WA, 1988

Alcan Lecture Series, Vancouver, British Columbia, Canada, 1988

California Polytechnic University, Pomona, CA, 1988

Texas A & M, College Station, TX, 1988

University of New Mexico, Albuquerque, NM, 1988

Rhode Island School of Design, Providence, RI, 1987

Columbia University, New York, NY, 1987

Tulane University, New Orleans, LA, 1987

University of Arkansas, Fayetteville, AR, 1987

American Institute of Architects: AIA Florida South, AIA Minnesota, AIA Kansas City, AIA Iowa, 1987

Harvard University, Cambridge, MA, 1987

Walker Art Center, Minneapolis, MN, 1987

University of Southern California, Los Angeles, CA, 1987

Yale University, School of Architecture, New Haven, CT, 1987

AIA National Convention, Orlando, FL, 1987

Calgary Architecture Alliance, Calgary, Alberta, Canada, 1986

San Francisco Museum of Modern Art, San Francisco, CA, 1986

Stanford Design Conference, Stanford University, Palo Alto, CA, 1986

University of Texas, School of Architecture, Austin Symposium: "New Regionalism" Austin, TX, 1986

Ohio State University, Department of Architecture, Cincinnati, OH, 1986

Association of Collegiate Schools of Architecture, New Orleans, LA, 1986

AIA Octagon Lecture Series, Seattle, WA, 1985

American Academy in Rome, Rome, Italy, 1985

Harvard University, Cambridge, MA, 1984

University of British Columbia, Vancouver, British Columbia, Canada, 1983

Centre Georges Pompidou, Paris, France, 1981

Technical University, Tokyo, Japan, 1973

SELECTED BIBLIOGRAPHY

A subset of the more than 1,200 books, magazines, newspaper, and online articles in which Antoine and his work have appeared.

BOOKS & MONOGRAPHS

ehmann, Steffen, *Reimagining The Library of the Future*, ro Editions, 2022, 187-188 *ibliotheca de Jalisco, Guadalajara, Mexico*

rooker, Arthur, *City Hall*, "Not a Buttoned-Down City Hall," 50-161, Schiffer Publishing, 2020 *Austin City Hall*

am, Elsa, Graham Livesay, *Canadian Modern Architecture, Fifty Year Retrospective From 1967 To The Present*, ov 2019, 63-64 *Canadian Museum for Human Rights*

rom Darkness To Light II, Stories Of Inspiration From the anadian Museum For Human Rights, Friesens 2018

aylor PhD, Anne & Cynthia Lewiecki-Wilson, PhD, *he Legacy of La Luz, Building Community With Respect or The Land*, Sunstone Press, 2018

00 Buildings 1900-2000, The Now Institute, izzoli International Publications, 2017, 236

rusco, Eduardo Delgado, *On The Border, Essay About ntoine Predock Drawings*, Tecnologico de Monterrey ampus Sonora Norte, 2017

ead, Christopher Curtis, *Drawing Into Architecture, he Sketches Of Antoine Predock*, UNM Press, 2016

usby, Karen, Adam Muller & Andrew Woolford, *The Idea of Human Rights Museum*, University of Manitoba Press, 2015

elzer, PhD,Richard, *Legendary Locals Of Albuquerque*, rcadia Publishing, 2015

iracle At The Forks, The Museum That Dares Make a ifference, Figure 1 Publishing Inc, 2014

rom Darkness To Light, The Building of The Canadian useum For Human Rights, Friesens, 2014

ead, Christopher Curtis, *Roadcut: The Architecture of ntoine Predock*, UNM Press, 2011

rkitektur Krop Rum, Kunstakademiets Arkitektskoles orlag, 2010

ael, Ronald, *Earth Architecture*, Princeton Architectural ress, 2009 *La Luz Community*

utagawa, Yukio, *GA Houses 107–Residential Masterpieces*, okyo, Japan: A.D.A. EDITA Tokyo Co., Ltd, 2008

eoni, Giovanni, *Architetturra Contemoranie, Stati Uniti, Vest Coast*, Il Sole 24 ORE Business Media srl, Milano, Italy, 008 *American Heritage Center*

ariations: The Architecture Photographs of Jenny Okun, hom Mayne, Henry T. Hopkins, and Michael Webb, ive Ties Publishing, New York, 2007 *lood Bank and Las Vegas Library*

iorentini, Pierluigi, *Antoine Predock, echi del deserto*, niversale architettura 173, Venice, Italy, Marsilio, ebbraio 2008

lancey, Jonathan, *Modern Architecture, The Structures hat Shaped the Modern World*, London, Carlton, 2007

anal, Maria Fernanda, *Analogias Arquitectura Mineral*, arcelona, Spain: Parramon Ediciones, S.A.. 2007 *pencer Theater for the Performing Arts*

he Collection of 2006 Awarded Projects in the World, alian University of Technology Press: China. 2007 *tudent Athletic and Recreation Center, Ohio State, lint RiverQuarium*

avies, Colin, *Key Houses of the 20th Century*, Laurence ing Publishing, Ltd. London, England, 2006 *Zuber House*

tern, Robert, David Fishman & Jacob Tilde, *New York 2000: rchitecture & Urbanism*, New York City: Monacelli. 2006 *int John the Divine, South Transept*

ollins, Brad, *Antoine Predock 4*, New York: Rizzoli ublishing Company. 2006 *Monograph*

akamatsu, Ena, Masayuki Fuchigami & Nobuyuki Endo, *Guide to Contemporary Architecture in America*, TOTO huppan. Tokyo, Japan. 2005 *Venice Beach House, housand Oaks Civic Arts Plaza, Tacoma Art Museum, as Vegas Central Library, Arizona Science Center, Nelson ine Arts Center, Spencer Theater for the Performing Arts, merican Heritage Center, Rio Grande Nature Center*

Moores, Jennifer, Jim Forni & Carol A. Monk, *The Sweet Spot* anum Entertainment, LLC. Solana Beach, California. 2004 *an Diego Padres Ballpark*

oldberger, Paul, Richard Schulman-Photos, *Portraits of the ew Architecture*, Assouline Publishing, Inc. New York City, ew York, 2004

ernie, David, *New Stone Architecture*, London, England: awrence King Publishing. 2003

he Creative Community—Designing for Life, Swaback, erdon D. Mulgrave, Victoria, Australia: Images Publishing roup Pty Ltd. 2003

acho Asensio, *Great Architects/Grandi Architerri/Grandes rquitectos*, Atrium Group. Barcelona, Spain. 2003 *Mesa Public Library*

eborah H. Dietsch, *Architecture for Dummies*, New York, ew York: Wiley Publishing, Inc. 2002

Aaron Betsky, *Landscrapers—Building with the Land*, New York: Thames & Hudson. 2002

Davis, Jodie & Diane Strong, *100 of the World's Best Houses*, Mulgrave, Victoria, Australia: Images Publishing Group Pty Ltd. 2002

Chan, Bernard, *Museums—Hundred Outstanding Architects*, Pace Publishing Ltd.: Hong Kong, China. 2002 *Arizona Science Center*

The House Book, Phaidon Press Inc. 2001

GA Houses Special—Masterpieces 1971-2000, Toyko: A.D.A. EDITA Tokyo Co., Ltd., November 2001

Monograph Antoine Predock, C3 Context, Seoul, Korea. 2001

Antoine Predock Architect 3 Houses, New York, Rizzoli, 2000

Cerver, Francisco Ascensio, *New Projects. Architecture*, Atrium International: Barcelona, Spain, 2000 *Mesa Public Library*

Slessor, Catherine, *4x4 Concrete Regionalism*, London: Thames & Hudson, 2000, 26-47, 121-122 *Nelson Fine Arts Center, Turtle Creek, Arizona Science Center, Rio Grande Nature Center*

Architect of the New Millenium, Mulgrave, Australia, Images Publishing Group Ltd., 2000

Wines, James, *Green Architecture*, Italy: Taschen. 2000

Herzog, Lawrence A., *From Aztec to High Tech*, Baltimore, Maryland, The John Hopkins University Press, 1999

Gelernter, Mark, *A History of Buildings in Their Cultural American and Technological Context to Architecture*, Great Britain: Manchester University Press. 1999

Lotus #102, Milan, Italy, Electa, 1999

Musei Architecture 1990-2000, Italy, Frederico Motta Editore, 1999

Giacoppo, Pierantonio, *l'Arcaedizioni*, Italy, l'Arca Edizioni, 1999

Castle, Helen, *Modernism and Modernization in Architecture*, Italy, John Wiley & Sons, 1999

Cerver, Francisco Asension, *Architects of the World*, Spain: Whitney Library of Design, 1998

Glancey, Jonathan, *20th Century Architecture*, New York, The Overlook Press, Peter Mayer Publishers, Inc., 1998

Lyon, Hortense, *American Contemporary Houses*, Paris, Telleri, 1998

Perresut, Luca Basso, *Musei per la Scienza/Science Museums*, Italy, Edizioni Lybra Immagine, 1998

Gili, Gustavo, *Antoine Predock: Architecture of the Land*, 1998

Collins, Brad, & Elizabeth Zimmerman, *Antoine Predock Architect 2*, New York, Rizzoli. 1998

Frampton, Kenneth, *Technology Place and Architecture: The Jerusalem Seminar in Architecture*, New York, Rizzoli, 1998

Predock, Antoine, *One House Series: Turtle Creek House*, New York, The Monacelli Press, 1998

Belsky, Aaron, ed., *Icons: Magnets of Meaning*, San Francisco: Chronicle Books, 1997, 236, 238, 240, 242-243 *Nelson Fine Arts Center, Atlantis Hotel and Casino*

Baker, Geoffrey, *Antoine Predock, Architectural Monograph No. 49*, Great Britain, Academy Editions, John Wiley & Sons., 1997

Loomis, John, *Dictonnaire de /'Architecture Moderne et Contemporaine*, Paris: Editions, 1997, 728-729 *Nelson Fine Arts Center, American Heritage Center*,

Antoine Predock Architect, Seoul, Korea, Korean Architects, 1997

Jodidio, Philip, *New Forms: Architecture in the 1990's*, Koln, Germany: Taschen. 1997

XII Prophecies for the XXI Century, Italy: l'Arca Edizioni, 1997

Kelm, Teresa, *Architektura Ziemi*, Warsaw, Poland: Murator, 1996

Hess, Alan, *Hyperwest: American Residential Architecture on the Edge*, New York: Whitney Library of Design, 1996

Dunlop, Beth, *Building a Dream: The Art of Disney Architecture*, New York: Abrams, 1996

Modern American Houses: Four Decades of Award-Winning Design in Architectural Record, New York, Harry N. Abrams, Inc., 1996

Ghirardo, Diane, *Architecture After Modernism*, New York: Thames & Hudson, 1996

LeBlanc, Sydney, *Whitney Guide to 20th Century American Architecture: A Traveler's Guide to 220 Key Buildings*, New York: WatsonGupthill, 1996, cover, 191, 195, 197. *Nelson Fine Arts Center, Las Vegas Central Library, Venice Beach House*

Predock, Antoine, *Architectural Journeys*, New York, Rizzoli, 1995

Fuchigami, Masayuki, *CrossCurrents: Fifty-One World Architects*, 1995

Tzonis, Alexander, *Architecture in North America Since 1960*, Boston, Bulfinch Press, 1995

Welsh, John, *Modern House*, London, Phaidon Press, 1995

Frampton, Kenneth & David Larkin, *American Masterworks; The 20th Century House*, New York, Rizzoli, 1995

Futugawa, Yukio, *Light & Space Modern Architecture*, Tokyo, A.D.A. Edita Tokyo Co., Ltd. 1994

Collins, Brad & Juliette Robbins, *Antoine Predock Architect*, New York, Rizzoli, 1994

Kultermann, Udo, *Architecture in the 20th Century*, New York, Van Nostrand Reinhold. 1993

Jodidio, Philip, *Contemporary American Architects*, Koln, Germany, Taschen, 1993

The Architect's Sketchbook: Current Practice, Exhibition Catalog, Montreal, Centre Canadien d'Architecture, 1992

Price, V. B., *A City at the End of the World Albuquerque*, V. B. Price, 1992, 33-35, 75, 78, 85, 92-93 *The Beach Apartments, La Luz Community, Albuquerque Museum*

Frankel, Jory & Felice, *Modern Landscape Architecture: Redefining the Garden*, Johnson, New York, Abbeville Press. 1991

Jencks, Charles, *The Language of Post-Modern Architecture*, The Sixth Edition, New York, Rizzoli, 1991

Lacy, Bill, *100 Contemporary Architects*, New York, Harry N. Abrams, Inc., 1991

Architectural Houses 9, Houses in the Mountains, Barcelona, Ediciones Atrium S.A., 1991 Betons Matière d'Architecture, Paris, Editions Régirex, 1991

Sa, Avi, *A&V Monografias de Arquitectura y Vivienda*, Madrid, Spain: Mercedes Medina

Wright, Sylvia Hart, *Sourcebook of Contemporary American Architecture: From Postwar to Post Modern*, New York, Van Nostrand, Reinhold, 1989

Plummer, Henry, *The Potential House: Three Centuries of American Dwelling*, Tokyo: A + U Publishing Co., Sept 1989, 244-57 *Fuller House*

Sacchi, Livio, *Il Disegno dell'architettura Americana*, Rome: Guis, Editori Laterza, 1989, 274-77 *Rio Grande Valley House, Fuller House, Tesuque House, The Beach Apartments, Desert Highlands*

Haber, Francine, *Contemporary Architecture 10*, Paris: Bibliotheque des Arts, 1988, 45-48 *Rio Grande Nature Center, La Luz Community, United Blood Services, The Beach Apartments, Lazarus House*

Studio Work, Harvard University Graduate School of Design, 1987-88, Cambridge: Harvard University Graduate School of Design, 1988

Wayne, Kathryn M., *Antoine Predock, FAIA: Selected Journals Published 1975 to the Present*, Illinois, Monticello Press: Vance Bibliographies, 1987

Predock, Antoine, *Italian Sketchbook*, Rome: Arti Grafiche Jasillo, 1985

Annual Exhibition Catalog, American Academy in Rome, 1985

McCoy, Esther & Barbara Goldstein, *Guide to U.S. Architecture 1940-1980*, Santa Monica, California, Arts + Architecture Press, 1982

Des Architectures De Terre, Paris, Centre Georges Pompidou/ CCI, 1981

The Architecture of the United States: The Plains States and Far West, G.E. Kidder-Smith with The Museum of Modern Art, New York. 1981

The Annual of American Architecture 1980, Washington D.C., The AIA Press, 1980

Low-Rise Housing in America: The Suburban Scene, Tokyo, Process Architecture Publishing Co., Ltd., 1980

Thompson, Elisabeth Kendall, *Houses of the West*, New York, McGraw-Hill. 1979

Gropp, Louis, *Solar Houses: 48 Energy Saving Designs*, New York, Pantheon Books, 1978

Modern Houses in America, Tokyo, Process Architecture Publishing Co., Ltd., 1978

A View of Contemporary World Architects, Japan, Shinkenchiku-Sha, 1977

Plumb, Barbara, *Houses Architects Live In*, London, Studio Vista, 1977

Macasi, John, *Housing*, New York: John Wiley & Sons, Inc., 1976, 445 *The Citadel Apartments*

Thompson, Elisabeth Kendall, *Apartments, Townhouses & Condominiums*, 1975

Davidson, Marshall B., *American Heritage History of Notable American Houses*, New York: American Heritage Publishing Co., Inc., 1971, 352-53 *La Luz Community*

MAGAZINES & NEWSPAPERS

Nyawara, Brenda, "Trinity River Audubon Centre, Dallas Texas By Antoine Predock And BRW Architects," *www.archute.com*, Aug 1, 2022

Betancourt, Matt,"The Mayor of Albuquerque declares June 24 Antoine Predock Day," *dailyalbuquerquenews.com*, June 28, 2021

Manifest no. 3 – Bigger than Big, Manifest Feature, Antoine Predock contributor, pp 166-167, Jan 2021

Belogolovsky, Vladimir, "My Buildings Are Rides, In Conversation With Antoine Predock," *ArchDaily.com*, June 16, 2020

Rybczynski, Witold, "A Brief History of Canadian Architecture," *Architect Magazine*, pp 91-98, Dec 2019

Hauser, "40 Best Houses, Scottsdale, AZ," *The Magazine for Architecture and Design*, pp 95, Issue 6, 2019 Dec/Jan'20 *Fuller House*

"Pushing the Limit, The Ascent of Architect Antoine Predock," *Western Art & Architecture*, Vol. 13, No. 4, Aug/Sep 2019

Riscica, Michael, " Keeping Your Flame Alive with Antoine Predock," *Young Architect Podcast*, July 2018

"Body & Motion, How the Motorcycle Has Influenced Architect Antoine Predock," *META Syndicate LLC*, Vol 12, Summer 2018

"Antoine Predock's Life in Architecture," *Fine Lifestyles Santa Fe and Albuquerque Magazine*, Spring 2018, Vol 4, Issue 1, April 2, 2018

"Viola Desmond makes civil-rights history with unveiling of new $10," *The Globe and Mail*, Vancouver, March 9, 2018 *Canadian Museum for Human Rights*

"Predock Brings Accessibility to Milwaukee School," *AIArchitect.com*, August 15, 2008, *Indian Community School*

"Designing a Legacy, Renowned architect Antoine Predock donates property, archives to UNM," Albuquerque Journal, Dec 4, 2017

"Sheika Moza inaugurates new NU-Q building," *Gulf Times*, May 2, 2017, p 28

"Architecture is a Ride, Antoine Predock," *McCall Magazine*, 2015, 24th Anniversary Issue

"Canadian Museum of Human Rights," *C3 Museum Spatial Journeys*, No. 364, Dec 2014

"Difficult Harmonies," *Canadian Architect*, Nov 2014

"A Mountain on the Prairies," *Winnipeg Free Press*, Sept 20, 2014 *Canadian Museum for Human Rights*

"The vision behind Winnipeg's Museum for Human Rights," *Maclean's*, Vol 127, Num 32 Aug 18, 2014

"Architect Predock elected Academician," *Albuquerque Journal Business Outlook*, Aug 11, 2014

"2012 Cocktail-Napkin Sketch Contest," *Architectural Record*, Oct 2012

Taiwan Architect, "Canadian Museum for Human Rights," 2012/03 NO. 447

THE magazine, "Roadcut: The Architecture of Antoine Predock," April 2011

"Studio Visit Antoine Predock Architect," *Architect*, March 2011

"Architecture's Alchemist," *New Mexico Daily Lobo*, Feb 17, 2011

"Roadcut, The Architecture Of Antoine Predock," *art ltd.*, Jan/Feb 2011

"Canadian Museum for Human Rights, A Portrait of the Artist," *Winnipeg Free Press*, Sept 4, 2010

"Architecture Survey," *Vanity Fair*, Aug 2010

"The World's 20 Greatest Designers of all Time," *Architectural Digest*, Jan 2010

"Poetry of the Earth–The Architecture of Antoine Predock," *Taiwan Architect*, 2009

"National Museum of African American History and Culture," *Architect*, May 2009

"National Palace Museum, Taibo City, Taiwan," *Detaili* (Bulgaria), April 2009

"George Pearl Hall, UNM School of Architecture, Albuquerque, NM," *Architect*, Nov 2008

"George Pearl Hall, UNM School of Architecture, Albuquerque, NM," *The Chronicle of Higher Education*, Nov 7, 2008

Vijayan, Sarita, "Conceptual Solutions=Summation of Myriad Details," *Indian Architect and Builder*, Sept 2008 *Canadian Museum for Human Rights, Highlands Pond, National Palace Museum, Turtle Creek, Tacoma Art Museum, Austin City Hall*

Wang Lu, "Antoine Predock Architect PC," *World Architecture*, Oct 2008 *Various Projects*

Dulin, Michael, "A Desert Touchdown from Outer Space," *Competitions*, Fall 2008 *Spaceport America*

Lopez, Carol Paeredo, "Access for All!," *PN*, Oct 2008 *Indian Community School*

"Canadian Museum for Human Rights," *Details*, Feb 2008

"Predock Brings Accessibility to Milwaukee School," *AIArchitect.com*, Aug 15, 2008, *Indian Community School*

Kontakt, "Expanding Culture Through Design," Allen, Art, August/September 2008 *McNamara Alumni Center*

"Diamonds are an Architect's Best Friend," *Competitions*, Spring 2008 *World Mammoth and Permafrost Museum*

Bernardi, Jose, "Dal Pueblo e dal Deserto," *Il Giornale dell'Architettura*, March 2008

"Place-Inspired Architecture," *Interior Architecture of China, Mind Exchange 2007 I*, Jan 2008

Giovannini, Joseph, "A Not So Log Cabin," *Architectural Digest*, Jan 2008 *Logjam House*

Kieran, Christopher, "Good Design is Good Business," *Architectural Record*, Nov 2007 *San Diego Padres Ballpark*

Mayfield, Dan, "Design Museum Salutes Antoine Predock's Western Vision," *Albuquerque Journal*, Oct 14, 2007

Mercado, Elvian Martinez, "Angulos sobresalientes," *El Nuevo Dia*, (Puerto Rico), Oct 7, 2007
Cooper-Hewitt Award, Austin City Hall and Public Plaza

"New Silk Road-Arabic Cultural Area," *Concept* (Korea), Oct 2007 *New Silk Road*

"National Palace Museum Southern Branch," *Concept* (Korea), Oct 2007 *National Palace Museum Southern Branch*

"World Mammoth & Permafrost Museum," *Concept* (Korea), Jeong, Ji-seong, Sept 2007
World Mammoth and Permafrost Museum

Eschliman, Dwight, "The Exhibitionists," *New York Times*, Fall 2007

"Report News: Cooper-Hewitt Announces National Design Awards," *Architect*, July 2007 *Cooper-Hewitt Award*

Paperny, Vladimir, "Antoine Predock-Portrait," *Architectural Digest* (Russia), July 2007 *Antoine Predock, various projects*

Amelar, Sarah, "The Architect's Hand-Antoine Predock's Vivid Journeys," *Architectural Record*, June 2007 *sketches*

Mayfield, Dan, "Predock Honored for Life's Work," *Albuquerque Journal*, June 3, 2007 *Cooper-Hewitt Award*

LeFort, Marie, "Coup de Foudre," *Numero* (France), May 2007 *Spencer Theater for the Performing Arts & American Heritage Center*

Berman, Jay, "Five New Ballparks We Love," *cityguides.msn.com*, April 12, 2007 *San Diego Padres Ballpark*

Solomon, Susan, "The Reinvention of a University Campus," *Competitions*, Spring 2007 *Rutgers Competition*

"National Palace Museum," *Future Arquitecturas* (Spain), Dec 2006 *National Palace Museum Southern Branch*

Levin, Dan, "East Village, Out West," *New York Times*, Dec 24, 2006 *San Diego Padres Ballpark*

Rinaldi, Paolo, "The Jade Mountain (La Montagna di Giada)," *OF ARCH*, Nov/Dec 2006-#93 *National Palace Museum*

von Hoffman, Nicholas, "A Fearless Vision," *Architectural Digest*, Oct 2006 *AIA Gold Medal*

Abdul-Alim, Jamaal, "A New Home For Long-Held Traditions," *Milwaukee Journal-Sentinel*, Sept 29, 2006
Indian Community School

Adler, Jerry, "Going Green," *Newsweek*, July 17, 2006
Austin City Hall and Public Plaza

Price, V.B., "Shaping the New Southwest," *Su Casa*, Summer 2006 *Zuber House, Kaminsky 2, Troy House & La Luz Community*

Montes, David, "Predock recibe la medalla de la AIA," *Arquitectura Viva*, #105-June 2006 *AIA Gold Medal*

Pearson, Clifford, "Antoine Predock Rides High With The Gold Medal," *Architectural Record*, June 2006 *AIA Gold Medal*

Jarmusch, Ann, "Golden in the West" & "Gold Standard," *San Diego Union Tribune*, Feb 5, 2006
AIA Gold Medal & San Diego Padres Ballpark

Gerfen, Katie,"Predock Wins AIA Gold Medal," *Architecture*, Jan 2006 *AIA Gold Medal*

"Antoine Predock Selected to Receive the 2006 American Institute of Architecture Gold Medal," *Dialogue* (Taiwan), 2006/1 & 2 *AIA Gold Medal*

Lubell, Sam, "AIA Gold Medal, Firm Award Goes to Antoine Predock," *Architectural Record*, Jan 2006 *AIA Gold Medal*

Jatras, Todd,"Super Geek Upgrades," *Wired*, Jan 2006
Turtle Creek House

Van Gelder, Lawrence,"Gold Medal Architect," *New York Times*, Dec 10, 2005 *AIA Gold Medal*

Hales, Linda, "Architecture's Natural Winner," *Washington Post*, Dec 9, 2005 *National Palace Museum Southern Branch*

Mayfield, Dan, "Antoine Predock Wins Gold Medal," *Albuquerque Journal*, Dec 9, 2005

Sari, Evi, "Groundbreaking of the National Palace Museum Southern Branch," *Dialogue* (Taiwan), Dec 2005-No.98
National Palace Museum Southern Branch

Hill, Steve, "Chinoiserie," *Identity* (United Arab Emirates), Nov 2005 *National Palace Museum Southern Branch*

Yang, Grace, "Ground Broken for NPM Southern Branch," *China Post*, Nov 20, 2005 *National Palace Museum*

Bernstein, Fred A., "Glass Adds Sheen to a Waterfront," *New York Times*, July 24, 2005 *Tacoma Art Museum*

Warson, Albert, "Canada Welcomes Major Museum Project," *Architectural Record*, June 2005
Canadian Museum for Human Rights

Betsky, Aaron,"Towards a Magic Mountain", *Competitions*, Spring 2005 *National Palace Museum Southern Branch*

Amelar, Sarah, "Flint RiverQuarium, Georgia," *Architectural Record*, May 2005

Haldeman, Peter, "The House of Shadows," *Architectural Digest*, May 2005 *Shadow House*

Lin, Evan J. S., "Special Issue-National Palace Museum Southern Branch," *Taiwan Architect*, March 2005

"American wins for Palace Museum design," *The China Post*, Nov 25, 2004

van Ryzin, Jeanne Claire, "You Can Really Plug In To The New City Hall," *Austin American-Statesman*, Nov 20, 2004

Ouroussoff, Nicolai, "Buildings Fit for a Parliament and a President," *New York Times*, Sept 12, 2004

"Scouting Two New Ballparks," *Newsweek*, May 3, 2004

Olson, Sheri, "Antoine Predock makes a landscape abstraction of the Tacoma Art Museum...," *Architectural Record*, Aug 2003

Hawthorne, Christopher, "Now Taking the Field: Bold Stadium Designs," *New York Times*, July 27, 2003

Covarrubias, Amanda, "Performing Arts Venue Now Winning Ovations," *Los Angeles Times*, Dec 2003

Pastier, John,"The Smell of Success," *Metropolis*, April 2003

Sanders, Eli, "Tacoma museum to evoke natural, ephemeral beauty," *The Seattle Times*, Jan 26, 2002

"Poesia em terras aridas," *Arquitectura & Urbanismo*, Dec 01/ Jan 02

"Antoine Predock La trascendencia en la arquitectura," *El Metropolitano*, Nov 10, 2001

"In the High Desert, An Oasis of Design," *The Washington Post*, Sept 30, 2001

"Predock Honored at May 12 Commencement," *Daily Lobo Campus News*, May 7, 2001

"Predock goes Upstate–The Quintessential Southwestern Architect Completes His First Building in the Northeast," *Metropolis*, May 2001

"Tang Shebang," *House & Garden*, April 2001

"Predock's Rock," *Minnesota, University of Minnesota Alumni Association*, Jan/Feb 2000

"Heavy Metal, A Cappella, and a Cake," *Skidmore Scope*, June 1999

"A Look at Stadiums to Come," *Architecture*, Nov 1998

"Ballpark Architect says Talk of Mission style Clearly is way off base," *San Diego Union Tribune*, Nov 29, 1998

"Big Museum on Campus," *New York Times*, Nov 6, 1998

"Alien Architect," *Tacoma City Paper*, May 21-27, 1998

"The Dramatic Forms of Antoine Predock's Spencer Theater are Drawn from the Natural Elements on its Isolated Southwestern Site," *Architectural Record*, May 1998

"Architect Seeks Soul of the Northwest," *The Seattle Times*, May 22, 1998

"Downtown, Art & Soul," *Washington Post*, May 2,1998

"Viewers Become Participants in New Predock Museum at Skidmore College," *Architectural Record*, April 1998

"Structures with Soul: Cubist Combinations of Multiple Fractured Images," *New York Times Magazine*, Jan 30, 1998

Bennett, David, "New Mexico Arts Center Impresses Jazz Legend," *El Paso Times*, Oct 4, 1997, B1
Spencer Theater for the Performing Arts

Chow, Phoebe, "Stanford Systems," *The Architectural Review*, Nov 1997, 50-53,
Center for Integrated Systems

Dillon, David "Playing the Competitions Game," *Architectural Record*, November 1997, 62-67
Danish National Archive, Atlantis Hotel and Casino & Nelson Fine Arts Center

Dixon, John Morris, "Due Recognition," *Harvard Design Magazine*, Summer 1997, 54 *La Luz Community*

Kai-sun, Katherine, "Predock Builds Dance Studio in Forest of Eucalyptus Trees," *Architectural Record*, Jan 1997
Dance Facility

Kruit, Caroline, "Architectonische expressie door constructieve vormgeving," *Architectuur & Bouwen*, Oct 1997, 3, 12-13
American Heritage Center, Museum of Science and Industry

"Rigsarkivet-landsarkivet," *Arkitekten #03*, February 1997, 23
Danish National Archive

Stein, Karen, "Two California campuses: Two different worlds," *Architectural Record*, August 1997, 66-75
Music School, Center for Integrated Systems

Connell, Michael, "Recapturing the Pride of Place," *Stanford Today*, September/October 1996, 48-55
Center for Integrated Systems

"Learning in Las Vegas," *Design Quarterly 168*, Spring 1996, 6-19 *Las Vegas Central Library*

Lopez, Margot. "El espiritu de\lugar," *Ta Lingo*, 1996, 16-21

Moller, Henrik Sten, "Tysk Bunke bryllup," *Pofitiken*, Dec 9, 1996 *Danish National Archive*

Oldenburg, Ann, "Do You Like This Building?," *USA Today*, June 24, 1996, 1D-2D

Pagnelli, Carlo, "In the Environment," *L'Arca*, April 1996, 16-23 *Museum of Science and Industry*

Wagner, Michael, "Housing Harmony," *Metropolis*, Oct. 1996, 79 *American Heritage Center*

Webster, Guy, "The Fun's in the Fin," *The Arizona Republic*, September 18, 1996, 4 *Arizona Science Center*

Bierman, Lindsay, "Freeway Acropolis," *Architecture*, March 1995, 84-93 *Thousand Oaks Civic Arts Plaza*

Castellano, Aldo, "Un borgo civico in California," *L'Arca*, October 1995, 24-31 *Thousand Oaks Civic Arts Plaza*

"Civic Arts Plaza in Thousand Oaks California," *Architektur + Wettbewerbe*, September 1995, 18-19

DellaFlora, Anthony, "Celebrity Architect Gets Triple Whammy," *Albuquerque Journal*, April 2, 1995, D12

"Dialogo Con la Naturaleza," *B.A. La Nacion Architectura*, June 21, 1995

Dietsch, Deborah, "Predock's Example," *Architecture*, March 1995, 15

Dillon, David, "American Visionary," *Architecture*, March 1995, 55-93

"Reading Circle," *Architecture*, March 1995, 68-73
Mesa Public Library

Giovannini, Joseph, "Planting Knowledge," *Architecture*, March 1995, 7 4-83 *Social Sciences and Humanities Building*

Goldberger, Paul, "Architecture: Antoine Predock-Variations on a Cube in Southern California," *Architectural Digest*, March 1995, 110-119 *Turtle Creek House*

"Houses as Art," *New York Times Magazine*, March 12, 1995, 46-47 *Rosenthal House*

Ivace, Fulvio, "A. Predock a Laramie Wyoming," *Abitare*, Feb 1995, 138-141 *American Heritage Center*

Kroloff, Reed, "Sculptural Sequence," *Architecture*, Nov 1995, 84-93 *Museum of Science and Industry*

Sicuso, Francisco, "A. Predock y sus Juegos Geometricos," *La Prensa*, March 6, 1995, 6 *Rosenthal House*

Von Lessing, Lukas, "Die Visioneneiner Wustenratte," *ADAC Special*, October 1995, 26-32
Rio Grande Nature Center, Las Vegas Central Library

Whiteson, Leon, "Through the looking glass," *Architecture*, March 1995, 125-129 *Rosenthal House*

Armando, Diego R, "Antoine Predock y el Teatro Mandel Weiss," *Consejo Profesionaf de Arquitectura y Urbanismo*, July 1994, 48-52 *Mandell Weiss Forum*

Bartolucci, Marisa, "Power," *Metropolis*, December 1994, 64-65 *Hotel Santa Fe*

Betsky, Aaron. "Latin Lessons," Metropolis, November 1994, 62-63 *Nelson Fine Arts Center*

"Curtain Up," *Los Angeles Times*, Oct 16, 1994
Thousand Oaks Civic Arts Plaza

"Geografia Cultural," *Arquitectura Viva*, Sept/Oct 1994, 46-49
American Heritage Center

Graaf, Vera, "Atlantis in der Neuen Welt," *Architektur & Wohen*, Dec 1994/Jan 1995, 101-109
Las Vegas Central Library & Atlantis Hotel and Casino

Kegel, "Zentrum fur das Amerikanische," *Architektur Innenarchitektur Technischer Ausbau*, July 8, 1994, 15
American Heritage Center

Andersen, Kurt, "Architecture: Antoine Predock, Serious Modernism in Dallas," *Architectural Digest*, March 1994, 104-11 *Turtle Creek House*

Gubitosi, Alessandro, "The Elemental Spirit," *L'Arca*, May 1994, 46-53

Pearson, Clifford A., "For the Birds," *Architectural Record: Record Houses*, April 1994, 76-83 *Turtle Creek House*

"Top 10 Best Design of 1993," *Time*, January 3, 1994, 72
Turtle Creek House

Betsky, Aaron, "Magic Marker," *Architectural Record*, Feb 1993, 62-69 *Classroom, Library and Administrative Building*

"World in Motion: Architect Antoine Predock Choreographs L.A.," *LA Weekly*, June 18-24, 1993, 30-31

"Western Frontiers: Myth and Spirit," *Architecture*, Dec 1993, 47-61 *American Heritage Center and Art Museum*

Webb, Michael, "Mandell Weiss Forum," *A+ U*, January 1993, 30-45 *Mandell Weiss Forum and La Jolla Playhouse*

Dietsch, Deborah K, "Desert Trails," *Architecture*, July 1992, 48-51 *Hotel Santa Fe*

Gustmann, Kurt, "Antoine Predock: Die Graben Architekten" *Hauser*, April 1992, 59-70

Horn, Miriam, "The Rise of the Desert Rat," *Vanity Fair*, March 1992, 112-22

"Hotel Santa Fe," *Connaissance des Arts*, April 1992, 46-51
Hotel Santa Fe

Kahn, Eve M, "Antoine Predock on Campus," *The Wall Street Journal*, Oct 23, 1992, A12
Classroom, Library and Administrative Building

McGuigan, Cathleen, "Apres Mickey, le Deluge," *Newsweek*, April 13, 1992, 16-18 *Hotel Santa Fe*

Morris, Roger, "New Star in Santa Fe," *Architectural Digest*, June 1992, 82-88 *Institute of American Indian Arts Museum*

"The New Nature of Architecture," *Metropolis*, April 1992, 45
Nelson Fine Arts Center, Las Vegas Central Library & Saint John the Divine South Transept

Rockwell, John, "At Euro-Disney Hotels, Another Fantasyland," *New York Times*, April 14, 1992 *Hotel Santa Fe*

Rybczynski, Witold, "A Good Public Building," *The Atlantic*, August 1992, 84-87 *Las Vegas Central Library*

"Six International Architects Discuss Their Design Approaches to Integrating Houses into the Natural Environment," *Architectural Digest*, September 1992, 48
Ship of the Desert & Troy House

Mulard, Claudine, "Las Vegas: Musee des enfants," *Architecture Interieure Cree*, Dec 1991-Jan 1992, 130-33
Las Vegas Central Library

Boissiere, Olivier, "Antoine Predock: Architect of the West," *Vogue Decoration*, Feb-March 1991, 53-61

Dibar, Carlos, & Diego Armando, "Antoine Predock: Filtrando imagenes," *Arquitectura e Urbanismo*, Feb-March 1991, 36-49
Nelson Fine Arts Center, Venice House, Fuller House, American Heritage Center

Dixon, John Morris, "Transcendence on the Beach," *Progressive Architecture*, April 1991, 92-95
Venice Beach House

GA Document 30, Tokyo: A.D.A. EDITA Tokyo Co., Aug 1991, 108-17 *Las Vegas Central Library*

GA Houses 31, Tokyo: A.D.A. EDITA Tokyo Co., March 1991, 59-61 *Rosenthal House*

GA Houses 32, Tokyo: A.D.A. EDITA Tokyo Co., July 1991, 116-25 *Zuber House*

Giordano, Michele Bazan, "La Cittadella dell'arte," *L 'Arca*, March 1991, 10-21 *Nelson Fine Arts Center*

Horn, Miriam, "Designing in Hues of Green," *U.S. News & World Report*, Feb 25, 1991, 58-59 *La Luz Community*

"A Master of Contradictions," *Graphis*, Nov-Dec 1991, 81-87

Mitchell, Shane, "Desert Mania," *Interiors*, Jan 1991, 110-11
Las Vegas Central Library

Posner, Ellen, "Supporting Role," *Architecture*, Sept 1991, 47-53 *Mandell Weiss Forum & La Jolla Playhouse*

Sainz, Jorge, "Con el mar en el salon, casa en la playa, Venice," *A&V(Monographias de Arquitectura & Vivienda)*, Nov-Dec 1991, 38-41 *Venice Beach House*

Boissiere, Olivier, "Antoine Predock," *L'Architecture d'Aujourd'hui*, Oct 1990, 177-87

Cecchetti, Maurizio, "Un Centro per la memoria collettiva," *L'Arca*, Oct 1990, 40-47 *American Heritage Center*

Cheek, Lawrence W, "Desert Blooms," *Architecture*, Jan 199[illegible] 92-97 *Nelson Fine Arts Center*

GA Houses 30, Tokyo: A.D.A. EDITA Tokyo Co., Dec 1990, 118-21 *Venice Beach House*

Goldberger, Paul, "Drawing the Past is Like Describing an Elephant," *New York Times*, Oct 7, 1990

"Speaking the Language of Desert and Mountain," *New York Times*, Jan 28, 1990, 37-38 *Nelson Fine Arts Center*

Lavin, Sylvia, "El Desierto edificado: Predock, centro de arte en Arizona," *Arquitectura Viva*, Nov-Dec 1990, 24-28
Nelson Fine Arts Center

"Magic and Power in the Landscape," *Landscape Architecture*, June 1990, 56-59 *Hotel Santa Fe*

Posner, Ellen, "Building with Desert, Mountains and Light," Wall Street Journal, March 6, 1990, A16
Nelson Fine Arts Center

Stein, Karen D, "Down the Strip," *Architectural Record*, Oct 1990, 68-75 *Las Vegas Library and Children's Museum*

Loriers, Marie-Christine, "Monts Et Merveilles," *Techniques & Architecture*, Dec 1989-Jan 1990, 90-95 *Nelson Fine Arts Center*

Mulard, Claudine, "Antoine Predock," *Architecture Interieure Cree*, Dec 1989-Jan 1990

Boles, Daralice D, "Magic Mountain," *Progressive Architecture*, June 1989, 65-77 *Nelson Fine Arts Center*

Moiraghi, Luigi, "Un Nuovo segno per Las Vegas," *L 'Arca*, Sept 1989, 52-59 *Las Vegas Central Library*

Andersen, Kurt, "An Architect for the New Age," *Time*, April 11, 1988, 72

Campbell, Robert, "Antoine Predock: Redefining the Traditional Hacienda Near Santa Fe," *Architectural Digest*, April 1988, 18-23 *Lazarus House*

Dillon, David, "Regionalism, But With Many Inventive Twists," *Architecture*, July 1988, 84-87 *Lazarus House*

Lemos, Paul, "Antoine's Altered States," *London Sunday Times Magazine*, June 19, 1988, 76-77
Fuller House, United Blood Services & Classroom, Library and Administrative Building

"Unity and Diversity," *L'Arca*, June 1988, 52-57
Classroom, Library and Administrative Building

Stein, Karen D., "Five Projects: Antoine Predock, Architect," *Architectural Record*, Oct 1988, 88-97

Freeman, Allen, "Forms As Rugged As Their Desert Setting," *Architecture*, May 1987, 128-133 *Fuller House*

GA Houses Special 2: The Emerging Generation in U.S.A. Tokyo: A.D.A. EDITA Tokyo Co., Nov 1987, 52-55 *Zuber House*

Geibel, Victoria, "The Allure of Water," *Metropolis*, July-Aug 1987, 39 -45 *Rio Grande Nature Center*

Morris, Roger, "Architecture: Antoine Predock," *Architectura[illegible] Digest*, August 1987, 90-97, 115 *Troy House*

Adams, Robert M., "Desert Spirit," *House & Garden*, Dec 1986, 132-41, 202-4 *Fuller House*

Crosbie, Michael, "'Vibrant' Italian Sketches," *Architecture*, Jan 1986, 23

Goldberger, Paul, "Architecture: Antoine Predock," *Architectural Digest*, Oct 1986, 178-83 *Tesuque House*

"The Beach," *Progressive Architecture*, Jan 1985, 108-9
The Beach Apartments

Crosbie, Michael J., "Kaleidoscope: Nature Center Stands in the Water Like a Sculpted Dam," *Architecture*, Dec 1984, 72-73 *Rio Grande Nature Center*

"La Luz-Stadt in der Sonne," *Hauser*, March 1984, 254-61
La Luz Community

Papademetriou, Peter C., "Blind Trust," *Progressive Architecture*, March 1984, 86 -90 *Rio Grande Nature Center*

Triglyph. Tempe: College of Architecture and Environmental Design, Arizona State University, Fall 1984, 24-27
Desert Highlands

"Post-Modernists: Out of the Glass Box," *Forbes Magazine* (Arabic Annual Issue), 1980, 29-31 *La Luz Community*

Hoyt, Charles K., "Even Small Banks Can Express A Regional Vernacular," *Architectural Record*, Sept 1976, 124-26
First National Bank: Sandia Plaza Branch

"Regionalism: The Southwest," *Progressive Architecture*, March 1974, 60-69 *La Luz Community, The Citadel Apartments, Kaminsky House, First National Bank: Sandia Plaza*

Predock, Antoine. "La Luz, Albuquerque, N.M.," *Architecture d'Aujourd'hui*, Sept 1971, 70-73 *La Luz Community*

"La Luz," *Architectural Forum*, July 1969, 65-70
La Luz Community

PHOTOGRAPHY CREDITS

Peter Aaron/OTTO
Hotel Santa Fe, Euro-Disney
200, 202 chronology

Glen Allison
Predock Compound
81 bottom left

Christine Bastin & Jacques Evrard
Predock Studio
65 chronology right, 673 chronology left
La Luz Community
112 chronology

Richard T. Bryant
Flint RiverQuarium
332 left, 333

JC Buck
School of Architecture, George Pearl Hall
396 chronology

Canadian Museum for Human Rights
491 chronology

Aaron Cohen
Canadian Museum for Human Rights
507 bottom right, 509

Columbia Pictures
GATTACA

Courtesy of Columbia Pictures
192 chronology

Patrick Coulie
School of Architecture, George Pearl Hall
396 top, 399 top left, 400 top, 402 top right, 403 bottom
South Plant
536-539

Education City Qatar
624 chronology left

Mary Elkins
United States Pavilion, Seville Expo
199 chronology
Baltimore Performing Arts Center
283 chronology

Arthur Evans
Tang Teaching Museum and Art Gallery
284 chronology

Alex Fradkin
Canadian Museum for Human Rights
cover, 486 top, 491 top & lower right, 492 top & right, 494 top & bottom, top right, 496, 497 left & right, 498 top, bottom left & right, 499 top, 500 right, 502, 504 bottom left & middle

Scott Frances/OTTO
Hotel Santa Fe, Euro-Disney
202 bottom
Turtle Creek House
200 top, 201 top

Joshua Freiwald
La Luz Community
4, 71, 76 top
First National Bank—Sandia Plaza
82-87

Kaminsky House
89, 90 top and left, 91, 92-93
Boulder House
94, 96 bottom, 97

Ken Gallard
Taos Skiing
103 bottom right

Kirk Gittings
Tang Teaching Museum and Art Gallery
314 bottom right
School of Architecture, George Pearl Hall
398 top, 399 middle left & right, 403 top
Science Canyon
463 chronology
Sage House
520-521
Aperture Center
528-535, all photos, except 532 left, 533 left & top right, 534 left top & bottom, 535 top & right

Jerry Goffe
La Luz Community
2, 73 top left & lower right, 77 top

Stephen Green-Armytage
La Luz Community
72 chronology, 73 lower right & chronology, 74 all, 75 chronology, 76 chronology, 78 top

Stanley Ira Hallet
Casa Malaparte
408-409

Mark M. Hancock
Trinity River Audubon Center
445

Dan Harper
Canadian Museum for Human Rights
501 chronology

©David Hewitt/ Anne Garrison
Dance Studio
297 top left, 298 right, 299 left middle & bottom middle

Michael Houghton, StudiOhio
Student Activity and Recreation Center
355 chronology, 356 top right

Timothy Hursley
Rio Grande Nature Center Master Plan and Visitors Center
6, 101-107 all photos, except 102 & 106 top
Fuller House
119-128 all photos
Robinson-Burney House
123 chronology
Nelson Fine Arts Center
149-165 all photos
Zuber House
166-167 all photos
Las Vegas Central Library and Children's Museum
168-173 all photos
American Heritage Center and Art Museum
4, 174-185 all photos, except 176, 177, 179 top, 183 right
Rosenthal House
187 top, 188 bottom, 189
Classroom, Library and Administration Building
190-195 all photos, except 191 top & bottom, 192 bottom, 194-195 bottom

Turtle Creek House
202 middle, 203 bottom
Mesa Public Library
206-211 all photos, except 207 bottom, 208 bottom
Venice Beach House
214-217, 220-221
Mandell Weiss Forum Theater
222-227 all photos
Thousand Oaks Civic Arts Plaza
228-233 all photos, except 228 bottom
Music Facility
234-235 all photos, except 234 bottom left, 236 bottom right, 236-237
Museum of Science and Industry
249-263 all photos, except 249
Social Science and Humanities
254-259 all photos, except 254 bottom left, 255 bottom right, 257 bottom right
Arizona Science Center
260-264 all photos, except 260 top, 261 top left & bottom middle, 264 bottom right
Ventana Vista Elementary School
278-283 all photos, except 278-283, 279 lower right, 281 bottom middle
Student Affairs and Administrative Services Building
278 chronology
Center for Integrated Systems
288 chronology

Spencer Theater for the Performing Arts
10, 26, 290-295 all photos, except 292 middle left, 290-291 bottom
Center for Nanoscale Science and Technology
294-295 chronology
Dance Studio
296-290 all photos, except 297 top left, 298 left & right, 299 left middle & bottom
McNamara Alumni Center (Gateway Center)
307-313 all photos
Tang Teaching Museum and Art Gallery
314-319 all photos, except 314 bottom right, 318 bottom right
Flint RiverQuarium
326-331 all photos, except 326 bottom, 327 bottom, 331 bottom right, 332 left & 333
Padres Ballpark
388 middle, 339-342, 343 top & middle right, 344-345
Student Activity and Recreation Center
349-357, 349 top, 350 top, except 356 top right, 355 chronology
Tacoma Art Museum
366-369 all photos, except 365 top right, 366 top right, 368 top left, top right
Robert Hoag Rawlings Public Library
370-373 all photos
Austin City Hall and Public Plaza
374-383 all photos, except 380 lower right, 382 top left
Cornell Parking Structure and Visitors Center
404-407 all photos

Page numbers refer to major project images. Chronology page numbers refer to images along the bottom of the page.
Every effort has been made to contact the holders of copyrighted material. Omissions will be corrected in future editions.

Highlands Pond House
412-439 all photos, except 423 bottom, 425 left middle, 426 bottom right, 434 bottom left

Trinity River Audubon Center
440-447 all photos, except 442 left, 443 right, 445

Indian Community School
448-457 all photos, except 449 right & bottom, 452 top left & bottom left, 454 bottom left, 455 bottom left & bottom right

Cornerstone Arts Center
524-527 all photos, except 526 top & bottom left, 527 middle right

Predock Studio
579 chronology, 674 chronology third from left, 675 chronology third from left

Instituto Tecnológico y de Estudios Superiores de Monterrey
633

©Christopher Mead
Roadcut Exhibition
568-569

Drawing into Architecture & Like A Signature Exhibitions
634-635

David Morton
Citadel Apartments
90 chronology

Mary E. Nichols, Architectural Digest ©Condé Nast
Rosenthal House
186-187

Venice Beach House
214-215

Michael Pratt
Canadian Museum for Human Rights
14, 485

Raven-Baker House Client
639 all photos

Robert Reck
World Map
28

Desert Highlands
114-118

Beach Apartments
120 chronology second from left

Lazarus House
134-135 chronology

Troy House
140 chronology

Landshark
171 chronology

American Heritage Center and Art Museum
176, 177, 179 top, 183 right, 181 chronology

Ship of the Desert
186-187 chronology

Winandy House
188-189 chronology

Turtle Creek House
196-197, 198-199, 200 bottom right, 202 top & bottom left, 203 top & middle, 207, 208 top

United States Pavilion, Seville Expo
199 chronology

Hotel Santa Fe, Euro-Disney
200 chronology

Disney Mediterranean Hotel
210-211 chronology, except first two

Institute of American Indian Arts Museum
228 chronology

Music Facility
234 bottom right

Texas Rangers Ballpark
236-237 chronology

Palm Bay Resort and Casino
238-246 all photos, except 242 bottom, 243 bottom & 244 bottom

Social Science and Humanities
254 bottom left & 255 bottom right

IBM Solana
258 chronology, except first & fifth images

Arizona Science Center
260-261 chronology

Bookstore and Parking Facility, UNM
262 bottom right

Hispanic Cultural Center
263 chronology

Massachusetts Bay House
264 chronology

Cathedral of Saint John the Divine South Transept
276-277

Ventana Vista Elementary School
279

Maryland Center for Performing Arts
282 chronology

Atlantis
284-289 all photos, except 285 top right

Spencer Theater for the Performing Arts
290-291 bottom

Danish National Archives
300-303

University Center (Northrup Hall), Trinity University
316 chronology

Shadow House, Architectural Digest ©Condé Nast
358-363 all photos

Logjam House
412-419 all photos

Canadian Museum for Human Rights
489 top left, 490 top & bottom left

Westside Studio
636-637 all photos

Antoine Predock Center for Design and Research
672-670 all photos

Lyle Stafford/ Winnipeg Free Press
486 chronology

James Steinkamp Photography
Doudna Fine Arts Center
384-386, 388 top right, 389 top, 391 top left 392 bottom, 393 top left & middle

Erik Stenbakken
School of Architecture, George Pearl Hall
398 bottom, 403 top left

©Lara Swimmer/Esto
Tacoma Art Museum
364, 366 top, 368 top left, top right

Bill Timmerman
Green Valley Performing Arts and Learning Center
320-323 all photos, except 322 left & right

Victory Jon
all action motorcycle shots unless otherwise noted

T. H. Weng
Jade Cascade
510 bottom left & right

University of Missouri
576 chronology

University of Wyoming
American Heritage Center
177 chronology

Wide Horizons Group
Gateway Arrival Building Arts Center
20, 593, 604 bottom right

Todd Winslow Pierce
Highlands Pond House
429 chronology left, 443 chronology left

All drawings, collages, and models by Antoine Predock

25
Km/h
VELOCIDAD
MAXIMA